RABI'A FROM NARRATIVE TO MYTH

RABI'A FROM NARRATIVE TO MYTH

THE MANY FACES OF ISLAM'S MOST FAMOUS WOMAN SAINT, RABI'A AL-'ADAWIYYA

RKIA ELAROUI CORNELL

ONEWORLD ACADEMIC

Oneworld Academic

An imprint of Oneworld Publications

Published by Oneworld Academic, 2019

Copyright © Rkia Elaroui Cornell 2019

The moral right of Rkia Elaroui Cornell to be identified as the Author of this work has been asserted by her in accordance with the Copyright, Designs, and Patents Act 1988

All rights reserved
Copyright under Berne Convention
A CIP record for this title is available from the British Library

ISBN 978-0-86154-900-9
eISBN 978-1-78607-522-2

Typeset by Siliconchips Services Ltd, UK

Oneworld Publications
10 Bloomsbury Street
London WC1B 3SR
England

Stay up to date with the latest books,
special offers, and exclusive content from
Oneworld with our newsletter

Sign up on our website
oneworld-publications.com

To my academic mentors,
Pieternella A. Van Doorn-Harder,
Hendrik M. Vroom and Carl W. Ernst.

And to my husband,
Vincent J. Cornell.

Without you this book would
never have been written.

Contents

Acknowledgments	xi
INTRODUCTION: RABI'A, "THE WOMAN WHO NEVER DIES"	1
I. *The Myth Of Rabi'a al-'Adawiyya As A Master Narrative*	4
II. *Key Premodern Sources and Modern Works on Rabi'a al-'Adawiyya*	12
III. *What Is a Myth?*	20
IV. *The Plan of this Work*	27
CHAPTER 1	
RABI'A THE TEACHER	33
I. *Who Was the "Real" Rabi'a?*	33
a. *Early Sources for the Historical Rabi'a*	34
b. *Alleged Students and Associates of Rabi'a al-'Adawiyya*	42
II. *Rabi'a in the Earliest Sources*	45
a. *Rabi'a the Arab*	45
b. *Rabi'a the Leader*	49
c. *Rabi'a the Sunni Muslim*	52
d. *Rabi'a the Eloquent*	53
III. *Rabi'a the Teacher and the Culture of* Adab *in Early Islam*	57
a. *Rabi'a and Sufyan al-Thawri*	60
b. *Ta'dib: The Art of Character Formation*	69
c. *Ta'dib and the "Manly" Virtues:* Muruwwa *and* Hilm	72
d. *Rabi'a's Way of* Ta'dib	75
CHAPTER 2	
RABI'A THE ASCETIC	83
I. *Conceptualizing Asceticism in Early Islam*	84
a. *The World/Nonworld Dichotomy*	84
b. *The Problem of Asceticism as a Theoretical Category*	87

II. Terms of Early Islamic Asceticism — 92
- a. Zuhd *(Renunciation)* — 92
- b. Wara' *(Ethical Precaution)* — 96
- c. Nusk *(Ascetic Ritualism)* — 104
- d. Faqr *(Poverty)* — 114

III. Traditions of Women's Asceticism in Basra — 121
- a. The Legacy of 'A'isha — 122
- b. The School of Mu'adha al-'Adawiyya and Instrumental Asceticism — 125
- c. The Weeping Women (al-Bakiyat) of Basra — 129

IV. The Asceticism of Rabi'a and Her Circle — 137
- a. Rabi'a's Alleged Students and Associates — 137
- b. From Instrumental Asceticism to Essential Asceticism — 140

CHAPTER 3
RABI'A THE LOVER — 147

I. From Historical Representation to Cultural Icon — 148

II. Asceticism and Love Mysticism in Early Islamic Basra — 150
- a. From Asceticism to Love Mysticism — 150
- b. Love of God in the Qur'an and Hadith — 154
- c. The Ascetic Lovers of Basra — 158
- d. The Question of Rabi'a's Celibacy — 167

III. Rabi'a the "Muslim Diotima?" — 179
- a. The "Incognito Presence" of Plato's *Symposium* — 179
- b. Rabi'a the Lover in Abu Talib al-Makki's *Qut al-Qulub* — 189

IV. Rabi'a the Love Poet — 196
- a. The Poem of the Two Loves — 196
- b. The Poem of the Intimate Gift — 208

CHAPTER 4
RABI'A THE SUFI — 213

I. The Lady Reconsidered: Can We See the Real "Rabi'a the Sufi"? — 213

II. Locating Rabi'a the Sufi: What Was A "Sufi" in Eighth-Century Islam? — 222

III. The Heart as a Metaphor in Early Islamic Mysticism — 234
- a. Scriptural Antecedents — 234
- b. Possible Paths of Transmission — 237
- c. The Metaphor of the Heart for Rabi'a al-'Adawiyya and Her Contemporaries — 243

IV. Rabi'a the "Knower of God" — 249

CHAPTER 5
RABI'A THE ICON (I): THE SUFI IMAGE — 261

I. *Rabi'a As A Literary Figure: Myth, Icon, and the "Reality Effect"* — 261
II. *From Visage to* Vita: *'Attar's Outline of the Rabi'a Myth* — 272
  a. *Composing the Background: 'Attar's Hagiographic Predecessors* — 272
  b. *'Attar's Portrayal of Rabi'a al-'Adawiyya in* Tadhkirat al-Awliya' — 278
III. *Every Picture Tells a Story: 'Attar's Emplotment of Rabi'a's* Vita — 294
IV. *Postscript: Where Is Rabi'a Buried?* — 321

CHAPTER 6
RABI'A THE ICON (II): THE SECULAR IMAGE — 325

I. *From Religious to Secular Narratives* — 325
II. *Rabi'a the Existentialist* — 328
III. *Rabi'a the Film Icon* — 352
IV. *Postscript: Rabi'a, The Phantom of the Television Series* — 364

EPILOGUE
RABI'A, THE MYTH AND THE NARRATIVE — 367

Bibliography — 379

I. *Sources in Arabic and Persian* — 379
II. *Sources in European Languages* — 382

Index — 395

Acknowledgments

This book has taken me fifteen years to write. It is hard to write a major academic study as a language teacher, especially when the subject of the study is outside the field of language pedagogy. It started as a Ph.D. project for VU University Amsterdam (Vrije Universiteit Amsterdam), when I was teaching Arabic at the University of Arkansas Fayetteville. It has ended up as a monograph in Atlanta, Georgia, where I still teach Arabic, as Professor of Pedagogy and Arabic Language Coordinator for the Department of Middle Eastern and South Asian Studies at Emory University. Doing language pedagogy at the proficiency level takes an enormous amount of time and energy, and often at the end of the day one is too tired to think of anything, much less switch gears to write a book in a different field. Consequently, it took me about a year (on average) to write each chapter of my dissertation, and about the same to write the chapters of this book. During this period, many people helped me in many different ways. Some are acknowledged in the pages that follow, such as the scholars from Iraq who struggled with me in Morocco to figure out where the "real" Rabiʿa al-ʿAdawiyya is buried, and Dr Ahmet Alibasic of the Faculty of Islamic Studies in Sarajevo, Bosnia-Herzegovina, who heard of this work from my husband and translated for me the *ilahi* "Hassan i Rabija" by Professor Džemaludin Latić. For those whom I have neglected to acknowledge or have forgotten along the way, please forgive me. The road to completion of this book has been long, and I am both happy and weary to have reached its end.

However, some people were so important for this project that I must acknowledge them up front. The first of these is the chair of my dissertation committee, Professor of Islamic Studies Dr Pieternella (Nelly) Van Doorn-Harder, of Wake Forest University and VU University Amsterdam. Nelly is one of four people without whom this book could never have been written. After reading my first book, *Early Sufi Women*, and hearing my proposed project on Rabi'a al-'Adawiyya during a visit to the University of Arkansas, she facilitated my entry into the Ph.D. program in theology at VU, and was a helpful and nurturing presence throughout the years that I wrote my dissertation. I will always be grateful for her friendship and support.

Another indispensable person was the late Dr Hendrik M. Vroom, Professor of Theology at VU University Amsterdam, who was also an important mentor for my dissertation. His firm, yet gentle guidance and critiques made my work much better than it would otherwise have been. As his other students would confirm, he was a true interlocutor and academic father figure who remained dedicated to his educational mission literally until the end. My last memory of him is of visiting with him shortly before his death at his home outside Amsterdam, where he strongly encouraged me to retain the integrity of the work I had produced and not sacrifice the manuscript for the sake of publication. He was a man of great faith, integrity, and love of God, and I will honor his legacy through my relationships with my students throughout my career.

The other people who were indispensable to this project are my two main American advisors. Carl W. Ernst, Kenan Professor of Islamic Studies at the University of North Carolina, Chapel Hill, was my third dissertation advisor and mentor. I have known Carl for more than twenty-five years, since I first started teaching Arabic at Duke University, and I have always cherished his kindness and wisdom. Before advising me on this project, he wrote the Preface for my book *Early Sufi Women*. I will never forget the maxim he taught me while I was writing my dissertation: "The perfect is the enemy of the good." I probably would never have finished this work without his wise advice.

Last, but by no means least, is my husband Vincent J. Cornell. Besides being my companion in life, he has been my mentor and partner throughout my academic career. He taught me the importance of personal integrity and not to produce anything under my name that was not the best that I could do. He gave me confidence in myself and supported me when others put me down. His faith in me has never wavered and he has always believed in my potential, even when I doubted it myself. His love and support has made me the person and the scholar that I am today. He also taught me the tradition of his teachers, both academic teachers in the US and Sufi teachers in Morocco. This tradition teaches that the best legacy for which a person can be remembered is the advancement of knowledge. The most honorable appellation for a family is *bayt al-'ilm*, "house of knowledge." As the Moroccan

Sufi Muhammad ibn Sulayman al-Jazuli (d. 1465 CE) stated, "God cannot bestow a calamity on a man greater than the ignorance of his family."

Other colleagues and teachers have also influenced this work in many ways. Janet Tucker, Professor of Russian Language and Literature at the University of Arkansas Fayetteville, first suggested the title, "Rabi'a from Narrative to Myth." Devin Stewart, Professor of Islamic and Middle Eastern Studies and Chair of the MESAS department at Emory University, went through the draft copy of the book with a fine-toothed editorial comb. I am also grateful for the support of other faculty colleagues at Emory, such as Professors Carrie Wickham, Ruby Lal, Kevin Corrigan and the members of the MESAS Faculty Writing Workshop, who read all or part of this work and gave me support and guidance. Thanks should also go to Dina Khapaeva, Professor of Russian at Georgia Tech, for her feedback, encouragement, and support. I should also thank the deans of the University of Arkansas and Emory University, who gave me institutional support for dissertation research and the completion of the book manuscript: this consisted of one sabbatical semester each at UA and Emory and a Winship Award at Emory. Thanks should also go to Bruce B. Lawrence, Marcus Family Humanities Professor of Religion Emeritus at Duke University, and the other members of my dissertation defense committee at VU University Amsterdam, who approved of my oral defense of the dissertation. I was so nervous at the time that I must have been nearly incoherent. Finally, I must not forget to thank the entire Faculty of Theology at VU University Amsterdam, who read the dissertation and voted unanimously to grant me the honor of a Ph.D. *Cum Laude*.

I have also received much help and support from my students and research assistants, both graduate and undergraduate. At the University of Arkansas, Mohammad Daadaoui, now Professor and Chair of Political Science at Oklahoma City University, helped me get this project underway by spending many hours collecting Arabic sources on Rabi'a al-'Adawiyya. My former Duke student Behdad Shahsavari, now a partner with BCG Digital Ventures in California, honored me by formally presenting me for my oral defense at VU University Amsterdam. Also standing up for me in Amsterdam was my niece Malika Berrahmo, who lives in Ghent, Belgium. At Emory, special thanks should go to my Islamic Civilizations Studies Ph.D. student Jeremy Farrell, who helped complete this book by sharing his deep knowledge of prosopographical sources on early Islam and Sufism and by helping me make sure that my coverage of research on early Islam was up to date.

Finally, I am grateful for the support of my family and extended family, in Morocco, the United States, and Europe. This includes my mother-in-law, Dr Eleanor Cornell, with whom I would often share ideas over strong coffee at her breakfast table, and my son-in-law Jens Klawiter, who patiently put up with our frequent family debates. However, greatest thanks must go to my daughter Sakina for patiently bearing two major sources of stress while growing up—having an academic mother and having a Moroccan mother. I will always cherish her love and support. Finally, I hope that when he is old enough to read this book, my grandson Adam Klawiter will find it to be a worthy legacy for him.

Introduction

Rabi'a, "The Woman Who Never Dies"

In October 1804 the Lewis and Clark expedition, which was organized to explore and map the lands along the Missouri River in the American West, entered the area where the Cannonball River and the Heart River join the Missouri River in present-day North Dakota. The expedition was following a map made by a member of the Mandan nation of Native Americans, who was asked to locate the sites of Mandan villages and important landmarks. The Mandan people called the region between the Heart and Cannonball Rivers "Heart of the Land" because it was the center of their world and the heartland of their culture. It was here that Lone Man, the first being, and First Creator, the Coyote, brought up mud from the Missouri River and its tributaries to build the Mandan villages. South of the Cannonball River was the home of Old Woman Who Never Dies. "Of all female life on earth I am the head," she said. "Cold and blizzard I subdue... I make whatever I plant to grow."[1]

Old Woman Who Never Dies originally came from a land far to the south of the Mandan homeland. When she heard about the villages that Lone Man and Coyote had created, she resolved to come north and make a female of each species so that life could continue. For the Mandan people, Old Woman Who Never Dies symbolized the female power of rebirth and regeneration; she was the spirit of vegetation and guaranteed the growth of agricultural crops. Her spirit also entered the body of the Rocky Mountains to make sure that the rivers would always flow. Her creative spirit entered into the body of the first woman to insure that females would always produce

---

1   Carolyn Gilman, *Lewis and Clark: Across the Divide* (Washington, DC and London: Smithsonian Books, 2003), p. 153.

children. Out of her spirit, she created the Holy Women of the Groves of the Four Directions.

The Holy Women had great power and acted as teachers for chosen men. In the sacred ceremonies of the Mandan people, both men and women performed special rituals for the Holy Women so that all women would be respected. Old Woman Who Never Dies maintained her immortality by bathing in the Missouri River and its tributaries. Each time she bathed in the river she came up younger, until she came up as a young girl.[2] According to some legends, she kept a second home far to the south of Mandan territory, where the Mississippi River empties into the Gulf of Mexico. There she lived in a hut beside the sea and ate corn porridge with spoons made of clamshells.[3]

When I was a young girl growing up in the Middle Atlas Mountains of Morocco, I had no idea about the Mandan people or Old Woman Who Never Dies. However, I did know something about holy people. I was born into a family that traced its origins to *murabitin*, holy people of the Moroccan countryside. My ancestors were the Banu Amghar, a family of Moroccan saints that created one of the first *ribats* or Sufi teaching centers in rural Morocco. This *ribat* was located near a sacred spring called Tit-n-Fitr, "Spring of Sustenance" in the Amazigh language. Known today as Moulay Abdellah, the *ribat* of Tit-n-Fitr can still be seen on the Atlantic coast of Morocco, just south of the city of El Jedida. Many legends are told about the holy men of the Banu Amghar, and even today, the festival of Abu 'Abdullah Muhammad Amghar (fl. 1133 CE) attracts thousands of visitors each year.[4]

Unlike most girls in rural Morocco in the 1960s, my father allowed me to leave my native town for school, first in the small city of Sefrou near Fez and later in the regional capital of Meknès. At an early age, I was taught the Qur'an because Qur'anic learning was my family's tradition. My father took his heritage seriously and tried to maintain the most important traditions of the family. During each vacation from school I would spend long hours with him, sharing what I had learned and listening to the stories and teachings that he related. I developed a reputation for being different from the other girls

---

2   Virginia Bergman Peters, *Women of the Earth Lodges: Tribal Life on the Plains* (Norman, Oklahoma: University of Oklahoma Press, 2000 reprint of 1995 first edition), pp. 31–4.
3   Alfred W. Bowers, *Mandan Social and Ceremonial Organization* (Lincoln, Nebraska and London: University of Nebraska Press, 2004 reprint of 1950 University of Chicago Press first edition), pp. 197–205.
4   For information on the Banu Amghar, see Vincent J. Cornell, *Realm of the Saint: Power and Authority in Moroccan Sufism* (Austin, Texas: The University of Texas Press, 1998), pp. 32–62. The *moussem* or festival of Moulay Abdellah Amghar has its own website: www.moulayabdellah.ma.

of my town. I read a lot, I kept to myself, and I did not think of marriage as a goal. Because I also had a serious inclination toward religion, the other girls of my town gave me a nickname that persisted throughout my childhood and adolescence: "Rabi'a al-'Adawiyya."

Despite being compared mockingly to Rabi'a al-'Adawiyya as a girl, it did not occur to me to write anything about her until I published my first book, *Early Sufi Women*, in 1999.[5] I only thought of writing about Rabi'a after I saw how she was depicted by the Persian Sufi Abu 'Abd al-Rahman al-Sulami (d. 1021 CE). Sulami portrayed Rabi'a very differently from most of the legends and accounts about her that I knew. Sulami's Rabi'a was not a dreamy and romantic Love mystic. Instead, she was a tough-minded and clear-headed teacher and spiritual master. Famous male ascetics respected her for the wisdom of her teachings. Some of these men were even her disciples. In addition, when I translated and published Sulami's Book of Sufi Women, I discovered that Rabi'a was not a unique figure in her time but instead represented a tradition of women's ascetic spirituality that went back more than a century before her. It was then that I resolved to write a book about Rabi'a and found my chance to do so in the pursuit of a doctoral degree at VU University Amsterdam.

However, as soon as I resolved to take on this project, I was faced with a major historiographical problem: What was I to say about a legendary figure like Rabi'a al-'Adawiyya? How could I find a framework of inquiry that explained the numerous and often contradictory narratives—both Sufi and non-Sufi—that have helped create the myth of Rabi'a as she is known in the Muslim world today? What metaphor could encapsulate the different "faces" of Rabi'a from medieval to modern times? In 2004, I found my inspiration on a visit to St Louis, Missouri during the Bicentennial Celebration of the Lewis and Clark expedition. At the St Louis Gateway Arch Bookstore, I found a copy of Carolyn Gilman's richly illustrated memorial volume, *Lewis and Clark: Across the Divide*. This book introduced me to the Mandan and Hidatsa legends of Old Woman Who Never Dies. I soon realized that this metaphor could also apply to the legend of Rabi'a al-'Adawiyya. Except for the Prophet Muhammad's daughter Fatima, more than any other woman in the history of Islam, Rabi'a is The Woman Who Never Dies.

---

5   Abu 'Abd ar-Rahman as-Sulami, *Early Sufi Women: Dhikr an-niswa al-muta'abbidat as-sufiyyat*, ed. and trans. Rkia E. Cornell (Louisville, Kentucky: Fons Vitae, 1999).

I. THE MYTH OF RABI'A AL-'ADAWIYYA AS A MASTER NARRATIVE

Because Rabi'a al-'Adawiyya is a figure of myth, she is not a normal subject of historical inquiry. In fact, she does not appear in most medieval histories or biographical works in the Islamic world. Instead, she mostly appears in hagiographic narratives and in Sufi doctrinal works. As the chapters of this book will demonstrate, her biography is largely—if not entirely—fictional. Her status as a subject of historical inquiry is mainly a product of the twentieth century. Because of this, she upsets the normal rules of historiographical method. In conventional historical studies, the scholar researches and assesses historical documents and archival sources and puts the conclusions of her research into writing.[6] However, with Rabi'a al-'Adawiyya, there are no sources to consult other than hagiographies or other literary works, and these are not historical documents in the normal sense of the term. As she is known today, Rabi'a is mostly a figure of literature and all the information that is known about her comes through literature. Thus, to write about her one must make use of literature and take literary forms of representation into account.

In the modern period, scholars of Islamic Studies in Europe, the US, and the Muslim world have tried to demythologize Rabi'a in order to write about her historically. This has created two major problems. First, some writers make the mistake of treating literary representations of Rabi'a uncritically as historical data or empirical facts.[7] Naively, they accept virtually everything that is written about her. This is clearly a mistake. As this book will reveal, not only is much of what is written about Rabi'a al-'Adawiyya governed by narrative tropes more than by documentary evidence but key elements of her story, especially her *vita* or life story, can be shown to be fictional, although they are most often believed to be factual today.

Second, in trying to avoid the naivety of the previous group of writers, other writers have been too skeptical. By trying to treat Rabi'a in a purely empirical manner, they diminish her as a religious and cultural figure by either dismissing her as a legitimate subject of history altogether or by ignoring the levels of symbolic meaning that have made her an important part of Islamic

---

6   Frank Ankersmit, *Meaning, Truth, and Reference in Historical Representation* (Ithaca, NY: Cornell University Press, 2012), p. 60.
7   This approach characterizes the great majority of works written on Rabi'a in the modern period, including a vast amount of Internet references that are too numerous to count.

cultural memory.⁸ As a figure of cultural memory, Rabiʻa al-ʻAdawiyya is not unlike the mythical figure of al-Khidr (The Green One), who in Muslim folklore reappears in every age to guide a new generation of seekers with his wisdom.⁹ As the phenomenologist of religion Mircea Eliade observed, myths and stories (including hagiographies and modern histories) often contain the same master plots and tropes, despite being expressed in different idioms. For Eliade, if the symbolic meaning of a story is paramount (or as he puts it, "whenever the essential precedes existence"), the story is a myth.¹⁰

Following Eliade's lead, but also making use of other theorists of narrative, historiography, and myth, this book examines the accounts, dicta, and stories that make up the myth of Rabiʻa al-ʻAdawiyya, both in terms of their content and in terms of their form and structure. Following a metaphor used by the theorist of narrative Roland Barthes, I approach the narratives that make up the Rabiʻa myth not as an "apricot" but as an "onion." In this metaphor, the apricot represents conventional historical narratives and the onion represents the Rabiʻa narratives. If the "fruit" of a historical narrative is the narrative content and the "pit" is the factual core, there is little that can be considered a "pit" or factual core in the Rabiʻa narratives. Thus, the Rabiʻa narratives cannot be compared to an apricot; rather, they are more like an onion. Like an onion, the narratives of Rabiʻa al-ʻAdawiyya consist of superimposed stories, layers of content, and different forms, with a "core" that can only be discerned when a new narrative version or image of Rabiʻa emerges from within.¹¹ For this reason, a thorough historical analysis of the Rabiʻa narratives must involve peeling back the multiple layers of content and form and rearranging them according to the most significant narrative tropes.

---

8   See for example, Julian Baldick, "The Legend of Rabiʻa of Basra: Christian Antecedents, Muslim Counterparts," *Religion*, 19, 1990. Baldick's view of the Rabiʻa narratives as fictional is apparent throughout this article. His concern is mainly to identify literary *topoi* that he can compare with Christian antecedents, without discussing their figural meaning or the role they have played in the construction of the Rabiʻa myth.
9   See Hugh Talat Halman, *Where the Two Seas Meet: The Qur'anic Story of al-Khidr and Moses in Sufi Commentaries as a Model of Spiritual Guidance* (Louisville, KY: Fons Vitae, 2013). Much like the present work, Halman's book examines the figure of al-Khidr both as a mythical figure and as a product of literature.
10 Mircea Eliade, *Myth and Reality*, trans. Willard R. Trask (Long Grove, IL: Waveland Press, 1998 reprint of 1963 original), p. 92.
11 Roland Barthes, "Style and Its Image," in idem, *The Rustle of Language*, trans. Richard Howard (New York: Hill & Wang, 1986), p. 99. For Barthes, an onion does not have a core. However, as any cook knows, the "core" of an onion becomes visible when a new onion plant starts to sprout from it.

According to the rules of conventional historiography, the study of a figure from the distant past like Rabi'a al-'Adawiyya is supposed to involve: (1) an examination of the factual information on the subject as she appears in premodern sources; and (2) a determination of what can be said about the "real" person as she lived out the events of her life. However, as mentioned above, there are no empirical source materials that can tell us conclusively what the "real" Rabi'a al-'Adawiyya was like. All we can know is how the figurative Rabi'a has been represented. A few purportedly eyewitness accounts exist in the literary record, but until more corroborating evidence can be found it is difficult to establish their reliability. Under these circumstances, separating the "real" Rabi'a from the figurative Rabi'a is virtually impossible.[12] Therefore, there is no recourse for the historian but to examine the *representations* of Rabi'a al-'Adawiyya in the narratives and the subsequent *interpretations* that have been made of her mythical image.

However, the narrative approach that I use in this book does not mean, "Anything goes." Rather, my motive for this methodology is, "Necessity is the mother of invention." Although evidence suggests that a well-known Muslim woman and ascetic by the name of Rabi'a lived in the region of Basra in southern Iraq in the eighth century CE, little else can be determined according to conventional historical methods. The normal approach of "fact-finding" followed by "history writing" cannot apply in this case. The unconventional nature of the archive demands a different approach. If one takes the position of Michel de Certeau, Hayden White, F.R. Ankersmit, and other scholars who believe that the sources of history can include literary forms of representation, then it becomes both possible and legitimate to study how the myth of Rabi'a al-'Adawiyya has been constructed through different forms of literature.

The historiographical approach that I use in this book is both narrativist and constructivist. According to the discursive model of constructivism advanced by Jonathan Potter, this approach is based on two premises: (1) descriptions and accounts construct our views of the world; (2) these descriptions and accounts are themselves constructed.[13] Such a perspective "suggests the possibility of assembly, manufacture. . . and the likelihood

---

12 The philosophy of historicism assumes the existence of a "kernel of truth," which defines the object that history reveals, like the pit in Barthes' apricot metaphor. Leopold von Ranke (1795–1886) called this kernel of truth a "seed." Unfortunately, there is no empirically discernible "seed" out of which to develop a conventional historical image of Rabi'a al-'Adawiyya. On this point see Ankersmit, *Meaning, Truth, and Reference*, p. 2.
13 Jonathan Potter, *Representing Reality: Discourse, Rhetoric, and Social Construction* (London: Sage Publications, second edition, 2012), p. 97.

that different materials will be used in the fabrication. It emphasizes that descriptions are human practices and that descriptions could have been otherwise."[14] Constructivism is a useful perspective from which to approach the historical study of Rabi'a al-'Adawiyya because everything that we know about her has been constructed. It enables us to ask questions of the available information that we could not ask otherwise. As Potter states, "If we treat descriptions as constructions and constructive, we can ask how they are put together, what materials are used, what sorts of things or events are produced by them, and so on."[15]

As the title, *Rabi'a from Narrative to Myth* implies, this book is more concerned with how Rabi'a al-'Adawiyya has been represented than with the alleged "facts" of her existence. The most important "fact" from this perspective is that her image has been constructed out of a variety of narrative forms for over 1200 years. Moreover, she exhibits through these narratives an identity that has inspired countless people in different times, places and cultures. Just as the Native American mythical figure of Old Woman Who Never Dies becomes a young girl again each time she bathes in the Missouri river, so too the mythical figure of Rabi'a al-'Adawiyya is revived by periodically "bathing" in new narratives or in new adaptations of former narratives. Today the Rabi'a narratives are popular among both Muslims and non-Muslims, and can be found in both Sufi and non-Sufi literatures, in local traditions, songs, movies, and even television miniseries.

The historical paradox of Rabi'a al-'Adawiyya is that her name is known by nearly everyone but the "real" Rabi'a is known by no one. In the term coined by the Belgian sociologist of religion Pierre Delooz, she is a "constructed saint"—a composite figure of legends, dicta, stories, poems, and hagiographic accounts that have taken on the aura of fact.[16] Both the details of Rabi'a's life and the meaning of her sainthood depend on narratives that vary according to differences in Sufi doctrine, literary convention, and authorial intent. These narratives are made up of religious, literary, and even philosophical tropes that when taken as a whole, portray her in figurative terms as the quintessential woman saint of Islam. Like a mirage in the desert, Rabi'a's mythical image is forever on the horizon. And like a mirage as well, she changes form according to the perspective from which she is viewed. The farther away one gets from

---

14 Ibid., 97–8.
15 Ibid.
16 Pierre Delooz, *Sociologie et Canonisations* (Liège, Belgium: Université de Liège Faculté de Droit, 1969), pp. 7–14.

the "real" Rabi'a, the more one believes one knows her. However, the closer one gets to the sources that are supposed to provide empirical information on her life and teachings, the less one finds consensus. Also like a mirage, Rabi'a's image dissolves when viewed at close range. However, when seen at a greater distance and from a different angle she reappears once again, clothed in yet another narrative that attracts a new group of admirers.

Defined most simply, a narrative is the representation of an event or a series of events.[17] The narratives of Rabi'a al-'Adawiyya refer to a *character* or a typified identity. Narratives are related to myths because like a myth a narrative starts as "a mode of verbal presentation and involves the linguistic recounting or telling of events."[18] Like myths as well, the events recounted in narratives occur in a time other than the present. Narratives vary according to their structure. Some narratives are compact and easily definable: these are the building blocks for larger narrative structures.[19] The short accounts and dicta that make up the earliest narratives of Rabi'a al-'Adawiyya are of this type. Other narratives are structurally more complex.[20] In the Rabi'a narratives, these more complex structures include longer accounts, different modes of representation, and the master narratives through which her story is told. Master narratives are associated with *types* or *tropes*. Tropes are universal character types that are integral to the narrative.[21] The tropes of the Rabi'a al-'Adawiyya master narrative are the main focus of this book.

Theorists of narrative differentiate between a story (the recounting of an event or a series of events) and a *narrative discourse* (how the recounting of the event is conveyed).[22] Narrative is related to historiography through the concept of narrative discourse. Theorists of history-as-narrative view history as a narrative because like a narrative, history is the representation of an event or a series of events. However, the representation of an event is not the same as "what really happened." For such theorists, history is a "mediated story" or "re-presentation" of what really happened. Because it is a form of representation, history also has something in common with myth. For the scholar of comparative religion Mircea Eliade, myth is a type

---

17 H. Porter Abbott, *The Cambridge Introduction to Narrative* (Cambridge, UK, Cambridge University Press, 2008), p. 13.
18 Ibid., p. 15.
19 Ibid., p. 14.
20 Ibid.
21 Ibid., p. 185.
22 Ibid., p. 15.

of sacred history. For the French literary theorist Roland Barthes, both myth and history are types of narrative discourse. In his landmark essay on narrative, Barthes stresses the fact that narrative is a universal form of human communication:

> The narratives of the world are numberless. Narrative is first and foremost a prodigious variety of genres, themselves distributed amongst different substances—as though any material were fit to receive man's stories. Able to be carried by articulated language, spoken or written, fixed or moving images, gestures, and the ordered mixture of all these substances; narrative is present in myth, legend, fable, tale, novella, epic, history, tragedy, drama, comedy, mime, painting... stained-glass windows, cinema, comics, news items, conversation. Moreover, under this almost infinite diversity of forms, narrative is present in every age, in every place, in every society; it begins with the very history of mankind and there nowhere is nor has been a people without narrative. All classes, all human groups, have their narratives, enjoyment of which is very often shared by men with different, even opposing, cultural backgrounds. Caring nothing for the division between good and bad literature, narrative is international, transhistorical, transcultural: it is simply there, like life itself.[23]

Because narrative is a form of communication, it has also been a major subject for theorists of Communications Studies. Scholars of this field would call the myth of Rabi'a al-'Adawiyya a *master narrative*, "a transhistorical narrative that is deeply embedded in a particular culture."[24] Because the name, "Rabi'a," stands for a master narrative, it conjures up an image based on a wide variety of stories and sayings that have been transmitted over many centuries. As I discuss below in Chapter 5, the association of Rabi'a al-'Adawiyya with master narratives may be compared to an Orthodox Christian icon. In the Orthodox icon, a single image can evoke a variety of symbolic associations. In this sense, one could say that Rabi'a is an icon too, except that her image is evoked through literature rather than through

---

23 Roland Barthes, "Introduction to the Structural Analysis of Narratives," in Susan Sontag (ed.), *A Barthes Reader* (New York: Hill & Wang, 1998), pp. 251–2.
24 Jeffry R. Halverson, H.L. Goodall, Jr., and Steven R. Corman, *Master Narratives of Islamist Extremism* (New York: Palgrave Macmillan, 2011), p. 14. See also, Walter R. Fisher, *Human Communication as Narration: Toward a Philosophy of Reason, Value, and Action* (Columbia, SC: University of South Carolina Press, 1989).

painting. However, now that she is represented in modern times through movies and television, her image also carries something of the visual aspect of an icon. As a master narrative, the myth of Rabi'a al-'Adawiyya is part of a dialectical process of composition: her master narrative both shapes other narratives and is shaped by them.

Scholars of Comparative Literature often refer to master narratives as "master plots." Master plots are narratives that reflect the dominant values of a society, such as the Horatio Alger story in American culture.[25] As the scholar of narrative H. Porter Abbott observes, master plots often appear as archetypes or barely conscious themes in historical narratives, such as when the "rags to riches" Horatio Alger master plot is used as a frame story for the biography of US President Abraham Lincoln. Based on this notion, I argue that the master plot of the Rabi'a al-'Adawiyya myth was first created by the Sufi Farid al-Din al-'Attar (d. ca. 1220 CE).[26] 'Attar's chapter on Rabi'a in the hagiographic anthology *Tadhkirat al-awliya'* (*Memorial of the Saints*) established the frame story for all subsequent versions of her life story. However, long before 'Attar other elements of the Rabi'a myth had already existed in the form of dicta and narrative tropes. Because dicta and narrative tropes do not fit the literary concept of "plot" very well, in this book I prefer the concept of master narrative to that of master plot.

I further argue in this book that the master narrative of Rabi'a al-'Adawiyya is composed of four major tropes or character types: Rabi'a the Teacher, Rabi'a the Ascetic, Rabi'a the Lover, and Rabi'a the Sufi. Each of these tropes may also be seen as a master narrative and each comprises a chapter of this book. Chapters 5 and 6, which discuss the concept of "Rabi'a the Icon," include all of the tropes mentioned above plus new tropes that emerged in the twentieth century from the adaptation of Rabi'a's *vita* by academic scholars, novelists, and dramatists. As part of a continuous process of re-presentation and re-interpretation, the mythical figure Rabi'a al-'Adawiyya emerges with a new or revised image in each period of narrative activity. This process has not only continued into the modern period but has been intensified as well. I discuss Rabi'a's biography, as it appears in medieval and modern literature and media, toward the end of the book rather than at the beginning because

---

25 Abbott, *The Cambridge Introduction to Narrative*, pp. 46–9.
26 The most thorough introduction to 'Attar and his works is Helmut Ritter's *Das Meer der Seele* (1955). This magisterial work is now available in English translation as Helmut Ritter, *The Ocean of the Soul: Men, the World, and God in the Stories of Farid al-Din 'Attar*, trans. John O'Kane and Bernd Radtke (Leiden and Boston: Brill, 2013).

this placement best illustrates the development of the Rabi'a narrative from master narrative to myth.

In order to become a master narrative, a narrative must pass two tests of validity or rationality. The first test of validity is of *narrative probability*, or whether the narrative is coherent and makes sense.[27] According to the communications theorist Walter R. Fisher, the information in a master narrative must be presented in a systematic way: "The stories must relate to one another in consistent ways, and carry a common theme [or related themes]. They must form a structure where one story reinforces, elaborates, or combines with another so that the whole is greater than the sum of the parts."[28] The second test of validity is of *narrative fidelity*, or whether the master narrative relates to the world as the audience understands it. Master narratives make sense out of the situations they relate by establishing archetypal characters, relationships, and standard actions that the audience can understand.[29] The tropes of the Rabi'a master narrative serve all of these functions.

However, passing the tests of narrative validity or rationality does not necessarily mean that the master narrative is true. It only has to seem true for audiences to accept it. The use of narrative tropes helps a master narrative pass these tests by enabling the audience to recognize familiar patterns in the way that characters and their actions relate to each other. This allows the audience to derive a common meaning for the master narrative. Major narrative tropes in the myth of Rabi'a al-'Adawiyya such as Rabi'a the Teacher, Rabi'a the Ascetic, Rabi'a the Lover, and Rabi'a the Sufi are also master narratives because each is made up of its own set of archetypal characters, relationships, and actions. Furthermore, each on its own can pass the tests of narrative probability and narrative fidelity. The narrative elements of these tropes are also related to elements in other tropes, such that it is possible to plot these relationships in a diagram. In this way, the narratives of the Rabi'a myth form a web or matrix of tropes or narrative types that make up the master narrative of Rabi'a al-'Adawiyya as a historical personage. In the chapters of

---

27   Fisher, *Human Communication as Narration* in Halverson, Goodall, and Corman, *Master Narratives of Islamic Extremism*, p. 24.
28   Ibid. Michael Cooperson has recently investigated narrative probability in Arabic biographies that were written around the same time that Rabi'a al-'Adawiyya first appears in literary sources. See idem, "Probability, Plausibility, and Spiritual Communication in Classical Arabic Biography," in Philip F. Kennedy (ed.), *On Fiction and Adab in Medieval Arabic Literature* (Weisbaden: Harrassowitz, 2005), pp. 69–84.
29   Fisher, *Human Communication as Narration*, in Halverson, Goodall, and Corman *Master Narratives of Islamist Extremism*, p. 24.

this book I will show how the elements of this matrix fit together and how the medieval narratives of Rabiʿa al-ʿAdawiyya became transformed into a myth that continues to inspire people today. Because the narrative elements of her story continue to be relevant for audiences across the centuries, one can refer to Rabiʿa figuratively as the Islamic version of the "Woman Who Never Dies."

II. KEY PREMODERN SOURCES AND MODERN WORKS ON RABIʿA AL-ʿADAWIYYA

The narratives of Rabiʿa al-ʿAdawiyya are too numerous to count. This situation has become even more problematical since the creation of the Internet. A Google search of the name "Rabiʿa al-ʿAdawiyya" comes up with nearly 29,000 entries. The name "Rabiʿa al-Basri" yields about 179,000 entries. The name "Rabiʿa" yields over 24 million entries because girls and women who are currently named Rabiʿa are also included. The trouble with this mass of information is that very little of it is useful. For the most part, the stories, quotations and anecdotes about Rabiʿa al-ʿAdawiyya recycle information contained in a handful of key narratives that span a 1200-year period from the mid-ninth century CE to the present. Because it is impossible to cover all of the works—even the premodern ones—that mention Rabiʿa al-ʿAdawiyya, I concentrate in this book on the medieval and modern narratives that were most influential in creating her myth.

For a figure about whom there seems to be so much information, it comes as a surprise to discover that there is no source on the life of Rabiʿa al-ʿAdawiyya from her own time. The first version of Rabiʿa's *vita* or life story was not written until 400 years after the approximate date of her death. Works that provide even a small amount of credible historical information on her are very rare. Only a handful of sources mention her in the century after her death. Since some of these sources are currently missing, information from them must be obtained by searching later sources for quotations and citations from these earlier works. The earliest extant mention of Rabiʿa al-ʿAdawiyya that I have been able to find is a statement attributed to her in the doctrinal work *al-Qasd wa-l-rujuʿ ila Allah* (*God as the Goal and the Return*), by the Sufi al-Harith ibn Asad al-Muhasibi of Baghdad (d. 857 CE). This reference to Rabiʿa is identified for the first time in this book. Another early Sufi work that contained information on Rabiʿa was *Kitab al-ruhban* (*The Book of Monks*), a work on ascetics by Muhammad ibn al-Husayn al-Burjulani of Baghdad (d. 852 CE). Several citations of Rabi'a from this work can be identified in later sources. Burjulani's citations of Rabi'a may actually be older than Muhasibi's; however, we cannot be certain of their date because the work itself has been lost. These citations by Muhasibi and Burjulani are the earliest references to Rabi'a in Sufi literature.

The earliest non-Sufi references to Rabi'a are in the works of two major literary figures of Abbasid-era Baghdad. The first of these authors is Abu 'Uthman al-Jahiz (d. 868 CE), a famous essayist and rhetorician who mentions Rabi'a in two works, *Kitab al-hayawan* (*The Book of Animals*) and *Kitab al-bayan wa-l-tabyin* (*On Demonstrative Proof and Elucidation*). Scholars have known about Jahiz's citations of Rabi'a for many years. However, scholars have not previously identified the references to Rabi'a in another important work from this period. This is *Kitab balaghat al-nisa'* (*Book of the Eloquence of Women*) by Ahmad ibn Abi Tahir Tayfur (d. 893 CE). *Balaghat al-nisa'* is the earliest extant work devoted entirely to women in Arabic literature. Ibn Abi Tahir Tayfur's references to Rabi'a have not been identified because this author does not refer to her as Rabi'a al-'Adawiyya or even as Rabi'a al-Qaysiyya, which is how Jahiz refers to her. Instead, he calls her *Rabi'a al-Musma'iyya*. However, we can be sure that this figure is Rabi'a al-'Adawiyya because some of the quotations that are attributed to her are the same as those attributed to her by Jahiz.

Rabi'a's identity is also an issue in another early work, *Kitab al-mahabba li-llah* (*Book of the Love of God*). This recently discovered work was written by Ibrahim ibn al-Junayd of Baghdad (d. 883–4 CE), who was a student of the Sufi Burjulani.[30] Here Rabi'a is mentioned in three accounts but is only referred to by her first name. However, we can know that this is Rabi'a al-'Adawiyya because one of the accounts is the same as that of Muhasibi. Ibn al-Junayd's references to Rabi'a are important historically for two reasons: first, his book is the earliest extant source on Rabi'a to provide documentation through chains of transmission (Ar. *isnad*); second, her inclusion in this work confirms, along with Muhasibi's citation, that Rabi'a was remembered as an ascetic lover of God in the period after her death.

The situation is similar for the early citations of Rabi'a transmitted by the traditionist Ibn Abi al-Dunya (d. 894 CE). Abu 'Abdullah Muhammad ibn Abi al-Dunya was a teacher of the Abbasid Caliph al-Muktafi' Billah (r. 902–8 CE). He is said to have composed several works on Muslim ascetics

---

30 Although this individual is known as "Ibn al-Junayd" in Sufi works, he was primarily known as "Ibrahim al-Khuttali" in Hadith circles.

and some of his collections of traditions are edited and in print today. Several references to Rabi'a can be found in the collection *Majmu'at rasa'il Ibn Abi al-Dunya* (*The Collected Letters of Ibn Abi al-Dunya*).[31] Like Ibn al-Junayd, Ibn Abi al-Dunya refers to Rabi'a only by her first name but he also provides detailed chains of transmission for his accounts. These can be useful for the historian in tracing oral traditions about Rabi'a from their origins in Basra to Baghdad, where Jahiz, Ibn al-Junayd, Ibn Abi al-Dunya, and Ibn Abi Tahir Tayfur all resided.

What historical information can be ascertained from the earliest sources on Rabi'a? As stated above, there is very little except to confirm that a Muslim woman ascetic and teacher named Rabi'a al-'Adawiyya or Rabi'a al-Qaysiyya (the name *'Adawiyya* refers to her clan and the name *Qaysiyya* refers to her tribe) lived in or around the city of Basra in southern Iraq in the eighth century CE. This is important because otherwise one might conclude that Rabi'a is merely a figure of literature. Even the exact dates of her birth and death are not known. The commonly accepted birth date of 717 CE and death date of 801 CE come from a much later period and the ultimate source of these dates is unclear. Thus, everything about Rabi'a al-'Adawiyya is tentative. However, the earliest sources mentioned above are valuable because of their proximity to her in time and place. Two early authors—Muhasibi and Jahiz—were born in Rabi'a's home city of Basra. Because of this, they were familiar with her reputation. This local reputation is the best empirical evidence we have that Rabi'a actually existed. In addition, Jahiz, Ibn Abi Tahir Tayfur, Ibn Abi al-Dunya, and Ibn al-Junayd are important sources on Rabi'a because they use her as a rhetorical example. These writers all regarded her as a figure of eloquence, although for Jahiz and Ibn Abi Tahir Tayfur, she was not part of their literary and intellectual milieu. They would not have used her in this way if her reputation had not been widely known, much as the reputation of Mother Teresa is widely known today.

In the classic historiographical study *Oral Tradition as History*, Jan Vansina defines oral traditions as "verbal messages which are reported statements from the past beyond the present generation."[32] According to Vansina, in

---

31 Abu 'Abdullah Muhammad ibn 'Ubayd al-Baghdadi, Ibn Abi al-Dunya, *Majmu'at rasa'il Ibn Abi al-Dunya*, ed. 'Abd al-Qadir 'Ata, 5 vols. (Beirut: Mu'assasat al-Kutub al-Thaqafiyya, 1993). I am grateful to my Ph.D. student Jeremy Farrell for making this source known to me.
32 Jan Vansina, *Oral Tradition as History* (London and Nairobi, Kenya: James Curry and Heinemann Kenya, 1985), p. 27; see also, idem, *Oral Tradition: A Study in Historical Methodology*, trans. H.M. Wright (New Brunswick, NJ and London: Aldine Transaction, 2009 reprint of 1965 original).

order to be used as historical evidence, an oral tradition must establish one or more links between the later record of a report (whether transmitted orally or in writing) and the original observation on which the tradition is based. If such a link does not exist, the tradition cannot be used as historical evidence. However, if such a link can be established, the tradition must not be dismissed as unhistorical. In the present context, this means that the oral traditions about Rabiʻa that are supported by chains of transmission, such as those cited by Ibn al-Junayd and Ibn Abi al-Dunya, should be regarded as legitimate historical information because the links between the written record and the original observation were preserved.

In Islamic historical, biographical and prosopographical literature, the links between the written record and oral narratives are often recorded as chains of transmission (Ar. *isnad*, pl. *asanid*, literally, "support"). In the culture of narrative in Islam, the chains of transmission that accompany oral accounts are taken as proofs of the authenticity of the narratives they support.[33] In other words, they are regarded as evidence, much like testimony in a court of law. In historical works, chains of transmission serve a function similar to that of source citations in modern scholarship. Jan Vansina views oral traditions in much the same way. According to him, the modern historian should view oral tradition "as a series of successive historical documents all lost except for the last one and usually interpreted by every link in the chain of transmission. It is therefore evidence at second, third, or nth remove, but it is still evidence unless it be shown that a message does not rely on a first statement made by an observer."[34] The same can be said of the traditions of Rabiʻa cited with *isnads* by Ibn al-Junayd and Ibn Abi al-Dunya. Although we must not make the mistake of treating oral traditions as if their narrative contents are fixed as in written documents, they can still provide important evidence of past events, people and ideas. For this reason, it is legitimate to take the citations and anecdotes of Rabiʻa in the early sources as circumstantial evidence of her existence.

However, to conclude that Rabiʻa probably existed does not make the voice that speaks through these early traditions entirely hers. She wrote no books and no account of her was written during her lifetime. Although certain poems have been attributed to her, these attributions are questionable at best.

---

33 Gregor Schoeler uses the term "aural" (i.e., heard) to refer to the interface between oral and written traditions in early Islamic sources. See Gregor Schoeler, *The Written and the Oral in Early Islam*, ed. James E. Montgomery, trans. Uwe Vagelpohl (London: Routledge, 2006).

34 Vansina, *Oral Tradition as History*, p. 29.

To date, no written body of work has been linked conclusively to Rabi'a al-'Adawiyya. In addition, narrative tropes can be found in some of the sources mentioned above. For example, I discuss in Chapter 1 how Jahiz used Rabi'a to exemplify the narrative trope of the "Person of *Bayan*." This is a trope from the Abbasid era that combined the concepts of eloquence and wisdom and which illustrated for Jahiz the virtue of practical reason. Another important narrative trope was "Rabi'a the Poet." I discuss in Chapter 3 how Ibn Abi al-Dunya might have been an early source for this trope.

The 200 years between the late ninth century CE and the beginning of the twelfth century CE comprise the period in which the most important Sufi tropes of Rabi'a al-'Adawiyya were developed. The process of turning the Sufi narratives of Rabi'a into tropes began in earnest in the tenth century CE. By this time the geographical location of the Sufis who related the Rabi'a narratives had expanded to include not only her homeland of Iraq but also Syria and Khorasan, a region that included eastern Iran and much of Central Asia. It was in Iraq, Syria and Khorasan that the tropes of Rabi'a the Teacher, Rabi'a the Ascetic, Rabi'a the Lover, and Rabi'a the Sufi were developed. Two Sufi writers were particularly important to this process.

The first of these Sufi writers was Abu Talib al-Makki (d. 996 CE), who uses the narrative trope of Rabi'a the Lover in his doctrinal work *Qut al-qulub* (*The Nourishment of Hearts*). Although Makki was born in Iran and lived in Baghdad, he spent a considerable amount of time in Rabi'a's home city of Basra.[35] Makki uses Rabi'a as a character type to exemplify his mystical theology of Love. Although statements on the love of God attributed to Rabi'a also appeared in the works of earlier Sufis such as Muhasibi and Ibn al-Junayd, the prominence that Makki gives to her in his book allows us to identify him as the creator of the trope of Rabi'a the Lover. For Makki, the figure of Rabi'a symbolized the highest degree of Love mysticism. I discuss in Chapter 3 how Makki's use of this character type was similar to Plato's use of the priestess Diotima of Mantinea in *The Symposium*. In Plato's work, Diotima initiates Socrates into the mysteries of Love, just as Rabi'a is used by Makki to initiate his readers into the Sufi theology of Love.

The second Sufi to use Rabi'a as a paradigmatic character type was Abu 'Abd al-Rahman al-Sulami (d. 1021 CE), who lived in the eastern Iranian city of Nishapur. Sulami was one of the greatest systematizers of Sufi doctrine.

---

35 On the life of Abu Talib al-Makki, see Atif Khalil, "Abu Talib al-Makki and *The Nourishment of Hearts* (*Qut al-Qulub*) in the Context of Early Sufism," *The Muslim World*, 102 (2), 2011, pp. 335–56.

He depicts Rabi'a al-'Adawiyya as the quintessential Sufi woman in his book *Dhikr al-niswa al-muta'abbidat al-sufiyyat* (*Memorial of Female Sufi Devotees*). This is the first extant Sufi work devoted entirely to women. For Sulami, the figure of Rabi'a symbolized the concept of *ta'abbud* (literally, "making oneself into a slave [of God]"), which for him was the key characteristic of Sufi women's spirituality. Sulami also used Rabi'a to symbolize the theology of servitude, which he viewed as the most important contribution of Sufi women to Sufism in general.[36]

Sulami's Book of Sufi Women is also important historiographically because like his predecessors Ibn al-Junayd and Ibn Abi al-Dunya, he cites chains of transmission for his accounts about Rabi'a. Some of the names in these chains of transmission are authors of written works that are now lost but would have been consulted by Sulami. In addition to Muhammad ibn al-Husayn al-Burjulani (mentioned above), he also cites other early authors of prosopographical works.[37] These include Abu Sa'id ibn al-A'rabi of Basra and Mecca (d. 952–3 CE), an important early Sufi who wrote a work titled *Tabaqat al-nussak* (*Generations of the Ascetic Ritualists*), and Ja'far al-Khuldi of Baghdad (d. 959 CE), a Sufi and traditionist who wrote a work titled *Hikayat al-awliya'* (*Stories of the Saints*) or *Hikayat al-masha'ikh* (*Stories of the Spiritual Masters*).

The most important step in the transformation of the Rabi'a narratives into a Sufi master narrative was taken around the beginning of the thirteenth century CE. Before this time no work that mentioned Rabi'a had established itself as the definitive model for subsequent narratives. Certain Sufi works, such as Makki's *Qut al-qulub* and Sulami's Book of Sufi Women, had created important narrative tropes. In addition, there is some evidence that short non-Sufi works devoted to Rabi'a al-'Adawiyya were also being written, which took material from Ibn Abi al-Dunya and other sources. However, since Rabi'a had already become recognized as an important figure in Islam, the lack of a *vita* for her hagiography is surprising.

All of this changed with the publication of Farid al-Din al-'Attar's *Tadhkirat al-awliya'* (*Memorial of the Saints*) in the first quarter of the thirteenth century. This was the most important single work for the development of the Rabi'a myth. The *vita* that 'Attar outlines in his chapter on Rabi'a al-'Adawiyya has become the source text for all subsequent versions of Rabi'a's life story. Because this *vita* has gained universal acceptance, no analysis of the Rabi'a

---

36 See Sulami, *Early Sufi Women*, pp. 54–60.
37 For a more detailed discussion of these authors and their works, see ibid., pp. 48–53.

myth is sufficient without discussing it in detail. 'Attar did more than just provide a new interpretation of the Rabi'a master narrative. Most if not all of the details of Rabi'a's life mentioned in *Tadhkirat al-awliya'* appear to have been created out of whole cloth. No tradition recounting the events that 'Attar describes can be found in any previous work known today. For this reason, his *vita* of Rabi'a must be viewed primarily as a work of fiction, whose message lies in its figurative meaning, not in its supposed "facts." In Chapter 5, I show how 'Attar employed the literary technique of verisimilitude to create a sense of historical reality in his *vita* of Rabi'a. In addition, I show how he opened the way for the popularization of the Rabi'a myth and enabled an icon for Sufis to become an icon for all Muslims. Because of the influence of 'Attar's work, no further major changes to the Rabi'a master narrative would be made until the twentieth century.

The adaptations to the Rabi'a narrative that were made in the twentieth century were influenced by the rise of historicism and the historical method. In the second half of this century, other tropes and narrative adaptations were introduced through the influence of existentialist philosophy and the dramatic requirements of entertainment media. The first modern historical works on Rabi'a also appeared in Europe and the Arab world at this time. Several of these works will be mentioned in the chapters below. However, two historical works stand out in particular because of their influence on subsequent versions of the Rabi'a master narrative. These are Margaret Smith's *Rabi'a the Mystic*, which was first published in 1928, and 'Abd al-Rahman Badawi's *Shahidat al-'ishq al-ilahi* (*The Martyr of Divine Love*), which was first published in 1948.

In terms of her importance to the development of the Rabi'a myth, the English historian Margaret Smith (1884–1970) has been as influential for the English-language tradition of works on Rabi'a as 'Attar has been for the Sufi tradition. In fact, one could say with only slight exaggeration that Margaret Smith was the "English 'Attar." Smith wrote the first detailed historical study of Rabi'a al-'Adawiyya. This book, *Rabi'a the Mystic A.D. 717–801 and Her Fellow Saints in Islam, Being the Life and Teachings of Rabi'a al-'Adawiyya al-Qaysiyya of Basra, Sufi Saint ca. A.H. 99–185, A.D. 717–801, Together with Some Account of the Place of Women in Islam*, has become the most widely read work on Rabi'a in English or any other European language.[38] In fact, if

---

38 Margaret Smith, *Rabi'a the Mystic A.D. 717–801 and Her Fellow Saints in Islam, Being the Life and Teachings of Rabi'a al-'Adawiyya al-Qaysiyya of Basra, Sufi Saint ca. A.H. 99–185, A.D. 717–801, Together with Some Account of the Place of Women in Islam*

translations of this work are included it may be the most widely read book on Rabi'a in any language.

Because Smith's book has influenced the scholarship on Rabi'a in so many ways, I could not confine my discussion of it to a single chapter. Instead, I refer to her contributions in various places throughout this work. In many ways, the present study of Rabi'a al-'Adawiyya is built on the foundations of Smith's pioneering scholarship. In other ways, however, it goes beyond her scholarship. One of the chief differences between my book and Smith's is in its initial premise. Whereas Smith was concerned with discovering the "real" or historical Rabi'a, I dispute the notion that the "real" Rabi'a could ever be represented in a way that corresponds to the ideals of conventional historiography. For this reason, I am more concerned with the *figural* Rabi'a— the Rabi'a of narrative and myth. Although in some chapters I discuss the religious, social and intellectual environments that the "real" Rabi'a might have lived in, the most I could accomplish with this method was to fill in the social and historical background for the tropes of Rabi'a the Teacher, Rabi'a the Ascetic, and Rabi'a the Sufi. There is no way to write a conventional biography of Rabi'a al-'Adawiyya with the source materials that currently exist. Therefore, as explained above, the only satisfactory way to approach her historiographically is to write the history of how she has been represented in the master narratives and tropes that comprise her myth.

When Margaret Smith wrote *Rabi'a the Mystic*, many of the premodern Islamic sources that are available today were not available to her. For example, although she had seen references to Sulami's Book of Sufi Women, the work itself had not been discovered. Without the discovery of Sulami's manuscript and the works of Ibn al-Junayd and Ibn Abi al-Dunya mentioned above, many of the early sources on Rabi'a based on oral tradition would still be lost. Because these works are now coming to light, the twenty-first-century scholar is in a position to make insights about Rabi'a and the Rabi'a narratives that Smith was not able to make in her time. In addition, Smith lived in an era when the field of Islamic Studies was dominated by philological scholarship and positivistic historiography. Today's scholars of Islam are able to draw from a greater variety of historiographical approaches.

(Cambridge, UK: Cambridge University Press, 1928). A reproduction of this work with the original title was published by The Rainbow Bridge in 1977. The most widely available edition today is Margaret Smith, *Rabi'a: the Life and Work of Rabi'a and Other Women Mystics in Islam* (Oxford, UK: Oneworld Publications, 1994). Page references to Smith's work in the pages below will cite both of these editions and will be referred to as *Rabi'a* (Oneworld) and *Rabi'a* (Rainbow Bridge).

For modern Arabic-speaking readers, the most influential historical work on Rabi'a has been 'Abd al-Rahman Badawi's *Shahidat al-'ishq al-ilahi, Rabi'a al-'Adawiyya* (*Rabi'a al-'Adawiyya the Martyr of Divine Love*).[39] This work is so important for contemporary Arabic studies of Rabi'a that if Margaret Smith can be called the "English 'Attar," then Badawi can be called the "Arab 'Attar." 'Abd al-Rahman Badawi (1917–2002) enjoys a high reputation in Western academia as a scholar of Islamic philosophy. However, in the Arab world he is also known as an important existentialist philosopher. Although Badawi's monograph on Rabi'a was written as a scholarly work, in many ways it has more in common with 'Attar's quasi-novelistic attempt to construct the Rabi'a myth than with empirical historical studies. Because of Badawi's frequent use of narrative adaptation and creative license, some Arab historians do not even list *Martyr of Divine Love* as part of his scholarly oeuvre.

Badawi's book on Rabi'a was one of the main inspirations for the 1963 Egyptian movie *Rabi'a al-'Adawiyya*. This well-known and widely popular film imaginatively chronicles Rabi'a's personal struggles, based on the existentialist model of Rabi'a's life as interpreted by Badawi. Badawi's book also inspired the Lebanese-Syrian author Widad El Sakkakini (1913–91) to write *al-'Ashiqa al-mutasawwifa* (*The Sufi Lover*), a novelistic biography of Rabi'a that was first published in 1955.[40] This work, which draws on the existentialist feminism of Simone de Beauvoir (1908–86), portrays Rabi'a as a heroine of feminist self-expression.

III. WHAT IS A MYTH?

The current study, *Rabi'a from Narrative to Myth*, begins with an early Muslim woman ascetic of Basra as a figure of narrative and ends with the Muslim saint Rabi'a al-'Adawiyya as a figure of myth. What does it mean to say that Rabi'a is a figure of myth? What definition of myth do I use in this book? Surprisingly, there is little consensus in current scholarship on what the term, "myth," means. To use a pun coined by the folklorist Alan Dundes, it is easy to fall victim to "myth-taken identity."[41] On one side are folklorists, such as

---

39   'Abd al-Rahman Badawi, *Shahidat al-'ishq al-ilahi Rabi'a al-'Adawiyya* (Kuwait: Wakkalat al-Matbu'at, 1978 reprint of 1948 first edition).
40   Widad al-Sakkakini, *al-'Ashiqa al-mutasawwifa, Rabi'a al-'Adawiyya* (Damascus: Dar Tlas li-l-dirasat wa-l-tarjama wa-l-nashr, 1989 reprint of the 1955 Cairo first edition).
41   Alan Dundes, *Sacred Narrative: Readings in the Theory of Myth* (Berkeley, Los Angeles, and London: University of California Press, 1984), p. ix.

Dundes himself, who advocate a very narrow definition of myth. They believe that this is the most scientifically valid approach to the subject. According to Dundes, "A myth is a sacred narrative explaining how the world and man came to be in their present form."[42] The term, "sacred narrative," means for Dundes that the ultimate meaning of a myth is religious. This is different from the folktale, for example, whose meaning is secular. For Dundes, a myth must also be about ultimate origins. Although he argues that a myth's story of origins should be taken as "true," this is because the myth serves a religious function, not because its narrative is empirically true. Dundes' definition of myth is based on a functional notion of truth: a myth is "true" because it is a story that serves a religious function. By contrast, a folktale is "fictional" because it has no such higher function: it is only a story.

Following a tradition in folklore studies that goes back to the Brothers Grimm, Dundes draws a distinction between three types of folk narratives: myths, legends and folktales. These three types correspond to the German terms *Mythen*, *Sagen* and *Märchen*, and the French terms *mythes*, *traditions populaires* and *contes populaires*.[43] Dundes regards these types of narrative as universal categories because similar types can be found in many different cultures. The differences among them depend on their content rather than on their form. Myths are sacred or religious stories that talk about origins; folktales are "once-upon-a-time" stories and thus are fictional; legends are in-between.[44] Legends may be either sacred or secular. Chronologically, their narratives take place after the time of origins but before the present time. Unlike myths, which are about origins, legends involve subjects that are relevant to present-day concerns. However, they do not have the truth-value of myths. For Dundes, stories of saints like Rabi'a al-'Adawiyya are legends, as are narrative tropes based on stereotypical figures, such as the tropes of the Flying Dutchman or the Wandering Jew. Thus, he would not agree with the contention made in this book that the Rabi'a narratives constitute a myth. For him, the Rabi'a narratives would be legends and the narrative tropes that they employ would be stories-within-a-story—rhetorical devices similar to those found in novels, short stories, or other types of fictional narrative. For Dundes, stories of saints are similar to the *Sagen* that were used as legendary

---

42   Ibid., p. 1.
43   See William Bascom, "The Forms of Folklore: Prose Narratives," in Dundes, *Sacred Narrative*, p. 25.
44   Ibid., pp. 5–6.

source materials by the German composer Richard Wagner (1813–83) for his operas.

G.S. Kirk, a scholar of myth from the field of Classics, rejects the definition of myth used by Dundes and other folklorists as too narrow: "[They] tend to exclude *prima facie* blocs of mythological material for no particular reason. Moreover, they tell us little about the nature of myths themselves; they simply isolate, not very accurately, one characteristic."[45] Kirk proposes a more inclusive definition of myth that is more relevant to the Rabiʿa narratives. For him, myths are "dramatically constructed tales" that are passed down from antiquity and incorporated in tradition.[46] Although they might contain supernatural elements, they are not necessarily religious or sacred. Even secular stories can be myths. For Kirk, the value of myths is to be found in their popular appeal and their openness to multiple forms of interpretation.

> [A myth's] narrative core or plot must be such as to allow different emphases and interpretations according to different customs, needs, and preoccupations. In one sense, a myth is always changing; in another its narrative structure persists. Many traditional oral tales... are what we term folktales or *Märchen*. [However,] it is sensible not to deny these the general title of myths, since their themes interact with those of more imaginative and pregnant types.[47]

Most of the premodern accounts of Rabiʿa discussed in this book correspond to Kirk's definition of myth. The same might also be said of Farid al-Din al-ʿAttar's *vita* of Rabiʿa al-ʿAdawiyya—but only if one accepts ʿAttar's contention that the stories he relates are based on actual traditions. For Kirk, unlike Dundes, the form or structure of a mythical narrative is just as important, if not more important, than its contents. He states, "The continuing factor... that receives the different qualities [of myth], is the narrative structure itself."[48]

Scholars of Religious Studies tend to agree with Kirk that the definition of myth is related to the form and structure of narrative. For example, Theodore H. Gaster defines myth as "any presentation of the actual in terms

---

45 G.S. Kirk, "On Defining Myths," in Dundes, *Sacred Narrative*, p. 55 (reprinted from *Phronesis: A Journal for Ancient Philosophy*, suppl. Vol. 1, 1973, pp. 61–9.)
46 Ibid., p. 56.
47 Ibid., pp. 57–8.
48 Ibid., p. 58.

of the ideal."⁴⁹ This definition recalls Mircea Eliade's statement that in myths, "the essential precedes existence." Because Eliade's writings on myth are so numerous and because he modified his views so often, it would take too much space to discuss them in detail here. At times, his view of myth is similar to that of Dundes.⁵⁰ However, at other times he seems to disagree with Dundes and support the idea that hagiographical narratives can be considered myths. For example, in *The Myth of the Eternal Return*, he states that the repetition of paradigmatic or archetypal acts (as in hagiographical accounts) is a major hallmark of myth.⁵¹ He argues that this is a key characteristic of the "mythicization of historical personages." To illustrate this concept, Eliade cites the example of the Serbian folk hero Marko Kraljević: "His historical existence is unquestionable, and we even know the date of his death (1394). But no sooner is Marko's historical personality received into the popular memory than it is abolished and his biography is reconstructed in accordance with the norms of myth."⁵² One could say much the same about the story of Rabiʿa al-ʿAdawiyya in the *vita* composed by ʿAttar. Circumstantial evidence indicates that she actually existed and her approximate lifespan is known. However, her biography as constructed by ʿAttar is clearly more mythical than historical.

For Eliade, the "mythicization of historical personages" is based on the trope of the folk hero. In Chapter 5, I discuss how ʿAttar's depiction of Rabiʿa was drawn in part from mythical images of the Virgin Mary and the Prophet Muhammad's wife ʿAʾisha. Although some may debate whether these female figures should be called "heroes," I argue that as paradigmatic female figures of Islamic scripture and history, the Virgin Mary and ʿAʾisha (along with the Prophet's daughter Fatima) can indeed be seen as Islamic folk heroes. In Muslim folklore, Rabiʿa al-ʿAdawiyya is often included as the fourth of these

---

49   Theodore H. Gaster, "Myth and Story," in Dundes, *Sacred Narrative*, p. 112; reprinted from *Numen*, 1, 1954, pp. 184–212.
50   See, for example, "Myth narrates a sacred history; it relates an event that took place in primordial Time, the fabled Time of the 'beginnings.' In other words, myth tells how, through the deeds of Supernatural Beings, a reality came into existence, be it the whole of reality, the Cosmos, or only a fragment of reality—an island, a species of plant, a particular kind of human behavior, and institution. Myth, then, is always an account of a 'creation': it relates how something was produced, began to *be*. Myth tells of that which *really* happened, which manifested itself completely. The actors in myths are Supernatural Beings." Eliade, *Myth and Reality*, pp. 5–6.
51   Mircea Eliade, *The Myth of the Eternal Return or, Cosmos and History*, trans. Willard R. Trask (Princeton, NJ: Princeton University Press, 1974 reprint of 1954 first edition), pp. 34–6.
52   Ibid., pp. 39–40.

paradigmatic women. Symbolically, it is significant that the name *Rabi'a*, means "fourth" in Arabic. Whether by chance or by design, Rabi'a's name is used to signify her status as the fourth of the paradigmatic female folk heroes of Islam. Given this coincidence, the following statement by Eliade on the relationship between oral tradition, myth and the hero is relevant to the story of Rabi'a from narrative to myth:

> Myth is the last—not the first—stage in the development of a hero... the recollection of a historical event or a real personage survives in popular memory for two or three centuries at the utmost. This is because popular memory finds difficulty in retaining individual events and real figures. The structures by means of which [myth] functions are different: categories instead of events, archetypes instead of historical personages. The historical personage is assimilated to this mythical model (hero, etc.), while the event is identified with the category of mythical actions... If certain epic poems preserve what is called "historical truth," this truth almost never has to do with definite persons and events, but with institutions, customs, landscapes.[53]

To further appreciate the relevance of Eliade's insights on myths to the Rabi'a myth, one need only recall that the development of major narrative tropes about her did not begin until two centuries after her death and that her *vita* was not composed until four centuries after her death. These facts lend support to Eliade's comments about the limited duration of historical memory. For Eliade, literary tropes and life stories do not become major parts of the repertoire of myth until the memory of oral tradition begins to fade away. Old traditions do not die or just disappear; instead, they are transformed into myths. Although Rabi'a al-'Adawiyya was not an epic hero like the Slavic warrior-heroes discussed by Eliade, she clearly provides an example of what he calls "the mythicization of historical personages."

Eliade's theory of myth is also relevant to the Rabi'a narratives when he talks about the reception of mythical stories by their audiences. In *Myth and Reality* (1963) he states:

> What is involved is not a commemoration of mythical events but a reiteration of them. The protagonists of the myth are made present; one becomes their contemporary. This also implies that one is no

---

53 Ibid., p. 43.

longer living in chronological time, but in the primordial Time, the time when the event *first took place*. This is why we can use the term the "strong time" of myth; it is the prodigious, "sacred" time when something *new*, *strong*, and *significant* was manifested.⁵⁴

The term, "reiteration," that Eliade uses in this passage recalls the narrative techniques of repetition, adaptation, appropriation and imitation that can be observed throughout the history of the Rabi'a narratives. The fact that Rabi'a lived in the "strong time" of early Islam was also significant for the development of her myth. In Muslim historical memory, Rabi'a is considered one of *al-Salaf al-Salih*, the "Righteous Predecessors" of early Islamic tradition, who are regarded as spiritual exemplars for later Muslims to follow. For Sunni Muslims, the generation of *al-Salaf al-Salih* is an exemplary generation, a notion that is reflected in the modern term, "Salafi Islam." For this reason, one is just as likely to hear someone speak about Rabi'a al-'Adawiyya in a Wahhabi mosque in Saudi Arabia as in a Sufi *zawiya* in Morocco. For Salafi Muslims, Rabi'a's status as one of *al-Salaf al-Salih* absolves her of the alleged doctrinal errors of the Sufis, who also include her as one of their own.⁵⁵

Although Eliade occasionally discusses European saints and Indian yogis in his writings on myth, to my knowledge he does not discuss Rabi'a al-'Adawiyya or any other Muslim figure. Instead of "tropes," he uses the term "clichés."⁵⁶ And when he discusses history, it is not in the way that history is conceived in this book. Instead, he contrasts empirical history and historicism negatively with so-called primordial worldviews. However, his willingness to consider the legends of heroes as myths points the way to a broader view of myth that is useful for the present study. In accord with this approach, I will take as a theoretical starting point for my view of myth the broad and inclusive definition proposed by Robert A. Segal, a prominent American scholar of

---

54 Eliade, *Myth and Reality*, p. 19; the italics are Eliade's.
55 In the 1990s, I once heard a Friday sermon on Rabi'a's teachings at a Saudi-sponsored mosque in Washington, DC. The Imam who gave the sermon was appointed by the Saudi government.
56 See, for example, Eliade, *Myth and Reality*, p. 117, where he speaks of Hindu narrative tropes or "clichés" that make the philosophical concept of the self more intelligible to uneducated audiences.

myth who is even cited approvingly by Alan Dundes.[57] Segal (2004) defines myth according to the following four characteristics:[58]

1. *A myth is a story about something significant.* Segal does not specify what the contents of a myth must be about because rigid, content-based definitions are too limiting. For example, if myth were only about creation as Dundes proposes, then most of the stories in the Bible apart from the Book of Genesis could not be counted as myths. In order to avoid such absurdities, says Segal, it is best to have a broad definition of myth. This notion of a broad definition also applies to the time of myths: a mythical story may take place in the past, the present, or even in the future. In addition, myths may include both religious beliefs and secular credos, such as the American Horatio Alger trope. Segal's term, "credo," is roughly equivalent to the "master plots" or "narrative tropes" discussed above.
2. *The main figures of myths are personalities, whether divine, human, or animal.* For Segal, mythical personalities may be either the agents or the objects of actions. If only divine agents were the protagonists of myths, then the stories of many characters in the Bible (such as Ruth or Rebecca) would be excluded from the category of myths. Such a narrow definition of myth would also exclude much of the Qur'an, since God is not always a direct agent in Qur'anic narratives.
3. *The function of a myth is weighty: the myth accomplishes something significant for its adherents.* Segal once again leaves this element of his definition open-ended on purpose. He refuses to specify what such accomplishments must entail in order to include as many types of significance and accomplishment as possible.
4. *To qualify as a myth, a story—which may convey a conviction—must be held tenaciously by its adherents.* In this part of his definition of myth Segal avoids the question of whether a myth is true or false. For Segal, it is irrelevant to the concept of myth whether a narrative is empirically true or advocates a clearly erroneous

---

[57] Robert A. Segal, *Myth: A Very Short Introduction* (Oxford, UK: Oxford University Press, 2004). On the back cover, Dundes endorses this work as "a concise, elegant, erudite overview of the major nineteenth and twentieth century theories of myth."
[58] Segal's definition of myth is summarized in ibid., pp. 4–6.

conviction, such as the belief that Elvis Presley is still alive. What is important for a myth is that it is tenaciously believed, that it says something significant about a personality, and that it is meaningful in some way for its adherents.

If the reader were to object that according to Segal's definition of myth, a wide variety of narrative forms could be called myths, this is precisely the point that he is trying to make. According to Segal, any definition of myth that aspires to universality must be as inclusive as possible. To be inclusive, this definition must also be minimalist rather than maximalist in its stipulations. Otherwise, narrative forms that are unique only to certain cultures might be excluded arbitrarily. Segal arrived at his minimalist definition of myth after studying myths cross-culturally for many years. If it seems less rigorous than other definitions, it is because experience has shown him that theoretically rigorous definitions of myth are too exclusive and that truly comprehensive definitions demand flexibility. The value of Segal's definition of myth as a starting point for the present work is that it allows me to discuss a wide variety of aphorisms, dicta, poems and stories associated with Rabi'a al-'Adawiyya as parts of a single mythmaking process.

IV. THE PLAN OF THIS WORK

Rabi'a From Narrative to Myth: The Many Faces of Islam's Most Famous Woman Saint combines the methodologies of history, narrative theory, and Islamic Studies. The aim of the book is to trace the representation of the woman ascetic and teacher from Basra known as Rabi'a al-'Adawiyya (ca. 717–801 CE) from narrative to master narrative and myth by examining in detail the most important tropes that have come to define her identity. Four main narrative tropes define Rabi'a al-'Adawiyya. These are Rabi'a the Teacher, Rabi'a the Ascetic, Rabi'a the Lover, and Rabi'a the Sufi. However, Rabi'a al-'Adawiyya is more to Muslims than just a myth; she is also revered as a saint. For this reason, another trope must be added to the list—Rabi'a the Icon. As an iconic figure, Rabi'a al-'Adawiyya is more of a literary icon than a visual icon because until the modern era her image was portrayed primarily through oral narratives and the written word. However, we can still consider her an icon because the name, "Rabi'a," evokes multiple meanings in the Muslim imaginary in the same way that an Orthodox religious icon evokes multiple meanings through a painted image. In the largely aniconic culture of Islam, Rabi'a al-'Adawiyya's image has mostly been "painted" with words. However, recently the notion of her as an icon has become more appropriate because her image is now represented pictorially through the visual media of paintings, motion pictures and television series.

Although this book is about the narrative depiction of Rabi'a, some chapters are more "historical" than others. In these "historical" chapters, I attempt to describe the social, cultural and intellectual milieus in which the "real" Rabi'a al-'Adawiyya might have lived in eighth-century CE Basra. This historically imagined figure is the woman ascetic on which the Rabi'a narratives were based. Although there is some evidence that she actually existed, her form remains hidden in the mists of time. Realizing that the "real" Rabi'a cannot be identified through conventional historiographical methods, I instead approach her indirectly—by investigating the types of spiritual and moral training, asceticism, and devotional practices that were current in her time. I use this information to shed indirect light on the woman who provided the inspiration for the subsequent myth of Rabi'a al-'Adawiyya. In figurative terms, this approach is similar to deciphering a palimpsest, in which one tries to read the faint traces of an earlier narrative on pages that were reused for a later work.[59] The chapters in which I attempt this approach are the closest that this book comes to conventional historiography.

Chapter 1, "Rabi'a the Teacher," is the first of these "historical" chapters. In it I discuss the earliest sources of information on the person identified by the mid-ninth century CE as "Rabi'a al-'Adawiyya" or "Rabi'a al-Qaysiyya." These sources recall her as a moral exemplar and teacher. In investigating the narrative trope of Rabi'a the Teacher, I focus in particular on Abu 'Uthman al-Jahiz's characterization of Rabi'a as a "person of *bayan*" and explore what this description meant in late Umayyad and early Abbasid Iraq. I also discuss the aphoristic teaching style attributed to Rabi'a and show how this pedagogical method was based on long-established traditions in the Mediterranean world of classical and late antiquity.

Chapter 2, "Rabi'a the Ascetic," is the second "historical" chapter of this book. In it I discuss Rabi'a al-'Adawiyya's reputation as a major figure

---

59   See Gérard Genette, *Palimpsests: Literature in the Second Degree*, trans. Channa Newman and Claude Doubinsky (Omaha: University of Nebraska Press, 1997). The metaphor of the palimpsest has also been used for the study of early Islamic literary culture by the Moroccan scholar Abdelfattah Kilito. See "Voice and Palimpsest," in idem, *The Author and His Doubles: Essays on Classical Arabic Culture*, trans. Michael Cooperson (Syracuse, NY: Syracuse University Press, 2001), pp. 91–9.

of early Islamic asceticism and assess the historical evidence for Muslim women's asceticism in eighth-century Basra and its environs. As part of this discussion, I offer new suggestions for how to think about early Islamic asceticism, drawing on recent studies of asceticism in late antiquity, early Christianity, and early rabbinic Judaism. I introduce three key concepts, drawn from descriptions of ascetic practices in the Umayyad and Abbasid periods. These are *instrumental asceticism*, in which ascetic renunciation is directed toward specific goals; *reactionary asceticism*, which arose as a form of countercultural protest against the unequal distribution of wealth in Abbasid society; and *essential asceticism*, in which the ascetic worldview is seen as integral to the spiritual life in general. I argue that essential asceticism is related doctrinally to the Love mysticism for which Rabi'a would become famous.

Chapter 3, "Rabi'a the Lover," is the first of the "literary" chapters of this book. Although every chapter discusses both history and literature, with the trope of Rabi'a the Lover it is impossible to separate the "real" Rabi'a in a meaningful way from her literary persona. In this chapter, I argue that both Rabi'a's Love mysticism and her alleged celibacy are doctrinally related to her essential asceticism. In early sources she is portrayed as practicing *vocational celibacy*, in which marriage and family life are viewed as impediments to the ascetic's true vocation, which is devotion to God. As noted earlier, the literary trope of Rabi'a the Lover appears to have been created by the Sufi Abu Talib al-Makki. I show through an analysis of Makki's discourse on love in the book *Qut al-qulub* that his portrayal of Rabi'a closely resembles Plato's portrayal of Diotima of Mantinea in *The Symposium*. I also discuss the trope of Rabi'a the Love Poet as an important corollary to the narrative trope of Rabi'a the Lover, although the "real" Rabi'a does not appear to have composed any poetry.

Chapter 4, "Rabi'a the Sufi," is the third "historical" chapter of this book. In it I argue that this narrative trope reads later Sufi doctrines anachronistically back into Rabi'a's time. The earliest accounts of Rabi'a al-'Adawiyya give no indication that she had a fully developed mystical doctrine. Instead, she most likely adhered to a form of "Proto-Sufism," which combined ascetic, social and spiritual outlooks and practices that are now seen as precursors of Sufism. A key concept that differentiated early Sufis from their ascetic predecessors was the importance of the heart as the locus of spiritual knowledge. This metaphor connects all the major tropes of the Rabi'a narratives. The wisdom of the heart that Rabi'a personified would eventually become an important part the Sufi theory of knowledge.

Chapters 5 and 6 return to the "literary" side of this study. In Chapter 5, "Rabi'a the Icon (I): The Sufi Image," I discuss the transformation of the Rabi'a narratives into a Sufi myth. Using Roland Barthes' concept of the "reality effect," I show how 'Attar's *vita* of Rabi'a al-'Adawiyya created a necessary backstory for her myth. The plot elements of this *vita* created a sense of verisimilitude by passing the tests of narrative probability and narrative validity. These plot elements are discussed in detail, with special attention given to their literary antecedents, figurative meaning, and use by later writers. Using the theory of myth of the Russian phenomenologist Aleksei Fyodorovich Losev, I show how the "faces" of Rabi'a that emerged from 'Attar's *vita* and earlier forms of narrative representation were used dialectically to create the iconic image of Rabi'a al-'Adawiyya as a mythical figure. Hence the notion of "Rabi'a the Icon." Chapter 5 concludes with a discussion of the mythical Rabi'a's purported burial sites. Although the "real" Rabi'a is likely buried in the al-Zubayr suburb of modern Basra, other tombs attributed to her can also be found in Jerusalem, Damascus and Cairo.

Chapter 6, "Rabi'a the Icon (II): The Secular Image," focuses on how in the twentieth century Rabi'a al-'Adawiyya became an object of secular attention. This was done by adapting 'Attar's *vita* to the narrative conventions of academic history, the modern novel, motion pictures and television. First I discuss 'Abd al-Rahman Badawi's representation of Rabi'a. By viewing her through the lens of Existentialist philosophy, he depicts her as a restless soul and an independent-minded individualist. This new "face" of Rabi'a was an inspiration for the Syro-Lebanese novelist Widad El Sakkakini, who combined elements of Simone de Beauvoir's feminism with the romantic trope of the "fallen woman" saint. Next I discuss "Rabi'a the Film Icon," a trope that was created by the Egyptian screenwriter Saniya Qurra'a, who popularized Badawi's depiction in a play for Radio Cairo, a published "historical study" and screenplay outline, and finally the script for the 1963 movie, *Rabi'a al-'Adawiyya*. The widespread popularity of this movie established the iconic image of Rabi'a that is best known in the Muslim world today.

This book ends with the Epilogue, "Rabi'a the Myth and the Narrative." By way of reflection more than conclusion, I return once again to the discussion of myth begun above. As seen from the vantage point of the present century, the myth of Rabi'a al-'Adawiyya has by now developed well beyond Robert A. Segal's introductory framework. Indeed, the process of mythmaking has never ended for Rabi'a, for it continues to develop dialectically in an open-ended chain of adaptations and re-presentations. Today just as in the past, the form and content of earlier narratives are used as raw materials for new myths constructed out of tropes and master narratives that have gone before. Because the mythical Rabi'a is more than the sum of her narrative parts, her historiography from narrative to myth now requires looking at myth from a symbolic perspective. In order to map out this new territory, the theoretical approaches of *semiology*—the study of forms and meanings—and *ideology*—the study of ideas-in-form—provide the researcher with better conceptual tools to take the study of the Rabi'a myth into new terrains. I use Roland Barthes' discussion of these concepts and his theory of myth to portray Rabi'a al-'Adawiyya in the twenty-first century as a "global sign." Like the Mandan guide who took Lewis and Clark to the lands beyond the Heart and Cannonball Rivers in their exploration of the American West, this approach points out new vistas ahead of us as we continue to seek the traces of Rabi'a al-'Adawiyya, The Woman Who Never Dies.

Chapter 1

Rabi'a the Teacher

"Take me to the teacher (*mu'addiba*). For when I am apart from her, I can find no solace."
—Sufyan al-Thawri (d. 778 CE), speaking about Rabi'a al-'Adawiyya in Sulami's *Dhikr al-niswa al-muta'abbidat al-sufiyyat* (*Memorial of Female Sufi Devotees*)

"He who is not educated by good behavior (*man lam yu'addibhu al-jamil*) is reformed by tribulations."
—Abbasid Caliph Harun al-Rashid (d. 809 CE) in Ibn 'Abd Rabbih, *al-'Iqd al-Farid* (*The Peerless Necklace*)

I. WHO WAS THE "REAL" RABI'A?

Who was the "real" Rabi'a al-'Adawiyya? As stated in the Introduction, the Rabi'a who is known by millions of Muslims and non-Muslims around the world is a "constructed saint," a composite image of female spirituality whose outline has been shaped through numerous sayings, stories, poems and other popular forms of expression. Rabi'a al-'Adawiyya is also a "master narrative": her identity is embodied in a trans-historical meta-narrative that is deeply embedded not only in the culture of Islam, but now in global culture as well. Thus, any serious attempt to study her representation through time must involve what Nicholas Wolterstorff has called the "archaeology of cultural memory"—"telling the story of how we got where we are in our thinking."[1]

---

[1] Nicholas Wolterstorff, *John Locke and the Ethics of Belief* (Cambridge, UK: Cambridge University Press, 1996), p. xiv.

However, Rabi'a al-'Adawiyya is not just a figure of literary representation and cultural memory. There was a real person at the beginning, a woman who lived in the Iraqi city of Basra roughly between the years 717 and 801 CE.[2] Although we know little in detail about her, we can surmise that she had a remarkable reputation. Otherwise, writers in the generations after her would not have mentioned her and used her as a rhetorical example. For this reason, the archeology of the tropes and narrative constructs that make up the building blocks of the master narrative of Rabi'a al-'Adawiyya must start where all archeological investigations begin, with the most concrete evidence at our disposal, no matter how scarce that evidence may be.

a. Early Sources for the Historical Rabi'a

Unlike an actual archeological investigation, the archeology of cultural memory of Rabi'a al-'Adawiyya can uncover no artifacts that can be attributed unquestionably to Rabi'a herself. She wrote no books and no prosopographical account was written about her during her lifetime.[3] In narrative terms, there is no "prior text" on which to base an outline of Rabi'a's life. What was to become the "prior text" of her life story was not written until the beginning of the thirteenth century CE, about 400 years after her death. How, then, are we to determine which of the many accounts of her actions, sayings, and teachings represent the "real" Rabi'a? Is there any way to sift through the accumulated narratives to find a trace of the person behind the myth? There is one way, although it is not foolproof. We can turn to the sources that provide what are purported to be the most contemporaneous views of Rabi'a extant in Islamic literature. However, one should not forget that even these sources were composed nearly fifty years or more after her death. The earliest extant references to Rabi'a come from five sources from the ninth century CE: (1) a single statement in a doctrinal work by al-Harith al-Muhasibi; (2) anecdotes reported by the prosopographer (compiler of collective

---

2   Although a few sources claim that Rabi'a died as early as 752-3 CE, this date is usually rejected on the basis of accounts attributed to her alleged students and associates, who flourished in the late eighth century and early ninth century CE.
3   The assumption by Margaret Smith and some other modern writers that Rabi'a left behind written works is based on the attribution of certain poems to her, such as the famous "Poem of the Two Loves," which will be discussed in Chapter 3. However, these poems were most likely not by Rabi'a herself but were composed by others. To date, no written work has been linked conclusively to Rabi'a al-'Adawiyya. Cf. Smith, *Rabi'a* (Oneworld), pp. 69 and 125-6 and (Rainbow Bridge) pp. 47 and 101-2.

biographical notices) Muhammad ibn al-Husayn al-Burjulani; (3) statements transmitted by Burjulani's student Ibrahim Ibn al-Junayd; (4) anecdotes reported by the Baghdad littérateurs Jahiz and Ibn Abi Tahir Tayfur; (5) statements attributed to Rabi'a by the traditionist Ibn Abi al-Dunya.[4]

Contemporary writers on Rabi'a tend to view non-Sufi accounts of her as more "objective" than Sufi accounts because they are presumed to be less colored by Sufi traditions. The earliest non-Sufi writer to provide information on Rabi'a was Abu 'Uthman al-Jahiz (d. 868 CE), a noted essayist and theologian whose writings covered a wide range of subjects.[5] Jahiz mentions Rabi'a in two of his works, *Kitab al-hayawan* (*The Book of Animals*) and *Kitab al-bayan wa-l-tabyin* (*Treatise on Demonstrative Proof and Elucidation*), where she is called "Rabi'a al-Qaysiyya." Jahiz's references to Rabi'a are significant because of his closeness to her in time and place. As a native of Basra, Rabi'a's home city, he could have known people who were personally acquainted with her. Clearly, he had heard stories about her and was well aware of her reputation. However, even at this early stage of collective memory formation, her image was not immune to the effects of figurative representation. In his works, Jahiz categorizes Rabi'a rhetorically and transforms her into what the historian of philosophy Pierre Hadot called a *figure*. Like a character sketch in a novel, a figure defines "what we think we know" about a historical personage. For Hadot, a figure is a constructed representation. However, because it encapsulates what we think we know about a personage, it is just as much a historical "reality" as the person herself. Hadot explains this phenomenon in the following way: "The *historical* Socrates is probably

---

4 By believing that the "real" Rabi'a can be (at least in part) the subject of empirical history, I disagree with Julian Baldick, who argues that early accounts of Rabi'a are "too allusive, and usually too late, to have any value for reconstructing her life and teachings." This may be true for the details of her life story, but not for all the statements attributed to her. In my opinion, Baldick holds the earliest sources on Rabi'a to an overly strict standard of objectivity that could not be met even by studies of some modern historical figures. See Julian Baldick, "The Legend of Rabi'a of Basra: Christian Antecedents, Muslim Counterparts," *Religion*, 19, 1990, p. 233.

5 The best overall study of Jahiz remains Charles Pellat, *The Life and Works of Jahiz*, trans. D.M. Hawke (London: Routledge and Kegan Paul and Berkeley: University of California Press, 1969). James E. Montgomery has replaced Pellat to a large extent as the main authority on Jahiz for the present generation of scholars. See James E. Montgomery, *Al-Jahiz: In Praise of Books* (Edinburgh: Edinburgh University Press, 2013) and idem, *Al-Jahiz: In Censure of Books* (Edinburgh: Edinburgh University Press, 2015). For a briefer overview of Jahiz's works, see also, James E. Montgomery, "al-Jahiz," in *Dictionary of Literary Biography Volume 311: Arabic Literary Culture, 500–925*, ed. Michael Cooperson and Shawkat M. Toorawa (Farmington Hills, MI: Thomson Gale, 2005), pp. 231–42; see also, Charles Pellat, "Djahiz," *EI*², 2, pp. 385–7.

an insoluble enigma. But the *figure* of Socrates, as it is sketched by Plato, Xenophon, and Aristophanes, is a well-attested historical fact."[6]

According to Michel de Certeau, the process of defining the identity of a saint starts by associating a personage with a place.[7] Since the time of Jahiz, Rabi'a has most often been associated with her city of origin. For this reason, she is often called "Rabi'a of Basra." As we shall see later on in this chapter, Jahiz also attempted to characterize Rabi'a rhetorically, by fitting her into his theory of *bayan*, a concept that refers to rhetorical excellence. Scholars consider *Kitab al-hayawan* and *al-Bayan wa-l-tabyin*, the works of Jahiz in which Rabi'a appears, to contain the most important discussions of his theology. This theology was rationalistic and relied on logical arguments to describe the nature of God.[8] Although Jahiz saw Rabi'a as different from himself in her approach to Islam, he nevertheless used her as a rhetorical example for his moral and theological arguments. By using the figure of Rabi'a rhetorically in this way, he played an important role in the creation of her narrative image.

Several modern scholars have remarked on the references to Rabi'a in Jahiz's works. However, no one has yet mentioned the references to her by another ninth-century literary figure, Ibn Abi Tahir Tayfur. Like Jahiz, Ahmad ibn Abi Tahir Tayfur of Baghdad (d. 893 CE) was a literary critic and cultural observer.[9] His most extensive work was a local history of Baghdad titled *Kitab Baghdad* (*The Book of Baghdad*). This work contained a description of Baghdad and accounts of events that occurred during the first century of Abbasid rule. Ibn Abi Tahir Tayfur supported himself as a book dealer and published other works on a wide variety of subjects. The most notable of these was *Balaghat al-nisa'* (*The Eloquence of Women*), which is the earliest extant work devoted to women in Islam.[10] In this work, Rabi'a is referred to as

---

6   Pierre Hadot, *Philosophy as a Way of Life*, ed. Arnold L. Davidson, trans. Michael Chase (Oxford and Malden, MA: Blackwell, 1995), p. 116 n. 80.
7   Michel de Certeau, *The Writing of History*, trans. Tom Conley (New York: Columbia University Press, 1988), p. 272.
8   Montgomery, "al-Jahiz," pp. 237–9.
9   See Shawkat Toorawa, *Ibn Abi Tahir Tayfur and Arabic Writerly Culture: A Ninth-Century Bookman in Baghdad* (London and New York: Routledge Curzon, 2005), and idem, "Ibn Abi Tahir Tayfur," in *Dictionary of Literary Biography Volume 311: Arabic Literary Culture, 500–925*, pp. 141–9. See also, Franz Rosenthal, "Ibn Abi Tahir Tayfur," *EI²*, 3, pp. 692–3. Ibn Abi Tahir Tayfur's *Balaghat al-nisa* is also discussed in Fadwa Malti-Douglas, *Woman's Body, Woman's Word: Gender and Discourse in Arabo-Islamic Writing* (Princeton NJ: Princeton University Press, 1991).
10 The depiction of women in *Balaghat al-nisa'* is discussed in Nancy N. Roberts, "Voice and Gender in Classical Arabic *Adab*: Three Passages from Ibn Abī Ṭayfūr's 'Instances of

Rabi'a al-Musma'iyya, which can be translated roughly as "Rabi'a the Woman Who Must Be Heard."[11] Although the exact meaning of this appellation is open to debate, it tells us, along with Jahiz's mention of her, that Rabi'a was remembered for "having something important to say" in the century after her death.[12]

The greatest amount of early information on Rabi'a al-'Adawiyya is to be found in Sufi works of prosopography. Some of these works claim to reproduce first-hand accounts that were transmitted by her students and contemporaries. Although these accounts have a strong aura of authenticity, they are historically problematical because most of them were written down 150 years or more after Rabi'a's death. Historiographically, Sufi prosopographical works are examples of *tabaqat* (levels, classes, or generations) literature. These are collections of sayings and biographical notices in which famous figures are classified either chronologically or according to their spiritual practices. The *tabaqat* genre originated in the field of Hadith studies out of the need to assess the reputation of transmitters of oral tradition.[13]

---

the Eloquence of Women,'" *Al-'Arabiyya*, 25, 1992, pp. 51–72; however, the references to Rabi'a are not mentioned in this article.

11 Ahmad ibn Abi Tahir Tayfur al-Khurasani, *Balaghat al-nisa'*, ed. Muhammad Tahir al-Zayn (Kuwait: Maktabat al-Sundus, 1993), p. 210.

12 On the term *musma'*, see E.W. Lane, *Arabic–English Lexicon* (Cambridge: The Islamic Texts Society, 1984 reprint of 1863 first edition), p. 1429. In the Book of Asceticism (*Kitab al-zuhd*) in *al-Bayan wa al-tabyin*, Jahiz mentions a man named 'Amr ibn al-Khawla, whose mother was called "Khawla of the Masami'a." The modern editor of *al-Bayan wa-l-tabyin* states in a footnote that *al-masami'a* referred to the descendants of a person named Masma' ibn Shihab ibn 'Umar. However, he cites no source for this information. It is possible that the Rabi'a to whom Ibn Abi Tahir Tayfur refers could be vocalized as "Rabi'a al-Masma'iyya" rather than Rabi'a al-Musma'iyya. However, I have not been able to find any independent confirmation of a clan of Masami'a in the major biographical works dealing with Iraq in the Umayyad and early Abbasid periods. In addition, it will become clear below that Ibn Abi Tahir Tayfur's accounts about Rabi'a match those of Jahiz quite closely. Therefore, we can conclude that both authors were talking about the same person. See Abu 'Uthman 'Amr ibn Bahr al-Jahiz, *al-Bayan wa al-tabyin*, ed. Ibrahim ibn Muhammad al-Daljamuni (Beirut: reprint of 1900 first edition, n.d.), vol. 3, p. 110, n. 2.

13 For an overview of the *tabaqat* genre, see Franz Rosenthal, *A History of Muslim Historiography* (Leiden: E.J. Brill, 1968), pp. 93–5; and Claude Gillot, "Tabakat," *EI²*, pp. 7–10. See also, Ibrahim Hafsi, "Recherches sur le genre 'Tabaqat' dans la litérature arabe," *Arabica*, xxiii, 1976, pp. 228–65, xxiv, 1977, pp. 1–41, 150–86; and R. Stephen Humphreys, *Islamic History, a Framework for Inquiry* (Princeton, NJ: Princeton University Press, 1991), pp. 187–208. Michael Cooperson argues against the Hadith origins of *tabaqat* literature in *Classical Arabic Biography: The Heirs of the Prophet in the Age of al-Ma'mun* (Cambridge, UK: Cambridge University Press, 2000). The most important recent work on this genre is Jawid Mojaddedi, *The Biographical Tradition in Sufism: The* Tabaqat *Genre from Sulami to Jami* (Richmond, Surrey: RoutledgeCurzon, 2001).

Most Sufi *tabaqat* works seek to link the Sufi tradition to the so-called "Righteous Predecessors" (*al-Salaf al-Salih*) of Islam, who were the Companions of the Prophet Muhammad and the following two generations of their successors. This category of individuals comprised the most important tradition-bearers of Islam. According to Tarif Khalidi, the publication of *tabaqat* works provided a sense of continuity between the generations of *al-Salaf al-Salih* and subsequent generations of Muslim religious figures: it linked the "then" to the "here and now."[14] Because they transmitted oral traditions, Sufi *tabaqat* works were often written in the style of Hadith collections. The most reliable of these relied on purportedly first-hand accounts that contained chains of oral and written transmission leading from the witness of an event to the author of the work in which the account of the event appeared.

The earliest prosopographical work to mention Rabi'a al-'Adawiyya was *Kitab al-ruhban* (*The Book of Monks*) by Muhammad ibn al-Husayn al-Burjulani of Baghdad (d. 852 CE).[15] This work appears to have focused on edifying statements and acts by early Muslim ascetics. Although no copy of the work is known to exist at the present time, information from it can be found in a number of later works. When chains of transmission are cited in these works, the appearance of the name "Muhammad ibn al-Husayn" often indicates that the account in question was transmitted by Burjulani and likely came from *Kitab al-ruhban*. The sayings and anecdotes about Rabi'a from Burjulani are extremely important because they represent some of the earliest accounts of her in existence.

Another work in this genre whose references to Rabi'a have not been mentioned previously is *Kitab al-mahabba li-llah* (*Book of the Love of God*) by Ibrahim Ibn al-Junayd of Baghdad (d. 883–4 CE).[16] This work consists of

---

14   Tarif Khalidi, *Arabic Historical Thought in the Classical Period* (Cambridge: Cambridge University Press, 1994), p. 46.
15   For information on Burjulani, see Tor Andrae, *In the Garden of Myrtles: Studies in Early Islamic Mysticism*, trans. Birgitta Sharpe, Introduction by Eric Sharpe (Albany, NY: SUNY Press, 1987), p. 32. See also, Louis Massignon, *Essay on the Origins of the Technical Language of Islamic Mysticism*, trans. Benjamin Clark (Notre Dame, IN: Notre Dame University Press, 1997), p. 160. See also, Abu Bakr Muhammad ibn 'Ali al-Khatib al-Baghdadi (d. 1071 CE), *Tarikh Baghdad aw Madinat al-Salam*, ed. Mustafa 'Abd al-Qadir 'Ata (Beirut: Dar al-Kutub al-'Ilmiyya, 1997), vol. 2, p. 219, where the traditionist Ahmad ibn Hanbal cites Burjulani as a reliable source of information on early Muslim ascetics.
16   Abu Ishaq Ibrahim b. 'Abdullah ibn al-Junayd al-Khuttali al-Samarra'i, *al-Mahabba li-llah subhanahu*, ed. 'Adil ibn 'Abd al-Shakur al-Zarqi (Riyadh: Dar al-Hadara li-l-Nashr wa-l-Tawzi', 2003). This work has also been translated into German: see Bernd Radtke

sayings on the love of God from *al-Salaf al-Salih* and the earliest generations of ascetics and Sufis. Ibn al-Junayd was a student of Burjulani.[17] The tenth-century bibliographer Ibn al-Nadim of Baghdad regarded him as a major authority on early Sufism and mentions that besides *Kitab al-mahabba*, he wrote works on the fear of God (*khawf*) and ethical precaution (*wara'*), plus another work titled *Kitab al-ruhban*.[18] The recent publication of *Kitab al-mahabba* is important for scholarship on early Islam because it provides crucial information on the links between early Sufism and other ascetic and pietistic traditions. As mentioned in the Introduction, the fact that Rabi'a al-'Adawiyya is called "Rabi'a" in this work indicates that by the time of Ibn al-Junayd's writing, she had become so well known that her first name was enough to identify her for his readers. In this sense, she could be called a religious "celebrity" in the way that a modern religious celebrity such as Mother Teresa is known today.

Another important early source on Rabi'a al-'Adawiyya was the traditionist Abu 'Abdullah Muhammad ibn Abi al-Dunya of Baghdad (d. 894 CE), who was a teacher of the Abbasid Caliph al-Muktafi' Billah (r. 902–8 CE). Several references to Rabi'a can be found in *Majmu'at Rasa'il Ibn Abi al-Dunya* (*The Collected Letters of Ibn Abi Dunya*) and in accounts attributed to him in later works.[19] Like Ibn al-Junayd, Ibn Abi al-Dunya provides detailed chains of transmission for his accounts. These chains of transmission can be useful in tracing the lineage of accounts about Rabi'a from their origins in Basra to Baghdad, where Burjulani, Jahiz, Ibn al-Junayd, Ibn Abi al-Dunya, and Ibn Abi Tahir Tayfur all resided.

The earliest Sufi writer to mention Rabi'a al-'Adawiyya appears to have been al-Harith ibn Asad al-Muhasibi of Baghdad (d. 857 CE).[20] In the treatise *al-Qasd wa-l-ruju' ila Allah* (*God as the Goal and the Return*), Muhasibi states: "Rabi'a al-'Adawiyya would say at the coming of night, 'The night has come, the darkness has mingled (*ikhtalata al-zalam*), and every lover is left alone

---

(ed.), *Materialien zur alten islamischen Frömmigkeit* (*Materials on Early Islamic Piety*) (Leiden: E.J. Brill, 2009).
17   Al-Khatib al-Baghdadi, *Tarikh Baghdad*, vol. 2, p. 219; see also Massignon, *Essay*, p. 160.
18   Abu al-Faraj Muhammad ibn Abi Ya'qub Ishaq al-Warraq al-Nadim, *Kitab al-fihrist*, ed. Ibn 'Ali ibn Zayn al-'Abidin al-Ha'iri al-Mazandarani (Beirut, 1988), p. 237.
19   Ibn Abi al-Dunya, *Majmu'at rasa'il Ibn Abi al-Dunya*, op. cit.
20   Although I consider Muhasibi an early Sufi or at least a Proto-Sufi, some writers on early Sufism do not consider him a Sufi because he does not refer to himself as such in his extant works.

with his beloved. Now I am alone with you, my Beloved.'"[21] No modern scholar has yet recognized this passage as the earliest extant reference to Rabiʿa. Muhasibi's mention of Rabiʿa is significant for three reasons. First, it is the earliest citation of her to date in any extant text. Second, he cites her full name, "Rabiʿa al-ʿAdawiyya." Third, like Jahiz, he spent the first part of his life in Basra, Rabiʿa's native city. Born in 781 CE, Muhasibi would have lived in Basra during Rabiʿa's lifetime and probably knew about her by reputation. In her book on Muhasibi, which was published seven years after *Rabiʿa the Mystic*, Margaret Smith agrees that Rabiʿa's fame "must certainly have come to [Muhasibi's] ears."[22] Smith also states that Muhasibi quoted Rabiʿa in one of his works; however, she provides no citation for this claim and the statement she reproduces is different from that given above.[23] Despite her extensive knowledge of Middle Eastern manuscript collections, *al-Qasd wa al-rujuʿ ila Allah* does not appear in Smith's bibliography of Muhasibi's writings.[24] However, we can be quite certain that this work is in fact Muhasibi's. ʿAbd al-Qadir ʿAta, the modern Arabic editor of Muhasibi's works, states that two manuscript copies of this work can be found in Istanbul.[25] He also confirms the work's authenticity by means of doctrinal and stylistic similarities with other, better-known examples of Muhasibi's writings.

The next Sufi treatise to mention Rabiʿa al-ʿAdawiyya was written more than a century after Muhasibi's. This is *al-Lumaʿ fi-l-tasawwuf*

---

21   Abu ʿAbdullah al-Harith ibn Asad al-Muhasibi, *al-Qasd wa-l-rujuʿ ila Allah*, ed. ʿAbd al-Qadir Ahmad ʿAta (Cairo: Dar al-Turath al-ʿArabi, 1980), p. 104. This account was also transmitted by Ibn al-Junayd, who says that Rabiʿa uttered the statement in a "sorrowful voice" (*sawt hazin*); *Kitab al-mahabba*, no. 190 and Radtke, *Materialien*, p. 143.
22   Margaret Smith, *An Early Mystic of Baghdad: A Study of the Life and Teaching of Harith B. Asad al-Muhasibi, A.D. 781–857* (London, UK: Sheldon Press, 1977 reprint of 1935 first edition), p. 215.
23   Ibid. In Smith's book, Rabiʿa is asked, "How did you attain to this station (of intimacy with God)?" She replies, "By abandoning what did not concern me, and seeking fellowship with Him Who is Eternal." This account comes from a later source and will be discussed in detail in Chapter 3.
24   Smith, *An Early Mystic of Baghdad*, pp. 44–59.
25   In the Introduction to his edition of Muhasibi's *Badʾ man anaba ila Allah* (*The Beginning of Penitence for the Sake of God*), the editor ʿAbd al-Qadir Ahmad ʿAta states that manuscript copies of *al-Qasd wa-l-rujuʿ ila Allah* can be found in the Jarallah (no. 1728) and Shehid Ali (no. 3319) manuscript collections in Istanbul. See Al-Harith ibn Asad al-Muhasibi, *al-Tawba*, ed. ʿAbd al-Qadir Ahmad ʿAta (Cairo: Dar al-Islah, 1982), p. 18. However, in his earlier (1980) edition of *al-Qasd*, ʿAta states that only one copy of this manuscript exists (Muhasibi, *al-Qasd*, p. 27). This work by Muhasibi is also mentioned in Gavin Picken, *Spiritual Purification in Islam: The Life and Works of al-Muhasibi* (London and New York: Routledge, 2011), pp. 82–3.

(*Flashes of Insight into Sufi*sm) by Abu Nasr al-Sarraj (d. 988 CE) of Tus in eastern Iran. In a section on the miracles of Muslim saints, Sarraj arranges early Sufis into a *tabaqat* list based on generations. One of the earliest generations includes Muhammad ibn Wasi' (d. 738 CE), Malik ibn Dinar (d. 745 CE), Farqad al-Sabakhi (d. 748–9 CE), Ayyub al-Sakhtiyani (d. 748–9 CE), 'Abd al-Wahid ibn Zayd (d. 793–4 CE), and Rabi'a al-'Adawiyya (d. 801 CE).[26] Significantly, all of these figures were from the city of Basra.[27] According to Sarraj, early scholars and the founders of schools of Islamic religious practice used them as major sources of tradition and confirmed what they had to say. The next generation of tradition-bearers included Sufyan al-Thawri (d. 778 CE), and Hammad ibn Zayd (d. 793 CE). These two figures also either came from Basra or spent time in that city. Sarraj states that neither of them was opposed to the doctrines of Rabi'a or her contemporaries in the previous generation: "They are our leaders in religion and confirm our knowledge of God's rules and regulations and our knowledge of what is permissible and forbidden. So how can we believe them in some of what they report and not believe them in other things?"[28] This statement thus provides further testimony of Rabi'a's reputation as an important figure of early Islam.

In the eleventh century CE, Abu 'Abd al-Rahman al-Sulami of Nishapur (d. 1021 CE) reproduced accounts from at least three lost ninth and tenth-century Sufi works in his prosopography of Sufi women, *Dhikr al-niswa al-muta'abbidat al-sufiyyat* (*Memorial of Female Sufi Devotees*). The earliest of these works is Burjulani's *Kitab al-ruhban*. In addition, he includes information from *Tabaqat al-nussak* (*Generations of the Ascetic Ritualists*) by Abu Sa'id ibn al- A'rabi of Basra (d. in Mecca, 952–3 CE) and *Hikayat al-masha'ikh* (*Stories of the Spiritual Masters*) by Ja'far al-Khuldi of Baghdad (d. 959 CE).[29] As noted previously, citations of Burjulani can be found in many Sufi prosopographical works and a portion of Ja'far al-Khuldi's book can be found in the *Fihrist* (*Bibliographical Catalogue*) of Muhammad ibn al-Nadim of Baghdad (d. 990 CE).[30] Sulami was conscientious about citing his sources

---

26 Abu Nasr 'Abdullah b. 'Ali al-Sarraj al-Tusi, *The Kitab al-Luma' fi'l-Tasawwuf*, ed. Reynold Alleyne Nicholson (London: Luzac & Co. Ltd., 1963 reprint of 1914 first edition), p. 322. Farqad al-Sabakhi is incorrectly cited as "Farqad al-Sinji" in this text. Cf. Christopher Melchert, "Farqad al-Sabakhi," *EI*³.
27 See Massignon, *Essay*, p. 114.
28 Sarraj, *The Kitab al-Luma'*, pp. 322–3.
29 On these works, see R. Cornell's Introduction to Sulami, *Early Sufi Women*, pp. 52–3 and notes.
30 See Bayard Dodge (trans.), *The Fihrist of al-Nadim: A Tenth-Century Survey of Muslim Culture* (New York: Columbia University Press, 1970), vol. 1, pp. 455–61.

of information and listed full chains of transmission whenever possible. However, while some of his accounts of Rabi'a's female contemporaries come from the works mentioned above, his notices on Rabi'a al-'Adawiyya do not. It is not clear why this is so, because Sulami includes a report about Rabi'a from Ja'far al-Khuldi in another work.[31]

The majority of references to Rabi'a al-'Adawiyya in Sufi works do not appear until nearly 150 years after her death. This underscores the importance of the references to her in the works of Muhasibi and Jahiz, who are separated from her by only half a century, and the works of Ibn al-Junayd, Ibn Abi al-Dunya, and Ibn Abi Tahir Tayfur, which were written a generation later. Ibn al-Junayd's *Kitab al-mahabba* and Sulami's Book of Sufi Women are the earliest extant works to give chains of transmission for reports about Rabi'a. None of the other Sufi works that predate Sulami's book provide chains of transmission. These include, besides Muhasibi's *al-Qasd wa-l-ruju' ila Allah* and Sarraj's *Kitab al-Luma'*, Abu Bakr al-Kalabadhi's (d. 990 CE), *Kitab al-ta'arruf li-madhhab ahl al-tasawwuf* (*Introduction to the Method of the Sufis*); Abu Talib al-Makki's (d. 996 CE), *Qut al-qulub* (*The Nourishment of Hearts*); and 'Abd al-Malik al-Khargushi's (d. 1016 CE), *Tahdhib al-asrar* (*The Primer of Secrets*). For this reason, according to modern standards of historical research, the citations of Burjulani, Muhasibi, Jahiz, Ibn Abi Tahir Tayfur, Ibn al-Junayd, and Ibn Abi al-Dunya should be considered especially valuable in that they are the closest we can get to first-hand information about Rabi'a al-'Adawiyya.

b. Alleged Students and Associates of Rabi'a al-'Adawiyya

What do the early sources tell us about the students and associates of Rabi'a al-'Adawiyya? For Sulami and later Sufi writers, the most important of Rabi'a's students was Sufyan al-Thawri (d. 776 CE), a key figure in the formative period of Islamic jurisprudence.[32] Although Sufis considered Thawri to be an

---

31 The account of Rabi'a from Khuldi ("Ja'far ibn Muhammad") can be found in Sulami's *Kitab 'uyub al-nafs wa mudawatuha* (*Book of the Faults of the Soul and their Cures*). See Nasrollah Pourjavady, *Majmu'at Athar Abu 'Abd al-Rahman al-Sulami* (Tehran: Tehran University Publishing Center, 2000), vol. 1, pp. 72–3. Each work of Sulami in this collection is paginated separately. Two of Ibn al-Junayd's accounts of Rabi'a are also cited by Sulami. However, Ibn al-Junayd is not cited as the source for them.

32 See Sulami, *Early Sufi Women*, pp. 74 and 76. The most extensive treatment of the life and teachings of Sufyan al-Thawri can be found in Abu Nu'aym al-Isfahani (d. 1038–9 CE), *Hilyat al-awliya' wa tabaqat al-asfiya'* (*The Adornment of the Saints and the Generations of*

important source of tradition, he was not a Sufi himself. For example, non-Sufi Sunni Muslims regard his commentary on the Qur'an as an important work of early Qur'anic exegesis.[33] Thawri was born and raised in Kufa but lived in Basra at the end of his life. He and Rabi'a were approximately the same age when they allegedly knew each other. Sulami reports that Thawri sought Rabi'a's advice on ethical matters and that he sought her spiritual counsel as well.[34]

Sulami also reports that Shu'ba ibn al-Hajjaj (d. 776–7 or 781–2 CE) transmitted Rabi'a's teachings.[35] Shu'ba was a Hadith scholar and friend of Thawri who resided in Basra. He also wrote an early commentary on the Qur'an.[36] Born in the Iraqi city of Wasit to a family of Persian origin, he was one of the many non-Arab clients (*mawla*, pl. *mawali*) of Arab clans who were beginning to rise to positions of importance in the early Abbasid period. Another Hadith scholar and companion of Thawri who is said to have known Rabi'a was Ja'far ibn Sulayman al-Dab'i (d. 794–5 CE).[37] In an *isnad* cited by Sulami, Dab'i confirms the contention of Abu Bakr al-Sarraj that Rabi'a knew Muhammad ibn Wasi', although she would have been in her early twenties at the time of Ibn Wasi''s death. Ibn Wasi' was a Hadith transmitter, Qur'an reciter, and ascetic who was a student of the famous Sunni theologian al-Hasan al-Basri (d. 728 CE).[38] Ibn Wasi' and other students of Hasan, such as Malik ibn Dinar, who is also mentioned along with Rabi'a by Sarraj, may have served as important links between Rabi'a and Hasan, with whom she is often associated anachronistically in later works. Although Rabi'a would have been too young to know al-Hasan al-Basri during his lifetime, it would have been possible for her to know his students.

---

the Pure), ed. Abu Hajar al-Sa'id ibn Basyuni Zaghlul (Beirut: reprint of the 1938 edition, n.d.), vol. 6, pp. 356–93 and vol. 7, pp. 3–143. See also, Steven C. Judd, "Competitive Hagiography in the Biographies of al-Awza'i and Sufyan al-Thawri," *Journal of the American Oriental Society*, 122 (1), 2002, pp. 25–37.

33 See Abu 'Abdullah Sufyan ibn Sa'id ibn Masruq al-Thawri al-Kufi, *Tafsir Sufyan al-Thawri*, ed. Imtiyaz 'Ali 'Arshi (Beirut: Dar al-Kutub al-'Ilmiyya, 1983 reprint of 1965 first edition). The Ranpur, India, manuscript on which this edition is based is the only known copy of this work. See also, Claude Gilliot, "The Beginnings of Qur'anic Exegesis," *The Qur'an: Formative Interpretation*, ed. Andrew Rippin (Aldershot, UK: Ashgate Publishing, 1999), p. 15.

34 Sulami, *Early Sufi Women*, p. 74.

35 Ibid., and Isfahani, *Hilya*, vol. 6, pp. 144–209.

36 See Charles Pellat, *Le Milieu Basrien et la formation de Gahiz* (Paris: Librarie d'Amérique et d'Orient Adrien-Maisonneuve, 1953), p. 83.

37 See Sulami, *Early Sufi Women*, p. 78 and Isfahani, *Hilya*, vol. 6, pp. 287–96; according to Massignon, Dab'i was a disciple of Farqad al-Sabakhi. See idem, *Essay*, p. 115.

38 Sulami, *Early Sufi Women*, p. 78 n. 16; see also, Isfahani, *Hilya*, vol. 2, pp. 345–57.

Ibn al-Junayd reports from Muhammad ibn al-Husayn al-Burjulani that Rabi'a also knew Riyah ibn 'Amr al-Qaysi (d. 796 CE).[39] Sulami also corroborates this claim, although from a different source.[40] Riyah al-Qaysi of Basra was an ascetic ritualist who practiced forms of bodily mortification that were more reminiscent of early Christian asceticism than the Muslim variety, such as wearing a heavy iron collar around his neck when he performed his nightly prayer vigils.[41] Despite his reputation for chastity, some heresiographers, such as the Hanbali scholar Ibn Khushaysh al-Nasa'i (d. 867 CE), accused him of belonging to a group of "spiritualists" (*al-ruhaniyya*), who believed that their intimate friendship with God (*khulla*) allowed them to take personal liberties with women and young boys.[42]

Sulami also mentions that Rabi'a had several female disciples and colleagues. These included Maryam of Basra (d. early ninth century CE), who is depicted as a love mystic.[43] Other reputed female colleagues included Sha'wana of al-Ubulla (d. ca. 770 CE), who had both male and female disciples like Rabi'a,[44] and Rabi'a al-Azdiyya of Basra (d. end of eighth century CE). Rabi'a al-Azdiyya has often been confused with Rabi'a al-'Adawiyya by later generations of Sufis.[45]

Surprisingly, Sulami cites none of these women as sources of information about Rabi'a al-'Adawiyya. This distinction belongs only to one woman, who is first mentioned by Ibn Abi al-Dunya and who also appears in *Sifat al-safwa* (*The Attribute of Purity*) by the Hanbali scholar Abu al-Faraj ibn al-Jawzi (d. 1200 CE).[46] Both Ibn Abi al-Dunya and Ibn al-Jawzi cite Rabi'a's

---

39 Ibn al-Junayd, *Kitab al-mahabba*, no. 236 and Radtke, *Materialien*, p. 171.
40 Sulami, *Early Sufi Women*, pp. 78–9.
41 Isfahani, *Hilya*, vol. 6, pp. 192–7. On the question of Qaysi's name, see Christopher Melchert, "Basran Origins of Classical Sufism," *Der Islam*, 82, 2006, p. 226 n. 24.
42 On Riyah al-Qaysi and the practice of *khulla*, see Carl W. Ernst, *Words of Ecstasy in Sufism* (Albany, NY: SUNY Press, 1985), pp. 100 and 118–22; see also, Massignon, *Essay*, pp. 150–2.
43 Sulami, *Early Sufi Women*, pp. 84–5.
44 Ibid., pp. 106–7; see also, Ibn al-Junayd, *Kitab al-mahabba*, nos. 18 and 223; Radtke, *Materialien*, pp. 55 and 162.
45 Ibid., pp. 128–9.
46 The most recent edited edition of this work is Abu al-Faraj 'Abd al-Rahman ibn al-Jawzi, *Sifat al-safwa*, ed. Mahmud Fakhuri and Muhammad Rawwas Qal'aji, 4 vols. (Beirut, 1986). In this study, references to *Sifat al-safwa* are from the Alexandria, Egypt, Dar Ibn Khaldun reprinted edition in two volumes (not dated). The section on Rabi'a al-'Adawiyya can be found in vol. 2, pp. 710–12 of the Alexandria edition. For a complete English translation of Ibn al-Jawzi's notice on Rabi'a see the Ibn al-Jawzi Appendix to Sulami, *Early Sufi Women*, pp. 276–83.

servant 'Abda bint Abi Shawwal as an important source of information.⁴⁷ According to an *isnad* provided by the Hanbali prosopographer Muhammad al-Dhahabi (d. 1374 CE), at least one account of 'Abda that was used by Ibn al-Jawzi came from Burjulani.⁴⁸ In these accounts, 'Abda claims to be present at Rabi'a's death and also recites dream narratives that recount posthumous conversations with her. The dream conversation is a common trope in Islamic hagiography, which serves to establish the divine acceptance of the person who speaks from beyond the grave.⁴⁹ Often, such conversations are not about the deceased, but about other famous people who were known to the deceased or her companions. In 'Abda's dream accounts, Rabi'a acts as a messenger from the beyond, which confirms her status as a respected transmitter of Sufi traditions.

II. RABI'A IN THE EARLIEST SOURCES

a. Rabi'a the Arab

Abu 'Uthman al-Jahiz mentions Rabi'a eight times in his works: four times in *Kitab al-hayawan* and four times in *al-Bayan wa-l-tabyin*. In these works she is not called "Rabi'a al-'Adawiyya," the name by which she has become famous, but "Rabi'a al-Qaysiyya." Although these appellations are different, they do not contradict each other. The name *Rabi'a al-'Adawiyya* refers to 'Adi ibn Qays, the Arab clan in Basra to which Rabi'a belonged. In Arabic, a man from 'Adi ibn Qays would be called *'adawi*; a woman would be called *'adawiyya*. *Qays* was the name of the tribe to which the 'Adi ibn Qays belonged. The Banu Qays ("Sons of Qays") belonged to a large tribal confederation called Mudar. Both Qays and the Prophet Muhammad's tribe of Quraysh were part of

---

47 See Sulami, *Early Sufi Women*, pp. 280–2, for an English translation of Ibn al-Jawzi's references to 'Abda bint Abi Shawwal. The original can be found in Ibn al-Jawzi, *Sifat al-safwa*, vol. 2, p. 712. Ibn al-Jawzi took at least one of these accounts from Ibn Abi al-Dunya's *Kitab al-Manamat (Book of Dreams)*. See also, idem, *Majmu'at Rasa'il*, vol. 3, p. 33 no. 21.
48 See the *isnad* from Burjulani via 'Abda bint Abi Shawwal in Shams al-Din Muhammad ibn Ahmad b. 'Uthman al-Dhahabi, *Siyar a'lam al-nubala'*, ed. Shu'ayb al-Arna'ut and Salih al-Sumr (Beirut: Mu'assasat al-Risala, 1996), vol. 8, p. 242.
49 See, for example, Leah Kinberg, *Morality in the Guise of Dreams: A Critical Edition of Kitab al-manam by Ibn Abi al-Dunya* (Leiden: E.J. Brill, 1994); Nile Green, "The Religious and Cultural Role of Dreams and Visions in Islam," *Journal of the Royal Asiatic Society*, 13 (3), 2003, pp. 287–313; Özgen Felek and Alexander D. Knysh (eds), *Dreams and Vision in Islamic Societies* (Albany, NY: SUNY Press, 2012).

Mudar. In early Islamic times, belonging to one of the tribes of Mudar meant that one was a northern Arab, as opposed to the "Yemenis" (also known as Qahtanis or Himyaris) who originally came from southern Arabia. Tribes of both northern and southern Arabian origin had been living in Iraq for two centuries before the Islamic conquest. Segments of the tribes of Mudar were numerous in southern Iraq and the region of Basra in particular. Most segments of Qays settled in the Jazira, a region west of the Euphrates River that stretched between Iraq and Syria. However, a group of Qays also settled in Basra, where they made up one "fifth" (*khums*) of the five original tribal groups that settled in that city. The fifth to which the 'Adi ibn Qays belonged was known as *Ahl al-'Aliyya* ("The People of Upper Arabia").[50] Yemeni Arabs were also numerous in Basra. One of the most important Yemeni tribes in Basra was Azd. The identity of this tribe is reflected in the name of Rabi'a's namesake, Rabi'a al-Azdiyya.[51]

Unlike some later writers, who depict Rabi'a as coming from a non-Arab background, Jahiz places her firmly within the Qays tribe and even suggests that she enjoyed a high status in her clan. In *al-Bayan wa-l-tabyin* he states: "Rabi'a al-Qaysiyya was asked, 'Could we ask the men of your clan to buy you a servant to do your household chores?' She replied, 'By God, I am ashamed to ask for the world from the One who owns the world. So how can I ask for the world from one who does not own it?'"[52] The same account also appears in *Kitab al-hayawan*, but in a slightly different version. Here Rabi'a is asked, "Would you give us permission to speak to your people so that they collect for you the price of a servant? He could be a support for you and be of sufficient service to you so that you could devote yourself to worship."[53] A third variant of this account appears in *Balaghat al-nisa'* by Ibn Abi Tahir Tayfur, where Rabi'a is told to ask the Sultan (i.e., the Abbasid governor of Basra) to repair her dwelling. Her response to this advice is the same as in Jahiz's account: "By God, I do not ask for the world from the One who owns it, so how can I ask for the world from one who does not own it?"[54]

---

50 Pellat, *Le Milieu Basrien*, p. 23.
51 For a concise overview of tribal factions in Umayyad Iraq, see Marshall G.S. Hodgson, *The Venture of Islam: Conscience and History in a World Civilization* (Chicago and London: University of Chicago Press, 1977), vol. 1, pp. 227–30. On Arab settlement patterns in the region of Basra, see Michael G. Morony, *Iraq after the Muslim Conquest* (Princeton, NJ: Princeton University Press, 1984), pp. 245–50.
52 Jahiz, *al-Bayan*, vol. 3, p. 66.
53 Abu 'Uthman 'Amr ibn Bahr al-Jahiz, *Kitab al-hayawan*, ed. 'Abd al-Salam Muhammad Harun (Beirut: Ihya' al-Turath al-'Arabi, 1969 reprint of 1949 first edition), vol. 5, p. 589.
54 Ibn Abi Tahir Tayfur, *Balaghat al-nisa'*, p. 205.

The context of this account provides an important clue about Rabi'a's likely standing within her clan and in Basra at large. In Jahiz's depiction, Rabi'a is highly respected by the leaders of her clan, who are concerned that her domestic duties might interfere with her religious vocation. By offering to buy her a servant or a slave to free her from her chores, they confirm that she was a highly valued person, despite the fact that she was a woman. In *al-Bayan wa al-tabyin*, it is suggested that the leaders of her clan should buy her a servant. In *al-Hayawan*, it is suggested that the clan members together should collect money to buy her a servant. In *Balaghat al-nisa'*, she is told by the leaders of her clan to ask the governor of Basra to rebuild her house. Obviously, this is something that a governor would not do for everyone. All three versions of this story make it clear that Rabi'a was highly respected in her community and was considered a valuable asset by her people. In the social context of the time, a woman who earned such a high level of respect was not likely to have been a slave or a servant herself. It is more likely that she was a *hurra*, a free woman of good standing in her clan.

Several non-Arab Sufis and even some Arab writers have depicted Rabi'a as a *mawlat*, a non-Arab client who was attached to an Arab tribe.[55] Up until the end of the Umayyad Caliphate (ca. 750 CE), a non-Muslim could only convert to Islam if she were sponsored by a patron from an Arab tribe, who either adopted the convert into the tribe or bound her to the tribe through a legal act of clientage (*muwalat*). The client was known as a *mawla* (fem. *mawlat*) and typically was either a freed slave or a free non-Arab (*'ajami*), who provided useful services for the patron or the patron's clan. Although it was possible under Islamic law for a freed slave or even a slave to own a slave herself, this was very rare, just as it was rare for a servant to employ another servant.[56]

While it is theoretically possible that the "real" Rabi'a was of non-Arab origin, the accounts of Jahiz and Ibn Abi Tahir Tayfur suggest otherwise. Although she might have been attached to her clan through clientage, she would have enjoyed such an unusually high status that she transcended the social restrictions normally placed on non-Arab clients in the Umayyad

---

55 See for example Sulami, *Early Sufi Women*, p. 74, where Rabi'a is depicted as a *mawlat* of the clan of Al 'Atik.
56 On the concept of clientage in pre-Islamic and early Islamic times, see Jacob Lassner, *The Shaping of 'Abbasid Rule* (Princeton, NJ: Princeton University Press, 1980), pp. 96–8; and Mahmood Ibrahim, *Merchant Capital and Islam* (Austin, TX: University of Texas Press, 1990), pp. 59–60 and 182–3.

period. A situation such as this would have been highly improbable.[57] In addition, some of the claims that Rabi'a was of non-Arab origin can be shown to be unlikely because they are based on incorrect information. For example, Sulami's claim that Rabi'a was a *mawlat* in his Book of Sufi Women is undermined by a mistake that would never have been made by a native of Basra. Although Sulami refers to Rabi'a as "Rabi'a al-'Adawiyya," he states that she was a *mawlat* of the Arab clan of Al 'Atik ("The People of 'Atik").[58] The appellation *'adawiyya* meant that Rabi'a belonged to the clan of 'Adi ibn Qays, which, as we have seen, was part of the north Arabian tribal confederation of Mudar. However, Al 'Atik was a clan of the South Arabian Azd Arabs. As a South Arabian clan, Al 'Atik could not have been related to either Qays or Mudar.[59] It would thus have been impossible for Rabi'a al-'Adawiyya to bear the name of a clan from Qays and to be bound through clientage to a clan of South Arabian origin. If she had been the client of a South Arabian clan, she would have borne that clan's name. We have already seen that there may have been two Rabi'as living in Basra in the same period: Rabi'a al-'Adawiyya and Rabi'a al-Azdiyya. Unlike Rabi'a al-'Adawiyya, Rabi'a al-Azdiyya's name indicates that she belonged to a tribe of South Arabian origin. Therefore, it is more likely to have been Rabi'a al-Azdiyya—not Rabi'a al-'Adawiyya—who was from Al 'Atik of the Banu Azd and who was a client of that South Arabian clan. While Sulami corrects some misinformation about Rabi'a al-'Adawiyya in his Book of Sufi Women, in this case he seems to have inadvertently contributed to a centuries-long confusion of identities over the two Rabi'as of Basra.[60]

---

57 The Umayyad-era poet Jarir once insulted the matriarch of a rival's clan by accusing her of being a *mawlat* and of being corrupted by her "foreign stink." Had Rabi'a been a non-Arab client, she would likely have been susceptible to similar abuse. See Allen Fromherz, "Tribalism, Tribal Feuds, and the Social Status of Women," in Amira El Azhary Sonbol (ed.), *Gulf Women* (Doha, Qatar: Bloomsbury Qatar Foundation Publishing, 2012), p. 60.
58 Sulami, *Early Sufi Women*, p. 74; unlike most of Sulami's information about Rabi'a, this claim is not supported by an *isnad*.
59 On 'Adi ibn Qays and Al 'Atik, see Pellat, *Le Milieu Basrien*, pp. 28 and 30. Pellat's information corrects the mistake in Sulami, *Early Sufi Women*, p. 74 n. 3, where Al 'Atik is linked both to 'Adi ibn Qays and to Quraysh. Like Sulami, Louis Massignon (*Essay*, p. 149 n. 458) also sees Rabi'a as a freedwoman of Al 'Atik, but "corrects" her tribal designation to make her a member of Azd. However, this does not help because it would make her the same person as Rabi'a al-Azdiyya.
60 The conflation of Rabi'a al-'Adawiyya and Rabi'a al-Azdiyya may have started as early as the publication of *Kitab al-ruhban* by Muhammad ibn al-Husayn al-Burjulani in the ninth century CE. The fourteenth-century prosopographer Muhammad al-Dhahabi, apparently following Sulami, makes the mistake of saying that Rabi'a al-'Adawiyya was a client of Al 'Atik. Dhahabi also cites an account about "Rabi'a" that Burjulani reported from a member of the Al 'Atik clan of Azd. This account states that Rabi'a refused to meet

b. Rabi'a the Leader

The *hurra*, the free Arab woman, played an important role in the culture of the Umayyad and early Abbasid periods. Unfortunately, until recently, little research has been done on this subject.[61] It is surprising, given today's widespread interest in Women's Studies, that one finds more references to Arab women of high standing in studies dating from the first half of the twentieth century than later. Margaret Smith, writing in 1928, states in *Rabi'a the Mystic*: "There is little doubt that the free Arab woman in Pre-Islamic and even early Islamic times held a more independent and even respected position than the Muslim woman of today."[62] She goes on to mention several notable women who lived in the pre-Islamic and early Islamic periods. Philip K. Hitti in *History of the Arabs*, published in 1937, mentions the Prophet Muhammad's great-granddaughter Sukayna bint al-Husayn (d. 735 CE), who was a patron not only of fashion and beauty, but also of literature.[63] He also notes that many women of the Caliphal household under the early Abbasids distinguished themselves as patrons of the literary and intellectual arts.[64] In *Two Queens of Baghdad*, published in 1946, Nabia Abbott discusses the philanthropy of Zubayda (d. 831 CE), the Arab wife of the Abbasid Caliph Harun al-Rashid. Zubayda made six pilgrimages to Mecca, endowed waterworks in that city, and trained 100 slave-girls to chant the Qur'an around the

---

with Sufyan al-Thawri. Since we know from Jahiz and other sources that Sufyan visited Rabi'a frequently, this early account by Burjulani is probably about Rabi'a al-Azdiyya rather than Rabi'a al-'Adawiyya. Dhahabi, *Siyar*, vol. 8, p. 241.

61 A recent exception to the lack of discussion about the influence of the *hurra* as transmitters of religious knowledge in the Umayyad and early Abbasid periods is Asma Sayeed, *Women and the Transmission of Religious Knowledge in Islam* (Cambridge, UK: Cambridge University Press, 2013), pp. 19–107.

62 See Smith, *Rabi'a* (Oneworld), p. 141 and (Rainbow Bridge), p. 111. Ironically, Smith's praise of the status of pre-Islamic and early Islamic Arab women was merely the prelude to a polemic she directed against Islam's subjugation of women in later periods. The statement quoted above ends with the assertion, "[The Muslim woman's] present degraded position is due to Islamic teaching which has prevailed since the second and third centuries of the Muslim era, to keep her in a position of almost complete subordination to the male sex." In a later passage Smith goes even further, adding, "The ultimate effect of [the Prophet Muhammad's] legislation was the degradation and enslavement of Muslim womanhood throughout the centuries up to the present time" (p. 156).

63 Philip K. Hitti, *History of the Arabs from the Earliest Times to the Present* (London: Macmillan Press, 1970 reprint of 1937 first edition), pp. 237–8.

64 Ibid., p. 333.

clock at the Caliphal palace in Baghdad.[65] She also endowed and maintained the *Darb Zubayda*, the main pilgrimage road from Baghdad to Mecca. Most relevant to the present discussion is the observation of Ahmad Amin in *Duha al-Islam* (*The Mid-Morning of Islam*), published in 1933, that although slave-girls were more highly valued as companions than free women in the early Abbasid period, some high-class Arab women distinguished themselves in spirituality and the religious sciences: "We find that many free women employed themselves in the sciences; however, the majority of those who employed themselves in this way were religiously motivated, such as many female Hadith scholars and Sufis."[66] In a recent article on free women in early Arabia, Barbara Stowasser agrees that the *hara'ir* of the Jahiliyya and Early Islamic periods were respected, but adds the following important caveat: "But this free... Arabian woman was also ideologically ensconced in her tribe, from which she derived her protection and to which she owed all her public activities."[67]

If Rabi'a was a *hurra*, as Jahiz and Ibn Abi Tahir Tayfur seem to indicate, and if she enjoyed so much respect from her clan that its leaders wanted to buy her a slave at their own expense, then it is highly likely that she was one of the religiously motivated and tribally protected *hara'ir* described by Ahmad Amin and Barbara Stowasser. Stowasser's observation also suggests that Rabi'a may have been regarded as a valuable asset by her clan of Banu 'Adi ibn Qays. It is important to note in this regard that Rabi'a's high status in her clan would not have contradicted her reputation for poverty and asceticism. Although women of high status in the early Islamic period were often wealthy, status and wealth were not directly related in Arab society at that time. It was possible for a woman of high status to devote herself to a life of asceticism and poverty and still retain or even exceed the power and influence that she would have enjoyed had she been wealthy. It was also not

---

65 Nabia Abbott, *Two Queens of Baghdad: Mother and Wife of Harun al-Rashid* (Chicago: University of Chicago Press, 1974 reprint of 1946 first edition), pp. 160 and 240–7.
66 Ahmad Amin, *Duha al-Islam* (Cairo: Egyptian National Book Organization, 1997 reprint of 1933 first edition), p. 117. Amin's positive view of the social position of the *hurra* in early Abbasid society is very different from that of Margaret Smith, who contended, "Muslim men preferred slaves as wives, because of the independent spirit of free Arab women." Idem, *Rabi'a* (Oneworld), p. 155 and (Rainbow Bridge), p. 126; Marlé Hammond tends to agree with Smith, noting the lack of poetry attributed to *hara'ir*, as opposed to slave-girls (sing. *jariya*). See idem, *Beyond Elegy: Classical Arabic Women's Poetry in Context* (Oxford: British Academy and Oxford University Press, 2010), pp. 10–19.
67 Barbara Freyer Stowasser, "Women and Politics in Late Jahili and Early Islamic Arabia: Reading Behind Patriarchal History," in Sonbol (ed.), *Gulf Women*, p. 76.

unusual in this period for a tribally protected woman of high status to have a male authority figure such as Sufyan al-Thawri as her associate. Early sources indicate that it would have been unlikely for Thawri to seek out a lowly, non-Arab *mawlat* for advice. According to the Sufi prosopographer Abu Nu'aym al-Isfahani (d. 1038–9 CE), Thawri refused to teach Hadith to the indigenous Aramaic-speaking people (*al-Nabat*) of Iraq or to people of the lower classes. He said, "Real Tradition is sought only among the Arabs. If knowledge is disseminated to the Aramaic-speaking people or the lower classes they will pervert it (*fa-qalabu al-'ilm*)."[68] For Thawri to come to a woman for instruction at all, it would only have been to a righteous Arab *hurra*.

Jahiz provides further confirmation of Rabi'a's high status in *Kitab al-hayawan*. In this work, she is classified as one of the "Ascetic Ritualists and Renunciants among the Prominent Sunni Women of Asceticism and Leadership" (*al-nasikat al-mutazahhidat min al-nisa' al-madhkurat fi-l-zuhd wa-l-riyasa min nisa' al-jama'a*).[69] Three terms in this statement are significant. The first term is *riyasa*, "leadership." Rabi'a is mentioned as a prominent figure by Jahiz along with Mu'adha al-'Adawiyya and Umm al-Darda', Sunni women ascetics of Basra who were known for their high standards of morality and ethics. Mu'adha al-'Adawiyya (d. 702 CE) came from the same Arab clan as Rabi'a. As we shall see in Chapter 2, her claim to leadership was based in part on her founding a school of women's asceticism in Basra.[70] Umm al-Darda', also known as "Umm al-Darda' *al-'Alima* (The Authority)," was the wife of Abu al-Darda' (d. 651–2 CE), a noted Companion of the Prophet Muhammad.[71] Abu al-Darda' was a member of the committee appointed by the Caliph 'Uthman to compile the official

---

68   Isfahani, *Hilya*, vol. 6, p. 369; according to Charles Pellat, *nabati* was a pejorative term that was applied both to the native residents of Basra and its environs, and to the residents of the Sawad marshlands, the ancestors of today's Marsh Arabs. See Pellat, *Le Mileu Basrien*, p. 22.
69   Jahiz, *al-Hayawan*, vol. 5, p. 589; for a discussion of my translations of *nasik* (fem. *nasika*) as "ascetic ritualist" and *mutazahhid* as "renunciant," see Chapter 2.
70   The earliest extant notice on Mu'adha al-'Adawiyya is in Muhammad ibn Sa'd (d. 845 CE), *al-Tabaqat al-kubra*, ed. Riyad 'Abdullah 'Abd al-Hadi (Beirut: Dar Ihya' al-Turath al-'Arabi, 1985), vol. 8, p. 483. This work portrays Mu'adha as teaching a group of women, who sit in a circle around her.
71   According to Asma Sayeed, there were two women named Umm al-Darda': Umm al-Darda' al-Kubra (the Elder) and Umm al-Darda' al-Sughra (the Younger). Umm al-Darda' al-Sughra is the more famous of the two and and was a noted transmitter of Hadith. Because many Syrian traditions locate her grave in Syria, Jahiz's reference to Umm al-Darda' of Basra may refer to Umm al-Darda' al-Kubra. See Sayeed, *Women and the Transmission of Religious Knowledge in Islam*, pp. 70–3 and n. 25.

version of the Qur'an.⁷² Both Muʻadha and Umm al-Darda' had impeccable Arab and Islamic credentials and were exemplars of piety and asceticism. Including Rabiʻa with this pair of religious notables meant for Jahiz that she shared their status as honored bearers of tradition. In addition, Rabiʻa shared with Muʻadha al-ʻAdawiyya the vocation of teaching, which also confirmed her prominence in her community.

c. Rabiʻa the Sunni Muslim

The second important term in Jahiz's categorization of Rabiʻa is *min nisa' al-jama'a*, which literally means, "of the women of the majority." This term refers to the fact that Jahiz considered Muʻadha al-ʻAdawiyya, Umm al-Darda' and Rabiʻa al-Qaysiyya as Sunni Muslims. The full title of the Sunni sect in Islam is *Ahl al-Sunna wa-l-Jama'a*, "The People of the Sunna and the Majority." Including Rabiʻa among other famous Sunni women meant that she was not considered a heretic and that her religious practices were within the bounds of Sunni piety. In *al-Bayan wa-l-tabyin* Jahiz distinguishes Muʻadha, Umm al-Darda', and Rabiʻa from other women who were Kharijites (*nisa' al-khawarij*) or extremist Shiites (*nisa' al-ghaliya*). Although these other women were also pious ascetics, they followed doctrines that were unacceptable to the majority.⁷³ Hence, they could serve as rhetorical models for Jahiz but they were not suitable to be religious or moral exemplars.

The third term of significance in Jahiz's categorization of Rabiʻa is *nasika*, "female ascetic ritualist." This term is further qualified by the word that comes after it, *mutazahhida*, "female renunciant." The Arabic root *n-s-k* is ambiguous, and carries meanings related to both worship and sacrifice.⁷⁴ With regard to worship, it implies a strict adherence to ritual. For example, the rites of the Hajj pilgrimage are known in Arabic as *manasik al-Hajj*. This meaning of *n-s-k* is also found in the Qur'an, where it appears in the verse, "My prayer and my ritual sacrifice (*nusuki*) and my life and my death are for God, the Lord of the Worlds" (Qur'an 6:162). This Qur'anic verse became a sort of motto for early Muslim ascetics, because it alludes to the self-sacrifice that comes from devoting oneself to God. Both Muʻadha al-ʻAdawiyya and

---

72 Dhahabi, *Siyar*, vol. 6, pp. 336–9.
73 Jahiz, *al-Bayan*, vol. 1, p. 194.
74 For an excellent discussion of the Qur'anic meaning of *n-s-k* see Rosalind Ward Gwynne, *Logic, Rhetoric, and Legal Reasoning in the Qur'an; God's Arguments* (London and New York: Routledge Curzon, 2004), pp. 14–16.

Umm al-Darda' were known for their self-sacrifice. Muʿadha's husband Sila ibn Ushaym al-ʿAdawi (d. 694–5 CE) died as a martyr in the wars of the Umayyad Empire against the Byzantines.[75] Umm al-Darda's husband Abu al-Darda' died in an epidemic. Umm al-Darda' also appears in Islamic texts as an advocate of the spiritual benefits of visiting graveyards.[76]

Although Rabiʿa was never married and never lost a loved one in battle, her celibacy was regarded as a sacrifice for the sake of God. Ibn Abi Tahir Tayfur is the earliest writer to testify to Rabiʿa's celibacy. In *Balaghat al-nisa'* she is asked, "Marriage is a requirement of God, the Glorious and Mighty. So why do you not marry?" Rabiʿa replies: "One obligation to God [i.e., devotion to God] prevents me from fulfilling another of his obligations."[77] Personal sacrifices such as these would have helped make Rabiʿa worthy to receive divine favor and would have legitimized her as a model of virtue. Jahiz reinforces this image in two passages in *Kitab al-hayawan*, where Rabiʿa's scrupulousness and self-discipline are cited as examples of the steadfastness of human nature.[78] Her exemplarity and reputation were so great that no one could imagine that she would fall victim to ordinary human weaknesses.

d. Rabiʿa the Eloquent

The final important reference to Rabiʿa in Jahiz's works is in *al-Bayan wa-l-tabyin*, where she appears in a section titled "Mention of the Ascetic Ritualists and Renunciants among the People of *Bayan*" (*dhikr al-nussak wa-l-zuhhad*

---

75 Alexander Knysh incorrectly states that Muʿadha al-ʿAdawiyya was the wife of the early ascetic ʿAmir ibn ʿAbd Qays (d. 670 CE). See idem, *Islamic Mysticism: A Short History* (Leiden and Boston: E.J. Brill, 2000), p. 26.
76 See Abu Muhammad ʿAbdullah ibn Qutayba al-Dinawari (d. 889–90 CE), *Kitab ʿuyun al-akhbar* (*The Wellsprings of Knowledge*), ed. Muhammad al-Iskandarani (Beirut: Dar al-Kitab al-ʿArabi, 1999), vols. 1–2 combined, p. 737. In this passage a man says to Umm al-Darda': "Verily in my heart I have found a disease for which there is no cure; I have found great suffering and have lost all hope." She replies, "Go up to the graveyard and contemplate the dead." This account originally came from Jahiz, *al-Bayan*, vol. 3, p. 81.
77 Ibn Abi Tahir Tayfur, *Balaghat al-nisa'*, p. 204; the person who transmitted this account was Muhammad ibn Bayan ibn Humran al-Madaʾini (fl. mid-ninth century CE). *Al-Madaʾin* (The Cities) was the Arabic name for the former Persian capital of Ctesiphon, near Baghdad. Madaʾini's father was a student of Sufyan al-Thawri. Thus, it is possible that Thawri himself was the original source of this account. For information on Madaʾini, see Baghdadi, *Tarikh Baghdad*, vol. 2, pp. 95–9.
78 Jahiz, *al-Hayawan*, vol. 1, p. 170 and vol. 6, p. 52.

min ahl al-bayan).⁷⁹ Here, Rabi'a again appears in the company of Mu'adha al-'Adawiyya and Umm al-Darda'. Once again, these three Sunni women are distinguished from Kharijite and Shiite women in the same category. In this latter passage, however, their names precede a list of "Men of *Bayan*," which includes preachers, poets, sages, leaders and teachers. Included among the Men of *Bayan* are "Sufis (*al-Sufiyya*) among the Ascetic Ritualists who are known for the fineness of their speech (*mimman yujidu al-kalam*)."⁸⁰ Obviously, the term *al-bayan* was important for Jahiz and it is significant that Rabi'a is characterized by it. What did Jahiz mean by *bayan* and what did it mean to include Rabi'a in this category?

The term *al-bayan* as used by Jahiz means "demonstrative argument." For Jahiz, this meaning is derived from the Qur'an, where *al-bayan* is used to characterize God's proofs for his existence. Muslim exegetes have also interpreted *al-bayan* to mean the ability to come to a clear understanding of the signs (*ayat*) of God as expressed in the Qur'an. Those who prefer this latter interpretation cite a passage from *Surat al-Rahman* (*The Beneficent*): "[God] created the human being; He taught him *al-bayan*" (Qur'an 55:34). Others have interpreted this passage to mean that God granted human beings the power of articulate thought and speech. For example, the modern Qur'an commentator Muhammad Asad uses this latter meaning of *bayan* in his English translation of the Qur'an. In a footnote to Qur'an 55:34, he explains that *bayan* means the ability to clarify God's teachings conceptually:

> The term *al-bayan*—denoting "the means whereby a thing is [intellectually] circumscribed and made clear" (Raghib [al-Isfahani])—applies to both thought and speech inasmuch as it comprises the faculty of making a thing or an idea apparent to the mind and conceptually distinct from other things or ideas, as well as the power to express this cognition clearly in spoken or written language (*Taj al-'Arus*); hence, in the above context, [the term means] "articulate thought and speech," recalling the "knowledge of all names" (i.e. the faculty of conceptual thinking) with which man is endowed.⁸¹

---

79   Jahiz, *al-Bayan*, vol. 1, p. 194.
80   Ibid., p. 195; the "Sufis" mentioned in this passage are Kilab, Kulayb, Hashim al-Awqas, Abu Hashim al-Sufi and Salih ibn 'Abd al-Jalil. They will be discussed in detail in Chapter 4.
81   Muhammad Asad, *The Message of the Qur'an* (Gibraltar: Dar al-Andalus, 1980), p. 824 n. 1.

In the opening chapter of *al-Bayan wa-l-tabyin*, Jahiz defines *bayan* as "the outward expression of the hidden meaning [of a concept]" (*al-dalala al-zahira 'ala al-ma'na al-khafi*).[82] This is not very different from Asad's understanding of the term as "the means whereby a thing is intellectually circumscribed and made clear." According to Jahiz, the connection between the concept of *bayan* and the clarification of meaning was already known to the Arabs before the revelation of the Qur'an. It was also known among certain groups of non-Arabs. Presumably, these non-Arabs included the Greeks, for Jahiz's discussion of *bayan* combines Arabic semantics with Aristotelian logic.[83] Jahiz additionally defines *bayan* as "a collective term for anything that intuitively (*dun al-damir*) expresses the obscured meaning [of a concept] and strips away the veils so that the hearer arrives at its true understanding."[84]

The concept of *bayan* for Jahiz was similar to the pre-Islamic Stoic concept of the True. For the Stoics, the most important truths were not always discovered through formal reasoning, but were sometimes revealed in flashes of insight.[85] Thus, the Stoic sage was considered both a Master of Truth, which is discovered through demonstration and argument, and a Master of the True, which is the immediate expression of that which is. According to A.A. Long, "[The Stoic sage] represents an ideal of language and rationality at one with reality, of truth discovered."[86] For Jahiz, the Master of *Bayan* served the same function. The similarities between the concept of *bayan* for Jahiz and the Stoic concepts of Truth and the True are striking and deserve further investigation.[87]

Thus, for Jahiz, *bayan* involved more than just the clarification of meaning. As both a hermeneutical and a rhetorical method, it combined the arts of interpretation and demonstration.[88] Therefore, *tabyin*, the act of doing *bayan*,

---

82 Jahiz, *al-Bayan*, vol. 1, p. 42.
83 See, for example, the discussion of Jahiz's hermeneutics in Khalidi, *Arabic Historical Thought*, pp. 104–8.
84 Jahiz, *al-Bayan*, vol. 1, p. 42.
85 The appropriation of the Stoic approach to knowledge by early Sufis may be reflected in the title of Abu Nasr al-Sarraj's *Kitab al-Luma' fi-l-tasawwuf* (*Flashes of Insight into Sufism*).
86 A.A. Long, "Dialectic and the Stoic Sage," in *The Stoics*, ed. John M. Rist (Berkeley and Los Angeles: University of California Press, 1978), p. 114.
87 *Bayan* is linked to Latin rhetorical concepts in James Montgomery, "Al-Jahiz's *Kitab al-Bayan wa al-Tabyin*," in Julian Bray (ed.), *Writing and Representation in Medieval Islam: Muslim Horizons* (London and New York: Routledge, 2006), pp. 91–152. For the Stoic philosopher Chrysippus, dialectics was "knowledge of demonstrative procedures," much like Jahiz's *bayan*. See Long, "Dialectic and the Stoic Sage," p. 107.
88 Jahiz, *al-Bayan*, vol. 1, p. 43.

required an aptitude for both logical analysis and rhetorical demonstration. For Jahiz, like the Stoics, the rhetorical arts of proof and persuasion depended on logic, whose original meaning in Greek was "persuasion with words."[89] The ability to persuade others with words was seen both as a mark of eloquence and as a way of revealing the truth. In a similar way, the logical processes employed in the arts of demonstration (*bayan*) and persuasion (*tabyin*) were two sides of the same coin. In order to be effective, both demonstration and persuasion had to rely on logic and reason.

For Jahiz, the opposite of *bayan* was *'iyy*, "inexpressiveness." This term connotes the lack of ability to formulate concepts and was used by Jahiz to characterize the discourse of the person who is unschooled in logic and rhetoric: "*Bayan* is sight whereas *'iyy* is blindness, just as knowledge is sight and ignorance is blindness. *Bayan* is a product of knowledge whereas *'iyy* is a product of ignorance."[90] Jahiz saw the process of *bayan* as a three-way relation in which logic (*mantiq*), knowledge (*'ilm*), and reason (*'aql*) work together to reveal the truth: "Reason is the motivator of the spirit (*al-'aql ra'id al-ruh*); knowledge is the motivator of reason (*al-'ilm ra'id al-'aql*); *bayan* is the interpreter of knowledge (*al-bayan tarjuman al-'ilm*)."[91] Because *bayan* is the "interpreter" of knowledge, it requires knowledge to be applied in practice, especially with respect to moral conduct and virtue. "The life of virtue lies in truthfulness; the life of the spirit lies in modesty; the life of wisdom lies in knowledge; the life of knowledge lies in *bayan*."[92]

Thus, for Jahiz to say that Rabi'a was one of the People of *Bayan* was highly significant. It meant that she was endowed with reason and possessed a unique ability to conceptualize and express important truths. For Jahiz, a person who does not possess both knowledge and reason in equal measure cannot practice *bayan*. In his works, Jahiz does not discuss Rabi'a's educational background. He does not say whether she studied under a teacher or whether she was self-educated. However, she clearly had accumulated enough knowledge of Qur'an, Hadith, and other Islamic teachings to comment authoritatively on them.[93]

---

89 Peter Kingsley, *Reality* (Inverness, CA: The Golden Sufi Center, 2003), pp. 141–4; the same sense of logic as deriving from "words" (Gr. *logoi*) can be found in the Arabic word for logic, *mantiq*. The root of this term is *n-t-q*, which means, "to utter, enunciate, or express."
90 Jahiz, *al-Bayan*, vol. 1, p. 43.
91 Ibid.
92 Ibid.
93 Margaret Smith believed that Rabi'a was self-educated (idem, *Rabi'a* [One World], p. 71 and [Rainbow Bridge], p. 47). As we shall see in Chapters 2 and 3, this assumption

Although Ibn Abi Tahir Tayfur does not refer to Rabi'a as a Person of *Bayan*, the image that he portrays of her is very similar to that of Jahiz. In *Balaghat al-nisa'*, Rabi'a is portrayed as one of the "Women of Authoritative Opinion" (*dhawat al-ra'y*).[94] This meant that she was considered qualified to give her own, independent interpretations of Islamic doctrines. Ibn Abi Tahir Tayfur's use of the term *ra'y* tells us that Rabi'a's teachings were not based on tradition alone but were also based on independent reasoning. Her teachings were considered authoritative, whether or not they were based on previous examples or precedents. This may be why he refers to her as *Rabi'a al-Musma'iyya*, "Rabi'a the Woman Who Must Be Heard." For those who came to Rabi'a for doctrinal and ethical advice, her teachings constituted an independent body of authoritative tradition. For Jahiz, a "woman who must be heard," and who embodied authoritative tradition was a "Person of *Bayan*." For Ibn Abi Tahir Tayfur, these same attributes epitomized Rabi'a as a "Woman of *Ra'y*."

III. RABI'A THE TEACHER AND THE CULTURE OF *ADAB* IN EARLY ISLAM

Jahiz's depiction of Rabi'a as a Person of *Bayan* and Ibn Abi Tahir Tayfur's depiction of Rabi'a as a Woman of *Ra'y* are important because they relate to one of the most important tropes of Rabi'a in the earliest sources. This is the trope of Rabi'a the Teacher. Rabi'a the Teacher and Rabi'a the Ascetic are the most important tropes of Rabi'a to appear in the earliest sources.[95] In his Book of Sufi Women Sulami relies on two principal informants for reports about Rabi'a the Teacher. One is Ja'far ibn Sulayman al-Dab'i (mentioned above), who is the main source for her relationship with Sufyan al-Thawri. The other is Shayban ibn Farrukh al-Ubulli (d. 850–1 CE), a respected traditionist of the generation after Dab'i.[96] Although Shayban may have met Rabi'a in his

---

is partly contradicted by the suggestion (albeit isolated) that she may have had at least one teacher.
94 See Ibn Abi Tahir Tayfur, *Balaghat al-nisa'*, p. 191. In this work, reports about Rabi'a appear in the chapter titled, "News of the Women of Authoritative Opinion and Their Witty Statements" (*Akhbar dhawat al-ra'y wa al-zarf minhunna*).
95 The "educative subject" (comprising the roles of both teacher and student) is one of the five modalities of ascetic subjectivity discussed by Richard Valentasis in his theory of asceticism. See idem, *The Making of the Self: Ancient and Modern Asceticism* (Eugene, OR: Cascade Books, 2008), pp. 45–6.
96 Dhahabi, *Siyar*, vol. 11, pp. 101–3. Shayban was said to have memorized over 50,000 hadiths.

youth he most often relates accounts from others who knew her. For example, he is the source for the statement in the epigraph to this chapter, wherein Sufyan al-Thawri says about Rabi'a: "Take me to the teacher (*mu'addiba*). For when I am apart from her, I can find no solace."[97]

Sulami's chapter on Rabi'a al-'Adawiyya in his Book of Sufi Women does not make use of Jahiz's term *bayan*. However, he supports Jahiz's depiction of Rabi'a as a Person of *Bayan* and Ibn Abi Tahir Tayfur's depiction of Rabi'a as a Woman of *Ra'y* by illustrating her aphoristic style of teaching and by confirming that she was a source of both ethical and spiritual advice for the jurist Sufyan al-Thawri. As portrayed by Sulami, most of Rabi'a's teachings are ethical in nature and consist of maxims or principles. This style of aphoristic teaching goes back to classical antiquity. Like Jahiz's concept of *bayan*, it was also associated with the Stoics. According to Pierre Hadot, Stoic teachers taught lessons in which their students learned "a fundamental principle which is formulable in a few words, and extremely clear and simple, precisely so that it may remain easily accessible to the mind, and be applicable with the sureness and constancy of a reflex."[98]

The Stoic style of teaching described by Hadot is very similar to Rabi'a's approach to pedagogy, in which ethical and theological principles are expressed in short, pithy sayings. In a recent book on the history of the aphorism, James Geary lists five "laws of aphorisms" that can be applied to Rabi'a's teaching method: (1) aphorisms are brief; (2) they are definitive; (3) they are personal; (4) they have a twist; (5) they are philosophical in nature.[99] Rabi'a's teachings, like aphorisms in general, were meant to challenge the thinking of those who learned them. Each statement requires a response from the learner. This response may either be the recognition of a shared insight or an outright rejection. Whatever the response, however, an aphoristic statement cannot be ignored. "Inside an aphorism," says Geary, "it is minds that collide and the new matter that spins out at the speed of thought is that elusive thing we call wisdom."[100] In this sense, Geary's view of the aphorism has much in common with Jahiz's understanding of *bayan*.

---

97   Sulami, *Early Sufi Women*, p. 76. This is the first account transmitted with an *isnad* in Sulami's chapter on Rabi'a. When I published *Early Sufi Women*, it was not yet clear to me that Shayban ibn Farrukh, which is the name found in the *isnad* of this report, and Shayban al-Ubulli were the same person.
98   Hadot, *Philosophy as a Way of Life*, p. 84.
99   James Geary, *The World in a Phrase: A Brief History of the Aphorism* (New York and London: Bloomsbury Publishing, 2005), pp. 8–20.
100 Ibid., p. 16.

In an essay on the maxims of La Rochefoucauld, the French literary theorist Roland Barthes also brings Jahiz's concept of *bayan* to mind when he discusses the "point" of the aphorism (what Geary calls its "twist").[101] For Barthes, the aphorism is effective as a teaching device because its "point" reveals the statement's "hidden oppositional seam." As Barthes puts it, the aphorism is a "two-faced being."[102] Sulami reports in his Book of Sufi Women that Rabi'a said to Sufyan al-Thawri, "Have you not learned that true safety from the world is to abandon all that is in it? So how can you ask for such a thing while you are still soiled with the World?"[103] This statement illustrates Barthes' contention that the "point" of an aphorism leads to an understanding of the essence of what it means to be a human being. In other words, it focuses the learner's attention on the question, "Who am I?" In Rabi'a's statement to Sufyan al-Thawri, the "oppositional seam" of the aphorism (you desire safety from the world/yet you are still soiled with the world) evokes a moral dichotomy between the World and the Nonworld. The "point" of the aphorism is that if Thawri truly desires peace and safety, then it can only be found by refocusing attention from the World to the Nonworld. As we shall see in the following section, this statement was not an idle platitude. For Thawri, the oppositional seam of Rabi'a's teaching ran along an existential boundary-line between two ways of life: one way of life led to safety and salvation, whereas the other way of life led to tragedy and death.

The example of this aphoristic lesson to Sufyan al-Thawri helps explain why in the Arabic language, a common term for aphorism is *hikma* (pl. *hikam*).[104] Because the term, *ḥikma*, in Arabic means "wisdom," this allows us to define the aphorism in the context of Arab culture as a "wisdom saying." Because the *ḥikma* conveys the meaning of a concept or teaching so concisely that it could sometimes be made into an equation, it also fits Jahiz's concept of *bayan*.[105] The aphorisms associated with the figure of Rabi'a in early Islamic

---

101 Roland Barthes, "La Rochefoucauld: 'Reflections on Sentences and Maxims,'" in idem, *New Critical Essays*, trans. Richard Howard (Evanston, IL: Northwestern University Press, 2009), p. 11.
102 Ibid., p. 21.
103 Sulami, *Early Sufi Women*, p. 76.
104 On the meaning and use of the term *hikma* as "maxim" or aphorism, see Dimitri Gutas, "Classical Arabic Wisdom Literature: Nature and Scope," *Journal of the American Oriental Society*, 101 (1), 1981, pp. 49–86.
105 Barthes, "La Rochefoucauld," p. 14. However, Barthes also points out that the effectiveness of the aphorism as a teaching method lies in the fact that the symmetry of the equation constituted by its semantic parts is a *false* symmetry: its "point" or message lies in the rupture of the logic of the equation. In Rabi'a's statement to Sufyan al-Thawri,

literature were most often lessons in practical wisdom. The themes of honesty, wisdom, and love of God that they conveyed provided the foundation for the trope of Rabi'a the Teacher as it was developed in later periods of Islamic history.

a. Rabi'a and Sufyan al-Thawri

When Sufayn al-Thawri said to Ja'far ibn Sulayman al-Dab'i, "Take me to the teacher," the word he used was not *ustadha*, the modern term for a woman teacher in Arabic, or *mu'allima*, "female instructor," but *mu'addiba*. The term *mu'addib* (fem. *mu'addiba*) has a rich history in Arab culture and identifies Rabi'a not only as a teacher but more importantly as a personal mentor and specialist in *ta'dib*, ethical training and character formation. Both *mu'addiba* and *ta'dib* are related to the Arabic word *adab*, which refers most commonly to literature and the arts. However, in Rabi'a's time *adab* also included everything that was relevant to the formation of the mature personality, including piety, comportment and ethics. Before discussing Rabi'a's depiction as a *mu'addiba* and the implications of the culture of *adab* on her role as a teacher, it is first necessary to look at the circumstances in which she and Sufyan al-Thawri might have come to know each other.

Sufyan al-Thawri was a noted jurist and traditionist, and was highly respected both inside and outside of early Sufi circles. An indication of his importance to Sufism can be seen in Abu Nu'aym al-Isfahani's *Hilyat al-awliya'* (*The Adornment of the Saints*), one of the most important works of Sufi prosopographical literature. In the modern edition of this work, the chapter on Thawri is nearly 180 pages long. For Isfahani, Thawri is an important link in the chain of authorities that connects the Sufi tradition to the generation of *al-Salaf al-Salih*. Therefore, it is not surprising to see that Isfahani portrays him as a traditionist. He stands firmly in the ranks of the Hadith scholars and is devoted above all to keeping the example of the Prophet Muhammad alive in the minds of Muslims. "Apart from fulfilling the requirements of religion," Isfahani quotes Thawri as saying, "there is no work more meritorious than seeking knowledge of traditions... We will keep on learning traditions as long as there are traditions left to learn."[106]

---

seeking the Nonworld does not lead directly to safety; to be truly safe (i.e. unconcerned with the World), one must ground one's existence in the Nonworld.

106 Isfahani, *Hilya*, vol. 6, p. 363.

However, Isfahani additionally portrays Sufyan al-Thawri not just as a traditionist but also as a traditionalist. He rejected religious innovation as heretical and believed that orthodox spirituality was dependent on scrupulous adherence to the example of the Prophet Muhammad and *al-Salaf al-Salih*. For Thawri, tradition was not history to be memorized; rather it was a set of behaviors to be lived. The bearer of tradition (*hamil al-'ilm*) was not only the Hadith scholar; this term also applied to those who lived according to the teachings of Hadith. To put it in more contemporary terms, the bearer of tradition was a religious activist who assimilated, applied and disseminated the Prophet's teachings. Thawri's motto with regard to this obligation was "Seek, Memorize, Act, Disseminate."[107] He was a popular teacher and attracted large crowds of both men and women to his lectures. During these lectures, he explained the meaning of problematical verses of the Qur'an, discoursed on Hadith, and interpreted points of law.[108] The "sound-bite" rhetorical style that he used in such gatherings is preserved in *Tafsir Sufyan al-Thawri* (*The Qur'an Commentary of Sufyan al-Thawri*). This work is less a formal exegesis of the Qur'an than a collection of comments on Qur'anic terms, phrases and verses by the Prophet, his Companions and their followers. Only seldom does one find the personal opinions of Thawri himself.[109]

When Thawri's traditionalism is considered along with his asceticism and uncompromising moralism, it becomes clear that he was one of those whom the historian of Islamic civilization Marshall Hodgson termed the "Piety-Minded"—"men and women for whom Islamic piety took precedence over any other interest."[110] In the early Abbasid period, the Piety-Minded formed, in Hodgson's words, an "exclusive and austere group" that demanded "a rigorous standard of public decency free of luxurious display or of other concessions to aristocratic culture that might be regarded, from an egalitarian viewpoint, as degenerate social corruption."[111] Traditionists like Thawri, the founders of the schools of Islamic jurisprudence, and ascetics like Rabi'a al-'Adawiyya were members of this group. Basic to their worldview was the belief that each generation after the Prophet Muhammad was worse than the previous one

---

107 Ibid., p. 362.
108 Ibid., p. 357.
109 Cf. Thawri's exegesis of Qur'an 2:96: Sufyan via a man (*'an rajulin*) from al-Hasan [al-Basri] on the statement of God, may He be exalted and glorified: "Our Lord, grant us good in this world and good in the Hereafter." [Hasan] said: "Good sustenance and beneficial work in the world;" ("And good in the Hereafter") [meaning] "until Heaven" (referring to verse 2:201). Thawri, *Tafsir Sufyan al-Thawri*, p. 65.
110 Hodgson, *Venture of Islam*, vol. 1, p. 250.
111 Ibid., p. 365.

and that the only way to maintain a truly Islamic way of life was to hold fast to the traditions of the Prophet and *al-Salaf al-Salih*. This was certainly the case for Thawri, whose stubborn adherence to ethical principles aroused the anger of the rulers of the day. By the time he allegedly met Rabi'a in Basra he had become cynical of the trappings of status and authority. His pessimistic moral vision is expressed in the following letter to his nephew, as related by Isfahani. Clearly, by this point in life Thawri had lost his taste for political and social activism and wanted nothing more than to be left alone.

> [The Prophet's generation] had knowledge that we do not have and they had a precedence that we do not have; so how are we to attain this [status] with our little knowledge, our little patience, our little support for the good, and with all the corruption among people and deceit in the world? So make the example (*amr*) of the first generation obligatory for yourself and hold fast to it; and require detachment from worldly affairs (*khumul*), for this is the time for detachment. Require withdrawal from society (*'uzla*) and mix with people very little; for [in normal times] when people meet each other, some learn from others; but today, this is gone from us and salvation is in rejecting human company, as you can see. Beware not to befriend or associate with princes and their affairs; and beware not to deceive, lest you be told to intercede in matters of corruption or the redress of damages; for this is one of the ruses of Iblis (Satan); the corrupt reciters of the Qur'an take this upon themselves without any objection. It used to be said: "Beware of the ignorant worshipper and the corrupt scholar, for the strife that they cause is the source of all unrest." Do not take personal advantage from giving legal opinions and *fatwas* or compete with others over them. Be not as one who desires to be followed in his teachings, who wishes to have his teachings disseminated, or to have them heard; instead, leave this to the one who is suited for it. Beware not to love personal authority (*riyasa*), for authority is more beloved to a man than gold or silver. It is a blind alley (*bab ghamid*); no one can see his way through it except one with insight among the most accomplished of scholars and you will lose yourself in it. So live by your intentions, and know that anything that brings people close to you will lead to such an affair that a man will wish he were dead.[112]

---

112 Isfahani, *Hilya*, vol. 6, pp. 376–7.

The contents of this letter indicate that when Thawri met Rabi'a he would likely have been a bitter and disillusioned man, which adds further meaning to the statement that when he was apart from her, he could find no solace.[113] Thawri's sojourn in Basra was short and took place only in the last three years of his life. The Hanbali scholar Ibn al-Jawzi reports that Thawri "went into hiding" in Basra during the reign of the Abbasid Caliph al-Mahdi.[114] Since the Caliphate of al-Mahdi started in 775 CE, and Thawri died in 778 CE, this meant that he could not have associated with Rabi'a for more than three years. The picture that Ibn al-Jawzi paints of Thawri is of a man who constantly fears death or torture, seems to suffer from either kidney disease or bladder cancer, and is prone to weeping.[115] In Basra, he appears to have had no home of his own but lived off the generosity of his students.[116] He was also known for constantly imploring God to grant him peace and security.[117] In several accounts, he blames his misfortunes on his status as a scholar, saying, "Were I not so learned, I would not be so sad."[118] Other authors, such as Isfahani, also mention Thawri's disillusionment with scholarship. In *Hilyat al-awliya'* Thawri complains, "He who increases his knowledge increases his pain." He also said, "I wanted to escape from this affair [i.e., scholarship] completely, so that it would neither harm me nor benefit me."[119]

In the period in which he would have known Rabi'a al-'Adawiyya, Thawri was a man at the end of his rope. He was both physically ill and on the run from the authorities. Why was this so? Why was he being hunted by the Abbasid state? Although the sources are not explicit on this matter, a number of clues can be found. Most sources indicate that Thawri's problems were political, and that his outspokenness only added to his misfortunes. The

---

113 Sulami, *Early Sufi Women*, p. 76.
114 Ibn al-Jawzi, *Sifat al-safwa*, vol. 2, p. 571; this is confirmed by Ibn al-Nadim. See Abu al-Faraj Muhammad ibn Abi Ya'qub Ishaq al-Ma'ruf bi al-Warraq, *Kitab al-Fihrist li-l-Nadim*, ed. Rida al-Tajaddud (Beirut: Dar al-Masira, 1988), p. 281.
115 Two accounts in Ibn al-Jawzi's *Sifat al-safwa* claim that Sufyan al-Thawri urinated blood. Ibn al-Jawzi attributes this to either Thawri's deep thinking ("Whenever he started to think, he urinated blood") or his deep sadness ("This man has destroyed his liver from sadness"). See idem, *Sifat al-safwa*, vol. 2, p. 570.
116 See, for example, Isfahani, *Hilya*, vol. 6, p. 371; Thawri's student 'Abd al-Rahman ibn Mahdi, in whose house Thawri died, found the words, "Allah will suffice for you" written on his teacher's body. Another account (ibid., p. 364) reports that in Basra Thawri had a map (*kharita*) written on his shirt. This may have helped him find safe houses in which to hide.
117 The original source for these accounts is Ibn Sa'd, *al-Tabaqat al-kubra*, vols. 5–6, pp. 538–9; see also, Sulami, *Early Sufi Women*, p. 76.
118 Ibn al-Jawzi, *Sifat al-safwa*, vol. 2, p. 569.
119 Isfahani, *Hilya*, vol. 6, p. 363.

most likely explanation for his political problems is that they were due to his Shiite sympathies and his disapproval of the ethics of the Abbasid regime. Some evidence for Thawri's pro-Shiite sympathies can be found in the text of *Tafsir Sufyan al-Thawri*. Although this work contains commentaries by many prominent Sunni Muslims, a few of them come from figures primarily associated with Shi'ism, such as Imam Muhammad al-Baqir (d. 731 CE). During Thawri's lifetime, the Abbasids were in a bitter dispute with the direct descendants of the Prophet Muhammad. If Thawri had truly been a supporter of the Abbasids as is claimed by Isfahani and other Sufi writers, it would have been rather unusual for him to report traditions from a Shiite Imam whose descendants were rivals of the Abbasids. One also gets the impression that the Hanbali scholar Ibn al-Jawzi's unflattering portrayal of Thawri was due to his mistrust of Thawri's professed loyalty to Sunni Islam.

The tenth-century CE bibliographer Muhammad ibn al-Nadim, who was a Shiite, claimed that Thawri belonged to the Zaydi sect of Shi'ism.[120] He also reports that many traditionists of the early Abbasid era were Zaydi as well.[121] Zaydi Shiites came in many varieties and are difficult to classify doctrinally. The main principle of Zaydism was that leadership in Islam was reserved for the descendants of the Prophet's daughter Fatima (d. 633 CE) and her husband 'Ali through either of their sons Hasan (d. 669 CE) or Husayn (d. 680 CE). Any descendant of 'Ali and Fatima who was learned, pious, and who raised his banner in defense of justice had the right to claim leadership in his time. Zaydi Shi'ism was named after Zayd ibn 'Ali (d. 740 CE), a son of the fourth Shiite Imam 'Ali Zayn al-'Abidin (d. 717 CE). Zayn al-'Abidin was the only male survivor of the massacre at Karbala in which his father Imam Husayn was killed. He lived quietly in Medina and did not take part in political disputes. However, his son Zayd led an unsuccessful revolt against the Umayyads. Unlike other Shiite groups, the Zaydis did not reject the Caliphs Abu Bakr (d. 634 CE) and 'Umar (d. 644 CE). Although they felt that 'Ali was better suited for leadership, they accepted the first two Sunni Caliphs because 'Ali himself had chosen not to oppose them.[122] In most of their doctrines, the Zaydis were little different from the Sunnis. In their practice

---

120 Dodge, *Fihrist*, vol. 1, p. 443; see also the Arabic edition of al-Nadim, *Kitab al-Fihrist*, al-Tajaddud, p. 226.
121 Ibid., p. 444, Arabic edition, p. 226.
122 For an introduction to Zaydi doctrines, see William Montgomery Watt, *The Formative Period of Islamic Thought* (Oxford: Oneworld Publications, 2002), pp. 162–6. This work was originally published in 1949 as *Free Will and Predestination in Early Islam*.

of jurisprudence and adherence to tradition they shared much in common with the piety-minded Sunni scholars discussed above.[123]

In the early Abbasid period, Zaydi Shi'ism provided an opportunity for the descendants of Imam Hasan to assert their claims to leadership. The Hasanids claimed that in coming to power the Abbasids had usurped the rights of the Prophet's immediate family. This dispute came to a head during the Caliphate of Abu Ja'far al-Mansur (r. 754–775 CE), and led to the arrest of many Hasanids, including 'Abdullah al-Kamil ("The Perfect"), who died in prison in 761 CE. Over the next two years, al-Mansur also had to deal with 'Abdullah al-Kamil's sons, who swore revenge for the death of their father. Muhammad al-Nafs al-Zakiyya ("The Pure Soul") revolted against al-Mansur in Medina and died in 762 CE; his brother Ibrahim was killed the following year and his other brother Idris escaped to Morocco, where he received the allegiance of the indigenous Amazigh (Berber) people. Idris was eventually assassinated on the orders of Caliph Harun al-Rashid (d. 809 CE).

Sunni sources that discuss Sufyan al-Thawri and his career ignore Ibn al-Nadim's claim that he was a Zaydi Shiite. However, since the Zaydi revolts occurred near the end of Thawri's life, they provide a likely context for the enmity of the Abbasid Caliphs toward him. Thawri's opposition to the Abbasids is unmistakable in the following account from *Ta'rikh Baghdad*, which indicates that he was under suspicion when he and his colleague, the Syrian jurist Abu 'Amr al-Awza'i (d. 773 CE) visited Mecca for the Hajj pilgrimage.

> Mufaddal ibn Muhalhal said: I went to perform the Hajj with Sufyan, and when we went to Mecca, Awza'i joined us. Awza'i and Sufyan gathered with us in our house. At that time 'Abd al-Samad ibn 'Ali al-Hashimi was responsible for the pilgrimage. He knocked at the door of the house and we said, "Who is it?" "The Emir," he replied. Then Thawri got up and went into the antechamber. Awza'i rose and greeted [the Emir] and 'Abd al-Samad ibn 'Ali said to him, "Who are you, oh Shaykh?" He said, "I am Abu 'Amr al-Awza'i." "May God make you live long and in peace!" he said. "Your letters have already reached us

---

123 On the importance of pious practices as a marker of identity in early Shi'ism, see Najam Haider, *The Origins of the Shi'a: Identity, Ritual, and Sacred Space in Eighth-Century Kufa* (Cambridge, UK: Cambridge University Press, 2011). Early Shiites such as Thawri often took on the identity of ascetic ritualists (*nussak*), like many of Rabi'a's other contemporaries. See Chapter 2 below for a detailed discussion of *nusk* as an ascetic practice.

and we have seen to your needs. But what has Sufyan al-Thawri done?" "He has gone into the antechamber," Awza'i replied. Then he went in after him and said, "This man wants only you." Sufyan came out with a frown on his face and said, "Peace be upon you. How are you?" 'Abd al-Samad ibn 'Ali said to him: "Oh Abu 'Abdullah, I have come to you so that I might record the proper rituals [of the pilgrimage] from you." Sufyan said to him: "Why don't I show you something that is better for you?" "What is that?" he asked. "Say what you really want." He said: "What am I to do about the Commander of the Believers Abu Ja'far [al-Mansur]?" Thawri replied: "If you really desire God, then God will take care of Abu Ja'far for you." Then Awza'i said to him, "Oh Abu 'Abdullah. These men are from the tribe of Quraysh and they don't want anything but praise from us." Thawri replied: "Oh Abu 'Amr. Verily we cannot beat them, so we have to train them (*fa-innama nu'addibuhum*) in the way that you see." Mufaddal said: Then I turned toward Awza'i and he said to me: "Let's get out of here. For I am sure that this one will send someone to put a rope around our necks." And what I predicted actually happened.[124]

Other accounts confirm that Thawri's opposition to the Abbasids caused him to be in danger of losing his life. Al-Khatib al-Baghdadi (d. 1071 CE) reports that in 775 CE the Caliph al-Mansur resolved to go to Mecca, where Thawri was then living, and crucify him for sedition. The carpenters had already started to construct the platform on which he would be executed. According to Baghdadi's account, when Thawri was called to present himself to the authorities, his head was in the lap of Fudayl ibn 'Iyad and his feet were in the lap of Sufyan ibn 'Uyayna. "Oh Abu 'Abdullah," they said to him, "Fear Allah and do not allow the enemy to deceive us." Thawri said, "We do not have to worry about Abu Ja'far [al-Mansur] ever entering Mecca." When Thawri later found out that al-Mansur had died before he could travel to Mecca, he denied that he had predicted the Caliph's death.[125]

The person in whose lap Thawri rested his head was the famous ascetic Fudayl ibn 'Iyad (d. 807 CE), of the Banu Tamim tribe of Kufa.[126] He was

---

124 Baghdadi, *Tarikh Baghdad*, vol. 9, p. 160. Although Awza'i eventually made peace with the Abbasids he was closely associated with the last rulers of the Damascus-based Umayyad dynasty of Caliphs, and lived under suspicion until the end of his life.
125 Ibid.
126 On Fudayl Ibn 'Iyad, see Knysh, *Islamic Mysticism*, pp. 23–4; Isfahani, *Hilya*, vol. 8, pp. 84–139; and Ibn al-Jawzi, *Sifat al-safwa*, vol. 2, pp. 237–47. Fudayl was one of

born, however, in Central Asia. Some accounts about Fudayl claim that he was a highwayman early in life.[127] Yet even as a highwayman, he had an ethical disposition. He would not rob a poor person or a caravan that carried a woman. After repenting and becoming an ascetic, he went first to Kufa and then to Mecca, where he spent the last decades of his life. Although Fudayl was not a Shiite, his ethics and concern for the poor were hallmarks of early Shi'ism. Thawri's attitude toward the poor was more equivocal. Despite Isfahani's claim that he refused to teach Hadith to Aramaic-speaking Iraqis and the lower classes, other reports say that he favored the poor over the rich in his teaching sessions. According to one account recorded by Isfahani, a person who attended Thawri's sessions said, "I have not seen the rich more reviled than at the session of Sufyan al-Thawri; and I have not seen the poor more glorified than at the session of Sufyan al-Thawri."[128]

The person in whose lap Thawri rested his feet was Sufyan ibn 'Uyayna (d. 814 CE), a *mawla* of the Banu Hilal tribe of Qays. Ibn 'Uyayna was born in Kufa. His father was a client of the Umayyad governor of Iraq, and he was forced to move to Mecca after his father's patron was deposed. Of possible Jewish origin, he was a major source of Jewish apocryphal accounts (*Isra'iliyyat*) that served as background material to Qur'an and Hadith in the early Islamic period.[129] In the *Fihrist*, Ibn al-Nadim identifies Ibn 'Uyayna as a Zaydi Shiite along with Thawri.[130] This claim is indirectly supported by his birth in Kufa, which was traditionally a Shiite city, although Sunnis could be found there too. Sufyan al-Thawri was also from Kufa. However, although Thawri may have been a Zaydi, he rejected the extremism of many Shiite groups and spoke out forcefully against them. At one point, he complained that the *Rawafid* (Shiite rejecters of the first three Sunni Caliphs) had gone so far in their extremism that he was ashamed even to mention the virtues of Imam 'Ali.[131]

This biographical information adds an important level of context to depictions of Sufyan al-Thawri's encounters with Rabi'a al-'Adawiyya. For example,

---

the most famous proto-Sufis and accounts of him can be found in many other sources as well.
127 Mun'im Sirry, "Pious Muslims in the Making: A Closer Look at Narratives of Ascetic Conversion," *Arabica*, 57 (4), 2010, pp. 437–54. Two versions of Fudayl's conversion story can be found on pp. 448–9.
128 Isfahani, *Hilya*, vol. 6, p. 365.
129 See Isfahani, *Hilya*, vol. 8, pp. 270–318 and Ibn al-Jawzi, *Sifat al-safwa*, vol. 2, pp. 231–7. See also, Morony, *Iraq after the Muslim Conquest*, p. 81, and Smith, *An Early Mystic of Baghdad*, pp. 75–6.
130 Dodge, *The Fihrist of al-Nadim*, vol. 1, p. 443; Tajaddud Arabic edition p. 226.
131 Dhahabi, *Siyar*, vol. 7, p. 253.

when Thawri and Dab'i go to Rabi'a in one account related by Sulami, Thawri raises his hands and prays, "Oh God, grant me safety!" Isfahani corroborates that this was a common habit of Thawri's. When he does this in Rabi'a's presence, however, she weeps. "What makes you weep?" Thawri asks. "You make me weep," she replies. "How?" he asks. She says, "Have you not learned that true safety from the world is to abandon all that is in it? So how can you ask for such a thing while you are still soiled with the world?"[132] Some readers may interpret this statement as a commentary on the virtues of the ascetic life. However, we can now see that it may have meant something quite different. Because of Thawri's opposition to the Abbasid regime, he might have been asking God for safety from those who sought to persecute him. Rabi'a might have wept out of real compassion for his misfortunes. Because they were nearly the same age, Thawri is depicted as seeking solace from Rabi'a as he would from a sister, and found comfort in her concern for his misfortunes. Nevertheless, Rabi'a does not spare Thawri the "tough love" that he needs. She informs him that the real tragedy is that he has brought his misfortune upon himself. Even in this desperate time, he is soiled with the affairs of the world. His political activism and confrontational attitude make him vulnerable to suffering, despite his denial of the world through his asceticism and high ethical standards.

In another account reported by Sulami, Thawri comes to Rabi'a and asks, "What is the best way for the slave to come close to God, the Glorious and Mighty?" Rabi'a weeps again and replies: "How can the likes of me be asked such a thing? The best way for the slave to come close to God Most High is for him to know that he must not love anything in this world or the Hereafter other than God."[133] In another account, Thawri comes to Rabi'a and complains, "How sorrowful I am!" Once again, Rabi'a cures his self-pity by rebuking him: "Do not lie!" she says. "Say instead: 'How little is my sorrow!' If you were truly sorrowful, life itself would not please you." "My own sorrow," Rabi'a explains, "is not from feeling sad. Rather, my sorrow is from not feeling sad enough."[134]

Some of Rabi'a's statements may be interpreted as moral lessons for Thawri. In one account, she comes across the body of a man who has been crucified. She says to the corpse, "Upon my father! With that tongue you used to say: 'There is no god but God!'" The narrator, who is named "Sufyan,"

---

132 Sulami, *Early Sufi Women*, p. 76.
133 Ibid., p. 80.
134 Ibid.

states, "Then she mentioned the good works that the man had done."[135] This lesson may have been meant as a consolation for Thawri. In effect, Rabi'a is saying that no matter how bad one's end may be, or for what crime one is punished, a person's good works will still be remembered after him. It also recounts the popular belief among Muslims that the mere act of saying the *Shahada*, "There is no god but God," leaves the door open to salvation, even for the worst sinners and criminals.

Sulami relates a similar account about Rabi'a and Salih al-Murri (d. 792–93 CE), a famous ascetic from Basra.[136] In this story, Murri comes to Rabi'a and paraphrases a statement by Jesus from the Sermon on the Mount (Matt. 7:7–8): "He who persists in knocking at the door will have it opened for him." Rabi'a replies: "The door is already open. But the question is, who wishes to enter it?"[137] In another version of this account, which appears in Sulami's *Kitab 'uyub al-nafs wa-mudawatiha* (*Book of the Faults of the Soul and Their Cures*), Rabi'a is much harsher with Murri: "The door, oh worthless one (*ya battal*), is open, but you run away from it! How will you arrive at a goal whose path has been laid out for you from the first step? How is the slave to save himself from the faults of his soul when his own desires have caused them? And how is one to save himself from following his desires when he cannot avoid acting in a contradictory manner?"[138] Rabi'a's message is clear: The door to your salvation is open. If you really want to enter, you know what you have to do.

b. Ta'dib: The Art of Character Formation

The style of teaching that Rabi'a used with Sufyan al-Thawri and Salih al-Murri in the accounts reproduced above was called *ta'dib*: literally, "training." A variant of this term is also used by Thawri when he explains how he intends to train the Abbasids by putting them in their place: "Verily we cannot beat them, so we have to train them" (*fa-innama nu'addibuhum*). The teacher

---

135 Ibid.
136 On Salih al-Murri see Isfahani, *Hilya*, vol. 6, pp. 165–77. On Murri's knowledge of the Qur'an see 'Abdullah Ibn al-Mubarak al-Marwazi, *Kitab al-zuhd wa yalihi Kitab al-raqa'iq*, ed. Habib al-Rahman al-'Azmi (Beirut: Dar al-Kutub al-'Ilmiyya, n.d.). Ibn al-Mubarak studied briefly under Sufyan al-Thawri and transmitted many of Thawri's exegetical comments on the Qur'an.
137 Sulami, *Early Sufi Women*, p. 80.
138 Pourjavady, *Majmu'at Sulami* (*Kitab 'uyub al-nafs*), pp. 72–3.

of *ta'dib* was the *mu'addib*, literally, "trainer." In the Umayyad and early Abbasid periods, this type of teaching supplemented other, more formal types of education. Sometimes, the term *ta'dib* was used metaphorically to describe the kind of training that comes from experience, what today would be called "the school of hard knocks." This is illustrated in the epigraph to this chapter, where the Abbasid Caliph Harun al-Rashid remarks: "He who is not educated by good behavior (*man lam yu'addibhu al-jamil*) is reformed by tribulations."[139] It can also be seen in the Arab saying, "Time suffices as a teacher; reason suffices as a guide (*kafa bi-l-dahri mu'addiban wa bi-l-'aqli murshidan*)."[140] The key verb in these aphorisms, *addaba*, is an Arabic cognate with *mu'addiba*, the word used by Thawri to describe Rabi'a the Teacher. The term *Rabi'a al-Mu'addiba* thus designates a female trainer, a woman who teaches *adab*. In the Umayyad and Abbasid periods, *adab* stood for an entire culture of conduct that combined Arab, Persian and Greek cultural ideals.[141]

According to the lexicographer E.W. Lane, the basic meaning of *adab* is "discipline of the mind and good qualities and attributes of the mind or soul." It "invites men to the acquisition of praiseworthy qualities and dispositions, and forbids them from acquiring such as are evil."[142] Under the influence of the Abbasid courtier Ibn al-Muqaffa' (d. 759 CE), who wrote two treatises on *adab*, the term came to be understood as an ethic of self-presentation, which included the virtues of eloquence, courtesy, prudence and self-restraint.[143] For Ibn al-Muqaffa', *adab* stood more for the character that one earned and the honor that one achieved than the position into which one was born. "If people honor you for money or power, it should not please you," he stated, "for honor can be lost with the loss of these things. Instead, it should please you only if they honor you for religion or for *adab*."[144] In his works on *adab* and advice to rulers, Ibn al-Muqaffa' created an ethic that sought to combine

---

139 Abu 'Umar Ahmad ibn Muhammad ibn 'Abd Rabbih al-Andalusi (d. 940 CE), *Kitab al-'iqd al-farid* (*The Unique Necklace*), ed. Ibrahim al-Abyari (Beirut: Dar al-Kitab al-'Arabi, 1990), vol. 5, p. 61.
140 Ibid., vol. 2, p. 237.
141 In *The Attainment of Happiness* (*Tahsil al-sa'ada*) the Islamic philosopher Abu Nasr al-Farabi (d. 950 CE) uses the term *ta'dib* to describe the training of the Young Guardians in Plato's *Republic*. Here the term means "character formation" and is contrasted with "instruction" (*ta'lim*). According to Joshua Parens, for Farabi, "the hallmark of *ta'dib* is 'habituation' (*ta'awwud*)." Joshua Parens, *An Islamic Philosophy of Virtuous Religions: Introducing Alfarabi* (Albany, NY: SUNY Press, 2006), pp. 32–3.
142 Lane, *Arabic–English Lexicon*, vol. 1, p. 35.
143 Michael Cooperson, "Ibn al-Muqaffa'," *Dictionary of Literary Biography Volume 311: Arabic Literary Culture, 500–925*, pp. 156–8.
144 Ibn 'Abd Rabbih, *al-'Iqd al-farid*, vol. 2, p. 412.

the best characteristics of Persian aristocratic culture and concepts of the noble self in pre-Islamic and early Islamic Arab culture. In subsequent generations, books on various types of *adab* were written following Ibn al-Muqaffa'*'*s model: there was an *adab* for princes, an *adab* for court officials, an *adab* of literature, and even an *adab* for seekers on the Sufi path (*adab al-sufiyya*). The Persian Sufi Sulami, who depicted Rabi'a al-'Adawiyya as the quintessential Sufi woman, wrote one of the first Sufi treatises on *adab*.[145]

In his discussion of *adab* in *The Venture of Islam*, Marshall Hodgson stressed the non-Arab roots of the culture of the *adib*, the courtly practitioner of *adab* as envisioned by Ibn al-Muqaffa'. Hodgson viewed *adab* as a form of secular culture; it drew heavily on pre-Islamic models of conduct that came from Greek philosophy and Persian aristocratic traditions. According to Hodgson, the secular culture of the *adib* was opposed by the Piety-Minded, who "looked to the moralistic and populistic strains in the Irano-Semitic background" for their models of behavior.[146] For Hodgson, the ideals of religion and *adab* stood at opposite cultural poles. Religion represented the moralism of Islam's Semitic origins, whereas *adab* represented the urbane and literate traditions of non-Semitic peoples, such as Greeks, Persians and Indians.

Unfortunately, Hodgson's view of *adab* was badly shortsighted. First of all, although he ascribes the religious values of the Piety-Minded to a combined "Irano-Semitic" cultural ethos, his more positive view of secular *adab* culture as Greek, Persian and Indian (i.e., Aryan) is arguably anti-Semitic. Second, his understanding of *adab* is accurate only in terms of high culture and belles-lettres. *Littérateurs* such as Ibn al-Muqaffa', who translated Indian works into Arabic, or Jahiz, who was a master stylist and was strongly influenced by court fashions, do in fact fit this pattern. However, Hodgson's emphasis on the non-Arab origins of *adab* caused him to overlook the important role that *adab* played in Arab society, both before and after the coming of Islam. Most crucially, his emphasis on the secular nature of this concept caused him to ignore the importance of *adab* among the Piety-Minded. Sources such as Isfahani's *Hilyat al-awliya'* and other early works on the ascetic tradition of Islam reveal that the Piety-Minded had their own version of *adab* culture. The trope of Rabi'a the Teacher, which comes from this culture, draws primarily from Arab and pietistic notions of *adab*. A deeper look at this tradition reveals that the *adab* of the religious teacher-trainer (*mu'addib*) may not have been the same as the *adab* of the *littérateur* (*adib*) as Hodgson imagined, but it

---

145 See Sulami, *Jawami' adab al-sufiyya*, ed. Nasrollah Pourjavady (op. cit.).
146 Hodgson, *Venture of Islam*, vol. 1, pp. 451–2.

was still part of the wider culture of *adab*. A fuller and more accurate picture of *adab* in the late Umayyad and early Abbasid periods emerges when one realizes that the discourse of *adab* was multivalent: a single term could have different meanings for different groups. While both the *littérateur* and the teacher-trainer cultivated *adab* through the pedagogy of *ta'dib*, the type of *adab* that was taught in each case was different.

c. Ta'dib *and the "Manly" Virtues:* Muruwwa *and* Hilm

In pre-Islamic Arabia, *adab* was associated with the virtue known as *muruwwa*.[147] In Arabic, *muruwwa* means "manliness"; hence, the term reflected a notion of virtue that was based on the ideal behavior of the mature male. Pre-Islamic *muruwwa* put a high value on the virtues of courage and loyalty, particularly toward one's clan or kin group. However, these virtues were not to be expressed rashly. Instead, they had to be tempered with the good judgment that came from maturity and experience. The key element in good judgment was sound reason. As a hadith of the Prophet Muhammad states, "He who does not have *adab* does not have reason (*'aql*)."[148] The set of virtues that was associated with *muruwwa* and the use of sound reason were expressed in Arabic by the term *hilm*. The *halim*, the possessor of *hilm*, was a person who exercised good judgment, had a calm and balanced mind, and practiced self-restraint. The opposite of the *halim* was the *jahil*, the ignorant and impetuous person, who was driven by the passions and was heedless of the consequences of his behavior.[149]

In the early Islamic period, the Arab moral concepts of *adab*, *muruwwa*, and *hilm* were assimilated to the Islamic religious concept of faith (*iman*). For the Japanese scholar of Islam Toshihiko Izutsu, *hilm* was so important to the early Islamic understanding of morality that he regarded this concept as "the pre-religious, pre-Islamic form of the concept of *islam* itself."[150] Although

---

147 On the concept of *muruwwa* in pre-Islamic Arabia, see Reynold A. Nicholson, *A Literary History of the Arabs* (Cambridge: Cambridge University Press, 1969 reprint of 1914 first edition), pp. 82–100. This term may also be transliterated as *muru'a*.
148 Ibn 'Abd Rabbih, *al-'Iqd al-farid*, vol. 2, p. 415.
149 Toshihiko Izutsu, *God and Man in the Koran: Semantics of the Koranic Weltanschauung* (Salem, NH: Ayer Company, 1987), p. 205; this work is a reprint of the 1964 first edition (Tokyo: The Keio Institute of Cultural and Linguistic Studies).
150 Ibid., p. 204; Charles Pellat reaches a similar conclusion to Izutsu's in the article, "Seriousness and Humour in Early Islam (*Al-Jidd wa 'l-Hazl fi Sadr al-Islam*)," *Islamic Studies*, 2 (3), 1963, pp. 353–62. On p. 353 he states, "[H]*ilm*, even if the Muslims

it connoted an ethic of restraint, *hilm* was not a passive quality. In Izutsu's words, "There can be no *hilm* where there is no power. It is essentially a quality of a man who governs and dominates others, and not of those who are governed and dominated."[151] In the Qur'an, God is called *al-Halim*. This attribute means that God, despite the fact that He is all-powerful, restrains Himself from acting tyrannically. In most places where this term is used in the Qur'an, the divine name *al-Halim* is accompanied by the divine name *al-Ghafur*, "The Forgiving" (cf. Qur'an 2:225). This pairing of concepts in the Qur'an indicates that the attribute of *hilm* was intended to be associated with restraint. According to the tenth-century Andalusian *littérateur* Ibn 'Abd Rabbih, the true person of faith (*mu'min*) is also a person of *hilm*: "Three things complete one's faith. When one is angry, his anger does not take him beyond the bounds of the truth. When he is pleased, his pleasure does not lead him toward oppression or immorality. When he has power he does not try to possess that which does not belong to him."[152] What is true of *hilm* is similarly true of *muruwwa*. Ibn 'Abd Rabbih quotes the Prophet Muhammad as saying, "There is no religion (*din*) without *muruwwa*."[153]

Virtues such as *muruwwa* and *hilm* were not just individual traits in pre-Islamic Arab culture. They were also seen as hereditary possessions that were acquired from one's ancestors, and certain tribes and clans were known for specific virtues. Among some groups of Arabs, such as the pre-Islamic Christian town-dwellers of Hira in Iraq, the store of virtues might include piety and asceticism. The Christian Arabs of Hira were known collectively as *al-'Ibad*, literally "Worshippers," and distinguished themselves by producing the oldest recorded poetry in the Arabic language.[154] Rabi'a's clan, 'Adi ibn Qays, were known for their asceticism as far back as the time of the Prophet Muhammad. In *Sifat al-safwa*, Ibn al-Jawzi reports that a contemporary of Rabi'a, the Basra traditionist Abu Sawwar al-'Adawi, boasted: "The people of Banu 'Adi are the most rigorous ascetics in this land! Here is Abu al-Sahba' [Sila ibn Ushaym al-'Adawi], who did not sleep during the night and did not eat during the day, and here is his wife Mu'adha bint 'Abdullah [al-'Adawiyya],

---

unconsciously practice it, must be regarded as a cardinal virtue in Islamic ethics, and we can at once see some sort of connection between the excellence of behaviour and seriousness of speech."
151 Izutsu, *God and Man in the Koran*, p. 207.
152 Ibn 'Abd Rabbih, *al-'Iqd al-Farid*, vol. 2, p. 264.
153 Ibid., p. 276; Ibn Qutayba, *'Uyun al-akhbar*, vol. 2, p. 340, attributes this saying to al-Hasan al-Basri.
154 Nicholson, *Literary History of the Arabs*, p. 138.

who did not look up at the sky for forty years!"[155] This account implies that the "real" Rabi'a al-'Adawiyya would have been honored among her clan not only because of her personal piety and asceticism, but also because her religious practices conformed to a clan-based tradition of asceticism. Paradoxically, her celibacy and asceticism, the characteristics that set her apart as an individual from other women of her day, were also "traditional" practices because they followed long-standing customs among her people. Some clans produced kings, some clans produced poets; the clan of Banu 'Adi ibn Qays produced ascetics.

This last point is an important reminder of the cultural differences that separated the late Umayyad and early Abbasid periods in which Rabi'a lived, from later eras of Islamic history. This is also important for the study of Sufism, because later Sufi writers tended to project the terminology and doctrinal usages of their own times back onto those, such as Rabi'a al-'Adawiyya, who were seen as the founding figures of the Sufi tradition. It is also important to remember that Rabi'a lived in a time when the term, "Sufism" (*tasawwuf*) was little known and when later Sufi technical terms, such as *al-tariqa* ("the way") were largely unknown. Perhaps the clearest example of this difference can be found in the popularity of the term *muruwwa* in early Sufism (ninth and tenth centuries CE). Within two centuries after Rabi'a's death, this ethical term of Arab origin would be replaced by *futuwwa*, an Arabized concept of Persian origin. Although the Arabic term *fata* ("youth") was often used and appears once in the Qur'an (Qur'an 21:60), the technical term *futuwwa* appears to have emerged as an Arabic calque on the Persian *javanmardi*, "young-manliness."[156]

The introduction of the term, *futuwwa*, paralleled the growing influence of Persian culture in Abbasid society. Its adoption by Sufis seems to have symbolized the replacement of an Arab cultural ethic that saw virtue embodied in maturity and the wisdom of experience with a Persian cultural ethic that saw virtue embodied in the ideals of youth and noble innocence. Although Sufi traditions trace the use of the term *futuwwa* as far back as the Shiite Imam Ja'far al-Sadiq (d. 765 CE), it does not come into historical view until the

---

155 Ibn al-Jawzi, *Sifat al-safwa*, vol. 2, p. 22; this passage is translated in the Appendix to Sulami, *Early Sufi Women*, p. 264.
156 On the origins of *futuwwa*, see the recent major study by Lloyd Ridgeon, *Moral and Mysticism in Persian Sufism: A History of Sufi Futuwwat in Iran* (London: Routledge, 2010).

ninth century CE and it was not used frequently until the tenth century CE.¹⁵⁷ It did not become prominent as a Sufi concept until after the publication of Sulami's *Kitab al-futuwwa* around the beginning of the eleventh century.¹⁵⁸

d. Rabi'a's Way of Ta'dib

In order to view the "real" Rabi'a the Teacher in the context of her own time and place, we must be careful not to project later Sufi terms and practices back onto the past. Instead, we should view the sayings and teachings attributed to Rabi'a in the context of the culture of *adab* that existed in the late Umayyad and early Abbasid periods. This culture retained many of the concepts of pre-Islamic Arabia, including the notion that the purpose of *adab* was to build moral character. This view of *adab* as a means of character development was prominent among the Umayyads, who sent their princes to the Syrian Desert for moral and physical training. In the second half of the Umayyad period, from the Caliphate of 'Abd al-Malik ibn Marwan (d. 705 CE), the *mu'addib* or personal mentor-trainer was a common figure at the Umayyad court. According to Philip Hitti, the qualities that the Umayyads sought to acquire from this training were courage, endurance, respect for the rights of neighbors, manly virtue (*muruwwa*), generosity, hospitality, respect for women, and the fulfillment of promises.¹⁵⁹

Among the Piety-Minded, the religious aspect of *ta'dib* as character formation was epitomized in a statement that has often been attributed to the Prophet Muhammad, although it does not appear in any of the six canonical Hadith collections: "Verily Allah has trained me and has ennobled my character" (*inna Allaha addabani fa-ahsana ta'dibi*).¹⁶⁰ Abu 'Abd al-Rahman al-Sulami cites as a source for this saying not the Prophet but the early Sufi Shaqiq al-Balkhi (d. 810 CE), a contemporary of Rabi'a al-'Adawiyya and a noted ascetic of Afghanistan and Central Asia.¹⁶¹ For practitioners of *ta'dib*

---

157 Muhammad Ja'far Mahjub, "Chivalry and Early Persian Sufism," in *Classical Persian Sufism: From its Origins to Rumi*, ed. Leonard Lewisohn (London and New York: Khaniqah-i Nimatullahi Publications, 1993), pp. 549–81.
158 For an English translation of this work, see Muhammad ibn al-Husayn al-Sulami, *The Book of Sufi Chivalry: Lessons to a Son of the Moment*, trans. Sheikh Tosun Bayrak al-Jerrahi al-Halveti (New York: Inner Traditions International, 1983).
159 Hitti, *History of the Arabs*, p. 253.
160 Sulami, *Jawami' adab al-sufiyya*, p. 343; another version of this hadith states: "Verily Allah has trained me and has improved my *adab*" (*inna Allaha addabani fa-ahsana adabi*).
161 On Shaqiq al-Balkhi see Isfahani, *Hilya*, vol. 8, pp. 58–73.

such as Rabi'a and Shaqiq, the Prophet was a "beautiful example" (*uswa hasana*, Qur'an 33:61) whose *adab* provided the model for all Muslims to follow. The early Sufi treatise *Kitab al-Luma'* by Abu Nasr al-Sarraj contains a chapter titled, "The Book of the Example and Emulation of the Messenger of God" (*Kitab al-uswa wa-l-iqtida' bi-Rasul Allah*). In this chapter, Sarraj encourages Sufis to follow the Sunna of the Prophet as thoroughly as possible, taking special care to acquire the Prophet's moral states and inner spiritual consciousness.[162] It was necessary for Sufis to pattern their conduct on the *adab* of the Prophet because, in the words of a famous hadith from *Sahih Muslim*, "The morals of the Messenger of God were of the Qur'an; he approved what it approved and he disliked what it disliked."[163]

Two centuries after Sarraj, the Andalusian jurist Qadi 'Iyad ibn Musa al-Yahsubi (d. 1150 CE) summarized the Prophet's *adab* in *Kitab al-Shifa' bi-ta'rif huquq al-Mustafa* (*The Antidote in Recognizing the Rights of the Chosen One*). Qadi 'Iyad was one of the foremost traditionists of the Islamic West and Chief Justice (*qadi al-jama'a*) of the cities of Granada in Spain and Sabta (Ceuta) in Morocco. His goal in writing the book was to restore the ethical values of Muslims by reorienting believers toward the practices of the early Muslim community. This work provides important details about the personal qualities that were prized by early Muslims, including those in Rabi'a's time. For Qadi 'Iyad, the chief significance of the Prophet's example—apart from his purely religious role—was the excellence of his character (*husn al-khuluq*). This was revealed in his "equanimity in strength of spirit" (*al-i'tidal fi quwwat al-nafs*), a trait that was fundamental to the concept of *muruwwa*. The practical wisdom (*hilm*) of the Prophet was revealed in his moderation (*tawassut*) and in his ability to prioritize issues and put them in their proper place. Other traits that made the Prophet an excellent example for Muslims also resulted from *muruwwa*. These included forbearance, generosity, bravery, fellowship, sympathy, humility, dignity, justice and the renunciation of worldly possessions. Assimilating these traits through *adab*, said Qadi 'Iyad, promises "eternal happiness to the person who patterns his conduct on them and makes them his own, for they are a portion of prophethood."[164]

---

162 Sarraj, *Kitab al-Luma'*, pp. 93–5.
163 See *Sahih Muslim*, Bab al-Musafirin, p. 139 for the first half of this hadith. Both the first and second portions of the hadith can be found in al-Qadi Abu al-Fadl 'Iyad al-Yahsubi, *al-Shifa' bi-ta'rif huquq al-Mustafa* (Beirut: Dar al-Kutub al-'Ilmiyya, 1979), vol. 1, p. 96. The Prophet's wife 'A'isha Bint Abi Bakr is often cited as a transmitter of this hadith.
164 Ibid., pp. 96–106.

Acquiring virtues such as these was the goal of the *ta'dib* that the "real" Rabi'a al-'Adawiyya would have imparted to her students and associates. For the Piety-Minded, *adab* was built on religiously based moral qualities that when properly assimilated gave rise to the maturity and wisdom of *muruwwa*. The acquisition of *muruwwa* led to the virtue of *hilm*, the combination of justice, forbearance and dignity that epitomized the mature personality of the righteous Muslim. The ultimate goal of *ta'dib* as character formation was the attainment of wisdom, which was revealed through the behaviors associated with *muruwwa* and *hilm*.

This view of Rabi'a's way of *ta'dib* agrees with Toshihiko Izutsu's description of ethical formation in early Islam. For Izutsu, this method of training "has in itself a latent possibility of being developed and elaborated philosophically into something close to the Hellenistic view of 'non-perturbation' based on the cultivation of autarchy [i.e., a fully independent self]."[165] Much like the "philosophy as a way of life" practiced by the pre-Islamic Hellenistic philosophers the way of *ta'dib* that Rabi'a would have used to train her students was a complete method of character formation. It was based on a regime of disciplines that led to the cultivation of religious and social virtues, moral uprightness, and practical wisdom. In later generations, Sufis would call such a regime of disciplines *al-Tariqa*, "the Way." However, for Rabi'a al-'Adawiyya, who lived before Sufism became an institutionalized practice (*madhhab*) in Islam, the term *tariqa* in this sense was unknown. For Rabi'a, her way of *ta'dib* was her *tariqa*. To put it another way, the *ta'dib* taught by Rabi'a the Teacher constituted the "*tariqa*" before the Sufi *Tariqa*.

The individual lessons of *ta'dib* in Rabi'a's time were made up of *masa'il* (sing. *mas'ala*), literally "topics" or "problems," which were to be solved in her teachings. This is what Sulami was referring to when he stated in his Book of Sufi Women that Sufyan al-Thawri sought *masa'il* from Rabi'a al-'Adawiyya.[166] For Muslims of the Umayyad and early Abbasid eras, *masa'il* were understood as sub-categories of knowledge: they contained important lessons in life, ethics, or spirituality. Students often learned them from their teachers in the form of aphorisms or other types of wisdom teachings.[167] Numerous

---

165 Izutsu, *God and Man in the Koran*, p. 211.
166 Sulami, *Early Sufi Women*, pp. 74–5. In the Introduction to *Early Sufi Women*, I stressed the jurisprudential meaning of the term *masa'il* and characterized Rabi'a as teaching a form of *fiqh al-mu'amalat* or the jurisprudence of interpersonal behavior (ibid., p. 63). Although this was not entirely incorrect, I now believe that the Proto-Sufi use of the term *mas'ala* is better understood in the pedagogical sense described above.
167 I am grateful to my colleague Devin J. Stewart of Emory University for this insight.

accounts from early Islam confirm that the term *mas'ala* bore a pedagogical meaning and that it was often used to designate lessons or exercises of a moral or ethical nature. In *Hilyat al-awliya'*, Abu Nu'aym al-Isfahani refers to the teachings of Rabi'a's contemporary Shaqiq al-Balkhi as *masa'il*. According to this understanding, *masa'il* were stepping-stones or stages on the path of ethical or spiritual wisdom. For example, Shaqiq al-Balkhi summarized the process of ethical formation as a five-step program of *masa'il*. He said, "One should not sit at the feet of any person of knowledge unless he teaches him how to advance from five *masa'il* to five *masa'il*:

1. From doubt to certainty (*min al-shakk ila al-yaqin*).
2. From enmity to constructive advice (*min al-'adawa ila al-nasiha*).
3. From arrogance to humility (*min al-kibr il al-tawadu'*).
4. From vanity to sincerity (*min al-riya' ila al-ikhlas*).
5. From desire [for God] to awe [of God] (*min al-raghba ila al-rahba*)."[168]

As an early Islamic program of character development, the way of *ta'dib* combined the Arab cultural tradition of practical wisdom with the spirituality of the Qur'an and the Sunna. In pedagogical terms, the teaching practices of the early Islamic *mu'addibun* belonged to a pan-Mediterranean cultural tradition that put Islam in dialogue with early Christianity and early rabbinic Judaism, and even with certain schools of Greek philosophy. Early Muslim writers were aware of the correspondences among these traditions. For example, Ibn 'Abd Rabbih (d. 940 CE), an Andalusian *littérateur* who lived about a century and a half after Rabi'a al-'Adawiyya, associated the way of *ta'dib* with the self-formation of Jesus: "It was asked of Jesus the Son of Mary, 'Who trained you (*man addabaka*)?' 'No one trained me,' Jesus answered. 'Rather, I saw that ignorance (*jahl*) was bad so I avoided it.'"[169] Ibn 'Abd Rabbih also cites a *mas'ala* about *adab* that he attributes to the Greek philosopher Diogenes (Ar. *Dijanis*, d. 323 BCE): "Diogenes was asked, 'What traits are most useful at the end of one's life?' He replied: 'Faith in God, the Glorious and Mighty, the righteousness of one's parents, love for the scholars, and the acceptance of *adab*.'"[170]

Despite the fact that this aphorism is too religiously Islamic to be authentic, Ibn 'Abd Rabbih's citation of Diogenes is important because this famous

---

168 Isfahani, *Hilya*, vol. 8, p. 72.
169 Ibn 'Abd Rabbih, *al-'Iqd al-Farid*, vol. 2, p. 438.
170 Ibid., p. 415.

Cynic philosopher was reputed to be an originator of the aphoristic style of teaching ascribed to Rabi'a and other early Sufis.[171] The Greek word for "training" is *askesis*. Likewise, the Arabic word *ta'dib* also means "training." For Hellenistic philosophers such as the Cynics and the Stoics, whose path to wisdom was based on a disciplined regime of character formation, philosophy was a form of *askesis*, a method of training for a complete way of life. Pierre Hadot summarizes this view of *askesis* in a way that resembles the concept of *ta'dib* as attributed to Rabi'a al-'Adawiyya in the earliest sources: "In their view, philosophy did not consist in teaching an abstract theory—much less in the exegesis of texts—but rather in the art of living. It is a concrete attitude and determinate life-style, which engages the whole of existence."[172]

The Roman Stoic philosopher Musonius Rufus (d. 101-2 CE) defined *askesis* as "the learning of the lessons appropriate to each and every excellence; practical training must follow invariably, if indeed from the lessons we have learned we hope to derive any benefit."[173] A similar view of pedagogy characterized the late Umayyad and early Abbasid approach to *ta'dib* as character development. In his treatise *On Askesis*, Musonius Rufus describes the character traits of the fully trained ascetic in a way that brings to mind early Islamic notions of *adab*, *hilm*, and *muruwwa*. These traits include moderation, temperance, self-control, and detachment from worldly affairs. Much as the figure of Rabi'a the Teacher might have stated about *ta'dib*, Musonius defines *askesis* as "a mental and moral discipline, a matter of knowledge and ethics that consists in training the mind to discern true good from true evil and to act accordingly."[174]

In *Hilyat al-awliya'* Shaqiq al-Balkhi is quoted as saying, "Befriend people the way that you befriend fire. Take what benefits you from them, but beware lest you get burned by them."[175] Diogenes the Cynic could have made a similar comment. In Sulami's Book of Sufi Women Rabi'a says, "I ask God's forgiveness for my lack of truthfulness in saying, 'I ask God's forgiveness.'"[176] The Stoic philosopher Epictetus (d. ca. 135 CE) might have agreed with this

---

171 Geary, *The World in a Phrase*, pp. 52-5.
172 Hadot, *Philosophy as a Way of Life*, p. 83.
173 James A. Francis, *Subversive Virtue: Asceticism and Authority in the Second-Century Pagan World* (University Park, PA: Pennsylvania State University Press, 1995), p. 11. See also, Valentasis, "Musonius Rufus and Roman Ascetical Theory," in *The Making of the Self*, pp. 279-98.
174 Francis, *Subversive Virtue*, p. 13.
175 Isfahani, *Hilya*, vol. 8, p. 73.
176 See Sulami, *Early Sufi Women*, p. 78. The earliest example of this statement is by the Sufi Abu Bakr al-Kalabadhi (d. 990 CE). See Abu Bakr Muhammad ibn Ishaq al-Bukhari

statement.¹⁷⁷ Many other examples can be found to suggest that the aphoristic teaching method of early Islamic sages such as Rabi'a al-'Adawiyya and Shaqiq al-Balkhi was part of a pan-Mediterranean pedagogical culture that inherited much from Hellenism. This has long been recognized as true for early Christianity and early rabbinic Judaism, so why should it not be true for early Islam as well? It should not be unthinkable to suggest that similarities between the pedagogical methods of Hellenistic *askesis* and early Islamic *ta'dib* might have provided a bridge between the cultures of classical antiquity, late antiquity, and early Islam. Richard Valentasis, a major scholar of Christian asceticism, has argued: "The definition of asceticism, dependent as it has been on Late Antique models, must now shift to authors and projects of the imperial period as models and systems of asceticism that preceded and perhaps even produced the later and more familiar asceticism of Late Antique Romans, Jews, and Christians."¹⁷⁸

The same might be said, I would argue, for *askesis* and *ta'dib* as character development. In the century after Rabi'a, the philosopher Abu Ishaq al-Kindi (d. 873 CE)—a descendant of the pre-Islamic Arab ruling family of Kinda in Iraq—wrote a short treatise titled, *On Dispelling Sorrows*. This work combines the Stoic and Cynic ethics of *askesis* with the early Islamic ethic of *ta'dib*. Kindi argues in this work that since God provides everything, sadness for the loss of one's possessions is irrational. One should train oneself not to desire anything; this leads to the acquisition of good habits. It is better to cure the soul through ascetic pursuits because the soul endures, whereas the body perishes. One should therefore be thankful for what one has because in truth, no one owns anything. To illustrate these ethical teachings, Kindi uses the figure of Socrates, who is portrayed more as a Stoic or a Cynic than as Plato describes him in the *Dialogues*.¹⁷⁹ Kindi also published a work on *The Sayings of Socrates*. This consists of 39 short anecdotes, many of which are aphoristic sayings. Peter Adamson notes in his translation of this work that the genre of "gnomic" or wisdom literature was one of the most important

---

al-Kalabadhi, *Kitab al-ta'arruf li-madhhab ahl al-tasawwuf*, ed. A.J. Arberry (Cairo: Maktabat al-Khanji, 1994 reprint of 1933 first edition), p. 64.

177 Epictetus is famous for saying, "God grant me the serenity to accept the things I cannot change, courage to change the things I can, and wisdom to know the difference." See Geary, *The World in a Phrase*, pp. 62–5.

178 Valentasis, *The Making of the Self*, p. 297.

179 Peter Adamson and Peter E. Pormann (eds.), *The Philosophical Works of al-Kindi* (Karachi: Oxford University Press, 2012), pp. 245–6; the Arabic title of *On Dispelling Sorrows* is not given in this source.

ways in which Greek ideas were disseminated in the early Islamic world.[180] Stylistically, many of the aphorisms in this work are similar to those attributed to Rabi'a al-'Adawiyya. Some are strikingly reminiscent of Rabi'a's statements: "An opulent man said to him: 'Socrates, how exceedingly poor you are!' Socrates replied: 'If you knew what poverty was, you would be too busy pitying yourself than lamenting for Socrates.'"[181] "One of his disciples said to him: 'Teacher, why do we see no signs of grief in you?' He replied: 'I own nothing which, were I to lose it, would make me sad.'"[182] "He used to say: 'Wisdom is the ladder leading up high; he who lacks it lacks closeness to his Creator.'"[183]

Because of examples like these, I would argue that whereas Richard Valentasis looks backward in time for antecedents of late antique Christian and Jewish ascetic concepts, one could just as well look forward to their continuation in the early Islamic period. Early Muslim ascetics and teachers such as Rabi'a al-'Adawiyya and Shaqiq al-Balkhi should be added to this genealogy. Historiographically, this contention supports Garth Fowden's argument that the end of late antiquity did not coincide with the coming of the Prophet Muhammad and the revelation of the Qur'an, as most scholars of early Christianity suppose. Instead, both Christian late antiquity and early Islam were part of a "long first millennium," which lasted, in Fowden's words, "from Augustus to Avicenna."[184] As Fowden states: "There are intellectual and spiritual benefits to be had from a contextualized approach to early Islam. It may, for example, uncover fertile dimensions of the tradition forgotten or misapprehended even by Muslims themselves."[185] Taking a more comprehensive and comparative approach to concepts such as *ta'dib* and *askesis* is one way to begin reading both Muslim and Christian "orthodoxies against the grain," as Fowden advocates.[186]

Garth Fowden's culturally inclusive approach to the historiography of late antiquity and early Islam suggests important implications for the historiography of Sufism and its relationship to pre-Islamic civilizations. Rather than

---

180 Ibid., p. 267.
181 Ibid., p. 268.
182 Ibid.
183 Ibid., p. 270.
184 Garth Fowden, *Before and after Muhammad: The First Millennium Refocused* (Princeton and Oxford: Princeton University Press, 2014). This new historiographic perspective was first suggested by Fowden in *Empire to Commonwealth: Consequences of Monotheism in Late Antiquity* (Princeton, NJ: Princeton University Press, 1993).
185 Fowden, *Before and after Muhammad*, p. 3.
186 Ibid.

seeing Sufism and its immediate antecedents as a set of practices unique to Islam, or as sharing elements with only the monotheistic religious traditions, Fowden's approach opens the door to comparisons between early Sufi and Proto-Sufi traditions and the ascetic practices and disciplinary regimes of pre-Islamic philosophies such as Cynicism, Stoicism and Neo-Platonism. However, just because some late pagan philosophers or Hellenized Christians practiced forms of spiritual training that resembled those of early Muslim sages, this does not necessarily mean that early Muslims directly borrowed philosophical or Christian models of spirituality as Margaret Smith and other scholars have surmised.[187] The mere existence of such similarities does not prove that early Muslims founded the concept of *ta'dib* on exactly the same principles as their late antique predecessors. However, the fact remains that the parallels between late antique and early Muslim practices of character formation are striking; thus, they should be studied seriously. In light of this evidence, it becomes important to ask the following questions: If the early Islamic concept of *ta'dib* was comparable to the late antique concept of *askesis*, how might this affect our understanding of early ascetical traditions in Islam and their relationship to Sufism? How might Fowden's attempt to extend the culture of late antiquity into the Abbasid period affect our understanding of the tropes of Rabi'a the Ascetic, Rabi'a the Lover, and Rabi'a the Sufi? These questions will be addressed in the next three chapters.

---

187 For Margaret Smith, "It was inevitable that Christianity should have its effect upon the religious development of Islam, and Christian elements were to be found even in the time of Muhammad, and in the Qur'an itself, as well as in the Traditions, and in the rules for religious observances accepted by the orthodox as having the authority, or being in accordance with the precepts, of the founder of their faith." Idem, *Studies in Early Mysticism in the Near and Middle East* (Whitefish, MT: Kessinger Publishing Company, reprint of 1931 first edition, n.d.), p. 125.

Chapter 2

Rabi'a the Ascetic

"I am ashamed to ask for the world from the One who owns the world. So how can I ask for the world from one who does not own it?"
—Rabi'a in Jahiz, *al-Bayan wa-l-tabyin* and
Ibn Abi Tahir Tayfur, *Balaghat al-Nisa'*

Rabi'a was asked, "Have you ever performed any work (*'amal*) that you knew would be accepted by God?" She replied, "If there were such a thing, it would be my fear that my works would be held against me."
—Rabi'a in Jahiz, *al-Bayan wa-l-Tabyin*

For most Muslims today, Rabi'a al-'Adawiyya is a lover of God. In Sufism, she is widely regarded as the founder of Islamic Love mysticism. However, as we have seen in the previous chapter, the Rabi'a of the earliest narratives is often different from the Rabi'a of later narratives. We shall see in Chapter 3 how the Sufi trope of Rabi'a the Lover developed from a few quotes related by al-Harith al-Muhasibi and Ibn al-Junayd into a theology of divine Love under the Sufi Abu Talib al-Makki and his successors. Eventually, this trope would develop into a romantic legend that had little to do with the "real" Rabi'a. By contrast, for Jahiz, Ibn Abi al-Dunya, and Ibn Abi Tahir Tayfur, Rabi'a was primarily an ascetic. Jahiz describes her in *Kitab al-hayawan* as one of the "ascetic ritualists and renunciants among the Sunni women of asceticism and leadership." In *al-Bayan wa-l-tabyin*, he refers to her as one of "the ascetic ritualists and renunciants among the People of *Bayan*." In the earliest stages of the development of her myth, the tropes of Rabi'a the Teacher and Rabi'a the Ascetic are much more important than that of Rabi'a the Lover.

I. CONCEPTUALIZING ASCETICISM IN EARLY ISLAM

a. The World/Nonworld Dichotomy

Margaret Smith, the most important writer on Rabiʿa al-ʿAdawiyya in the English language, characterized Rabiʿa as "an ascetic of extreme otherworldliness."[1] More recently, Alexander Knysh observed, "Rabiʿa's whole life was marked by extreme asceticism and self-denial."[2] Early accounts about Rabiʿa agree that she focused more on the world to come than on the here-and-now. A useful way to conceptualize this worldview is through what Belgian anthropologist Jacques Maquet has termed the "World/Nonworld Dichotomy." For Maquet, the World/Nonworld Dichotomy is a cultural universal that is at once conceptual, behavioral, and institutional.[3] The "World" in this dichotomy refers to the social and economic networks along which human society is organized. It also refers to a set of values that are considered worldly. Comparing ascetical works in Christianity, Hinduism, and Buddhism, Maquet notes that worldly values are much the same regardless of the religion in which they appear—"pleasure and wealth, prestige and power."[4] The "Nonworld," by contrast, is an alternative worldview that liberates the ascetic from normal economic and social constraints and from the pursuit of worldly values.[5] Maquet's model of the World/Nonworld Dichotomy applies very well to asceticism in early Islam. The concept of asceticism as a form of mastery over worldly concerns and as a path of liberation from economic and social constraints was important for Rabiʿa and other early Muslim ascetics. As Rabiʿa says to Sufyan al-Thawri in Sulami's *Book of Sufi Women*, "Liberation from the world is to abandon all that is in it (*al-salama min al-dunya tark ma fiha*)."[6] This saying supports both Maquet's concept of the World/Nonworld Dichotomy and Richard Valentasis's more recent assertion that asceticism is focused on the construction of a countercultural identity: "Ascetic reality is by definition a resistant reality within a dominant system."[7]

---

1   Smith, *Rabiʿa* (Rainbow Bridge), p. 82 and (Oneworld), p. 105.
2   Knysh, *Islamic Mysticism*, p. 27.
3   Jacques Maquet, "The World/Nonworld Dichotomy," in *The Realm of the Extra-Human, Volume 2, Ideas and Actions*, ed. Agehananda Bharati (The Hague: Mouton, 1976), p. 56.
4   Ibid., p. 57.
5   Ibid., p. 58.
6   See Sulami, *Early Sufi Women*, pp. 76–7. In my edition of this work, I originally translated *salama* as "safety." I now believe that "liberation" from the world is a more meaningful translation of this term.
7   Valentasis, *The Making of the Self*, p. 54.

Although Maquet did not include Islam in his article on the World/Nonworld Dichotomy, this worldview has long been present in Islam, where it is expressed by the dichotomy of *al-dunya* ("the World") versus *al-akhira* ("the Afterlife" or "Nonworld").[8] This dichotomy is based on a fundamental opposition of values, just as Maquet found it to be in Christianity, Hinduism and Buddhism. The following verses of the Qur'an reflect this opposition of values and exemplify the World/Nonworld Dichotomy in Islam:

> Alluring to human beings is the love of worldly desires for women, children, weight upon weight of gold and silver, for branded horses, cattle, and tillable land. These are the pleasures of the life of *al-dunya*, but the most beautiful of all goals is with God. (Qur'an 3:14)

> Oh you who believe! What is the matter with you that when you are called to go forth in the Way of God, you cling heavily to the earthly world (*al-ard*)? Do you prefer the life of *al-dunya* to that of *al-akhira*? The pleasure of the life of *al-dunya* is but a paltry thing when compared with the life of *al-akhira*. (Qur'an 9:38)

> The life of *al-dunya* compared to *al-akhira* is nothing but a fleeting pleasure. (Qur'an 13:26)

> What is this life of *al-dunya* but an amusement and a game? Verily, the house of *al-akhira* is the true means of livelihood, if only they knew. (Qur'an 29:64)

> Nay, but you love this fleeting existence (*al-'ajila*) and avoid *al-akhira*. (Qur'an 75: 20–1)

As these verses indicate, Muslim ascetics did not have to go beyond the literal meaning of the Qur'an to find support for their renunciation of the World. The Qur'an is full of verses warning against the World and prescribing renunciation of it.[9] Real life is the life to come, whereas the World is but a fleeting pastime.

---

8   The Andalusian traveler and geographer Ibn Jubayr (ca. 1185 CE) called Muslim ascetics *rijal al-akhira* ("Men of the Nonworld/Afterlife"). See Josef Dreher, "Étude sur l'Origine et le Sens du Mot *'Uzla* dans la Littérature ascétique et mystique," *Mélanges de l'Institut dominicain d'Études orientales du Caire (MIDEO)*, 23, 1997, pp. 199–200.
9   See Toshihiko Izutsu, *Ethico-Religious Concepts in the Qur'an* (Montreal and London: McGill-Queen's University Press, 2002), especially pp. 45–54 ("The Pessimistic Conception of Earthly Life") and pp. 105–18 ("The Basic Moral Dichotomy").

God has charged His Messengers with the mission of informing humanity of the mercurial nature and false pleasures of the World. God's message, as portrayed in the Qur'an, warns believers to avoid the World's temptations and cautions against the assimilation of worldly values. The Muslims who took the concept of the World/Nonworld Dichotomy most to heart were those whom Marshall Hodgson called the "Piety-Minded"—those "for whom Islamic piety took precedence over any other interest."[10] As ascetically inclined Hadith transmitters, jurists and theologians, the Piety-Minded sought to preserve conformity to key beliefs, standard rituals, and elementary morality, and protected the integrity of Islam from outside influences.[11] However, the ascetics among the Piety-Minded went further by making the Nonworld a true vocation. By interiorizing scripture and tradition, they attempted to develop a new Islamic identity, an ascetic self that replaced the World with the Nonworld according to the teachings of the Qur'an and the Sunna of the Prophet Muhammad.[12] Whoever the real person was behind the trope of Rabi'a the Ascetic, she would have inhabited this Nonworld dimension and advocated its values.

However, merely to say that the trope of Rabi'a the Ascetic had to do with the World/Nonworld Dichotomy and the ethos of the Piety-Minded is not enough to describe the asceticism that Rabi'a al-'Adawiyya likely practiced. Detaching oneself from the World and attempting to inhabit the Nonworld is a complex process that requires a variety of ascetic attitudes and types of behavior. In the early Islamic period, each stage of this process was conceptualized differently and was designated by a specific term that expressed a particular approach to the construction of an ascetic identity. In order to understand the asceticism that Rabi'a may have practiced, it is necessary to examine the key terms of early Islamic asceticism in order to arrive at a clearer understanding of the concepts that lay behind the trope of Rabi'a the Ascetic. However, up till now there has not been a systematic study of asceticism in Islam, as has been attempted for early Christianity. Therefore, before discussing the trope of Rabi'a the Ascetic, it is first necessary to map the conceptual terrain of asceticism in early Islam.

In this chapter, I will attempt to sketch the preliminary outlines of this terrain by identifying the most important ascetic practices in Rabi'a's time.

---

10   Hodgson, *The Venture of Islam*, vol. 1, p. 250.
11   Ibid., p. 251.
12   My perspective here agrees in general with that of Gavin Flood, who considers the ascetic self "formed by tradition and internalizes tradition and its goals." See Gavin Flood, *The Ascetic Self: Subjectivity, Memory, and Tradition* (Cambridge, UK: Cambridge University Press, 2004), p. 3.

Only after this task is completed will it be possible to assess the ascetic practices that the "real" Rabi'a may have followed. As we shall see below, saying that someone was an ascetic in Rabi'a's time meant more than just one thing. Asceticism is a broad category that includes more than just a rejection of the World in favor of the Nonworld. For example, the *zahid* deeply explored the practices and attitudes of renunciation. The *wari'* took special precautions to avoid ethical failings. The *nasik* used a ritualized approach to renunciation to attain specific goals. These types of ascetic also lived in a state of *faqr*, poverty, as a general condition of their lives and practices. The trope of Rabi'a the Ascetic included all of these notions and more.

b. The Problem of Asceticism as a Theoretical Category

The terms "ascetic" and "asceticism" come from the Greek word *askesis*, which literally means, "training," as in the training of an athlete. In the Greco-Roman world asceticism comprised both a philosophy of life and a culture of practices that were considered "ascetic." We saw at the end of Chapter 1 that the term *askesis* for Stoic philosophers referred to a regime of character formation that sought to instill the virtues of moderation, temperance, self-control and detachment from worldly affairs. In this respect, *askesis* was similar to the early Islamic concept of *ta'dib*, which also meant character formation. In Rabi'a's time, the Arabic terms *hilm* and *muruwwa* stood for the virtues of patience, self-control, and detachment from petty affairs that character formation was supposed to develop. The *ta'dib* associated with the trope of Rabi'a the Teacher was a set of practices that trained the student for ethical and spiritual maturity. Because *ta'dib* and the Stoic version of *askesis* resulted in the formation of similar values, I suggested that early Islam perpetuated a culture of ethical training that was inherited from late antiquity.

Another issue that linked Rabi'a and her contemporaries to the worldview of late antiquity was the idea that ethical philosophy was not just a set of precepts but a way of life, a concept stressed by the French historian of philosophy, Pierre Hadot. Classical philosophers used the Greek term *bios* ("life") for this concept, whereas early Christians used the Greek term *hodos* ("way" or "path").[13] The notion of a way of life as a spiritual path provides a bridge, not only between Rabi'a and her non-Muslim predecessors, but also

---

13   Gail P. Corrington-Streete, "Trajectories of Ascetic Behavior," in *Asceticism*, ed. Vincent L. Wimbush and Richard Valentasis (Oxford and New York: Oxford University Press, 1998), p. 119.

between Rabiʿa and the Sufis who followed her in later generations. The fact that the ascetics of early Islam saw themselves as following a path of training for the spiritual life was a major reason why later systematizers of Sufism such as Abu ʿAbd al-Rahman al-Sulami and Abu Nuʿaym al-Isfahani considered them "Sufis," even if most early Muslim ascetics did not use this term themselves. Furthermore, because this path was based more on moral and spiritual character formation than on mystical doctrines, it was respected even by those who were opposed to mysticism, such as the late twelfth-century Hanbali scholar Ibn al-Jawzi. Despite the centrality of mystical doctrines in Sufism, the development of moral character has always been important to the Sufi Way. The Sufi systematizers of the tenth and eleventh centuries CE saw piety and ethics as the core values of Sufism and considered them the most important link between Sufism and the Sunna of the Prophet Muhammad.[14] This is why I concluded at the end of Chapter 1 that the discipline of *taʾdib* associated with the figure of Rabiʿa the Teacher amounted to "the *Tariqa* ("the Way") before the Sufi *Tariqa*."

This aspect of the culture of asceticism corresponds closely to Pierre Hadot's concept of philosophy as a way of life. Unfortunately, this notion has not been accepted universally by the academic discipline of philosophy and remains largely unknown in the field of Islamic Studies. In general, the lack of an adequate theoretical framework for comparison has held back the study of asceticism in Islam. Even outside the study of Islam, asceticism is seldom viewed as a philosophy; instead, it is seen as a (usually extreme) set of ritual practices within a religion. It has only recently become an object of comparative study in the field of Religious Studies and its main concepts are still not sufficiently understood. Before the publication of the edited volume *Asceticism* in 1998 by Vincent L. Wimbush and Richard Valentasis, the only other treatment of this subject that was comparative across all major religions was the survey of asceticism by James Hastings in the 1909 edition of the *Encyclopaedia of Religion and Ethics*.[15] In her book *Reading Renunciation*, Elizabeth A. Clark notes that despite numerous meetings throughout the 1980s, the Society of Biblical Literature Group on Ascetic Behavior in

---

14 For a discussion of Sufi ethics based on the writings of Sulami, see Kenneth Lee Honerkamp, "Sufi Foundations of the Ethics of Social Life in Islam," in *Voices of Islam, Volume Three: Voices of Life: Family, Home, and Society*, ed. Vincent J. Cornell (General Editor) and Virginia Gray Henry-Blakemore (Westport, CT and London: Praeger Publishers, 2007), pp. 181–96.

15 Vincent L. Wimbush and Richard Valentasis, "Introduction," in idem, *Asceticism*, p. xxii.

Greco-Roman Antiquity could not reach a consensus on the definition of asceticism. She reports, "Group members disagreed as to whether they should stress deprivation, pain, and the 'shrinking of the self' as definitive components of asceticism—or, conversely, the liberation of true 'human nature.'"[16] Participants in this group finally settled on a definition of ascetic behavior rather than of asceticism per se, retreating, as Clark says, from the "thing-in-itself" to the safety of observable practices.

However, this retreat into observable practices has not solved the theoretical problem of asceticism. The best summary of the Group on Ascetic Behavior's conclusions is Walter O. Kaelber's definition of asceticism in the current edition of *The Encyclopedia of Religion*: "[Asceticism is] a voluntary, sustained, and at least partially systematic program of self-discipline and self-denial in which immediate, sensual or profane gratifications are renounced in order to attain a higher spiritual state or a more thorough absorption in the sacred."[17] This definition views asceticism as a religious practice and differentiates asceticism from other forms of training, such as athleticism or bodybuilding.[18]

A different and more inclusive perspective can be found in the definition of asceticism recently proposed by Richard Valentasis, who rejects Kaelber's distinction between religious and secular forms of ascetic behavior. For Valentasis, asceticism is a counterculture. Furthermore, it can be found in any disciplined set of performances designed to create an alternative identity (Valentasis prefers the term "subjectivity"), lifestyle, or worldview:

> Asceticism consists of any performance resistant to an externally projected or subjectively experienced dominant social or religious context specifically intended... and purposefully performed in order to inaugurate a new and alternative subjectivity. This new subjectivity may be understood both inter-subjectively (those people and events constituting the social self of the individual) and intra-subjectively (those with whom the agent interacts beyond the individual social body). Social relationships must be transformed in order to support

---

16   Elizabeth A. Clark, *Reading Renunciation: Asceticism and Scripture in Early Christianity* (Princeton, NJ: Princeton University Press, 1999), p. 14.
17   Walter O. Kaelber, "Asceticism," in *The Encyclopedia of Religion*, ed. Mircea Eliade (New York and London: Macmillan & Co., 1987), vol. 1, p. 441, cited in Clark, *Reading Renunciation*, p. 15.
18   See also, the section titled "Athletes Are Not Ascetics," in Flood, *The Ascetic Self*, pp. 216–18.

the new and alternative subjectivity. The symbolic universe or construction of reality must be adapted and changed in order to explain and sustain the resistant subjectivity.[19]

Geoffrey Galt Harpham, whose view of asceticism influenced Valentasis, similarly regards what he calls the "ascetic imperative" as a universal human tendency that is expressed both religiously and non-religiously and in many different forms. For him, asceticism is a set of disciplined practices that represents the values of a culture: "[Asceticism is] a kind of MS-DOS of cultures, a fundamental operating ground on which the particular culture, the word processing program itself, is overlaid. Where there is culture there is asceticism."[20]

Unfortunately, these recent attempts to improve Kaelber's definition of asceticism are both too broad and too narrow to be of much use in unpacking the trope of Rabi'a the Ascetic. Despite their universalistic pretensions, Harpham's notion that asceticism can be found in every culture and Valentasis's notion that "true" asceticism must express a form of cultural resistance are too grounded in the cultural milieu of the West to be fully applicable to the premodern Islamic world. In these definitions, one cannot help but suspect that theory has become an end in itself and that the concept of asceticism has been taken too far from how it was understood by its premodern practitioners. As Gavin Flood has observed, premodern asceticism cannot be understood in its own context without giving due consideration to the concepts of tradition and transcendence: "The residues of ascetic practice in our culture have become mere technique without the accompaniment of tradition and an articulated idea of transcendence."[21] A less ethnocentric approach to the study of asceticism can be found by heeding Catherine Bell's methodological warning about the study of ritual: "Rather than impose categories of what is or is not [asceticism], it may be more useful to look at how human activities establish and manipulate their own differentiation and purposes—in the very doing of the act within the context of other ways of acting."[22]

---

19   Valentasis, *The Making of the Self*, pp. 101–2; this definition of asceticism is a 2005 revision of the definition that Valentasis first proposed in 1995.
20   Geoffrey Galt Harpham, *The Ascetic Imperative in Culture and Criticism* (Chicago and London: The University of Chicago Press, 1987), p. xi.
21   Flood, *The Ascetic Self*, p. 1.
22   Catherine Bell, *Ritual Theory, Ritual Practice* (New York and Oxford: Oxford University Press, 1992), p. 74. Bell's observation is relevant in this context because ascetic practices are themselves ritualized forms of behavior. Thus, we can read her statement as a warning against the essentialist, "thing-in-itself" definition of asceticism that Elizabeth A. Clark

In heeding Catherine Bell's advice, the student of early Islamic asceticism must be careful to avoid falling into the trap of anachronism, not only with respect to modern theoretical discourses but also with respect to later Sufi discussions of asceticism. The relationship between Sufism and earlier practices of asceticism still remains unclear. Thus, it is advisable for students of asceticism in early Islam to adhere closely to the statements of early ascetics themselves and avoid as much as possible the formulations of later theorists. The works of Sufi theorists such as Abu Nasr al-Sarraj (d. 988 CE), Abu Bakr al-Kalabadhi (d. 990 CE), Abu 'Abd al-Rahman al-Sulami (d. 1021 CE), and Abu al-Qasim al-Qushayri (d. 1074 CE) provide a mixed blessing. On the one hand, they offer some of the earliest discussions of Sufi concepts and practices, including asceticism. On the other hand, these authors tended to project their own understandings of Sufi doctrines and practices onto the past. In doing so, they created the impression that the concept of asceticism never changed and that the doctrines and practices of early ascetics such as Rabi'a al-'Adawiyya were little different from later Sufi doctrines and practices. This redefinition of concepts is a normal part of doctrinal formation. As Gavin Flood observes, "Tradition is not passively received but actively reconstructed in a shared imagination and reconstituted in the present as memory."[23] However, because of this tendency, anachronistic reconstructions based on later traditions of Sufi asceticism are likely to undermine historical inquiry by bestowing a false coherence on earlier concepts and practices.

For this reason, in order to accurately map the conceptual boundaries of Islamic asceticism in Rabi'a's time, it is helpful to focus on the key terms by which early Muslim ascetics characterized their ascetic practices. Four of the most important terms will be discussed below. The first two terms, *zuhd* ("renunciation") and *wara'* ("ethical precaution"), remained in use for many centuries and denoted widespread practices both within and outside of Sufism. The third term, *nusk* ("ascetic ritualism"), was a characteristic of early Islamic asceticism but fell out of favor in later periods. The fourth term, *faqr* ("poverty"), denoted the condition of the ascetic life, but was not regarded as a formal Sufi practice until about a century after Rabi'a's death. Eventually, this term became so popular that it is now used as a virtual synonym for "Sufism" itself.

---

refers to. As Bell points out, definitions of religious practices that are not based on actual behaviors frequently impose concepts that are either culturally alien or anachronistic.
23   Flood, *The Ascetic Self*, p. 8.

II. TERMS OF EARLY ISLAMIC ASCETICISM

a. Zuhd *(Renunciation)*

Zuhd is the Arabic term most commonly defined as "asceticism." It is also the broadest and most general term for asceticism in Islam, since other terms for asceticism are often regarded as subcategories of *zuhd*. The term *zuhd* is derived from the Arabic root *z-h-d*, which means, "to shun, avoid, abandon, or abstain." The practitioner of *zuhd* is called a *zahid* ("one who avoids or abstains") or a *mutazahhid* ("one who makes himself avoid or abstain"). The meaning of *zuhd* thus revolves around the idea of renunciation, whether it is active renunciation through avoidance or passive renunciation through abstention. In general, the *zahid* is a renunciant, who rejects the World, avoids it, abstains from it, or holds it in little regard. This understanding of *zuhd* is supported by the Qur'an, where in *Surat Yusuf* (Qur'an 12:20) the Prophet Joseph's brothers sell him as a slave for a paltry price, thus demonstrating how little they value him (*wa kanu fihi min al-zahidin*, "They held him in little regard").[24]

As an ethico-religious concept, *zuhd* reflects the values of the World/Nonworld Dichotomy discussed above. As a ritualized form of separation from worldly life it is, in the words of Jonathan Z. Smith, "an assertion of difference above all else."[25] As such, the life and worldview of the *zahid* are fundamentally different from those of the ordinary person.[26] A common synonym for *zahid* in early Islam was *munqati'*, "one who is cut off" from the

---

[24] Christopher Melchert compares *zuhd* to the Greek term *apatheia* ("indifference" or "unconcern") and translates the Qur'anic phrase, *wa kanu fihi min al-zahidin*, as "indifferent about him." I would argue, however, that an active rather than passive connotation of *zuhd* is more appropriate, both in the Qur'anic passage and in the extensive literature on *zuhd* that advocates renunciation in early Islam. A better equivalent for *apatheia* as "indifference" would be the Arabic term *khumul*, which was sometimes used by Sufis to refer to indifference to the World. See Christopher Melchert, "Origins and Early Sufism," in *The Cambridge Companion to Sufism*, ed. Lloyd Ridgeon (Cambridge, UK: Cambridge University Press, 2014), p. 11.

[25] See ibid., p. 102; see also, Jonathan Z. Smith, *To Take Place: Toward Theory in Ritual* (Chicago: University of Chicago Press, 1987), p. 109.

[26] Richard Valentasis agrees with Jonathan Z. Smith that asceticism is the ritualized assertion of difference—in his terms, between "the rejected subjectivity" and the "desired subjectivity." The focus of ascetical formation is not the rejected subjectivity but the "*emergent* person, the victorious athlete who becomes visible in the fruits of ascetic labor." Valentasis, *The Making of the Self*, p. 42.

World or conventional society. Sometimes, the renunciant who cut herself off from the World also practiced *'uzla*, physical withdrawal or separation from the World and its affairs. However, ascetic withdrawal should not be mistaken for quietism, but instead should be seen as an active and self-empowered form of renunciation.[27] A contemporary of Rabi'a al-'Adawiyya and noted writer on asceticism, 'Abdullah Ibn al-Mubarak of Merv (d. 797 CE), devotes much of his book, *Kitab al-zuhd wa-l-raqa'iq* (*The Book of Renunciation and the Refinements of Worship*), to the concept of *zuhd* and the World/Nonworld Dichotomy.[28] The ascetic practices mentioned in this work include renunciation of the World (*al-'ard min al-dunya*), making little of the World (*al-taqallul min al-dunya*), disrespect for the World (*hawan al-dunya*), and condemnation of the pleasures of the World (*dhamm al-tana'um fi-l-dunya*).[29] All of these practices are covered by the term *zuhd*. In the words of another contemporary of Rabi'a, the Proto-Sufi and ascetic Fudayl Ibn 'Iyad, "If evil were a house, the key to it would be desire for the World. If good were a house, the key to it would be renunciation of the World (*al-zuhd fi-l-dunya*)."[30]

Numerous statements of early Muslim ascetics also relate *zuhd* to the theological concept of *al-thiqa bi-llah* (also called *tawakkul*), complete trust in God's providence.[31] Margaret Smith's description of the practitioner of *tawakkul* (*al-mutawakkil 'ala Allah*) as the "true dependent," who "knows that his Lord's provision for him is better than his own for himself" is a useful way to think of this concept.[32] Fudayl ibn 'Iyad said, "The root of *zuhd* is satisfaction with whatever comes from God."[33] The theological relationship between the concepts of providence and destiny that is reflected in this statement was

---

27 Academic research on asceticism over the last thirty years has conclusively demonstrated that whatever else it may be, asceticism is an active and goal-oriented form of self-discipline. Thus, Margaret Smith's contention that early Sufism "consisted of asceticism carried to the point of quietism" is both conceptually wrong and historically inaccurate. Smith, *Rabi'a* (Oneworld), p. 100 and (Rainbow Bridge), p. 76.
28 For a short overview of Ibn al-Mubarak and his teachings, see Knysh, *Islamic Mysticism*, pp. 21–2.
29 Ibn al-Mubarak, *Kitab al-zuhd*, pp. 15–21, 175–7, 177–94, 262–81.
30 Abu 'Abd al-Rahman al-Sulami, *Tabaqat al-sufiyya*, ed. Nur al-Din Shurayba (Cairo: Maktabat al-Khanji, 1986), p. 13.
31 On the concept of *tawakkul*, see Benedikt Reinhart, *Die Lehre vom Tawakkul in der klassischen Sufik*, Studien sur Sprache, Geschichte und Kultur des islamischen Orients 3 (Berlin: W. de Gruyter, 1968).
32 Smith, *Rabi'a* (Rainbow Bridge), p. 80 and (Oneworld), p. 104.
33 Sulami, *Tabaqat al-sufiyya*, p. 10.

widely understood by early Muslim ascetics. Shaqiq al-Balkhi attributed his practice of *tawakkul* to a lesson about destiny that he learned from a Buddhist monk. Shaqiq states that in his youth he was a merchant among the Turks in what is now northeastern Afghanistan. On one of his trading journeys, he came across a group he called "The Specialists" (*al-khususiyya*), who were distinguished by their beardless faces, shaved heads and red robes. This description fits the Buddhist monks of Tibet, who in the eighth century CE were consolidating their control over Tibetan society.[34] After Shaqiq mocked their idolatry, one of the monks said to him, "You traveled all the way out here to seek your provision. Do you not know that the source of your provision out here is the same as your provision back there? So relax and let go of your worries."[35] Struck by this admonition, Shaqiq returned home to Balkh and became a "true renunciant" (*al-zahid al-haqiqi*). Shaqiq's path of asceticism recalled the Buddhist model in its emphasis on mendicant wandering, the abandonment of financial means of support, and complete trust in providence.[36] He stated, "No one is able to practice *zuhd* without trust in God (*illa bi-l-thiqa bi-llah*)."[37]

Many statements about *zuhd* in early Islamic literature support the idea that the root of asceticism is ethical formation, which is achieved through a regime of personal development.[38] This links the concept of *zuhd* to the early Islamic concept of *ta'dib*, since the practice of *zuhd* in early Islam also included a wider regime of moral training.[39] This highlights an important point

---

34 See Robert A.F. Thurman, "Tibetan Buddhist Perspectives on Asceticism," in Wimbush and Valentasis, *Asceticism*, pp. 113–17.

35 Isfahani, *Hilya*, vol. 8, p. 59.

36 Ibid., p. 58. The story of Shaqiq al-Balkhi and the Buddhist monk should not necessarily be taken as evidence of Buddhist influence on early Sufi ascetical practices. Instead, it better supports Jacques Maquet's contention that the World/Nonworld Dichotomy is a cultural universal. Shaqiq was able to learn from Buddhist monks because the concept of the World/Nonworld dichotomy was shared by both traditions.

37 Abu al-Qasim 'Abd al-Karim ibn Hawazin al-Qushayri, *al-Risala al-Qushayriyya fi 'ilm al-tasawwuf*, ed. Ma'ruf Zurayq and 'Ali 'Abd al-Hamid Baltarji (Beirut: Dar al-Jil, 1990), p. 117.

38 Wimbush and Valentasis, "Introduction" in idem, *Asceticism*, p. xxix.

39 In *The Making of the Self*, Richard Valentasis distinguishes asceticism, which he defines as countercultural, from formation, which he says reinforces cultural norms (pp. 80–100). In my opinion, this distinction goes too far. First, it threatens to divorce asceticism from the concept of training (i.e., formation), which is the root meaning of *askesis*. Second, it begs the question of why—if asceticism is culturally subversive—early Christian and Islamic states allowed so many ascetics to practice freely. Finally, the distinction made by Valentasis seems to ignore the important role of formation in the development of ascetical institutions.

that is often overlooked by critics of asceticism, whether they are secularists, Protestant Christians, or Muslim modernists: ethical self-discipline cannot be achieved without the ascetical practices of renunciation and withdrawal. All self-discipline requires ascetic withdrawal in some form or another. This might be in the form of a physical separation from worldly life, or it might be in the form of avoidance of what is harmful to the body or the spirit. This is the universal aspect of asceticism on which advocates of universal asceticism such as Geoffrey Galt Harpham and Richard Valentasis base their arguments. One of the most important insights conveyed by Max Weber's *The Protestant Ethic and the Spirit of Capitalism* is that despite the anti-monastic ethic of Protestantism, a strong sense of asceticism continued to govern the Protestant worldview.[40]

A similarly anti-monastic attitude can also be found in Islam, where the Qur'an states that Christians invented monasticism (*rahbaniyya*) for themselves despite the fact that God did not prescribe it for them (Qur'an 57:27). The verb used in the Qur'an to describe the invention of monasticism is *ibtada'a*, which comes from the same root as *bid'a*, the term used in Islam to characterize the unauthorized innovation of religious practices or doctrines.[41] It is common today for Muslim modernist reformers to claim that *zuhd* is an unauthorized innovation in Islam since, like monasticism, it is not enjoined on believers in the Qur'an. However, premodern commentators on Qur'an and Hadith largely agreed that the prohibition of monasticism applied only to celibacy; it did not apply to asceticism in general.[42] In addition, Qur'an 57:27 and the verse that follows it make it clear that despite the Qur'anic rejection of monasticism, Muslims are expected to adhere to some of the most important religious attitudes associated with asceticism, such as awareness of God's presence (*taqwa*) and observance of the rights due to God (*haqq al-ri'aya*) (Qur'an 57:28). For early Muslim ascetics, observance of the rights of God was fundamental to both their ethical outlook and their practice of renunciation. This is the basis of Rabi'a al-'Adawiyya's statement in the epigraph to this chapter: "I am ashamed to ask for the world from

---

40 See Chapter 4, "The Religious Foundations of Worldly Asceticism" in Max Weber, *The Protestant Ethic and the Spirit of Capitalism*, trans. Talcott Parsons with Introduction by Anthony Giddens (London and New York: Routledge & Co., 1996), pp. 95–154.
41 See Umar F. Abd-Allah, "Creativity, Innovation, and Heresy in Islam," in *Voices of Islam, Volume Five: Voices of Change*, ed. Vincent J. Cornell (General Editor) and Omid Safi (Volume Editor) (Westport, CT and London: Praeger Publishers, 2007), pp. 1–22.
42 This was the opinion, for example, of the Hadith transmitter Abu Dawud al-Sijistani (d. 888–9 CE), the compiler of *Sunan Abi Dawud*.

the One who owns the world. So how can I ask for the world from one who does not own it?"

b. Waraʿ (Ethical Precaution)

The pious caution expressed in the above statement by Rabiʿa is an example of *waraʿ*, a concept that stood for the ethical aspect of asceticism in early Islam.[43] According to Jahiz, Rabiʿa was an exemplar of *waraʿ* and later writers continued to affirm this claim.[44] The term *waraʿ* comes from the Arabic root *w-r-ʿ*, which means "to pause, to hesitate, to be cautious, to refrain, to abstain." Thus, the concept of *waraʿ* in Islamic asceticism adds the notions of precaution and avoidance to the concept of *zuhd* as ascetic renunciation. Abu Sulayman al-Darani (d. 830 CE), who founded an early school of Sufism in Syria but lived in Basra while Rabiʿa was still alive, regarded *waraʿ* as fundamental to the practice of ascetic renunciation (*al-waraʿ awwal al-zuhd*).[45] As an early Islamic ascetic practice, *waraʿ* was most often expressed as a ritualized form of avoidance—specifically, the avoidance of substances, actions, or possessions that had the potential of being ethically polluting. The *wariʿ*, literally "the abstemious person," often went to great lengths to avoid contact with anything that was ethically questionable.[46]

---

43   Knysh (*Islamic Mysticism*, p. 357) defines *waraʿ* as "scrupulousness in discerning between the permitted and the prohibited." For other recent discussions of this concept, see Christoph Pitschke, *Skrupulöse Frömmigkeit im frühen Islam: das "Buch der Gewissenfrömmigkeit"* (Kitab al-Waraʿ) *von Ahmad b. Hanbal: annotierte Übersetzung und thematische Analyse* (Weisbaden: Otto Harassowitz, 2010); Christopher Melchert, "Exaggerated Fear in the Early Islamic Renunciant Tradition," *Journal for the Royal Asiatic Society*, 21 (3), 2011, pp. 283–300 (on the related concept of *khawf*). Pitschke translates *waraʿ* (in German) as "scrupulous piety" or "conscience-piety."
44   Jahiz, *al-Hayawan*, vol. 1, p. 170. Margaret Smith does not discuss the concept of *waraʿ* in her treatment of Rabiʿa's asceticism in *Rabiʿa the Mystic*. This is a curious omission, both because of the importance of this practice in early Islamic asceticism and because it is mentioned by Jahiz, one of the earliest writers on Rabiʿa. One wonders whether Smith omitted *waraʿ* because it was not comparable enough to early Christian forms of asceticism.
45   Qushayri, *al-Risala*, p. 110.
46   The Lutheran Bishop and Orientalist scholar Tor Andrae saw *waraʿ* as an expression of religious anxiety rather than of precaution. For this reason, he translated the Arabic term *al-wariʿun* as "anxiously pious ones." According to Andrae's account, this interpretation was due to his personal experiences with "Old Pietist" Lutheran traditionalists in Sweden, whose acts of "pious anxiety" reminded him of early Sufis. See Andrae, *In the Garden of Myrtles*, pp. 40–1.

In the culture of *waraʿ* as a form of asceticism, the notions of ritual purity and ethical purity were seen as interrelated. For early Muslim ascetics, the practice of *waraʿ* marked the believer's commitment to the pure world of the sacred and the abandonment of the impure world of the profane. The Persian Sufi ʿAli al-Hujwiri (d. 1071 CE) described this commitment as a "double purification" because ethical awareness combined "the tongue's observance with the heart's belief."[47] Similarly reflecting the ethical values of *waraʿ* and the concern of early ascetics for ritual purity, the Sufi Abu Bakr al-Shibli (d. 945 CE) stated, "Whenever I neglect any rule of purification, some vain conceit always arises in my heart."[48]

Sufi women were particularly likely to regard *waraʿ* as a ritualistic act of pollution avoidance. The *waraʿ* of Sufi women was based on the belief that the body of the ascetic was a vessel for the divine presence. This attitude was also shared by early Christians. According to Peter Brown, in early Christianity the body was viewed as a microenvironment. "It was a vehicle through which the spirit adjusted to its present material environment as a whole."[49] In this microenvironment, body and soul were in a state of delicate balance. Upsetting the body could upset the soul and vice-versa. Muslim practitioners of *waraʿ* had a similar view of body and soul. A major danger for the soul, especially for women, was the defilement of the soul's inner purity through the body's contact with the World. Thus, the practice of *waraʿ* among Sufi women included rituals of avoidance that were designed to protect the soul from sources of ethical pollution that came from the outside. As a response to the dangers of the World, the practice of *waraʿ* by Sufi women was often expressed as a sort of "dramatic play" that inscribed the ethical boundaries of the World/Nonworld Dichotomy on the ascetic body.[50]

However, although the early Islamic view of the ascetic body was similar in some ways to the early Christian view of the body as a temple for the Holy Spirit, the Islamic ethos of *waraʿ* actually had more in common with philosophical notions of purification by means of avoidance (Gr. *hagneia*)

---

47 ʿAli b. ʿUthman al-Jullabi al-Hujwiri, *The Kashf al-Mahjub, the Oldest Persian Treatise on Sufiism*, trans. Reynold A. Nicholson (London: Luzac and Company, 1976 reprint of 1911 first edition), p. 292.
48 Ibid., p. 293.
49 Brown uses the term, "microclimate" rather than microenvironment. See Peter Brown, *The Body and Society: Men, Women, and Sexual Renunciation in Early Christianity* (New York: Columbia University Press, 1988), pp. 170–1.
50 On asceticism as a form of "dramatic play," see Corrington-Streete, "Trajectories of Ascetic Behavior," in Winbush and Valentasis, *Asceticism*, p. 119.

than with Christian notions of purity.[51] Peter Brown describes *hagneia* as "a visceral reflex of avoidance, by which the pious strove to preserve charged boundaries between their bodies and all forms of polluting, anomalous mixture."[52] In his description of this practice, Brown cites the Neo-Platonic Syrian philosopher Porphyry (d. 305 CE), but it could apply just as well to the early Muslim practitioner of *wara'*. A key difference between Christian and Islamic views of bodily impurity had to do with how impurities entered the body. For early Christians, impurities were believed to enter the body through the sexual organs. This is one reason why celibacy was such a crucial practice for Christian ascetics. By contrast, Muslim practitioners of *wara'*, along with pagan Neo-Platonists, believed that impurities were more likely to enter the body through the mouth than through sexual activity.[53] For this reason, early Muslim ascetics tended to be more concerned with food pollution than with sexual pollution.

Early ascetics in Islam believed that the ascetic body could become unfit for the divine presence through neglect of worship or through contact with ritual or ethical impurities. Major sources of ethical impurity were desire (*shahwa*) and greed (*tama'*). Desire and greed were linked to the appetites both literally and metaphorically. The mouth was seen as the primary source of impurity because it was through the mouth that the most basic appetite, the appetite for food, was gratified. Eating food that was ritually or ethically impure was believed to pollute the body inwardly, making it unfit for worship and other forms of divine service. This belief is reflected in the following statement by one of Rabi'a's most famous predecessors among the women ascetics of Basra. Mu'adha al-'Adawiyya, the founder of the Basra school of women's asceticism, admonishes her student Umm al-Aswad not to spoil the pure breast-feeding she had given her as a child by taking forbidden substances into her mouth. She scolds, "Do not spoil the breast-feeding I have given you by eating forbidden food (*akl al-haram*), for when I was nursing you I made every effort to eat only what was lawful (*akl al-halal*). So make every effort after this to eat only what is lawful. Perhaps you will succeed in your service

---

51 In early Christianity, the term *hagneia* primarily denoted celibacy. Giulia Sfameni Gasparo, "Asceticism and Anthropology: *Enkrateia* and 'Double Creation' in Early Christianity," in Wimbush and Valentasis, *Asceticism*, p. 127. In early Islam, celibacy as a sign of inner purity was more important for women than for men.
52 Brown, *The Body and Society*, p. 182.
53 The Sufi Sahl al-Tustari (d. 896 CE) said, "When one eats that which is forbidden, the members of his body become disobedient, whether he wants it so or not. But when one eats only permitted food, his members become obedient and disposed to do good." Andrae, *In the Garden of Myrtles*, p. 38.

to your Lord and in your acceptance of His will." Upon recounting this story, Umm al-Aswad said, "I would not eat anything suspicious lest it cause me to miss either a prescribed prayer or an extra invocation."[54]

To use a concept from ritual studies developed by Catherine Bell, the *wara'* of Mu'adha al-'Adawiyya and other early Muslim ascetics "ritualized" the Islamic legal distinction of lawful versus unlawful (*halal* vs. *haram*) in terms of the World/Nonworld Dichotomy. That which is unlawful or impure binds the soul to the World, whereas the lawful or ethically pure releases the soul to seek its true abode in the Nonworld. Bell's concept of ritualization allows the student of Islamic asceticism to distinguish ethical precaution (*wara'*) from ascetic renunciation (*zuhd*) by defining *wara'* as the "ritualization" of ascetic renunciation in ethical terms.[55] As the ritualized expression of ethical difference, *wara'* drew a symbolic line in the sand between actions and substances that were lawful, pure and sacred and those that were unlawful, impure or profane. In the asceticism of avoidance that characterized *wara'*, the legally or ethically forbidden was regarded as unclean and hence was untouchable as a source of pollution. Contact with the unclean was believed to rub off on the person who was exposed to it in the way that a disease could be transferred from one person to another. This meant that for the Muslim ascetic who was committed to both inward and outward purity, even things of doubtful origin (*shubuhat*) had to be avoided, lest they make the ascetic impure in both body and spirit. For the practitioner of *wara'*, what was unlawful or ethically impure was more than just polluting: it was also toxic for the development of a spiritual way of life.

In stories about Rabi'a al-'Adawiyya, one of the clearest illustrations of how an ethically polluting substance affects both inward and outward purity can be found in Farid al-Din al-'Attar's *Ilahi Nama* (*God Book* or *Book of Theology*). In this story, al-Hasan al-Basri comes to visit Rabi'a in the wilderness. He finds her surrounded by mountain goats, gazelles and other animals. However, when the animals see Hasan, they immediately take fright and run away. When Hasan asks Rabi'a why the animals are afraid of him but not of her, she asks him what he has eaten. "Onions fried in animal fat," he replies. "You have eaten the fat of these poor creatures," she says, "so how could they not run away from you?" Then Rabi'a admonishes Hasan and tells him that if he ate just a little like an ant—perhaps one date each day—his body would be safe from the worms of the grave. She says: "Nothing are you, oh man,

---

54 Sulami, *Early Sufi Women*, p. 166.
55 On the concept of ritualization, see Bell, *Ritual Theory, Ritual Practice*, pp. 88–93.

without the latrine and the kitchen. Has your heart not been taken away by these two hells? From one hell to another you go; from the latrine to the kitchen you go... You were told to purify your soul, but you are always filling your body. You must always respect the inner (*batin*), yet you only serve the outer (*zahir*)."[56]

Major sources of ethical pollution in premodern Islamic society were Bedouins and the government. Trade with Bedouins was suspect because Bedouins often obtained their goods by raiding and stealing from others. If the food given to an ascetic came from a Bedouin, it might have been obtained illegally. The same concern applied to government officials and to the premodern state. Governments were often seen as sources of extortion and oppression and governmental officials were constantly looking for new sources of revenue. It was widely felt that the state was unjust by nature and that ethical persons should avoid governmental service. Consequently, Muslim hagiographical collections are full of stories about religious figures that refused to serve in legal or administrative positions. In such cases, the practice of *wara'* may reflect an attitude of political dissidence, as suggested for asceticism in general by Richard Valentasis. However, one should be careful before concluding that every practitioner of *wara'* was a dissident. In many cases, complaints about the lack of governmental ethics in Muslim hagiographical narratives are generic and are not directed against specific regimes or individuals. An example of this can be seen in *Risala fi-l-tasawwuf* (*The Treatise on Sufism*) by Abu al-Qasim al-Qushayri. In this work, Qushayri states that Rabi'a once tried to mend her torn garment by the light of a lamp that was maintained by the government (*fi daw' shu'lat al-sultan*). "She lost her heart for a time until she realized why. Then she tore her garment and found her heart."[57] In this anecdote, the "heart" stands for moral equilibrium or spiritual balance. What caused Rabi'a to lose her equilibrium was the

---

56 Shaykh Farid al-Din 'Attar Nishapuri, *Ilahi nama*, ed. Fu'ad Ruhani (Tehran: Intisharat Zavvar, 1961), pp. 96–7. The passage reproduced above was translated by Vincent J. Cornell. See also, John Andrew Boyle, *The Ilahi-nama or Book of God of Farid al-Din 'Attar* (Manchester: Manchester University Press, 1976), pp. 115–16. Some modern observers see this story as evidence that Rabi'a was a vegetarian. On the vegetarian website Compassionate Spirit, a shortened and altered version of the story states that Hasan ate meat but that Rabi'a ate only dried bread: "The animals recognized that Rabi'a was a vegetarian and that Hasan was not." http://www.compassionatespirit.com/spiritual-trends-and-veg.htm

57 Qushayri, *al-Risala*, p. 114.

possibility that the money used by the government to install and maintain the public lanterns of Basra may have been obtained by unlawful means.[58]

Unlike the term *zuhd*, the term *wara'* or its derivatives do not appear in the Qur'an. However, later Sufi writers tried to portray the practice of *wara'* as in agreement with the Qur'an and the Sunna by tracing it back to the Prophet Muhammad and his Companions. For example, 'Abd al-Malik al- Khargushi of Nishapur (d. 1016 CE) cites the following hadith of the Prophet: "The excellence of knowledge is better than the excellence of worship; the excellence of your religion is *wara'*."[59] In Qushayri's *Risala*, the Prophet is quoted as saying, "Be a practitioner of *wara'* and you will be the most devout among people."[60] A hadith with a similar meaning is also related by Abu Bakr al-Sarraj in *Kitab al-luma'*. "What is truly yours of your religion (*milku dinikum*) is *wara'*."[61]

According to Louis Massignon, the establishment of *wara'* as a form of Islamic ascetic practice was due to the influence of al-Hasan al-Basri (d. 728 CE), an important theologian and ascetic who is often depicted as Rabi'a's companion in Sufi legends.[62] Hasan's interest in *wara'* was in agreement with his ethical view of piety, which held that a life of honesty accompanied by prayer is better for salvation than prayer alone.[63] The Sufi Khargushi describes Hasan's understanding of *wara'* as based on the virtues of absolute truthfulness (*sidq*) and sincerity (*ikhlas*).[64] Qushayri states that Hasan learned from one of the Shiite Imams that the essence of Islamic

---

58 Other accounts attribute this story to Mukhkha (Marrow or Essence), the sister of the early Sufi Bishr al-Hafi (The Barefoot) of Baghdad (d. 840 CE). These accounts claim that Mukhkha supported herself by spinning wool, and that she would continue spinning by the light of the moon even after the lamps of Baghdad had gone out. See, for example, 'Abd al-Malik ibn Muhammad al-Khargushi, *Tahdhib al-asrar*, ed. Bassam Muhammad Barud (Abu Dhabi: al-Majma' al-Thaqafi, 1999), p. 108. Two centuries later, the Hanbali scholar Ibn al-Jawzi attributed this story to Mudgha (Embryo), another purported sister of Bishr al-Hafi. See idem, *Sifat al-Safwa*, vol. 2, pp. 525–6 and the Appendix to Sulami, *Early Sufi Women*, p. 324. On Khargushi's *Tahdhib al-asrar*, see Sara Sviri, "The Early Mystical Schools of Baghdad and Nishapur or: In Search of Ibn Munazil," *Jerusalem Studies in Arabic and Islam*, 30, 2005, pp. 451–6. For an attribution of this story to Bishr al-Hafi himself, see Cooperson, *Classical Arabic Biography*, p. 176.
59 Khargushi, *Tahdhib al-Asrar*, p. 108; this hadith does not appear in the six canonical collections. The earliest mention of it that I am aware of is in Ahmad ibn Hanbal, *Kitab al-zuhd*, ed. 'Abd al-Rahman ibn Qasim (Beirut: Dar al-Kutub al-'Ilmiyya, 1976), p. 108.
60 Qushayri, *al-Risala*, p. 110.
61 Sarraj, *al-Luma'*, p. 44.
62 Massignon, *Essay*, p. 131.
63 Ibid., p. 129; see also, Watt, *The Formative Period of Islamic Thought*, pp. 79–81.
64 Khargushi, *Tahdhib al-asrar*, p. 109.

religious practice is *wara'*. Hasan was so impressed with this teaching that he proclaimed, "A grain's weight of pure *wara'* is better than a hundredweight of fasting and prayer."[65]

One of the most important advocates of *wara'* in the generation after Rabi'a was al-Harith al-Muhasibi (d. 857 CE).[66] Muhasibi, who was born and raised in Basra but later moved to Baghdad, seems to have been in many respects Rabi'a's doctrinal successor. As we saw in Chapter 1, his citation of a statement on love by Rabi'a is the earliest reference to her in any extant work. The concept of *wara'* was fundamental to Muhasibi's practice of *muhasaba*, from which his nickname (Ar. *kunya*) al-Muhasibi was derived. Muhasibi defined *muhasaba* as a "contract with the conscience" (*al-'aqd bi-l-damir*), in which the sincere Muslim resolves to examine all of her actions critically before they are performed.[67] This process of critical self-examination shares much in common with the practice of *wara'* as ethical precaution. Muhasibi considered *wara'* to be so central to Islamic spirituality that he wrote a treatise on the subject titled, *Kitab al-makasib wa-l-wara' wa-l-shubha wa bayan mubahiha wa mahzuriha wa akhlaq al-nas fi-talabiha wa-l-radd 'ala al-ghaliyin fiha* (*Treatise on Earnings, Ethical Precaution, and Ethical Doubt with an Explanation of What is Permissible about Them, What is Forbidden about Them, the Ethics of Seeking Them, and a Refutation of Those Who Are Excessive in Seeking Them*).[68] In this work, Muhasibi defines *wara'* as "the avoidance of everything that God dislikes, whether in speech or in action or

---

65   Qushayri, *al-Risala*, p. 112.
66   For major works in English on Muhasibi, see Picken, *Spiritual Purification in Islam* and Smith, *An Early Mystic of Baghdad*. Two other important studies of Muhasibi are 'Abd al-Halim Mahmud, *Al-Muhasibi: Un Mystique Musulman Religieux et Moraliste* (Paris: Librairie Orientaliste Paul Geuthner, 1940); and Josef Van Ess, *Die Gedankenwelt des Harith al-Muhasibi* (Bonn: Selbstverlag des Orientalischen Seminars des Universität Bonn, 1961).
67   Al-Harith ibn Asad al-Muhasibi, *Kitab al-Makasib* in *al-Masa'il fi a'mal al-qulub wa-l-jawarih wa al-Makasib wa al-'Aql*, ed. 'Abd al-Qadir Ahmad 'Ata (Cairo: 'Alam al-Kutub, 1969), p. 200.
68   This work is available in two Arabic editions. The full title of the work as given above comes from a photograph of the title page of the manuscript in the University of Cairo Library. See al-Harith ibn Asad al-Muhasibi, *al-Rizq al-halal wa haqiqat al-tawakkul 'ala Allah* (*Lawful Gain and the Reality of Trusting in God*), ed. Muhammad 'Uthman al-Khisht (Cairo: Maktabat al-Qur'an, 1984), p. 25. The editor of this work changed the original title to fit his view of its contents. A more trustworthy version can be found in a collection of three of Muhasibi's works by 'Abd al-Qadir 'Ata, the premier editor of Muhasibi's writings. See *al-Masa'il fi a'mal al-qulub wa-l-jawarih wa al-Makasib wa al-'Aql*, pp. 171–234.

in the heart or the limbs; and caution against neglecting what God has made obligatory for either the heart or the limbs."[69]

For Muhasibi, the relationship of *muhasaba* to *wara'* was that of a means to an end. Critical self-examination is the most effective technique by which the ascetic can practice *wara'* in daily life. Muhasibi's best-known written work was *al-Ri'aya li-huquq Allah wa-l-qiyam biha* (*The Care for and Establishment of the Rights of God*). The relationship between *wara'* and asceticism is discussed in the final chapter of this book, "The Training of Disciples" (*ta'dib al-muridin*). Muhasibi's frequent use of the term *ta'dib* in his works demonstrates that this was still the way that early Sufis conceived of ethical and spiritual training in the generation after Rabi'a's death. Muhasibi refers to *ta'dib* as *al-ta'dib li-l-nafs*, "the training of the soul."[70] For Muhasibi, *wara'* is an important aspect of *al-ta'dib li-l-nafs* because it fosters self-awareness and prevents moral backsliding. It is especially important in business (*tijara*) and the marketplace (*suq*). Muhasibi considered the marketplace so full of ethical pollution that "those who seek purity in their actions" (*ahl al-safwa min al-a'mal*) are enjoined to practice *wara'* as a type of moral armor whenever they enter a place where goods are sold.[71]

However, for Muhasibi the mere avoidance of ethical impurities was not enough by itself to make ascetics immune from the World. Besides putting on the armor of *wara'*, ascetics also had to conduct an active defense against ethical pollution through the remembrance and invocation of God (*dhikr Allah*).[72] For Muhasibi, the invocation of God created a sort of spiritual force field that shielded the God-fearing person from the pollution of the World. His addition of ritualized formulas of remembrance to the practice of asceticism takes asceticism out of the domain of *wara'* as ethical avoidance and into the domain of *nusk*, asceticism as a set of formally ritualized practices.

---

69   Muhasibi, *al-Makasib* in *al-Masa'il*, p. 200; for a summary of the contents of this work see Smith, *An Early Mystic*, pp. 50–2.
70   Muhasibi, *al-Makasib* in *al-Masa'il*, p. 225.
71   Abu 'Abdullah al-Harith ibn Asad al-Muhasibi, *al-Ri'aya li-huquq Allah*, ed. 'Abd al-Qadir Ahmad 'Ata (Beirut: Dar al-Kutub al-'Ilmiyya, fourth printing, n.d.), pp. 503–19. The phrase, "those who seek purity in their actions" comes from idem, *al-Makasib* in *al-Masa'il*, p. 222.
72   Muhasibi, *al-Ri'aya*, p. 513.

c. Nusk *(Ascetic Ritualism)*

Nusk was the most visible form of ascetic practice in Rabi'a's time. However, this concept is often overlooked in studies of Islamic asceticism because the term *nusk* is commonly equated with *zuhd*.[73] One of the reasons for this is that while the *nasik*, the practitioner of *nusk*, is often mentioned in early Islamic texts, one seldom finds discussions of *nusk* as a concept.[74] For example, when Jahiz describes Rabi'a as a renunciant (*mutazahhida*), he also describes her as a *nasika* but he does not say what this means. Clearly, for Jahiz, the concept of *nusk* was self-evident. Although he devotes an entire chapter of his book *al-Bayan wa-l-tabyin* to the subject of *zuhd*, he gives no such attention to *nusk*.[75] Apparently, the *nasik* was such a common figure in early Islamic society that writers did not feel the need to explain what the term signified. The contemporary student of early Islamic asceticism is thus faced with a dilemma. Although *nusk* was an important concept of early Islamic ascetic practice, its meaning is hidden within its historical context. It is important that this concept be clarified if we are to fully understand the trope of Rabi'a the Ascetic.

As mentioned briefly in Chapter 1, *n-s-k*, the Arabic root of the word *nusk*, is ambiguous, and carries meanings that range from rituals of worship to ritual sacrifice, and even to reclusive withdrawal.[76] The common element in all of these definitions is the notion of ritualistic behavior. Most of the verses of the Qur'an that contain the root *n-s-k* deal with ritual observances. For example, Qur'an 2:128 states: "Our Lord! Put us in a state of submission to you; make of our children a community that submits to you; show us the rites/rituals we are to perform (*wa-arina manasikana*), and redeem us (*wa tub 'alayna*)." The term *manasik* in this verse refers to Islamic rituals and sacrifices, such as the rituals of the Hajj pilgrimage and the sacrifice at Mina

---

73 A partial exception is Julian Baldick, "Asceticism," in Jane Dammen McAuliffe (ed.), *Encyclopedia of the Qur'an* (Brill Online), where the term is briefly mentioned and is voweled as *nask*. Knysh (*Islamic Mysticism*) speaks of *nussak* ("devout men") but not of *nusk* per se. The concept of *nusk* is also discussed in the context of Mamluk Egypt in Megan R. Reid, *Law and Piety in Medieval Islam* (Cambridge, UK: Cambridge University Press, 2013), p. 21f.

74 Early Islamic religious texts that are extant today include works on ritual practices (*manasik*) written by Hadith specialists, such as *Kitab al-manasik* (*The Book of Ritual Practices*) by Sa'id ibn Abi 'Uruba (d. 773 CE) and *Kitab al-manasik al-kabir* (*The Big Book of Ritual Practices*) by Ahmad ibn Hanbal (d. 855 CE). However, these works are only descriptions of ritual practices, not discussions of *nusk* as a concept.

75 Jahiz, *al-Bayan*, vol. 3, pp. 81–122.

76 Gwynne, *Logic, Rhetoric, and Legal Reasoning in the Qur'an*, p. 15.

that is one of the concluding acts of the pilgrimage. In her study of the logic of the Qur'an, Rosalind Gwynne defines the meaning of *n-s-k* as the ritual fulfillment of God's covenant. She draws this conclusion from the use of this root in another Qur'anic verse, "My prayer and my ritual sacrifice (*nusuki*) and my life and my death are for God, the Lord of the Worlds" (6:162). This verse comes after a passage in the Qur'an (6:151–2) that describes the ritual observances (*manasik*) required by God and ends with the command to fulfill God's covenant (*wa bi-'ahdi Allahi ufu*).[77]

Gwynne's definition of *nusk* as the fulfillment of covenantal responsibility provides an important bridge between the ascetical understanding of *nusk* in Rabi'a's time and the related term *nusuk*, meaning ritual sacrifice, that appears in the Qur'anic verse quoted above. It is likely that early practitioners of *nusk* thought of their austerities as ritualized forms of self-sacrifice. Both *nusk* and *nusuk* involve the fulfillment of God's covenant by means of ritual acts. In fact, the correct performance of ritual is so important in Islam that it is said to comprise half of the Shari'a.[78] Islamic jurisprudence (*fiqh*) is divided into *fiqh al-mu'amalat*, which deals with social actions, and *fiqh al-'ibadat*, which deals with rituals of worship. Early legal works such as *al-Muwatta'* (*The Trodden Path*) by Malik ibn Anas (d. 795 CE) discuss the root *n-s-k* primarily in terms of ritual sacrifice and prescribe rituals of expiation (*fidya*, literally "ransom") for neglecting their observance.[79] This further suggests a link between *nusk* and the concept of self-sacrifice.

However, the meaning of *nusk* became broader and less specific in later centuries. For example, the medieval Arabic dictionary *Lisan al-'Arab* (*The Tongue of the Arabs*) by Jamal al-Din ibn Manzur (d. 1321 CE) defines *nusk* as "anything that brings a person close to God." Ibn Manzur defines the *nasik* broadly as a "worshipper [of God]" (*'abid*). However, when he gives examples of *nusk*, most of these examples involve the observance of required rituals.[80] In the most suggestive passage for the use of this term among Muslim ascetics, Ibn Manzur states that the sincere worshipper of God is called a *nasik*

---

77   Ibid., pp. 14–15.
78   The Prophet Muhammad stated: "If there is something defective in [a believer's] prayers, the Lord (glorified and exalted be He) will say, 'See if my servant has any supererogatory prayers which might replace what was defective in his obligatory prayers. Then the rest of his actions will be judged in a similar fashion.'" *Forty Hadith Qudsi*, translated and selected by Ezzeddin Ibrahim and Denys Johnson-Davies (publisher's information and date not given), pp. 26–7; I have changed the translation slightly so that it is less awkward.
79   See, for example, Malik ibn Anas, *Kitab al-Muwatta'*, ed. Faruq Sa'd (Beirut: Dar al-Afaq al-Jadida, 1981), pp. 345–9.
80   Ibn Manzur, *Lisan al-'Arab*, vol. 10, p. 498.

because he purifies himself from the pollution of sin in the same way that gold or silver is purified by extracting the pure metal from impure alloys. Following this analogy, the *nasik* can be seen as an ascetic who purifies himself by performing ritualized acts to signify his renunciation of the World.[81] When we put Ibn Manzur's definitions in modern theoretical terms, this leads us to suggest that *nusk* is best defined as the ritualization of Islamic asceticism, either in terms of renunciation (*zuhd*) or ethical precaution (*wara'*), or both.

Ibn Manzur's understanding of *nusk* as a process of ritual purification is similar to that of the eleventh-century Persian Sufi 'Ali al-Hujwiri, who as we saw above, gave great importance to the concept of ritual purity. For Hujwiri, the most important form of *nusk* was *mujahada*, which literally means "disciplined struggle." Although this term may also be defined as "self-mortification," it would be a mistake to think of it in this way without qualification. For Hujwiri, *mujahada* as a type of *nusk* entailed any form of ritualized discipline, from rituals designed to develop the ascetic self to rituals required for the practice of Islam in general. He said, "The most important act of *mujahada* is to observe the outward rules of discipline (Pers. *adab-i zahir*) assiduously in all circumstances."[82] To illustrate this point, Hujwiri cites the example of Sufyan al-Thawri, who suffered from rectal discharges during his final illness. Once, he performed sixty ablutions before a single prayer, saying, "I shall at least be clean when I leave this world."[83] In a similar way, the early Sufi Abu Yazid al-Bistami (d. 874 CE) said, "Whenever the thought of the World comes to me, I perform an act of ritual purification (*tahara*) and whenever the thought of the Afterlife comes to me, I perform a full ritual ablution (*ghusl*)."[84] For Abu Yazid, the contemplation of the Afterlife required a ritual washing because it was like a preparation for death. Just as a corpse requires a full washing to cleanse it of impurities before burial, the body of the ascetic requires a ritual washing to prepare it for the renunciation of the World and the fulfillment of God's covenant.[85]

The covenantal meaning of *nusk* highlighted by Rosalind Gwynne suggests an interesting parallel with Syrian Christianity. Early Muslim ascetics

---

81 Ibid., p. 499.
82 Hujwiri, *Kashf al-mahjub*, p. 292.
83 Ibid., p. 293.
84 Ibid.
85 For a description of the cleansing ritual of the dead in Islam, see Rkia E. Cornell, "Death and Burial in Islam," *Voices of Islam Vol. 3, Voices of Life: Family, Home, and Society*, ed. Vincent J. Cornell (General Editor) and Virginia Gray Henry-Blakemore (Volume Editor) (Westport, CT and London: Praeger Publishers, 2007), pp. 163–7.

were in frequent contact with Aramaic-speaking Christians and some Muslim practitioners of *nusk* were even called "monks" (*ruhban*).⁸⁶ In the early Syrian Church, certain lay ascetics belonged to a group that was known in Western Aramaic as *bnay qiyama*, "children of the covenant." These men and women pledged themselves to Christ at the time of their baptism and lived distinctive lives in their communities. The key member of the *bnay qiyama* was the *ihidaya* (Syr.), the "single, solitary, or unique one." This person was "singled out" from the majority of believers by practicing celibacy, living separately from the opposite sex, and by practicing the imitation of Christ through various forms of self-sacrifice.⁸⁷ The Western Aramaic term *ihidaya* is close in meaning to the Arabic term *munfarid*, which similarly denoted the "unique" or "solitary" ascetic who was singled out from the multitude because of his ascetic practices. Rabi'a the Ascetic is often portrayed as a *munfarida*. Like the Syrian Christian *ihidaya*, she practiced celibacy, lived separately from the opposite sex, and followed a regime of ascetic disciplines.⁸⁸

The most characteristic practice of the Syrian Christian solitary ascetic was *abila*, a Western Aramaic term that connotes "sorrow" or "mournful penitence" (Ar. *huzn*).⁸⁹ This spiritual attitude is closely related to repentance. The Greek word for repentance, *metanoia*, means "turning" or "redirection."⁹⁰

---

86 The root of the word *ruhban* (*r-h-b*) connotes fear or trepidation. Thus, the Arabic term for monk, *rahib*, literally means "God-fearing." The early Qur'an commentator Muqatil ibn Sulayman (d. 767 CE) stated that whenever Muslims hear the term *ruhban* they should understand it to mean, "believers who practice their religion with zeal" (*mujtahidun fi dinihim*). See Massignon, *Essay*, pp. 98–9.
87 On the *bnay qiyama* and *ihidaya*, see Sidney H. Griffith, "Asceticism in the Church of Syria: the Hermeneutics of Early Syrian Monasticism," in Wimbush and Valentasis, *Asceticism*, p. 238.
88 'Abd al-Wahid ibn Zayd (d. 793–94 CE), a reputed associate of Rabi'a and founder of a hermitage for ascetics at 'Abbadan in what is now Iran, stated in verse, "The way of truth is solitary/ and those who enter the way of truth are alone and unique (*afrad*)." See Massignon, *Essay*, p. 148. The paradox of "solitaries" in Eastern Christian and early Islamic asceticism who are nonetheless visible to the general public confirms Richard Valentasis's observation that novelty is an important part of the attraction of asceticism to lay people. For Valentasis, the uniqueness of the solitary ascetic both highlights the separation of the ascetic from society and conveys the image of a new "avant-garde" subjectivity—"a harbinger, an experimental prototype, the cutting-edge... Novelty makes asceticism attractive, desirable: the newness of the reconstructed self, society, and world creates the desire that provides the energy and impetus for transformation and ascetical performance." See Valentasis, *The Making of the Self*, pp. 41–2.
89 Griffith, "Asceticism in the Church of Syria," pp. 234–5.
90 According to the Greek Orthodox writer John Chryssavgis, "The whole of the Christian life (is) a repentance; (the Greek word 'meta-noia') implies reorientation and redirection from death to life, from sin to grace." Cited in Hannah Hunt, *Joy-Bearing*

In Islam, the penitent (Ar. *al-ta'ib*, literally, "the one who turns") also turns toward God in repentance (*tawba*) and performs ritualized acts of prayer and self-sacrifice in the hope of receiving forgiveness.[91] Redemption, the divine acceptance or favor that is the fruit of repentance, is depicted in the Qur'an as a bargain that is based on reciprocal "turning." In other words, God turns toward the worshipper to the extent that the worshipper turns toward God. "Show us the rituals (*manasik*) that we must perform and grant us redemption" (*tub 'alayna*, literally "turn toward us,"), says Qur'an 2:128. The use of the term *manasik* in this verse implies that ritual acts in Islam are viewed as outward signs of the "turning toward God" that must take place before redemption is granted. Later on in the same Sura, repentance is also depicted as requiring purification: "Verily God loves the penitents (*tawwabin*) and those who make themselves pure (*mutatahhirin*)" (Qur'an 2:232). The twelfth-century Andalusian Sufi Abu Madyan (d. 1198 CE) quotes Rabi'a al-'Adawiyya as describing penitents in a similar way: "The signs of true repentance are remorse and a heart that is fearful, pure, and submissive — one that is a dwelling place for obedience."[92]

The Sura of Repentance (Qur'an 9, *al-Tawba*) depicts the path to redemption as a contract of sale (*bay'*) (Qur'an 9:111–12). In this Sura, certain categories of believers are depicted as "selling" the World to God in return for the Nonworld: these are the penitents (*ta'ibun*), worshippers (*'abidun*), praisers (*hamidun*), wanderers (*sa'ihun*), bowers (*raki'un*), prostrators (*sajidun*), those who command the right and forbid the wrong (*al-amiruna bi-l-ma'ruf wa al-nahuna 'an al-munkar*), and those who observe the limits set by God (*al-hafizuna li-hudud Allah*). In Rabi'a's time, the term *nasik* applied to all Muslims who made a vocation of the ritual practices mentioned in this Qur'anic passage. Social activists who added the requirement to command the right and forbid the wrong and by doing so, helped maintain the legal and ethical boundaries of Islamic morality were also regarded as *nussak* (plural of *nasik*). Both *nusk* and *wara'* involved the ritualization of ascetic attitudes and practices. However, whereas *nusk* primarily involved the ritualization of

---

Grief: Tears of Contrition in the Writings of the Early Syrian and Byzantine Fathers (Leiden and Boston: E.J. Brill, 2004), p. 33.
91   For a fuller discussion of the Sufi concept of *tawba*, see Atif Khalil, "*Tawba* in the Sufi Psychology of Abu Talib al-Makki (d. 996)," *Journal of Islamic Studies*, 23 (3), 2002, pp. 294–324.
92   Vincent J. Cornell, *The Way of Abu Madyan: Doctrinal and Poetic Works of Abu Madyan Shu'ayb ibn al-Husayn al-Ansari (c. 509/1115-15—594/1198)* (Cambridge, UK: Islamic Texts Society, 1996), pp. 108–9.

practices of worship and symbolic acts of renunciation, *wara'* involved the ritualization of social behaviors. The significance of *nusk* for early Islamic asceticism was that it added an extra dimension of care or observance to the rites that were required for every Muslim. *Wara'* accomplished much the same thing for the observance of ethical distinctions.

According to Gavin Flood, "The ascetic self is constructed through ritual and *entextualizes* the body through ritual (my emphasis)."[93] Flood's notion of the "entextualization" of bodily actions through ritual performance helps us understand why Jahiz and other writers in early Islam so often equated asceticism in general with the practice of *nusk*. *Manasik* rituals, from prayer, to funeral rites, to the rites of the Hajj pilgrimage, provide some of the clearest connections in Islam between the ritualized disciplines of the body that are associated with asceticism and the scriptural traditions of the Qur'an and Sunna. Supplementing *manasik* rituals with supererogatory ascetic performances highlights these scriptural connections even further. As Flood explains, every act of asceticism is a ritual performance, "but a performance entails a particular kind of competence or cultural knowledge that flows through the generations."[94] In the ascetic culture of early Islam, the practitioners of *nusk* "entextualized" the values of the Qur'an and Sunna through dramatic acts of worship and self-denial. Since the actions of the *nussak* were often visible for all to see, one could say that the *nussak* were the "performance artists" of Islamic asceticism.[95]

Sometimes taking their practices to extremes, early Muslim *nussak* sought God's favor by exerting themselves far beyond the minimum of the required forms of worship. The *nussak* of early Islam also practiced a form of asceticism that was goal-directed and instrumental and viewed their devotions as an investment of spiritual capital. As Eliezer Diamond has observed about the ascetics of early rabbinic Judaism, the *nussak* of Rabi'a's time saw their exertions "as an investment in a spiritual bank account, as it were, being held in one's name."[96] The motto of the *nasik* was the famous "Hadith of Supererogatory Devotions" (*Hadith al-Nawafil*): "My slave continues to draw near to me with supererogatory devotions so that I shall love him. When I

---

93 Flood, *The Ascetic Self*, p. 214.
94 Ibid., p. 215.
95 Richard Valentasis also stresses the performative aspect of asceticism, although he uses theatrical performance as an example instead of performance art. See idem, *The Making of the Self*, pp. 8–10.
96 Eliezer Diamond, *Holy Men and Hunger Artists: Fasting and Asceticism in Rabbinic Culture* (Oxford and New York: Oxford University Press, 2004), p. 60.

love him, I am his hearing with which he hears, his seeing with which he sees, his hand with which he strikes, and his foot with which he walks. Were he to ask [something] of me, I would surely give it to him and were he to ask refuge of Me, I would surely grant it."[97] A similar notion of spiritual capital is expressed in a statement by Rabi'a al-'Adawiyya to Sufyan al-Thawri: "You are but a numbered set of days. When one day goes, a part of you goes as well. And when the part is lost, the whole is sure to be lost too."[98] In other words, the ascetic self is defined by acts of devotion to God, which are limited in number. Losing days from one's devotion to God is like losing part of oneself.

A more elaborate account attributed to Rabi'a expresses a similar ethic. This account appears in *Masari' al-'ushshaq* (*Battlefields of the Lovers*) by Ja'far ibn Ahmad al-Sarraj of Baghdad (d. 1106 CE). It recounts the story of a dream in which Rabi'a is chastised by a *houri* of Heaven for neglecting her nighttime prayers (*tahajjud*) and night-vigils (*qiyam al-layl*). These nightly devotions are so often associated with the *nasik* in early Islamic literature that they can be regarded as typical markers of ascetic ritualism:

> Rabi'a al-'Adawiyya said: "I was struck by an illness that prevented me from doing my night-vigils. So, instead, I read a section of the Qur'an during the daytime for some days, for it is stated that reading one-thirtieth (*juz'*) of the Qur'an every day [so as to finish it in a month] is equivalent to performing night-vigils."
>
> She continued: "Then Allah Most High and Exalted, granted me my health. During the period of my sickness, I became accustomed to reading one-thirtieth of the Qur'an [every day] and found solace in doing so. I stopped my night-vigils, and one night during my sleep I had a vision in my dream, as if I were lifted up to a green garden (*rawda*) with palaces and beautiful vegetation. While I was walking around it and marveling at its beauty, I saw a green bird and a slave-girl (*jariya*) chasing the bird, as if she wanted to catch it. Her beauty preoccupied me from the bird's beauty and I said to her, 'What do you want from him? Leave him alone, by God, for I have never seen a bird more beautiful than this!'
>
> "'Indeed!' the girl replied. Then she took me by the hand and led me around the garden until we reached the door of the palace within. She

---

97 Ibrahim and Johnson-Davies, *Forty Hadith Qudsi*, p. 68. This hadith can also be found in Bukhari's *Sahih*.
98 Ibn al-Jawzi, *Sifat al-safwa*, in Sulami, *Early Sufi Women*, pp. 278–9.

asked for it to be opened, and it opened for her. Then she said, 'Open for me the House of Instantaneous Vision (*iftahu-li bayta lamqa*)!'" [Rabiʿa said]: "A door opened for her from which emanated brilliant rays, whose light illuminated what was in front of me and what was behind me. Then the girl said to me, 'Enter!' And I entered a house whose brilliance and beauty bewildered the sight. I do not know of anything in this world comparable to it. As we were walking around the house, a door rose before us that opened into an enclosed garden (*bustan*). The girl descended toward it and I with her. We were met by serving-girls (*wusafaʾ*), with faces like pearls, holding braziers in their hands. The girl asked them: 'What is your destination?' They said, 'We are seeking someone who died as a martyr at sea.' The girl said, 'Will you not anoint this woman [meaning me] with your incense?' They replied, 'She had the chance to receive it but she gave it up.' Then the girl let go of my hand, turned toward me, and said in verse:

'Your prayers are light when people are asleep,

'But your sleep is the sworn enemy of prayer.

'Were you to consider for just a moment, you would see your life as a treasure,

'Eternally moving, departing, and passing away.'

[Rabiʿa said]: "Then she disappeared from my sight, and I awoke at the appearance of dawn. By God, each time I recall her or imagine her, I lose my mind and hate myself." Then Rabʿia fell into a faint.[99]

In this account, the ascetic self is defined by ritualized acts of devotion to God, which are limited in number and thus can be lost forever. Night-vigils and prayers are portrayed as an investment that produces definite and tangible rewards. If Rabiʿa ceases to make "deposits" of prayers and night-vigils into her spiritual "bank account," she cannot hope to profit from it.

The balance sheet of ritualized acts that characterized the ascetic practices of the *nasik* symbolizes the instrumental aspect of early Islamic asceticism.

---

99 Abu Muhammad Jaʿfar ibn Ahmad b. al-Husayn al-Sarraj al-Qariʾ, *Masariʿ al-ʿushshaq* (Beirut: Dar Sadir, n.d.), vol. 1, pp. 207–8. This anecdote is attributed to "Rabiʿa al-ʿAdawiyya the Sufi." However, because it is supposed to have come from Muhammad ibn al-Husayn al-Burjulani via a source from the Syrian city of Aleppo, this leaves open the possibility that it may originally have been about Rabiʿa bint Ismaʾil of Damascus (d. before 845 CE). For more on Rabiʿa bint Ismaʾil see the discussion below and Chapter 4. For traditions on nighttime prayers and night-vigils in early Islam, see ʿAbdullah ibn Abi al-Dunya, *Kitab al-tahajjud wa qiyam al-layl*, ed. Musʿad ʿAbd al-Hamid Muhammad al-Saʿdani (Cairo: Maktabat al-Qurʾan, n.d.).

The *nasik* performed ritualized acts with specific goals in mind. According to Catherine Bell, ritual practice is both situational and strategic: "It is a ceaseless play of situationally effective schemes, tactics and strategies."[100] The *nasik* was constantly in search of effective schemes, tactics, and strategies in order to earn God's favor. This search was often visible to the public. As the "performance artists" of Islamic asceticism, the *nussak* were sometimes regarded in the popular imagination as the "monks" (*ruhban*) of Islam. Like the Syrian Christian *ihidaya*, they often exhibited a mournful demeanor and were sometimes called "weepers" (*bakka'un*) for making the ritualized expression of sorrow part of their path.

Some *nussak* performed their struggles against the World by engaging in acts of "warfare" against the ego known as *mujahada* (sometimes also called *ijtihad* or *juhd*). Displaying a literalistic understanding of struggle (the term *mujahada* is related in meaning to *jihad*), they put their bodies on the line as ascetic "warriors" in God's service, subjecting themselves to physical mortifications or giving up their lives on the battlefield against the unbelievers. In his typology of the ascetic self, Richard Valentasis includes the *combative subject*, in which the ascetic moves from a deconstructed former identity to a new ascetic identity through constant struggle or warfare.[101] Textual evidence suggests that the combative ascetic subject was just as common in early Islam (where it was identified by the term *mujahid mujtahid*) as it was in early Christianity.[102] One of the most famous representatives of this type was 'Utba ibn Aban al-Ghulam, a disciple of al-Hasan al-Basri who lived in Basra during Rabi'a's lifetime. Like the Syrian Christian *ihidaya*, he was noted for his penitence and sorrowful demeanor and mortified his flesh by fasting and binding himself in chains. In the end, he attained his desire to be a witness to God's truth (*shahid*) by being martyred in battle against the Byzantines.[103] Because of the zealousness of *nussak* such as 'Utba al-Ghulam, the rationalist

---

100 Bell, *Ritual Theory, Ritual Practice*, p. 82. I disagree with Bell's opinion that ritual practice always involves a lack of intentionality or a misrecognition of what it is meant to accomplish. While this may be true for some religious rituals, the ritualization of ascetic practice in Islam must be both conscious and intentional in order to be acceptable to God.
101 Richard Valentasis, *The Making of the Self*, pp. 44–5.
102 For examples of militant asceticism in early Syrian Christianity, see Thomas Sizgorich, *Violence and Belief in Late Antiquity: Militant Devotion in Christianity and Islam* (Philadelphia: University of Pennsylvania Press, 2009). See also, Arthur Voobus, *History of Asceticism in the Syrian Orient* (Louvain, Belgium: Catholic University of America and Catholic University of Louvain, 1958), vol. 1, p. 13.
103 Massignon, *Essay*, p. 114 and n. 158; there is no clear death date for 'Utba al-Ghulam in the sources.

Mu'tazilite theologian Jahiz distrusted such combative ascetics and tended to regard them as extremists. Although he admired Rabi'a's reputation, by discussing her and other female Sunni ascetics along with Kharijite and Shiite women who met their deaths through gruesome forms of execution, he implied that the practices of the *nussak* sometimes went beyond the limits of what was religiously appropriate.[104]

For the Sufi Abu 'Abd al-Rahman al-Sulami, *nusk* was the most characteristic form of asceticism practiced by Rabi'a al-'Adawiyya and her contemporaries. In particular, *nusk* constituted for him the outward sign of the spirituality of Sufi women. Sulami's Book of Sufi Women is full of *nasikat*, and in one case, the term *nusk* itself even appears.[105] For Sulami, the designation of a Sufi woman as *'abida* ("worshipper") or *muta'abbida* (literally, "one who acts like a slave") indicated that she was also a *nasika*. For example, in his Book of Sufi Women a woman from Jerusalem named Lubaba is called both *muta'abbida* and *nasika*.[106] She is described as a specialist in *nusk* and combative asceticism (*mujahada*), and is also portrayed as a ritual specialist who prescribes prayers for men the way a doctor might prescribe medicine. The instrumentality of Lubaba's approach to spirituality is revealed in her statement that the goal of making invocations to God is that "[God] will be pleased with you, that He will make you attain the station of those who find their satisfaction in Him, and that He will magnify your reputation among His protégés (*awliya'*)."[107] However, Lubaba was not just an outward ritualist. Like Rabi'a, she also practiced an inner-wordly asceticism that was revealed by her practice of *wara'* and her sense of shame at being preoccupied with anything other than God: "I am ashamed lest God see me preoccupied with anything other than Him." For Sulami, this was a sign that Lubaba had attained *ma'rifa*, the Sufi concept of mystical knowledge of God. However, like other *nasikat*, her spiritual method was more a way of action than a way of contemplation. According to Sulami's account of Lubaba, it is only in action where she finds repose: "The more I am a *mujtahida* in worship, the more comfortable I become with its practice. When I become weary of human company, [my *mujahada*] allows me to find intimacy in the invocation

---

104 See, for example, Jahiz, *al-Bayan*, vol. 1, p. 194.
105 This is in the second of Sulami's notices on Lubaba al-'Abida (or al-Muta'abbida) of Syria. See the discussion below and Sulami, *Early Sufi Women*, pp. 124–5.
106 Ibid., pp. 82–3 and 124–5.
107 Ibid., p. 82.

of God. When I get tired of talking to people, I find rest in my dedication to God and in fulfilling my service to Him."[108]

d. Faqr *(Poverty)*

The concept of *faqr* ("poverty" or "need") has become so important to Sufism that Annemarie Schimmel characterized it as "the central attitude in Sufi life."[109] Words that express this concept, such as the Arabic term *faqir* ("fakir") or the Persian term *darvish* ("dervish") have come to stand for the Sufi in European languages. Similarly, the image of a life of poverty and self-denial has become so important to the contemporary trope of Rabi'a the Ascetic that one could also call her "Rabi'a the *Faqira*." As Margaret Smith stated, "Rabi'a al-'Adawiyya was an ascetic who followed the path of poverty and self-denial with unwavering steps to the end."[110] In the prosopographical collection *Sifat al-safwa*, Jamal al-Din ibn al-Jawzi (d. 1201 CE) includes a striking description of Rabi'a the Ascetic that confirms her reputation as a person who lived in extreme poverty.

> Muhammad ibn 'Amr said: I visited Rabi'a when she was an old woman of eighty years of age. She looked like a shrunken, old water-skin and appeared to be on the verge of collapsing. In her house, I saw a worn rectangular mat and a clothes rack made of Persian reeds, extending about two spans up from the floor. The door to the house was covered by a skin, perhaps made from mullet. There were also a jar, a mug, and a piece of felt that served as her bed and prayer rug. On the clothes rack made of reeds, she had hung her burial shrouds.[111]

The Arabic term *faqr*, "poverty," comes from the root *f-q-r*, which means, "to pierce, to bore [holes in something], to perforate." Thus, when *faqr* is used as a term for poverty, it connotes both affliction and need. In other words,

---

108 Ibid., Arabic text p. 83; I have changed the translation of this statement somewhat from what is in the original version.
109 Annemarie Schimmel, *Mystical Dimensions of Islam* (Chapel Hill, NC: University of North Carolina Press, 1986 reprint of 1975 first edition), p. 120.
110 Smith, *Rabi'a* (Rainbow Bridge), p. 20 and (Oneworld), p. 40.
111 Ibn al-Jawzi, *Sifat al-safwa*, vol. 2, p. 711 and Appendix to Sulami, *Early Sufi Women*, pp. 276–7; this account cannot be taken as a first-hand description of Rabi'a's physical condition because there is no chain of transmission (*isnad*) to support its attribution to "Muhammad ibn 'Amr." I have not been able to identify this latter person.

the poor person (*faqir*) is like a sieve: "pierced full of holes" by the affliction of poverty, the *faqir* has nothing and is unable to possess anything. It is from this sense of the root *f-q-r* that Sufis derived the meaning of *faqr* as an existential state of insufficiency or need. This is also the way *faqr* is expressed in certain verses of the Qur'an. In the Qur'an, humanity is portrayed as poor or needy (*fuqara'*). "Poor" humanity is contrasted with God, who is "The Self-Sufficient" (*al-Ghani*, literally, "the One who needs nothing"). One of the clearest Qur'anic verses that links poverty to humanity's need for God is the following: "Oh humanity! You are in need of God (*antum al-fuqara' ila Allah*) but God is the Self-Sufficient (*al-Ghani*), the Praiseworthy (*al-Hamid*)" (Qur'an 35:15). Clearly, it was not a major step for Sufis to define *faqr* as existential neediness rather than as mere physical or material deprivation.

However, despite the close connection in the Qur'an between the concept of poverty and humanity's need for God, the intentional cultivation of poverty as a spiritual path does not seem to have been practiced widely in Rabi'a's time. Although this assertion may seem surprising, since some early ascetics such as Ibrahim ibn Adham were famous for giving up their wealth for a life of poverty, a close examination of early Islamic sources on asceticism indicates that those who intentionally cultivated poverty were the exception rather than the rule.[112] In addition, the treatises of early systematizers of Sufi doctrine, which often discuss poverty as an important aspect of Sufism, cite few authorities on the spiritual path of poverty that lived in the first two centuries of Islam. In these works, one finds citations of the Qur'an and traditions of the Prophet or his Companions that discuss the poverty of early Muslims; however, few citations from Rabi'a's time can be found that equate asceticism with the intentional cultivation of poverty. To give but one example: the Persian Sufi Khargushi of Nishapur opens his chapter on poverty and wealth in *Tahdhib al-asrar* with the following tradition: "Everything has two keys. The key to heaven is love for the economically poor (*al-masakin*). Those who are patient in their poverty (*al-fuqara' al-subbar*) will sit with God Most High on the Day of Judgment." This tradition praises the attributes of compassion and patience in the face of poverty but it does

---

[112] I recognize that this view of the practice of poverty goes against most introductions to Sufism and discussions of early Islamic asceticism that are currently available in European languages. While I acknowledge that Isfahani's *Hilyat al-awliya'* and other works contain significant anecdotal evidence of ascetics and Proto-Sufis who practiced intentional poverty, I argue that the weight of evidence indicates that the intentional practice of poverty (such as constant fasting or intentional food deprivation) was rarer in early Islam than poverty as a by-product of the ascetic life.

not advocate the intentional cultivation of poverty as a way of life.[113] This curious lacuna in the sources requires some discussion.

Early accounts and statements attributed to Rabi'a al-'Adawiyya follow a similar pattern. For example, in *Balaghat al-nisa'* Ibn Abi Tahir Tayfur reproduces an account of Rabi'a going to an *'Id* prayer with Muhammad ibn Wasi'. Ibn Wasi', who is wearing his finest clothes for the occasion, asks Rabi'a, "What do you think of my attire?" "What should I say to you?" Rabi'a replies. "You go out among people to revive the Sunna and eliminate innovation. However, I see by your boasting about God's grace that you have caused harm to the poor (*adkhaltum 'ala al-faqir madarratan*)."[114] In this statement, Rabi'a's reference to the poor is about the economically poor, not about those who have made themselves poor for spiritual reasons. She tells Ibn Wasi' that by dressing in his finest clothes he has made the economically poor feel ashamed for their poverty.

However, when this story was passed on in later centuries, both the content and the meaning of Rabi'a's rebuke of Ibn Wasi' were changed from Ibn Abi Tahir Tayfur's original version to fit later doctrines and attitudes. For example, in *Mir'at al-zaman* (*Mirror of the Times*) by the Hanbali historian Sibt Ibn al-Jawzi (d. 1257 CE), Rabi'a's concern for the feelings of the poor is replaced by a statement about the hypocrisy of religious figures who affect piety while displaying wealth: "You displayed a love of luxury and soft living and thereby you brought humiliation upon the Muslims."[115] The story was changed even more dramatically when it got into Sufi hands. In Kalabadhi's *Kitab al-ta'arruf*, which was written about a century after Ibn Abi Tahir Tayfur's *Balaghat al-nisa'*, Rabi'a disappears from the story entirely. She is replaced by the male Sufi Abu al-Husayn al-Nuri (d. 907–8 CE), who recites a poem about the existential meaning of poverty as it came to be understood in later Sufi doctrine.[116]

Early Islamic treatises on asceticism also tended to discuss poverty as a state of material privation rather than as an intentional ascetic practice. In these works, the traditions used to extol poverty describe poverty more as an opportunity to practice patience (*sabr*) than as an intentional practice of deprivation. Perhaps most significantly, the infliction of physical pain through

---

113 Khargushi, *Tahdhib al-asrar*, p. 154.
114 Ibn Abi Tahir Tayfur, *Balaghat al-nisa'*, p. 210.
115 Smith, *Rabi'a* (Oneworld), p. 42 and (Rainbow Bridge), p. 22.
116 Kalabadhi, *al-Ta'arruf*, p. 67 and Arberry, *The Doctrine of the Sufis*, p. 87.

poverty, which some scholars such as Elizabeth A. Clark have seen "as part of the very definition of asceticism," is rare in early Islamic ascetical works.[117]

The most characteristic spiritual attitude that one finds in early Islamic discussions of poverty is patient acceptance of God's will. For example, 'Abdullah Ibn al-Mubarak opens the chapter on *faqr* in *Kitab al-zuhd wa-l-raqa'iq* by quoting the Prophet Muhammad's Companion 'Abdullah ibn Mas'ud (d. 653 CE): "The two most hateful things are death and poverty, but what is more due to God than wealth and poverty? I have no idea which of them I should reject because God has ordained an obligation for each. In the case of wealth, it is compassion and in the case of poverty, it is patience."[118] One of the lessons of this tradition, which sets the stage for the discussion of poverty in Ibn al-Mubarak's book, is that there is little value in seeking poverty for its own sake. Rather, one must accept both poverty and wealth as God's will and be prepared to fulfill the moral obligations required for each. A statement by Ibn al-Mubarak cited by the Persian Sufi Khargushi makes a similar point: "The appearance of wealth in poverty is better than poverty itself" (*izhar al-ghina' fi-l-faqr ahsan min al-faqr*).[119]

The interrelationship between poverty and patience that characterizes Ibn al-Mubarak's treatment of poverty brings to mind another observation about the concept of *faqr* in early Islam. To the extent that poverty was viewed as part of asceticism, it was only one of several indicators of the ascetic life. Poverty was undoubtedly very common among early Muslim ascetics, but it was not necessarily seen as the quintessence of *zuhd*. Although the term *faqir* ("the poor one") eventually became a synonym for *Sufi*, it does not appear originally to have been a synonym for *zahid*, "ascetic." As we saw in the previous section, the *zahid* in early Islam was more often equated with the *nasik*, the ascetic ritualist. This understanding is reflected in one of the most important early works on Islamic asceticism, *Kitab al-zuhd* (*The Book of Renunciation*) by Abu Mas'ud al-Mu'afa ibn 'Imran (d. 801 CE).

Mu'afa was a student of Sufyan al-Thawri and knew Ibn al-Mubarak. He was born in Mosul in northern Iraq and died in the same year as Rabi'a al-'Adawiyya. His book provides one of the clearest available pictures of Islamic asceticism in Rabi'a's time. For Mu'afa, poverty as an aspect of asceticism consisted primarily in avoiding the moral pitfalls of wealth and in traveling

---

117 See, for example, Elizabeth A. Clark, "The Ascetic Impulse in Religious Life," in Wimbush and Valentasis, *Asceticism*, p. 507.
118 Ibn al-Mubarak, *Kitab al-zuhd*, p. 199.
119 Khargushi, *Tahdhib al-asrar*, p. 157.

lightly through life (*khiffat al-hal*).[120] In his opinion, the proper attitude toward poverty was to regard oneself as God's slave and submit to God's will with patience and humility. However, if God decreed that one was to be rich, wealth was to be borne with patience and humility. The chief value of poverty was that it made it easier for the ascetic to resist temptation. The less one possessed, the less one would be called to account for one's moral failings (*la hisaba 'alayhi*).[121] When Mu'afa cites a hadith from the Prophet stating, "The poor (*al-fuqara'*) among the believers will enter heaven forty years before the rich," the point of the lesson is not to advocate poverty per se. Rather, it is to remind the reader of the moral burdens of wealth and power.[122]

Ascetic fasting—the systematic inducement of hunger as part of the path of poverty—was an important practice for early Christian ascetics. However, this practice appears only rarely in early Islamic discussions of asceticism. Some early Muslim ascetics are depicted as practicing severe forms of fasting, but this is most often discussed as part of ascetic ritualism (*nusk*). For example, in *Kitab al-makasib*, al-Harith al-Muhasibi describes some ascetics in Basra as practicing what he calls "preventative hunger" (*ju' al-man'*). This practice involved periodic abstention from food in order to prevent desire or foster humility.[123] According to Muhasibi, other ascetics in Basra also cultivated hunger as a means of training the soul (*al-ta'dib li-l-nafs*).[124] However, these Basra ascetics should not be confused with Christian anchorites. A number of early Muslim writers criticized Christian-style ascetic fasting for endangering the health.[125] In *Kitab al-makasib*, Muhasibi strongly criticizes ascetics who practice extreme fasting and likens Christian-style anchoretic fasting to suicide. For Muhasibi, such practices are immoral because they are contrary to human nature. In a statement that disagrees with later Sufi advocates of

---

120 Abu Mas'ud al-Mu'afa ibn 'Imran al-Mawsili, *Kitab al-zuhd*, ed. 'Amir Hasan Sabri (Beirut: Dar al-Bashir al-Islamiyya, 1999), p. 202.
121 Ibid., pp. 202–3.
122 Ibid., p. 204.
123 Muhasibi, *al-Makasib* in *al-Masa'il*, pp. 226–7.
124 Ibid., p. 226.
125 The ascetic al-Aswad b. Yazid ibn Qays (d. 694–5 CE) of Kufa was said to have mortified his flesh so severely from fasting that it became "green and yellow." He also became blind in one eye as a result of his fasting. For this practice, his contemporaries called him "one of the monks" (*rahib min al-ruhban*). His uncle, the traditionist 'Alqama ibn Qays al-Nakha'i (d. 682 CE), criticized al-Aswad for these practices because they harmed his health. See Isfahani, *Hilya*, vol. 2, pp. 102–5 and Ibn al-Jawzi, *Sifat al-safwa*, vol. 2, pp. 507–8.

fasting, he argues, "One who encourages people to fast disobeys God, for he knows that hunger kills."[126]

Much like Muhasibi, 'Abdullah Ibn al-Mubarak also associates poverty with hunger but he does not advocate fasting as a method for inducing poverty through hunger. Instead, he is mostly concerned about overeating. In one of the more humorous accounts in *Kitab al-zuhd*, the Caliph 'Umar ibn al-Khattab (d. 644 CE) is making the Hajj pilgrimage with the future Umayyad Caliph Mu'awiya ibn Abi Sufyan (d. 680 CE). During their journey, 'Umar criticizes Mu'awiya for having a stomach so big that it "almost touches the sun."[127] The point of this story is to contrast 'Umar's ascetic simplicity with the gluttony of Mu'awiya, whose Umayyad successors were criticized for their love of the World. Ibn al-Mubarak praises abstention from food as a sign of simplicity, but not as a means to induce spiritual poverty through hunger. Significantly, there is no chapter on fasting in his book. Although Ibn al-Mubarak encourages Muslims to follow a life of abstinence and simplicity, he does not advocate fasting to induce a state of permanent hunger or poverty. This appears to be because he viewed fasting primarily as a ritual observance.

Ibn al-Mubarak's view of fasting as a ritual observance follows that of the Qur'an. In one Qur'anic verse, fasting is described as a means of instilling awareness of God's power: "Oh you who believe! Fasting is prescribed for you even as it was prescribed for those before you, so that you may become aware of God" (Qur'an 2:183). After the tenth century CE, Sufis would use this verse to justify fasting as a means to attain spiritual poverty. However, fasts are more often described in the Qur'an as having a ritual value: they are mandated as expiations (*kaffara*) for sins, such as the two-month fast for involuntary manslaughter (Qur'an 4:92), or the three-day fast for breaking an oath (Qur'an 5:98). The Qur'an also mentions fasting as part of a vow, such as when the Virgin Mary vows a fast to God in order to avoid having to speak to men during her pregnancy (Qur'an 19:26). Other ritualistic fasts are mentioned in the Hadith, such as fasting three days out of every month, fasting on alternate days (which the Prophet called the "Fast of David"), fasting on the Day of 'Arafa during the Hajj pilgrimage, and fasting on Mondays and Thursdays.[128]

---

126 Muhasibi, *al-Makasib* in *al-Masa'il*, p. 227.
127 Ibn al-Mubarak, *Kitab al-zuhd*, p. 203.
128 See, for example, Muslim ibn al-Hajjaj al-Nisaburi, *Sahih Muslim*, trans. 'Abdul Hamid Siddiqi (New Delhi: Kitab Bhavan, 1978), vol. 2, pp. 548–53 and 561–70.

Qur'anic verses and Hadith accounts also insist on moderation in rituals concerning food, which further distances the practice of fasting from its use as an inducement to poverty. For example, the Qur'an alludes to Jewish Kosher regulations when it criticizes the People of the Book for being excessive in their religious practices (*la taghlu fi dinikum*) (Qur'an 2:171). Similarly, the Prophet Muhammad specifically forbade continuous fasting, saying, "Your wife has a right over you, your visitor has a right over you, and your body has a right over you."[129] Thus, despite the fact that some early Muslim ascetics practiced extreme forms of fasting, it was difficult for them to justify this practice in the face of stipulations in the Qur'an and Hadith that argued for moderation. Because they strictly adhered to these scriptural teachings, early writers on asceticism such as Ibn al-Mubarak and Mu'afa ibn 'Imran conceived of fasting as one of the ritual obligations of Islam. To the extent that fasting had anything to do with asceticism, it was primarily as part of *nusk*, ascetic ritualism.

The importance of fasting to the practice of asceticism was to change significantly in later centuries, when some Sufis adopted fasting as a way of inducing a greater sense of God-consciousness. For example, the Andalusian Sufi Abu Madyan considered fasting so important to the Sufi Way that he begins his Sufi manual *Bidayat al-murid* (*Basic Principles of the Sufi Path*) with a discussion of this practice. Abu Madyan required his disciples to perform a fast called "The Fast of Intimate Union" (*sawm al-wisal*), whose origins he traced to the Prophet Moses. This was a set of ritualized ascetic practices (i.e., a form of *nusk*), lasting up to forty days, which combined retreat, ascetic fasting, and the constant practice of invocations.[130] To justify this fast, Abu Madyan cites Rabi'a as an advocate of hunger as a spiritual practice. "Someone asked Rabi'a al-'Adawiyya, 'By what is the Intimate united to God Most High?' 'By hunger,' she replied. Then she was asked, 'So what is hunger?' She said, 'Hunger is the act of keeping oneself away from

---

129 Ibid., pp. 562–3 (hadiths 2587 and 2588).
130 V. Cornell, *The Way of Abu Madyan*, pp. 30–1. The Fast of Moses that Abu Madyan refers to was based on the forty-day fast performed by Moses on Mount Sinai before he received the divine revelation of the Ten Commandments. However, according to Eliezer Diamond, "Moses' abstention from food was not a true fast; it appears not to have been a decision taken consciously on his part but rather was a natural result of his being in God's presence" (Diamond, *Holy Men and Hunger Artists*, p. 95). Diamond's view of abstention from food as a by-product of God-consciousness is similar to that of early Muslim ascetics. A more fitting biblical precedent for Abu Madyan would have been the fast of Elijah in I Kings 19, who modeled his practice after that of Moses as well, but fasted for forty days with the explicit intention of obtaining a vision of God (ibid., p. 182 n. 23).

worldly delights. One who keeps away from the delights of the World attains his goal in the Hereafter.'"[131]

Abu Madyan's depiction of Rabiʿa as an advocate of hunger does not appear in any other extant source. Although on the surface this account seems to confirm that Rabiʿa was one of Muhasibi's hunger artists of Basra, one could also argue that she is not advocating the literal practice of hunger, as Abu Madyan thought she was. Rather, she might be saying that all acts of renunciation are metaphorically a form of hunger, since they conform to the World/Nonworld Dichotomy. A similar sentiment can be found in Muʿafa ibn ʿImran's *Kitab al-zuhd*. Muʿafa cites an early ascetic of Basra named ʿAmir ibn ʿAbd Qays (d. ca. 680 CE), who stated that the World consists of four desires: money, women, sleep, and food. ʿAmir claimed to have completely removed women and money from his life by renouncing them outright. However, sleep and food were another matter. They were so necessary for life that he could not decide which of them was more harmful. ʿAmir's solution to this problem was to do the opposite of whatever his body desired. "My struggle (*juhdi*) is that when it is night I stand [in prayer] and when it is day I sleep and fast."[132] ʿAmir was one of the minority of early Muslim ascetics who seems to have practiced a combination of poverty, celibacy and ascetic fasting as integral aspects of his asceticism. However, none of these practices was an end in itself. Rather, like the fast of Abu Madyan, they were ritualized behaviors associated with the practice of *nusk*.

III. TRADITIONS OF WOMEN'S ASCETICISM IN BASRA

In *Essay on the Origins of the Technical Language of Islamic Mysticism*, Louis Massignon calls the eighth century CE the high point of Islamic asceticism.[133] During this period, which coincides with Rabiʿa al-ʿAdawiyya's life, the asceticism of those whom Marshall Hodgson called the Piety-Minded became deeply embedded in the social life of the urban centers of Iraq and Syria, especially in Basra and its environs. In my book *Early Sufi Women*, I identified a tradition of Muslim women's asceticism in Basra that flourished during this period.[134] In that work, I suggested that the use of educational

---

131 V. Cornell, *The Way of Abu Madyan*, pp. 60-1.
132 Ibn ʿImran al-Mawsili, *Kitab al-zuhd*, p. 312.
133 Massignon, *Essay*, p. 113.
134 R. Cornell, Introduction to Sulami, *Early Sufi Women*, pp. 60-3.

terms such as *tilmidha* ("female student") and *mu'addiba* ("female mentor or trainer") in accounts about Rabi'a and her contemporaries could be taken as circumstantial evidence for the existence of a school of women ascetics in the Basra region.[135] This means that as the representative of a century-long tradition of female ascetics, the "real" Rabi'a would not have been unique in her asceticism. In addition, it would not be accurate to think of Rabi'a as the founder of women's ascetic spirituality in Islam. Rather, in the figure of Rabi'a the Ascetic, she should more accurately be seen as the foremost exemplar of women's asceticism. In this sense, as a symbolic figure, she stands between the asceticism and Proto-Sufism of her contemporaries and the more theologically based Sufism that developed in the tenth century CE. We shall see in Chapter 4 that the interiorization of ascetic practice marked an important difference between asceticism and what I call Proto-Sufism. However, before discussing this aspect of Rabi'a's identity, we must first understand the wider tradition of women's asceticism to which she belonged. As noted in the Introduction, this tradition does not start with Rabi'a herself but goes back to the first decades of Islam.

a. The Legacy of 'A'isha

'A'isha bint Abi Bakr (d. 678 CE), the widow of the Prophet Muhammad, appears to have been an inspiration for the Basra tradition of women's asceticism.[136] 'A'isha herself did not found this tradition. However, Mu'adha al-'Adawiyya, who is credited with founding the "school" of women's asceticism in Basra, was 'A'isha's handmaiden and companion and is mentioned by Muslim historians as a transmitter of Hadith accounts via 'A'isha. 'A'isha established a political base in Basra in the months before the Battle of the Camel in 656 CE. During this period, she and another widow of the Prophet Muhammad, Hafsa bint 'Umar, called on related clans and allies to support Talha and Zubayr, Companions of the Prophet who opposed the murder of the Caliph 'Uthman (d. 656 CE) and the accession to the Caliphate of the Prophet's cousin and son-in-law 'Ali ibn Abi Talib (d. 661 CE). The Battle of the Camel took place in December 656 CE and is named after the camel from

---

135 See ibid., and the notice on Unaysa bint 'Amr al-'Adawiyya, pp. 102–3. These terms are also discussed in Chapter 1.
136 On 'A'isha's importance as a source of Islamic traditions, see Sayeed, *Women and the Transmission of Religious Knowledge in Islam*, pp. 26–34.

which 'A'isha directed an attack against 'Ali's forces.[137] Among her strongest supporters in this battle were Rabi'a's clan of Banu 'Adi ibn Qays. The Banu 'Adi were also related to Hafsa and her father the Caliph 'Umar.[138] In this battle, 'A'isha and the rebels of Basra were defeated by the forces of 'Ali, and Talha and Zubayr, the pretenders to the Caliphate, were killed. After the battle, 'A'isha retired to Medina where she spent the rest of her life. However, many of those who supported her in Basra remained active in the city.

'A'isha was noted for asceticism during the final twenty years of her life. Although she spent this period in the Arabian Peninsula, her legacy remained in Basra through the influence of Mu'adha al-'Adawiyya. Denise Spellberg, the author of an important study on the historical depiction of 'A'isha in Islam, sees the tropes of 'A'isha "the sage" and Rabi'a "the saint" as exemplifying "the two main paths of faith in medieval Islam."[139] However, Spellberg does not specify what these tropes entailed. Simply labeling 'A'isha a sage and Rabi'a a saint is of little help because both figures are honored as both sages and saints by Sunni Muslims. In addition, Spellberg does not compare 'A'isha's and Rabi'a's asceticism. On this subject, she instead compares 'A'isha's asceticism after the Battle of the Camel with the Virgin Mary's distress in giving birth to Jesus as depicted in the Qur'an. According to Spellberg, "Both Maryam and 'A'isha wish for complete oblivion during moments of personal trial: Maryam in the throes of childbirth ([Qur'an,] 19:23) and 'A'isha at the end of her life."[140]

---

137 For a good synopsis of historical accounts of the Battle of the Camel and 'A'isha's career after the death of the Prophet, see Nabia Abbot, *Aishah the Beloved of Mohammed* (London: Al Saqi Books, 1985 reprint of 1942 first edition), pp. 82–176. Allen L. Fromherz calls 'A'isha an "Islamic Lady of Victory" in this battle because he sees her as enacting in the Battle of the Camel a pre-Islamic Arab tradition in which noble women were used as guarantors of honor and bravery: "The battle would rage around these women until the day was decided and the feud was lost or won. The capture of a chief Lady of Victory meant the end of the battle. No man with a vestige of honor would allow a rival tribesman to approach his Lady of Victory without fighting him to the death." Idem, "Tribalism, Tribal Feuds, and the Social Status of Women," in Sonbol (ed.), *Gulf Women*, pp. 50–3.
138 Abbot, *Aishah the Beloved of Mohammed*, p. 160.
139 Denise A. Spellberg, *Politics, Gender, and the Islamic Past: the Legacy of 'A'isha Bint Abi Bakr* (New York: Columbia University Press, 1994), p. 58.
140 The Qur'anic statement of Mary in the throes of childbirth, "Would that I had died before this and had been forgotten without a trace" (*ya laytani mittu qabla hadha wa kuntu nasyan mansiyyan*), is almost identical to a statement reported of 'A'isha after the Battle of the Camel: "I wish that I had been forgotten without a trace" (*wadidtu anni kuntu nasyan mansiyyan*). See ibid., pp. 167–8. For the original version of this account, see Ibn Hanbal, *Kitab al-zuhd*, p. 164.

By contrast, Nabia Abbot's biography of 'A'isha, which was written fifty years before Spellberg's study, provides a fuller account of 'A'isha's asceticism. Abbot observes that numerous traditions "bear witness to the almost ascetic simplicity of her life."[141] She notes that 'A'isha wore patched clothing and sometimes rebuked the Prophet's Companions for their extravagance. During her time in Medina, she was noted for "tearful readings of the Qur'an and long periods of fasting and prayers." At the end of her life, says Abbot, "she could not bear to live in comfort, let alone luxury, as long as she remembered the hardships and poverty of Mohammed's life."[142] However, Abbot undermines the ascetic image that she constructs of 'A'isha by casting doubt on its authenticity. She remarks, "Aishah neither stinted herself on worldly goods nor allowed her piety to curtail her social freedom."[143]

This statement is odd because many Sunni accounts contrast 'A'isha's asceticism with the behavior of her co-wife Hafsa Bint 'Umar, who was fond of comfort and luxury.[144] Although Abbot paints a contradictory picture of 'A'isha's commitment to asceticism, she admits that "Moslem traditions came in time to draw a picture of an ascetic and devout Aishah whose guiding principle in life was to live in the faith, hope for its rewards, and practice freely its charities."[145] The question left unanswered by such accounts is whether the asceticism that 'A'isha practiced at the end of her life was a consequence of her remorse for causing the disaster of the Battle of the Camel or whether she advocated asceticism as part of a new approach to spirituality. Ibn Hanbal lends support to the remorse hypothesis by quoting 'A'isha as saying after the battle, "I wish that I were a barren tree and had never been born!"[146] By contrast, both Ibn al-Mubarak and Mu'afa ibn 'Imran—who were Rabi'a al-'Adawiyya's contemporaries—mention 'A'isha as the source of a teaching on sincerity that later traditionists such as Ibn Hanbal attributed to the Prophet

---

141 Abbot, *Aishah*, p. 212.
142 Ibid., Abbot's references to 'A'isha's asceticism are taken from Ibn Sa'd. See idem, *al-Tabaqat al-kubra*, vol. 7, pp. 271–84.
143 Abbot, *Aishah*, p. 213.
144 See, for example, Mu'afa ibn 'Imran, *Kitab al-zuhd*, p. 279, where Hafsa urges her father the Caliph 'Umar to take better care of himself. This account may be contrasted with another from the same source (p. 287), where 'A'isha testifies to the simplicity of the Prophet Muhammad's dress and demeanor. See also, Ibn Hanbal, *Kitab al-zuhd*, p. 116, where Hafsa asks her father to allocate a greater share to his family from the public treasury.
145 Abbot, *Aishah*, pp. 213–14.
146 Ibn Hanbal, *Kitab al-zuhd*, p. 164.

himself: "Do not show off in your acts of worship. Instead, practice humility, for humility is the most excellent act of worship."[147]

b. The School of Mu'adha al-'Adawiyya and Instrumental Asceticism

The first "school" of women's asceticism in Basra appears to have been founded by Mu'adha bint 'Abdullah al-'Adawiyya (d. 702 CE). Mu'adha was the wife of Sila ibn Ushaym al-'Adawi (d. 694–5 CE), a noted ascetic and *mujahid*, who died as a martyr along with their son.[148] In her younger days, Mu'adha was a companion and political supporter of 'A'isha in Basra and transmitted Hadith reports from 'A'isha to important male religious figures such as al-Hasan al-Basri. As her name indicates, Mu'adha belonged to the same clan of Banu 'Adi ibn Qays as Rabi'a al-'Adawiyya. An account in Ibn al-Jawzi's *Sifat al-safwa* states that she and her husband were early exemplars of the tradition of asceticism for which the clan of Banu 'Adi ibn Qays was famous.[149] My theory that the group of female ascetics who gathered around Mu'adha made up a school is partly based on Sulami's notice on Mu'adha's disciple Unaysa bint 'Amr al-'Adawiyya (d. ca. 720 CE). In this account, Unaysa is called Mu'adha's "student" (*tilmidha*).[150] The image of a school that this appellation implies is reinforced by another account from Ibn Sa'd's *al-Tabaqat al-kubra*, where Mu'adha is depicted with her legs drawn up (*muhtabiya*) and teaching a group of women, who sit in a circle around her.[151]

Mu'adha al-'Adawiyya also appears to have been responsible for introducing the way of disciplined servitude (*ta'abbud*) that for Sulami epitomized the spiritual path of women's Sufism. As one would expect from an early leader of the Piety-Minded, her approach to religion was moralistic and her religious practices stressed prayer and the performance of night-vigils. She is depicted as praying 600 prostrations in a twenty-four hour period and reading the Qur'an at night in a standing position.[152] The importance given

---

147 Mu'afa ibn 'Imran, *Kitab al-zuhd*, pp. 249–50 and n. 4; Ibn al-Mubarak's version is slightly different: "Verily you forget that the most excellent form of worship is humility." See idem, *Kitab al-zuhd*, p. 122.
148 Ibn al-Jawzi, *Sifat al-safwa*, vol. 2, p. 707; see also, Appendix to Sulami, *Early Sufi Women*, pp. 266–9.
149 Ibid., p. 22 and Sulami, *Early Sufi Women*, p. 264.
150 Sulami, *Early Sufi Women*, pp. 102–3.
151 Ibn Sa'd, *al-Tabaqat al-kubra*, vol. 8, p. 483.
152 Ibn al-Jawzi, *Sifat al-safwa*, vol. 2, p. 707 and Appendix to Sulami, *Early Sufi Women*, p. 264.

to such practices in prosopographical literature indicates that Mu'adha was an early *nasika*, a practitioner of ascetic ritualism. Her name, *Mu'adha*, may be symbolic because it refers to the custom of seeking divine protection (*isti'adha*) against external enemies such as Satan. The use of symbolic names also appears to have been common among her followers. Ghufayra al-'Abida (d. after 720 CE), who was one of Mu'adha's most celebrated disciples, also had a symbolic name. The term *ghufayra* refers to the forgiveness of sins (*ghufran*), while the term *'abida* means "worshipper."[153] Likewise, the name of Mu'adha's disciple Unaysa means "Little Female Intimate [of God]."[154]

The most important ascetic characteristic of Mu'adha al-'Adawiyya and her followers was their instrumental approach to asceticism. The term *instrumental asceticism* was coined by Eliezer Diamond to describe the ascetic practices of early rabbinic Jews. For Diamond, these practices involved "the passionate commitment to a spiritual quest so consuming that one feels it necessary to minimize or eliminate worldly pursuits and pleasures because they detract from or distract one from one's godly objectives."[155] In the context of early Islamic asceticism, however, a more appropriate reason for describing such practices as instrumental is that they were focused on the attainment of specific goals or objectives. In many cases, the practices of ascetics in early Islam were in pursuit of concrete and identifiable goals. Often, early Muslim ascetics sought to obtain a specific reward for their ascetic practices as part of a bargain or transaction with God.[156] The instrumentality of Mu'adha al-'Adawiyya's asceticism can be seen in the following statement that she is

---

153 In the edited version of Ibn al-Jawzi's *Sifat al-safwa* (vol. 2, p. 714), Ghufayra's name is given as *'Afira* or *'Ufayra*. Since the Arabic word *'affara* means "dusty," *'Ufayra* would mean "The Little Dusty One." However, this does not seem to be a likely appellation. *Ghufayra* is a more probable name, in that it derives from the well-established Islamic notion of *ghufran* (forgiveness). The literal meaning of *Ghufayra* is "The Little Woman Who Grants Forgiveness." This fits Ibn al-Jawzi's description of Ghufayra as a religious figure who was sought out by people for intercessory prayers. The apparent mistake in rendering her name could have been the result of an early copyist eliminating a single dot, which marks the difference between the letter *'ayn* (for 'Ufayra) and the letter *ghayn* (for Ghufayra).

154 As the diminutive of *anisa*, Unaysa could also mean "Little Girl." Symbolic names may also have been literary tropes bestowed by later writers. However, even if this were the case, they would still be important as symbolic references to distinctive individual attributes.

155 Diamond, *Holy Men and Hunger Artists*, pp. 12–13.

156 Instrumental asceticism also existed in premodern Christianity. In Latin Christianity the term *instrumentum satisfactiones* was used to refer to ascetic practices that were intended as instruments of salvation. See Sebastian Brock, "Early Syrian Asceticism," in idem, *Syriac Perspectives on Late Antiquity* (London: Variorum Reprints, 1984), p. 8.

alleged to have made to her disciple Umm al-Aswad bint Zayd al-'Adawiyya: "By God, my daughter! My desire to continue living in this world is neither for the sake of luxury nor of relaxation. By God, I desire to continue living only so that I may get closer to my Lord the Glorious and Mighty through acts of worship, in the hope that He will grant me the pleasure of joining [my husband] Abu al-Sahba' and his son in heaven."[157] In this statement, Mu'adha explains that she practices asceticism primarily for the purpose of convincing God to let her join her husband and son in the Afterlife.

Like Eliezer Diamond's early rabbinic ascetics, Mu'adha al-'Adawiyya and her disciples rejected the World not only because it was a source of temptation and sin, but also because worldly affairs distracted them from God. Mu'adha was noted for minutely managing her day in order to leave little time for anything but religious practices. According to Sulami, she did not lift her gaze up to the sky for forty years. She did not eat during the day and did not sleep at night. When told that she was causing harm to herself with these practices, she excused herself by saying, "I have merely postponed one time for another. I have postponed sleep from night until day and have postponed food from day until night."[158] In other words, Mu'adha used ritualized ascetic practices (*nusk*) to turn the daytime fasts and nighttime prayers that are normally associated with the month of Ramadan into a daily routine. If she were overcome by the need for sleep during her nighttime vigils, she would wander around her house saying, "Oh soul! Eternal sleep is ahead of you. If I were to die, your repose in the grave would be a long one, whether it was sorrowful or happy."[159]

The early Muslim women ascetics of Basra also shared with early Jewish and Christian ascetics the belief that sincere piety demanded separation from humanity in both word and deed. *Perishut*, the Hebrew word most often translated as "asceticism," connotes separation, especially from things or people that are regarded as impure.[160] Mu'adha's disciple Unaysa bint 'Amr al-'Adawiyya was a practitioner of what Abu Hamid al-Ghazali (d. 1111 CE) called *al-zuhd fi-l-halal*, a type of ascetic perfectionism that involved the

---

157 Ibn al-Jawzi, *Sifat al-safwa*, vol. 2, p. 708 and Sulami, Appendix to *Early Sufi Women*, p. 268.
158 Sulami, *Early Sufi Women*, p. 88.
159 Ibid. A similar statement is attributed to Rabi'a al-'Adawiyya by Ibn Abi al-Dunya. See, "Kitab al-Manamat" in *Majmu'a*, vol. 4, pp. 43–4, no. 51: "Oh soul/self (*nafs*)! How long will you sleep? And how long will it be before you awaken? Your sleep is nearly as deep as the sleep from which you will only awaken when the trumpet heralds the Day of Resurrection!" This account was transmitted by Rabi'a's servant 'Abda Bint Abi Shawwal.
160 Diamond, *Holy Men and Hunger Artists*, pp. 85–6.

renunciation even of things that were permissible for the ordinary believer.[161] This practice is also found in Jewish asceticism, where *qedusha* (Heb.) "holiness," similarly results from foregoing even what is permitted.[162] Similarly, in Syrian Christianity, the *qaddish* or holy man was "someone apart from his surroundings, someone who has alienated himself from, and is unattached to the world he lives in."[163]

For the scholar of asceticism Richard Valentasis the concept of difference, along with the ritualized practices of separation and withdrawal that symbolize it, is important for the ascetic's construction of a countercultural identity. Valentasis describes the ascetic as a *tertium quid*, a person who is always "in transit, in process, in motion toward a new subjectivity. The early Christian monks, for example, experienced themselves as neither fully human, nor fully divine, as embodied angels, or disembodied humans, as living corpses, who lived in society and yet did not, who withdrew from society in order to create another so that at once they existed in a non-existence."[164]

Although this description might also be used to describe Muʿadha al-ʿAdawiyya and her disciples, Valentasis overlooks the possibility that sometimes the ascetic's act of separation from her former identity may paradoxically involve entering *into* social relations instead of withdrawing from them. For a few Basra women ascetics, separation from the lives of ordinary women involved earning a living in public, something that most Muslim women at that time did not do. In an account transmitted by the ninth-century prosopographer Muhammad ibn Husayn al-Burjulani, Muʿadha's disciple Unaysa bint ʿAmr is quoted as saying, "My spirit has never resisted anything that I compelled it to do more strongly than the avoidance of eating what is permissible and earning a living (*kasb*)."[165] From this statement it seems that Unaysa's practice of asceticism led her to act in ways that were contrary to what was normal for most Muslim women. This is a counterintuitive example of difference in asceticism, in which separation is not expressed as withdrawal from society but as involvement in a sphere of activity that would normally have been avoided.

---

161 See Abu Hamid Muhammad al-Ghazali, *Ihya' ʿulum al-din* (Beirut: Dar al-Maʿrifa reprint, n.d.), vol. 4, p. 229 (Kitab al-faqr wa al-zuhd); in this passage, Ghazali attributes the origin of this practice to Ibrahim ibn Adham.
162 Diamond, *Holy Men and Hunger Artists*, pp. 81–2.
163 Brock, "Early Syrian Asceticism," p. 9; see also, Voobus, *History of Asceticism in the Syrian Orient*, vol. 1, pp. 104–6.
164 Valentasis, *The Making of the Self*, p. 43.
165 Sulami, *Early Sufi Women*, p. 102.

c. The Weeping Women (al-Bakiyat) of Basra

Regardless of the religious tradition in which it occurs, instrumental asceticism is the product of a cultural environment in which the marketplace provides the primary model for the moral economy of divine rewards and punishments. In early rabbinic asceticism, says Eliezer Diamond, "Man *owes* God obedience, and every sin, whether of commission or of omission, is a defaulted obligation, a debt."[166] In Christianity, Paul of Tarsus says in his Letter to the Romans, "The wages of sin is death" (Romans 6:23). *Surat al-Baqara* of the Qur'an asks, "Who will grant Allah a generous loan? He will repay him many times over" (Qur'an 2:245). Behind each of these examples is the notion that a moral economy governs the relationship between righteousness and sinfulness on the one hand, and reward and punishment on the other. In this economy of faith and morals, says Diamond, "God has created a system of debits, credits, rewards and punishments and he operates within its confines."[167]

In both rabbinic Jewish and early Islamic instrumental asceticism, the moral economy of divinely bestowed rewards and punishments was seen as a zero-sum game, in which the portions allotted to the believer in this life and the Hereafter were strictly controlled. In rabbinic Judaism, this led to the belief that any pleasure enjoyed in the World might be deducted from the store of rewards being held on account in the next world.[168] The same notion of limited goods lies behind the statement of Rabi'a al-'Adawiyya to Sufyan al-Thawri that was cited in the section on *nusk* above: "You are but a numbered set of days. When one day goes, a part of you goes as well. And when the part is lost, the whole is sure to be lost too." In such an environment, the ascetic fears the consequences of even the least of her actions because each mistake or sin of omission is likely to diminish her reward in heaven. In early Islamic asceticism, this belief caused the awareness of God's power (*taqwa*) to be felt as fear (*khawf*) of retribution and led to such practices as obsessive preoccupation with ritual observances (*nusk*) or extreme caution with regard to issues of moral doubt (*wara'*). Among some ascetics of Basra—both male and female—this ethic also led to weeping (*buka'*). Ascetic weeping was such a widespread practice in Rabi'a's time that the jurist Malik ibn Anas devoted an entire chapter of *al-Muwatta'* to "The Excellence of Weeping

---

166 Diamond, *Holy Men and Hunger Artists*, p. 67.
167 Ibid.
168 Ibid., p. 68.

out of Fear of God."[169] Rabi'a's contemporary Ibn al-Mubarak believed that if newly learned information about God does not move the ascetic to weep it is of no benefit at all.[170]

Religious weeping is justified in Islam by a verse of the Qur'an that mentions weeping as a sign of the recognition of divine truth: "When the Qur'an is recited to those who were given knowledge before it... they fall down on their faces weeping, and it increases them in humility" (Qur'an 17:109). Although Hadith reports disapprove of lamentations and hiring professional mourners at funerals, weeping while recalling the inevitability of death is approved.[171] The practice of weeping appears to have been particularly widespread among the ascetics of Basra during the Abbasid revolution against the Umayyad Caliphate in the mid-eighth century CE. Louis Massignon cites several residents of Basra during this period that he identifies as *Bakka'un* (Weepers), including Salih al-Murri (d. 792–3 CE), who is often mentioned as an associate of Rabi'a al-'Adawiyya.[172]

William Chittick rejects Massignon's category of Weepers and states, "Despite the opinions of some of the Orientalists... there is no evidence that there was a group of people known by this label."[173] However, this claim is incorrect. In his Book of Sufi Women, Abu 'Abd al-Rahman al-Sulami characterizes the late eighth-century ascetic Sha'wana of al-Ubulla as "one of the weepers (*al-bakiyat*), and one who induces others to weep (*al-mubkiyat*)."[174] Clearly, if Sulami saw the need to classify weepers into two separate categories, a well-established tradition of ascetical weeping must have existed in his time and probably much earlier as well.[175] Three women ascetics of the

---

169 Malik, *al-Muwatta'*, p. 176.
170 Ibn al-Mubarak, *Kitab al-zuhd*, p. 41. This important work was overlooked by William C. Chittick in his article, "Weeping in Classical Sufism," in *Holy Tears: Weeping in the Religious Imagination*, ed. Kimberley Christine Patton and John Stratton Hawley (Princeton and Oxford: Princeton University Press, 2005), pp. 132–44. This oversight caused Chittick to conclude incorrectly that the early Sufi tradition did not devote much attention to the practice of weeping.
171 Chittick, "Weeping in Classical Sufism," p. 143 n. 4.
172 Massignon, *Essay*, p. 114.
173 Chittick, "Weeping in Classical Sufism," p. 133.
174 Sulami, *Early Sufi Women*, pp. 106–7. Sha'wana also appears in Ibn al-Junayd, *Kitab al-mahabba*, nos. 18 and 223 (Radtke, *Materialien*, pp. 55 and 162), where she is called *Sha'wana al-'Abida* (Sha'wana the Worshipper). She is also depicted in this source as being of non-Arab origin, because one of her statements is translated from Persian.
175 Women making people cry by enunciating beautiful truths is attested as far back as the pre-Islamic period in the tradition of elegiac *ritha'* dirges in Arabic poetry. See for example, Shawqi Dayf, *al-Ritha'* (Cairo: Dar al-Ma'arif, 1968) and Hammond, *Beyond Elegy: Classical Arab Women's Poetry in Context*, pp. 48–57.

Basra region, spanning the period between Mu'adha al-'Adawiyya and Rabi'a, illustrate this tradition and its role in early Islamic asceticism.[176]

We have already seen that Ghufayra al-'Abida was an important disciple of Mu'adha al-'Adawiyya. According to Muhammad ibn al-Husayn al-Burjulani, (ninth century CE), Ghufayra wept until she became blind.[177] Ghufayra's nickname, *al-'Abida*, means "The Worshipper" and refers to the fact that she was a practitioner of ascetic ritualism (*nusk*). Ascetic ritualists were instrumental ascetics who believed that the relationship between the human being and God was framed in terms of obligations and debts. This is illustrated by Ghufayra's response when someone sympathizes with her for her blindness: "Being veiled from God is worse [than blindness]. And the blindness of the heart from understanding what God desires from His commands is even greater."[178] In this statement, Ghufayra complains that ignorance of God is a sin because it prevents the ascetic from knowing the extent of her obligations toward God, even before trying to fulfill them.

Ibn al-Jawzi's account of Ghufayra in the book *Sifat al-safwa* (late twelfth century CE) provides further evidence that her weeping was due to the fear that her balance sheet of pious and virtuous acts would come up short on the Day of Judgment. "I have sinned against you, oh God, with each of my extremities. By God, if you aid me, I will do my best to obey you with every extremity with which I have disobeyed you."[179] Elsewhere, we find that for Ghufayra, weeping was a way of adding extra credit to her balance sheet. When asked if she becomes depressed from crying so much, she replies, "How could someone who has fallen ill from something become weary of that which contains the cure for her illness?"[180] Nothing, even the sight of her favorite nephew, could cause Ghufayra to forget the trials she had to undergo in order to pass from this world to the next: "By God, I cannot find any place for joy in my heart while I am thinking of the Hereafter. The news

---

176 The Egyptian writer Su'ad 'Ali 'Abd al-Raziq, quoting her uncle, Shaykh al-Azhar Mustafa 'Abd al-Raziq (d. 1950), claims that Rabi'a al-'Adawiyya was "the first to place the principles of love and sorrow in the temple of Islamic mysticism." However, this claim is more romantic than historically valid. See Su'ad 'Ali 'Abd al-Raziq, *Rabi'a al-'Adawiyya bayn al-ghina' wa-l-buka'* (*Rabi'a al-'Adawiyya between Wealth and Weeping*) (Cairo: Anglo-Egyptian Book Shop, 1982), p. 129.
177 See Sulami, *Early Sufi Women*, who cites Burjulani in the *isnad* of this account, p. 96.
178 Ibid.
179 Ibn al-Jawzi, *Sifat al-safwa*, vol. 2, p. 714 and Appendix to Sulami, *Early Sufi Women*, p. 286.
180 Ibid., p. 287; this account also cites Burjulani as a source.

of my nephew's arrival reminded me of the day of my encounter with God. So I find myself between joy and devastation."[181]

A similarly fear-based asceticism motivated the weeping of 'Ubayda (Little Female Worshipper) bint Abi Kilab (d. after 745 CE), a noted woman ascetic from a village outside of Basra who lived in the generation after Ghufayra. Sulami refers to 'Ubayda as "sound in judgment" (*'aqila*), which indicates that she was not considered insane or hysterical for her weeping.[182] For twenty years, she associated with Malik ibn Dinar (d. 745 CE), a noted disciple of al-Hasan al-Basri. 'Ubayda would often visit Ibn Dinar in the company of 'Abd al-'Aziz ibn Salman, a preacher who practiced pious retreats in an underground cell (*sardab*) beneath his house.[183] Ibn Salman's spiritual practices were also based on the fear of God. Whenever he mentioned the Day of Judgment in his sermons, he would cry out, and his audience would respond to him by also crying out. Sometimes, we are told, people in his audience would drop dead from heart attacks out of fear of God's judgment.[184] Motivated by a similar fear of divine judgment, 'Ubayda wept for forty years until she became blind. The self-mortification that she practiced led her to hope for death, both as a form of martyrdom through spiritual combat and to release herself from the moral dangers of the World: "By God, every morning I get up fearing that I will commit a sin against myself that will lead to my perdition on the Day of Judgment!"[185]

The notion of asceticism as martyrdom is a characteristic of instrumental asceticism because martyrdom is sought instrumentally as a key to heaven. In the market-based culture of limited goods that 'Ubayda inhabited, every day carried the danger of sins of omission and commission that might cause her moral account to end up with a negative balance.

What might be described as a "science of weeping" characterized the practice of Sha'wana (d. ca. 770 CE), a contemporary of Rabi'a who was the most important early woman ascetic of the Iraqi port city of al-Ubulla. Accounts of Sha'wana's weeping confirm Massignon's contention that the Weepers of the Basra region made up a special category of ascetics and that

---

181 Ibid.
182 Sulami, *Early Sufi Women*, pp. 134–5.
183 Ibn al-Jawzi, *Sifat al-safwa*, vol. 2, p. 715 and Appendix to Sulami, *Early Sufi Women*, p. 290.
184 Isfahani, *Hilya*, vol. 6, pp. 243–5. One of those who may have dropped dead from 'Abd al-'Aziz ibn Salman's sermons was Rabi'a's (alleged) disciple Maryam of Basra. See Sulami, *Early Sufi Women*, p. 84.
185 Ibn al-Jawzi, *Sifat al-safwa*, vol. 2, p. 715 and Sulami, *Early Sufi Women*, p. 290.

they were seen as different from other practitioners of asceticism. In his notice on Sha'wana, Sulami informs us that she preached to the public and that her lectures were attended by several different categories of the Piety-Minded. These included renunciants (*zuhhad*), worshippers (*'ubbad*), intimates of God (*mutaqarribun*), so-called "masters of hearts" (*arbab al-qulub*), and female practitioners of combative asceticism (*mujahidat*).[186] As for Sha'wana herself, Sulami describes her as self-sacrificing (*min al-mujtahidat*), God-fearing (*min al-kha'ifat*), a weeper (*min al-bakiyat*), and an inducer of weeping (*min al-mubkiyat*).[187]

The more detailed but later account of Sha'wana by Ibn al-Jawzi supports another of Massignon's theories: that weeping as an ascetic practice in Basra was related to al-Hasan al-Basri's teachings on sorrow (*huzn*).[188] A major source of information on Sha'wana was Malik ibn Daygham, the son of Daygham ibn Malik, a student of al-Hasan al-Basri and one of the first people to refer to himself as a Sufi.[189] Daygham was curious about Sha'wana but, because of his advanced age, he could not travel from Basra to al-Ubulla to see her. Therefore, on several occasions he sent his son Malik, who reported to him on Sha'wana's condition. Often, her bouts of weeping were so severe that her guests became embarrassed and had to leave. One ascetic complained that he stopped attending Sha'wana's gatherings because her profuse weeping made it impossible to understand what she wanted to say. Sha'wana defended herself from such criticism saying, "Any one of you who is able to weep should weep or at least be compassionate toward the one who weeps. For the weeper only weeps because of his awareness of what has affected his soul."[190] At one point, she was so overcome by grief that she could neither pray nor perform other acts of worship. Then a visitor came to her in her dreams and recited the following verses:

---

186 Richard Valentasis, *The Making of the Self*, pp. 44–5.
187 Sulami, *Early Sufi Women*, pp. 106–7. Sha'wana's weeping is not mentioned by Ibn al-Junayd in *Kitab al-mahabba*. However, in account no. 18 of this work she exhibits pious anxiety by admonishing a male ascetic for not worrying enough that he might not be worthy of God's love.
188 Massignon, *Essay*, p. 114 n. 158.
189 See Ibn al-Jawzi, *Sifat al-safwa*, vol. 2, pp. 682–4. Ibn al-Jawzi suggests that Daygham ibn Malik's ascetic ritualism was learned from his mother, who was a Bedouin. He was said to be unique in his sadness and the extent to which he afflicted his body with austerities. He said, "If I knew that it would bring about God's satisfaction, I would call upon the cleaver to cut my flesh into pieces."
190 Ibn al-Jawzi, *Sifat al-safwa*, vol. 2, pp. 727–9 and Sulami, *Early Sufi Women*, p. 300.

> Scatter tears from your eyes if you are truly distressed,
> For wailing heals the sorrowful.
> Strive, stand, and fast steadfastly at all times,
> For steadfastness comes from obedience.[191]

The most interesting accounts of Sha'wana are detailed analyses of her tears. In one account, she says: "By God, I want to weep until I run out of tears. Then I will weep blood until not a single drop of blood is left in my body. This is how far I am from real weeping!"[192] One day, Daygham ibn Malik received a man from al-Ubulla who described Sha'wana's weeping. Daygham asked detailed questions about her weeping: "How does she begin her weeping?" "Whenever she begins a session of invocation, you will see tears pouring from her eyelids like rain." "Which are more abundant—the tears coming from the inner corner of the eye beside the nose, or the tears coming from the outer corner of the eye beside the temple?" "Her tears are too numerous to distinguish one from another. From the moment she begins her invocations, they flow, all at once, from the four parts of her eyes." Then Daygham wept and said, "It seems to me that fear has burned up her entire heart! It has been said that an increase or decrease of tears is proportional to the extent of the burning of the heart. When the heart has been fully consumed, the sorrowful ascetic (*al-hazin*) can weep whenever he wants to do so. Thus, the smallest amount of invocation will cause him to weep."[193]

Daygham's assessment of Sha'wana's weeping provides yet another illustration of the highly ritualized asceticism practiced by early Muslim instrumental ascetics. It would not have been possible to assess Sha'wana's weeping in such a way unless this tradition was formalized enough to create a checklist of weeping behaviors. This account also brings to mind Herbert W. Basser's discussion of weeping in rabbinic Judaism. According to Basser, tears are an important supplement to prayer because penitential tears stir up divine passions.[194] In Jewish traditions God weeps, the angels weep, and the Prophets Abraham, Isaac, Jacob and Moses weep. Weeping is also a common theme in the Book of Psalms. Tears, says Basser, are the medium of an unspoken theology: "The mystery of crying is that through tears the

---

191 Ibid., vol. 2, p. 728 and Sulami, *Early Sufi Women*, p. 302.
192 Ibid., vol. 2, pp. 727–8 and Sulami, *Early Sufi Women*, p. 300.
193 Ibid., vol. 2, p. 727 and Sulami, *Early Sufi Women*, p. 298.
194 Herbert W. Basser, "A Love for all Seasons: Weeping in Jewish Sources," in Patton and Hawley, *Holy Tears*, p. 180.

outside worlds and the interior worlds merge deep inside the human spirit."[195] The tears of Shaʿwana, like the tears of the sages in rabbinic literature, may express either remorse or despair, but in either case, they express deep religious convictions. In the rabbinic tradition, much as in early Islamic asceticism, a distinction was made between the oily upper tear and the watery lower tear.[196] When Shaʿwana's tears flowed "all at once, from the four parts of her eyes," this was a sign of divine union, in which the divine and human waters flowed together to quench a burning heart.

Shaʿwana's weeping also brings to mind the Eastern Christian tradition of weeping (Gr. *penthos*). For early Christians, the practice of weeping revealed "the purified passion experienced by the penitent who, through the pricking of conscience, accepts his or her need to repent in order to be restored to God."[197] Eastern Christians used the Greek term *penthountes* ("mourning" or "wailing") or the Western Aramaic term *abiluta* ("mourning") to describe a state of repentance that was expressed through lamentations and the continuous shedding of tears.[198] In early Christianity, the grief that led to penitential weeping was called "joy-bearing grief" because the penitent's approach to God ultimately led to redemption and salvation.

Bishop Kallistos Ware describes a science of tears and redemptive weeping in Orthodox Christianity that is similar to what is described for Shaʿwana in early Islam. In the Orthodox tradition of weeping, the tears of the ascetic are both "bitter" and "sweet." Bitter tears, which flow from the lower part of the eye, express contrition for sin and act as a form of purification. Sweet tears, which flow from the upper part of the eye, reflect a "transfiguring spiritualizing of the senses" and act as a type of illumination. This is because they express joy at the reconciliation of the penitent ascetic with God.[199]

However, just because the Islamic tradition of ascetic weeping shared similarities with rabbinic Jewish weeping and Christian penitential weeping, this does not necessarily mean that the Weepers of Basra directly copied their practices from Jews or Christians. On the one hand, correspondences between Sufi statements and the teachings of early Church figures

---

195 Ibid., p. 185.
196 Ibid., p. 187.
197 Hunt, *Joy-Bearing Grief*, p. 3.
198 Ibid., p. 8.
199 See Kallistos Ware, *The Orthodox Way* (Oxford: Oxford University Press, 1979) and idem, "The Orthodox Experience of Repentance," *Sobornost*, 2 (1), 1980, pp. 18–28, cited in Hunt, *Joy-Bearing Grief*, p. 32 and n. 142.

do not necessarily imply that the Christian tradition of monasticism had a "pervasive" or directly formative influence on the development of Islamic asceticism, as Albert Hourani and other Christian scholars of Islam have asserted.[200] On the other hand, the opposite is not necessarily true for the assumed differences between these traditions. Not enough comparative research has been done on Jewish, Christian and Muslim ascetic weeping for Hannah Hunt to conclude that Muslim weeping "is devoid of the joy-bearing grief of *penthos*."[201] This latter comment has less to do with empirical research than with the dubious assumption that Islam, as a "religion of the Law," does not share the same depth of feeling as Christianity, which is a "religion of the Spirit."

The earliest Muslim writers on asceticism and Sufism do not include Rabi'a al-'Adawiyya among the Weepers of the Basra region. Rabi'a the Weeper is a trope that appears to have been introduced by the Hanbali theologian Ibn al-Jawzi in the late twelfth century CE. For Ibn al-Jawzi, Rabi'a's weeping is more an expression of feminine emotionalism than a ritualized ascetic practice. In one account that he relates, a male observer states, "I began to hear the sound of Rabi'a's tears falling on [her prayer mat] like pouring rain. Then she became agitated and cried out. At that point, we got up and left."[202] This account contains two tropes that are typical of Ibn al-Jawzi's depiction of Rabi'a the Weeper: first, she weeps uncontrollably; second, she becomes agitated. Ibn al-Jawzi also depicts Rabi'a as reacting to unexpected visitors hysterically—sometimes agitated, sometimes shrieking, and sometimes cringing against a wall. Often, her male observers, who are made uncomfortable by her actions, take leave of her. In the book *Holy Tears*, Kimberley Christine Patton and John Stratton Hawley observe that not only in Islam but also in other religions, male hagiographers often announce the entry of women onto the public stage with "emotional discourse-breaking acts" such as weeping. Men, on the other hand, are more commonly characterized by ceremonial behaviors that perpetuate and reconstitute the prevailing social system.[203]

---

200 See, for example, Albert Hourani, *A History of the Arab Peoples* (Cambridge, MA: Belknap Press of Harvard University Press, 1991), pp. 72–3.
201 Hunt, *Joy-Bearing Grief*, p. 18.
202 Ibn al-Jawzi, *Sifat al-safwa*, vol. 2, pp. 710–12 and Appendix to Sulami, *Early Sufi Women*, pp. 276–83.
203 Patton and Hawley, *Holy Tears*, p. 13.

IV. THE ASCETICISM OF RABI'A AND HER CIRCLE

a. Rabi'a's Alleged Students and Associates

In his Book of Sufi Women, Sulami discusses ten women ascetics who were contemporaries of Rabi'a al-'Adawiyya in Basra and the surrounding region. Of these women, only one is specifically mentioned as a disciple of Rabi'a. This is Maryam of Basra (d. before 801 CE), who made statements on divine love (*wa kanat tatakallamu fi-l-mahabba*) and went into fits of ecstasy whenever Love was mentioned. Her ascetic practices included night-vigils and the entrustment of all her personal affairs to God (*tawakkul*).[204] Sulami's notice on Maryam of Basra seems unusually reminiscent of Christian spirituality. Possible Christian referents include Maryam's name (Mary), her exclusive focus on Love as a spiritual method, and the verse of the Qur'an that she is said to have recited in her night-vigils: "Gracious is God toward his servants" (Qur'an 42:19). This verse describes God's love for His servants in a way that recalls the Christian theological concept of divine grace.[205] Also possibly reminiscent of Christianity is Maryam of Basra's practice of celibacy. The practice of celibacy by a number of early Muslim ascetics including Rabi'a al-'Adawiyya is one reason why Western scholars such as Margaret Smith have often sought the origins of Islamic asceticism in early Christianity. Rabi'a's celibacy will be discussed in detail in Chapter 3. Finally, it is perhaps also significant that Maryam of Basra does not appear in the early text of Ibn al-Junayd's *Kitab al-mahabba li-llah*. If she existed as more than just a character in a hagiographic tradition, one would expect such an important teacher of Love mysticism to appear in this important work on ascetics motivated by the love of God.

Another reputed servant of Rabi'a was 'Abda ("Slave" or "Servant") bint Abi Shawwal. 'Abda is a much better attested figure than Maryam of Basra. Not only is she named as the source of three traditions about Rabi'a in Ibn al-Jawzi's *Sifat al-safwa* but she also appears in a much earlier work, *Kitab al-Manamat* (*Book of Dreams*), by the late ninth-century traditionist Ibn Abi

---

204 Sulami, *Early Sufi Women*, pp. 84–5.
205 The early fifth-century CE Christian ascetic Makarios the Great stated: "Manifold are the patterns of grace, and most varied are the ways it leads the soul. Sometimes, as God decides, grace gives rest to the soul, at other times it puts it to work." John Anthony McGuckin, *The Book of Mystical Chapters: Meditations on the Soul's Ascent, from the Desert Fathers and other Early Christian Contemplatives* (Boston and London: Shambhala Books, 2003), pp. 146–7.

al-Dunya (d. 894 CE). Ibn al-Jawzi follows Ibn Abi al-Dunya in reporting that 'Abda was the source of accounts about Rabi'a's death and tells the story of a dream vision, in which 'Abda sees Rabi'a in a bright green dress and wearing a veil made of green silk brocade. Rabi'a says to 'Abda in the dream that the original shroud and woolen veil with which her body was wrapped for burial were taken up to the Heaven of *'Illiyyin* (Qur'an 83:18–21).[206] Finally, one can also cite the tradition of Jahiz, mentioned in Chapter 1, in which the leaders of Rabi'a's clan raise money to purchase a slave or servant for her to do her household chores.[207] This servant may have been 'Abda.

A unique account in an unusual source provides the only extant reference to a possible teacher of Rabi'a. This is Hayyuna, a woman ascetic of the second half of the eighth century CE. Hayyuna lived in the port city of al-Ubulla and may also have been a teacher or associate of Sha'wana al-'Abida, the famous practitioner of ascetic weeping. Hayyuna appears in a work entitled *'Uqala' al-Majanin* by al-Hasan ibn Muhammad al-Nisaburi (d. 1016 CE). The phrase *'uqala' al-majanin* literally means "wise fools" or "the rationally insane." It refers to individuals who were considered mad by the general public but whose supposed madness actually concealed profound wisdom.[208] The twelfth-century Hanbali scholar Ibn al-Jawzi probably read this work because he uses the term *'uqala' al-majanin* to describe several of the women ascetics who appear in *Sifat al-safwa*.[209]

Rabi'a al-'Adawiyya does not appear as one of the "rational madwomen" in Nisaburi's book. However, Hayyuna does figure prominently in this work and is depicted as an important teacher of Love mysticism.[210] What made her appear to be a madwoman was her tendency to go into raptures because of her love of God. According to Nisaburi, Rabi'a used to visit Hayyuna regularly. One night, in the middle of her devotions, Rabi'a fell asleep and Hayyuna kicked her awake, saying, "Get up! The wedding of the Guided Ones

---

206 Ibn al-Jawzi, *Sifat al-safwa*, vol. 2, p. 712 and Appendix to Sulami, *Early Sufi Women*, p. 280; Ibn Abi al-Dunya, "Kitab al-Manamat," in *Majmu'a*, vol. 4, pp. 43–4 (no. 51). The dream account can also be found in Kinberg, *Morality in the Guise of Dreams*, pp. 33–5.
207 Jahiz, *al-Bayan*, vol. 3, p. 66.
208 For an extensive discussion of *'Uqala' al-majanin* and its author, see Michael W. Dols, *Majnun: The Madman in Medieval Islamic Society*, ed. Diana E. Immisch (Oxford: Clarendon Press of Oxford University Press, 1992), pp. 349–65.
209 Rayhana "The Enraptured" (*al-waliha*), who flourished in the middle of the eighth century CE, is mentioned by Ibn al-Jawzi as one of "The Rationally Insane of al-Ubulla." See idem, *Sifat al-safwa*, vol. 2, p. 729 and Appendix to Sulami, *Early Sufi Women*, p. 306.
210 See al-Hasan ibn Muhammad ibn Habib al-Nisaburi, *'Uqala' al-majanin*, ed. Muhammad Bahr al-'Ulum (Najaf, Iraq: al-Maktaba al-Haydariyya, 1968), p. 149.

('*urs al-muhtadin*) has come! Oh, One who beautifies the Brides of the Night (*'ara'is al-layl*) by means of night-vigils!"[211]

Although Hayyuna does not appear in any of the earliest sources on Rabi'a that are currently available, the account of her in *'Uqala' al-majanin* is important because it possibly contains hints about the "real" Rabi'a's doctrines. Hayyuna's references to the "wedding of the Guided Ones" and "Brides of the Night," recall the earliest extant citation of Rabi'a by Muhasibi (also cited by Ibn al-Junayd), which states, "Rabi'a al-'Adawiyya would say at the coming of night, 'The night has come, the darkness has mingled, and every lover is left alone with his beloved. Now I am alone with you, my Beloved.'"[212] These accounts suggest that the "real" Rabi'a's asceticism may have included the concept of sacred marriage. As Richard Valentasis observes, "the metaphor of marriage with the divine articulates the intimate union experienced by advanced ascetics in their quest for complete absorption into the divine."[213] As such, it represents "the apex of ascetical effort" and provides a doctrinal link between asceticism and mysticism.[214] The metaphor of divine marriage was prominent in early Christian asceticism and continues to be important in both Western and Eastern Christianity. For example, the fourth-century Eastern Christian ascetic Makarios the Egyptian stated, in language much like that attributed to Hayyuna, "One kneels down in prayer and at once his heart is filled with the power of God. And his soul exults with the Lord as a bride with the bridegroom according to that which Isaiah the Prophet said: 'As the bridegroom will take delight in the bride, so the Lord will take delight in thee (Isaiah 62:5).'"[215]

For Valentasis, the spiritual goal of Eastern Christian asceticism is the transformation of the natural human subjectivity into a supernatural subjectivity. The active performance of ascetic disciplines that characterizes the aspirant is replaced through the stages of ascetic formation by a more

---

211 Ibid. The trope of a God-fearing woman kicking a sleeping student or spouse awake is fairly common in stories of Muslim ascetics. Sulami uses it in an account about Kurdiyya bint 'Amr, who was reputed to be the servant of Sha'wana. Sha'wana kicks Kurdiyya awake saying, "This is not the abode of sleep! Verily, sleep is reserved for cemeteries!" Ibn al-Jawzi also uses this trope in an account of the wife of Rabah al-Qaysi (d. 796 CE), who kicks her husband awake, saying, "The night has left and with it the army of the righteous, while you were asleep. I fear that you have deluded me, oh Riyah (*sic*)!" See Sulami, *Early Sufi Women*, p. 116 and Ibn al-Jawzi, *Sifat al-safwa*, vol. 2, p. 721.
212 Muhasibi, *al-Qasd wa-l-ruju' ila Allah*, p. 104; see also, Ibn al-Junayd, *Kitab al-mahabba*, no. 190 and Radtke, *Materialien*, p. 143.
213 Valentasis, *The Making of the Self*, p. 61.
214 Ibid. This thread will be picked up again in Chapter 3, "Rabi'a the Lover."
215 Ibid., p. 70.

passive attitude of receptivity, which allows the ascetic to take divine grace into herself and receive the "imprint of divinity" that marks her as permanently transformed and regenerated by spiritual marriage. Valentasis describes this process of transformation as follows: "The Eastern tradition... affirms the ability to achieve union through ascetic effort that creates both longing and desire for union. Such longing and desire results in a complete union, a communion and mystical knowledge of God in which God penetrates the very being of the ascetic to effect union."[216]

For the student of Sufism, this process seems remarkably similar to the Sufi Way. If Rabi'a al-'Adawiyya actually used the metaphor of spiritual marriage as Muhasibi and Ibn al-Junayd indicate, this would represent a major example of the dialogue of religions in Middle Eastern late antiquity. Equally importantly, the concept of spiritual marriage provides a link between asceticism and mysticism as well as a connection between asceticism and the spiritual path of divine Love. The doctrinal relationship between asceticism and Love will be explored in Chapter 3. In the following section, we will examine the concept of essential asceticism, which provides another connection to Love mysticism.

b. From Instrumental Asceticism to Essential Asceticism

In the discussion of Mu'adha al-'Adawiyya above, the concept of *instrumental asceticism* was introduced to characterize ascetic practices that were directed toward specific and identifiable goals. Instrumental asceticism was closely related to the ascetic ritualism of *nusk*, which saw the worshipper's relationship with God as a set of ritual obligations and moral duties. Rabi'a's contemporary 'Ajrada the Blind (*al-'Amiya*) exemplifies this type of asceticism. She fasted continuously for sixty years, wept and lamented constantly, and passed the night in prayer-vigils. Although a modern observer might view these behaviors as signs of depression, they were not spontaneous or uncontrolled actions. Rather, they were intentional performances and were part of a competition among ascetics for divine favor and spiritual status. The more carefully and more often one performed such behaviors, the higher one could rise in the hierarchy of the holy. This can be seen in the following supplication, in which 'Ajrada speaks of a competition among ascetics and asks to be ranked among God's intimates: "For your sake, oh

---

216 Ibid., p. 77.

God, the worshippers cut themselves off from the World in the darkness of night, glorifying you from nightfall until the predawn hours, competing for (*yastabiquna ila*) your mercy and the favor of your forgiveness. So through you, my God, and none other, I ask you to put me in the first rank of the Foremost, that you raise me up to the level of your Intimates, and that you count me among your righteous servants."[217]

Another type of asceticism that was important in Rabi'a's time was asceticism as a form of social protest, particularly against the unequal distribution of wealth in the Abbasid Empire. This type of asceticism, which was central to the moral outlook of the Piety-Minded as described by Marshall Hodgson, can be termed *reactionary asceticism*.[218] The French historian Maurice Lombard paints a vivid portrait of social and economic conditions in the early Abbasid period, which he derived in part from the writings of contemporary Christian observers. One of these observers was Pseudo-Denys of Tell Mahre, who was a contemporary of Rabi'a al-'Adawiyya. According to Lombard, the economic life of early Abbasid society was affected by a major influx of gold and a rise in the production of consumer goods. These economic pressures caused long-term price inflation, which benefited court circles and the merchant class but caused hardship for the lower classes.[219] Great numbers of the landless poor migrated from the countryside to the urban centers of Iraq. Because of this growth in the supply of available labor, the salaries of workers could not keep up with the rising prices caused by inflation. As more and more country people moved to the cities, merchants and government officials bought up rural land at discount prices. Lomabard calls this process an "urban invasion of the countryside," which resulted in the breakup of traditional patterns of land tenure. According to Lombard, "Wealth began to be expressed in chattels instead of real estate. . . This disintegration of the domanial structure brought with it social upheaval: the uprisings of the humbler country-folk matched the slave and plebeian uprisings in the cities."[220]

---

217 Ibn al-Jawzi, *Sifat al-safwa*, vol. 2, pp. 712–13 and Appendix to Sulami, *Early Sufi Women*, p. 284.
218 For Richard Valentasis, reactionary asceticism, as a "resistant subjectivity," is the essence of all asceticism. In fact, he goes so far as to say, "[O]nly performances intending to inaugurate a new, resistant subjectivity may properly be classified as ascetical." Idem, *The Making of the Self*, pp. 103–7.
219 Maurice Lombard, *The Golden Age of Islam*, trans. Joan Spencer (Princeton: Markus Wiener Publishers, 2004 reprint of the first translated edition, 1975), pp. 146–57. This work was originally published posthumously in 1971 as *Islam dans sa première grandeur*.
220 Ibid., p. 147.

However, despite these unsettled conditions, great fortunes could be made. The cargo of a single ship from China docking at the port of al-Ubulla might be worth 500,000 gold dinars.[221] "The merchant lived on a grandiose scale in his stately townhouse, surrounded by a host of slaves and hangers-on, in the midst of his collections of books, travel souvenirs, and rare ornaments."[222] By contrast, the towns and villages around the urban centers were full of dispossessed farmers and poor rural laborers. Tax farmers and money-lenders in the cities forced small landowners off their lands for defaulted loans and non-payment of taxes, "which grew in proportion with the fall of the purchasing power of the currency... The only recourse was to run away from the villages. Everywhere there were refugees, displaced persons wandering aimlessly in an attempt to evade the taxes and their urban creditors, and gradually slipping into brigandage."[223] The ascetic and former highwayman Fudayl ibn 'Iyad may have been one of these displaced persons. Also during this period, the local Aramaic-speaking people of Iraq began to show signs of unrest and occasionally rose in revolt. Sometimes, these revolts took on the color of pre-Islamic Iranian forms of religious revivalism.[224] At other times, they expressed Kharijite or Shiite aspirations.[225]

Al-Mu'afa ibn 'Imran's *Kitab al-zuhd* confirms Lombard's picture of economic transformation and social crisis in the early Abbasid period. By contrast with later works in this genre, it is almost entirely devoted to reactionary asceticism. The book opens with a chapter on the advantages of having little wealth and few offspring (*fi fadl qillat al-mal wa-l-walad*).[226] Unlike today, where wealth is conceived almost entirely in terms of money, for Mu'afa wealth consisted not only in gold and silver, but also in land, farm animals, women, and slaves. Children, literally "sons," were also included in this list because boys provided labor and added to the strength of one's lineage. Less positively, children required wealth, and hence involvement in the World, for

---

221 Ibid., p. 148.
222 Ibid., p. 149.
223 Ibid., p. 151.
224 See Patricia Crone, *The Nativist Prophets of Early Islamic Iran: Rural Revolt and Local Zoroastrianism* (Cambridge, UK: Cambridge University Press, 2014).
225 For early Shiite revolts in Iraq, see William F. Tucker, *Mahdis and Millenarians: Shi'ite Extremists in Early Muslim Iraq* (Cambridge, UK: Cambridge University Press, 2008).
226 Mu'afa's pessimism may have been related to the fact that he lost both his wealth and his two sons during the Abbasid conquest of Mosul. See the notice in Ibn al-Jawzi, *Sifat al-safwa*, vol. 2, p. 804.

their maintenance.²²⁷ For Mu'afa, all forms of wealth belonged to the World in the World/Nonworld dichotomy of Islamic asceticism. Mu'afa demonstrates his reactionary approach to asceticism by citing Hadith reports of the Prophet Muhammad that warn against the accumulation of excess wealth.²²⁸ The Caliph 'Umar is said to have wept at the thought of the harm that an increase in wealth would bring to the Muslims.²²⁹ The Prophet's Companion 'Abdullah ibn Mas'ud is quoted as saying that there would be a time when people would want to free themselves from the World so much that they would seek out death for themselves.²³⁰ In this and similar accounts, the World is described as a source of strife (*fitna*) that must avoided at all costs. In what is perhaps Mu'afa's harshest condemnation of worldly values, the ascetic Khalid ibn Maymun (d. 753 CE) states that in the time in which he lived, it was better to raise a dog or a puppy than to raise a child.²³¹

Much of *Kitab al-zuhd* is devoted to the condemnation of fame, status, honor, and the trappings of power. Mu'afa reports that when the Caliph 'Umar wanted to appoint the ascetic Sa'id ibn 'Amir al-Jumahi (d. 640 CE) as governor of Caesaria in Palestine, Jumahi protested, saying, "Fear God, 'Umar, and don't put me in turmoil!" Jumahi's fear of the moral dilemmas caused by the exercise of power is presented as a rebuke against those who sought power for personal gain.²³² In a Hadith report that would later be popularized by Ahmad ibn Hanbal, Mu'afa quotes the Prophet Muhammad as saying: "Four things remain in my community from the Time of Ignorance (*al-Jahiliyya*) that people do not want to give up. These are arrogance about social position (*al-fakhr fi-l-ahsab*), cursing a person for his lineage (*al-ta'n fi-l-ansab*), using the stars to forecast rain (*al-istisqa' bi-l-nujum*), and wailing [at funerals] (*al-niyaha*)."²³³ The only way to overcome such problems and return to the original values of Islam, says Mu'afa, is to make the humility of the Prophet the standard of conduct: "He visited the sick; he followed funerals;

---

227 Muslim ascetics in this period often viewed children as an impediment to the spiritual life because they had to earn a living in order to care for them. Nusiyya bint Salman, the wife of an ascetic preacher and disciple of Sufyan al-Thawri named Yusuf ibn Asbat al-Shaybani (d. 814–15 CE), complained of her duties as a wife and mother in terms that would be understood by a modern career woman today: "Oh Lord, you do not see me as someone worthy of your worship. So because of this you have preoccupied me with a child!" See Sulami, *Early Sufi Women*, p. 92.
228 Mu'afa ibn 'Imran, *Kitab al-zuhd*, p. 185.
229 Ibid., p. 179.
230 Ibid., p. 189.
231 Ibid., p. 188.
232 Ibid., p. 206.
233 Ibid., p. 262; a separate chapter in *Kitab al-zuhd* is devoted to each of these faults.

he answered the petitions of slaves; he rode a donkey; and he allowed his slave to ride with him."[234]

Although Muʿafa ibn ʿImran does not advocate fasting, he calls for humility in dress and diet. Surprisingly, the level of renunciation that he encourages is more moderate than one might expect from a work of reactionary asceticism. Instead of advocating extreme forms of self-mortification, he merely warns against overeating, advises moderation in the consumption of meat, and recommends eating barley bread and whole grains instead of wheat bread or white bread. Ironically, such practices today would not be considered asceticism. Rather, they would be seen as part of a balanced diet and healthy lifestyle.

In the book *Holy Men and Hunger Artists*, Eliezer Diamond contrasts instrumental asceticism with *essential asceticism*, an asceticism that entails "explicit renunciation of some aspect of conventional existence because self-denial itself is seen as inherently spiritually salutary."[235] For Diamond, essential asceticism is governed by a "dynamic imperative," which causes the ascetic to see the path of renunciation as governing every aspect of life.[236] This approach goes beyond the balance sheet of goal-oriented actions that characterizes instrumental asceticism. For the essential ascetic, the path of asceticism is not supererogatory to religion; rather, it is an integral part of religion itself, in the sense of a fully engaged submission to God.[237] As such, it is characterized more by indifference to the World than by renunciation of the World. This spiritual attitude is illustrated by a famous statement attributed to Rabiʿa al-ʿAdawiyya. When asked how she attained her high spiritual station, she replied, "By leaving aside all that does not concern me and by cleaving to Him who always is" (*bi-tarki ma la yaʿnini wa unsi bi-man lam yazal*).[238]

---

234 Ibid., pp. 238–9.
235 Diamond, *Holy Men and Hunger Artists*, p. 12.
236 Ibid., p. 11.
237 The concept of essential asceticism can be compared to Richard Valentasis's *integrative* model of ascetic subjectivity, in which "the ascetic subject achieves a transformation or enlightenment that enhances and enriches the subject's life within the dominant culture. In the integrative model the emphasis remains on the development and maturing of the subject over a period of time, without a strong bifurcation of old and new subjectivities, without setting up a conflict between old and new identities, but while encouraging the growth and development of the subject into a more perceptive or aware mode of existence." Valentasis, *The Meaning of the Self*, p. 45.
238 Khargushi, *Tahdhib al-Asrar*, p. 81. Khargushi's book is the earliest source for this saying that I have been able to find. Margaret Smith traces it to Muhasibi, but she does not say in which work it appears (idem, *An Early Mystic*, p. 215). Smith is probably referring

A common theme in Sufi accounts of Rabi'a's asceticism is her tendency to criticize outward forms of religious practice in order to reveal the inner meaning of ascetic worship. Often this included criticism of instrumental asceticism. For example, in the chapter on repentance in Khargushi's *Tahdhib al-asrar*, Rabi'a says, "Our repentance is in need of its own repentance." She also says, "Seeking the forgiveness of God by the tongue alone is the repentance of liars."[239] She explains the meaning of these statements in a third anecdote. A man said to Rabi'a, "Verily, I have committed many sins and acts of disobedience. Do you think that God will forgive me if I repent to him?" "No," Rabi'a replied. "If God had wanted to forgive you, you would already have repented. God the Glorious and Mighty has said, '[God has already] forgiven them so that they might repent'" (Qur'an 9:118).[240]

Perhaps the clearest example of Rabi'a's critique of instrumental asceticism is in an account from Abu Talib al-Makki's *Qut al-qulub* (*The Nourishment of Hearts*), which relates one of the lessons that she teaches to Sufyan al-Thawri. Thawri states the problem to be discussed in a formal way, as if he is asking for a legal opinion: "Every act of worship has a rule behind it and every act of faith has an inner meaning. What is the meaning of your faith?" Rabi'a says, "I do not worship God out of fear of God. If I did, I would be like the disobedient slave-girl who only works when she is afraid. Nor [do I worship God] out of a love for heaven. If I did, I would be like the disobedient slave-girl who only works when she is given something. Instead, I worship God out of love for him alone and out of yearning for him."[241] This statement is important because Rabi'a's rule of worship

---

to the fact that the statement appears in Abu Nu'aym al-Isfahani's chapter on Muhasibi in *Hilyat al-awliya'*. However, a careful reading of this passage reveals that the authorial voice in the saying is Isfahani's, not Muhasibi's. It is part of an argument to demonstrate that Muhasibi's approach to asceticism was shared by other early Sufis, including Rabi'a, 'Abd al-Wahid ibn Zayd, and Dhu al-Nun al-Misri. See Isfahani, *Hilya*, vol. 10, p. 108.
239 Khargushi, *Tahdhib al-asrar*, p. 95.
240 Ibid., p. 97.
241 Muhammad ibn 'Ali b. 'Atiyya Abu Talib al-Makki, *Qut al-qulub fi mu'amalat al-Mahbub wa wasf tariq al-murid ila maqam al-tawhid*, ed. Basil 'Uyun al-Sadr (Beirut: Dar al-Kutub al-'Ilmiyya, 1997), vol. 2, p. 94. This statement is reminiscent of a passage in the Jewish *Mishnah*, which dates to the fourth century CE. Chapter 1 of *Mishnah Pirkei Avot* (*The Wisdom of the Worshippers*) contains the tradition: "Antigonus of Socho received the Torah from Shimon the Righteous. He used to say: Be not like servants who minister unto their master for the sake of receiving a reward, but be like servants who serve their master not upon the condition of receiving a reward; and let the fear of Heaven be upon you." Rabi'a's statement differs from this tradition only in stressing the love of God more than the fear of God as the basis of her asceticism. I would like to thank my colleague Gordon Newby of Emory University for this reference.

subordinates the spiritual attitudes of fear (*khawf*) and service (*khidma*), which are central to instrumental asceticism, to the attitudes of love (*mahabba*) and knowledge (*ma'rifa*), which are more important to essential asceticism. In Rabi'a's essential asceticism as portrayed by Sufi writers, the outward forms of worship and divine service that are associated with instrumental asceticism are subordinated to their inner meaning. To the extent that the body is transcended through acts of ascetic discipline, the heart as a locus for spiritual knowledge grows in importance.

Chapter 3

Rabi'a the Lover

Long ago, exchanging greetings and salutations,
the two Sufis met in Basra.

As soon as she saw him behind the gate,
she revealed her face to the beautiful young man.

Her face was wrinkled and her eyes were faded,
beneath the black face-veil and under the white lace.

Hassan bowed his head with a deep sigh,
and responded to the salutation of this dear guest.

"What are you doing Rabi'a, for God's sake?"
The lover asked, his chin trembling.

[Rabi'a said,] "If only 'Hassans' would walk the beautiful streets of Basra,
Oh God, how decent human nature would be!

If only people like him walked our streets,
I would never have to wear the veil!"

—Bosnian *Ilahi*, "Hassan i Rabija," by Džemaludin Latić[1]

---

1   Džemaludin Latić is Professor of Qur'anic Exegesis (*tafsir*) at the Faculty of Islamic Studies in Sarajevo, Bosnia-Herzegovina. The song was recorded by the popular Bosnian *ilahi* singer Aziz Alili. I am grateful to Dr Ahmet Alibasic of the Faculty of Islamic Studies in Sarajevo for translating this song and providing information about its author.

I. FROM HISTORICAL REPRESENTATION TO CULTURAL ICON

The Rabi'a that is depicted in this *ilahi* (Islamic religious song) by the Bosnian scholar, poet and politician Džemaludin Latić never existed as an actual person. Even more, the "real" Rabi'a al-'Adawiyya most likely never met al-Hasan al-Basri.[2] If she had done so, their ages would have been reversed. Hasan would have been an old man and Rabi'a would have been a young girl. It is difficult to imagine the famous Rabi'a al-'Adawiyya as a Sufi sage in her pre-teen years. Al-Hasan al-Basri died in 728 CE and Rabi'a died more than seventy years after him, around 801 CE. Thus, from a strictly historical perspective, one has to conclude that this encounter is fictional and that Rabi'a as she appears in the song is a trope. Like the Native American myth described in the Introduction, the figure of Rabi'a in Latić's *ilahi* is another example of "The Old Woman Who Never Dies."

However, the historical accuracy of the friendship between al-Hasan al-Basri and Rabi'a al-'Adawiyya is not an important issue for the Bosnians who love this song, memorize its lyrics, and post it on numerous websites.[3] What is most important is not its historical accuracy but its message, which alludes to the religious and political conflicts that have caused the nation of Bosnia-Herzegovina to suffer for decades. The song recalls a better time in the past when goodness and beauty (*hasan* in Arabic means both "good" and "good-looking") were easier to find. The phrase, "beautiful streets of Basra," in the song evokes nostalgically the streets of Sarajevo and other Bosnian cities and towns in an earlier time of peace and tranquility. Latić uses the figures of Rabi'a and Hasan, who love each other because of their shared love for God, to evoke this bygone world. As Lynda L. Coon has observed about the subject-matter of hagiography in general, the evocation of these two figures depends not on historical facts, but on "*topoi*, literary inventions, and moral imperatives."[4]

---

2 As far as can be known today, the trope of Rabi'a's friendship with al-Hasan al-Basri seems to have first appeared in Farid al-Din al-'Attar's *Tadhkirat al-awliya'* (*Memorial of the Saints*). Over time, it spread throughout the Islamic world. See Chapter 5 and the translated passages on Rabi'a and Hasan in Michael A. Sells, *Early Islamic Mysticism: Sufi, Qur'an, Mi'raj, Poetic, and Theological Writings* (Mahwah, New York: Paulist Press, 1996), pp. 160-2.
3 See, for example, http://bosnamedia.com/media/cat6.stm.
4 Lynda L. Coon, *Sacred Fictions: Holy Women and Hagiography in Late Antiquity* (Philadelphia: University of Pennsylvania Press, 1997), p. xv.

The key motif of "Hassan i Rabija" is the depiction of al-Hasan al-Basri and Rabiʿa al-ʿAdawiyya as lovers of God. By evoking the trope of Rabiʿa the Lover, the song is related to other narratives, both premodern and modern, which have used this trope for purposes far beyond what the "real" Rabiʿa probably ever imagined. The romantic image of Rabiʿa the Lover has evoked more examples of poetic license than any of her other master narratives. For example, when imagining Rabiʿa in her book *al-ʿAshiqa al-mutasawwifa* (*The Sufi Lover*), the Lebanese–Syrian author Widad El Sakkakini keeps the following vision in her mind's eye: "I see Rabiʿa as an apparition, shimmering like a wave: not unsteady with a walking-stick and in ancient and worn-out garments and sandals, but running toward the shores of heaven in a halo of light."[5] In *Doorkeeper of the Heart*, a reflection on Rabiʿa that was inspired by the English translation of El Sakkakini's book, Charles Upton offers a similarly romantic view. For him, the love poems attributed to Rabiʿa are precursors of the love poetry of the Persian Sufi Jalal al-Din Rumi (d. 1273 CE): "If Rumi is the Ocean, Rabiʿa is the Well... Rabiʿa... has the virtues of maidenly simplicity, and the virgin blade; along with the taste of wine, she carries also the taste of water—a far more precious substance, when you live, like Rabiʿa did, in the desert of God."[6]

As we can see from these modern evocations, the tropological image of Rabiʿa the Lover is both complex and contradictory. She lives in the city and in the desert; she is an old woman and a virgin maiden; she walks beside the "shimmering waves" of Basra in a haloed garment but she also walks in the "desert of God," playing a reed flute that recalls the opening lines of Rumi's *Masnavi*.[7] As if this were not enough, a recent French evocation of Rabiʿa the Lover, in the book *Rabiʿa: Les Chants de la Recluse* (*Rabiʿa: the Songs of the Recluse*), depicts her as a reformed sinner: "Her genius was that of Mary Magdalene. She was much loved."[8]

---

5   Widad El Sakkakini, *First among Sufis: The Life and Thought of Rabia al-ʿAdawiyya the Woman Saint of Basra*, trans. Nabil Fatih Safwat (London: Octagon Press, 1982), p. 62; idem, *al-ʿAshiqa al-Mutasawwifa* (*The Sufi Lover*) (Damascus: Dar Tlas li-l-Dirasat wa-l-Tarjamat wa-l-Nashr, 1989 reprint of 1955 original), p. 98.
6   Charles Upton, *Doorkeeper of the Heart: Versions of Rabiʿa* (New York: Pir Press, 2003), p. vii.
7   "Listen to the reed flute how it tells a tale, complaining of separation/ Saying, 'Ever since I was parted from the reed-bed, my lament hath caused man and woman to moan/ I want a bosom torn by severance, that I may unfold the pain of love-desire.'" Reynold A. Nicholson (ed. and trans.), *The Mathnawi of Jalaluddin Rumi* (London: Luzac & Co., Ltd., 1977 reprint of 1926 original), vol. 1, p. 5.
8   Mohammed Oudaimah and Gérard Pfister, *Rabiʿa: Les Chants de la Recluse* (Mesnil-sur-l'Estrée, France: Éditions Arfuyen, 2006), p. 7.

The many "faces" of this trope support Lynda L. Coon's view of hagiography as an "exalted" form of discourse, which fixes the representation of a saint in the cultural imaginary.[9] For this reason, more than with the tropes of Rabi'a the Teacher and Rabi'a the Ascetic, the investigation of Rabi'a the Lover has to be more "literary" than "historical." Although there is evidence that the "real" Rabi'a spoke of love in her teachings, there is no way to be sure how much her actual teachings conformed to our present understanding of Sufi Love mysticism. The most that can be said with certainty is that the trope of Rabi'a the Lover has persisted for many centuries and has been, in the words of the French North African writer Jamal-Eddine Benghal, "a point of reference and a model for many men and women taken by purity and love."[10] Thus, in this chapter I will not spend as much time trying to distinguish the "real" Rabi'a from her figurative persona, as I have done in the previous two chapters. Instead, most of the chapter will focus on how the trope of Rabi'a the Lover has been represented in Sufi and Sufi-inspired literature. By using this approach, I hope to shed significant light on the importance of this trope in the cultural imaginary of the Muslim world.

II. ASCETICISM AND LOVE MYSTICISM IN EARLY ISLAMIC BASRA

a. From Asceticism to Love Mysticism[11]

Rabi'a's contemporary and fellow master of spiritual training Shaqiq al-Balkhi taught that the path of asceticism has four stages. The first is renunciation of the World (*zuhd*), the second is fear of God (*khawf*), the third is desire for Heaven (*al-shawq ila al-janna*), and the fourth is love of God

---

9 Coon, *Sacred Fictions*, p. 1.
10 Jamal-Eddine Benghal, *La Vie de Rabi'a al-'Adawiyya, une sainte musulmane du VIIIème siècle* (Paris: Editions Iqra, 2000), p. 8.
11 In this book, I use the term "mysticism" according to the definition recently proposed by Lloyd Ridgeon: "[Islamic mysticism refers] to the belief among some Sufis that experience of some form of intimacy with God was possible in their own lifetimes (whether it was an apprehension of ontological unity or else a vision of ultimate reality), which went beyond the piety of many Muslims who engaged in 'normative' Islamic ritual activity and who accepted 'orthodox' forms of belief." See Lloyd Ridgeon, "Mysticism in Medieval Sufism," in idem, *The Cambridge Companion to Sufism*, p. 126.

(*al-mahabba li-llah*).¹² This doctrine is important to the present discussion for several reasons. First, Shaqiq defines asceticism as a way of truthfulness and sincerity (*sidq*). In doing so, he reaffirms the close relationship between asceticism and ethical formation.¹³ Second, by asserting that asceticism culminates in the love of God, he lends support to the view of Bishop Kallistos Ware and other religiously inspired modern scholars of asceticism that the practice of asceticism is a positive attempt to find God and is not merely a negative rejection of the World. For Shaqiq, desire motivates the ascetic to attain the ultimate goal of asceticism, which is closeness to God. This agrees with an important statement that Bishop Ware makes about asceticism in Orthodox Christianity: "Desire, employed aright, impels us to love God; jealousy (or *zelos* [zeal]) spurs us on to make greater efforts in the spiritual life. . . our objective is not the *nekrosis* (mortification) of the passions but their *metathesis* (transposition)."¹⁴ This rather optimistic view of asceticism is quite different from the pessimistic view made famous by the German philosopher Friedrich Nietzsche (1844–1900). For Nietzsche, the asceticism of the saints is reactionary, passive-aggressive, and self-indulgent, "a pretext for hibernation, their *novissima gloriae cupido*, their peace in nothingness ('God'), their form of madness."¹⁵

Shaqiq al-Balkhi also believed that the key to the transformation of the self in asceticism was the conquest of fear. The conquest of fear marks the transition from asceticism viewed as a form of renunciation to asceticism viewed as a form of affirmation. Freed from preoccupation with the World's desires and cares, the ascetic opens herself up to the Nonworld and seeks her ultimate fulfillment in God. Fulfillment in God—not rejection of the World—is the true goal of the ascetic path. It is also the goal of the mystical path. According to Averil Cameron, a noted scholar of early Christian

---

12   Shaqiq al-Balkhi, "Manazil al-Sidq," in Paul Nwyia, *Trois Ouevres inédites de mystiques musulmans, Šaqīq al-Balhī, Ibn 'Atā, Niffarī* (Beirut: Dar al-Machreq, 1972), p. 17. See also, Balkhi's discussion of the stages of love in Carl W. Ernst, "The Stages of Love in Early Persian Sufism, from Rabi'a to Ruzbihan," in *Classical Persian Sufism*, ed. Lewisohn, pp. 439–41. Alexander Knysh (*Islamic Mysticism*, pp. 32–5) ignores Shaqiq's comments on Love mysticism and stresses instead his asceticism and involvement in *jihad*, describing him as "a curious hybrid of Ibrahim b. Adham and Ibn al-Mubarak" (p. 33).
13   Wimbush and Valentasis consider ethical formation to be the basis of asceticism. This also links asceticism to the concept of *ta'dib*, discussed in Chapter 1. see, "Introduction" in idem, *Asceticism*, p. xxix.
14   Kallistos Ware, "The Way of the Ascetic: Negative or Affirmative?" in Wimbush and Valentasis, *Asceticism*, p. 12.
15   Friedrich Nietzsche, *The Genealogy of Morals*, trans. Horace B. Samuel (New York: Boni and Liverlight, 1918), p. 94.

asceticism, by reorienting desire away from the World and toward God, the ascetic expresses "the freest form of desire in his or her individual relation with God."[16] The theorist of asceticism Geoffrey Galt Harpham explains this paradox in the following way: "Asceticism does not exclude desire, it complicates it; it proposes gratifications which are represented as both 'anti-desire' and yet (and for this reason) are more desirable than desire because they do not insult the conscience."[17] For Shaqiq as well, a desire that is "more desirable than desire" inspires the ascetic "to love what God loves and to hate what God hates until nothing becomes more beloved than God and what pleases Him. God watches over and blesses the one who strives for the love of God and bestows Love upon him."[18]

As we saw in Chapter 2, there were three main approaches to Islamic asceticism in Rabi'a's time. The first was *instrumental asceticism*, a form of asceticism that was directed toward specific goals. Instrumental asceticism was related to the practice of ascetic ritualism (*nusk*), which led the ascetic to conceive of her relationship with God as a balance sheet of religious and moral obligations. God's virtues are always greater than human virtues. Thus, there was theoretically no limit to how far the instrumental ascetic of Rabi'a's day might go in her pursuit of ritual and moral perfection. At times, such ascetics even competed with each other to attain the highest possible rank in the hierarchy of virtue. The majority of ascetics in Rabi'a's day were instrumental ascetics.

The second type of asceticism in Rabi'a's time was *reactionary asceticism*. This was an expression of social and ethical protest against the unequal distribution of wealth in the Abbasid Empire. The perspective of reactionary asceticism was illustrated in Chapter 2 by Mu'afa ibn 'Imran's *Kitab al-zuhd*, a book written during Rabi'a's lifetime, which was as much concerned with asceticism as a form of social protest as it was with asceticism as an approach to God. Although reactionary asceticism had a different focus than instrumental asceticism, it was not fundamentally different from the latter because it too was instrumental. Often, these two approaches to asceticism could be found together, as seen in the following statement from *Kitab al-zuhd*:

---

16 Averil Cameron, "Ascetic Closure and the End of Antiquity," in Wimbush and Valentasis, *Asceticism*, p. 154.
17 Harpham, *The Ascetic Imperative*, p. 46.
18 Shaqiq al-Balkhi, "Manazil al-Sidq," in *Trois Oeuvres inédite*, ed. Nwyia, p. 20; the verb translated as "strive for" in the above passage is *ibtagha*, which comes from an Arabic root that connotes "desire."

"Your wealth calls you to hellfire but your poverty calls you to heaven."[19] This statement reflects the ethics of reactionary asceticism because it rejects wealth as a moral danger and affirms poverty as a sign of worthiness for heaven. However, it also reflects the ethics of instrumental asceticism because salvation depends on the renunciation of wealth as a means to an end. Since wealth leads to hellfire and poverty leads to heaven, rejecting wealth averts hellfire and makes the ascetic's attainment to heaven possible.

Rabi'a al-'Adawiyya is most often portrayed as a practitioner of the third type of asceticism in this period, *essential asceticism*. In essential asceticism, the ascetic attains the Nonworld not by rejecting the World but by treating it as unimportant. The essential ascetic avoids the World not because it is evil per se but because it is a distraction from God. Essential asceticism is in agreement with normative Islam because it reflects the Qur'anic message of complete submission to God. Rabi'a's essential asceticism was illustrated in Chapter 2 by her statement that asceticism consists in "leaving aside all that does not concern me and by cleaving to the One that always is." This statement implies that a major goal of essential asceticism is the love of God, because the ascetic cleaves to that which is most fundamental for her existence. Since we all depend on God for our existence, closeness to God is the worthiest of all goals. Rabi'a is also reported to have said, "I do not worship God out of fear of God. If I did, I would be like the disobedient slave-girl who only works when she is afraid. Nor [do I worship God] out of love for heaven. If I did, I would be like the disobedient slave-girl who only works when she is given something. Instead, I worship God out of love for Him alone and out of desire for Him."[20] God is the worthiest object of our love because He is the source of all that is important to us. This statement agrees with Geoffrey Galt Harpham's assertion that the ascetic's desire for God is "more desirable than [ordinary] desire." The same notion is reflected in another aphorism attributed to Rabi'a: "The best way for the slave to come near to God Most High is for him to know that he must not love anything in this world or the Hereafter other than Him."[21]

---

19 Mu'afa ibn 'Imran, *Kitab al-zuhd*, p. 185.
20 Makki, *Qut al-qulub*, vol. 2, p. 94; see also, Abu Hamid al-Ghazali, *Love, Longing, Intimacy, and Contentment: Kitab al-mahabba wa'l-shawq wa-l-uns wa'l-rida, Book XXXVI of The Revival of the Religious Sciences* Ihya' 'ulum al-din, trans. Eric Ormsby (Cambridge, UK: Islamic Texts Society, 2011), p. 52. Ghazali seems to have taken this quote from Makki's book.
21 Sulami, *Early Sufi Women*, pp. 80–1.

b. Love of God in the Qur'an and Hadith

Mahabba, the Arabic term for love that is used in the above aphorisms, appears only once in the Qur'an. However, its use is significant, because it occurs in a verse that instructs the believer to put her trust completely in God, which is an important aspect of essential asceticism. In this verse, the mother of Moses is ordered by God to put her baby in a chest and cast him into the River Nile in order to save him from Pharaoh's men. God tells her not to worry about Moses' safety, "for I have put my love (*mahabba*) upon him and he will be formed under my care" (Qur'an 20:39). God assures the mother of Moses that her trust will be rewarded by His love and care for her son.

Another woman in the Qur'an who entrusts herself to God is Mary the Mother of Jesus, who "had faith in the words of her Lord and His books, and was one of the obedient" (Qur'an 66:12). When the pain of childbirth drives Mary to seek refuge under a palm tree, she cries out to God for help. In response, God provides her with ripe dates and running water to sustain her (Qur'an 19:23–26). Although the term *mahabba* does not appear in the Qur'anic verses about Mary, the same concepts of obedience and trust apply to her relationship with God as in the verse about the mother of Moses. The Qur'an's description of Mary as "one of the obedient" (*min al-qanitin*), connotes devotion and surrender to God.[22] Mary's devotion to God leads her to entrust her life completely to her Lord, an act that Tor Andrae, the Swedish scholar of Sufism, called "the sum of all devotion."[23] Some early Sufis followed Mary's path of entrustment to God (*tawakkul*) and refused to earn a living because, like Mary, they depended on God to provide for all of their needs.[24]

Verses that discuss the love of God in the Qur'an stress the importance of reciprocity between the believer's love of God and God's love for the believer. "Say: If you love God, follow [the Prophet Muhammad] so that God will love you" (Qur'an 3:31). "Soon God will bring forth a people whom He will love and they will love Him" (Qur'an 5:54). A sense of reciprocity can also

---

22 See Aliah Schleiffer, *Mary the Blessed Virgin of Islam* (Louisville, Kentucky: Fons Vitae, 1998), p. 56.
23 Andrae, *In the Garden of Myrtles*, p. 110.
24 The Iraqi Sufi Ibrahim al-Khawwas (d. 904 CE), who was a famous practitioner of *tawakkul*, even refused to beg for food from others. He said, "It is not part of Sufi conduct to have means upon which to rely in case of need, nor something that can be accepted by another [as payment], nor sight nor tongue with which to beg if one is hungry, nor a word by which to beseech human beings in case of misfortune." See Abu Madyan, "Bidayat al-murid," in V. Cornell, *The Way of Abu Madyan*, pp. 31 and 64.

be found in the numerous references to love of God in Hadith. "When I [i.e., God] love someone, I am the hearing by which he hears, the sight by which he sees, the tongue by which he speaks, and the hand by which he grasps."[25] Ascetic ritualists (*nussak*) in early Islam used this tradition to argue that the amount of love that God gives the believer is directly related to the amount of pious observances that the believer gives back to God. Hadith accounts also distinguish between love that is given altruistically and without hope of reward and love as a form of recompense for specific acts of devotion. For example, the notion of love as a form of recompense can be seen in the following tradition from the *Musnad* of Ahmad ibn Hanbal: "Renounce the World (*izhad fi-l-dunya*) so that God will love you."[26] However, despite its mention of love, this hadith is a justification for instrumental asceticism because devotion is not altruistic; it depends on a cause-and-effect relation between the practice of asceticism and divine favor. By contrast, a more altruistic concept of love can be seen in the following hadith from *Sunan al-Tirmidhi*: "God is an intimate friend (*rafiq*) and He loves intimate friendship (*rifq*)."[27] This hadith argues for essential asceticism rather than instrumental asceticism because God gives love altruistically, irrespective of the believer's ability to respond in kind.

However, one must be careful when using Hadith accounts to understand the notion of ascetical love in Rabi'a's time. Just because a statement appears in a Hadith collection, it does not necessarily mean that the Prophet Muhammad said it. The most widely used Hadith collections were compiled after Rabi'a's time and more than 200 years after the death of the Prophet Muhammad. For example, Ahmad ibn Hanbal died in 855 CE, half a century after Rabi'a and 223 years after the Prophet. Thus, the traditions about love and renunciation in his *Musnad* may reflect the views of asceticism in his own time more than the views of the Prophet himself. Abu 'Isa al-Tirmidhi, the compiler of *Sunan al-Tirmidhi*, died almost a century after Rabi'a, in 892–93 CE. Nearly 260 years separate him from the Prophet Muhammad. Similarly, the traditions that support altruistic love in his Hadith collection may reflect notions of altruistic love that were popular in the Abbasid age but may not have been as popular in the time of either Rabi'a or the Prophet.[28]

---

25 *Sahih al-Bukhari*, Kitab al-Riqaq (*Book of Ritual Practices*), p. 38.
26 *Musnad Ibn Hanbal*, Kitab al-Zuhd (*Book of Renunciation*), p. 1.
27 *Sunan al-Tirmidhi*, Kitab al-Birr (*Book of Virtue*), p. 77.
28 Recent research has demonstrated that some Hadith traditions can in fact be dated to the Prophet's time. See, for example, Harald Motzki, "Dating Muslim Traditions: A Survey," *Arabica*, 52, 2005, pp. 204–53.

Nevertheless, Hadith collections can still be used to provide answers for more limited questions. For example, the modern researcher can use Hadith to get a sense of whether or not the terms for love used in later Sufi accounts about Rabi'a were authentic to Rabi'a's era. The use and meaning of key terminology can help date an account's origin. A survey of statements about the love of God in Hadith accounts reveals that the word *mahabba*—which was to become a key technical term for the practice of love as a spiritual method in Sufism—was a generic term for love in the early Islamic period.[29] This supports the belief that statements of early Sufis that use this term may be genuine. In one hadith from Ibn Hanbal's *Musnad*, the Prophet explains that the Qur'anic phrase "bonds of the womb" (*silat al-rahim*, Qur'an 4:1) means, "love for one's family" (*mahabbatan fi-l-ahl*).[30] Here, the term *mahabba* is used as a synonym for *hubb*, the most common word for love in Arabic. The Prophet could have used the phrases *hubban fi-l-ahl* and *mahabbatan fi-l-ahl* interchangeably.

Further support for the idea that early Muslims used the terms *mahabba* and *hubb* interchangeably can be found in a statement attributed to Rabi'a's contemporary Ibrahim ibn Adham. "Do not seek the love of God (*hubb Allah*) along with the love of money or honor (*mahabbat al-mal wa-l-sharaf*)."[31] This statement is significant because it reverses the expected use of the terms *hubb* and *mahabba*. In later generations, Sufis would use the term *mahabba* for the love of God but not for the love of worldly things. The more common term *hubb* was used for the love of worldly things. However, in Ibn Adham's time, this distinction does not appear to have been important: *mahabba* is used for love of the World whereas *hubb* is used for the love of God. Numerous examples such as these provide evidence that the terms *hubb* and *mahabba* were synonymous in Rabi'a's time.

However, this was not the case for *'ishq*, another Sufi term for the love of God, which does not seem to have been used widely in early Islam.[32] This term, which means, "desire," has often been used by Sufis as a synonym

---

29 The Abbasid-era *littérateur* Jahiz, a contemporary of Ibn Hanbal, also affirmed that *mahabba* was a common term for love in early Islam. See Joseph Norment Bell, *Love Theory in Later Hanbalite Islam* (Albany, NY: SUNY Press, 1979), p. 36.
30 *Musnad Ibn Hanbal*, 2:374 and *Sunan al-Tirmidhi*, Kitab al-Birr, p. 49.
31 Sulami, *Tabaqat al-sufiyya*, p. 35.
32 This contention is also supported, mostly from Persian sources, by Joseph E.B. Lumbard, "From Hubb to 'Ishq: The Development of Love in Early Sufism," *Journal of Islamic Studies*, 18 (3) 2007, pp. 345–85.

for *mahabba*.³³ Unlike *mahabba*, *'ishq* cannot be found in any of the major Hadith collections. Only its cognate verb, *'ashiqa*, appears in Hadith, and then only once. This is in the *Musnad* of Ibn Hanbal, where *'ashiqa* refers to physical desire, such as a man's desire for a woman.³⁴ Louis Massignon asserted that the first religious figure to use the term *'ishq* for the love of God in Islam was Rabi'a's contemporary 'Abd al-Wahid ibn Zayd (d. 793 CE).³⁵ According to Massignon, Ibn Zayd refused to use the term *mahabba* because it "presumed too much confidence in divine favor."³⁶ Massignon's opinion was challenged by the Egyptian scholar 'Abd al-Rahman Badawi, who points out that the French scholar cites no evidence for this assertion.³⁷ According to Badawi, the term *'ishq* did not become part of Sufi vocabulary until the mid-ninth century CE, a generation or so after Rabi'a and around the time of the appearance of the root *'ashiqa* in Ibn Hanbal's *Musnad*. Consequently, the use of this term likely reflects a later stage in the development of Sufi Love mysticism.³⁸

Overall, the evidence of Hadith and the earliest Sufi and ascetical works in Islam support Badawi's contention that the use of *'ishq* as a term for the love of God was a later development. This seems to suggest that statements attributed to Rabi'a and other early Sufis and ascetics that use the term *'ishq* are not authentic to their period. In further support of this assertion, one

---

33   For Jahiz, *'ishq* was a type of *mahabba*. See Bell, *Love Theory*, p. 36. On *'ishq* as excessive or mad love see Dols, *Majnun*, pp. 313–19.
34   *Musnad Ibn Hanbal*, 5:164.
35   On 'Abd al-Wahid ibn Zayd, see Knysh, *Islamic Mysticism*, pp. 16–18. In some Sufi texts, Rabi'a al-'Adawiyya, 'Abd al-Wahid ibn Zayd, and Riyah al-Qaysi (d. 796 CE) appear as members of a Basra Sufi Love Trio. In this trope, Rabi'a is depicted as the founder of the doctrine of *mahabba*, Riyah al-Qaysi is the founder of *khulla* (intimate friendship), and Ibn Zayd is the founder of the doctrine of *'ishq*. See my discussion of this trope in Rkia Elaroui Cornell, "Rabi'ah al-'Adawiyyah (circa 720–801)," in Cooperson and Toorawa, *Arabic Literary Culture, 500–925*, p. 294.
36   Massignon, *Essay*, p. 135.
37   In ibid., p. 135, n. 346, Massignon cites a manuscript by the Hanbali theologian Ibn Taymiyya (d. 1328 CE), as the source for this claim about Ibn Zayd. However, he does not give the title. Badawi, *Shahidat al-'ishq al-ilahi*, pp. 61–3.
38   Textual evidence to support Badawi's opinion can be found in Ibrahim ibn al-Junayd's late ninth-century *Kitab al-mahabba*. In this work, the terms *'ishq* (desire) and *'ashiq* (desirer) appear only once, in a group of teachings that summarize the relationship between ascetic rejection of the World and the love of God. These teachings were transmitted by Ibn al-Junayd's teacher, Muhammad ibn al-Husayn al-Burjulani, who flourished in the mid-ninth century. For Ibn al-Junayd, *'ishq* connoted mournful desire (*innama yazidu al-'ishq li-l-huzn*). Similarly, the term *'ashiq* stands for the lover whose yearning or desire causes pain or sorrow. See Ibn al-Junayd, *Kitab al-mahabba*, no. 247 and Radtke, *Materialien*, p. 179.

might also add that the basic meanings of *'ishq* and *mahabba* in Arabic are different. The term *'ishq* connotes love as desire whereas the term *mahabba*, like *hubb*, connotes love as affection.[39] In addition, it can be argued, contrary to Massignon, that in Rabi'a's period, love as affection (*mahabba*) would have been a more "appropriate" way of expressing the ascetic's love for God than love as desire (*'ishq*). Where, then, did the Sufi term *'ishq*, meaning, "desire for God," come from? We shall see later on in this chapter that a likely source for this term was the Greek word *eros*, which, like *'ishq*, means both "love" and "desire."

c. *The Ascetic Lovers of Basra*

In the previous chapter, asceticism was defined as "a voluntary, sustained, and at least partially systematic program of self-discipline and self-denial in which immediate, sensual or profane gratifications are renounced in order to attain a higher spiritual state or a more thorough absorption in the sacred." Both goals of asceticism, the attainment of a higher spiritual state and a more thorough absorption in the sacred, were part of the essential asceticism attributed to Rabi'a al-'Adawiyya. Asceticism and mysticism come together as spiritual paths at the point where the goals of both practices are attained—in the "thorough absorption" in God that is the goal of essential asceticism.

In her book *Studies in Early Mysticism in the Near and Middle East*, Margaret Smith locates the meeting-point between asceticism and mysticism in the notion that "none can attain direct knowledge of God except by purification from self. The soul must be stripped of the veils of selfishness and sensuality if it is to see clearly the Divine Vision."[40] Recent comparative research on asceticism confirms Smith's hypothesis. It is now understood that a major goal of ascetic practice in all religions is to purify the self in order to aspire to a higher reality.[41] However, as Bishop Kallistos Ware and others

---

39 In *'Atf al-alif al-ma'luf 'ala al-lam al-ma'tuf* (*The Conjunction of the Attached Letters Alif and Lam*), Abu al-Hasan 'Ali al-Daylami (d. ca. 1001–2 CE) defines love (*hubb*) as "a term for affection that is pure." See Abu'l-Hasan 'Ali b. Muhammad al-Daylami, *A Treatise on Mystical Love*, trans. Joseph Norment Bell and Hassan Mahmood Abdul Latif Al Shafie (Edinburgh, UK: Edinburgh University Press, 2005), p. 24.
40 Smith, *Studies in Early Mysticism*, p. 5. This work, which is little known today, was published in 1931, three years after *Rabi'a the Mystic*. It remains the best available comparative study of early Christian and Islamic mysticism in the Middle East.
41 Although Smith located the meeting-point of asceticism and mysticism in the active purification of the self that leads to the vision of God, she continued to maintain the

have pointed out, asceticism as a form of active spirituality involves more than just renunciation and precaution; it requires both withdrawal from the World and an approach to God beyond the World.

The most common approach to God for early Muslim ascetics was through the practice of instrumental asceticism. Through ritualized acts of devotion, early Muslim ascetics sought to make themselves worthy of God. However, a more effective means of approach to God was the essential asceticism associated with Rabi'a al-'Adawiyya. Through essential asceticism, devotion to God could be transformed into love of God. Margaret Smith regarded Love as the "guide and inspiration of the soul" that motivates the ascetic's approach to God. "He that does not love does not know God; for God is Love," she states, quoting the New Testament (I John 4:8).

> The Oriental mystic, seeking to get rid of that element of not-being, which is opposed to true Being, the Divine Reality, finds that self, the great hindrance, can be overcome by Love alone. Love alone can perfectly purify the soul and set it free from the bonds of self-seeking and the fetters of the flesh and so enable it to pass on its upward way, to look upon God as He is in truth, and to realize that it is itself one with the Divine Goodness, one with that Reality which is also Everlasting Love.[42]

The type of transcendent Love-mysticism that Smith describes has been a hallmark of Sufi theology since the mid-tenth century CE and is often attributed to Rabi'a al-'Adawiyya. This has led both medieval Sufi writers and modern scholars to assert that Rabi'a was important—perhaps even the key figure—in introducing Love mysticism to Islam.[43] However, the most recent evidence indicates that just as Rabi'a was not the first Sufi woman in

---

mistaken view that both asceticism and mysticism are passive forms of spirituality. In *Rabi'a the Mystic*, she contends that early Sufism "consisted of asceticism carried to the point of quietism." See Smith, *Rabi'a* (Rainbow Bridge), p. 76 and (Oneworld), p. 100.

42 Smith, *Studies in Early Mysticism*, pp. 5–6. In this passage, the phrase, "Oriental mystics" refers to Muslim and Eastern Christian mystics alike.

43 'Abd al-Rahman Badawi (*Shahidat al-'ishq al-ilahi*, p. 63) claims that no Muslim mystic used the term *mahabba* for divine love before Rabi'a. Numerous citations in Ibrahim ibn al-Junayd's *Kitab al-mahabba* clearly refute this claim. The idea that Rabi'a was the first Love mystic in Islam goes back in modern works to Margaret Smith's *Rabi'a the Mystic*. For more recent versions of this assumption, see Ahmet T. Karamustafa, *Sufism: The Formative Period* (Edinburgh, UK: Edinburgh University Press, 2007), p. 4, and Knysh, *Islamic Mysticism*, pp. 26–32, who ascribes to Rabi'a the Sufi "doctrine of pure love (*'ilm al-mahabba*)."

Islam, she was also not the first Sufi lover. Although she may have been an important figure in the development of Islamic Love mysticism, she was not the first Muslim ascetic to focus on the love of God. Ibn al-Junayd's *Kitab al-mahabba* is full of ascetics who were contemporaries or predecessors of Rabi'a and who stressed the importance of the love of God. One of the earliest of these was the male ascetic 'Amir ibn 'Abd Qays (d. ca. 680 CE) of Basra. Ibn al-Junayd quotes him as exclaiming, "By God, I love nothing that God does not love!"[44]

According to the modern Egyptian historian Su'ad 'Ali 'Abd al-Raziq, 'Amir ibn 'Abd Qays was "the first lover of God (*muhibb*) in Islam."[45] Other members of his clan also focused on the love of God. Sulami's Book of Sufi Women mentions a woman named 'Afiya of the clan of 'Abd Qays, who was called "The Infatuated" (*al-Mushtaqa*) because she focused on the love of God (*mahabba*) and the desire for God (*shawq*) in her teachings. Sulami quotes 'Afiya as saying, "The lover (*al-muhibb*) never wearies of intimate discourse (*munajat*) with the Beloved, and nothing is of interest to him other than the Beloved. Oh, may I always desire Him!"[46] This statement could just as easily have come from Rabi'a al-'Adawiyya. Both Rabi'a's clan of 'Adi ibn Qays and 'Amir's and 'Afiya's clan of 'Abd Qays were part of the same Arab tribe of Qays 'Aylan. Is it possible that the combination of asceticism and love of God that has been attributed to Rabi'a reflected different aspects of her tribe's spiritual traditions? Were both traditions, so to speak, "all in the family?"

In attempting to answer this question, however, it is important to keep in mind a major difference between the love doctrines of 'Amir ibn 'Abd Qays and his later kinswoman 'Afiya. For the seventh-century ascetic 'Amir, the love of God does not seem to have led to a transcendent knowledge of God. Instead, his love of God was instrumental. In *Hilyat al-awliya'*, Abu Nu'aym al-Isfahani quotes him as saying, "I love God, the Glorious and Mighty, with a love that eases every problem for me and God has shown his pleasure with me by granting my every wish."[47] This statement describes the love of an instrumental ascetic. 'Amir's devotion to God is instrumental because he expects tangible rewards: each investment of devotion or service leads to a problem solved or a wish granted. By contrast, 'Afiya's love of God, which

---

44 Ibn al-Junayd, *Kitab al-mahabba*, no. 186; Radtke, *Materialien*, p. 141; this source also contains a long statement on love via 'Amir ibn 'Abd Qays from the prophet David (no. 233, pp. 168–9).
45 'Abd al-Raziq, *Rabi'a al-'Adawiyya*, p. 117.
46 Sulami, *Early Sufi Women*, pp. 98–9.
47 Isfahani, *Hilya*, vol. 2, p. 89.

causes her to see nothing in the world except the Divine Beloved, recalls the essential asceticism attributed to Rabi'a al-'Adawiyya. A change of focus seems to have taken place in the love doctrines of Basra ascetics in the hundred years between 'Amir ibn 'Abd Qays and Rabi'a.

A survey of the statements of Basra ascetics in early Sufi sources suggests that the concept of essential asceticism started to become more prominent around the second half of the eighth century CE. In this period, one can find examples of both instrumental and non-instrumental asceticism. For example, Abu Muhammad Habib al-Farisi, better known as Habib al-'Ajami (both terms refer to his Persian origin), frequented Basra around the time of the Abbasid conquest of Iraq in 750 CE. Habib al-'Ajami was famous for "ransoming his soul from God" (*ishtara nafsahu min Allah*) through ritualized acts of devotion.[48] It was so widely believed that his bargains with God would be fulfilled that people gave him money to distribute as alms in symbolic down payment on their dwellings in paradise.[49] Ransoming one's soul back from God and putting down payments on dwellings in paradise are unmistakable signs of instrumental asceticism.

In contrast to Habib al-'Ajami's instrumental asceticism was the more altruistic asceticism of Malik ibn Dinar (d. 745 CE). Ibn Dinar was a student of al-Hasan al-Basri who served as an important link between the ascetics of Hasan's and Rabi'a's generations. Some hagiographers even claimed that Ibn Dinar and Rabi'a knew each other.[50] The key principle of Ibn Dinar's asceticism was to accept whatever God willed. He would say, "Verily the heart of the lover of God loves hardships for God's sake."[51] Unlike Habib al-'Ajami and 'Amir ibn 'Abd Qays but more like Rabi'a al-'Adawiyya and 'Afiya of 'Abd Qays, he viewed his altruistic service to God as a *mimesis* of God's own altruism. This can be seen in the following quotation: "I read in some book that God the Glorious and Mighty said, 'Oh son of Adam, my goodness descends on you and your evil rises up to me. I show my love to you by granting you grace (*ni'ma*) but you show your dislike of me through your disobedience. Yet I am still a generous king who turns aside his face from your ugly behavior.'"[52] The altruism expressed in this tradition reflects the spiritual perspective of essential asceticism. However, even though Malik

---

48 Ibid., vol. 6, p. 149.
49 Ibid., p. 151.
50 See, for example, the account related by Malik ibn Dinar in 'Attar's *Tadhkirat al-Awliya'* reproduced in Sells, *Early Islamic Mysticism*, pp. 167–8.
51 Isfahani, *Hilya*, vol. 6, p. 263.
52 Ibid., p. 277.

ibn Dinar viewed his devotion to God altruistically, he did not conceive of divine love as a form of intimacy between the lover and the Beloved. Rather, his love for God was more an expression of the affection of a grateful client for a generous and forgiving patron. Because of this social distance, it still fell short of true Love mysticism.

By contrast, the love of God attributed to Rabi'a al-'Adawiyya made greater use of the language of intimacy. The earliest recorded quotation of Rabi'a by al-Harith al-Muhasibi speaks of the relationship between God and the ascetic in terms that are more intimate in a personal sense than those used by Malik ibn Dinar: "The night has come, the darkness has mingled, and every lover is left alone with his beloved. Now I am alone with you, my Beloved." Besides Rabi'a, several other women ascetics of the Basra region are also depicted as combining essential asceticism with a personal and intimate love of God. Among the most notable of these are three women of the port town of al-Ubulla, whom we have met in Chapter 2. These are Rayhana, Hayyuna and Sha'wana. Rayhana was a slave.[53] However, despite her lowly status, she was also a noted poet. Sulami's notice on Rayhana in his Book of Sufi Women contains verses that clearly express her personal and intimate love of God:

> You are my intimate companion, my aspiration, and my happiness,
> And my heart refuses to love anything but you.
>
> Oh my dear, my aspiration, and the object of my desire (*muradi*),
> My desire (*shawqi*) is endless! When will I finally encounter you?
>
> My request is not for Heaven's pleasures (*min al-jinani ni'ama*).
> I only want to be together with you![54]

The portrayal of Rayhana by Sulami and other early Sufi writers includes two major tropes that would later appear in narratives about Rabi'a al-'Adawiyya. First, Rayhana is portrayed as a slave: this depiction first appears in Nisaburi's *'Uqala' al-majanin*, which was written around the same time as Sulami's Book of Sufi Women. Two centuries later, Farid al-Din al-'Attar would also portray Rabi'a al-'Adawiyya as a slave in *Tadhkirat al-awliya'* and it remains

---

53 Nisaburi, *'Uqala' al-majanin*, p. 147.
54 I have changed the above translation slightly from my original translation in Sulami, *Early Sufi Women*, p. 94–5.

a major part of the Rabi'a myth today. Second, Rayhana is portrayed as a love poet. This too was to become an important part of the Rabi'a myth. As we shall see later in this chapter, the trope of Rabi'a the Poet first becomes prominent in Abu Talib al-Makki's *Qut al-qulub*, which was written about a generation prior to Sulami's and Nisaburi's works. Might their portrayals of Rayhana have been related to the later tropes of Rabi'a the Slave and Rabi'a the Poet? The possibility is worth considering although, as we shall see in the section on "Rabi'a the Love Poet," there is evidence to support a different hypothesis.

What is most important about Rayhana's poetry to the concept of essential asceticism is that it expresses a "desire more desirable than desire," which Geoffrey Galt Harpham has identified as the goal of the ascetic's approach to God. In the verses translated above, Rayhana rejects even the pleasures of heaven for an intimate encounter with God. She expresses a similar sense of altruistic love in a statement reproduced by Ibn al-Jawzi in *Sifat al-safwa*: "The lover subsists with the object of his hopes (*al-ma'mul*), with a presence that causes the heart to take flight out of happiness."[55] In a poem from Nisaburi's *'Uqala' al-majanin*, Rayhana describes her devotion to God as a love that demands complete sacrifice of the self:

It is enough for the lover that the Beloved knows
That the lover is cast down (*matruh*) at his door.

The heart within [the lover] sighs in the darkness of night,
Pierced through and wounded by the arrows of passion (*hawa*).[56]

The love that is expressed in these verses is so single-minded that the lover is willing to make any sacrifice in order to be with her Beloved. Even though Rayhana is mortally wounded by passion, she remains at the Beloved's door, sighing her last breaths and hoping to be let in.

A similar connection between essential asceticism and Love mysticism can be found in aphoristic statements attributed to Rabi'a al-'Adawiyya. In one early anecdote, which first appears in Ibn al-Junayd's *Kitab al-mahabba*, she is asked, "How is your love for the Prophet?" She replies, "Verily, I love him. However, my love for the Creator has distracted me from love for

---

55   Ibn al-Jawzi Appendix in ibid., pp. 306–7; I have changed the present translation of this verse somewhat from the original version.
56   Nisaburi, *'Uqala' al-majanin*, p. 147.

created beings" (*shaghalani hubb al-khaliq 'an hubb al-makhluqin*).⁵⁷ Fifty years later, the Sufi prosopographer Abu Sa'id ibn al-A'rabi (d. 952–53 CE), would explain Rabi'a's words in the following way: "What she meant was this: I love the Messenger of God with faith, belief, and conviction, because he is the Messenger of God and because God loves him and has commanded us to love him. However, my love for God demands preoccupation with constant remembrance of God, intimate converse with him, and constant delight in the sweetness of his speech and in his looking into men's hearts, while still remembering his blessings."⁵⁸ One could hardly ask for a clearer example of the devotional aspect of essential asceticism.

Another woman ascetic of al-Ubulla who appears to have combined essential asceticism with Love mysticism was Hayyuna. As noted in Chapter 2, Hayyuna is the only figure to appear in premodern sources as a teacher of Rabi'a al-'Adawiyya. She also appears in some sources as the teacher of Rayhana. A major source of information about Hayyuna seems to have been the early ascetic Ibrahim ibn Adham.⁵⁹ This suggests that Hayyuna flourished at the same time as Ibn Adham in the mid-eighth century CE. An elaborate statement on Love attributed to Hayyuna can be found in Nisaburi's *'Uqala' al-majanin*. In this account, Hayyuna gives a detailed analysis of the states of love (*ahwal al-mahabba*), which suggests that her path of Love was a well-defined spiritual method:

> One who loves [God] becomes intimate (*man ahabba anisa*). One who is intimate becomes joyful (*man anisa tariba*). One who is joyful becomes desirous (*man tariba ishtaqa*). One who is desirous becomes infatuated (*man ishtaqa waliha*). One who is infatuated serves [the Beloved] (*man waliha khadima*). One who serves [God] attains the goal (*man khadima wasala*). One who attains the goal attains union (*man wasala ittasala*). One who attains union comes to know [the Beloved]

---

57 Ibn al-Junayd, *Kitab al-mahabba*, no. 65 and Radtke, *Materialien*, p. 77; see also, Sulami, *Early Sufi Women*, pp. 78–9. Another version of this anecdote can be found in Daylami's *'Atf al-alif*; see Daylami, *A Treatise on Mystical Love*, p. 112.

58 Daylami, *A Treatise on Mystical Love*, p. 112. Because of the implication that God's words are more important than those of the Prophet, this statement led Rabi'a to be accused of heresy by some opponents of Sufism. Ironically, one of those who defended her against these accusations was the Hanbali jurist Ibn Taymiyya, who was otherwise bitterly opposed to Sufism. See Taqi al-Din ibn Taymiyya, *Majmu'at al-Rasa'il wa al-masa'il*, ed. Muhammad 'Ali Baydun (Beirut: Dar al-Kutub al-'Ilmiyya, 2000), vol. 1, pp. 76 and 94–7.

59 See, for example, the account attributed to Ibn Adham in Nisaburi, *'Uqala' al-majanin*, p. 150.

(*man ittasala 'arafa*). One who knows [the Beloved] becomes close [to Him] (*man 'arafa qaruba*). One who is in a state of closeness cannot sleep and experiences moments of profound sorrow (*wa tasawwarat 'alayhi bawariq al-ahzan*).[60]

Hayyuna is also reported to have made the following supplication: "Oh God! Grant me peace in my heart through my commitment (*'aqd*) to trust only you. Make all of my thoughts, ideas, and inclinations agree with your acceptance of me. Do not allow these to deprive me of you. Oh, hope of those who hope!"[61] In this statement, Hayyuna's asceticism is likened to a spiritual marriage, as discussed for Rabi'a al-'Adawiyya in Chapter 2. She makes a "contract" (*'aqd*) of commitment to God that recalls a contract of marriage (*'aqd al-zawaj*). This contract leads her to expect that God will reciprocate her commitment to Him, just as with a legal marriage contract. In another quotation from *'Uqala' al-majanin*, Hayyuna seems to admonish God for taking her love for granted and not fulfilling His part of the bargain: "You know that I am infatuated with you. So, my Lord, why don't you protect me from the harshness of the sun?"[62] Although it is about spiritual love, this statement still has overtones of instrumental asceticism because Hayyuna feels that God "owes" her a practical sign of recompense for her devotion.

Another important similarity between Hayyuna and Rabi'a in Islamic literature can be seen in her vocation as a teacher-trainer (*mu'addiba*). Hayyuna was famous for giving "tough love" to her students and associates, just as Rabi'a did with Sufyan al-Thawri. In one account from *'Uqala' al-majanin*, she is depicted as criticizing the famous male ascetic and preacher 'Abd al-Wahid ibn Zayd. Much as Rabi'a chastises the jurist Thawri for his worldliness, Hayyuna chastises the moralist Ibn Zayd for his hypocrisy.

> One day Hayyuna was present at one of 'Abd al-Wahid ibn Zayd's sessions. Upon hearing him finish speaking, she stood up and shouted, "Oh so-called theologian (*mutakallim*)! Critique yourself instead! By God, if you were to die, I would not attend your funeral!" "Why?" Ibn Zayd asked. She replied, "You criticize people and then you seek their company. I can only compare you to a child in the first stages

---

60 Ibid.
61 Ibid.
62 Ibid., p. 149.

of learning. His way of learning is to memorize things in his mother's house in the evening and he forgets them completely by daybreak. This causes his teacher to discipline him by hitting him. So go, 'Abd al-Wahid! Chastise yourself with an abundance of discipline (*adab*). Sustain yourself with the nourishment of sufficiency in God, and earn your true reputation by applying to yourself what you say about other people!"[63]

The third woman ascetic of al-Ubulla who is depicted as combining asceticism and Love mysticism was Sha'wana. As we saw in Chapter 2, Sha'wana was most famous as a practitioner of ascetic weeping. An explicit reference to how Sha'wana's asceticism was related to the love of God appears in an account attributed to the Persian Sufi Muhammad ibn Khafif of Shiraz (d. 982 CE).[64] According to Ibn Khafif, Sha'wana wept at having neglected her devotions "because she had been distracted by Love for so long." Later, a figure appears to her in a dream and says to her in verse:

Let your eyes flow with the tears you were holding back,
For lamentations can cure the grief-stricken.

Be diligent; keep vigils, and fast always and forever,
For wasting away is an attribute of the obedient.[65]

This account supports the contention, also discussed in the previous chapter, that early Muslim ascetics regarded tears as a way of arousing divine passion. According to this view, weeping helps the ascetic cross the threshold between the World and the Nonworld. As Herbert W. Basser explains for rabbinic Jewish asceticism, "The mystery of crying is that through tears the outside worlds and the interior worlds merge deep inside the human spirit."[66] For early Muslims as well, the merging of the outside and the interior worlds was a major goal of both asceticism and mysticism.

---

63   Ibid., pp. 149–50; Ibn Zayd was a noted preacher whose sermons were famous for their evocations of Judgment Day and his "emphasis on humility and scrupulosity in food and conduct" (Knysh, *Islamic Mysticism*, p. 16). Thus, Hayyuna's criticism of Ibn Zayd for hypocrisy chastises him for the very sin he warned others against.
64   On Ibn Khafif see Florian Sobieroj, *Ibn Ḥafīf aš-Šīrāzī und seine Schrift zur Novizenerziehung (Kitāb al-Iqtiṣād): biographische Studien, Edition, und Übersetzung* (Stuttgart: Franz Steiner Verlag, 1998).
65   Daylami, *A Treatise on Mystical Love*, p. 199.
66   Basser, "A Love for all Seasons," p. 185.

d. The Question of Rabi'a's Celibacy

Celibacy is an important ascetic practice in Hinduism, Buddhism, and Christianity. Likewise, most premodern Muslim sources describe Rabi'a al-'Adawiyya as having been celibate. In her chapter on Rabi'a's celibacy in *Rabi'a the Mystic*, Margaret Smith cites several sources for this claim and notes that Rabi'a was said to have refused proposals of marriage from the ascetic 'Abd al-Wahid ibn Zayd, the Abbasid governor of Basra, and even from al-Hasan al-Basri, who died seventy years before her.[67] For Smith, stories of Rabi'a's celibacy suggested parallels with early Christianity. "Like her Christian sisters in the life of sanctity," she writes, "Rabi'a espoused a heavenly bridegroom and turned her back on earthly marriage."[68] Smith believed that Rabi'a's celibacy was based on the Christian concept of divine marriage. We have seen that certain statements attributed to Rabi'a and Hayyuna reflect this concept as well. However, Smith's explanation for Rabi'a's celibacy was objectionable to some modern Muslim writers, who sought to distance Rabi'a from parallels with Christianity. For example, Widad El Sakkakini countered Smith's view by arguing that Rabi'a created a new Islamic version of celibacy: "Rabi'a's love was not like the love known to the Greeks, which came from the teachings of Plato; nor like the pre-Islamic love familiar to the monks. Her uniquely woven model entered the Islamic creeds as a concept of beauty dissociated from the body."[69]

The Egyptian historian Su'ad 'Ali 'Abd al-Raziq also attempted to separate Rabi'a from the Christian model of celibacy. However, instead of saying that Rabi'a created a new model of celibacy, she domesticated her by making her a pious housewife. According to 'Abd al-Raziq, Rabi'a started her adult life as a married woman who struggled to combine her physical duties to her husband with her spiritual devotion to God: "[Rabi'a] did not practice celibacy like Christian nuns. Rather, the actual sources state that she was married and that every night she used to cook and attend to her husband, saying, 'Do you have a need?' When she had fulfilled them and left him, she would purify herself and bend her knees in prayer."[70] In 'Abd al-Raziq's view, Rabi'a was able to commit herself to celibacy and asceticism only after her husband had died. This story is based on an account in Ibn al-Jawzi's *Sifat al-safwa*. However,

---

67   Smith, *Rabi'a* (Oneworld), pp. 29–39 and *Rabi'a* (Rainbow Bridge), pp. 10–19.
68   Ibid. (Oneworld), p. 32 and (Rainbow Bridge), p. 13.
69   El Sakkakini, *First among Sufis*, p. 62; *al-'Ashiqa al-mutasawwifa*, p. 98.
70   'Abd al-Raziq, *Rabi'a al-'Adawiyya*, p. 57.

in Ibn al-Jawzi's account, the woman in question is not Rabi'a al-'Adawiyya. Instead, it is the unnamed wife of Rabi'a's contemporary Riyah al-Qaysi (d. 796 CE).[71] Some later writers have claimed that Rabi'a herself was married to Riyah al-Qaysi in order to resolve this discrepancy.

'Abd al-Raziq's denial of Rabi'a's celibacy can be criticized on at least three grounds. First, her concern to avoid Christian comparisons ignores a long-standing tradition in Sufism that characterizes the Muslim mystic's intimate union with God as a type of spiritual marriage.[72] As noted previously, the earliest citation of Rabi'a by Muhasibi reflects this concept. Even today, in many parts of the Muslim world, the death of a Sufi saint or Muslim martyr is referred to as a "wedding" ('urs). On this evidence, Margaret Smith was justified in suggesting a possible parallel between the Christian concept of celibacy as marriage to God and the well-established Sufi notion of union with God as a form of spiritual marriage.

Second, 'Abd al-Raziq's contention that Rabi'a only became celibate after her husband had died makes her revisionist account seem ironically more "Christian" than the accounts of Rabi'a's celibacy. Although Muslim widows, like many women, sometimes refuse to remarry after the death of their husbands, this is not a recommended practice in Islam. Rather, practicing celibacy after the death of a husband is more in conformity with Christian teachings. For example, St Paul of Tarsus states in his letter to Timothy that Christian widows should take a vow of celibacy after their husbands have died (1 Tim. 5:9–12). If 'Abd al-Raziq had not been so concerned to avoid all comparisons with Christianity—even those that are historically and culturally valid—she might have avoided this error.

Finally, 'Abd al-Raziq cites only two sources to back up her story of Rabi'a's marriage and eventual widowhood and both sources are chronologically much later than those that assert Rabi'a's celibacy. Furthermore, both sources come from Egypt. The earlier of these sources is *al-Rawd al-fa'iq* (*The Splendid Garden*) by the Mamluk-era Egyptian writer Shu'ayb ibn Sa'd al-Hurayfish (d. 1398 CE). In Hurayfish's account, al-Hasan al-Basri comes to Rabi'a after her husband has died and inquires whether she wants to marry

---

71   See Ibn al-Jawzi, *Sifat al-safwa*, vol. 2, p. 721.
72   The trope of the marriage of the ascetic soul to God has a long history. Some scholars trace it to the Jewish Hellenistic philosopher Philo of Alexandria (d. 45 CE). See for example, Pierre Hadot, *Plotinus or the Simplicity of Vision*, trans. Michael Chase with Introduction by Arnold I. Davidson (Chicago and London: University of Chicago Press, 1993), p. 55 and n. 12.

again.⁷³ This account can be rejected as anachronistic because Hasan died when Rabi'a was still a young girl. Most of Hurayfish's stories about Rabi'a were adapted from her *vita* in Farid al-Din al-'Attar's *Tadhkirat al-awliya'* (*Memorial of the Saints*). However, Hurayfish adds new features to this *vita*, such as the claim of Rabi'a's marriage and widowhood, which cannot be found in 'Attar's work.⁷⁴ The second historical source that 'Abd al-Raziq cites is *al-Kawakib al-durriyya* (*The Pearly Spheres*), by Muhammad 'Abd al-Ra'uf al-Munawi (d. 1621 CE).⁷⁵ This hagiographical work from Ottoman Egypt is notorious for its inaccuracies, such as the claim that Rabi'a lived in both Basra and Egypt.⁷⁶ If these two works are the best that 'Abd al-Raziq can find in the way of "actual historical sources," then her denial of Rabi'a's celibacy stands on very shaky ground.

Premodern accounts that attest to Rabi'a's life-long commitment to celibacy are both more numerous and chronologically much earlier than accounts of her marriage and widowhood. The earliest extant reference to Rabi'a's celibacy is in *Balaghat al-nisa'* by Ibn Abi Tahir Tayfur (d. 893 CE). In this account, an unnamed person asks Rabi'a, "Marriage is a requirement of God, the Glorious and Mighty. So why do you not marry?" She replies, "One requirement of God prevents me from fulfilling another of His requirements."⁷⁷ This account is significant not only because it attests to Rabi'a's celibacy less than a century after her death but also because it associates her practice of celibacy with essential asceticism, in which devotion to God is an all-consuming vocation. Because Ibn Abi Tahir Tayfur was both an early source on Rabi'a and a non-Sufi, his claim that she was celibate is more credible than the much

---

73   Al-Shaykh ['Abdullah Shu'ayb ibn Sa'd] al-Hurayfish, *al-Rawd al-fa'iq fi-l-mawa'iz wa-l-raqa'iq* (Cairo: Maktabat al-Jumhuriyya al-'Arabiyya, 1970), p. 183. Margaret Smith also traces Hurayfish's *vita* of Rabi'a to 'Attar's *Tadhkirat al-awliya'*. In her book, she cites a passage in which Hasan al-Basri says to Rabi'a, "I desire that we should marry and be betrothed" (*Rabi'a* [Oneworld], p. 31 and [Rainbow Bridge], p. 13). However, in the actual passage from the Persian edition of *Tadhkirat al-awliya'*, Hasan asks, "Do you desire to take a husband?" (Pers. *Raghibti shawhar koni?*). The passage is mixed, with both Arabic and Persian words. Nowhere does Hasan indicate that he is the intended suitor. See Shaykh Farid al-Din Muhammad 'Attar Nishaburi, *Tadhkirat al-awliya'*, ed. Muhammad Isti'lami (Tehran: Intisharat Zavar, 14th edition, 2005 reprint of 1967 original), p. 47.
74   For another dubious assertion by Hurayfish, see Jonathan Berkey, *Popular Preaching and Religious Authority in the Medieval Islamic Near East* (Seattle: University of Washington Press, 2001), where he adds a new plot twist to a story about Jesus (p. 49 n. 73).
75   Muhammad 'Abd al-Ra'uf al-Munawi, *al-Kawakib al-durriyya fi tarajim al-sadat al-sufiyya* (Beirut: Dar al-Sadir, 1999), vol. 1, p. 288.
76   Ibid., p. 285; A tomb that is purported to be Rabi'a's can still be found in Cairo today.
77   Ibn Abi Tahir Tayfur, *Balaghat al-nisa'*, p. 204.

later Egyptian Sufi accounts of her marriage and widowhood cited by ʿAbd al-Raziq. He thus provides important evidence that the "real" Rabiʿa was in fact, to borrow a term from Susanna Elm, a "virgin of God."[78]

Another Egyptian historian, Taha ʿAbd al-Baqi Surur, agrees that Rabiʿa was celibate but also argues that she was viewed by her contemporaries as a consecrated virgin. For Surur, Rabiʿa's practice of celibacy was directly linked to her radical other-worldliness. In his view, she could never have married because as a committed ascetic she was psychologically detached from her body: "She had left creation in its entirety. She had left the world in its entirety. She was spirit and not body. So what could men want of her?"[79] Surur's argument raises the question of how the celibacy of Muslim ascetics was perceived in Rabiʿa's time. Was it seen as similar to the Christian concept of marriage with God as Margaret Smith assumed, or was it seen as a radical expression of the World/Nonworld dichotomy, in which the ascetic is psychologically detached from worldly norms and practices?[80]

The Qur'an criticizes monasticism (Ar. *rahbaniyya*)—and by implication celibacy—in *Surat al-Hadid* (57:27). Here Christians are described as creating monasticism on their own, despite the fact that God did not prescribe it for them. The verb used in this verse to characterize the invention of monasticism is *ibtadaʿa*, which comes from the same root as *bidʿa*, the term used in Islam for the unauthorized innovation of religious practices or doctrines.[81] However, in this verse, it is not clear exactly which aspects of monasticism are being called into question. The Arabic root of the term *rahbaniyya*, *r-h-b*, means "to fear." Thus, a *rahib*, or monk, is literally "a God-fearing person." Clearly, the problem with monasticism was not the fear of God, which is praised many times in the Qur'an. Rather, the question is how far one should go in expressing such fear. The remainder of verse 57:27 states that although Christians created the tradition of *rahbaniyya* for the sake of God's pleasure, they exceeded the limits that God intended for them (*illa ibtighaʿa ridwani*

---

78 See Susanna Elm, *Virgins of God: The Making of Asceticism in Late Antiquity* (Oxford, UK: Clarendon Press, 1996).
79 Taha ʿAbd al-Baqi Surur, *Rabiʿa al-ʿAdawiyya wa-l-hayat al-ruhiyya fi-l-Islam* (Cairo: Dar al-Fikr al-ʿArabi, 1957), p. 51.
80 For an overview of the question of celibacy in Islam, see Shahzad Bashir, "Islamic Tradition and Celibacy," in *Celibacy and Religious Traditions*, ed. Carl Olson (New York: Oxford University Press, 2007), pp. 133–50.
81 For a detailed discussion of this verse, see Sara Sviri, "*Wa-rahbāniyyatan ibtadaʿūhā*: An analysis of traditions concerning the origin and evaluation of Christian monasticism," *Jerusalem Studies in Arabic and Islam*, 13, 1990, pp. 195–208.

Allahi fa-ma ra'awha haqqa ri'ayatiha). Celibacy is merely one of several ways in which God's limits might be exceeded.

The question of celibacy in Islam is also problematical in Hadith. In the major Hadith collections there are numerous accounts in which the Prophet Muhammad encourages Muslims to marry but only a few accounts that discuss celibacy or monasticism per se. For example, the term *rahbaniyya* only occurs three times in the major Sunni Hadith collections and only in sources that are relatively late: (1) "Jihad is prescribed for you, for it is the *rahbaniyya* of Islam" (*Musnad ibn Hanbal*, 3:86 and 3:266); (2) "Verily, I [Muhammad] was not commanded to practice *rahbaniyya* (*Sunan al-Darimi*, Kitab al-Nikah, no. 3); (3) "Verily, *rahbaniyya* was not prescribed for us (*lam tuktab 'alayna*)" (*Musnad Ibn Hanbal*, 6:226).[82]

As in the Qur'anic passage cited above, it is unclear which monastic practices are being referred to in these Hadith traditions. The collections in which they appear—the *Musnad* of Ahmad ibn Hanbal (d. 855 CE) and the *Sunan* of Muhammad al-Darimi al-Samarqandi (d. 869 CE)—date to the mid-ninth century CE, well after the time of Rabi'a al-'Adawiyya. Therefore, they were compiled long after the development of the early Islamic ascetic practices discussed in Chapter 2 and also after the publication of major works on asceticism, such as *Kitab al-zuhd wa-l-raqa'iq* by Ibn al-Mubarak (d. 796 CE) and *Kitab al-zuhd* by al-Mu'afa ibn 'Imran (d. 801 CE). It is at least worth suggesting that the practice of celibacy may not be the real issue in these traditions. Instead, they might refer to controversies over the excesses of ascetic ritualism (*nusk*), of which the practice of celibacy was only one part.

Support for this hypothesis can be found in the fact that in modern discussions of celibacy in Islam, there is hardly any mention—either in published works or on the Internet—of Hadith traditions that discuss the practice of *tabattul*. This is the Arabic term that most clearly reflects the notion of celibacy as a form of *nusk* or ritualized ascetic practice. The verb *tabattala* means, "to cut oneself off," "to devote oneself to something completely," or "to practice virginity."[83] The root of the term also appears in a common appellation given to the Virgin Mary in Islam. Muslims refer to Mary as *al-Batul*, "The Virgin" or "The Consecrated One." In the Hadith collections

---

82 A.J. Wensinck and J.P. Mensing, *Concordance et Indices de la Tradition Musulmane* (Istanbul: Çagri Yayinlari, 1986), vol. 2, p. 312.

83 See, for example, how the imperative (*tabattal*) and verbal noun forms (*tabtil*) of this root are used in Qur'an 73:8: "Keep the remembrance of the name of your Lord with complete and utter devotion" (*wa-udhkur isma Rabbika wa tabattal ilayhi tabtila*).

of Sunni Islam, the term *tabattul*, rather than *rahbaniyya* (monasticism), is most often associated with unequivocal prohibitions of celibacy. For example, several versions of the following tradition can be found in *Musnad Ibn Hanbal*: "Verily the Messenger of God (May God bless and preserve him) forbade *tabattul*" (3:158 and 230, 5:17, 6:125, etc.). A similar prohibition appears in *Sahih al-Bukhari*: "The Messenger of God (May God bless and preserve him) rejected *tabattul*" (Kitab al-Nikah, 8).[84] The most detailed prohibition of *tabattul* as a ritual practice can be found in *Sahih Muslim*: "Sa'id b. al-Musayyib reported: I heard Sa'd [ibn Abi Waqqas] say that 'Uthman b. Maz'un's desire to practice *tabattul* was rejected. For if [the Prophet] had allowed him to do it they (*sic*) would certainly have been castrated (*wa law adhina lahu la-akhtasayna*)."[85]

In this last hadith, the reason for the prohibition of *tabattul* is quite specific and focuses on its literal meaning, "ritually consecrating oneself as a virgin." It appears that 'Uthman ibn Maz'un and his unnamed companion were planning to ritually castrate themselves in order to preserve their virginity. This hadith thus provides important circumstantial evidence for the suggestion that the main concern with celibacy in early Islam was not about refraining from marriage per se but about preventing Muslims from engaging in extreme acts of ascetic ritualism (such as castration). Significantly, 'Abdullah Ibn al-Mubarak, the noted specialist on ascetic practices in Islam, is cited as a transmitter of this hadith in its chain of transmission (*isnad*) to Imam Muslim.[86]

Despite the apparent ambiguity of Islamic scriptural sources, the criticism of monasticism in the Qur'an and Hadith and the proscription of *tabattul* in Hadith are clearly in opposition to the support given to celibacy in early Christianity. In the New Testament, celibacy is prescribed for full-time priests in the Book of Matthew (Matt. 19:12). Also in the Book of Matthew, women are advised to forsake childbearing for the sake of God (Matt. 19:29). Matthew 22:30 states that the bond of marriage does not apply in heaven. In the First Letter to the Corinthians, St Paul of Tarsus argues that it is best for a man not to take a wife (1 Cor. 7:1). In the same letter, Jesus is portrayed as wishing that all men would follow his example of celibacy (1 Cor. 7:7), and that men should avoid marriage in order to resist worldly temptations (1 Cor. 7:27).

---

84 Wensinck and Mensing, *Concordance et Indices de la Tradition Musulmane*, vol. 1, pp. 142–3.
85 *Sahih Muslim*, 8 ("Kitab al-Nikah"), nos. 3,237–3,239 (variant readings). For the Arabic text, see: http://www.iium.edu.my/deed/hadith/muslim/008_smt.html.
86 Ibid.

At this juncture, it is important to note that although the Qur'an criticizes monasticism, it sometimes refers to celibacy with approval. For example, John the Baptist is described as chaste or celibate (*hasur*, Qur'an 3:39). Similarly, the Virgin Mary is praised for preserving her chastity (*ahsanat farjaha*, Qur'an 21:91 and 66:12). In addition, some verses of the Qur'an even criticize family and children as worldly temptations, such as the following: "Verily, your possessions and your children are trials for you" (Qur'an 64:14).

In the time of Rabi'a al-'Adawiyya, a number of well-known Muslim ascetics refused to marry. Sometimes, this was due to the misanthropic attitude of reactionary asceticism. In the previous chapter, we saw how the pessimism of works such as al-Mu'afa ibn 'Imran's *Kitab al-zuhd* led to exhortations against having children in a dangerous and sinful world. This prejudice against having a family (*ta'ahhul*) can be seen in a statement attributed to Ibrahim ibn Adham, one of the most famous celibate ascetics of Rabi'a's day: "If a Sufi marries, his example is like that of a man who travels on a boat; if he has children, he is sunk."[87] At other times, Muslim ascetics expressed their objections to marriage or family life as part of a cynical attitude toward social relations. The Prophet's cousin Ibn 'Abbas (d. 688 CE) asked rhetorically, "Can anyone ruin people other than other people?"[88] The Basra ascetic Malik ibn Dinar stated, "A man will not attain the station of the true believers until he casts his wife aside as if she were a widow and takes refuge in garbage dumps frequented by dogs."[89] Ibn Dinar was reputedly so averse to marriage that he exclaimed, "If I could, I would divorce myself!"[90] Although Ibrahim ibn Adham also rejected marriage as a matter of principle, he was more pragmatic about the subject. When asked why he did not marry, he replied, "What would you say about a man who deceives and cheats on his wife? If I were to marry a woman, she would ask from me what women ask. Yet I have nothing to do with women."[91] Abu Sulayman al-Darani, a celibate ascetic and early Sufi of Basra who later moved with his disciples to Syria, rejected marriage because he disliked women in general. Seeing women as the embodiment of the World, he forbade his followers from marrying them as a form of ethical precaution (*wara'*). Darani felt that companionship with

---

87 Sarraj, *al-Luma'*, p. 199.
88 Khargushi, *Tahdhib al-asrar*, p. 307.
89 Isfahani, *Hilya*, vol. 2, p. 259.
90 Ibid., p. 295.
91 Ibid., vol. 8, p. 21; This account contains a similar trope as the "Why do you not marry?" account of Rabi'a in Ibn Abi Tahir Tayfur's *Balaghat al-nisa'*. Other examples can be found in Isfahani, *Hilya*, vol. 2, p. 261 and 'Attar, *Tadhkirat al-awliya'*, pp. 47–8.

women made men ignorant (*jahil*) and stupid (*safih*). Therefore, all men who sought the presence of God should avoid women as much as possible.[92]

However, the negative attitude toward marriage and association with women on the part of male Muslim ascetics did not apply to women ascetics. Despite their disapproval of women in general, many celibate male ascetics—including Darani—frequently visited women ascetics such as Rabi'a al-'Adawiyya and her contemporaries. In fact, not only did they visit them but they also visited them alone and after dark. This practice, which is attested to by many Sufi writers, has troubled modern Muslim moralists. To cite just one example: Su'ad 'Ali 'Abd al-Raziq's concern about the impropriety of al-Hasan al-Basri spending the night alone in prayer with Rabi'a seems to be what caused her to try to save Rabi'a's reputation by marrying her off to a husband.[93]

Clearly, ascetic women were exceptions to the normal category of women in early Islam. As 'Attar famously states about Rabi'a in *Tadhkirat al-awliya'*, "When a woman is on the path of God Most High, she becomes a man."[94] Because the reputation of ascetic women was based on their virtues and celibacy was a major sign of virtue in early Islamic society, it is not surprising to find that many of Rabi'a's female colleagues practiced celibacy as she did. Among the female ascetics in the region of Basra in Rabi'a's time, only Sha'wana of al-Ubulla is mentioned in premodern sources as having been married.[95]

In light of the abundant textual evidence attesting to the practice of celibacy in early Islam, and because the criticism of this practice in the Qur'an and Hadith appears to have been focused primarily on the faults of excessive ascetic ritualism, it is necessary to find a more nuanced way to compare early

---

92 Makki, *Qut al-qulub*, vol. 2, pp. 413–14. As a woman, it is difficult to read about Darani's attitude toward women without thinking of the following statement of the feminist writer Helène Cixous: "Is that me, a phantom doll, the cause of sufferings and wars, the pretext, 'because of her beautiful eyes,' for what men do, says Freud, for their divine illusions, their conquests, their havoc?" Helène Cixous and Catherine Clément, *The Newly Born Woman*, trans. Betsy Wing (Minneapolis and London: University of Minnesota Press, 1986), p. 69.
93 'Abd al-Raziq, *Rabi'a al-'Adawiyya*, p. 59; To underscore the moral problem of Rabi'a and Hasan being alone together, 'Abd al-Raziq cites a hadith in which the Prophet Muhammad forbids a man to be alone with a woman, "even if they are the Virgin Mary and John the Baptist."
94 'Attar, *Tadhkirat al-awliya'*, p. 41.
95 See Ibn al-Jawzi Appendix in Sulami, *Early Sufi Women*, pp. 304–5. The earliest mention of Sha'wana being married is Ibn al-Junayd, *Kitab al-mahabba*, no. 223; Radtke, *Materialien*, p. 162.

Christian and Islamic approaches to celibacy than has been the case until now. Although modern Muslim moralists try to deny that celibacy has been an accepted practice in Islam, it is undeniable that celibacy was at least widely tolerated, if not fully approved, in the early Muslim world. Even more, most, if not all, of the varieties of celibacy that were practiced in early Christianity were also practiced in early Islam.

For example, in 325 CE the Council of Nicaea forbade Christian priests and other celibate males from taking into their houses *synesaktoi*—women who lived with men as fictive "sisters" in a sort of pseudo-marriage.[96] Despite this prohibition, many Christian ascetics continued this practice, especially in Syria.[97] Muslim pseudo-marriages are also sometimes mentioned in early Sufi accounts from Syria. For example, Abu Nasr al-Sarraj mentions a male Muslim ascetic from Syria who contracted a marriage but still had not consummated his union after thirty years.[98] Another example of this practice can be found in Ibn al-Jawzi's *Sifat al-safwa*, where relations between the Sufi Ahmad ibn Abi al-Hawari (d. 845 CE) and his wife Rabi'a bint Isma'il of Damascus are described in terms that are reminiscent of the practices of Syrian Christian *synesaktoi*. In this account, which was originally transmitted by Ibn Abi al-Dunya, Rabi'a of Damascus says to her husband, "I do not love you in the way that married couples do; instead, I love you as one of the Sufi brethren. I wanted to be with you only in order to serve you, and I desired and hoped that my fortune would be consumed by someone like you and your brethren."[99]

A comparative examination of celibacy as an ascetic practice in late antique Christianity and early Islam reveals that celibacy was expressed in two major forms, which I shall call "principled" and "vocational." *Principled celibacy* is a form of celibacy that is based on scriptural foundations and is seen as fundamental to the practice of asceticism in general. Celibacy in early Christianity can be characterized as principled celibacy because it was sanctioned by scripture and was a key practice of both anchoretic (individual) and cenobitic (group) asceticism. In general, it was very difficult to call oneself an ascetic in early Christianity unless one practiced

---

96 Elm, *Virgins of God*, pp. 48–51.
97 Ibid., p. 206.
98 Sarraj, *al-Luma'*, Arabic text, p. 199.
99 Ibn al-Jawzi Appendix to Sulami, *Early Sufi Women*, pp. 316–17. Because the source of this account, Ibn Abi al-Dunya, lived only a generation after the protagonists, it seems to argue against Julian Baldick's assertion that Rabi'a bint Isma'il of Damascus never existed. See Baldick, "The Legend of Rabi'a of Basra," p. 237.

celibacy. Other examples of principled celibacy can be found in Hinduism and Buddhism. However, celibacy in Judaism and Islam was conceived differently. Celibacy among early rabbinic Jewish and Muslim ascetics is best characterized as *vocational celibacy*. In late antique Judaism and early Islam, celibacy was not a universal practice for ascetics because the scriptures did not prescribe it. Celibacy was tolerated but it was not required as part of the ascetic life style. It was not seen as fundamental to the practice of asceticism itself. This type of celibacy can be termed vocational because it was based on individual choice and because it viewed marriage and family as impediments to the ascetic's principal vocation, which is devotion to God.

Vocational celibacy was closely related to the practice of essential asceticism. This can be seen in Rabi'a's description of her celibacy as recorded by Ibn Abi Tahir Tayfur: "One requirement of God prevents me from fulfilling another of His requirements." In other words, the undivided attention the ascetic gives to God leaves little room for anyone or anything else. Abu Talib al-Makki makes a similar point in his chapter on Love in *Qut al-qulub*: "He who wants to be loved by God must reject the World and must not even contemplate the love of God unless he renounces the World."[100] For the ascetic who follows the way of essential asceticism, marriage and family can be unacceptable distractions because they are likely to divert the attention of the lover of God from the Beloved.

The concepts of essential asceticism and vocational celibacy can also be seen in the stories that recount Rabi'a al-'Adawiyya's refusal of marriage proposals. In the original version of the account reproduced by Hurayfish, in which al-Hasan al-Basri asks Rabi'a if she will marry again after her husband has died, the Persian hagiographer 'Attar depicts Rabi'a as "belonging to" God. However, unlike Margaret Smith, who sees Rabi'a as the bride of God, 'Attar sees Rabi'a as the ward or protégé of God. In 'Attar's original Persian account Rabi'a explains to Hasan: "I am not my own. I belong to [God] and I am under His command. Permission for a betrothal can come only from Him."[101] The basis of this statement is the rule in Islamic law that a bride can only be given away in marriage by her guardian. For 'Attar, God is the guardian (*wali*) of his ascetic devotees; if the ascetic is celibate, it means that God has chosen to withhold permission for his ward to marry.[102] In the story,

---

100 Makki, *Qut al-qulub*, vol. 2, p. 92.
101 'Attar, *Tadhkirat al-awliya'*, p. 47 and Sells, *Early Islamic Mysicism*, pp. 161–2; Sells' translation states, "You must ask permission from him."
102 This notion also corresponds to the Qur'anic view of God as the *wali* (guardian or protector) of the believers. See, for example, Qur'an 2:257: "God is the guardian of

Hasan approves of Rabi'a's statement because it correctly portrays the close relationship between the essential ascetic and her divine guardian. However, it is also necessary to point out that although this story is about marriage, it is not about love. Although the moral of 'Attar's story is the close relationship between Rabi'a and God, this relationship is based on guardianship and dependency, not on love and intimacy. As 'Attar describes it, essential asceticism has not yet become Love mysticism.

The themes of essential asceticism and vocational celibacy can also be found in two other accounts of marriage proposals to Rabi'a. These stories first appear in Abu Talib al-Makki's *Qut al-qulub*, a work that was written at the end of the tenth century CE, around 200 years after Rabi'a's death. In the first story, Rabi'a is petitioned for marriage by the Abbasid governor of Basra, Muhammad ibn Sulayman al-Hashimi (fl. ca. 762 CE), who offers her 100,000 gold *dinars* as a bride price and 10,000 *dinars* a month as maintenance. Rabi'a refuses this offer with the following words: "It does not please me that you should be my slave and that all you possess should be mine, nor that you should distract me from God for a single moment."[103] Since Rabi'a was born around 717 CE, she would have been around forty years old at the time of the governor's proposal. Although it is possible that the governor, who was a kinsman of the Abbasid Caliph, might have thought of marrying a famous woman ascetic as a political act, such a scenario is unlikely. Once again the moral of the story is Rabi'a's refusal of the proposal, which expresses the idea that marriage, especially to a government official, would be a distraction for an ascetic who was devoted to the service of God.

In the second story of Rabi'a's rejection of a marriage proposal in *Qut al-qulub*, the proposal is made by the famous ascetic and preacher 'Abd al-Wahid ibn Zayd. As noted previously, Ibn Zayd was an important disciple of al-Hasan al-Basri.[104] As a preacher, he was famous for the quality of his sermons, which stressed moral virtue, sincerity and the solitary life. Given his high moral reputation, it comes as a surprise to find that he is sometimes portrayed as being rebuked for hypocrisy by Sufi women (see, for example, Hayyuna's rebuke of Ibn Zayd in the previous section of this chapter). In Makki's story, Rabi'a acts as if Ibn Zayd has insulted her by making a marriage proposal: "Oh lustful one! Seek a lustful woman like yourself! What did you

---

those who believe; He takes them out of the darkness toward the light" (*Allahu waliyyu alladhina amanu, yukhrijuhum min al-zulumati ila al-nur*).
103 Makki, *Qut al-qulub*, vol. 2, p. 94; see also, Smith, *Rabi'a* (Oneworld), p. 29 and (Rainbow Bridge), p. 10.
104 Massignon, *Essay*, pp. 147–8.

see in me that aroused your desire?"[105] This statement once again reaffirms Rabi'a's reputation for essential asceticism. The point of her rebuke is that Ibn Zayd's desire could only have been aroused if he had been distracted from the devotion that he had committed to God.

In his book *Plotinus, the Simplicity of Vision*, Pierre Hadot associates the Love mysticism of the Egyptian Neo-Platonic philosopher Plotinus (d. 270 CE) with a type of asceticism that closely resembles the essential asceticism of Rabi'a al-'Adawiyya. Hadot characterizes Plotinus's ideal of Love as "an invasion of the soul by a presence which leaves no room for anything but itself."[106] This statement could just as well describe Rabi'a's essential asceticism and her vocational celibacy. Her devotion to God reinforces her practice of asceticism and celibacy because nothing but God is important to her—neither the eschatological goals of instrumental asceticism nor the ideal of marriage as a social norm.

As Richard Valentasis points out in *The Making of the Self: Ancient and Modern Asceticism*, the ascetic self is always a work in progress. Ascetic practices are performed in a liminal space between one's former (worldly) identity and one's future (otherworldly) identity. Through her practices, the early Muslim ascetic acknowledged that the subjectivity to which she aspired was still beyond herself, whether it was defined ethically, as in reactionary asceticism, or eschatologically, as in instrumental asceticism.[107] In all forms of asceticism, the ultimate goal of the ascetic is to attain nearness to God. However, according to Valentasis, being in proximity to God is not the same as being in union with God. Being in proximity to God means that the divine presence is close at hand but is still not fully attainable. However, when the goal of asceticism is expressed through the symbolic idioms of Love or spiritual marriage, as has been described for Rabi'a al-'Adawiyya—when the lover's soul, in Pierre Hadot's words, is "invaded by a presence which leaves no room for anything but itself"—the ascetic's liminal state between her former and desired subjectivities begins to change. In her new state of intimacy with God, the consciousness of the ascetic comes close enough to the desired ideal to attain the mystical experience of a single subjectivity, in which union with God replaces proximity to God. I suggest that it is at this point—when the formerly externalized subjectivity of the ascetic becomes internalized—that the practice of asceticism is transformed into the practice

---

105 Makki, *Qut al-qulub*, vol. 2, p. 94.
106 Hadot, *Plotinus*, p. 55.
107 Valentasis, *The Making of the Self*, p. 43.

of mysticism. For Abu Talib al-Makki and the Sufis who followed his description of this process, the internalization of the ascetic identity and its transformation into a mystical subjectivity was symbolized by the image of Rabi'a the Lover.

III. RABI'A THE "MUSLIM DIOTIMA?"[108]

a. The "Incognito Presence" of Plato's Symposium

Rabi'a al-'Adawiyya is often portrayed as both the founder and the quintessential teacher of Sufi Love mysticism. Although we have seen that other Muslim ascetics followed the spiritual path of Love before her, this has made little difference to the Sufi tradition of Love mysticism. As Carl W. Ernst observes, "It is striking that the Sufi tradition unanimously credits Rabi'a with these insights into love and regards her as the example of the pure lover of God."[109] Even the great Andalusian Sufi Muhammad (Muhyiddin) Ibn al-'Arabi (d. 1240 CE), who composed a famous collection of poems on love titled *The Interpreter of Desires* (*Tarjuman al-ashwaq*), noted that Rabi'a "analyzes and classes the categories of love to the point of being the most famous interpreter of love."[110] In the Arabic-language tradition of Sufism, credit for the trope of Rabi'a the Lover can be traced to Abu Talib al-Makki (d. 996 CE), who underwent much of his Sufi training in Rabi'a's home city of Basra.[111] In the Persian-language Sufi tradition, the trope of Rabi'a the Lover can be traced to Farid al-Din al-'Attar (d. 1220 CE).[112] Carl Ernst summarizes Rabi'a's reputation in the Sufi tradition of Love mysticism in the following way: "Regardless of the difficulty of ascertaining her exact formulations, we

---

108 Some of the material in this section was previously published in Rkia E. Cornell, "The Muslim Diotima? Traces of Plato's *Symposium* in Sufi Narratives of Rabi'a al-'Adawiyya," in *Religion and Philosophy in the Platonic and Neoplatonic Traditions: from Antiquity to the Early Medieval Period*, ed. Kevin Corrigan, John D. Turner and Peter Wakefield (Sankt Augustin, Germany: Akademie Verlag, 2012), pp. 235–56. However, much of what follows is different from the published article.
109 Ernst, "The Stages of Love," p. 439.
110 Ibid.
111 See Atif Khalil, "Abu Talib al-Makki and the *Nourishment of Hearts* (*Qut al-qulub*) in the Context of Early Sufism," *The Muslim World*, 102 (2), 2012, pp. 10–17.
112 See, for example, Smith, *Rabi'a* (Oneworld), p. 124 and (Rainbow Bridge), pp. 99–100.

may still invoke Rabi'a as the figure who stands for the first intensive meditations on the nature of mystical love in Islam."[113]

Shortly after 'Attar presented what was to become the paradigmatic version of Rabi'a's life story in *Tadhkirat al-awliya'*, a scholar and Sufi from Jerusalem named 'Izz al-Din ibn 'Abd al-Salam al-Maqdisi (d. 1279 CE) composed a hagiographical work titled *Kitab sharh al-awliya'* (*The Description of the Saints*).[114] One of the chapters of this work bears the title, "The Description of Rabi'a's Spiritual State" (*Sharh hal Rabi'a*). In this chapter, Maqdisi portrays Rabi'a as teaching the following lesson on the mystery of Love:

> Between the lover and the beloved, there is no separation. Love is an expression of desire (*nutq 'an shawq*). It is the description of an experience (*dhawq*, literally, "taste") and only the one who has "tasted" it knows it. He who expresses it cannot be defined by it (*man wasafa fa-ma ittasafa*). How can one express a thing whose presence is absence, whose existence melts away, whose appearance is fleeting, whose sobriety is intoxication, whose emptiness is fullness, and whose happiness is infatuation? The awe it causes deprives the tongue of speech. The senselessness it causes makes the coward act courageously. The jealousy it causes veils the sight from anything else. The perplexity it causes prevents reasoned thought. What else is left but everlasting astonishment, permanent bewilderment, hearts that are perplexed, secrets that are hidden, and bodies that are forever wasting away? Such is Love (*mahabba*), the Ruler of Hearts under her harsh regime (*bi-dawlatiha al-sarima fi-l-qulub hakima*)![115]

In the next section of the chapter, Maqdisi comments on the mystery of Love in a poem. At the end of this poem, he eulogizes Rabi'a in both verse and prose:

---

113 Ernst, "The Stages of Love," p. 439.
114 On 'Izz al-Din ibn 'Abd al-Salam al-Maqdisi (also called Ibn Ghanim), see, Jalal al-Din al-Suyuti, *Nazm al-'iqyan fi a'yan al-a'yan*, ed. Philip Hitti (Beirut: al-Maktaba al-'Ilmiyya, 1927), p. 129 no. 112. Although he is not described as a Sufi in this source, Suyuti identifies him as a Shadhili Sufi in idem, *Tanbih al-ghabi fi takhti' at Ibn 'Arabi*, ed. 'Abd al-Rahman Hasan Mahmud (Cairo: Maktabat al-Adab, 1990).
115 This selection from Maqdisi's book are reproduced in Badawi, *Shahidat al-'ishq al-ilahi*, pp. 177–8; According to Badawi, the manuscript of *Kitab sharh al-awliya'* can be found in Bibliothèque Nationale, Paris, *fonds Arabes*, no. 1641.

Have mercy on the desirers (*al-'ashiqin*), whose hearts
Are bewildered and lost in the vast wilderness of Love (*mahabba*)!

The resurrection of their desire *('ishq)* has taken place. Their souls
Arise, with an endless and everlasting humility,

Leading either toward gardens of eternal union
Or toward a fire that blocks hearts and keeps them aflame!

Oh Rabi'a! You are a wonder in the domain of Love! How is it that the "face" of the Cataclysmic Event [i.e., the sudden unveiling of the Divine Reality] (*surat al-waqi'a*), came to be called "Rabi'a"? If the state [of Love] is one, then from whence come this sharing of two (*sharika*) and union of many (*mujama'a*)? She said: "Oh people! Harmony is a rule of companionship. Do you not see that the Children of Desire and Awe are not fulfilled unless they drink from the Sea of Love with Love's own drink? I saw him saying to his companion in the cave, 'Do not despair, for God is with us.' What do you think of 'two' when God is the third of two? Then, I advanced toward the solitude of the cave with true commitment. But Jealousy cried out from inside the cave: 'Who is this infatuated and anxious woman who removes the veil of contentment and yet is content with us alone?'"[116]

This remarkable passage from Maqdisi's chapter on Rabi'a contains several important literary allusions. The first allusion is to *Surat al-Waqi'a* in the Qur'an (Qur'an 56, "The Cataclysmic Event"). This *sura* contains some of the best-known Qur'anic descriptions of the rewards of heaven that await the righteous and the punishments of Hell that await the sinful in the Hereafter. In the passage, Maqdisi makes a pun out of this Qur'anic reference: instead of *sura* with the letter *sin*, meaning, "Qur'anic discourse," he uses *sura* with the letter *sad*, meaning, "face" or "image." In doing so, he portrays Rabi'a as the "face" or symbolic image of *Surat al-Waqi'a*. In his reading, the "cataclysmic event" referred to by the Qur'an becomes the mystical revelation of Divine Reality. Another literary allusion in the passage is to the cave on Mount Thawr near Mecca, where the Prophet Muhammad and his Companion Abu Bakr hid for three days during their flight from Mecca to Medina. In popular accounts of this story, the Prophet tells Abu Bakr not to fear that their pursuers will

---

116 Ibid., p. 178.

discover them, for "God is with us."[117] For Maqdisi, the point of this story is that one who trusts in the Divine Beloved is never alone; whether in solitude or in a crowd, God is always present.

However, along with these Islamic literary allusions, the passage also contains other literary allusions, which evoke the Greek philosopher Plato as much as they evoke the Qur'an or the Prophet Muhammad. One indication of Platonic influence can be seen in Maqdisi's conflation of love-as-affection (*mahabba*) with love-as-desire (*'ishq*). As noted at the beginning of this chapter, the original connotation of spiritual love in early Islam was affection, which corresponds to the Arabic terms *hubb* and *mahabba*. Only later was spiritual love expressed as *'ishq*, which connotes mournful longing or desire. In Plato's *Dialogues*, the Greek term *eros*, which connotes physical desire, was primarily used for the concept of Love as a principle. Because the term *'ishq* began to appear as a synonym for *mahabba* in Islamic texts around the same time as Greek philosophical texts were first being translated into Arabic, some scholars have suggested that *'ishq* originally entered into Islamic discourse as the Arabic translation of *eros*.[118] According to some other scholars, the Abbasid inquisition of Baghdad Sufis in 885 CE, which resulted in the blacklisting or imprisonment of many of the most prominent early mystics of that time, was due to their use of the term *'ishq* to discuss the divine–human relationship. During this inquisition, Sufis were accused

---

117 This popular version of the story of the cave does not appear in *Sirat Rasul Allah* (*Biography of the Messenger of God*) by Muhammad ibn Ishaq (d. 768 CE) or in the later recension of this work by Ibn Hisham (d. ca. 833 CE). See Arnold Guillaume, *The Life of Muhammad: A Translation of Ibn Ishaq's Sirat Rasul Allah* (Lahore: Oxford University Press, 1970 reprint of 1955 first edition), pp. 224–5. Many Muslims believe that Sura 29 of the Qur'an, *al-'Ankabut* (*The Spider*), refers to a spider's web that hid the Prophet and Abu Bakr from their pursuers by being stretched across the mouth of the cave. However, the title of the *sura* actually refers to the vain hopes of those who take worldly powers instead of God for protection. These hopes are likened to the thinness of a spider's web (Qur'an 29:41).

118 See, for example, Bell, *A Treatise on Mystical Love*, who uses the construct "*'ishq* (eros)" in his translation of Daylami's *'Atf al-alif*. Richard Walzer also draws a contrast between the terms *'ishq* and *eros* (Gr. "love-as-desire") and *mahabba* and *philia* (Gr. "love-as-affection"). Walzer attributes the use of *'ishq* in Sufi works and Islamic Love treatises to the influence of the Arabic translation of the sixth book of Plotinus' *Enneads* (Ar. *Uthulujiya Aristatalis*), which deals in part with the concept of divine love. See idem, "Commentary" to Abu Nasr al-Farabi, *On the Perfect State* (*Mabadi' ara' ahl al-madinah al-fadilah*), ed. Richard Walzer (Chicago: Kazi Publications, 1998 reprint of 1985 Oxford University Press original), p. 352.

of advocating love between human beings and God and condoning sexual misconduct.[119]

Maqdisi's "Description of Rabi'a's Spiritual State" contains other examples of the influence of Plato as well. For example, Rabi'a's personification of Love as a great feminine ruler may allude to Plato's personification of Love as the goddess Aphrodite or to Phaedrus' description of Love as a "mighty god" in the *Symposium*.[120] In addition, Maqdisi's description of Love as a paradox recalls Plato's discussion of the spirit of Love in the *Symposium*, which he describes as occupying a liminal space between the human and divine realms.[121] Other possible echoes of the *Symposium* can be found in Rabi'a's statement about the harmony of souls that Love seeks to create. This brings to mind Eryximachus' description of Love in the *Symposium* as the creator of harmony among the elements.[122] Maqdisi's depiction of the lover as the Child of Desire and Awe brings to mind another mythological part of the *Symposium*, where Eros is portrayed as the Child of Poverty and Plenty.[123] Another possible allusion to Plato is in the passage where Jealousy cries out from "inside the cave" and asks, "Who is this infatuated and anxious woman who removes the veil of contentment and yet is content with us alone?" This statement brings to mind the Myth of the Cave in Book VII of Plato's *Republic* and the figure of the priestess Diotima of Mantineia, who teaches the higher mysteries of Love to Socrates in the *Symposium*.[124]

Clearly, there seem to be a number of allusions to Plato's *Symposium* in Makdisi's "Description of Rabi'a's Spiritual State." Might this allow us to suggest that Rabi'a al-'Adawiyya was for Maqdisi a sort of "Muslim Diotima?" If so, then it might be possible to find further traces of Plato's *Symposium* in other Sufis' descriptions of Rabi'a's teachings on Love. Although she does not discuss this subject directly, the same thought appears to have occurred to Margaret Smith, for she includes a passage from Plato's *Symposium* in the chapter on Love mysticism in *Rabi'a the Mystic*.[125] She also makes a statement

---

119 See, for example, Khalil, "Abu Talib al-Makki and *The Nourishment of Hearts*," pp. 5–6.
120 Plato, *The Symposium*, in *The Dialogues of Plato in Four Volumes*, ed. B. Jowett (Boston and New York: The Jefferson Press, 1871), vol. 1, p. 473 (178a).
121 See Louis A. Ruprecht Jr., *Symposia: Plato, the Erotic, and Moral Value* (Albany, NY: SUNY Press, 1999), pp. 48–57, and Plato, *Symposium*, in Jowett, vol. 1, p. 495 (202c–203a).
122 Plato, *The Symposium*, in Jowett, vol. 1, p. 481 (187a–187c).
123 Ibid., pp. 495–6 (203b–203e).
124 On Diotima of Mantineia, see ibid., p. 494 (201d); on the Myth of the Cave, see Plato, *The Republic*, in Jowett, vol. 2, pp. 841–7 (514a–519c).
125 Smith, *Rabi'a* (Oneworld), p. 119 and (Rainbow Bridge), pp. 94–5.

that would not make sense unless she were thinking of a comparison between Rabi'a and the figure of Diotima in the *Symposium*: "[Plato] makes Diotima of Mantineia set forth the doctrine of love leading to the beatific vision, and foreshadow the ideals of the mystics of all creeds who were to come after her, and who were to seek the way to God through love."[126]

As Plato describes her, Diotima of Mantineia was "a wise woman in [Love] and many other branches of knowledge."[127] The Sufi Abu Talib al-Makki makes a similar comment about Rabi'a when he introduces her in *Qut al-qulub*. Makki's book is the earliest Sufi treatise to employ the trope of Rabi'a the Lover extensively. He states, "[Rabi'a] was noted for her expertise in the doctrine of Love" (*idh kana laha fi-l-mahabba qadama sidqin*).[128] Plato also describes Diotima as a religious sage and teacher, who initiated male students into the truth that lies behind the sacred mysteries. The same could be said for the figure of Rabi'a the Teacher, discussed in Chapter 1. Another important similarity between the literary depictions of Diotima and Rabi'a, as Kevin Corrigan and Elena Glazov-Corrigan have observed about Diotima, is that both figures are portrayed as "a dialectical image, not thrice removed from the original, but a paradigm herself through which one may see the truth she represents and of which she speaks."[129] The Greek word for "image" is *ikon* (Ar. *sura*, "face," "form," or "image") and both Diotima and Rabi'a have come down to us through history as literary and cultural icons whose significance transcends the limitations of time and space.

Despite these important similarities, however, the problem with thinking of Rabi'a as a Muslim Diotima is that no conclusive evidence yet exists that Muslims were acquainted with Plato's *Symposium* in detail before the modern period. According to the historian of Islamic philosophy Dimitri Gutas, "Plato's *Symposion* (sic) was very little known in the medieval Arab world. As far as it can be ascertained, no direct translation of the full Greek text was ever made; the Arab bibliographers say nothing on the subject, and no verbatim quotations that might derive from such a translation have ever been recovered."[130] Gutas characterizes the *Symposium* as an "incognito

---

126 Ibid. (Oneworld), p. 120 and (Rainbow Bridge), p. 95.
127 Plato, *Symposium*, in Jowett, vol. 1, p. 494 (201d).
128 Makki, *Qut al-qulub*, vol. 2, p. 95. The phrase, *qadama sidqin*, comes from Qur'an, 10:2 and literally means "sure-footedness."
129 Kevin Corrigan and Elena Glazov-Corrigan, *Plato's Dialectic at Play: Argument, Structure, and Myth in the* Symposium (University Park, PA: Pennsylvania State University Press, 2004), p. 115.
130 Dimitri Gutas, "Plato's *Symposion* in the Arabic Tradition," in idem, *Greek Philosophers in the Arabic Tradition* (Aldershot, Hampshire, UK and Burlington, VT: Ashgate-Variorum, 2000), IV, p. 36.

presence" in Islamic thought, and claims that Muslims first came to know about it either through a paraphrase by the Arab philosopher Abu Ya'qub al-Kindi (d. 866 CE) or through "gnomic fragments current in Graeco-Arabic wisdom literature."[131] Indirect evidence to support Gutas's contention can be found in the fact that most of the extant allusions to the *Symposium* in medieval Islamic literature discuss theories that Plato rejects in this work, such as the myth of Aristophanes that souls were originally created round or that Love consists of the soul's search for completeness by finding its missing half.[132] Nowhere does one find Diotima mentioned by name, nor does one find detailed references to her teaching the higher states of Love, which is the real message of the *Symposium*.

However, as the historian of Islamic philosophy John Walbridge has noted in another context, one can respond to Gutas's skepticism about the existence of an Arabic *Symposium* with a different but equally true observation: "There is no unambiguous evidence of a complete Arabic translation of *any* Platonic dialogue before modern times."[133] In other words, if the existence of a complete premodern Arabic translation of Plato's *Symposium* is the main criterion by which to consider the influence of this text on Islamic thought, then the argument used by Gutas to dismiss the influence of the *Symposium* can be applied to every other dialogue of Plato as well.[134] Clearly, this would be absurd. Examples of the influence of Plato's *Phaedo* and *Timaeus* are too numerous to mention and major Islamic philosophical works have been based on Plato's *Republic* and *Laws*. Furthermore, as Walbridge points out, it is impossible to prove a negative; the lack of mention of a full translation of the *Symposium* in extant Arabic sources does not necessarily mean that such a translation never existed.[135]

---

131 Ibid., pp. 37–8.
132 See Plato, *Symposium*, in Jowett, vol. 1, pp. 483–4 (190e–191e). Extant references to the myth of Aristophanes first appear in Arabic literature in the late ninth and early tenth centuries CE. See, for example, Abu Bakr Muhammad ibn Dawud al-Isfahani (d. 910 CE), *al-Nisf al-awwal min Kitab al-zahra*, ed. Louis Nichol Al Bouhaymi and Ibrahim 'Abd al-Fattah Tuqan (Beirut: Jesuit Printing House, 1932), p. 15.
133 John Walbridge, *The Leaven of the Ancients: Suhrawardi and the Heritage of the Greeks* (Albany, NY: SUNY Press, 1999), p. 88; emphasis added.
134 Franz Rosenthal went so far as to doubt that any complete dialogue of Plato would ever be found in medieval Arabic sources. This was because of the reliance, going back to late antiquity, on paraphrases of Plato's works by Galen, Themistius, and other Neoplatonic writers. See idem, "On the Knowledge of Plato's Philosophy in the Islamic World," *Islamic Culture*, XIV (4), 1940, pp. 393 and 395.
135 Walbridge, *The Leaven of the Ancients*, On the Knowledge of Plato 88.

Indeed, there is evidence that an Arabic translation or at least a fairly detailed paraphrase of Plato's *Symposium* existed in the early Abbasid period. Ihsan Abbas (1920–2003), the noted Palestinian scholar of medieval Arabic literature, argued that Plato's *Symposium* was in fact translated into Arabic and was known in the Abbasid capital of Baghdad by the end of the second century AH (eighth century CE).[136] If this were true, then knowledge of the *Symposium* in Arabic would date to around the time of Rabi'a's death in 801 CE. Thus, it is not far-fetched to suggest that this work might have provided the rhetorical model for the Sufi depiction of Rabi'a as the Muslim Diotima.

Abbas bases his argument for an Arabic translation of the *Symposium* on a chapter in *Muruj al-dhahab* (*The Pastures of Gold*) by the Abbasid-era historian 'Ali ibn al-Husayn al-Mas'udi (d. 958 CE). This chapter contains the account of an intellectual salon (*majlis*) on the subject of Love that was organized by the Abbasid vizier Yahya ibn Khalid al-Barmaki (d. 805 CE). According to Abbas, the very institution of the *majlis* (literally, "sitting" or "assembly") in medieval Islamic society was based on the model of the symposium, which became known in the Middle East through the influence of Hellenism.[137] Historical sources mention the existence of elite Arabic literary salons as far back as the second half of the Umayyad period. Sukayna bint al-Husayn (d. 738 CE), the great-granddaughter of the Prophet Muhammad, was famous for hosting such salons.[138] According to Samer M. Ali, a contemporary expert on the medieval Arabic literary salon, the concept of the intellectual *majlis* was introduced into Muslim elite circles by Nestorian Christian physicians from the Sassanian learning center of Gondishapur, located near present-day Dezful in Iranian Khuzestan.[139] Ihsan Abbas believed that the Barmakid gathering mentioned by Mas'udi was mainly devoted to Plato's *Symposium*. This is because nearly all of the references to the subject matter of the *majlis* in *Muruj al-dhahab* are paraphrases of Plato's text.[140]

---

136 Ihsan Abbas, Introduction to Ibn Hazm al-Andalusi, *Tawq al-hamama fi-l-ulfa wa-l-alaf*, ed. Ihsan Abbas (Sousse, Tunisia: Dar al-Ma'arif li-l-Tiba'a wa al-Nashr, reprint of 1980 first edition, n.d.), p. 9.
137 Ibid.
138 See Amira El Zein, "Love Discourse in Hijazi Society under the Umayyads: A Study in Class and Gender," in *Gulf Women*, ed. Sonbol, p. 117–19.
139 Samer M. Ali, "Literary Salons: From Ancient *Symposion* to Arabic *Mujalasat*," in idem, *Arabic Literary Salons in the Islamic Middle Ages* (Notre Dame, IN: Notre Dame University Press, 2010), pp. 13–32.
140 Abbas, Introduction to Ibn Hazm, *Tawq al-hamama*, p. 11.

Whether or not Abbas was correct to conclude that the Barmakid *majlis* was based on Plato's *Symposium*, Mas'udi's discussion of this gathering refutes Gutas's contention that the philosopher Kindi first introduced the *Symposium* to the Muslim world. Since Kindi flourished more than a generation after this event took place, it is not likely that he composed the first Arabic paraphrase of the *Symposium*. One would have to believe that Mas'udi's account was completely false to reject his references to Plato's *Symposium*. No less than three direct references to the *Symposium* can be found in Mas'udi's description of the Barmakid *majlis*. The clearest example is a paraphrase of the discourse of Aristophanes:

> One of [the guests] said: God created every soul round in the shape of a ball. Then He divided them into portions and made every body out of one half. Therefore, when a body encounters the body that was the half that was originally cut away from it, love-as-desire (*'ishq*) occurs by necessity between the two of them because of their primordial relationship.[141]

Mas'udi also reproduces a two-part statement that he attributes to Plato (*Aflatun*) by name: "I do not know what Love (*hawa*, another Arabic term for love-as-desire) is, other than an excess of passion. Also, Love is neither praiseworthy nor blameworthy."[142] This statement recalls Diotima's teaching to Socrates in the *Symposium*, in which she states that Love is a spirit that is neither fair nor foul.[143]

The best evidence for the existence of a translation or major paraphrase of Plato's *Symposium* in Mas'udi's description of the Barmakid *majlis* is in the paragraph after the paraphrase of the statement of Aristophanes quoted above. The opening sentence of this paragraph states, "Those who are responsible for this discourse (*maqala*) have made other statements that expand on the subject we have just discussed."[144] Ihsan Abbas interprets this statement as alluding to the existence of a translation or at least an extensive paraphrase of the *Symposium*. Although Abbas sometimes seems to draw hasty conclusions

---

141 Abu al-Husayn 'Ali ibn al-Husayn b. 'Ali al-Mas'udi, *Muruj al-dhahab wa ma'adin al-jawhar*, ed. Mufid Muhammad Qumayha (Beirut: Dar al-Kutub al-'Ilmiyya, 1985), vol. 3, p. 457.
142 Ibid., p. 458; The Greek physician Hippocrates (*Buqrat*) is also quoted by Mas'udi as saying that Love is the mingling of two souls (p. 456).
143 Plato, *Symposium*, in Jowett, vol. 1, p. 498 (206b).
144 Mas'udi, *Muruj al-dhahab*, vol. 3, p. 457.

from the available evidence, this statement by Mas'udi seems to confirm that some of the topics covered in the *Symposium* were subjects of discussion and debate in the early Abbasid period. His work *Muruj al-dhahab* was published about fifty years before Abu Talib al-Makki, who also resided in Baghdad, expanded on the trope of Rabi'a the Lover in *Qut al-qulub*. Thus, it is not unreasonable to suggest that Makki, who was well acquainted with the literary arts of his day, would have had at least a second-hand knowledge of Plato's *Symposium*.

Many scholars, both inside and outside the Muslim world, have discussed the influence of Neo-Platonism on Sufi mysticism. It is not necessary to repeat these observations here. However, in light of the present discussion it is worth suggesting that this emphasis on Neo-Platonism may have obscured the influence of Plato's works on the Sufi tradition. Now that it can be argued that the contents of the *Symposium* were better known in the period after Rabi'a's death than Gutas and other skeptics have assumed, it becomes possible to suggest parallels between Plato's depiction of Diotima and the depiction of Rabi'a the Lover in Sufi literature. As we shall see below, the similarities between the literary depictions of Diotima in Plato's *Symposium* and the depictions of Rabi'a al-'Adawiyya in Makki's *Qut al-qulub* are significant enough to make their chance occurrence unlikely.[145]

However, it must be conceded that the figure of "Rabi'a the Muslim Diotima" is likely to always be an "incognito presence" in Sufi literature. Gutas's observation about the *Symposium* applies quite well in this latter case. Even if a medieval Arabic translation of Plato's *Symposium* were eventually to be found, we are still not likely to find explicit references to it or to Diotima in Sufi works. On the contrary, because Sufism has been criticized as heretical for so much of its history, Sufi authors have tended to downplay non-Muslim sources in their writings. Until now, no explicit reference to Diotima has been found in any Sufi text, nor is the modern researcher likely to find one. However, the parallels between Diotima and Rabi'a as iconic women teachers

---

[145] Traces of Plato's *Symposium* can be found in early Christian texts too. Elizabeth A. Clark has similarly identified traces of Diotima in two of Gregory of Nyssa's fourth-century CE works, *Life of Macrina* and *On the Soul and the Resurrection*. See Elizabeth A. Clark, *History, Theory, Text: Historians and the Linguistic Turn* (Cambridge, MA and London: Harvard University Press, 2004), pp. 178–9. These works from the Capadoccian tradition of Christian hagiography would also have been available in Iraq in the Abbasid period. If it turns out that Gutas is correct, and that no Arabic translation or major paraphrase of Plato's *Symposium* ever existed, then Christian works such as these might have provided the Diotima trope—"at six degrees of separation," so to speak—for medieval Sufi writers.

of men are too significant to overlook, and they have reappeared over and over again in Sufi depictions of Rabiʿa the Lover from the tenth century CE through modern times.

b. Rabiʿa the Lover in Abu Talib al-Makki's Qut al-Qulub

Given the importance of Makki's *Qut al-qulub* to the development of the trope of Rabiʿa the Lover, it should not be a surprise to find that several points of comparison can be found between Plato's portrayal of Diotima of Mantineia and Makki's portrayal of Rabiʿa al-ʿAdawiyya. What is more surprising, however, given the importance of *Qut al-qulub* to Sufi theology, is the lack of significant modern studies devoted to this work. Most studies of Makki's book in European languages are article-length only and barely scratch the surface of its contents. Even the recent monograph on *Qut al-qulub* by the Japanese scholar Saeko Yazaki is a very thin volume. It consists of a short biography of Makki, a summary of the section of the book on the Sufi concept of the heart, and notes on later Muslim writers who were influenced by Makki.[146] This treatment does not give *Qut al-qulub* the attention it deserves as one of the most important early treatises on Sufism.

The main topics discussed in Makki's book are revealed in the title: *Qut al-qulub fi muʿamalat al-Mahbub wa wasf tariq al-murid ila maqam al-tawhid* (*The Nourishment of Hearts Through the Encounter with the Beloved and Description of the Way of the Seeker to the Station of Divine Unity*). We can see from the title that Makki intended the work to be a Sufi manual and that its principal aim was to show the seeker the way to the spiritual realization of divine unity. The narrative of the book focuses most of its attention on three subjects: the Sufi concept of the heart, the mystical experience of encounter with God the Beloved, and the theological concept of oneness or divine unity (*tawhid*). The key to the work as a whole is hidden in the middle of its title: "The Encounter with the Beloved." Makki's discussion of this experience is the *tertium quid* of his argument for knowledge of divine unity. Logically, it is the "third element" that connects the concept of the heart, which is known by most people only conventionally but not spiritually, with the concept of divine oneness, which is also known conventionally, through the exoteric

---

146 Saeko Yazaki, *Islamic Mysticism and Abu Talib al-Makki: The Role of the Heart* (London and New York: Routledge, 2013).

doctrines of Islam.¹⁴⁷ The Sufi's mystical encounter with the Beloved on the path of Love awakens the heart of the seeker to the true inner meaning of the theological concept of divine oneness.

The importance of the heart in Makki's approach to Sufism is that it is the site of the soul's encounter with the Beloved. The intimate knowledge of God in His oneness is the fruit of this encounter. Because the Sufi seeks spiritual knowledge both outwardly and inwardly, Makki begins his book with a discussion of outward spiritual practices, such as prayer and invocation, and then moves on to more specialized forms of devotion, such as the practices associated with asceticism. The narrative then turns to the inner dimensions of Sufi practice and the spiritual and psychological states and stations through which the seeker must pass as she begins to encounter the Beloved in her heart. The discussion of the remaining outward practices of Islam are reserved for the final section of the book, for only when the seeker has developed herself spiritually can she understand the deeper meaning of required religious behaviors. Symbolically, the experience of reading *Qut al-qulub* as a Sufi text is designed to follow the ancient literary trope of the soul's quest or journey into itself in order to find enlightenment. The seeker's journey starts first in the outside world (the *via activa*); next it goes deep into the interior world in order to plumb the mine of secrets (the *via contemplativa*); finally, the seeker returns in a more enlightened state to the world of conventional reality. This trope has deep roots in Hellenistic antiquity, and can be found in Plato's Parable of the Cave, The Orphic Mysteries, and Hermetic texts like the Emerald Tablet. By implication, it would also have applied to Diotima's teaching of Socrates in the *Symposium*.

For Makki, the spiritual path that the seeker travels on her way to the encounter with the Beloved culminates in the Station of Certainty (*maqam al-yaqin*). To convey to the reader that this station is the final stage of the seeker's quest, he devotes nearly one-fourth of *Qut al-qulub* (253 pages in the latest edition) to its discussion. It is also significant that the discussion of this station is located in the middle of the text. In other words, it is the "heart" of the narrative, and just as the heart is situated in the middle of the human body, Makki's discussion of the Station of Certainty is situated in the middle of his "body of work." In rhetorical terms, the placement of this discussion

---

147 The Latin term *tertium quid* (Gr. *tríton ti*, "third thing"), is a concept of logic whose textual origin can itself be found in the works of Plato. In the *Sophist* Plato states, "Being must therefore be a *tertium quid*, apart from motion and rest, not the sum total of those two items." See George Grote, *Plato and the Other Companions of Sokrates* (London: John Murray, 1888), vol. 2, p. 418.

serves as another *tertium quid*. Located in the human heart (the center of the body), and also being the "heart" of Makki's narrative, the Station of Certainty is the goal of the Sufi path and the site of the soul's spiritual transformation through the encounter with God.

Because the narrative structure of *Qut al-qulub* follows the model of a spiritual journey or quest, the seeker cannot reach the Station of Certainty all at once, as in a flash of insight. Instead, she must progress through nine spiritual and psychological states (*ahwal*) on the way to the Beloved, until she finally reaches her goal. These states are likened to way stations or caravanserais on the *via contemplativa*, the inner part of the quest for the secret of Divine Unity. Each of these stations must be experienced separately and the wisdom found within them must be learned fully before certainty can be attained. Makki identifies these spiritual and psychological states as follows:

(1) Repentance (*tawba*)
(2) Patience (*sabr*)
(3) Thankfulness (*shukr*)
(4) Hope (*raja'*)
(5) Fear (*khawf*)
(6) Renunciation (*zuhd*)
(7) Complete Trust in God (*tawakkul*)
(8) Satisfaction with God's Will (*rida'*)
(9) Love (*mahabba*).

As the ninth and final state, Love is the "peak experience" of the self's Encounter with God. Makki describes this as the most exalted state in the Station of Certainty, the most advanced way station on the journey to God, and the final stop on the Sufi Way. Here one experiences "the Love of the spiritual elites (*mahabbat al-khusus*) and the Love of the Beloved (*mahabbat al-mahbub*)."[148]

Most of Makki's references to Rabi'a al-'Adawiyya in *Qut al-qulub* are contained in his discussions of the states of Satisfaction (*rida'*) and Love (*mahabba*), the two highest states in the Station of Certainty. By situating his references to Rabi'a the Lover at the end of his discussion of these stations, he indicates to the reader that she stands for or symbolizes the culmination of the Sufi way and is the personification of divine wisdom (*hikma*). He informs

---

148 Makki, *Qut al-qulub*, vol. 1, p. 317.

the reader that Rabi'a earned God's special regard through her perfection of Love as a spiritual practice and her intimate knowledge of Divine Unity. When Makki first introduces Rabi'a as "one of the lovers" (*wa kanat ihda al-muhibbin*), this is not an offhand or casual remark.[149] This description identifies her as a paragon of intimate knowledge of God. Like the priestess Diotima of Plato's *Symposium*, she is uniquely qualified through her combination of knowledge and experience to teach others about the spiritual practice of Love and the reality of the theological concept of Divine Unity.

In Plato's *Symposium*, Diotima is similarly described as teaching the way of "True Love." Also like Rabi'a, she is the teacher of the "True Order" of spiritual ascent that leads to the mystical vision of "true divine beauty. . . pure and clear and unalloyed, not clogged with the pollutions of mortality."[150] Like Rabi'a the Teacher, her lessons go directly to the heart of the matter by stripping away the veils of rhetoric that hide the truth and by revealing its inner meaning. In *Qut al-qulub*, Makki describes Rabi'a as having "truly experienced the ecstasy of the lovers" (*wajd al-muhibbin al-muhiqqin*).[151] By using the Arabic term *muhiqq* ("one who has fully actualized a teaching or a doctrine"), he informs the reader that Rabi'a is a master practitioner of the Sufi doctrine of Love. Like Diotima for Plato, she is also the personification of divine wisdom (Ar. *hikma*, Gr. *Sophia*). As we shall see in Chapter 5, for the Persian Sufi Farid al-Din al-'Attar, whose treatment of Rabi'a two centuries later was to turn Makki's trope of Rabi'a the Lover into a literary icon, her wisdom even transcends the limitations of identity and gender: "In unity, how can your existence and mine remain, much less 'man' and 'woman'?"[152]

In their study of the rhetoric of Plato's *Symposium*, Kevin Corrigan and Elena Glazov-Corrigan highlight the importance of dialectical cross-examination as Diotima's method of teaching.[153] Jahiz noted the same characteristic of Rabi'a when he described her as a "Person of *Bayan*" in *Kitab al-bayan wa-l-tabyin*. For Jahiz, and for the Sufi Sulami, the use of this pedagogical method was a sign of the true teacher and sage. In the *Symposium*, Plato suggests that it was Diotima who taught Socrates the dialectical method of inquiry for which he became famous. In Sulami's Book of Sufi Women, Sufyan al-Thawri says about Rabi'a to his companion, "Take me to my

---

149 Ibid., vol. 2, p. 94.
150 Plato, *Symposium*, in Jowett, vol. 1, p. 508 (211e).
151 Makki, *Qut al-qulub*, vol. 2, p. 95.
152 Sells, *Early Islamic Mysticism*, p. 155, and 'Attar, *Tadhkirat al-awliya*', p. 41.
153 Corrigan and Glazov-Corrigan, *Plato's Dialectic at Play*, p. 108.

mentor. For when I am apart from her, I can find no solace."[154] Socrates calls Diotima his "instructress" in the *Symposium*.[155] The Arabic term *mu'addiba*, which Thawri uses to describe Rabi'a as his mentor, can also be translated as "instructress." As discussed at length in Chapter 1, this term refers to *ta'dib*, a type of training that made use of both dialectical and aphoristic methods. Diotima's method of teaching was based on the cultivation of knowledge through dialectical questioning. This process was meant to instill mystical knowledge, social virtues, righteousness, and wisdom. Rabi'a al-'Adawiyya also instilled these characteristics through her practice of *ta'dib*. According to Plato, such methods are important for training disciples in the spiritual life because they are the pedagogical methods used by Love itself.[156]

Plato's account of Socrates' encounter with Diotima introduces the reader of the *Symposium* to a mystical doctrine of Love. This is contrasted with the other theories of Love that Plato presents in this work, which are mythological, medical, or ethical in nature.[157] Diotima speaks of Love as possessing lesser and greater mysteries, and, like Makki in *Qut al-qulub*, Plato provides a doctrinal ladder by which one can ascend conceptually to the higher states of the mysteries.[158] Makki's discussion of Rabi'a the Lover similarly stresses Rabi'a's role as a teacher who initiates her disciples into the mysteries of Love. Medieval Islamic works on Love borrowed thematic elements from Greek philosophical and medical texts as well as from the cultural traditions of the Arabs, and like Plato, discussed medical, ethical, and even mythological theories of Love.[159] Makki takes great pains to convince his readers that "the Love that comes from God" (*al-mahabba min Allah*) is not like other kinds of love. These other kinds of love arise from personal needs. Ordinary types of love, he states, arise from seven possible causes: (1) a natural inclination; (2) the desire for sexual procreation; (3) self-interest; (4) an inherited trait or tendency; (5) the instinct of lust; (6) the need for

---

154 R. Cornell, *Early Sufi Women*, p. 76.
155 Plato, *Symposium*, in Jowett, vol. 1, p. 494 (201d).
156 On the "Science of Beauty," see ibid., pp. 502–3 (211b): "He who is under the influence of true love rising upward from these, begins to see that beauty is not far from the end."
157 Corrigan and Corrigan, *Plato's Dialectic*, p. 108. Unlike the Corrigans, Pierre Hadot sees no mysticism in Plato's doctrine of Love ("Platonic love thus is not, properly speaking, a 'mystical transport.'" Hadot, *Plotinus*, p. 54). In my opinion, Hadot overstresses the irrational element in the concept of mysticism. This is the only way that one could fail to see Plato's doctrine of higher love as mystical.
158 Plato, *Symposium*, in Jowett, vol. 1, pp. 502–3 (211d).
159 For a discussion of medieval Islamic theories about what today might be called the "pathology" of love, see the chapter on "The Romantic Fool," in Dols, *Majnun*, pp. 313–48.

compassion; (7) the emotional need to feel close to God.[160] By contrast, the higher Love of God is not sought on the basis of personal needs; instead, it depends on the transcendence of need. The path of self-transcendence starts with transcendence of the World through ascetic renunciation and leads to the transcendence of the more subtle aspects of the ego, as illustrated by the example of Rabi'a's actions and teachings. The selfless longing for God (*shawq*) that motivates the Sufi's search for the higher Love arises out of the renunciation of self-interest (*ithar*) and the desire of the soul for inner peace and tranquility (*sakina*).[161]

At the end of her part of the *Symposium*, Diotima speaks of the higher Love as a state of peaceful communion, where images of beauty are beheld in their full realities, and where the initiate into the mysteries subsists with Beauty as the "immortal friend of God."[162] In his description of Rabi'a's Love mysticism in *Qut al-qulub*, Makki says much the same thing. Similarly to Plato, he mentions that the "friends of God" (*awliya' Allah*) and "God's intimates" (*al-muqarrabun*) are to be found in the Station of Certainty. He also describes their abode in the Gardens of the Righteous, where the fruits of Love's mysteries are brought together, just as knowledge and action are combined in the Qur'an and Sufi doctrine. Also like Plato in the *Symposium*, Makki describes the state of higher Love as a visionary experience (*ru'ya*), a view of Certainty which only those who have attained to divine intimacy can behold: "Only the intimates shall behold it" (*yashhaduhu al-muqarrabun*).[163]

In the *Symposium*, Plato demonstrates that he conceives of Love as a way of knowledge by announcing at the beginning of the dialogue that Diotima will speak of "a *logos* pertaining to Love."[164] The Greek word *logos*, like the Arabic word *kalima*, can mean "word," "discourse," "reason," or "knowledge," depending on the context. In her discourse in the *Symposium*, Diotima addresses the subject of knowledge by asking Socrates to define the mean or middle point between ignorance and wisdom. The correct answer to this question, "right opinion" (*ortho-doxa*, conventional knowledge or religion), cannot be called true knowledge because it is based more on opinion than

---

160 Makki, *Qut al-qulub*, vol. 2, p. 86.
161 Ibid., p. 91.
162 Plato, *Symposium*, in Jowett, vol. 1, p. 503 (211c).
163 Makki, *Qut al-qulub*, vol. 2, pp. 93–4; the original of this phrase is in Qur'an, 83:21.
164 Corrigan and Corrigan, *Plato's Dialectic*, p. 114.

on reason. However, it is not complete ignorance either, because it contains part of the truth.[165]

The tropes of Rabi'a the Teacher and Rabi'a the Lover similarly depend on the idea that true knowledge transcends both religious dogma and tradition. As a teacher of wisdom (*hikma*), Rabi'a's knowledge, like Diotima's, must go beyond both ordinary belief or opinion (Ar. *zann*, Gr. *dogma*) and orthodox creed or belief (Ar. *'aqida*, Gr. *doxa*). For Plato, the key to achieving true knowledge through Love is the practice of remembrance, for as Diotima says, knowledge must be renewed periodically by remembrance or else it is lost.[166] The greatest mysteries of both Love and knowledge are attained through the practice of remembrance. A paradox of the contemplation of Absolute Beauty, which is the goal of the initiatory path for Plato, is that the knowledge of Beauty consists in the recollection of what one already knows. In Sufism as well, the practice of remembrance—both as a spiritual practice (*dhikr*) and as a form of recollection (*tadhakkur* or *tafakkur*)—is fundamental to the pursuit of knowledge. For Makki, Love and knowledge are two sides of the same coin. Because of this correspondence, just as the gnostics or "knowers" of God (*al-'arifin*) are ranked according to the extent of their knowledge, so too the Lovers of God (*al-muhibbin*) are ranked according to the extent of their knowledge. At the highest stage, the different approaches to knowledge merge into one. Makki describes the relationship between Love and knowledge in the following way: "The elite knowers of God (*khusus al-'arifin*) practice a special kind of Love (*khassat al-mahabba*), whereas the ordinary knowers of God practice an ordinary kind of love (*wa li-'umumihim 'umum al-mahabba*)."[167] However, the seeker can only reach the Station of Certainty if her knowledge of God (*ma'rifa*) is confirmed by her knowledge of Love (*mahabba*).

Makki states that the knowledge embodied by Rabi'a al-'Adawiyya is based on the clarity of vision that Love provides through the "Eye of Certainty" (*mushahadat 'ayn al-yaqin*). He contrasts this with the conventional attainment of knowledge by means of "tradition or confirmed hearsay" (*khabar wa sam' tasdiq*). Switching from his own voice to that of Rabi'a, he summarizes her encounter with the Beloved in the Station of Certainty in words that could just as well have been spoken by Diotima in Plato's *Symposium*: "My love for you is through a vision that brought me closer to you, made

---

165 Plato, *Symposium*, in Jowett, vol. 1, p. 494 (201d).
166 Ibid., p. 500 (208a).
167 Makki, *Qut al-qulub*, vol. 2, p. 86.

me hurry toward you, preoccupied me with you, and cut me off from everything other than you. Before that, I had scattered passions, but when I truly witnessed you, all of my passions merged into one and you became the entirety of the heart and the totality of Love" (*fa-sirta anta kulliyata al-qalb wa jumlat al-mahabba*).[168]

IV. RABI'A THE LOVE POET

The statement on Love that Makki attributes to Rabi'a al-'Adawiyya is reminiscent of the end of the section on Diotima in Plato's *Symposium*, where she states: "What if man had eyes to see the true beauty—the divine beauty, I mean, pure and clear and unalloyed, not clogged with the pollutions of mortality, and all the colors and vanities of human life—thither looking, and holding converse with the true beauty divine and simple, and bringing into being and educating true creations of virtue and not idols only?"[169] In this statement Diotima speaks of two loves—a passionate love that corresponds to the lesser mysteries of love, and a higher love of the remembrance and contemplation of divine beauty that corresponds to the "greater and more hidden mysteries." The concept of two loves is a key part of Diotima's teaching on Love in the *Symposium*. Although the lesser mysteries of Love are accessible to anyone with understanding, the bridge that leads to the greater mysteries of Love, "which are the crown of these," is crossed by only a few. A similar concept of two loves is also central to Rabi'a's Love theory as portrayed in Sufi narratives from Makki's time to the present. Theologically, this notion is linked to the famous verse of the Qur'an, which states, "God did not create two hearts for man in his breast" (Qur'an 33:4). As a literary trope, it most famously appears in the "Poem of the Two Loves," which was first attributed to Rabi'a by Abu Talib al-Makki.

a. The Poem of the Two Loves

Makki introduces the final section of his discussion of Love in *Qut al-qulub* with a poem that he claims was attributed to Rabi'a al-'Adawiyya "by the

---

168 Ibid., p. 95.
169 Plato, *Symposium*, in Jowett, vol. 1, p. 503 (211e).

people of Basra and others."¹⁷⁰ This poem has become known over time as the "Poem of the Two Loves." Among the sources for its attribution to Rabi'a, Makki cites four respected male ascetics, who have often been associated with Rabi'a in Sufi texts. These are Sufyan al-Thawri (d. 778 CE), Hammad ibn Zayd (d. 793 CE), 'Abd al-Wahid ibn Zayd (d. 793–4 CE), and Ja'far ibn Sulayman ad-Dab'i (d. 794–5 CE).¹⁷¹ As noted in Chapter 1, these figures lend credibility to Makki's attribution of the poem to Rabi'a because all of them are associated with the city of Basra and all of them lived in Rabi'a's time. However, no extant source prior to Makki mentions either Rabi'a or any of these individuals in connection with this poem. At the present time, it is impossible to determine who actually composed the Poem of the Two Loves. Abu Bakr al-Kalabadhi (d. 990 CE), writing a short time before Makki in the Central Asian city of Merv, reproduces a slightly different version of the poem in his treatise *al-Ta'arruf li-madhhab ahl al-tasawwuf* (*Understanding the Doctrines of the Sufis*). Unlike Makki, however, he does not attribute the poem to Rabi'a al-'Adawiyya. He only states, "One of [the Sufis] recited [it]."¹⁷²

Because of the uncertainty about its origins, the Poem of the Two Loves cannot be attributed conclusively to Rabi'a al-'Adawiyya. The best one can say is that it belongs to the tradition of Sufism as a whole as much as to Rabi'a herself.¹⁷³ Makki's attribution of this poem to Rabi'a and his commentary on it were largely responsible for the notoriety it was to attain as part of the Rabi'a myth. Today it is one of the most famous poems of the Sufi tradition. A Google search of the phrase, "The Poem of the Two Loves by Rabi'a," yields 36,300 web entries. This is not far behind "Rumi's *Masnavi*," which yields 51,400 web entries. I have translated Makki's version of the poem below, retaining as much of the literal sense of the Arabic text as possible.

> I love you with two loves: a passionate love,
> And a love of which only you are worthy.

---

170 Makki, *Qut al-qulub*, vol. 2, p. 94.
171 Ibid.
172 See Kalabadhi, *al-Ta'arruf*, p. 80 and Arberry, *The Doctrine of the Sufis*, p. 103.
173 G.J.H. van Gelder claims to have identified the source of the Poem of the Two Loves in a secular poem of the Abbasid period. See idem, "Rabi'a's Poem of the Two Kinds of Love: A Mystification?," in *Verse and the Fair Sex: A Collection of Papers Presented at the 15th Congress of the UAEI*, ed. Frederick de Jong (Utrecht, The Netherlands: 1993), pp. 66–76; cited in Knysh, *Islamic Mysticism*, p. 31 n. 74.

As for the passionate love,
It has preoccupied me with the remembrance of you beyond all else.

And as for the love of which only you are worthy,
Your parting of the veils allows me to see you.

No praise is mine for either one or the other,
But all praise is yours for this [love] and the other.[174]

The Poem of the Two Loves has appeared in many different versions over the past millennium, with some versions differing significantly from others. The different versions of the poem go back to the very origins of its transmission. For example, in the earliest extant version, in Kalabadhi's *al-Taʿarruf*, the second line of the third verse reads, "I do not see the world of existence unless I see you" (*fa-lastu ara al-kawna hatta araka*). In Makki's version, the same line reads, "Your parting of the veils allows me to see you" (*fa-kashfuka li-l-hujubi hatta araka*). Although these two versions seem to convey a similar meaning, their theological implications are quite different.[175] Kalabadhi's, "I do not see the world of existence unless I see you," conveys a pantheistic theology because the poet sees God in the world of existence. The poet either sees the world through God or she sees God in everything. This perspective is problematical for orthodox Muslims, who prefer to keep God and the world ontologically separate. By contrast, Makki's version of the poem is more ambiguous and thus is theologically less problematical. "Your parting of the veils allows me to see you," may be interpreted to mean, "You have enabled me to see you as the cause of all things." This corresponds quite closely to the Qurʾanic description of God as the Creator of All Things (Qurʾan 13:16). The theological problem of Kalabadhi's pantheistic version of the poem has been a point of contention throughout Islamic history. As recently as 2005, it was discussed as the subject of a *fatwa* by the Qatar Mufti Yusuf al-Qaradawi.[176]

Kalabadhi does not attribute the Poem of the Two Loves to Rabiʿa or to any other person, but instead quotes it anonymously. For the most part, he avoids the mention of women, whether Sufi or otherwise, in *Kitab al-taʿarruf*.

---

174 Makki, *Qut al-qulub*, vol. 2, p. 94.
175 See also my discussion of this issue in R. Cornell, "Rabiʿah al-ʿAdawiyyah," pp. 294–5.
176 For Qaradawi's *fatwa*, see http://www.ghrib.net/vb/archive/index.php/t-12042.html (*Islam Light*).

Rabi'a is the only Sufi woman whom Kalabadhi mentions by name in his book. Unlike Makki, however, who depicts Rabi'a as one of the key figures of Sufi Love mysticism, he gives the final word in his chapter on Love to a man, a certain Ibn 'Abd al-Samad, who is the author of two other poems about Love. Kalabadhi's placing of Ibn 'Abd al-Samad and his poems at the end of his chapter on Love lessens the rhetorical impact of the Poem of the Two Loves. To borrow the title of a famous movie by Alfred Hitchcock, one could say that in Kalabadhi's treatment of this poem, "the lady vanishes." Unlike Makki, he obscures the importance of the poem, as well as its attribution to Rabi'a, within his narrative.

In the twentieth century, the Poem of the Two Loves became famous because of the prominent treatment that Margaret Smith gave to it in her book *Rabi'a the Mystic*.[177] In 1935, some seven years after the publication of *Rabi'a the Mystic*, the British Orientalist A.J. Arberry mentioned "Miss M. Smith's" book on Rabi'a in connection with Kalabadhi's version of the Poem of the Two Loves in his English translation of *Kitab al-ta'arruf*.[178] Ironically, in this work Arberry obscures Smith's voice in a way that parallels Kalabadhi's failure to acknowledge Rabi'a al-'Adawiyya or any other Sufi woman as the author of the poem. For some unknown reason, Arberry chose not to translate the poem himself nor did he account for the textual difference between Kalabadhi's and Makki's versions. Instead, in a footnote, he criticizes Smith's "literal" translation of the poem and states that he will use the "excellent version" of his doctoral advisor, Reynold A. Nicholson. By using Nicholson's translation instead of Smith's, Arberry chose an interpretation of the Poem of the Two Loves that took major liberties with both Kalabadhi's and Makki's versions. Instead of following the Arabic text of either version of the poem closely, Nicholson chose to rhyme the poem in English and then shaped his translation to fit a stereotyped image of Victorian-era poetry. In Nicholson's awkward rendition of the Poem of the Two Loves, which appears in Arberry's translation of Kalabadhi's book, not one but two ladies now vanish. Both Rabi'a as the possible author, and Margaret Smith, without whom the Poem of the Two Loves would not have been known in the West, are silenced and exiled to a footnote. This makes room for the discordant rhymes of R.A. Nicholson, who had the advantage of being Arberry's doctoral advisor and a famous male authority on Sufism. This example of academic favoritism makes the reference to "selfish love" in his translation particularly ironic.

---

177   Smith, *Rabi'a* (Oneworld), pp. 126–33 and (Rainbow Bridge), pp. 102–10.
178   Arberry, *The Doctrine of the Sufis*, p. 103 n. 1.

> Two ways I love Thee; selfishly,
> And next, as worthy is of Thee.
>
> 'Tis selfish love that I do naught
> Save think on Thee with every thought;
>
> 'Tis purest love when Thou dost raise
> The veil to my adoring gaze.
>
> Not mind the praise in that or this,
> Thine is the praise in both, I wis.[179]

The tendency to indulge in unethical conduct with regard to the Poem of the Two Loves was not unique to Arberry and Nicholson. Even Margaret Smith's treatment of the poem in *Rabi'a the Mystic* is marred by this problem. In her book, Smith imagines Rabi'a reciting the poem in a scenario that she attributes to Sulami's Book of Sufi Women. However, Sulami does not cite the Poem of the Two Loves in his Book of Sufi Women. Even more, although Smith speculates about its existence, she could not have seen an actual copy of Sulami's book because it was not discovered until after her death.[180] Under these circumstances, one can only conclude that her story of the poem's attribution to Rabi'a and the circumstances of its recitation are false. Smith is also wrong in claiming that Makki states in *Qut al-qulub* that the four male transmitters of the poem were its authors.[181] Makki never makes such a claim in his book. Smith also misinterprets Makki's commentary on the poem by paraphrasing it in an anthropomorphic way that does not correspond to the actual Arabic text. As we shall see in Chapters 5 and 6, this use of poetic license to fill in empty spaces in the Rabi'a narrative is an aspect of her myth that has persisted from medieval times to the present. Although this phenomenon is interesting from a literary point of view, it seriously complicates the academic study of Rabi'a al-'Adawiyya.

---

179 Ibid., p. 103.
180 Smith, *Rabi'a* (Oneworld), p. 125 and (Rainbow Bridge), p. 102. Smith assumed incorrectly that Sulami's Book of Sufi Women was a lost portion of his *Tabaqat al-sufiyya*. The Iraqi scholar Mahmud Muhammad al-Tanahi discovered Sulami's Book of Sufi Women in 1991 in the Muhammad ibn Saud University library in Saudi Arabia. It was first published in Arabic in 1993. See Abu 'Abd al-Rahman al-Sulami, *Dhikr al-niswa al-muta'abbidat al-Sufiyyat*, ed. Mahmud Muhammad al-Tanahi (Cairo: Maktabat al-Khanji, 1993).
181 Smith, *Rabi'a* (Oneworld), pp. 125–6 and (Rainbow Bridge), p. 102.

One of the key interpreters of the Poem of the Two Loves in medieval Islam was the Sunni theologian and Sufi Abu Hamid al-Ghazali (d. 1111 CE). Ghazali drew much material from Makki's *Qut al-qulub* when writing his masterwork, *Ihya' 'ulum al-din* (*The Revival of the Religious Sciences*). Following Makki, he attributes the Poem of the Two Loves to Rabi'a in this work and uses it in his discussion of the Sufi's intimate knowledge of God (*ma'rifa*). This discussion appears in Book 36 of the *Ihya'*, "Love, Longing, Intimacy, and Contentment." In this chapter, Ghazali does not use the usual Sufi term, "taste" (*dhawq*), to refer to mystical experience but instead uses the term "pleasure" (*ladhdha*), which is closer to Plato's *Symposium* than to most Sufi discourses.[182] Also like Plato, he portrays the higher form of love—which the poem calls the "love of which only [God] is worthy"—as a peak aesthetic experience, and says that it reflects the divine attributes of Beauty (*jamal*) and Glory (*jalal*).[183] Ghazali's description of mystical union in this chapter as an act of communion with divine Beauty is also reminiscent of Plato's *Symposium*. It recalls the last part of Diotima's discourse, in which she says to Socrates, "Do you not see that in communion only, beholding beauty with the eye of the mind, he will be enabled to bring forth, not images of beauty, but realities? For he has hold not of an image, but of a reality; and bringing forth and educating true virtue to become the friend of God and be immortal, if mortal man may."[184] Although Ghazali would not call the fully realized "knower of God" immortal as Plato does, he would certainly agree with Plato in referring to him as a "friend of God" (Ar. *wali Allah*).

Sufi writers after Ghazali who attributed the Poem of the Two Loves to Rabi'a al-'Adawiyya frequently reproduced his discussion of the trope of Rabi'a the Lover in the *Ihya'*. This was also often the case for non-Sufi writers who were influenced by Ghazali. For example, the Andalusian vizier and essayist Lisan al-Din ibn al-Khatib (d. 1374 CE) paraphrases Ghazali's comments in Book 36 of the *Ihya'* in his treatise on Love, *Rawdat al-ta'rif bi-l-hubb al-sharif* (*The Garden of Knowledge of the Noble Love*). However, Ibn al-Khatib only reproduces the first verse of the Poem of the Two Loves, retaining the Platonic trope of two loves but rejecting its mystical theology.[185]

---

182 See Eric Ormsby's translation in Ghazali, *Love, Longing, Intimacy, and Contentment*, pp. 51–5.
183 Ghazali, *Ihya'*, vol. 4, pp. 310–11 and Ghazali-Ormsby, *Love, Longing, Intimacy, and Contentment*, p. 52.
184 Plato, *Symposium*, in Jowett, vol. 1, p. 503 (212c).
185 Lisan al-Din Ibn al-Khatib, *Rawdat al-ta'rif bi-l-hubb al-sharif*, ed. 'Abd al-Qadir Ahmad 'Ata (Beirut: Dar al-Fikr al-'Arabi, n. d.), p. 427.

By contrast, the full text of the poem, along with Ghazali's comments on it, were reproduced by the Yemeni Sufi Muhammad Murtada al-Zabidi (d. 1790 CE) in his commentary on Ghazali's *Ihya'*.[186] In this work, Zabidi not only reproduces both Makki's and Ghazali's commentaries on the poem but also adds background narratives as well, such as the stories of marriage proposals to Rabi'a by 'Abd al-Wahid ibn Zayd and the governor of Basra.

As we have already seen in the case of Kalabadhi's *Kitab al-ta'arruf*, a second Sufi tradition exists that does not attribute the Poem of the Two Loves to Rabi'a al-'Adawiyya. Unlike the Ghazalian tradition, this alternate tradition does not seem to have a single origin. Although Kalabadhi's discussion of the Poem of the Two Loves is the earliest example of this tradition that currently exists, it is seldom cited in subsequent versions. For example, Muhammad al-Nisaburi, writing only a few decades after Kalabadhi, mentions the Poem of the Two Loves in *'Uqala' al-majanin*. In this work, he does not mention Kalabadhi but cites as his source for the poem the Sufi of Baghdad, Abu al-Qasim al-Junayd (d. 910 CE). In what is presented as the verbatim account of an oral tradition, Junayd states that the poem was composed by a *shaykh* that he met in a hospital in Egypt. We are not told whether the term, *shaykh*, refers to an old man, a Sufi master, or a doctor. However, it is clear that the hospital is an asylum for the insane. In medieval Islam, passionate love, whether of the physical or the spiritual kind, was often associated with mental illness. Just as in Ghazali's later discussion of the poem, Nisaburi's account reveals the influence of Platonic Love theory, in that the more rational of the two loves is prompted by a vision of the Good:

> I entered a hospital (*dar al-marda*) in Egypt and saw a *shaykh* who said to me, "What is your name?" "Junayd," I replied. "Are you Iraqi?" he asked. "Yes," I said. "Are you one of the Folk of Love (*min ahl al-mahabba*)?" he asked. "Yes," I said. "Then what is Love (*al-hubb*)?" he asked. "Preferring the Beloved over everything else (*ithar al-mahbub 'ala ma siwahu*)," I answered. He said, "Love is two loves; a love that has a cause and a love that has no cause. As for the love that has a cause, it is the vision of the Good (*ru'yat al-ihsan*). As for the love that has no cause, it is because it is worthy of being loved for itself (*fa-li-annahu ahlun li-an yuhabb*)." Then he recited:

---

186 See the selections from Zabidi, *Ithaf al-sadat al-muttaqin fi sharh Ihya' 'ulum al-din* in Badawi, *Shahidat al-'ishq al-ilahi*, pp. 119–21.

I love you with two loves, a passionate love
And a love of which only you are worthy.

As for the passionate love,
It is a love that preoccupies me with you beyond all else.

But as for the love of which only you are worthy,
I do not see life (*fa-lastu ara al-'aysh*) unless I see you.

Despite that without which there is no life for me,
All praise is yours in both the one and the other.[187]

Besides the attribution to Junayd, Nisaburi's story of the Poem of the Two Loves differs from other versions because the non-rational form of Love described in the poem has more to do with the literary trope of "the romantic fool" than with Sufi doctrine. Although spiritual love is not ruled out in Nisaburi's version, in general the story conforms to Arabic and Persian literary traditions about profane forms of romantic love. This can be seen in the third verse of the poem, which reads, "I do not see life unless I see you." A similar statement is made in the fourth verse, "Despite that without which there is no life for me/ All praise is yours in both the one and the other." The metaphor of both finding and losing one's life in Love's passion recalls the romance of *Layla and Majnun*, the classic story of the romantic fool in Arabic literature. Although the story of Majnun's "mad" love for Layla was used by Sufis to refer metaphorically to the mystic's love of God, it was popular in non-mystical and secular literature as well.

In the posthumously published study, *Majnun: the Madman in Medieval Islamic Society*, Michael Dols traces the trope of the romantic fool in Islamic literature as far back as the ninth century CE. He explains that this trope drew from a combination of Arab cultural notions of passionate love and the writings of Greek authorities on Love theory, such as Plato, Ptolemy, and Galen.[188] The influence of Plato on Nisaburi's account is apparent in the shaykh's explanation that the love that has a cause is stimulated by the vision of the Good. This is similar to Socrates' description of Love in the *Symposium* as "the love of the everlasting possession of the Good."[189] For Plato as well as

---

187 Nisaburi, *'Uqala' al-majanin*, p. 173.
188 Dols, *Majnun*, pp. 313–19.
189 Plato, *Symposium*, in Jowett, vol. 1, p. 498 (206a).

for the Egyptian protagonist of this story, love of the Good is a lesser form of Love; the greatest Love leads to the vision of Pure Beauty. This must be so because Pure Beauty is the archetype of which the Good is only a reflection. Although Nisaburi attributes his story of the Poem of the Two Loves to the Iraqi Sufi Junayd, there is nothing particularly "Sufi" about the meaning of the poem in this story. Rather, it is more reminiscent of secular discussions of Love in the medieval period and thus belongs to a different genre of Arab–Islamic literature.

Another interesting version of the Poem of the Two Loves also provides a background story that is traced to Egypt but draws on tropes that are found in Christian hagiographies. This version appears in *Masari' al-'ushshaq* (*Battlefields of the Lovers*), by Ja'far ibn Ahmad al-Sarraj of Baghdad (d. 1106 CE).[190] This collection of anecdotes about passionate love combines elements from both religious and non-religious types of literature. For this reason, it has been compared to Ibn al-Khatib's *Rawdat al-ta'rif*, which also discusses both sacred and profane views of Love.[191] In his book, Sarraj traces the origin of the Poem of the Two Loves to another famous Sufi, Dhu'l-Nun al-Misri ("The Egyptian," d. 859 CE). The figure of Dhu'l-Nun is well known in Sufi literature, both for his mystical teachings and for his encounters with Sufi women.[192] However, most of the women that he meets in these stories are not named, and thus must be seen as literary tropes. Such is also the case for the unnamed woman ascetic that Dhu'l-Nun meets on the coast of the Mediterranean Sea in Sarraj's story.

> [Dhu'l-Nun said:] One day I was walking along the edge of the sea when I saw a slave woman (*jariya*) wearing garments of hair; she was emaciated and had a withered appearance. I drew close to her to hear what she was saying and saw that she was overcome with sadness and grief. Suddenly, a wind blew up and roiled the waves, so that some fish appeared. The woman screamed and fell to the ground. When

---

190 See the reference to this work in Bell, *Love Theory in Later Hanbalite Islam*, pp. 9–10. See also, Mustafa 'Abd al-Wahid, *Dirasat al-hubb fi-l-adab al-'arabi* (Cairo: Dar al-Ma'arif, 1972), vol. 2, pp. 311–408.

191 While Bell (ibid.) recognizes the influence of *Masari' al-'ushshaq* on Hanbali writers such as Ibn al-Jawzi, he considers it haphazardly organized and ignores both its Sufi content and Sarraj's use of chains of transmission for its anecdotes. While some of these chains of transmission may be spurious, the possibility remains that they could provide important new information on a number of Sufi traditions.

192 See, for example, R. Cornell's Introduction to Sulami, *Early Sufi Women*, pp. 15–16, and Knysh, *Islamic Mysticism*, pp. 39–42.

she awoke, she cried out weeping and said: "My Lord! Through you the Near Ones attain intimacy in their places of retreat. For the sake of your greatness the fish swim in the swelling sea. For the sake of the glory of your holiness the pounding waves crash on the shore. You are the one before whom the dark of night, the light of day, the encircling sphere, the swelling sea, the shining moon, and the glistening stars all prostrate themselves. Everything has its appointed measure, because you are the Most High, the All-Conquering!"[193]

After saying these words, the woman on the beach next recites two poems about Love. The second poem is the Poem of the Two Loves. Sarraj's version of this poem is much the same as Makki's, except that the phrase "passionate love" (*hubb al-hawa*) in Makki's version is replaced by "affectionate love" (*hubb al-widad*) in the later version. Both versions, however, teach the same lesson: this is to differentiate a greater form of love from a lesser form of love. Sarraj's account ends with the statement that after reciting the poem, the woman "gasped and then left the world" (*thuma shahiqat shahqatan fa-idha hiya faraqat al-dunya*). While Dhu'l-Nun stands in surprise over the woman's body, a group of women suddenly appear and prepare her for burial. At the end of the story, Dhu'l-Nun leads the women in a funeral prayer for the deceased ascetic on the beach.[194]

The hagiographical tropes in this account from *Masari' al-'ushshaq* are reminiscent of the "fools for Christ" stories of early Christianity. When a woman appears in these Christian stories, she is most often an ascetic and a penitent, a former sinner who has renounced the World for the love of God. A number of such stories appeared in the seventh century CE and became widely popular in the Middle East.[195] One of the most famous of these stories is the legend of Pelagia of Antioch. The description of the woman ascetic's hair shirt and emaciated body in Sarraj's account recalls a passage in the *Life of Pelagia* where James the Deacon describes Pelagia in the following way: "The joints of her holy bones, all fleshless, were visible beneath her skin through emaciation brought on by ascetic practices. Indeed the whole

---

193 al-Sarraj, *Masari' al-'ushshaq*, vol. 1, p. 274.
194 Ibid., p. 275.
195 Patricia Cox Miller, "Is There a Harlot in This Text? Hagiography and the Grotesque," in Dale B. Martin and Patricia Cox Miller, *The Cultural Turn in Late Ancient Studies: Gender, Asceticism, and Historiography* (Durham, NC and London: Duke University Press, 2005), p. 88; the *vitae* of Mary of Egypt and Pelagia of Antioch were translated into several languages and were well known in the early Islamic Middle East.

complexion of her body was coarse and dark like sackcloth, as the result of her strenuous penance."[196] The all-consuming love of God of the woman on the beach also brings to mind other Christian women ascetics such as Shirin of Iraq. It was said of Shirin: "Despising the whole world out of love for God and considering it as mere refuse, in order to gain Christ she rejected and pushed aside everything else, attaching herself totally to him with a love that was without any guile as she lived out the perfect life of asceticism in all its rigor."[197]

The depiction of the woman ascetic on the beach as a female slave is also a trope that appears in Christian writings on asceticism. As Dale B. Martin notes in his book *Slavery as Salvation*, the trope of slavery conveys a dual meaning. First, it symbolizes the ascetic's former enslavement to worldly passions. Second, the ascetic transforms her passions through acts of self-denial into a new form of "liberated" slavery in the service of God.[198] Once the female fool for Christ is "discovered" by a male observer, she dies and is prepared for burial. This too happens in Sarraj's account when a group of women appear in order to bury their holy sister.[199]

A revised version of this story would appear a century later in *al-Kawkab al-durri fi manaqib Dhi'l-Nun al-Misri* (*The Glistening Sphere in the Exploits of Dhu'l-Nun the Egyptian*) by the famous Andalusian Sufi Muhammad (Muhyiddin) Ibn al-'Arabi (d. 1240 CE). This little-known work of hagiography, which was translated into French by Roger Deladrière in 1988, was written by Ibn 'Arabi as a testimonial to Dhu'l-Nun, whom he viewed as one of the founders of his approach to Sufism. In Ibn 'Arabi's version of the story, Dhu'l-Nun and a male companion meet what they believe to be a male ascetic in the "desert of the Israelites" (*tih Bani Isra'il*). After discovering that the ascetic is in fact a woman, a lively exchange ensues, at the end of which the woman explains her doctrine of Love in the following way:

---

196 Sebastian Brock and Susan Ashbrook Harvey (eds and trans.), *Holy Women of the Syrian Orient* (Berkeley, Los Angeles, and London: University of California Press, 1987), p. 60.
197 Ibid., p. 179.
198 See Dale B. Martin, *Slavery as Salvation: The Metaphor of Slavery in Pauline Christianity* (New Haven, CT and London: Yale University Press, 1990). See also, R. Cornell's Introduction to Sulami, *Early Sufi Women*, pp. 54–8. In this work, I discuss the "theology of servitude," a concept which was shared alike by early Christian lovers of Christ and Muslim lovers of Allah.
199 This trope can be seen in several of the *vitae* recounted in Brock and Harvey, *Women of the Syrian Orient*. In the story of Mary of Egypt, a lion appears to help the monk Zosimas bury the saint. See also Miller, "Is There a Harlot in This Text?," p. 89.

"For me, Love is a beginning and an attainment. Its beginning is when the heart is fervently given over to the remembrance of the Beloved; it consists of a constant sadness and an ardent desire without end. When [the lovers] attain the summit of Love, and are put to the test in their solitude, they are released from most acts of obedience."[200] Just as in the version of the story from *Masari' al-'ushshaq*, in Ibn 'Arabi's version the woman collapses and dies after reciting the Poem of the Two Loves. However, the version of the Poem of the Two Loves that is reproduced in Ibn 'Arabi's story is not that of Sarraj, but of Makki.

Ibn 'Arabi's rendition of the story of Dhu'l-Nun and the woman on the beach appeared once again in the fourteenth century CE in the hagiographical anthology *al-Rawd al-fa'iq* (*The Excellent Garden*) by the Egyptian prosopographer Sa'id al-Hurayfish.[201] Hurayfish's version of the story is identical to Ibn 'Arabi's up to the point where the woman ascetic explains her doctrine of Love to Dhu'l-Nun. This part of the story, which is central to Ibn 'Arabi's version, is left out by Hurayfish, probably because of the suggestion in the original that the enraptured lovers of God can ignore the Law ("they are released from most acts of obedience"). Another difference between these versions is in the Poem of the Two Loves itself. For some unknown reason, Hurayfish eliminates the reference to two loves in the first verse while retaining the suggestion of two loves in the remainder of the poem.

Hurayfish's version of the Poem of the Two Loves also differs from other versions in that he rearranges the verses in a way that transgresses the original poem's poetic style. He changes the first verse of the poem to read, "Your love is the Beloved of the Folk of Passion/ and a love for which only you are worthy." He also changes the middle of the poem to describe the lesser form of Love as a form of remembrance that preoccupies the lover with the Beloved to the exclusion of everything else. This creates some confusion as to the poem's ultimate meaning. Remembrance (*dhikr*), which Plato associates with the higher form of Love, now seems to be associated with the lower form of love, whereas passion is associated with the higher form of love. Finally, at the end of the poem Hurayfish adds two additional verses, most likely of his own composition: "Oh Beloved of the Heart, I have nothing without you/ So

---

200 Ibn 'Arabi, *La Vie merveilleuse de Dhu-l-Nun l'Égyptien*, trans. Roger Deladrière (Paris: Éditions Sindbad, 1988), pp. 256–8; Ibn 'Arabi seems to indicate in a note that follows this story that the anecdote originated with Ibn al-Jawzi. However, it is not contained in *Sifat al-safwa*, Ibn al-Jawzi's major work on hagiography. Whether or not it can be found in another of his works, I cannot say with certainty.
201 Hurayfish, *al-Rawd al-fa'iq*, p. 183.

have mercy today on the sinner who comes to you. Oh my hope, my solace, and my happiness/ My heart has refused everything but you." Although Hurayfish does not say explicitly that Rabi'a al-'Adawiyya composed the Poem of the Two Loves, this is strongly implied by its inclusion in the section on Rabi'a in *al-Rawd al-fa'iq* and by the fact that the woman who is depicted as composing the poem does not die after she recites it to Dhu'l-Nun.

b. The Poem of the Intimate Gift

The second famous poem on Love that has been attributed to Rabi'a al-'Adawiyya was originally attributed to Rabi'a bint Isma'il of Damascus, the wife of the Sufi Ahmad ibn Abi al-Hawari.[202] Ibn Abi al-Hawari was a disciple of Abu Sulayman al-Darani (d. 830 CE), a famous early Sufi who was originally from Basra but later moved to Daraya, a village near Damascus.[203] Ibn Abi al-Hawari was also from Basra and moved to Syria with his teacher. After their arrival in Syria, Darani, a celibate ascetic who normally forbade his disciples from marrying, allowed Ibn Abi al-Hawari to marry Rabi'a bint Isma'il, a rich widow who was the disciple of a woman ascetic named Hukayma. Hukayma was Rabi'a al-'Adawiyya's contemporary and seems to have played a similar role as a teacher in Damascus to that of Rabi'a in Basra. According to the short notice on her in Sulami's Book of Sufi Women, she taught a path of asceticism, celibacy and devotion to God that was very similar to Rabi'a's. Sulami refers to her as *ustadh*, the masculine Arabic term for "teacher." This unusual term, which may imply that she had a school of disciples, is equivalent in many ways to the term *mu'addiba*, by which Sulami refers to Rabi'a al-'Adawiyya.[204]

Because of the similarity of their names, accounts of Rabi'a bint Isma'il of Syria are often mistaken for accounts of Rabi'a al-'Adawiyya. In fact, in some accounts Rabi'a of Basra's name is given as "Rabi'a bint Isma'il."[205]

---

202 Ahmad ibn Abi al-Hawari was known for transmitting traditions about Christian ascetics. See Sulami, *Tabaqat al-sufiyya*, pp. 98–102; Isfahani, *Hilya'* vol. 10, pp. 5–33; Ibn al-Jawzi, *Sifat al-safwa*, vol. 2, pp. 836–7, and Massignon, *Essay*, pp. 152–8.
203 For information on Abu Sulayman al-Darani, see Smith, *An Early Mystic of Baghdad*, pp. 76–7; Massignon, *Essay*, pp. 152–4; Sulami, *Tabaqat al-sufiyya*, pp. 75–82; Isfahani, *Hilya'*, vol. 9, pp. 254–80, and Ibn al-Jawzi, *Sifat al-safwa*, vol. 2, pp. 828–34.
204 Sulami, *Early Sufi Women*, pp. 126–7. The fact that the term *ustadh* appears in the masculine form indicates that Hukayma attained the status of a "man" in her wisdom.
205 Ibn al-Jawzi claims that Sulami said that the fathers of both Rabi'a's were named Isma'il. However, this claim seems to be false because it does not appear in Sulami's Book

Abu Talib al-Makki drew attention to the separate existence of the two Rabi'as in *Qut al-qulub*, saying of Rabi'a bint Isma'il, "Her excellence among the people of Syria is comparable to that of Rabi'a al-'Adawiyya among the people of Basra."[206] Rabi'a bint Isma'il's first marriage may have been the source of mistaken reports about Rabi'a al-'Adawiyya's marriage and widowhood, as claimed by Hurayfish and others. Makki describes Rabi'a bint Isma'il as a widow and says that she donated her inheritance of 300,000 gold dinars to Abu Sulayman al-Darani and his disciples.[207] Ibn al-Jawzi, who relied on an earlier source for his information, puts Rabi'a bint Isma'il's inheritance at the lower but still significant figure of 7,000 silver dirhams.[208] As noted earlier in this chapter, one of the most significant features of Rabi'a bint Isma'il's asceticism was her adherence to the Syrian Christian practice of pseudo-marriage, in which she and Ibn Abi al-Hawari lived not as husband and wife, but as "brother" and "sister." This practice is reported by Ibn al-Jawzi in *Sifat al-safwa*. An important early source for the information transmitted by Ibn al-Jawzi on Rabi'a bint Isma'il was the traditionist Ibn Abi al-Dunya (d. 894 CE). It is from Ibn Abi al-Dunya that we learn via Ibn al-Jawzi that Rabi'a al-'Adawiyya and Rabi'a bint Isma'il may have been confused with each other as early as the second half of the ninth century CE.[209]

After the Poem of the Two Loves, the "Poem of the Intimate Gift" is the most famous poem attributed to Rabi'a al-'Adawiyya. Unlike the Poem of the Two Loves, whose text varies from version to version, the Poem of the Intimate Gift has been transmitted in a standardized version that hardly ever varies. This may indicate that it originally came from a written source. For example, in the recently published *Diwan Rabi'a al-'Adawiyya* by the Syrian Muwaffaq Fawzi al-Jabr (1999), as well as in the popular biography *Rabi'a al-'Adawiyya* by the Egyptian Muhammad 'Atiyya Khamis (1955), one finds the same version of the poem that appears in Ibn al-Jawzi's *Sifat al-safwa* from twelfth-century Baghdad.

---

of Sufi Women. See R. Cornell, *Early Sufi Women*, pp. 138–41 and Ibn al-Jawzi Appendix, pp. 314–15.
206 Makki, *Qut al-qulub*, vol. 2, p. 413.
207 Ibid.
208 Ibn al-Jawzi Appendix to Sulami, *Early Sufi Women*, pp. 316–17.
209 This can be inferred from Ibn Abi al-Dunya's careful specification of their names. See the comment in Ibn al-Jawzi, *Sifat al-safwa*, Appendix to Sulami, *Early Sufi Women*, pp. 314–15.

I have made you the one who speaks to me in the depths of my soul,
But I made my body lawful for the one who desires to be with me.

My body is my intimate gift to my worldly companion,
But my heart's beloved is my true intimate in the depths of my soul.[210]

The main difference between the modern versions of the Poem of the Intimate Gift and that of Ibn al-Jawzi is that most modern accounts attribute the poem to Rabi'a al-'Adawiyya of Basra whereas Ibn al-Jawzi attributes the poem to Rabi'a bint Isma'il of Damascus. Although we cannot be certain without further textual evidence, Ibn al-Jawzi may have derived this attribution from Ibn Abi al-Dunya. However, if the Poem of the Intimate Gift was attributed to Rabi'a bint Isma'il at such an early date, why have so many writers attributed it to Rabi'a al-'Adawiyya? What might have been the source for the attribution of this poem to the wrong Rabi'a? Abu 'Abd al-Rahman al-Sulami mentions both Rabi'a al-'Adawiyya and Rabi'a bint Isma'il in his Book of Sufi Women but attributes no poetry to either of them. However, a possible source for the confusion between the two Rabi'as can be found in a work that was contemporaneous with Sulami's Book of Sufi Women and was written in the same city of Nishapur. This work is *Tahdhib al-asrar* (*The Primer of Secrets*) by 'Abd al-Malik al-Khargushi (d. 1016 CE). Khargushi was an important Sufi of Nishapur who appears to have been a rival of Sulami.[211] *Tahdhib al-asrar* is currently the earliest extant source for the Poem of the Intimate Gift because it predates Ibn al-Jawzi's *Sifat al-safwa* by nearly two centuries. In his chapter on the Sufi doctrine of Intimacy (*uns*), Khargushi states: "Ahmad ibn Abi al-Hawari said: Rabi'a used to experience many spiritual states (*ahwal*). Sometimes Love (*hubb*) overcame her; sometimes Intimacy (*uns*) overcame her; sometimes Fear (*khawf*) overcame her." The reader is not told which Rabi'a is meant in this passage. The report then goes on to cite three poems by Rabi'a, one for each of the three spiritual states

---

210 Appendix to Sulami, *Early Sufi Women*, pp. 316–17 and Ibn al-Jawzi, *Sifat al-safwa*, vol. 2, pp. 871–2; see also, Muwaffaq Fawzi al-Jabr, *Diwan Rabi'a al-'Adawiyya wa akhbaruha* (Damascus: Dar Ma'add and Dar al-Namir, 1999), pp. 57, 78–9, and Muhammad 'Atiyya Khamis, *Rabi'a al-'Adawiyya* (Cairo: Dar Karam, 1955), p. 62.
211 The rivalry between Khargushi and Sulami can be inferred from the similarity of their teachings and their use of the same sources, as well as by the fact that only Sulami's father but not Sulami himself is mentioned in *Tahdhib al-asrar*.

mentioned by Ibn Abi al-Hawari. The Poem of the Intimate Gift is Rabi'a's poem for the state of Intimacy.[212]

It is easy to imagine how a reader who was unfamiliar with Ahmad ibn Abi al-Hawari and Rabi'a bint Isma'il might mistake Khargushi's account of an unspecified Rabi'a as referring to Rabi'a al-'Adawiyya. In fact, it has long been common for Sufi authors to attribute any unspecified reference to a Sufi woman named Rabi'a to Rabi'a al-'Adawiyya. A similar attribution of the Poem of the Intimate Gift to an unspecified Rabi'a appears in the treatise *'Awarif al-ma'arif* (*The Ways of Discernment*) by Abu Hafs 'Umar al-Suhrawardi (d. 1234 CE).[213] Suhrawardi was head of the Sufis of Baghdad and was an ambassador and advisor for the Abbasid Caliph al-Nasir (d. 1225 CE).[214] Because of his influence on the development of orthodox mystical doctrines in Islam, *'Awarif al-ma'arif* was often attached as an appendix to Ghazali's *Ihya' 'ulum al-din*. Like Khargushi, Suhrawardi gives no indication that the Rabi'a who composed the Poem of the Intimate Gift was anyone other than Rabi'a al-'Adawiyya. Thus, the uninformed reader is led to assume that Rabi'a of Basra wrote the poem. Because of the wide popularity of *'Awarif al-ma'arif* throughout the Islamic world, it is reasonable to suppose that this work may have been another source for the misattribution of the Poem of the Intimate Gift to Rabi'a al-'Adawiyya.

However, the misattribution of this poem to the wrong Rabi'a reveals more than just a case of mistaken identity. It also illustrates the uncritical attitude toward tradition that has characterized Sufi literature for centuries. Upon careful consideration of the text of the Poem of the Intimate Gift, it makes little sense to attribute it to Rabi'a al-'Adawiyya. The second line of the poem, "I made my body lawful for the one who desires to be with me," alludes to a sexual experience and possible marriage that would be alien to the celibate Rabi'a al-'Adawiyya as she appears in early Sufi literature. We have already seen in this chapter how the earliest accounts of Rabi'a agree that she was celibate and that she practiced an ascetic form of devotion that left no room for anyone but God. The third line of the poem, "My body is my intimate gift to my worldly companion," confirms that the author of the

---

212 Khargushi, *Tahdhib al-asrar*, p. 80.
213 See, for example, Abu Hafs 'Umar al-Suhrawardi, *'Awarif al-ma'arif*, appended to various editions of Ghazali, *Ihya' 'ulum al-din*. The attribution of The Poem of the Intimate Gift to an unspecified "Rabi'a" appears in Chapter 61, *Dhikr al-ahwal wa sharhiha* (*Mention of the Spiritual States and Their Explanation*).
214 On Abu Hafs 'Umar al-Suhrawardi and his influence on Sufi doctrine, see Schimmel, *Mystical Dimensions of Islam*, pp. 244-7.

poem most likely had a worldly companion and that she was intimate with him. By contrast, early Sufi traditions concur that Rabi'a al-'Adawiyya was celibate and that her male students such as Sufyan al-Thawri were not intimate with her in this way.

Clearly, the only Rabi'a whose life story provides a fitting background for the Poem of the Intimate Gift is Rabi'a bint Isma'il of Damascus. If Makki and Ibn al-Jawzi are correct, the Syrian Rabi'a did in fact have a male companion for whom she made her body lawful. This was her first husband, whose inheritance she gave to Abu Sulayman al-Darani and his disciples. Significantly, Darani's disciple Ibn Abi al-Hawari is the source for the account about the Poem of the Intimate Gift in Khargushi's *Tahdhib al-asrar*. The later account by Ibn al-Jawzi depicts Rabi'a bint Isma'il as unsure about how to balance her obligations to her husband and her obligations to God. She tries to resolve this conflict by encouraging her second husband to take another wife so that she can maintain their spiritual pseudo-marriage without compromising herself sexually. A similar sense of conflict is expressed in the Poem of the Intimate Gift. The author of the poem allows her body to be possessed by her worldly companion; however, only God, her "true intimate," has the right to possess her heart. The appeal of this poem for many generations of Sufis, both male and female, is that it eloquently expresses the dilemma of the devotee who struggles to give the proper measure of devotion both to God and to a worldly partner at the same time. How is a Sufi woman to give herself completely to both God and her husband without the dilemma of what the Qur'an refers to as "two hearts in one body"?

Chapter 4

Rabiʿa the Sufi

"Verily, the Knower of God (*ʿarif*) asks God to grant him a heart. So [God] grants it to him from Himself. When he possesses the heart, he then offers it back to his Lord and Master, so that in [God's] repossession of it he will be protected and will be veiled in its concealment from created beings."
—Rabiʿa al-ʿAdawiyya in Khargushi, *Tahdhib al-asrar*

"The fruit of true knowledge (*maʿrifa*) is constant orientation toward God (*iqbal*)."
—Rabiʿa al-ʿAdawiyya in Khargushi, *Tahdhib al-asrar* and Sulami, *Dhikr al-niswa al-mutaʿabbidat al-sufiyyat*

I. THE LADY RECONSIDERED: CAN WE SEE THE REAL "RABIʿA THE SUFI"?

In a famous 1998 article titled "The Lady Vanishes," the scholar of early Christianity Elizabeth A. Clark argued that the depiction of women saints in early Christian hagiography exhibited a "reality effect" that gave these depictions an aura of factuality that was due more to the literary tropes they employed than to actual facts.[1] Hayden White has also argued that the authors

---

1 Elizabeth A. Clark, "The Lady Vanishes: Dilemmas of a Feminist Historian after the 'Linguistic Turn,'" *Church History*, 67 (1), 1998, pp. 1–31; the term "reality effect" (*l'effet du réel*) comes from the French literary theorist Roland Barthes. This concept will be taken up again in Chapter 5, in the discussion of Farid al-Din al-ʿAttar's *vita* of Rabiʿa.

of historical works are often more concerned with the moral of the story than with the details of the story, and thus may endow certain events or depictions with special symbolic or ideological significance.[2] A similar phenomenon can be seen when Muslim hagiographers construct the mythical image of a saint such as Rabi'a al-'Adawiyya. As Clark states in her article, "Readers are... led to ascribe considerable truth to the account because so many 'effects of the real' have been summoned up."[3] The concept of the "reality effect" is similar to the concept of "narrative validity" that was discussed in the Introduction to this book. The mutual reinforcement of the elements of a master narrative and the archetypal characters, relationships and situations they invoke often conspire to give the narrative an aura of validity or factuality that may not be objectively real.

The argument that Elizabeth Clark makes in her article is especially relevant to the study of the Rabi'a narratives because the particular "reality effect" that she focuses on is the tendency of early Christian writers to depict women saints as teachers of wisdom. As we saw in Chapter 1, the trope of Rabi'a as a teacher of wisdom is also a central theme of the Rabi'a narratives. As an example of the "reality effect," Clark examines Gregory of Nyssa's (d. 395 CE) description of his sister St Macrina. Gregory calls Macrina "my teacher," just as Sufyan al-Thawri does for Rabi'a in Sulami's Book of Sufi Women. Like Rabi'a as well, Macrina is depicted as caring for the human condition and the life of the soul, and her approach to God is based on a theology of Love.[4] Perhaps the most striking similarity between these two figures can be seen in the following observation made by Clark: "Macrina is modeled on Socrates' muse Diotima of the *Symposium*, while her words in the dialogue *On the Soul and the Resurrection* owe much to Plato's *Phaedo*."[5]

As we have seen in the previous chapter, virtually the same assertion can be made about the trope of Rabi'a the Lover as expressed by Abu Talib al-Makki. Clark argues that the trope of "Wisdom As A Woman" in Christian hagiography originated with the classical Greek concept of *Sophia* (a personified feminine term for wisdom) and *hochmah*, the Hebrew term

---

2   See Hayden White, "The Fictions of Factual Representation," in idem, *Tropics of Discourse*, pp. 121–34.
3   Clark, "The Lady Vanishes," p. 21.
4   Ibid., p. 23.
5   Ibid., p. 24. I came up with my own theory of the parallels between Diotima and Rabi'a al-'Adawiyya independently, before discovering Elizabeth Clark's article.

for wisdom, which is also feminine.⁶ Since early Christian literary culture drew from both Greco-Roman and Jewish antecedents, it makes sense to suggest that early Christian writers would feminize the concept of wisdom just as their predecessors did. Because of this trope, Clark argues, one could characterize the theology expressed in works such as Gregory of Nyssa's dialogues of Macrina as "Sophialogy."⁷ The wisdom expressed in the tropes of Rabi'a the Teacher and Rabi'a the Lover could easily be called "Sophialogy" as well.

However, Elizabeth Clark's article also raises an important historiographical question. She concludes from the literary origins of the Woman as Wisdom trope that the "reality effect" it creates obscures the actual women in early Christian hagiography from view. For Clark, Gregory of Nyssa's depiction of St Macrina says very little about the "real" Macrina. Instead, it reveals Gregory appropriating his sister's voice by "writing as a woman."⁸ Clark sees the Woman as Wisdom trope as merely designed to legitimate the philosophical, theological, or political agendas of male hagiographers. In other words, the trope provides a cover behind which men can "think through various troubling intellectual and theological problems that confronted male theologians."⁹ On this basis, Clark concludes that the female teachers of wisdom in early Christian hagiography are not real women at all; rather, they are figural "women." Rather than a real person, the "wise woman" in such stories is merely the "inversed alter ego" of the male writer.¹⁰ If we apply Clark's theory to the case of Rabi'a al-'Adawiyya, we once again are faced with the key historiographical question discussed at the beginning of this book: Is there any way to see the "real" Rabi'a behind her figural representation?

I believe that one way to answer this question is to recall a point made by Hayden White but has been overlooked by many of his readers: Just

---

6   If one were to follow Garth Fowden's suggestion discussed in Chapter 1 and extend the periodization of late antiquity through the first centuries of Islam, then one could also add *hikma*, the Arabic term for wisdom, to Clark's pair of *sophia* and *hochmah*.
7   Clark, "The Lady Vanishes," p. 24.
8   Ibid., p. 27.
9   Ibid.
10 Ibid., p. 26. The Moroccan scholar of Arabic literature Abdellatif Kilito makes a similar point when he speaks of the need in medieval Arabic literature to attach a statement "to a speaker universally accepted as an authority. A text is thus an utterance both authorized and authoritative, solidly moored to an author." The men who wrote as women in medieval Islamic literature could not speak for themselves. Thus, the "wise women" through whom they spoke became their figurative "doubles." See Kilito, *The Author and His Doubles*, p. 6.

because some historians employ literary tropes and quasi-novelistic forms of representation, this does not necessarily mean that their works are fictional. Fiction is defined more by content than by form. In the essay, "The Question of Narrative in Contemporary Historical Theory," White stresses the the fact that history writing and fiction writing start from different premises:

> What distinguishes "historical" from "fictional" stories is first and foremost their content, rather than their form. The content of historical stories is real events, events that really happened, rather than imaginary events, events invented by the narrator... The form of the discourse, the narrative, adds nothing to the content of the representation; rather, it is a simulacrum of the structure and process of real events ... The story told in the narrative is a mimesis of the story lived in some region of historical reality, and insofar as it is an accurate imitation, it is to be considered a truthful account thereof.[11]

I understand this passage to mean that both reality (in the sense of an accurate representation of an event) and the "reality effect" can coexist in the same narrative. Students of history and hagiography—which, despite the opinion of some positivists, is a genre of history—should not allow the ideal of objectivity to lead them into the blind alley of artificial and overly simplistic "either–or" dichotomies. It is not always the case that historical representation is either true or false. Because historical representation is a matter of interpretation, the actual situation is more often "both–and."[12] According to Hayden White's view of historiography, one can argue that the use of tropes and other literary devices in hagiographical accounts does not necessarily mean that everything said about a "wise woman" such as Rabi'a al-'Adawiyya or St Macrina is untrue. The figurative construction of the narrative does not by itself imply that the content of the narrative is false. Even a trope may have some basis in fact. For example, although the trope of Rabi'a the Lover was developed two centuries after Rabi'a's death by Abu Talib al-Makki, the fact that al-Harith al-Muhasibi cited a statement about love by Rabi'a 150 years

---

11 Hayden White, *The Content of the Form: Narrative Discourse and Historical Representation* (Baltimore: Johns Hopkins University Press, 1987), p. 27.
12 On the basis of this argument, I disagree with Jawid Mojaddedi's contention that the authors of Muslim hagiographies were not concerned with "the preservation and transmission of material in its original form." As we have seen in the previous chapters, this statement is belied by the reliance on *isnads* by Sufi prosopographers like Ibn al-Junayd and Sulami. See idem, *The Biographical Tradition in Sufism*, pp. 180–1.

before Makki can be taken as evidence that the "real" Rabi'a probably did practice some kind of Love mysticism. Therefore, we must acknowledge that some element of the real exists in the story, even if it is embellished for narrative purposes. If history is understood to be a matter of representation and interpretation, then the question to be asked of the figural representation of a saint or other half-legendary figure is not only whether it contains anything real at its core but also, if some aspect of reality exists in the representation, how does it relate to the work's rhetorical form?

Elizabeth Clark bases her argument about the figurative nature of St Macrina on Gregory of Nyssa's reproduction of her statements in formal, classical styles of rhetoric that she could not have learned without an advanced education. Since she did not have such an education, Clark concludes that what Macrina supposedly "says" in Gregory's narratives are actually Gregory's words and not her own. The same can also be said about many of the statements that have been attributed to Rabi'a al-'Adawiyya. In the previous chapters, I have noted several instances in which Sufi writers made up statements that were supposedly by Rabi'a without reference to any original text. However, other accounts about Rabi'a do not show the same evidence of fictionalized composition. For example, some early prosopographers from both Sufi and non-Sufi backgrounds (such as Ibn al-Junayd and Ibn Abi al-Dunya) cite full or nearly full chains of transmission for their information. This tells us that they based their portrayals of Rabi'a on oral and/or written testimony. Thus, they saw themselves as traditionists more than storytellers, and their different portrayals of Rabi'a were not matters of "fact" versus "fiction."

Although it is true that some accounts of Rabi'a—like those of St Macrina—were due to men "thinking through various troubling intellectual and theological problems," we should not automatically dismiss all hagiographical accounts of her as factually unreliable. Doing so would amount to committing the type of category mistake that critical historiography is supposed to avoid. Just because we cannot prove that an account is true does not necessarily mean that it is false. When Makki created the trope of Rabi'a the Lover to illustrate his theory of Love as a form of knowledge, he was indeed "a man writing a woman," just as Gregory of Nyssa wrote the trope of St Macrina the Wisdom Teacher. However, as noted previously, the much earlier account of Muhasibi suggests that the trope of Rabi'a the Lover was partly based on "real" evidence, even if Makki's representation went beyond the evidence itself. The same process of tropological construction continues in the Rabi'a narratives today. For this reason, when assessing these narratives, it is important to make a distinction between the early accounts that recorded her sayings on the basis of oral traditions and later narratives that were designed to make a theoretical point (like Makki's) or that embellished earlier accounts to create a fictional life story (as we shall see with 'Attar).

Despite Elizabeth Clark's useful warning about the unreliability of tropological and gendered discourses, one should not automatically assume that just because a man wrote about a woman, the woman herself could not be seen. Although Rabi'a's female gender may have played a role in her portrayal as a teacher of Love instead of other aspects of Sufi doctrine, it would be a mistake to draw the conclusion that Abu Talib al-Makki made Rabi'a into a love mystic only because she was a woman. Feminist theory on the politics of gender and representation is a double-edged sword. On the one hand, it correctly warns women historians not to allow our interest in creating a hermeneutic of remembrance ("the lady must not vanish") to blind us to the fact that what seem to be women's voices are sometimes not women's voices at all.[13] On the other hand, we must ask ourselves: Were notable women in premodern times always destined to be merely the mouthpieces of male ghostwriters?

When I first began my research for this book I assumed that Rabi'a al-'Adawiyya was only a narrative construct. Like Elizabeth Clark with St Macrina, I did not expect to find an actual person behind the myth. However, I now regard the Rabi'a master narrative as it has developed over the centuries as something like a biographical novel produced by a writer's collective. Evidence suggests that a real woman ascetic from eighth-century Basra lies at the heart of the story but the character constructed through the master narrative is significantly different. Over time, the figure of Rabi'a the ascetic and spiritual mentor of Basra that emerged from oral traditions achieved a more mythical and universal status through the tropes of Rabi'a the Teacher, Rabi'a the Ascetic, Rabi'a the Lover, and Rabi'a the Sufi. However, despite the numerous acts of creative license that have embellished and revised her story, the faint outlines of a distinct person can still be found behind the persona of Rabi'a al-'Adawiyya. Despite the myth that was created, a "real" Rabi'a of Basra actually did teach, did practice asceticism, and did develop a mystical doctrine that was based (at least in part) on the love of God. This historical figure of Rabi'a is what emerges from the earliest accounts. In

---

13 For a more detailed discussion of the concept of "hermeneutic of remembrance" and its application to Sufi *tabaqat* literature, see R. Cornell, *Early Sufi Women*, pp. 48–53.

historiographical terms, to assume that Rabi'a was nothing but a myth would be to deny the very possibility of using tradition as a source for history.

However, the tropes of Rabi'a the Lover and Rabi'a the Sufi must be treated differently from the tropes of Rabi'a the Teacher and Rabi'a the Ascetic. This is because with these former tropes the ascetic and teacher of oral tradition has been replaced to a significant extent by a "new and improved" Rabi'a that is the product of Sufi doctrine. This "doctrinal" Rabi'a is considerably different from the "historical" Rabi'a of oral tradition. Although we know from Muhasibi that the "real" Rabi'a most likely spoke of love and spiritual marriage, the trope of Rabi'a the Lover owes much more to the tenth-century CE interest in Platonically inspired Love theory and Abu Talib al-Makki's Sufi theology of Love. In a similar way, the trope of Rabi'a the Sufi was created retrospectively by later generations of Sufi writers. During Rabi'a's lifetime, the appellation, "Sufi," while not entirely unknown, was seldom used. And when it was used, it did not mean what it means today. Thus, the question to be asked in this chapter is whether there is any empirical validity to the trope of Rabi'a the Sufi? Could the "real" Rabi'a have been what I call in this chapter a "Proto-Sufi?" If so, what did it mean to say that Rabi'a was a "Proto-Sufi?" How was "Proto-Sufism" similar to or different from "Sufism" as it developed in the tenth and eleventh centuries CE?[14]

Despite Rabi'a's reputation as a major figure of early Sufism, such questions are not easy to answer. Margaret Smith avoided them entirely when writing *Rabi'a the Mystic*. In the chapter "The Sufi Doctrine," she does not discuss what Sufism meant in Rabi'a's time. Instead, she provides the reader with an anachronistic discussion of Sufism based on the definitions of Orientalist scholars and Sufi doctrines that were developed long after Rabi'a's death.[15] When referring to Rabi'a's Sufism elsewhere in her book, she similarly analyzes Rabi'a's sayings with concepts formulated by later Sufi writers. Of the five key tropes of the Rabi'a master narrative that are examined in this study, only Rabi'a the Lover and Rabi'a the Ascetic receive significant attention in *Rabi'a the Mystic*.

---

14 In *Islamic Mysticism* Alexander Knysh also uses the term, "proto-Sufi" (p. 9ff.). However, apart from associating the term vaguely with Love mysticism, he does not define it, as I attempt to do in this chapter.
15 See Smith, *Rabi'a* (Oneworld), pp. 71–6 and (Rainbow Bridge), pp. 47–52. Instead of using Rabi'a's own statements, Smith uses quotations from the later Sufis Makki (d. 996 CE), Munawi (d. 1621 CE), Abu Sa'id Abu al-Khayr (d. 1041 CE), Rumi (d. 1273 CE), and Mahmud al-Shabistari (d. 1320 CE). She also uses quotations from the Orientalists R.A. Nicholson and E.J.W. Gibb, and even an early Christian mystic.

Smith's tendency to discuss Rabi'a's Sufism anachronistically and on the basis of later doctrines is by no means unique. Most medieval Sufi hagiographers and almost everyone who has written about Rabi'a after Smith have done the same thing. When Abu 'Abd al-Rahman al-Sulami called Rabi'a a Sufi at the beginning of the eleventh century CE, he assumed that his readers already knew what the term meant. However, recent scholarship has demonstrated that many of the doctrines that characterized Sufism for Sulami were not developed until the ninth and tenth centuries CE, long after Rabi'a's death. Most contemporary historians of Sufism agree that one cannot speak meaningfully about Sufism as a tradition until at least the second half of the ninth century CE.[16]

In this chapter, I shall argue that the essential asceticism ascribed to Rabi'a and some of her contemporaries provided an important bridge between the ascetic pietism of her era and Sufism as it was developed doctrinally in the ninth and tenth centuries CE. Essential asceticism was a key practice of Proto-Sufism. As we saw in the previous chapter, the essential ascetic's devotional focus on God is similar to that of the Love mystic. In addition, the goals of the essential ascetic and the Love mystic are much the same: both strive to attain a close relationship with God. This connection highlights an important aspect of the early Rabi'a narratives. Rather than leading from one trope to another serially as in a teleological chain of development, the tropes of the Rabi'a narrative are more like a cluster or a bundle. It is difficult to conceive of Rabi'a as characterized by any one trope without the others. The tropes of Rabi'a the Ascetic, Rabi'a the Teacher, and Rabi'a the Lover all share important characteristics in common. As this chapter will demonstrate, these tropes also had an intertextual role to play in the development of the trope of Rabi'a the Sufi. Although it is too reductionistic to derive from this intertextuality a "transition theory" from asceticism to Sufism, the phenomenon is significant nonetheless.[17]

---

16 See, for example, Bernd Radtke, "Tasawwuf" in *EI²*; Karamustafa, *Sufism: The Formative Period*, p. 1; Christopher Melchert, "Origins and Early Sufism"; and Knysh, *Islamic Mysticism*, pp. 43–67. Nile Green does not see Sufism becoming a tradition or even a coherent movement until well into the tenth century CE. Idem, *Sufism, A Global History* (Malden, MA and Oxford, UK: Wiley-Blackwell, 2012), p. 22.
17 For "transition theories" of the development of Sufism, see for example, Peter J. Awn, "Sufism," in *The Encyclopedia of Religion, Second Edition*, ed. Lindsay Jones and Charles J. Adams (Mircea Eliade), 15 vols. (Detroit: Macmillan Reference USA, 2005), 13:8809–8825; Radtke, "Tasawwuf" in *EI²*; and Melchert, "Origins and Early Sufism," *op. cit.*

However, there is also another way to view this intertextuality that is less literary and more focused on the relationship between the concept of knowledge and ascetic practices. From an epistemological perspective, essential asceticism, Love mysticism, and Sufism can all be seen as ways of knowledge. On the path to knowledge that begins with essential asceticism, the servant-devotee of God is led by her devotion to focus on God exclusively. As an essential ascetic, all of her practices are for the sake of God, the object of her devotion. Because she is not distracted by instrumental goals, the focus of her asceticism shifts from renunciation of the World to detachment from the World. She comes to realize that any involvement with the World—even to renounce it—is a distraction from God. As her goals change from renunciation for the sake of eschatological rewards (instrumental asceticism) to closeness or intimacy with God (essential asceticism), the rhetoric of Love becomes more appropriate as a form of expression for her asceticism. When her essential asceticism becomes combined with Love mysticism, she takes on a new identity and becomes a "gnostic" or "knower" of God (*al-'arifa bi-llah*). In an aphorism related by Sulami, Rabi'a describes this state as follows: "For everything there is a fruit and the fruit of knowledge is constant orientation [toward God] (*li-kulli shay'in thamaratun wa thamarat al-ma'rifa al-iqbal*)."[18] In this statement, the Arabic term *iqbal* stands both for the ascetic's "turn" toward God and God's "turn" toward the ascetic. In the terminology of Love mysticism, one could say that both lover and Beloved are equally present for each other. Another story that reflects this state describes Rabi'a's comment on the famous aphorism of Jesus from the Sermon on the Mount: "Knock and the door will be opened" (Matt. 7:7–8). "The door is already open," says Rabi'a. "But the question is, who wishes to enter?"[19] Rabi'a's knowledge that the door to God is always open comes from the intimate knowledge of God (*ma'rifa*) that is the goal of both essential asceticism and Love mysticism. It is a special form of knowledge that goes beyond the traditional knowledge associated with the Shari'a or religious dogma (*'aqida*).

I will argue in this chapter that the interrelationship between essential asceticism, Love mysticism, and knowledge of God is the key to understanding the trope of Rabi'a the Sufi. It is also a key part of the concept of Proto-Sufism. As such, it implies that Sufism is most accurately described as a way of knowledge and that this has been the case from its very foundation. This theory is not new, nor is it restricted to Western scholarship. The late

---

18   Sulami, *Early Sufi Women*, pp. 76–7.
19   Ibid., p. 80.

tenth-century CE Sufi Abu Nasr al-Sarraj made the same assertion in *Kitab al-luma' fi-l-tasawwuf*. In this work, Sarraj argues that the Sufis have a special status among the scholars of Islam because of their distinctive approach to knowledge (*wa li-l-sufiyya aydan takhsisun min tabaqat ahl al-'ilm*). Unlike more conventional "knowers of God" (*'ulama'*), they seek out the noblest virtues, conduct research into the loftiest spiritual states and the most excellent practices, and delve deeply into (*mustanbatat*) the most difficult matters of doctrine.[20] According to Sarraj, Sufism was a legitimate doctrinal countercurrent in Islam, in which the specialized knowledge (*ma'rifa*) of the Sufis was contrasted with the more traditional forms of knowledge (*'ilm*) held by exoteric Islamic scholars. Viewing Sufism like Sarraj as a sort of "loyal opposition" or legitimate countercurrent to conventional Islam provides a way for contemporary scholars to take the countercultural aspects of both early Sufism and early Islamic asceticism seriously without necessarily branding these movements as dissident or antinomian.[21]

II. LOCATING RABI'A THE SUFI: WHAT WAS A "SUFI" IN EIGHTH-CENTURY ISLAM?

In a recently published introduction to Sufism Nile Green observed, "It would scarcely be an exaggeration to say that more academic ink has been spilt over the origins of the Sufis than over any other question in Sufi history."[22] A lively debate over Sufi origins has continued in Western scholarship from the beginning of the twentieth century until today. One reason for this debate is because etymological theories of the origin of the term, *Sufi*, do not provide a clear answer to this question. A common theory states that the term originally referred to ascetics who wore woolen (*suf*) garments; another claims that it referred to religious devotees who patterned their lifestyle after the "people of the porch" (*ahl al-suffa*), early Muslim ascetics who prayed and invoked God at the Prophet Muhammad's mosque in Medina; other theories

---

20 Sarraj, *The Kitab al-Luma'*, pp. 13–14.
21 See, for example, Radtke, "Tasawwuf" in *EI²*, who views the *al-sufiyya* of the eighth century CE as a fringe group: "A fringe group of the movement was called Ṣūfiyya in the 2nd/8th century. As opposed to the *religiosi*, antinomian, antisocial and anti-governmental tendencies became noticeable among them." Christopher Melchert ("Origins and Early Sufism," p. 13) characterizes the *al-Sufiyya* as "disreputable, marginal figures, often involved with political opposition and certainly not demonstrably mystics."
22 Green, *Sufism, A Global History*, p. 16.

claim that it referred to those who followed a path of moral and ethical purity (*safa*), or that it referred to those who patterned their spirituality on the Greek philosophical concept of wisdom (Gr. *Sophia*).²³ Not only have Western writers advanced such theories but they can also be found in premodern Muslim works as well, both inside and outside of the Sufi tradition.²⁴ Even the *Sophia-Sufiyya* etymology, which many contemporary Muslims assume to have been the creation of Western Orientalists, was first thought up by a Muslim: its origin can be traced to Abu Rayhan al-Biruni's (d. 1048 CE) *Kitab al-Hind* (*Book of India*).²⁵

Modern attempts to clarify the meaning of the term "Sufi" by relying on generalized definitions of Sufism have also been of little help. For example, Annemarie Schimmel defines early Sufism in *Mystical Dimensions of Islam* (1975) as follows: "Sufism meant, in the formative period, mainly an interiorization of Islam, a personal experience of the central mystery of Islam, that of *tawhid*, 'to declare that God is One.'"²⁶ One problem with Schimmel's definition is that she does not explain what she means by the "formative period." Another problem is that her notion of the interiorization of *tawhid* relies on a theological definition of Sufism that was not developed until relatively late—around the beginning of the tenth century CE.²⁷ A third problem is that the term "Sufism" is itself a Western concept, being a translation of the Arabic word *tasawwuf*, which has its own problematic genealogy.²⁸

---

23 See, for example, Göran Ogén, "Did the Term '*ṣūfī*' Exist before the Sufis?," *Acta Orientalia*, 43, 1983, pp. 33–48. Ogén demonstrates from Syriac texts that the wearing of wool was a common pietistic practice in late antique Christian communities.

24 R.A. Nicholson claimed to have found 78 etymologies for the term "Sufi" in Muslim sources. See R.A. Nicholson, "A Historical Inquiry Concerning the Origin and Development of Sufism," *Journal of the Royal Asiatic Society*, 1906, pp. 303–48.

25 According to Biruni, the term "Sufi" was derived from an incorrect understanding of the Greek word *sophia*, which Muslims linked etymologically to the Arabic terms *suf* and *al-suffa*, explained above. See Ainslee Embree (ed.), *Alberuni's India*, trans. Edward C. Sachau (New York: W.W. Norton and Company, 1971), pp. 33–4.

26 Schimmel, *Mystical Dimensions*, p. 17.

27 The notion that Sufism involves the internalization of *tawhid* as a mystical experience is commonly associated with the figure of Abu al-Qasim al-Junayd (d. 910 CE), who is often credited with being the first Sufi theologian. It can also be found in the contemporaneous doctrines of Sahl al-Tustari (d. 896 CE), a resident of Basra whose teachings influenced Abu Talib al-Makki. In his writings, Tustari speaks of the mystic's encounter with God as a recompense for the internalization of *tawhid*. See Gerhard Böwering, *The Mystical Vision of Existence in Classical Islam: The Qur'anic Hermeneutics of the Sufi Sahl At-Tustari (d. 283/896)* (Berlin and New York: Walter de Gruyter, 1980), pp. 172–5.

28 See Carl W. Ernst, *The Shambhala Guide to Sufism* (Boston and London: Shambhala Books, 1997), pp. 1–31, especially the section, "The Orientalist 'Discovery' of Sufism," pp. 8–17. One should also point out that the term *tasawwuf*, which in Arabic literally

The concept of mysticism has a problematical genealogy too, especially when compared with asceticism.²⁹ Finally and most importantly, Schimmel's definition is not supported by the earliest references to the term "Sufi" in Islamic sources. Although Schimmel's theological definition of Sufism is shared by many Sufis and scholars today, it is not accurate when applied to the origins of Sufism.

Among the earliest extant treatises on Sufism, Sarraj's *Kitab al-luma'* is the most explicit in affirming the problematic genealogy of the term "Sufi." After a section detailing some of the etymologies mentioned above, Sarraj adds another section, "Refutation of one who says that we have not heard mention of [the term] *al-Sufiyya* in the past because it is a neologism" (*al-Radd 'ala man qala lam nasma' bi-dhikri al-sufiyya fi-l-qadim wa huwwa ismun muhdath*).³⁰ The very presence of this discussion proves that the authenticity of Sufism was called into question early in its history. Sarraj acknowledges that the term *al-sufiyya* did not exist in the first two generations of Islam. However, he maintains that the practice of *tasawwuf* in his time was dependent on the Sunna of the Prophet Muhammad, his Companions, and their Successors. As for the term *al-Sufiyya* being a neologism, he says that some people claimed that this term was first coined in Baghdad. Sarraj refutes this assertion by claiming that the early Basra theologian al-Hasan al-Basri (d. 726 CE) once reported seeing a "Sufi" at the Ka'ba in Mecca. When he tried to give the man some money, the "Sufi" refused the gift, saying, "I have four *dawaniq* (3/4 of a dirham) with me and this is sufficient."³¹

This story is important because it indicates that early systematizers of Sufism such as Sarraj dated the first use of the term "Sufi" to the eighth century CE, the same period in which Rabi'a al-'Adawiyya lived. In addition, Sarraj

---

means "doing *suf*" or "practicing woolliness," is meaningless when taken out of the context of Sufism as a tradition. Due to the modern influence of the Western academic field of Religious Studies, today *tasawwuf* is used in Arabic to mean "mysticism" in general.

29 See Gert H. Mueller, "Asceticism and Mysticism: A Contribution Towards the Sociology of Faith," in *International Yearbook for the Sociology of Religion 8: Sociological Theories of Religion/Religion and Language*, ed. Günter Dux, Thomas Luckman and Joachim Matthes (Opladen: Westdeutscher Verlag, 1973), pp. 68–132, cited in Melchert, "Origins and Early Sufism," p. 14 n. 70. For an essay that links the terms *zuhd* and *nusk* (discussed in Chapter 2) with the term "*Sufi*," see Bernd Radkte, "Von den hinderlichen Wirkungen der Extase und dem Wesen der Ignoranz" (On the Debilitating Effects of Ecstasy and the Essence of Ignorance), *Neue kritische Gägne. Zu Stand und Aufgaben der Sufikforschung / New Critical Essays: On the Present State and Future Tasks of the Study of Sufism* (Utrecht: M. Thn. Houstma Sichting, 2005), pp. 251–92.

30 Sarraj, *The Kitab al-Luma'*, Arabic text pp. 21–2.
31 Ibid., p. 22.

associates the earliest Sufis with an ascetic lifestyle, which is well established for Rabi'a. Sarraj further confirms this indirect connection to Rabi'a when he cites a tradition in which Rabi'a's student Sufyan al-Thawri states, "Were it not for Abu Hashim the Sufi, I would not have learned about the worthlessness of ostentation (*daqiq al-riya'*)."[32] This tradition tells us that Sarraj also associated the early "Sufis" with ethical and moral training. It also recalls Rabi'a's pedagogy of *ta'dib*, which formed the basis of the trope of Rabi'a the Teacher discussed in Chapter 1.

Thawri's reference to Abu Hashim "al-Sufi" (d. ca. 776 CE) identifies perhaps the earliest ascetic in Islam to refer to himself as a Sufi. According to Louis Massignon, Abu Hashim was the first person in Islam to refer to himself as a Sufi.[33] This person also appears in Jahiz's treatise *al-Bayan wa-l-tabyin*, which was written nearly 150 years before Sarraj's *Kitab al-luma'*. In Jahiz's book, Abu Hashim is mentioned along with other Sufis named Kilab, Kulayb, Hashim al-Awqas and Salih ibn 'Abd al-Jalil.[34] Jahiz, who was not a Sufi himself, refers to these individuals as ascetic ritualists (*nussak*) and includes them in his book because of the eloquence of their speech.[35] In Chapter 1 it was noted that Jahiz regarded Rabi'a in much the same way, although he did not call her a Sufi. Other information on Abu Hashim can be found in the hagiographical anthology *Hilyat al-awliya'* (*The Ornament of the Saints*) by Abu Nu'aym al-Isfahani (d. 1037 CE). Among the sources that Isfahani consulted were two of the earliest Islamic works on ascetics: *Kitab al-ruhban* by Muhammad ibn al-Husayn al-Burjulani (d. 852 CE) and *Tabaqat al-nussak* by Abu Sa'id ibn al-A'rabi (952–3 CE).

Abu Hashim appears under two different headings in *Hilyat al-awliya'*, which indicates that Isfahani was not sure whether both sets of accounts referred to the same person. In neither entry, however, is he called a Sufi. In one notice, which is based on Ibn al-A'rabi's *Tabaqat al-nussak*, he appears

---

32 Ibid.; Sarraj also reports that before the Prophet Muhammad began to preach Islam, a person known as a "Sufi" once came in from the desert to visit Mecca outside of the normal pilgrimage season; he performed the ritual of circumambulating the Ka'ba and then went back into the desert. This pattern of behavior recalls a common trope in the stories of early Christian anchorites. By recording this story Sarraj seems to suggest that before Islam the term *Sufi* was regarded as a synonym for *hanif* (unaffiliated monotheist).
33 Massignon, *Essay*, p. 105; Massignon reports that Abu Hashim was born in Kufa. Kufa was also the home of Sufyan al-Thawri, Fudayl ibn 'Iyad, and Sufyan ibn 'Uyayna (see Chapter 1). Perhaps for this reason Massignon also assumes that Kufa was the first place where the term "Sufi" was used.
34 Jahiz, *al-Bayan*, vol. 1, p. 195.
35 Ibid., p. 194.

as "Abu Hashim Fadim." In the other notice, which is based on Burjulani's *Kitab al-ruhban*, he appears as "Abu Hashim the Renunciant" (*al-Zahid*). As an ascetic and renunciant, Abu Hashim was a firm believer in the World/Nonworld Dichotomy discussed at the beginning of Chapter 2. This is clearly visible in the following statement of Abu Hashim, which originally came from Burjulani: "God Most High has characterized the World as desolate (*inna Allaha wasama al-dunya bi-l-wahsha*) so that those who seek Him will find solace in its opposite and that those who find satisfaction in Him will reject it. The Folk of the Knowledge of God are alienated [from the World] and are desirous of the Hereafter" (*fa-ahl al-ma'rifa bi-llah fi-ha mutawahhishun wa ila al-akhira mushtaqun*).[36] Abu Hashim is also reported to have said, "If the World is all palaces and gardens and the Hereafter is nothing but caves, the Hereafter would still be more desirable than the World because of its permanence compared with the impermanence of the other."[37] Abu Hashim's use of the term *ahl al-ma'rifa bi-llah*, "The Folk of the Knowledge of God," is significant. Besides providing support for Sarraj's contention that a defining characteristic of Sufism was a distinctive approach to knowledge, it tells us that a group that identified themselves as possessing this type of knowledge existed in Rabi'a's time.

In contrast to Sarraj and Isfahani, al-Harith al-Muhasibi (d. 857 CE) focuses less on knowledge and more on practice when discussing early ninth-century Sufis in *Kitab al-makasib* (*The Book of Outcomes*). This treatise, which was written only a generation or so after Rabi'a's death, is one of the earliest extant works to mention the Sufis as a distinct group. In this work, Muhasibi uses two different terms for the Sufis: *al-sufiyyin*, the plural of *al-sufi*, and *al-mutasawwifa*, literally, "practitioners of *tasawwuf*."[38] The use of this latter term indicates that a distinctive set of "Sufi" doctrines and/or practices had already been conceptualized by the first half of the ninth century CE. Together, both terms tell us that a group of people called "Sufis" existed in the early ninth century and that Muhasibi singled them out from other groups for acting and/or thinking "Sufistically." Muhasibi's reference is of great importance to the historical question of Sufi origins because most recent scholarship has tended to dismiss earlier theories that traced the development of Sufism to this period. For example, Nile Green asserts forcefully in his history of Sufism that "[What]

---

36 Isfahani, *Hilya*, vol. 10, p. 225.
37 Ibid.
38 See, for example, Muhasibi, *Kitab al-makasib*, pp. 205–12. On p. 205 Muhasibi mentions "organized groups of scholars, Hadith transmitters, Qur'an reciters, and practitioners of Sufism" (*asnaf min al-'ulama' wa ahl al-hadith, wa-l-qurra' wa-l-mutasawwifa*).

we do not have yet [in the mid-800s] is a Sufi movement, a characteristic set of doctrines and still less a tradition, all of which would develop only later. For this reason, it makes little sense to speak of 'Sufism' as though such an entity had any meaningful existence at this time."[39] But if this were the case, and Sufism had no meaningful existence in the early 800s, then how could Muhasibi speak of the doctrines and practices of *al-mutasawwifa*?

For Muhasibi, the term "Sufi" referred to renunciants and ascetic ritualists (*zuhhad* and *nussak*), who also specialized in ethical precaution (*wara'*). *Kitab al-makasib* was written as a treatise on ethical precaution and Muhasibi's references to the Sufis mostly appear in the section titled, "Practices of Ethical Precaution among the Predecessors" (*Madhahib al-salaf fi-l-wara'*).[40] A key attribute of the Sufis described in this section is the pursuit of both outward and inward purity. This indicates that the notion of a difference between outward (*zahir*) and inward (*batin*) ascetic practices also existed in the early ninth century CE. Recent scholars of Sufism have suggested that an "inward turn" or a turn toward "the inward life" was a major token of distinction between the "ascetics" and the early "Sufis."[41] Muhasibi's focus on purity also suggests that he was more inclined to link the etymology of the term "Sufi" to *safa*, the Arabic word for purity, than to *suf*, the Arabic word for wool.

In *al-Makasib* Muhasibi identifies three types of ethical precaution (*wara'*) that conform to the Sunna of the Prophet Muhammad and his Companions: (1) a purely social form of *wara'* that entails avoiding all discussion of people and their affairs; (2) a more symbolic form of *wara'* that requires the ascetic to avoid everything that is not unambiguously licit or illicit (*halal* or *haram*) or about which there is moral or ethical doubt (*shubuhat*); (3) a more subtle form of *wara'* that is based on the following hadith of the Prophet Muhammad: "You will not be among the truly God-fearing until you leave aside everything in which there is no harm, out of fear of the harm that may be in it."[42] Those who followed one or more of these practices, says Muhasibi, included an elite group of religious scholars, specialists in Hadith, devotees of the Qur'an, and the "Sufis." He also notes that some sects (*tawa'if*) of Muslims in the city of Basra made the avoidance of morally doubtful things (option 2 above) the basis of their asceticism.

---

39 Green, *Sufism, A Global History*, p. 16.
40 Muhasibi, *Kitab al-makasib*, pp. 205–12.
41 See, for example, Karamustafa, *Sufism, the Formative Period*, p. 2; Melchert calls this inward turn the "Protestant solution." Melchert, "Origins and Early Sufism," p. 13.
42 Muhasibi, *Kitab al-makasib*, p. 205.

Because Muhasibi does not mention Rabi'a al-'Adawiyya in *al-Makasib*, it is not possible to determine which of these practices she may have followed. However, most of the "Sufis" that he identifies followed the third, most inward and subtle form of *wara'*. This practice corresponds to what the Sufi and theologian Abu Hamid al-Ghazali would later refer to as "the renunciation of the permissible" (*al-zuhd fi-l-halal*).[43] Muhasibi particularly liked this form of ethical precaution because it forbade mendicant begging. In his book he associates begging, of which he strongly disapproves, with Rabi'a's eastern contemporary Shaqiq al-Balkhi (see Chapter 1).[44] In fact, many of the individual practices of *wara'* discussed in *al-Makasib* concern the prohibition of actions (like begging) that are deemed inappropriate but are not legally forbidden in Islam. Muhasibi refers to this type of *wara'* as "avoiding that in which there is no explicit harm" (*tark ma la ba's bi-hi*).

Although Muhasibi does not provide a definition of Sufism in *al-Makasib*, it is evident from his references to *al-sufiyyin* and *al-mutasawwifa* that he considered early Sufis to be devoted to the pursuit of both outward and inward purity. This can be seen both in his critiques and in his approval of certain "Sufi" practices. Much of Muhasibi's ethical concern is with the subject of spiritual arrogance. For example, he criticizes as "great ignorance and error" the refusal of some Sufis to take alms if this could be understood as profiting the recipient in any way. The point of his criticism is that these individuals considered themselves too morally pure to accept assistance from anyone.[45]

Muhasibi's portrayal of early Sufis as advocates of ethical purity fits the image of another figure who is often identified as one of this group, Salih ibn 'Abd al-Jalil. Although there is no clear death date for this individual, traditions make him a contemporary of the Abbasid Caliph al-Mahdi, who ruled from 775–85 CE. This would also make Salih a contemporary of Rabi'a al-'Adawiyya, who is alleged to have associated with Sufyan al-Thawri during

---

43   Ibid., pp. 205–6; see also, Ghazali, *Ihya'*, vol. 4, p. 229 (Kitab al-faqr wa al-zuhd); Ghazali attributes the origin of this concept to Ibrahim ibn Adham (d. 778 or 790 CE), an ascetic who also appears prominently in *al-Makasib*. Ghazali's approach to Sufism was strongly influenced by Muhasibi's ethics. For a discussion of this influence, see Smith, *An Early Mystic of Baghdad*, pp. 269–91.
44   According to Muhasibi, Shaqiq al-Balkhi taught that striving to earn a living was forbidden (*haram*) for ascetics because it implied a lack of trust in God. See idem, *al-Makasib*, pp. 194–9.
45   Ibid., p. 207.

the first three years of al-Mahdi's reign (see the discussion in Chapter 1). In fact, an account in Ibn al-Jawzi's *Sifat al-safwa* depicts Salih as visiting Rabi'a, although the lack of a chain of transmission makes it impossible to consider this account as a reliable source.[46] In *Essay on the Origins of the Technical Language of Islamic Mysticism*, Louis Massignon mentions a group of "Shiite Sufiyya" from Kufa, who included the figures Kilab and Kulayb. These same individuals are also identified as "Sufis" by Jahiz along with Abu Hashim al-Sufi and Salih ibn 'Abd al-Jalil.[47] In *Kitab al-bayan wa-l-tabyin* Jahiz reproduces an address by Salih to the Caliph al-Mahdi. This address is worth reproducing in full because some of the terminology that is used seems to confirm Massignon's hypothesis about a group of "Shiite Sufiyya."

> Salih ibn 'Abd al-Jalil came to see the Caliph al-Mahdi and asked him if he could be allowed to speak. "Speak, " al-Mahdi said. Salih said: "Since access to you has been made much easier for us than it has been for others, I will take this opportunity to speak on their behalf as well as on behalf of the Prophet. This is by virtue of the burden around our necks that requires us to command the good and forbid evil, and because the excuse of concealing the truth (*taqiyya*) no longer applies to us, and especially because you seem to be a person of humble demeanor and have vowed to God and those who bear His word that you will privilege the truth above everything else. You and I have been brought together in this inquest in order to fulfill what we have promised God we would deliver. We are bound to accept the consequences of our promise; otherwise, God will look into our inner and outer intentions and see that we are clothed in garments made of lies. The Prophet's Companions used to say: 'When God conceals His knowledge from someone, such a person is tortured by ignorance.' However, an even worse torture is reserved for one who is given the opportunity to take knowledge from God, but turns his back on it. When God grants knowledge to a person and he neglects to put what he has been given to use, he has indeed ignored God's gift to him and has belittled it. Therefore, accept the gift that God has given you

---

46 See Ibn al-Jawzi, *Sifat al-safwa* in Sulami, *Early Sufi Women*, pp. 278–9.
47 Massignon, *Essay*, p. 116. According to Massignon, Kulayb wrote a book titled *Kitab al-mahabba wa-l-waza'if* (Book of Love and Invocations). According to Ibn al-Jawzi (*Sifat al-safwa*, vol. 3, p. 381), he was also one of the "weepers" (*bakka'un*) of Basra. Kulayb also accompanied Salih on the visit to Rabi'a cited above.

through our speech truly and sincerely, but not as an excuse to boost your vanity and promote your reputation. Rest assured that we will not condemn you for what you do not know, and we will not belittle what you do know or remind you of what you have forgotten. For God granted the Prophet peace and security in the face of what befell him, and protected him from overstepping the limit, for He always shows the way to every exit. God said: 'If [at any time] an incitement to discord is made to you by the Evil One, seek refuge in God, for He is the All-Hearing, the All-Knowing' (Qur'an 41:36). So let God be the watcher over your heart so that by means it other hearts may be enlightened through your privileging the truth and disavowing the passions. If you do not do this it will not only result in your actions being exposed as a failure, but it will also reveal the effects of God's command on you as well. There is no strength and no power other than through God!"[48]

Because Jahiz does not provide background information for this anecdote, it is not clear whether Salih had been brought to al-Mahdi's inquest under duress or came of his own accord. However, the very fact that he appeared before a formal tribunal, along with his reference to *taqiyya*—a practice associated with Shi'ism in which one conceals one's true beliefs out of fear of harm to oneself or one's family—supports the possibility that he was one of the "Shiite Sufiyya" mentioned by Massignon.

In *Hilyat al-awliya'*, Abu Nu'aym al-Isfahani similarly portrays Salih ibn 'Abd al-Jalil as a person who was not afraid to speak his mind. He quotes him as saying, "The people of insight (*ahl al-basa'ir*) look upon the kings of the World disparagingly, whereas the folk of the World look upon them adoringly and with awe."[49] Unlike Jahiz, however, Isfahani does not call Salih a Sufi. Instead, he characterizes him as one who takes pleasure in obedience to God (*al-mustaladhdh bi-l-ta'a*) and adds that he was noted for his unquestioning acceptance of God's will (*tawakkul*). He also states that a group called "God's Obedient Ones" (*al-muti'un li-llah*) were to be found in Iraq in the second half of the eighth century CE. Could this group have been Massignon's "Shiite Sufiyya"? In support of this possibility, the

---

48   Jahiz, *al-Bayan*, vol. 2, pp. 222–3.
49   Isfahani, *Hilya*, vol. 8, p. 317; this statement also recalls Marshall Hodgson's concept of the Piety-Minded.

following statement by Salih may indicate that he was a member of such a group: "God's Obedient Ones have lost their taste for both the life of the World and the Hereafter. God will say to them on the Day of Judgment, 'I have caused you to suffer for my sake in the World on account of your desires and have made this known to you today. By my glory, I created the Heavenly Garden (*al-jinan*) only for you!'"[50]

The notion that "God's Obedient Ones" have lost their taste for both the World and the Hereafter because of their love for God recalls two of the best-known statements attributed to Rabi'a al-'Adawiyya. In a statement that first appears in Makki's *Qut al-qulub*, Rabi'a says: "I do not worship God out of fear of God. If I did, I would be like the disobedient slave-girl who only works when she is afraid. Nor [do I worship God] out of love for heaven. If I did, I would be like the disobedient slave-girl who only works when she is given something. Instead, I worship God out of love for him alone and out of yearning for him."[51] In a statement that first appears in 'Attar's *Tadhkirat al-awliya'*, Rabi'a says: "Oh Lord, if I worship you out of fear of Hell, burn me in Hell. If I worship you in the hope of Heaven, forbid it to me. But if I worship you for your own sake, do not deprive me of your eternal beauty."[52] Because neither of these statements appears in the earliest sources on Rabi'a, it is impossible to determine if the "real" Rabi'a actually said them. However, they reflect the essential asceticism and devotionalism that characterized the practices of both Rabi'a and the early "Sufis" of Abbasid Iraq.[53]

Although references to individuals and groups called "Sufi" before the late ninth century CE are scattered and inconsistent in Islamic sources, the meaning of this term nonetheless seems to have revolved around a common and identifiable set of spiritual attitudes and practices. Because of this, one can use early accounts in the works of Muhasibi, Jahiz, Isfahani and other Sufi and non-Sufi writers to draw a rough outline of what I shall call "Proto-Sufism." This set of beliefs and practices in Rabi'a's time formed the foundation for what would become a more theologically oriented Sufism

---

50 Ibid.
51 Makki, *Qut al-qulub*, vol. 2, p. 94.
52 'Attar, *Tadhkirat al-awliya'*, p. 74; see also, Sells, *Early Islamic Mysticism*, p. 169.
53 Christopher Melchert has also remarked on the possibility of "a single-minded concentration on God" as providing a bridge between asceticism and mysticism for early Sufis. See idem, "Origins and Early Sufism," p. 15.

in the tenth and eleventh centuries CE. These beliefs and practices can be summarized as follows:

1. The Proto-Sufis were ascetics, whose worldview was defined by the World/Nonworld Dichotomy.
2. The Proto-Sufis were dedicated to the pursuit of outward and inward purity.
3. Because the path of the Proto-Sufis was based more on practice than on theology, some but not all of them, were also practitioners of ascetic ritualism (*nusk*).
4. The Proto-Sufis internalized their ascetic practices through essential asceticism and Love mysticism.
5. The social practices of the Proto-Sufis were characterized by moralism and ethical precaution (*wara'*), which were combined with a highly disciplined regime of moral and spiritual training (*ta'dib*).
6. The practice of ethical precaution (*wara'*) led many Proto-Sufis to criticize the pursuit of worldly gain, although most do not appear to have been political dissidents.

When viewed in light of this set of Proto-Sufi beliefs and practices, the earliest accounts of Rabi'a al-'Adawiyya suggest that she could be considered a Proto-Sufi, even if she was not called a "Sufi" in the earliest sources. The most historically verifiable tropes of the Rabi'a narrative—Rabi'a the Ascetic and Rabi'a the Teacher—conform closely to the beliefs and practices outlined above. The trope of Rabi'a the Lover can also be seen to fit this model, so long as one confines it to what appears prior to Makki's theological depiction of Rabi'a's Love mysticism in *Qut al-qulub*. With respect to the debate over Sufi origins, this summary of beliefs and practices suggests that the difference between asceticism and Proto-Sufism was not based on the interiorization of theology, as Annemarie Schimmel supposed; rather, it was based on the interiorization of ascetic practice. This emphasis on practice over theory is reflected in an account of Rabi'a that appears in Jahiz's *al-Bayan wa-l-tabyin*. In this account Rabi'a is asked, "Have you ever performed any action that you knew would be accepted by God?" She replies, "If there were anything, it would be my fear that my works would be held against me."[54] As this saying indicates, Rabi'a's asceticism was "essential" because it involved the interiorization of ascetic attitudes and practices. In essential asceticism,

---

54 Jahiz, *al-Bayan wa al-tabyin*, vol. 3, p. 108.

renunciation of the World is transformed into detachment from the World and ascetic practices are interiorized because the ascetic has come into sight of the ultimate goal of asceticism: this is to attain what Walter O. Kaelber described in *The Encyclopaedia of Religion* as "a more thorough absorption in the sacred."

From the perspective of essential asceticism, the goal of the essential ascetic is much the same as the goal of the mystic. This is because asceticism and mysticism are both approaches to God. The essential ascetic seeks proximity to God and the mystic seeks union with God. The difference between these two approaches depends on how one defines the concept of "closeness." As discussed in Chapter 3, proximity—the goal of the ascetic—is different from union—the goal of the mystic—although the two concepts are closely related. Proximity maintains a measure of social distance through a master-servant or patron-client relationship whereas in union the relationship between the lover and the Beloved is more egalitarian. In both cases, however, once the ascetic's relationship with God has become close enough, there is no longer any need to conceive of asceticism as instrumental renunciation because the World has lost its importance. All that matters is the relationship with God. This attitude is reflected in Rabi'a's famous statement that her asceticism entailed "leaving aside all that does not concern me and cleaving to the One that always is."[55] A generation later, Abu Sulayman al-Darani (d. 830 CE) would critique the practices of asceticism in his time in similar terms: "Some say [*zuhd*] is leaving off meeting people, some say it is leaving off desires, and some say it is leaving off satiety. Their definitions are similar to one another. I think that renunciation (*zuhd*) is leaving off whatever distracts you from God."[56] Besides expressing essential asceticism, both of these statements illustrate how the path of asceticism can be seen as related to the mystical path of Love. Rabi'a's phrase, "cleaving to the One that always is," expresses the ascetic's devotion to God in terms of the more egalitarian relationship of Love mysticism. This statement also alludes to the fact that the end of the path of asceticism involves a spiritual reorientation, which is central to the notion of Sufism as a path of knowledge. In the next section of this chapter we shall see how for Rabi'a and her fellow Proto-Sufis the heart was conceived as the meeting-place of love and knowledge and the site where the transformation of self that is essential to spiritual realization takes place.

---

55 Khargushi, *Tahdhib al-asrar*, p. 81 and Isfahani, *Hilya*, vol. 10, p. 108.
56 Melchert, "Origins and Early Sufism," p. 15 (quoting Isfahani, *Hilya*, vol. 9, p. 258).

III. THE HEART AS A METAPHOR IN EARLY ISLAMIC MYSTICISM

a. Scriptural Antecedents

For Abu Nasr al-Sarraj and the Sufi writers who came after him, knowledge, love and wisdom find their meeting place in the heart. In *Kashf al-mahjub* (*Unveiling the Veiled*), an influential manual of Sufism from the second half of the eleventh century CE, the Persian Sufi 'Ali al-Hujwiri quotes 'Ali al-Isfahani, an associate of the famous Baghdad Sufi and theologian Abu al-Qasim al-Junayd (d. 910 CE), as saying about the heart: "From the time of Adam to the Resurrection people cry, 'The heart, the heart!' I wish that I might find someone to describe what the heart is or how it is, but I find no one. People in general give the name of 'heart' to that piece of flesh, which belongs to madmen and ecstatics and children, who really are without heart. What, then, is this heart, of which I hear only the name?" Hujwiri explains, "That is to say, if I call intellect the heart, it is not the heart; and if I call spirit the heart, it is not the heart. All the evidences of the Truth subsist in the heart, yet only the name of it is to be found."[57]

The word "heart" (*qalb*) in either its singular or plural form is mentioned 134 times in the Qur'an. It is also used frequently in the Hadith, and since Rabi'a's time it has become one of the most important spiritual symbols of Sufism. The fact that the Sufi heart is primarily a symbol, and not a physical "thing," lies at the root of 'Ali al-Isfahani's frustration in the quotation from *Kashf al-mahjub*. This is because a symbol has no essential meaning. As Hujwiri explains, one can summarize the ways in which the word "heart" is used; however, because it is a symbol one can never find a single, essential definition for the concept.[58]

However, the heart is not just a Sufi symbol; it is also an important symbol in the Qur'an. In the Qur'an, the heart most often symbolizes the seat of the conscience or moral and emotional states: it may be haughty and tyrannical (*qalb mutakabbir jabbar*, Qur'an 40:35); it may be repentant (*qalb munib*, Qur'an 50:33); it may be hardened (*qasat qulubuhum*, Qur'an 2:74); it may

---

57 Hujwiri, *Kashf al-Mahjub*, p. 144.
58 Most accurately, the Sufi heart is both a symbol and a synechdoche; as a synechdoche the term is understood immediately to mean the whole person or the essential self. Roland Barthes would call the Sufi concept of the heart a *global sign*, "the first term of a greater system which it builds and of which it is only a part." Roland Barthes, "Myth Today," in idem, *Mythologies*, trans. Annette Lavers (New York: Hill & Wang, 1972), pp. 114–15.

be diseased (*fi qulubihim marad*, Qur'an 33:12); it may be anxious or fearful (*fi qulubihim al-ru'b*, Qur'an 33:26); it is at peace when it possesses faith (*qalbuhu mutma'inun bi-l-iman*, Qur'an 16:106). The Qur'an also describes the heart of the Prophet Muhammad as the site of divine revelation, whether through the agency of the angel Gabriel (Qur'an 2:97), or through a spiritual being called "The Trustworthy Spirit" (*al-Ruh al-Amin*, Qur'an 26:194). The heart may also be described, like the human being in general, as God-fearing (*taqwa al-qulub*, Qur'an 22:32); also like the human being, it is capable of remembering God's teachings (*lahum qulubun ya'qiluna bi-ha*, Qur'an 22:46). Conversely, when reflecting the negative aspect of humanity, the heart may be blind (Qur'an 22:42) or otherwise veiled from the truth (Qur'an 4:155). Often the heart is described as the seat of knowledge and understanding; because it is the site of the person's most secret feelings and thoughts (Qur'an 32:51), it is predisposed to recall eternal truths (*dhikra li-man lahu qalb*, Qur'an 50:37). For the ordinary Muslim, just as for the Prophet Muhammad, a heart that is purified is potentially a receptacle for the divine presence: "[God] it is who has revealed His presence to the hearts of the believers (*anzala al-sakinata fi-l-qulub al-mu'minin*), that they may add faith to their faith" (Qur'an 48:4).

All of these examples allude to the heart as symbolizing the place where the conventional or ordinary self is united with the transcendental Self. It is the place where God "inscribes" faith on the believers and strengthens them with His spirit (*kataba fi qulubihim al-iman wa ayyadahum bi-ruhin minhu*, Qur'an 58:22). When the Qur'an states, "God did not create two hearts in a man's body" (*ma ja'ala Allahu li-rajulin min qalbayni fi jawfihi*, Qur'an 33:4), it is saying that all notions of the "divided self" are either false or deluded. The true human self is not only unified metaphorically; rather, it is an integral unity, undivided within itself and spiritually united with God.[59]

The use of the heart as a symbol in the Qur'an is similar in many ways to its use in the Hebrew Bible and the New Testament. In these earlier scriptures the heart also symbolizes the self and is the site of the deepest thoughts, feelings and intentions of the human being. In Hebrew, the word "heart" (Heb. *lev*) can refer both to the physical heart and to the concepts

---

[59] This interpretation is borne out by the remainder of the discourse in Qur'an 33:4, which compares the metaphor of two hearts in one body with legal fictions that were accepted as realities by the pagan Arabs, such as the *zihar* divorce, in which a husband's wife is called his "mother" to prevent remarriage and the practice (common in the West today but forbidden in Islam) of calling one's adopted children one's "own;" i.e., children by blood.

of emotion and understanding.⁶⁰ The word "heart" is used 833 times in the Hebrew Bible.⁶¹ Its most frequent use is in the Book of Psalms, where it appears 125 times in 121 verses. In the Psalms, the heart appears not only as the seat of the emotions, but also as the speaker's alter ego and as a metaphor for the personality. In this sense, the Hebrew word *lev* is similar in meaning to the Arabic term *lubb* or "kernel," which in Sufi usage denotes the spiritual self or the inner essence of the personality. Thus, it is not surprising to find that virtually all of the metaphors for which the heart is used in the Qur'an can also be found in the Psalms. In the Psalms, as in the Qur'an, one finds the unitary heart used as a metaphor for the unified self: "Teach me your way, oh Lord; I will walk in your Truth; unite my heart to fear your Name" (Ps. 86:11). One can also find in the Psalms a foreshadowing of the Sufi symbolism, in which the heart stands for all aspects of the human personality, including both body and soul: "My soul longs, even faints for the presence of the Lord, and my heart and my flesh cry out for the living God" (Ps. 84:2).

In the Christian New Testament the heart (Gr. *kardia*, Aramaic *lebba*) is described as something that can think (Mark 2:8), reflect (Luke 2:19), and understand (Matt. 13:15). The New Testament also describes the heart as the seat of the morals and the conscience. When the heart is pure, the believer's morals are pure; when the heart is sullied, the moral life is sullied as well: "The good person out of the good treasure of his heart produces good, and the evil person out of his evil treasure produces evil, for out of the abundance of his heart his mouth speaks" (Luke 6:45). Matthew 5:8 states, "Blessed are the pure in heart." In Paul's Letter to the Romans there is even a reference to God inscribing or "writing" on the heart as in the Qur'an: "They show that the work of the Law is written on their hearts, while their conscience also bears witness, and their conflicting thoughts accuse or even excuse them" (Romans 2:15). Also as in the Qur'an, Paul of Tarsus describes the heart as the place where the Holy Spirit resides: "He who searches hearts knows what is the mind of the Spirit because the Spirit intercedes for the saints according to the will of God" (Romans 8:27).

---

60 *Biblical Hebrew E-Magazine*, http://www.ancient-hebrew.org/emagazine/009.html. (Accessed November 2004.)
61 *Strong's Concordance with Hebrew and Greek Lexicon*, http://www.eliyah.com/lexicon.html. (Accessed June 2016.)

b. Possible Paths of Transmission

When Islam first came on the scene in the Middle East, the region of Iraq had large Jewish and Christian populations. Most scholars of rabbinic Judaism date the Babylonian Talmud to the sixth century CE, about a century before the coming of Islam. Besides talking with Jews, Muslims in Rabiʻa's time may also have "compared notes" on the heart with Christian interlocutors who read the Aramaic Gospels.[62] Starting in the seventh century CE, Christian mystics in Iraq, Palestine, Egypt and Syria began to make symbolic use of the heart in ways that recall the aphorisms of Muslim ascetics and Proto-Sufis. The Christian ascetic Hesychios of Sinai (fl. late sixth or early seventh century CE) stated, "When the heart has acquired stillness, it will look upon the heights and depths of knowledge, and the intellect, once quieted, will be given to hear wonderful things from God."[63] Similar correspondences with Sufi statements about the heart can be found in the aphorisms of "Makarios" the Great, an anonymous monk and mystic who lived in Syria sometime between the fourth and sixth centuries CE.[64] Much like Rabiʻa's alleged teacher Hayyuna, Makarios conceived of the heart as a bridal-chamber where the soul of the ascetic lover of God unites with the divine Beloved. In the following passage, he describes the heart as a place of spiritual transformation where the soul of the perfected or purified believer is enabled to "see" God:

> What did the Lord mean when he said, "Blessed are the pure in heart, for they shall see God?" Or again when he said, "Be perfect as your heavenly Father is perfect?" Did he not promise to us in these words a state of final purification from all wickedness? And is this not the final setting aside of our ignoble obsessions and our ascent to the perfections of the highest plane of virtues, which is itself the ultimate purification and sanctification of our heart by means of its communion with the divine and perfect spirit of God?"[65]

---

62 See Emran El Badawi, *The Qur'an and the Aramaic Gospel Traditions* (London: Routledge, 2013).
63 McGuckin, *Book of Mystical Chapters*, pp. 118–19.
64 Massignon, *Essay*, p. 39; unlike Tor Andrae and Margaret Smith, Massignon considered most correspondences between Christian and Muslim mystical doctrines and practices to be fortuitous. Although he recognized that a "genealogical kinship" might exist between Christian and Muslim practices, he felt that specific instances had to be proven rather than assumed.
65 McGuckin, *Book of Mystical Chapters*, pp. 155–6; "Makarios" also said with respect to the doctrine of Love, "It was God's own desire to have communion with the human

Of particular relevance to the mystical language of Sufism are the teachings of Isaac of Nineveh, a Nestorian Christian monk from Beth Qatreya (in modern Abu Dhabi), who briefly served as Bishop of Nineveh sometime between the years 660 and 680 CE. The teachings of Isaac are important because he lived through the Muslim conquest of Iraq and flourished under the Rightly Guided Caliphs and the first Umayyads. Often, both the form and content of his lessons and aphorisms appear suggestive of Sufi teachings. For Isaac, as it was for Rabi'a and her Proto-Sufi contemporaries, the heart was the locus of the spiritual intellect and the source of wisdom that transcends the limitations of normal thought. The transparency or clarity of the purified heart—*shafyut lebba* in Aramaic—was an important subject of discussion for ascetics of the Syrian Christian tradition, both for the Orthodox and for Nestorians like Isaac. For Isaac, the heart that is cleansed of impurities makes visible the forms of divine truths that are obscured by the rational mind and the material world. For this early Christian Neo-Platonist, the heart took the place of the head in the Greek philosophical tradition. The head, which contains the rational faculty, is the highest part of the body; however, the heart, as a metaphor for the deepest part of the soul, is more profound and thus "higher" than the head, just as the immortal soul, which is located in the body, is both "deeper" and "higher" than the mortal body. As the following passage from Isaac's *Third Discourse* demonstrates, the depth of the heart allows it—through the mediation of ascetic practices—to protect itself from the impurities that would otherwise affect the soul through the body:

> Of what does the difference between purity of mind and purity of heart consist? Purity of mind is different from purity of heart, just as there is a difference between a member of the body and the whole body. The mind is indeed one of the senses of the soul. But the heart is the ruler of the internal senses; that is, the sense of senses, which is the root. If the root is holy, so also are all the branches. But the root is not holy even if in one of the branches there is holiness. The mind indeed with a little study of the Scriptures and a little labor in fasting and stillness forgets its former musing and is made pure, in that it becomes free from alien habits. The heart, however, is purified with great sufferings and by being deprived of all mingling with the world, together with complete mortification in everything. When it has been

---

soul, and this was why he espoused it to himself as a royal bride and why he purified it from all uncleanliness" (p. 155).

purified, however, its purity is not defiled by contact with inconsequential things. That is, it is not afraid of violent battles, for it has a strong stomach which easily digests all foods hard for others who are ill in their abdomens... Every purification which is achieved easily, quickly, and with little labor is easily defiled. But the purity acquired with great troubles over a long period and by the highest part of the soul does not fear insignificant contact with worldly things.[66]

The trope of the heart as the ruler of the senses and the seat of the personality goes back to Greek philosophy, where it can be observed in the works of Plato.[67] In the ascetic tradition of Islam, the use of the heart as a metaphor for the personality has traditionally been traced to al-Hasan al-Basri. Hasan was a gifted orator and Jahiz's *al-Bayan wa-l-tabyin* contains a number of selections from his sermons. Among these selections, two statements on the heart are particularly noteworthy. In the first statement, Hasan despairs of humankind, much like Diogenes the Cynic centuries before him: "Ah! If only I could find life in your hearts! Men have become like specters; I perceive a murmur, but I see nothing that loves. Tongues are brought to me in abundance, but I am looking for hearts. Your intellects go astray, seeking the butterflies of hell and the flies of covetousness!"[68] In the second statement recorded by Jahiz, Hasan's advice sounds more like Rabi'a's: "Converse with your hearts and maintain them, for they are quick to rust. Humble your carnal souls, for they tend to raise themselves up!"[69]

Sufi traditions claim that al-Hasan al-Basri's teachings on the heart were passed on to later generations by his disciple Malik ibn Dinar (d. 745 CE). Since Ibn Dinar lived in Basra during the first half of Rabi'a's life, it is not unreasonable to speculate that he was influential in establishing the heart as a symbol for Rabi'a and her contemporaries. In Chapter 2 it was noted that 'Ubayda bint Abi Kilab, a woman ascetic and weeper from the Basra region, is alleged to have been a disciple of Malik ibn Dinar. Ibn Dinar was also an early teacher of Love mysticism and some later hagiographers, such as Ibn

---

66 St. Isaac of Nineveh, *On Ascetical Life*, trans. Mary Hansbury (Crestwood, NY: St. Vladimir's Monastery Press, 1989), pp. 50–1.
67 In the *Republic*, Plato states, "The good, then, is the end of all endeavor, the object on which every heart is set, whose existence it divines, though it finds it difficult to grasp just what it is; and because it can't handle it with the same assurance as other things it misses any value those other things have." Plato, *The Republic*, trans. Desmond Lee (London: Penguin Group, 1955), p. 230.
68 Massignon, *Essay*, p. 133, citing Jahiz, *Bayan*, 3:69.
69 Ibid., citing Jahiz, *Bayan*, 1:162.

al-Jawzi and 'Attar, suggested that Rabi'a knew him.[70] This is theoretically possible, since their lives overlapped enough for Rabi'a to have encountered Ibn Dinar early in her career as an ascetic. If they did know each other, Ibn Dinar might have been an important influence on Rabi'a, both in her doctrine of Love mysticism and in her use of the heart as a symbol. In addition, this might also suggest why Sufi legends place Rabi'a anachronistically together with al-Hasan al-Basri more often than with Ibn Dinar, who was her more probable associate. Since Ibn Dinar was reputed to be an exceptionally faithful transmitter of al-Hasan al-Basri's doctrines, it is understandable that traditionists and storytellers would conflate the identity of the lesser-known pupil with his more famous teacher.

The same situation might also explain why some statements that were originally attributed to al-Hasan al-Basri later ended up as "Rabi'a's" statements. For example, in Ibn al-Jawzi's biographical dictionary *Sifat al-safwa*, we are told that Rabi'a said to Sufyan al-Thawri, "You are but a set number of days. When one day goes, a part of you goes as well."[71] Although this aphorism seems to be authentic because its purported transmitter, Abu Sulayman al-Dab'i, related accounts about Sufyan al-Thawri's encounters with Rabi'a, there is no chain of transmission to support it. This lacuna is important because a century and a half before Ibn al-Jawzi, Abu Nu'aym al-Isfahani attributed the same aphorism to al-Hasan al-Basri in *Hilyat al-awliya'*.[72] In this earlier version the reporter of the story is Salih al-Murri, another ascetic who has been linked to Rabi'a. Although Isfahani also fails to provide a chain of transmission, his attribution is corroborated by the earlier account of Jahiz, who attributes this aphorism to al-Hasan al-Basri in *al-Bayan wa-l-tabyin*.[73] Because of Jahiz's greater proximity in time and place to both Rabi'a and

---

70   See, for example, Ibn al-Jawzi in Sulami, *Early Sufi Women*, pp. 278–9. Farid al-Din al-'Attar's accounts of meetings between Rabi'a and Ibn Dinar should only be taken as rhetorical constructs. In one account, 'Attar has Ibn Dinar relating a tradition about Rabi'a. This would have been highly improbable, since at the time of his death, Ibn Dinar would have been much more famous than Rabi'a, who was then only in her twenties. In another account, 'Attar has al-Hasan al-Basri, Ibn Dinar, and Shaqiq al-Balkhi all visiting Rabi'a at the same time. In actuality, Balkhi died nine years after Rabi'a and Hasan died when Rabi'a was only eleven years old. Therefore, it would have been impossible for such a cast of characters to assemble at the same time. See Sells, *Early Islamic Mysticism*, pp. 167–8.
71   Ibid. See also, Chapter 2 above, where this statement is used to illustrate instrumental asceticism.
72   Isfahani, *Hilya*, vol. 2, p. 148.
73   Jahiz, *al-Bayan*, p. 94.

Hasan, one must conclude that if either of these two figures actually made this statement, it is much more likely to have been Hasan than Rabi'a.

Besides providing a possible doctrinal connection between Rabi'a al-'Adawiyya and al-Hasan al-Basri, Malik ibn Dinar is also important because he was a transmitter of aphorisms and wisdom traditions from Christian and Jewish sources. For example, the section devoted to his memory in Isfahani's *Hilyat al-awliya'* contains numerous references of this kind. The most interesting of these refer to Ibn Dinar "reading" Christian or Jewish texts. In one account he states, "I read in the Torah: 'Oh Son of Adam! Do not be discouraged to stand weeping in my presence while you pray; for I am the God that is close to your heart and through the unseen you saw my light!'" [74] In another account he says, "I read this in the Psalms (*al-Zabur*): 'With the arrogance of the hypocrite the poor person is burned.'"[75] Elsewhere he says, "I was informed that Jesus (peace be upon him) said, 'Make your bodies endure hunger, thirst, nakedness, and exposure to the elements, so that your hearts might come to know [God].'"[76] What might Ibn Dinar have been "reading" to come up with such aphorisms? If he read Christian or Jewish texts, the language in which he read them would have been Aramaic—either Syriac or Hebrew Aramaic. However, it is important to note that for the most part Ibn Dinar's quotations are not actually from the Torah, the Psalms, or the Gospels. Instead, they are apocryphal traditions that probably circulated orally among the indigenous non-Muslim inhabitants of southern Iraq. As such, Ibn Dinar could just as likely have learned them in Arabic instead of Aramaic.

Another early transmitter of Christian traditions was Ahmad ibn Abi al-Hawari (d. 845 CE), a student and disciple of the Sufi Abu Sulayman al-Darani (d. 830 CE).[77] In the previous chapter it was noted that Darani originally lived in Basra but later moved to a village outside of Damascus in Syria.[78] Ibn Abi al-Hawari was also from Basra and moved to Syria with his teacher. After his arrival in Syria, he married the wealthy woman of Damascus, Rabi'a bint Isma'il (d. before 845 CE), who appears in Sufi hagiography as the most famous namesake of Rabi'a al-'Adawiyya. In exchange for giving her wealth

---

74 Isfahani, *Hilya*, vol. 2, p. 357.
75 Ibid., p. 376.
76 Ibid., p. 370.
77 For information on Ahmad Ibn Abi al-Hawari see Sulami, *Tabaqat al-sufiyya*, pp. 98–102; Isfahani, *Hilya*, vol. 10, pp. 5–33; Ibn al-Jawzi, *Sifat al-safwa*, vol. 2, pp. 836–7; and Massignon, *Essay*, pp. 152–8.
78 Abu Sulayman's *nisba*, "al-Darani," came from the name of this village. See Sulami, *Tabaqat al-sufiyya*, pp. 75–82, Isfahani, *Hilya*, vol. 9, pp. 254–80, and Ibn al-Jawzi, *Sifat al-safwa*, vol. 2, pp. 828–34.

away to Darani and his disciples, she compelled her husband to practice a celibate form of marriage that was popular among the lay ascetics of early Syrian Christianity.

Darani and Ibn Abi al-Hawari are significant historically because they were connected in various ways to the most important centers of early Sufism in Iraq, Syria and Khorasan (present-day eastern Iran, Afghanistan and Central Asia). Circumstantial evidence also suggests that when they lived in Basra, they were aware of Rabi'a al-'Adawiyya and her associates. For example, in his Book of Sufi Women Sulami cites Ibn Abi al-Hawari as the source of an account about Maryam of Basra, an alleged disciple of Rabi'a who was noted for her practice of Love mysticism.[79] Both Sulami and Ibn al-Jawzi also cite accounts from Ibn Abi al-Hawari about Bahriyya, a piety-minded woman ('*abida*) and "knower of God" ('*arifa*) from Basra who was a disciple of Shaqiq al-Balkhi.[80]

In *Hilyat al-awliya'*, Isfahani claims that Abu Sulayman al-Darani was a teacher of the famous early Egyptian Sufi Dhu'l-Nun al-Misri (d. 859 CE).[81] Darani was also a close associate of Salih ibn 'Abd al-Jalil, who was discussed above as one of the first ascetics to call himself a "Sufi." In the *Hilya*, Darani is cited as the source of a statement by Ibn 'Abd al-Jalil (different from the statement quoted above), concerning God's blessings on "God's Obedient Ones."[82] Might this reference lend credibility to the suggestion that Massignon's "Shiite Sufiyya," "God's Obedient Ones," and Muhasibi's "Pure Ones" were all from the same group? At this point, there is not enough evidence to say. However, genealogical connections such as these demonstrate that more research needs to be done on the links between Proto-Sufis and self-designated "Sufis" in the eighth and ninth centuries CE.

A number of accounts attributed to Ahmad ibn Abi al-Hawari also describe personal encounters with Christian monks or relate traditions that could only have come from Jewish sources. In *Hilyat al-awliya'* Ibn Abi al-Hawari relates the following teaching on renunciation from a monk at the Syrian monastery of Dayr Harmila: "We find in our books that the body of the Son of Adam is created from earth but his soul is created from the heavenly realm (*malakut*

---

79 See Chapter 1 and Sulami, *Early Sufi Women*, pp. 84–5.
80 Ibid., pp. 148–9 and Ibn al-Jawzi Appendix to ibid, pp. 296–7; Ibn al-Jawzi claims without attribution that Bahriyya led gatherings of invocation at her house in Basra (*wa kana laha majlisun tudhakkiru fihi*).
81 If this report were true, Dhu al-Nun would have studied with Darani in Syria. See Isfahani, *Hilya*, vol. 9, pp. 254–5.
82 Ibid., p. 255.

al-sama'). When the body is made hungry and naked and suffers deprivation, the soul is freed to go back up to the place from which it came. However, when the body has food, water, sleep and rest it fixes itself permanently in the place in which it was born, for there is nothing more beloved to it than the World."[83] In another account, Ibn Abi al-Hawari relates a saying from the Prophet Joseph: "My God, verily I turn toward you with the righteousness of my father Abraham Your Friend, Isaac Your Sacrifice, and Jacob Your Israel." Then God revealed to him: "Oh Joseph, did you turn toward me with the grace that I bestowed on all of them?" Because Ibn Abi al-Hawari is unclear about the meaning of this tradition, he takes it to his teacher to inquire about it. Darani explains the tradition in the following way: "Verily God approaches him first with the love of His friends, then He comes to him according to the spiritual station with which his heart is occupied."[84]

c. The Metaphor of the Heart for Rabi'a al-'Adawiyya and Her Contemporaries

The use of the heart as a metaphor for the self in the explanation recounted above illustrates a motif that appears repeatedly in the notices on Abu Sulayman al-Darani in *Hilyat al-awliya'*. Among the Sufis of his generation, Darani is most often associated with statements about the heart in Isfahani's book. Although he was not the only early Sufi to use the heart as a metaphor, his prominence in the *Hilya* indicates that Isfahani regarded him as one of the most important specialists on the heart in early Sufism.[85] Abu Sulayman al-Darani's statements about the heart can be seen as an early form of personality theory, in which the heart stands for the self and the states of the heart correspond to what we today would call personality traits. As such, his doctrine of the heart can be seen as a possible precursor to the more fully

---

83 Ibid., vol. 10, p. 5; the doctrine of the soul as expressed by this Christian monk is Platonic in origin. According to Pierre Hadot, early Christian teachers frequently borrowed ideas from the writings of pagan Neo-Platonists, such as in the following statement by St. Ambrose of Milan: "A blessed soul it is which penetrates the secrets of the Word. For awakening from the body, becoming a stranger to everything else, she seeks within herself and searches, so as to find out whether she can, in some way, reach divine being." Hadot, *Plotinus*, p. 25 n. 5.
84 Isfahani, *Hilya*, vol. 10, p. 9.
85 The section on Abu Sulayman al-Darani in the most recent edition of the *Hilya* comprises 26 pages and is one of the longer sections in the volume in which it appears. See ibid., vol. 9, pp. 254–80.

developed personality theory of al-Harith al-Muhasibi, a fellow native of Basra, whose "science of hearts" (*'ilm al-qulub*) was to have a long-lasting influence on Sufism through the writings of Ghazali.[86]

Based on Isfahani's record of his teachings, Darani's doctrine of the heart was based on three central themes or motifs:

1. *The preoccupation of the heart*, expressed by the metaphors of "filling" the heart (*'imarat al-qalb*) and "emptying" the heart (*khawa' al-qalb*).
2. *The condition of the heart*, expressed by metaphorical references to the "place" or station of the heart (*manzilat al-qalb*) and the cohesiveness of the heart (*ijma' al-qalb*).
3. *The knowledge of the heart*, expressed by metaphorical references to the "awareness" of the heart (*ittila' al-qalb*), the "vision" of the heart (*basar al-qalb*), and the "light" of the heart (*nur al-qalb*).

The first of Darani's themes, the "preoccupation of the heart," closely accords with the concept of asceticism as renunciation. Here, "filling" the heart does not mean that the heart is filled with God, as in essential asceticism; instead, it means being preoccupied with material concerns or passions. This metaphor reflects a Platonic ethic and is also reminiscent of early Christian teachings, in which renunciation or "emptying the heart" is equated with purification. Darani explains this metaphor in the following way: "Sinful suggestions (*al-wasawis*) only come to a heart that is full. Have you ever seen a thief going to empty ruins, scrutinizing them and entering them from any door that he wishes? No. A thief only comes to houses with material goods locked inside of them, seeking to open them so that he might steal what is in them."[87]

In another account Darani describes the preoccupation of the heart in terms of the World/Nonworld Dichotomy. Here the dichotomy between the World and the Nonworld is described in terms of a fundamental moral opposition: "When the World (*al-dunya*) comes to the heart, the Nonworld (*al-akhira*) moves away from it; and if the World is in the heart, the Nonworld

---

86   See Gavin Picken, *Spiritual Purification and Islam: The Life and Works of al-Muhasibi* (London: Routledge, 2009).
87   Isfahani, *Hilya*, vol. 9, p. 257.

will never come to it. This is because the World is depraved (*la'ima*) whereas the Nonworld is honorable (*'aziza*)."[88]

In yet another account, Darani explains the metaphor of emptying the heart in terms of the heart's "hunger" and "thirst": "When the heart is made hungry or thirsty, it is purified and made valuable; but when it is satiated, it is rendered blind and worthless."[89] This reference to the purifying effects of hunger and thirst allude to the practice of systematic fasting as a form of bodily mortification which, as we have seen in Chapter 2, was more representative of Christian than early Muslim asceticism. Although Darani's reference to the "hunger" and "thirst" of the heart may refer to a regime of inward purification, it more likely indicates that he and his followers practiced fasting as part of their ascetic disciplines.[90]

This last statement by Darani also links the "preoccupation of the heart" with the "condition," "station," and "knowledge" of the heart described in other aphorisms. For Darani, it is not enough just to empty the heart of the World; each stage of filling the heart with the divine presence calls for greater responsibilities for the ascetic and hence a greater risk of earning God's displeasure: "For each level that the station (*manzila*) of the heart is raised, the opportunity for divine punishment increases."[91] In order not to fail in these responsibilities, one must maintain strict ascetic discipline and associate only with those whose company strengthens one's resolve on the path to God. The "cohesion of the heart" (*ijma' al-qalb*) or coherence of the self depends on the complete transformation of the personality. This is to be accomplished with the help of one's brethren among the Piety-Minded and the pursuit of illuminative knowledge through the practices of meditation

---

88 Ibid., p. 260.
89 Ibid., p. 266.
90 The frequent references to hunger by Darani in the *Hilya* might suggest that the statements about hunger attributed to Rabi'a by the Andalusian Sufi Abu Madyan originated among the Sufis of Syria. As noted in Chapter 2, the statements about hunger in Abu Madyan's *Bidayat al-murid* are unique in the Rabi'a narratives. Throughout the period of Umayyad rule in Spain (755–1031 CE), Andalusian Islam was strongly influenced by Syrian doctrines and practices. Since Darani and Ibn Abi al-Hawari were major Sufi figures in Syria, it is possible that when reports about Darani reached Muslim Spain, they were conflated with reports about Rabi'a bint Isma'il of Damascus, who Andalusian transmitters thought was Rabi'a al-'Adawiyya. The doctrinal and *tabaqat* works of Abu Sa'id ibn al-A'rabi, a student of Ibn Abi al-Dunya, were well known and influential in Islamic Spain and would likely have been a source for these traditions. See Manuela Marin, "Abû Sa'îd Ibn al-A'râbî et le développement du soufisme en al-Andalus," *Revue du monde musulmane et de la Mediterranée: Minorités religieuses dans l'Espagne médievale*, 63/64, 1992, pp. 28–38.
91 Isfahani, *Hilya*, vol. 9, p. 257.

and retreat: "Reject all pride in the mind's knowledge (*radd sabil al-'ajab bi-ma'rifat al-nafs*)," says Darani. "Instead, dedicate yourself to the cohesion of the heart by committing few errors, seek the flawlessness of the heart (*riqqat al-qalb*) by sitting with the God-fearing, procure the illumination of the heart through constant sorrow, seek the way to sorrow through constant meditation (*tafakkur*), and seek the presence of meditation through the practice of retreat (*khalwa*)."[92]

Many of the metaphors that were used by Darani to speak about the heart can also be found in statements attributed to Rabi'a al-'Adawiyya. For example, Kalabadhi cites the following statement by Rabi'a in *al-Ta'arruf*: "A group of people came to visit Rabi'a in order to console her for some complaint. They said to her, 'What is your condition?' She replied, 'By God! I know of no cause for my illness, except that Paradise was revealed to me, and my heart was drawn toward it. I think that my Lord was jealous of me, so He reproached me; for only He can make such a reproach.'"[93] In this tradition, Rabi'a's physical condition is analogous to the condition of her heart. Echoing Darani's concern for the heart's purity, she likens her heart's preoccupation with Paradise (a reference to instrumental asceticism) to baser and more material preoccupations with the World. Her "illness" comes from the realization that even Paradise is a created thing; therefore, the only proper approach for the ascetic is toward God Himself, without regard for anything else, including Heaven (a reference to essential asceticism). God, as the jealous Beloved, reproaches Rabi'a, troubling her heart and leaving her soul in an agitated state. This state is comparable to *al-nafs al-lawwama*, the "self-blaming soul" that would become an important part of Muhasibi's Sufi psychology.

A similar depiction of the heart as a metaphor for the self can be found in an account from *Hilyat al-awliya'* about Rabi'a's contemporary Ibrahim ibn Adham. In this account Ibn Adham states: "View all of creation in your heart without discrimination: preoccupy yourself with your sins instead of judging others for their sins and make sure to utter beautiful words from a humble heart for the sake of God Most High. Reflect on your sins and repent them to your Lord. Doing so will establish ethical precaution (*wara'*) in your heart, so do not be greedy for anything other than your Lord."[94] For Ibn

---

92   Ibid., p. 266.
93   Kalabadhi, *al-Ta'arruf*, p. 121; Arberry, *The Doctrine of the Sufis*, p. 159.
94   Isfahani, *Hilya*, vol. 8, p. 16; a later version of this account can be found in Qushayri's *Risala* (p. 258), where Rabi'a states, "I looked with my heart at Heaven (*nazartu bi-qalbi*

Adham, just as it was for Rabiʿa and Darani, the heart is the seat of spiritual judgment and its condition affects the ability of the ascetic to "see" spiritual realities. However, in this account the heart is also depicted as the site of moral judgments; thus, it requires the ethical precaution of *waraʿ* in order to become properly oriented toward God as the ultimate reality. For Ibn Adham, essential asceticism is the perfect realization of *waraʿ* because it empties the heart of all things but God.

In his Book of Sufi Women, Sulami mentions a group of people that he calls *arbab al-qulub*, "The Masters of Hearts," or specialists in the doctrine of the heart.[95] Just as with his references to "weepers" and "those who cause others to weep" discussed in Chapter 2, this reference to early Sufi "heart specialists" indicates that when Sulami and other systematizers of Sufi doctrine looked back on the Proto-Sufis and ascetics of Rabiʿa's generation, they noticed that some individuals relied more heavily than others on the heart as a metaphor in their teachings. One of the early Sufi women that Sulami highlights as a "Master of Hearts" is Hukayma of Damascus, who was the teacher of Rabiʿa al-ʿAdawiyya's Syrian namesake, Rabiʿa bint Ismaʿil. In a teaching that anticipates Darani's metaphor of the "empty" heart, Hukayma interprets the Qurʾanic passage, "Except one who comes to God with a sound heart" (Qurʾan 26:89), in the following way: "It means that when one encounters God, there should be nothing in his heart other than Him."[96] Darani is said to have approved of this statement because he felt that the only truly "healthy" heart (*qalb salim*) was one that had been emptied of the World and was thus ready to receive knowledge directly from God. Hukayma's teaching also expresses a similar sentiment to one of the most famous statements attributed to Rabiʿa al-ʿAdawiyya: "Love for the Creator (*al-Khaliq*) has preoccupied me from love for created beings (*al-makhluqin*)."[97] For both Rabiʿa and Hukayma, a heart that is spiritually sound is empty of all but God and is oriented toward God alone.

One of the most important Sufi sources for Rabiʿa al-ʿAdawiyya's teachings and aphorisms is *Tahdhib al-asrar* (*The Primer of Secrets*) by ʿAbd al-Malik

---

ila-l-janna) and [God] corrected me, for He is the only one to do so. Therefore, I will never do this again."

95 See, for example, the notice on Shaʿwana of al-Ubulla in Sulami, *Early Sufi Women*, pp. 106–7.
96 Sulami, *Early Sufi Women*, pp. 126–7.
97 Khargushi, *Tahdhib al-asrar*, p. 60; see also Sulami, *Early Sufi Women*, pp. 78–9. Later versions of this tradition changed the key phrase from *hubb al-makhluqin* ("love for created beings") to *hubb al-makhluq* ("love for creation or that which is created"). This opened the statement to more abstract and theological interpretations.

al-Khargushi (d. 1016 CE). As we saw in the previous chapter, Khargushi lived in Nishapur at the same time as both Sulami and al-Hasan al-Nisaburi, the author of *'Uqala' al-majanin*. Taken together, the works of Khargushi, Sulami and Nisaburi provide some of the most important information currently available on eighth-century Proto-Sufism and the circle of women around Rabi'a al-'Adawiyya. Like Sulami's Book of Sufi Women, Khargushi's *Primer of Secrets* portrays Rabi'a as a Sufi. In the following account from this work, which is also one of the epigraphs to this chapter, Rabi'a describes the heart and the knowledge it contains as God's personal possessions: "Verily, the Knower of God (*'arif*) asks God to grant him a heart. So [God] grants it to him from Himself. When he possesses the heart, he then offers it back to his Lord and Master, so that in [God's] repossession of it he will be protected and will be veiled in its concealment from created beings."[98]

Unfortunately, no chain of transmission is given for this account, so there is no way to verify whether it is reliable. However, if it did come from Rabi'a, it would be significant because theologically it goes beyond other expressions of the heart as a metaphor, including those of Darani, who also spoke of the heart's knowledge. Its closest analogue among the sayings of other Proto-Sufis is a tradition from Nisaburi's *'Uqala' al-majanin* that is attributed to Hayyuna. In this account, Hayyuna asks God to grant her stillness of heart and bestow divine acceptance upon her: "Oh God, grant me stillness of heart through the contract of my complete trust in you (*hab li sukun al-qalb bi-'aqd al-thiqa bi-ka*). Make all of my thoughts, ideas, and inclinations accord with your acceptance of me. Do not make my fate deprive me of you. Oh hope of those who seek hope!"[99]

In these statements by Rabi'a and Hayyuna, the heart is portrayed as God's property and the ascetic possesses her heart on loan from God as the result of a binding agreement or contract. Hayyuna refers to a contract of trust (*'aqd al-thiqa*), whereas Rabi'a speaks of giving the heart back to God as if it were the repayment of a loan. Both statements refer to the concept of complete trust in God (*tawakkul* or *al-thiqa bi-llah*), which, as we saw in Chapter 2, was an important spiritual attitude for early Islamic ascetics. Since both Hayyuna and Rabi'a combined their asceticism with Love mysticism, it is possible to think of Hayyuna's metaphor of a contract as based on the Islamic contract of marriage (*'aqd al-zawaj*), and to think of Rabi'a's metaphor of a loan or a gift as alluding to the female lover's gift of her heart to her male beloved. In

---

98 Khargushi, *Tahdhib al-asrar*, p. 53.
99 Nisaburi, *'Uqala' al-majanin*, p. 150.

both of these cases, the relationship between the ascetic and God is analogous to a spiritual marriage. The metaphor of marriage and the portrayal of the ascetic devotee as God's "bride" are further supported by references to veiling (*hijab*) and concealment (*sitr*) in Rabi'a's statement and by the desire for God's pleasure (*rida'*) in Hayyuna's prayer. In both traditions the heart is a type of spiritual domicile. Just as in an Islamic marriage, the bride takes up residence in the husband's home, where she is concealed and protected from the gaze of outsiders. By virtue of the contracted relationship between husband and wife, she becomes "Mistress of the House," although the real owner of the house is her husband. Just as the bride knows that her status is dependent on her husband's pleasure, the "knower" of God (*al-'arif bi-llah*) is aware that the condition of the heart as a home for the spirit similarly depends on God's pleasure. This is why Hayyuna asks God to ensure that the preoccupations of her heart are in agreement with the desires of her heavenly bridegroom. Rabi'a's statement is more altruistic than Hayyuna's but the meaning of it is more or less the same. Just as a successful marriage depends on mutual trust between husband and wife and the maintenance of a quiet and peaceful home, so the gift of God's knowledge depends on a devoted and trusting heart.

IV. RABI'A THE "KNOWER OF GOD"

Amy Hollywood, a major scholar of medieval Christian hagiography, has observed that in hagiographical accounts, when God is represented as the male Beloved in contrast to the ardent female soul, "the cultural association of women with eroticism is accepted, spiritualized, and, in part, subverted."[100] The marital motifs in the statements of Hayyuna and Rabi'a given above can be seen as an Islamic version of this trope. However, as Hollywood also notes, the presence of Love mysticism or erotic imagery in a hagiographical text does not necessarily mean that women are really speaking. Often, the use of such imagery turns out to be an example of "men writing women," as Elizabeth Clark observed with Gregory of Nyssa and his sister St Macrina. As Catherine M. Mooney has noted about the hagiographic depiction of Christian women saints in the Middle Ages, the presence of erotic imagery in

---

100 Amy Hollywood, *The Soul as Virgin Wife: Mechthild of Magdeburg, Marguerite Porete, and Meister Eckhart* (Notre Dame, IN and London: University of Notre Dame Press, 1995), p. 7.

"male hagiographic texts describing women's relationship with God appears to reflect a particularly male concern that is not similarly echoed in many women's self-representations."[101] According to Mooney's research, domestic imagery is much more representative of the voices of actual women than erotic imagery.[102] This observation is echoed by Caroline Walker Bynum, who claims that in the writings and statements of medieval Christian women, "all women's central images turn out to be continuities [with domestic life]."[103] In other words, rather than rejecting the values of the dominant society as Leila Ahmed has claimed for Sufi women mystics, medieval Christian women mystics were more likely to frame their depictions of spiritual life in terms of ordinary life experiences.[104]

The use of marital imagery in the statements of Rabi'a and Hayyuna suggests that in Sufi hagiographies as well, male authors may have been speaking through the voices of famous women. In the statements reproduced above, it is possible that we are hearing Khargushi's and Nisapuri's interpretations of the Sufi doctrine of the heart as much as Rabi'a's or Hayyuna's. One of the most important contributions of Amy Hollywood's research to the feminist study of hagiography has been to demonstrate that not only the affirmation but also the subversion of women's stereotypes in hagiographical texts often has more to do with men than with women. We shall see a major example of this in 'Attar's *vita* of Rabi'a in the next chapter. At times, male writers have found it useful to subvert gender stereotypes in order to make a doctrinal point. Famous examples of this practice include the Andalusian Sufi Ibn 'Arabi and the German mystic Meister Eckhart.[105] Such twists and turns of rhetorical form make it hard to draw conclusions about authentic women's voices, either from the statements of female Christian saints or from Sufi women. As Hollywood's analyses of hagiography and feminist theory demonstrate, to indulge in "universal claims [about gender and

---

101 Catherine M. Mooney, "Voice, Gender, and the Portrayal of Sanctity," in C.M. Mooney (ed.), *Gendered Voices: Medieval Saints and Their Interpreters* (Philadelphia: University of Pennsylvania Press, 1999), p. 12.
102 Ibid.
103 Caroline Walker Bynum, "Women's Stories, Women's Symbols," in idem, *Fragmentation and Redemption: Essays on Gender and the Human Body in Medieval Religion* (New York: Zone Books, 1992), p. 48.
104 Leila Ahmed, *Women and Gender in Islam* (New Haven and London: Yale University Press, 1992), p. 96.
105 On Ibn 'Arabi see Sadiyya Sheikh, "In Search of *al-Insan*: Sufism, Islamic Law, and Gender," *Journal of the American Academy of Religion*, 77 (4), 2009, pp. 781–822. On Eckhart, see Hollywood, *The Soul as Virgin Wife*.

voice] made with regard to particular historical places, times, and evidence, is dangerous both to scholarship and to feminist political and ethical aims, for it works to obscure crucial differences between women themselves, as well as between men."[106]

This warning is especially important for the study of Rabi'a al-'Adawiyya because the "point" of her depiction in medieval hagiography is more often about knowledge than gender. Whatever else the "real" Rabi'a al-'Adawiyya may have been, she was seen as a woman whose knowledge and opinions were worth heeding. In Sufi writings, the trope of "Rabi'a the Knower of God" (*Rabi'a al-'arifa bi-llah*) is closely related to the trope of Rabi'a the Lover. The reason for this is simple: (male) Sufi authors would ask, "Who would know the (male) divine Beloved better than His most ardent (female) lover?" The theme of knowledge—whether it be rational knowledge or intimate knowledge—is a common thread that links early representations of the trope of Rabi'a the Teacher in Muhasibi, Jahiz, Burjulani, Ibn Abi Tahir Tayfur, and Ibn al-Junayd to later representations of the trope of Rabi'a the Lover in Makki, Sulami, Ghazali, and 'Attar. The conceptual relationship between Love and knowledge has a pedigree that goes back long before the coming of Islam. As we saw in the previous chapter, no matter what other literary influences might have existed, the trope of "a woman wise in the ways of love" would have been enough by itself to allow the figure of Rabi'a al-'Adawiyya to be compared with the figure of the priestess Diotima in Plato's *Symposium*.

When medieval male writers of Islamic hagiography used gender-based stereotypes in their depictions of Rabi'a, she is often portrayed as emotional or even hysterical. For example, Ibn al-Jawzi depicts her as crying, weeping and fainting.[107] Such images reinforce the long-held Muslim stereotype of women as deficient in intellect and emotional stability.[108] Such portrayals undermine the image of Rabi'a al-'Adawiyya as a wise sage and cause the reader to treat her aphorisms skeptically, "with a grain of salt," so to speak. However, modern male writers in the West are just as likely to use gender-based stereotypes

---

106 Hollywood, *The Soul as Virgin Wife*, p. 197.
107 See, for example, Ibn al-Jawzi's chapter on Rabi'a from *Sifat al-safwa*, reproduced in Sulami, *Early Sufi Women*, pp. 276–83.
108 On the Muslim trope of women's innate deficiencies, see Rkia E. Cornell, "Soul of A Woman Was Created Below: Woman as the Lower Soul (*Nafs*) in Islam," in *Probing the Depths of Evil and Good: Multireligious Views and Case Studies*, ed. Jerald D. Gort, Henry Jansen and Hendrik M. Vroom (Amsterdam and New York: Editions Rodopi, 2007), pp. 257–80.

as their medieval Muslim counterparts. In particular, contemporary New Age depictions of Rabi'a are replete with gendered stereotypes. The only difference is in the details. For example, in contrast to Ibn al-Jawzi, who depicts Rabi'a as a hysterical eccentric, the New Age writer Charles Upton portrays Rabi'a as a dreamy romantic, a Sufi version of the Hippie-era flower child. In his book *Doorkeeper of the Heart*, he turns the medieval "Poem of the Intimate Gift" into a more modern adaptation:

> I set up house for you in my heart
> As a friend that I could talk with.
>
> Gave my body to someone else,
> Who wanted to embrace it.
>
> The body, all in all, is good enough for embracing.
> But the Friend who lives in my house
> Is the Lover of my Heart.[109]

In this poem, Upton evokes the 1960's Hippie-era ethic of free love. In the first verse, the reader is presented with an image of youthful domesticity, in which Rabi'a, the "girlfriend," sets up house with her divine "boyfriend." It is not hard to imagine the two of them sharing intimate converse over a cup of herbal tea. The second verse informs the reader in a rather offhanded way that Rabi'a has given her body to another and that furthermore, she may do so again. In this and the following verse, the romantic Hippie ethic of free love trumps the moral issues of betrayal and sexual promiscuity that are raised by this scenario. Rabi'a's gift of her body to another is ultimately of no major concern because her body is less authentically "hers" than her heart. Like the disposable husk of a seed, her body is "good enough for embracing." What is most important in the naive romanticism of this poem is the bond of true friendship that Rabi'a maintains with "the Lover of my Heart," for her heart is the core of her being. In Upton's poem, Rabi'a cohabits spiritually with her divine lover in a sort of "open marriage."

'Attar, whose representation of Rabi'a al-'Adawiyya lies behind the romanticized image of Rabi'a used by New Age writers like Upton, sought to avoid morally ambiguous scenarios by reminding his readers that she was not like ordinary women: "When a woman is on the path of God Most High, she is a

---

109 Upton, *Doorkeeper of the Heart*, p. 4.

man and cannot be called a woman."[110] Abu 'Abd al-Rahman al-Sulami had a similar idea in mind when he portrayed Rabi'a as the quintessential Sufi woman. Although he does not call Rabi'a an honorary man as 'Attar does, he makes a point of stressing that some of the most respected male scholars of her day sought out her knowledge and advice.[111] Sulami reverses the gender stereotypes of his era by portraying Rabi'a's spiritual knowledge as fully equal to that of a male Sufi master. In one account, he portrays Rabi'a as coming upon a crucified criminal. Rather than cringing or turning away at the grisly sight (as an ordinary woman might do), she looks directly at the crucified man and says, "Upon my father! With that tongue you used to say, 'There is no god but God!'"[112] This story illustrates what Amy Hollywood has called the "ethics of detachment," which is often found in hagiographic literature. In this trope, the saint refuses to make a personal moral judgment but rather affirms God's justice by allowing it to proceed in its own way.[113] Feminist theory, says Hollywood, has tended to regard such tropes as gendered expressions of the "male bias toward rationality, disembodiment, and justice."[114] However, she argues against this critique by stating that there is no necessary correlation between gender identity and either rationality or justice, nor is there a gendered correlation "between disinterestedness and rationality, or between the ideal of justice and a rule-based ethical system."[115]

Like the feminist historian Leila Ahmed, the scholar of Sufism Marcia Hermansen characterizes Sufi women as "culture-critiquing female heroes."[116] Although this is an appealing image, it is unfortunately an exaggeration. Most Sufi women are depicted in hagiographical accounts as supporting the status quo, including gender distinctions, rather than opposing them. Amy Hollywood's research into medieval Christian hagiography has made it clear that most often it was male writers, not the women they wrote about, who

---

110 'Attar, *Tadhkirat al-awliya'*, p. 61 and Sells, *Early Islamic Mysticism*, p. 155; the most recent major work on Rabi'a—Jean Annestay, *Une Femme Soufie en Islam: Rabi'a al-'Adawiyya* (Paris: Éditions Entrelacs, 2009)—provides a good example of how modern romantic narratives continue to depend on 'Attar. Although Annestay acknowledges in several places that 'Attar's accounts are historically anachronistic, he nevertheless reproduces them as if they were true.
111 Sulami, *Early Sufi Women*, pp. 74–5.
112 Ibid., pp. 80–1.
113 Hollywood, *The Soul as Virgin Wife*, pp. 193–6.
114 Ibid., p. 197.
115 Ibid., p. 198.
116 Marcia Hermansen, "The Female Hero in the Islamic Religious Tradition," in *The Annual Review of Women in World Religions*, ed. Arvind Sharma and Katherine K. Young (Albany, NY: SUNY Press, 1992), vol. 2, p. 130.

were the real culture critics. In this respect Muslim hagiography is no different. However, certain female figures are sometimes regarded as transcending gender stereotypes, even if the men who wrote about them could not always maintain this image consistently. Rabi'a al-'Adawiyya is a figure of this type. The ethics of detachment that she exhibits in Sulami's story of her encounter with the crucified man reflects the ostensibly "male" virtues of *muruwwa* (an ethic of mature behavior) and *hilm* (forbearance and practical wisdom). As we saw in Chapter 1, these characteristics are key elements of the trope of Rabi'a the Teacher. The cultural importance of these virtues during the Umayyad and Abbasid periods was that they signified the presence of intellect and reason, properties that in patriarchal Islamic society were attributed to men more than to women. For the Persian Sufis Sulami and 'Attar, Rabi'a was a unique woman who displayed the maturity, knowledge and judgment of a man. This is why 'Attar placed her outside the gender category of women. As Toshihiko Izutsu reminds us, *muruwwa* and *hilm* were culturally associated with men in early Islam because they are not passive virtues. Rather, they refer to "a [person] who governs and dominates others, and not of those who are governed and dominated."[117] In exemplifying these characteristics, Rabi'a al-'Adawiyya was thus more "male" than "female" because she exercised moral authority over men.

For Makki, Sulami, Khargushi and other Sufis who wrote about Rabi'a from the standpoint of institutionalized Sufism, she was seen as a figure of authority because her unique knowledge of God gave her the ability to make important insights into Sufi doctrines. However, for the trope of Rabi'a the Sufi, the knowledge that conveyed this ability went beyond what was expressed by mature reason and judgment. Sufi mystical theology acknowledges the importance of reason (*'aql*) and good judgment (*hilm*), which characterizes the trope of Rabi'a the Teacher, but it privileges knowledge that goes beyond such reasoning. Epistemologically, it is not enough to know about something (Ar. *'ilm* or *khibra*, "expertise"). Rather, it is more significant to *know the ways of knowing*—to be conversant with the "ins and outs" of knowledge itself (Ar. *ma'rifa*). For Makki and the Sufi theologians who followed him, Rabi'a al-'Adawiyya was able to impart remarkable insights to her students because she possessed this deeper type of knowledge. As discussed in the previous chapter, the root of this knowledge was in her combination of essential asceticism and Love mysticism. For the Sufi hagiographers who wrote about her, it did not matter whether or not she was called a "Sufi" in

---

117 Izutsu, *God and Man in the Koran*, p. 207.

her lifetime. Because the weight of evidence demonstrated that she possessed the type of knowledge that was seen as a hallmark of Sufism, she could only have been a "Sufi." That is to say, from the standpoint of major Sufi writers such as Makki, Sulami, Ghazali, or 'Attar, the distinction made in this chapter between "Rabi'a the Sufi" and the other master narratives in which she appears is somewhat artificial. For them the tropes of Rabi'a the Teacher, Rabi'a the Ascetic, and Rabi'a the Lover were all integral parts of the master narrative of Rabi'a the Sufi.

Although he was not a Sufi himself, the Abbasid-era *littérateur* Abu 'Uthman al-Jahiz was also thinking in much the same way when he described Rabi'a as a "Woman of *Bayan*." For Jahiz, the true intellectual was one who understood things "from their roots to their branches." As a Sufi theorist, Abu Talib al-Makki similarly indicated that Rabi'a possessed this kind of knowledge when he referred to her as a *muhiqqa*. By using this term he meant that she knew how everything "worked" or "fit together" in both the inner and outer dimensions of reality.[118] Through the wisdom of her teachings she could strip away the veil of appearances and reveal the true nature of things. For both Jahiz and Makki, as well as for their successors, this type of wisdom was exemplified by Rabi'a's use of the aphorism as a pedagogical tool. In other words, she personified James Geary's definition of the aphoristic way of knowledge: "Inside an aphorism it is minds that collide and the new matter that spins out at the speed of thought is that elusive thing we call wisdom."[119] Jahiz and Makki were well aware that creating a good aphorism takes more knowledge and skill than creating a good argument. This is because teaching by way of aphorisms requires a deeper and more thorough type of understanding than teaching by way of formal arguments. In order to convey a meaningful paradox to others one must possess a full understanding of paradoxical knowledge.[120] As Makki states about Rabi'a al-'Adawiyya in *Qut al-qulub*, in figurative terms, this type of knowledge resides in the heart rather than in the head.

The ability to teach with aphorisms was not the only type of advanced knowledge associated with the trope of Rabi'a the Sufi. As a *muhiqqa*, Rabi'a also had a deep understanding of moral conduct and the Shari'a. By understanding the proper balance between what pertains to God (*huquq Allah*) and what pertains to the human being (*huquq al-insan*), she was credited

---

118 Makki, *Qut al-qulub*, vol. 2, p. 95.
119 Geary, *The World in a Phrase*, p. 16.
120 For a comparison of the Sufi aphorism and the Zen *koan*, see Ernst, *Words of Ecstasy*, p. 133f.

with the paranormal ability to act in an appropriate way at all times and in all contexts. In the ethical worldview of Umayyad and early Abbasid Islam, this sense of innate appropriateness was an important sign of *hilm*. In the hagiographical tradition, Rabi'a's ability to accord everything its proper right or due allowed her to cast a critical eye on human behavior. This concept is expressed by the Arabic verb *haqqa*, the root of the term *muhiqqa*, by which Makki characterizes Rabi'a the Lover as Rabi'a the Sufi. The statement of Rabi'a recorded by Jahiz, 'By God, I am ashamed to ask for the world from the One who owns the world, so how can I ask for the world from one who does not own it?" also expresses this type of judgment. Thus, it is in terms of prioritizing moral and ontological truths (Ar. *tahqiq*) rather than of modern feminist theory that one is most justified in calling Rabi'a al-'Adawiyya a "culture-critic."

In Sufism, knowledge of the outward aspect of things (Ar. *zahir al-ashya'*) is indicated by the term *'ilm*, whereas knowledge of the inner nature of things (Ar. *batin al-ashya'*) is indicated by the term *ma'rifa*.[121] The term *ma'rifa* does not appear in the Qur'an, nor does it figure prominently in Hadith. By contrast, the word *'ilm* appears about 750 times in the Qur'an and includes all forms of knowledge, with special emphasis given to understanding the revelations and signs of God. Although the term *ma'rifa* is not used in the Qur'an, words derived from the Arabic verb *'arafa* ("to know" or "to be familiar with") are used more than 70 times and revolve semantically around the concept of knowledge as recognition.[122] Sometimes, the past participle *ma'ruf* ("known") is used to designate acts that are both lawful and morally transparent, such as in the phrase, "commanding the good (*al-ma'ruf*) and forbidding evil" (Qur'an 9:71).

The word *ma'rifa* as a term for inner knowledge first began to be used in Rabi'a al-'Adawiyya's lifetime, around the second half of the eighth century CE. Evidence for the use of *ma'rifa* as a technical term in this period can be found in the statement of Abu Hashim al-Sufi (d. 776 CE) that was discussed earlier in this chapter: "Those who truly know God (*ahl al-ma'rifa bi-llah*) are alienated from [the World] and are desirous of the Hereafter." In this

---

121 John Renard distinguishes these terms by defining *'ilm* as "discursive knowledge," "acquired knowledge," or "traditional knowledge," whereas *ma'rifa* is "experiential knowledge," "infused knowledge," "intimate knowledge," or "mystical knowledge." See idem, *Knowledge of God in Classical Sufism: Foundations of Islamic Mystical Theology* (New York and Mahwah, NJ: Paulist Press, 2004), p. 7.
122 Ibid., pp. 13–14; note that knowledge-as-recognition is considered philosophically to be a "Platonic" concept.

statement, Abu Hashim uses a phrase that can also be translated as the "People of the *Ma'rifa* of God." In this sense, the term *ma'rifa* denotes both knowledge and familiarity: those who know God in this way are also by implication the "friends" or "protégés" of God (*awliya' Allah*, Qur'an 10:63). This statement and others like it also imply that in Rabi'a's time *ma'rifa* was used to describe the knowledge obtained through essential asceticism, thus providing a connection between Proto-Sufism and Islamic ascetic traditions.[123]

A discussion of *ma'rifa* that comes close to how it was likely understood by the "real" Rabi'a al-'Adawiyya can be found in 'Ali al-Hujwiri's Sufi treatise, *Kashf al-mahjub*.[124] This work has already been cited for its discussion of the concept of the heart. Hujwiri's treatment of Sufi knowledge (which he terms *ma'rifat Allah*) is also useful for this discussion because he retains the distinction between inward and outward forms of knowledge that characterized the Proto-Sufism of Rabi'a's generation. For Hujwiri, *al-'ilm bi-llah*, outward knowledge of God, is essential for understanding the outward aspects of religion, such as Islamic law and dogmatic theology. In this sense, it is foundational for all religious knowledge in Islam. By contrast, *ma'rifa* or inward knowledge is a more advanced form of knowledge that comprises the in-depth knowledge of things and their attributes (*ma'rifa 'ilmiyya*), as well as the knowledge of states, contexts and conditions (*ma'rifa haliyya*). In summary, *ma'rifa* thus stands for both in-depth knowledge of the world and metaphysical states of being. It is superior to *'ilm* because it is the most comprehensive form of knowledge. For this reason, it leads the believer to the deepest understanding of God. Although the exoteric *al-'ilm bi-llah* is "the foundation of all blessings in this world and the next," it is spiritually of lesser value than the esoteric *ma'rifat Allah* because "the worth of everyone is in proportion to *ma'rifat Allah*, and he who is without *ma'rifa* is worth nothing."[125]

---

123 John Renard places the first Sufi use of *ma'rifa* in the ninth century CE. He identifies al-Harith al-Muhasibi as the first to make "a systematic effort to establish the foundations of Sufi thought as a legitimate religious discipline" (Ibid., p. 22). However, accounts of Proto-Sufis in works such as Isfahani's *Hilyat al-awliya'* make it clear that an understanding of *ma'rifa* that was very close to the eventual Sufi concept had been developed by the second half of the eighth century CE.

124 See Hujwiri, *Kashf al-mahjub*, pp. 266–77. In what follows, I depart from R.A. Nicholson's English translation of some of Hujwiri's concepts. For example, he translates *'ilm* as "cognition" and *hal* as "feeling." I find these translations to be superficial, and thus they do not accurately convey the meaning expressed by Hujwiri in the original Arabic-inflected Persian.

125 Ibid., p. 267.

Hujwiri also states that *'ilm* is a deficient form of knowledge epistemologically because it requires one to "turn away" or distance oneself from the object of knowledge in order to know it. For this reason, all that can be known theologically about God through *'ilm* are the outward manifestations of divinity, such as His laws, dogmas and divine attributes. However, in *ma'rifat Allah*, knowledge of God is not limited in this way. As with *'ilm*, the knowledge denoted by *ma'rifa* requires a "turning away;" however, in this case knowledge of God is gained not by turning away from the object of knowledge but by "turning away from everything that is *not* God [as the object of knowledge]." Thus, the one who possesses *ma'rifat Allah* achieves a greater degree of objective distance by turning away from the perspective of the World and by turning toward the perspective of true reality (*al-haqiqa*). In this sense, the epistemological meaning of *ma'rifa* as a form of in-depth knowledge shares much in common with the intimate knowledge gained by *mahabbat Allāh*, or the Love of God.[126]

Hujwiri's discussion of *ma'rifat Allah* is also helpful for understanding the aphorisms of Rabi'a al-'Adawiyya that express her essential asceticism. For example, when Rabi'a is asked in Khargushi's *Tahdhib al-Asrar* how she has attained her high spiritual station, she replies: "By leaving aside all that does not concern me and by cleaving to the One who always is."[127] According to Hujwiri's theory of *ma'rifa*, this act would be an excellent example of "turning away from everything that is *not* God." According to Rabi'a's statement, the essential ascetic must reposition herself with respect to the World in order to achieve a more profound perspective on the World.

Hujwiri's discussion of *ma'rifa* also helps explain another of Rabi'a's aphorisms: "For everything there is a fruit and the fruit of *ma'rifa* is orientation toward God."[128] According to this statement, true knowledge is both a goal and a return. Although orientation toward God is the "fruit" or goal of *ma'rifa*, it is also the beginning of *ma'rifa* because one cannot know God until one has turned away from everything other than God. The Sufi notion of orientation toward God is expressed by the verbal noun *iqbal*, which means "turning toward something" or "orienting oneself toward something." Semantically, this term is related to the Arabic noun *tawba* or "repentance," which similarly comes from a root that means, "to turn." For Sufis like Hujwiri as well as for Proto-Sufis like Rabi'a al-'Adawiyya, "turning to God in repentance" is the

---

126 Ibid., pp. 269–71.
127 Khargushi, *Tahdhib al-Asrar*, p. 81.
128 Sulami, *Early Sufi Women*, pp. 76–7 and Khargushi, *Tahdhib al-Asrar*, p. 49.

first step on the path of essential asceticism. Turning away from the World only makes sense spiritually if one turns toward God in place of the World. In the circular logic of this aphorism, "turning" or spiritual orientation has neither a beginning nor an end. Although the act of turning toward God is supposed to come before knowledge of God, the increase in knowledge of God reinforces and makes permanent the essential ascetic's "turn" toward the divine.

Sufi doctrinal and hagiographical works that convey traditions about early ascetics and Proto-Sufis indicate that along with the concept of *ma'rifa*, the practice of the invocation of God (*dhikr Allah*) also began to gain importance in the second half of the eighth century CE. Various forms of the verb *dhakara* ("to mention," "to recall") occur 290 times in the Qur'an. In addition, several Qur'anic verses in which the noun *dhikr* ("invocation" or "remembrance") is used, employ this term in ways that resemble Sufi concepts. Two such verses will suffice as examples here: "We did not send down before you aught but a man; so ask the Folk of Remembrance (*ahl al-dhikr*) if you do not know" (Qur'an 16:43); "It is only in the remembrance of God that the heart is at peace" (*ala bi-dhikri Allahi tatma'innu al-qulub*, Qur'an 13:28). The first of these verses refers to a group of people known as the "Folk of Remembrance." Sufis have long taken this appellation as referring to themselves. As for the second Qur'anic verse, Sufis see it as divine authorization for their practice of *dhikr* as invocation, which is a key characteristic of Sufi devotionalism.

Although most references to *dhikr* as a formal practice in Sufi sources were written after the mid-ninth century CE (nearly fifty years after Rabi'a al-'Adawiyya's death), several early ascetics, including Rabi'a herself, have been credited with establishing the practice of *dhikr* as a spiritual discipline. For example, in the chapter on Remembrance and Invocation in *Tahdhib al-asrar*, 'Abd al-Malik al-Khargushi quotes Rabi'a as making the following supplication: "My God, I ask you to make my aspiration in the World my remembrance (*dhikr*) of you in the World; and [to make my aspiration of you] in the Hereafter the vision (*ru'ya*) of you."[129] Khargushi also quotes Abu Sulayman al-Darani as saying, "One who knows his Lord (*man 'arafa rabbahu*) finds that his heart is panicked because of the recollection (*dhikr*) of Him. It is preoccupied in service to Him, and it weeps at its mistakes."[130] Ibrahim ibn Adham is quoted as saying: "One who does not find three habits (*mawatin*) in his heart finds the door to God locked before him. [These are]:

---

129 Khargushi, *Tahdhib al-asrar*, p. 318.
130 Ibid.

recitation of the Qur'an; remembrance (*dhikr*) of God the Great and Glorious; and prayer (*salat*)."[131]

These traditions are important both for what they say and for what they do not say. First, Darani's use of the verb *'arafa* indicates that the concept of *ma'rifa* in the sense of "knowing God deeply" may already have been established as a spiritual goal by the time of Rabi'a's death. The same can be said of the correspondence between the knowledge of God (*ma'rifat Allah*) and the remembrance of God (*dhikr Allah*). The fact that Khargushi cites Darani as speaking of *dhikr* is significant, because the early Sufi who is most often quoted on the practice of *dhikr* is Dhu al-Nun al-Misri (d. 859 CE). As we have seen, some early writers allege that Dhu al-Nun was Darani's student. However, it is also important to note that the early mystics of Rabi'a's time do not yet seem to have settled on a common understanding of the meaning of *dhikr* or on how the concept of *dhikr* relates to the concept of *ma'rifa*. Rabi'a's understanding of *dhikr* in the above quotation has to do primarily with the recollection of God's actions in the World. Here *dhikr* connotes remembrance through observation and reflection; as such, it is related to the concept of *tafakkur* ("consideration," "reflection," or "meditation"), which also appears in the discourses of Proto-Sufis around this time. Darani, on the other hand, thinks of *dhikr* as an act of momentary recollection—as if God suddenly comes to mind and startles the worshipper into the awareness of His presence. This is more like a flash of insight. By contrast, for Ibrahim ibn Adham *dhikr* is clearly a form of invocation, for he speaks of *dhikr* as a practice to which the heart becomes accustomed. Nonetheless, despite such differences, all of these statements agree on the implication that *dhikr* occurs in the heart, which is the seat of the spiritual intellect. This provides important circumstantial evidence that the concepts of heart, knowledge, and remembrance were already defining elements of Proto-Sufism at the end of the eighth century CE.

---

131 Ibid.

Chapter 5

Rabi'a the Icon (I): the Sufi Image

"All classical culture lived for centuries on the notion that reality could in no way contaminate verisimilitude; first of all because verisimilitude is never anything but *opinable*: it is entirely subject to (public) opinion; as [Pierre] Nicole said: 'One must not consider things as they are in themselves, nor as they are known to be by one who speaks or writes, but only in relation to what is known of them by those who read and hear'. . . In verisimilitude, the contrary is never impossible, since notation rests on a majority, but not an absolute opinion. The motto implicit on the threshold of all classical discourse (subject to the ancient idea of verisimilitude) is: *Esto* (*Let there be, suppose. . .*)."
—Roland Barthes, "The Reality Effect" (1968),
in *The Rustle of Language*

"Wholeness is something we impose on narratives, rather than something we find in them."
—H. Porter Abbott, *The Cambridge Introduction to Narrative*

I. RABI'A AS A LITERARY FIGURE: MYTH, ICON, AND THE "REALITY EFFECT"

In the previous chapter I introduced Roland Barthes' concept of the "reality effect" (*l'effet du réel*) in Elizabeth A. Clark's article, "The Lady Vanishes: Dilemmas of a Feminist Historian after the 'Linguistic Turn'." Clark used this concept to show how in early Christian hagiography tropes and other narrative elements work together to give the story of a saint an aura of factuality that may not be deserved. As an aspect of narrative, the reality effect is a product of the interrelationship between the narrative structure and the master plots, characters, relations, and actions in the story. As such, it is related to the concepts of narrative probability and narrative fidelity discussed in the Introduction. This phenomenon can also be found in Islamic hagiography. As we saw in Chapter 3, as a result of the reality effect, the narrative motif of Rabi'a al-'Adawiyya as the founder of Sufi Love mysticism has become such a part of the historical memory of the Sufi tradition that doctrines related to this concept have been read back anachronistically into her narratives.[1] It is not an exaggeration to say that the trope of Rabi'a the Lover owes more to the reality effect than to the actual evidence of her teachings.

As Barthes explains this concept, the reality effect creates an imaginary sense of "paper time" that replaces the chronological time of history with "a reminiscence or a nostalgia, a complex, parametric, non-linear time whose deep space recalls the mythic time of the ancient cosmogonies."[2] Under the influence of the reality effect, tropes based on narratives take the place of historical memory and transform historical persons and events into myths. Master narratives such as the tropes of Rabi'a al-'Adawiyya discussed in this book constitute what Barthes calls "referential illusions." Referential illusions are narrative constructs that take on the appearance of reality and thus have the ability to change historical memory. For Barthes, because these illusions appear to be real, they are comparable to myths; thus, the writers that use them can be viewed as agents or propagators of myth.[3]

Barthes first introduced the concept of the reality effect in the essay, "Le Discours de l'Histoire" (The Discourse of History), in his book *Informations sur les sciences sociales* (1967).[4] In this essay, he shows how the reality effect functions in historical writing. His description of this process suggests certain similarities with Hayden White's theory of tropology. First, Barthes and White both use the linguistic theories of Roman Jakobson (1896–1982) to conduct structural analyses "of the universals of discourse... in the form of units and

---

1 This process still continues today. In a chapter in *The Cambridge Companion to Sufism* (2015), Rabi'a is called "the supreme mistress of the Sufi Religion of Love." See Leonard Lewisohn, "Sufism's Religion of Love from Rabi'a to Ibn al-'Arabi," in Ridgeon (ed.), *The Cambridge Companion to Sufism*, p. 151.
2 Roland Barthes, "The Discourse of History," in idem, *The Rustle of Language*, pp. 130–1.
3 Ibid., pp. 131–2.
4 Ibid., pp. 127–40.

general rules of combination."⁵ Second, both theorists separate the form of historical discourse from the content and argue that the form of a narrative discourse can provide new content on a meta-level that is revealed within the structure of the text. What White refers to as the "content of the form" can be seen in what Barthes calls the "arrangement of the thematic units" of historical narratives. White calls these thematic units "tropes," as in the title of his book *Tropics of Discourse* (i.e., "Trope-ics of Discourse"). Although tropes or themes can be found in all historical narratives, for Barthes they are especially visible in premodern historical works, which do not correspond to modern Western notions of empirical history.⁶ According to Barthes, a looser or more "fluid" approach to the question of historical accuracy is typical of premodern historical literature. As recent research on the historiography of sainthood has demonstrated, few genres of premodern historical writing were more "fluid" and hence susceptible to tropological construction than hagiography or "sacred biography."

Thomas J. Heffernan, the historian of sainthood who introduced the concept of sacred biography, defines this genre as "a narrative text of the *vita* of the saint written by a member of the community of belief. The text provides a documentary witness to the process of sanctification for the community and in so doing becomes itself a part of the sacred tradition it serves to document."⁷ Clearly, many of the narratives dedicated to the memory of Rabi'a al-'Adawiyya, both premodern and modern, can be characterized as sacred biography according to Heffernan's definition. It is also evident that the narratives that make up sacred biography often depend for their effectiveness on the reality effect as discussed by Barthes. At times, Heffernan discusses sacred biography in semiotic terms that are very reminiscent of Barthes: "Narrative in this genre is primarily a medium for symbolic representation, since the essential thing (*res*) being signified (the presence of the divine in the saint) exists outside a system where sign and signified can be empirically validated. It follows that our reading and interpretation of such narrative should take seriously its symbolizing structures."⁸ According to this statement, it seems as if Barthes and Heffernan are arguing from the same theoretical position.

---

5   Ibid., p. 127.
6   Ibid., p. 134.
7   Thomas J. Heffernan, *Sacred Biography: Saints and Their Biographers in the Middle Ages* (New York and Oxford, UK: Oxford University Press, 1988), p. 16.
8   Ibid., p. 11.

However, on closer examination we can see that this is not really the case. Heffernan's approach to sacred biography is not based on narrative or linguistic theory, as Barthes' is. Instead, it is based on the French *Annales* tradition of historiography, which regards texts as documents rather than as literature. According to this perspective (*pace* Barthes), hagiographic accounts are not myths. As Heffernan states, the hagiographic text provides "documentary witness" to empirically verifiable social facts and mentalities that exist outside of the text. Even if one cannot objectively prove the truth-claims of hagiographical accounts, some kind of objective truth is still present beyond the text. In *Annales*-type studies of sainthood, the subjective belief that God is acting through the saint is replaced by the objective reality of public opinion as expressed through the hagiographic text. As Heffernan puts it, the reality of public opinion is "witnessed" by the text, and the text is to be read by the historian as evidence of this reality. For Heffernan, the hagiographic text reflects an image of the saint that is socially generated. Thus, the "truth" of a saint is not to be found in the structures of hagiographic narratives as in Barthes' approach but rather in how the community views the saint in the collective memory that it constructs of her. In this type of historiography, the form of the hagiographic narrative, which is centrally important for Roland Barthes and Hayden White, is less important than the public perception of celebrity or reputation.

While the *Annales*-based historiography of Thomas Heffernan deserves much credit for opening sacred biography to systematic study, it only tells part of the story. It is indeed important for historians to recognize that hagiographic texts can provide insights into popularly held beliefs; these should neither be overlooked nor trivialized. However, it is also important not to overlook the fact that hagiographic texts may *create* public opinion as well as reflect it. To illustrate this point, I will give an example from personal experience.

In 2007, I was at a conference in Morocco that was attended by Iraqi scholars from the Al-Khoie Foundation in London. While most of these scholars were from Baghdad, two of them were from Basra. During one of the breaks in the conference, I told them of my research on Rabi'a al-'Adawiyya and asked if any of them knew the location of Rabi'a's tomb in Basra. Since the site of Basra in Rabi'a's time was some distance away from the city of Basra today, a heated discussion took place in which several locations around Basra were mentioned as possible sites of her tomb. Unfortunately, I did not write down the names of these locations and forgot about them until about six months later. At that time, I tried to contact the scholars from Basra to see if they could recall the places they had mentioned. The reply that I received was surprising. First of all, they had completely forgotten the locations that they had mentioned at the conference. However, even more surprisingly, they referred me for information on the location of Rabi'a's tomb to *Wafayat al-a'yan* (*Death Notices of the Notables*), a thirteenth-century historical work by Abu al-'Abbas Ahmad ibn Khallikan (d. 1282 CE). Although Ibn Khallikan was born in the Iraqi city of Erbil, he spent most of his life in the Syrian city of Damascus. As we shall see later in this chapter, in this work he conflates accounts of Rabi'a al-'Adawiyya of Basra and Rabi'a bint Isma'il of Damascus and claims that Rabi'a al-'Adawiyya was buried not in Basra but in Jerusalem. Having forgotten our discussion in Morocco, the scholars from Basra insisted that Rabi'a al-'Adawiyya was buried in Jerusalem, just as Ibn Khallikan claimed. Because of Ibn Khallikan's authoritative reputation as a chronicler of famous notables, they valued his mistaken information above local knowledge and other accounts that placed the tomb of Rabi'a in the Basra region.

Jerusalem is not the only alternative site for Rabi'a al-'Adawiyya's tomb. Some premodern writers have her buried in Egypt and a tomb ascribed to Rabi'a can be seen today in Cairo. Other alternative sites exist as well, including tombs in Damascus and Afghanistan. This is despite the fact that the earliest accounts of Rabi'a all agree in locating both her residence and her burial place in Basra. However, as Roland Barthes states in the epigraph to this chapter, empirically verifiable truth is largely irrelevant to myths. Verisimilitude—the appearance of truth—is what matters most. Barthes quotes the seventeenth-century French essayist Pierre Nicole (1625–95) as saying, "One must consider things only in relation to what is known of them by those who read and hear." This quotation helps explain the story of my strange experience with the scholars from Basra. For these scholars, the verisimilitude of an account in a respected medieval text from Syria was so great as to cause them to forget the location of a tomb that was actually in the vicinity of their own city. To this day, I still have not found anyone from Basra who can tell me exactly where Rabi'a al-'Adawiyya is buried.[9] This does not necessarily mean that her burial place has been forgotten. However, it

---

9   Local tradition in Basra claims that Rabi'a al-'Adawiyya's grave is somewhere in the cemetery adjoining the tomb of al-Hasan al-Basri in the suburb of al-Zubayr, which was the site of Basra in Rabi'a's time. Also in this cemetery are said to be the graves of Mu'adha al-'Adawiyya, Maryam of Basra, Shu'ba ibn al-Hajjaj, and the Umayyad-era poet al-Farazdaq.

does illustrate the power of verisimilitude to create new "facts," even at the expense of other information that is likely to be more accurate.

According to Barthes' theory of the reality effect, the misplacement of Rabi'a's tomb by the scholars of Basra was due to a "referential illusion" created by a highly respected historical source. This source was Ibn Khallikan's book *Wafayat al-a'yan* and the referential illusion was the conflation of Rabi'a al-'Adawiyya and Rabi'a bint Isma'il that led to the misplacement of Rabi'a's tomb in Jerusalem. Because this referential illusion came from a "classical" and hence respected source, it influenced the scholars from Basra so much that the illusion took the place of more accurate information. Because Ibn Khallikan's reputation as an Islamic historian is so well established, the believability of his erroneous information was greater than that of local knowledge, even for these modern residents of Rabi'a's home city. For these scholars of Basra, the Rabi'a of literature was indistinguishable from the Rabi'a of history. Thus, they became another link in the chain of "agents of myth" of the Rabi'a narrative that extends from the present day back into medieval times.

Barthes further explains that the reality effect is the result of a dialectical process in which "the extrusion of the signified outside the 'objective' discourse," leads to a confrontation between the real and its alternative expression. This confrontation creates a new meaning that is taken for the real itself. Because all historical memory depends in part on the reality effect of narratives, Barthes is pessimistic about the ability of history to relate empirically verifiable facts: "Historical discourse does not follow the real, it merely signifies it, constantly repeating *this happened*, without this assertion ever being anything but the signified *wrong side* of all historical narration."[10]

In the story of Rabi'a from narrative to myth, the hagiographic text that best illustrates the power of the reality effect is the chapter on Rabi'a al-'Adawiyya in Farid al-Din al-'Attar's *Tadhkirat al-awliya'* (*Memorial of the Saints*). From the time it was written at the beginning of the thirteenth century CE, 'Attar's chapter has been the source text for nearly all subsequent versions of Rabi'a's story, including modern works of historical scholarship. Because of this, 'Attar has become the most important agent of the Rabi'a myth. For most Muslims today, the "truth" of 'Attar's version of Rabi'a's life has become so obvious as to call for neither comment nor critique. In Barthes'

---

10   Barthes, "The Discourse of History," p. 139; italics in the original.

terminology, the verisimilitude of 'Attar's depiction of Rabi'a inhabits the realm of the "falsely obvious."[11]

However, as Barthes would hasten to add, Rabi'a is more than just a figure of narrative. She is also a myth. As I argued in the Introduction, a theory of myth is just as important for understanding the story of Rabi'a al-'Adawiyya as a theory of narrative. Barthes' semiological theory of myth can be of great help in understanding the symbolic aspects of the Rabi'a myth. A discussion of this theory will make up a significant part of the Epilogue. However, other theorists may be better for helping us understand the phenomenological aspects of the Rabi'a myth. One of the best theorists for this purpose is the Russian philosopher and historian Aleksei Fyodorovich Losev (1893–1988). Although Losev was one of the most important Russian intellectuals of the twentieth century, he remains largely unknown in the West because his works were banned by the Soviet Union for most of his life. Losev's first published book was on the subject of myth. This work, *The Dialectics of Myth* (1930), was banned by Soviet authorities because it was based on the prohibited doctrines of phenomenology and philosophical idealism and also because Losev was a believer in Russian Orthodox mysticism.[12]

Like Barthes, Losev was more interested in the structure of myth than in its contents. Also like Barthes, he did not consider myth to be an exclusively religious phenomenon: "Myth as such, pure mythical nature as such, does not necessarily have to be religious in principle... Religion brings into myth a specific content that makes it a religious myth, but the *structure* of myth itself by no means depends on whether it is filled with religious or some other content."[13] Losev further agreed with Barthes that myth has an expressive function. However, he explores this aspect of myth phenomenologically and existentially rather than linguistically: "Myth is not the substantial, but an *energistic* self-affirmation of a person. It is the assertion of a person not

---

11 Roland Barthes, 1957 Introduction to *Mythologies*, trans. Annette Lavers (New York: Hill & Wang, 1972), p. 11.
12 See the biography of Losev in the Introduction to Aleksei Fyodorovich Losev, *The Dialectics of Myth*, trans. Vladimir Marchenkov (London and New York: Routledge, 2003), pp. 1–15. After publishing this work, Losev was arrested and condemned to a labor camp. He soon became blind and was lucky to survive his ordeal. In 1931 Maxim Gorky criticized Losev for being a "blind, insane, and illiterate professor who had failed to die in a timely fashion" (p. 14). Ironically, his sentence was suspended in 1933 at the intercession of Gorky's wife, who was then the head of the Soviet Red Cross.
13 Ibid., p. 92; the italics in this and other quotations come from the published text.

in her deepest and ultimate root, but in her *manifestational* and *expressive* functions."[14]

According to Losev, when a historical personage is turned into a mythical figure, she becomes an idealized image: "Myth is a *depiction* of a person, i.e., her pictorial emanation, her image."[15] However, this ideal image is not a philosophical ideal but an existential phenomenon. As phenomena, both the myth and the person behind the myth occupy the same space in the mind of the believer. As Losev expresses it, "Myth is not a person as such, but her face; and this means that the face is inseparable from the person, i.e., myth is inseparable from her."[16] If one were to apply Losev's theory of myth to the myth that emerges from the Rabi'a narratives, one could say that the "face" of Rabi'a—the mythical identity that she possesses—has become the dominant reality of Rabi'a al-'Adawiyya over time. For those who keep her memory, the mythical identity of Rabi'a expresses an objective reality, no matter how much contrary evidence is provided. We have already seen how this concept applied to the scholars of Basra who thought that Rabi'a was buried in Jerusalem. One could also cite as an example the Bosnian Muslims who are fans of the *ilahi*, "Hassan u Rabija," introduced at the beginning of Chapter 3. For these people, the historical anachronisms in the lyrics of the song are not important. It makes no difference to them that the ages of al-Hasan al-Basri and Rabi'a al-'Adawiyya should be reversed or that these two figures most likely never met. In mythological narratives, the teacher must always be older than the student. Since in the *ilahi* Rabi'a is the teacher of Hasan, the idealized "face" of Rabi'a must therefore be older than that of Hasan. For Losev, tropological constructs such as these are common characteristics of "myth in history." Each new narrative adaptation of a myth engages dialectically with previous narratives in a never-ending process of interpretation. In this process, new "faces" or identities are continually generated without resolving the contradictions between the myth and the empirically "real" person behind the myth.

However, in this Venetian masked ball of tropes, character types, and mythological identities, a phenomenologically "real" Rabi'a can still be found behind the idealized image of Rabi'a al-'Adawiyya, even if she is not real in an empirical sense. This is because the myth of Rabi'a al-'Adawiyya has its own form of historical reality. Like Pierre Hadot's "figure," discussed

---

14　Ibid., p. 93.
15　Ibid.
16　Ibid.

in Chapter 1, the mythological image of Rabi'a is just as much a historical reality—if not more so—than the image of the empirically "real" Rabi'a that we have tried to discern in the previous chapters. This notion of phenomenological reality is how Losev approaches Barthes' concept of the reality effect and it helps explain how myths can create new historical "truths." Even the Egyptian atheist philosopher 'Abd al-Rahman Badawi was able to discern the phenomenological truth of the Rabi'a myth, although he could not acknowledge its objective reality. In the book *Shahidat al-'ishq al-ilahi* (*The Martyr of Divine Love*), he tells about his visit to the alleged tomb of Rabi'a in Damascus in December 1947. He describes how an old man who had been a devotee of the tomb for fifty years insisted that Rabi'a had protected the neighborhood of the tomb from a French air raid during the Damascus revolt of 1925. Rather than deny that the "real" Rabi'a had anything to do with the event or was even buried in the tomb, Badawi accepts the reality of her myth as the old man experienced it and states at the end of the story: "And still the memory of Rabi'a al-'Adawiyya lives on universally in the souls of the people of Damascus and Syria!"[17]

Losev accounts for the phenomenological reality that Badawi noticed by explaining that the "face" or persona of a mythicized historical figure is both "real" and "unreal" at the same time:

> Dialectics demands a *simultaneous* recognition that a person is *identical* to her manifestations and energies, and at once *different* from them. There is *one* thing, *one and the same thing*—a person with living functions, but this does not prevent the person as such being different from her own states and energies... The face, the mythical visage, is inseparable from the person and is therefore the person herself. But the person herself is different from her own mythical visages, and therefore she is neither her own face, nor her own myth, nor these mythical visages.[18]

Losev approaches the subject of myth from two perspectives simultaneously—from the perspective of narrative and from the perspective of the audience. This enables him to understand myth as the product of a dialectical relationship between narrative and audience. As a historian of sainthood, he provides a bridge between Barthes and Heffernan. While

---

17 Badawi, *Shahidat al-'ishq al-ilahi*, p. 100.
18 Losev, *The Dialectics of Myth*, p. 93.

Barthes examines the structure of the hagiographical narrative to see how it can create an alternate reality, Losev steps away from the narrative to see how the audience experiences this reality. In this sense, he is more like Heffernan than Barthes. However, when Losev speaks about mythical representation, his approach is semiotic, like that of Barthes. The key metaphor that he uses for the mythical representation of a historical figure is the *icon*. In the context of the Rabi'a myth, Losev would say that Muslims approach the narrative image of Rabi'a in much the same way that Christians approach the painted icon of a saint in an Orthodox Church. In fact, this can be observed in many representations of Rabi'a in contemporary literature. To give but one example: the Lebanese–Syrian writer Widad El Sakkakini describes Rabi'a in her novelistic biography *The Sufi Lover* (*al-'Ashiqa al-mutasawwifa*), as if she were describing an Orthodox icon: "I am looking at Rabi'a al-'Adawiyya as if through eternity, or at the door of the infinite. In her right hand, she is holding a thick book of pages without blemish, the first of which she is about to turn. She goes over it contemplatively and tenderly."[19] Like the image of a saint in an Orthodox icon, El Sakkakini's vision of Rabi'a is not the same as the "real" Rabi'a but it is not completely unreal either. When she imagines Rabi'a, she makes the details of her vision conform to the deeper reality that the image represents.

The Dutch scholar of religion Hendrik M. Vroom has similarly observed that religious stories cause the audience to "see otherwise," or better yet, "to see more truly."[20] Vroom argues that religious narratives can make truth claims on four different levels at the same time:

1. *Historical truth claims* relate an allegedly historical event.
2. *Fictional truth claims* tell the story not as it empirically occurred but "as what could have happened in order to yield insight."[21]
3. *Moral truth claims* provide the background lesson, or the "moral" of the story.
4. *Religious truth claims* provide insight into the story as it is connected to God.

---

19 El Sakkakini, *First Among Sufis*, p. 9; idem, *al-'Ashiqa al-mutasawwifa*, p. 10.
20 See Hendrik M. Vroom, "Religious Truth: Seeing Things As They Really Are, Experience, Insight, and Religious Stories," in Frederiek Depoortere and Magdalen Lambkin, *The Question of Theological Truth: Philosophical and Interreligious Perspectives* (Amsterdam and New York: Rodopi Press, 2012), pp. 115–35.
21 Ibid., p. 128.

According to Vroom, none of these truth claims necessarily excludes the others. For example, the fact that a religious story is empirically untrue (i.e., that an event did not happen in the way that the historical truth claim asserts) makes no difference to the moral and religious truth claims of the narrative. Because the story appeals to a higher truth, the insights that the narrative provides are still "real." In fact, with respect to moral and religious truth claims, the meaning of a fictional narrative might even be "truer" than what actually happened. Losev would not have disagreed with Vroom on this point. As a Russian Orthodox mystic, he was fully aware of the value of truth claims that cannot be assessed empirically. Unlike the secular Barthes, he would not have claimed that the mythical visage of a saint portrayed through the reality effect was "falsely obvious" or less real than the actual living person.

Unlike Thomas Heffernan, who argues that the image of a saint is a reflection of public opinion, for Losev, "Myth is in no sense any kind of reflection. It is always a manifestation, immediate and naive reality, a seen and tangibly felt sculptural quality of life."[22] For Heffernan and Vroom, the theologies that underlie the religious truth claims of hagiography are dogmatic: they act as thematic frameworks for how the saint is to be perceived. For example, Vroom might use this argument to explain why the faces of saints in Russian Orthodox icons all seem to look alike. His explanation would be that the faces of Orthodox saints look the same because they reflect symbolically the same dogmatic theologies. For Losev, however, myth is not dogmatic but creative. Because hagiographic narratives refer to specific times and places, the myths that they create are situated in time. Theological dogma, which Losev calls the "absolutization" of myth, stands outside of time. Myth, however, remains a part of time (and thus of history) because it expresses a type of becoming.

To illustrate what he means by the "historical" aspect of myth, Losev uses the example of the Russian myth of the blossoming fern on St John's Eve. According to Orthodox Christian tradition, St John's Eve marks the birthday of St John the Baptist. For the Russian Orthodox believer, finding a blossoming fern on St John's Eve is a lucky event: it can help one find hidden treasures and perform other extraordinary acts. However, if one takes away the "historical" event of St John the Baptist's birthday, the fern becomes like any other object, "any stone lying along the road with other refuse."[23] For Losev, the

---

22 Losev, *The Dialectics of Myth*, p. 100.
23 Ibid., pp. 101–2.

association of the myth of the blossoming fern with a specific event—even if that event is itself mythological—proves that the myth is inseparable from history. Its power is based on a historical truth claim: it symbolizes the birth of St John the Baptist, a "real" historical figure. For the myth to be meaningful it must have a historical context, even if that context only exists in what Barthes would call "paper time." Similarly, the Rabiʿa myth is grounded in the historical truth claims of the Rabiʿa al-ʿAdawiyya master narrative. In Losev's terminology, her myth is traced in the *visages, forms, images,* and *outlines* of narratives that portray her at different moments in "historical" time.

II. FROM VISAGE TO *VITA*: ʿATTAR'S OUTLINE OF THE RABIʿA MYTH

a. Composing the Background: ʿAttar's Hagiographic Predecessors

In the jargon of narrative theory, Roland Barthes' concept of the reality effect, Hayden White's theory of the "tropics of discourse," Hendrik Vroom's theory of the levels of truth in religious narratives, and Aleksei Fyodorovich Losev's dialectics of myth all deal in one way or another with the concept of the *implied author*. This concept refers to the feeling of sensibility or personality that the reader finds in a written narrative: it is "that combination of feeling, intelligence, knowledge, and opinion that accounts for the narrative."[24] Readers of narratives believe that they have found the implied author when they identify a set of views that appears to be consistent with all the elements of the narrative discourse, as they understand it.[25] Barthes', White's, Vroom's and Losev's theories may also be described as examples of *symptomatic reading*. In other words, "the narrative is seen to expose symptomatically the conditions out of which it comes."[26] To a greater or lesser degree, these theories also involve *deconstructive reading*. That is, they deconstruct the *intentional reading* or surface meaning of the narrative to find an underlying or background reading that the real or implied author

---

24 Abbott, *The Cambridge Introduction to Narrative*, p. 84. The concept of the implied author comes from Wayne Booth. See idem, *The Company We Keep: An Ethics of Fiction* (Berkeley: University of California Press, 1988), especially the chapter, "Implied Authors as Friends and Pretenders", pp. 169–98.
25 Abbott, *The Cambridge Introduction to Narrative*, p. 84.
26 Ibid., p. 105.

may or may not have been conscious of constructing.[27] These approaches offer new interpretations for the story in order to fill in perceived gaps or resolve contradictions that appear in the narrative discourse. The danger involved in such readings is the problem of *overreading*: the tendency to find qualities, moods, motives, ideas and judgments for which there is no direct evidence in the discourse.[28] This is especially a problem with symptomatic and deconstructive readings.

However, sometimes the implied author turns out to be the true author and sometimes what at first seems to be unconscious in a narrative discourse turns out to be intentional. As we have seen in the previous chapters, this is the case for many of the Rabi'a narratives. In the premodern historiography of the Rabi'a al-'Adawiyya master narrative, three Sufi authors stand out for developing the most durable character types or tropes. The first of these authors is Abu Talib al-Makki, who was primarily responsible for the trope of Rabi'a the Lover. As we saw in Chapter 3, creating this trope did not mean that Makki was the first to associate Rabi'a with Love mysticism. This connection had already been made in the mid-ninth century CE by al-Harith al-Muhasibi. Makki took Muhasibi's and other early depictions of Rabi'a and made adaptations of them in light of the Platonically inspired Love theory that was popular in his time. By portraying Rabi'a as a Muslim Diotima in his book *Qut al-qulub*, he highlighted the mystical elements of Plato's Love theory and wove them into a theory of Sufi knowledge. By using the figure of Rabi'a to stand for the mystic who had attained the station of Certainty, he not only established her as one of the greatest Love mystics in Islam but he also enshrined her as the icon of this tradition. Whatever the actual content of her Love teachings might have been, Rabi'a's mythical visage henceforward would always include the trope of Rabi'a the Lover.

The character type of Rabi'a the Lover as depicted by Makki and the Sufis who followed him constitutes what the Moroccan scholar of Arabic literature Abdelfattah Kilito—a student of Roland Barthes—calls an *exemplary figure*. This concept has much in common with Pierre Hadot's concept of the *figure*, discussed in Chapter 1. However, more like Barthes than Hadot, Kilito describes the exemplary figure as "an empty shell with a yawning mouth, filling itself with whatever new content it can swallow, the new content

---

27 Ibid.
28 Ibid., p. 89.

being always reminiscent of the old."[29] He goes on to explain what he means by this dramatic metaphor:

> Because he is familiar to both author and reader, the exemplary figure can be evoked with the most sparing of details. His name refers directly to an instantly recognizable background. Like the transparent anecdote, the exemplary anecdote permits the construction of a series of tales featuring the same protagonist; it wears a sort of cloak that can be stretched in any direction. No attribution of words or actions to the exemplar can ever have unpleasant consequences, either for the exemplar or for the person making the attribution. The salient property of the figure is its transcendence of time and place. Joseph is always beautiful and Nestor was never young.[30]

Besides Hadot's concept of the figure, Kilito's exemplary figure also brings to mind Losev's concept of the "face" or "visage." Kilito explains that the exemplary figure is illustrated by *exemplary anecdotes* that depict the character's key attributes:

> [The exemplary anecdote] depicts a character whose name, by some subtle transformation, becomes the sign of a moral quality or some other attribute such as beauty, stupidity, generosity, or stinginess. The actions and statements attributed to such a character conform to and extend the function he exemplifies, and prepare the ground for a proliferation of numberless bastard offspring. Once this proliferation has begun, no standard permits us to distinguish between legitimate and bastard children.[31]

To illustrate the use of the exemplary figure in premodern Arabic literature, Kilito uses selections from Jahiz's *Book of Misers* (*Kitab al-bukhala'*). This is a fortuitous example because as we saw in Chapter 1, in two other works—*Kitab al-hayawan* and *Kitab al-bayan wa-l-tabyin*—Jahiz portrays Rabi'a as a "Person of *Bayan*" in much the same way that Kilito describes the exemplary figure. In addition, Jahiz provided "exemplary anecdotes" for Rabi'a that

---

29 Abdelfattah Kilito, *The Author and His Doubles: Essays on Classical Arabic Culture*, trans. Michael Cooperson (Syracuse, NY: Syracuse University Press, 2001), p. 60.
30 Ibid., pp. 60–1.
31 Ibid., pp. 59–60.

helped establish the tropes of Rabi'a the Teacher and Rabi'a the Ascetic. For Kilito, the exemplary anecdote is a sub-category of the *transparent anecdote*. Transparent anecdotes are so closely associated with a subject that "the mere mention of them instantly betrays the identity of that subject."[32] These anecdotes serve as references to an *anchoring name*, which not only heightens the power of the anecdote but "also opens up a vast field of related anecdotes, all of which have the same figure as their hero."[33] For Jahiz, the appellation "Rabi'a al-Qaysiyya" was such an anchoring name. The simple mention of this name, along with a transparent anecdote like, "I am ashamed to ask for the world from the one who owns the world. So how can I ask for the world from one who does not own it?" conjured up the exemplary figure of Rabi'a of Basra as a Person of *Bayan*.

In the early development of the Rabi'a master narrative, the exemplary anecdotes transmitted by writers such as Jahiz, Ibn Abi Tahir Tayfur and Makki and by traditionists such as Burjulani, Ibn al-Junayd and Ibn Abi al-Dunya clustered around the anchoring name of Rabi'a al-'Adawiyya and gave rise to the exemplary figures or tropes of Rabi'a the Teacher, Rabi'a the Ascetic and Rabi'a the Lover. The interrelationship between anchoring name, trope and master narrative additionally gave birth to what Kilito calls "bastard children"—new generations of anecdotes and narratives. As these "children" proliferated, the point was reached where the sheer number of narratives began to be taken as evidence of the historical reality of the character type that they portrayed. By this stage, which was reached around the beginning of the eleventh century CE, all that was needed to turn the trope of Rabi'a al-'Adawiyya into a myth was to link her to the origins of Sufism as a developing institution and to provide a *vita* or "backstory" that would add verisimilitude to her tropological identity.

Abu 'Abd al-Rahman al-Sulami (d. 1021 CE) was the most influential author to link the exemplary figure of Rabi'a al-'Adawiyya to the origins of Sufism. Although Sulami has long been known as an important hagiographer and writer on Sufi doctrines, his reputation has increased in recent years due to the edition and publication of many of his works. We now know that his doctrinal works were Sufi "best-sellers" of their day and that he was one of the most influential early systematizers of Sufi doctrines and practices.[34]

---

32   Ibid., p. 59.
33   Ibid.
34   On the popularity of Sulami's works in his time see al-Khatib al-Baghdadi, *Ta'rikh Baghdad*, vol. 2, p. 245.

Although he had a low opinion of ordinary women, he believed that Sufi women deserved a hermeneutic of remembrance, so that their contributions to Islam could be appreciated. Sulami's solution for this problem was to compose the first hagiographical work on Sufi women, *Dhikr al-niswa al-muta'abbidat al-sufiyyat* (*Memorial of Female Sufi Devotees*). Significantly, Rabi'a al-'Adawiyya is the first Sufi woman mentioned in this work. By highlighting her in this way as an exemplary figure that stands for an entire tradition, Sulami took a major step in establishing the trope of Rabi'a the Sufi. This move was not entirely unprecedented. Abu Talib al-Makki could not have depicted Rabi'a the Lover as he did unless he too thought of her as a major figure of Sufism. For Sulami, Rabi'a personified better than any other exemplary figure the theology of servitude that he saw as the defining characteristic of Sufi women's spirituality.[35]

In his depiction, Sulami stressed Rabi'a's knowledge as much as her practices. Each of the exemplary anecdotes that he used to construct the trope of Rabi'a the Sufi Woman helped prove that she had attained an advanced state of knowledge of God. By reaffirming Makki's portrayal of her as one who knows God both intimately and deeply, Sulami also confirmed for his readers that Rabi'a was equal in rank to the ascetics and mystics that were mentioned in his more widely known hagiography of male Sufis, *Tabaqat al-sufiyya* (*Generations of the Sufis*). In his Book of Sufi Women he portrays Rabi'a as proficient in all of the moral and spiritual virtues normally associated with men, including truthfulness, critical self-awareness, devotion to God, and doctrinal expertise.

At the same time, however, Sulami did not try to hide Rabi'a's femininity, nor did he assert, as 'Attar would later do, that she should be regarded as an honorary man. Unlike some Sufi women in his book, who are identified as teachers by the masculine term *ustadh*, Rabi'a al-'Adawiyya is identified by the feminine term *mu'addiba* (female trainer). Sulami also allowed her to display stereotyped female traits, such as weeping and expressing her love for God emotionally. However, these traits are not portrayed as signs of weakness, nor do they diminish Rabi'a's reputation as a Sufi teacher. Her weeping is not for herself but for others and her love of God is not a matter of emotion but the sign of a highly developed form of Love mysticism. The overall impression that one gets from Sulami's portrayal of Rabi'a is of a wise, independent, and self-confident teacher, who remains a woman despite taking on roles that are

---

35   For a detailed discussion of Sulami's theology of servitude, see R. Cornell, *Early Sufi Women*, pp. 54–60.

normally associated with men. Her value for Sufism is proven by the fact that as a woman she is accepted in a man's world.

Unfortunately, Sulami's relatively positive view of Sufi women was not to last. An important difference between the earliest Sufi portrayals of Rabi'a al-'Adawiyya, which culminate in the eleventh-century CE representations of Sulami, Khargushi and Ghazali, and later medieval portrayals, which begin to appear about a century later, is that later writers tended to pay more attention to Rabi'a's gender. One of the first to do this was the Hanbali theologian Jamal al-Din ibn al-Jawzi (d. 1200 CE). Ibn al-Jawzi's highly gendered portrayal of Rabi'a stands in sharp contrast to that of Sulami. Unlike Sulami, who was not very concerned about the sexuality of Sufi women because their spiritual vocation made them immune to physical passions, Ibn al-Jawzi felt the need to negate Rabi'a's sexuality in order to make her more acceptable as an exemplar for men. For this reason, he depicts her as an old woman (*'ajuza*), "who looked like a shrunken, old water-skin and appeared to be on the verge of collapsing."[36]

Ibn al-Jawzi's attempt to neutralize Rabi'a's femininity by portraying her as an aged and emaciated ascetic was also a common rhetorical device in Christian hagiography. For example, in the *vita* of St Pelagia of Antioch (ca. fifth century CE), the saint at the end of her life is portrayed in a way that is similar to Ibn al-Jawzi's depiction of Rabi'a al-'Adawiyya:

> I failed to recognize her because she had lost those good looks I used to know; her astounding beauty had all faded away, her laughing and bright face that I had known had become ugly, her pretty eyes had become hollow and cavernous as the result of much fasting and the keeping of vigils. The joints of her holy bones, fleshless, were visible beneath her skin through emaciation brought on by ascetic practices. Indeed, the whole complexion of her body was coarse and dark like sackcloth, as the result of her strenuous penance.[37]

Ibn al-Jawzi's notice on Rabi'a in the prosopography *Sifat al-safwa* (*The Attribute of Purity*) contains only a small number of the accounts that he originally included in a lost work devoted entirely to her.[38] Thus, we have no

---

36 Ibn al-Jawzi, *Sifat al-safwa*, in R. Cornell, *Early Sufi Women*, pp. 276–83 and idem, *Sifat al-safwa*, vol. 4, pp. 22–4.
37 Brock and Harvey, *Holy Women of the Syrian Orient*, p. 60.
38 Ibn al-Jawzi mentions this work himself. See Cornell, *Early Sufi Women*, pp. 282–3.

way of knowing which other themes from Christian hagiography he might have used in his portrayal. Such themes would have been readily available to him because the stories of early Christian saints were popular in the Christian communities of his native city of Baghdad. However, in *Sifat al-safwa* there are some indications of what we might find in this lost work. For example, the theme of repentance, which is central not only to the story of St Pelagia but also to the hagiographies of other famous Christian women ascetics such as St Mary of Egypt and St Thaïs of Alexandria, is more apparent in Ibn al-Jawzi's depiction of Rabi'a than in other accounts of her.[39] Also, by stressing Rabi'a's emotionalism he implies that the level of her reason or rationality was less than that of her male counterparts. Ibn al-Jawzi portrays Rabi'a as weeping constantly and as practicing a high-strung form of piety that borders on hysteria.[40] For Ibn al-Jawzi she is forever imprisoned in what Simone de Beauvoir called "The Eternal Feminine." As part of this character type, women are portrayed as acting subjectively whereas men are portrayed as acting objectively. Through her emotional outbursts and by being moved more by feelings than by reason, Ibn al-Jawzi's Rabi'a exemplifies what de Beauvoir refers to as a woman "thinking through her hormones."[41]

b. *'Attar's Portrayal of Rabi'a al-'Adawiyya in* Tadhkirat al-Awliya'

Farid al-Din al-'Attar (d. ca. 1220 CE) deserves special mention in the story of Rabi'a al-'Adawiyya from narrative to myth because he was responsible for the *vita* or life story of Rabi'a that everyone knows today. Ironically, his life is as much of an enigma as that of Rabi'a herself. As the Iranian scholar of Islam Navid Kermani writes, "Hardly anything is known about the life of Attar. Neither his teachers nor his friends are known, nor even the people he dealt with. His everyday life is as much of a secret as his exact dates of birth and death, his social status, or his standing among the

---

39 See, for example, Benedicta Ward, *Harlots of the Desert: A Study of Repentance in Early Monastic Sources* (Kalamazoo, MI: Cistercian Publications, 1987), pp. 26–56 and 76–84. As we shall see in Chapter 6, Widad El Sakkakini recalls the story of St Thaïs in her biography of Rabi'a.

40 R. Cornell, *Early Sufi Women*, pp. 276–83. The motifs of repentance and personal weakness are stressed so much by Ibn al-Jawzi that it is hard to avoid the impression that he believed in the concept of original sin for women. In a way that is quite different from the ascetic weeping discussed in Chapter 2, Ibn al-Jawzi's Rabi'a seems to weep for the sins of all the daughters of Eve.

41 Simone de Beauvoir, *The Second Sex*, trans. Constance Borde and Sheila Malovany-Chevallier (New York: Vintage Books, 2011), pp. 4–5.

mystics of the period. There are no sources to tell us whether he had a wife and children, what his full name was, what his parents were called, or in which of the Sufi chains of initiation, if any, he stood. Among the classics of Persian literature there is no one whose life is as much of a mystery as Faridoddin Attar (sic)."[42]

Although 'Attar was born in Nishapur like Sulami, his portrayal of Rabi'a in the hagiographic anthology *Tadhkirat al-awliya'* (*Memorial of the Saints*) is different not only from Sulami's portrayal but also from that of Makki. At first glance, the highly gendered tone of his portrayal brings to mind Ibn al-Jawzi's depiction of Rabi'a, which was written at roughly the same time. However, 'Attar's and Ibn al-Jawzi's narratives in reality share little in common. While both writers conform to the oral model of narrative established by their traditionist predecessors, 'Attar is more a storyteller who uses tradition primarily as a rhetorical device. Because he adds so many new elements to the Rabi'a narrative it is best to think of 'Attar's chapter on Rabi'a as a unique and original work.

First, 'Attar's chapter on Rabi'a is unique because it is the earliest hagiography of Rabi'a in the Persian language. Second, it is unique because most of the stories that 'Attar relates in it cannot be found in any previous work. One can find partial traces of earlier accounts here and there in 'Attar's chapter, but the stories in which they appear are quite different from the originals.[43] Some of the most famous stories—such as the those of Rabi'a's encounters with al-Hasan al-Basri—are anachronistic and appear to have been invented by 'Attar himself. A third important difference between previous depictions of Rabi'a and 'Attar's version is that 'Attar portrays Rabi'a as a miracle-worker. His depiction of Rabi'a is the first extant narrative in which miracles are used as proofs of her sainthood. Finally and most importantly, 'Attar's chapter on Rabi'a is unique because for the first time in Islamic literature he provides a background narrative—what Losev calls an *outline*—for Rabi'a's life. In other words, it is a true *vita* in the sense of hagiography as "sacred biography."

In providing the outline for Rabi'a's life story, 'Attar filled in the gaps that he saw in the previous master narratives. One could argue that this was a case of overreading because he added ideas, judgments and events for which there was no direct evidence in the previous narratives. As H. Porter

---

42 Navid Kermani, *The Terror of God: Attar, Job, and the Metaphysical Revolt* (Cambridge, UK: Polity Press, 2011), p. 25.
43 One exception is an anecdote which relates how a bird once supplied Rabi'a with onions for her soup. An earlier version of this story was transmitted by Ibn Abi al-Dunya. See Sells, *Early Islamic Mysticism*, p. 160.

Abbott observes, "Our minds seem to abhor narrative vacuums. We try to fill them in."[44] He adds, "Overreading is a phenomenon that is frequently cued by the masterplots in which our fears and desires are most engaged."[45] For a Sufi storyteller like 'Attar, one could also say that overreading may be cued by the tropes and master narratives in which one's moral, theological and philosophical ideals are engaged. Clearly, 'Attar was trying to bring a sense of closure to the Rabi'a narrative. To quote Abbott once again, "If a narrative won't close by itself, one often tries to close it, even if it means shutting one's eyes to some of the details or imagining others that aren't there, underreading and overreading."[46] One could hardly imagine a more accurate description of what 'Attar does with the Rabi'a narratives in *Tadhkirat al-awliya*'.

From the perspective of fiction, 'Attar's revision of the Rabi'a master narrative demonstrates that a story may be capable of many different realizations. One might say that 'Attar discovered a new "crux" of her story, which enabled him to affect how subsequent generations would interpret the Rabi'a narratives. However, from the perspective of empirical history, 'Attar's revision of the Rabi'a master narrative is less justifiable. Does the fact that he made up most if not all of the stories in his chapter on Rabi'a entitle us to call him a forger? In one sense 'Attar can be called a forger because most of the accounts of Rabi'a in the chapter are falsely presented as authentic traditions. Clearly, he wanted his readers to believe that the stories in his chapter were true, even if they were not. However, because (with one exception) he does not attribute these accounts to other authorities, he technically cannot be accused of forging another person's work.

In my opinion, it is most productive to think of 'Attar from the perspective of empirical history as a Sufi version of the traditional Middle Eastern storyteller. This role is designated in Arabic by the term *qass*. In the Arab and Iranian cultural traditions of storytelling, it was an expected practice for storytellers (*qussas*) to embellish their tales with new and original elements. As the Arabic root *qassa* ("to cut," "to trim," "to shear") implies, storytellers "cut and pasted" old and new narrative elements into their stories in order to better entertain their audiences. In his works, 'Attar reveals his genius as a popular Sufi teacher and as a poet and storyteller. As Roland Barthes has observed, in oral narratives the "author" is not only the person who invents the stories but also "the person who best masters the code which is practiced

---

44 Abbott, *The Cambridge Introduction to Narrative*, p. 89.
45 Ibid.
46 Ibid.

equally by his listeners."⁴⁷ Much of the effectiveness of 'Attar's *Tadhkirat al-awliya'* as a classic of Sufi literature is due to the fact that it straddles the boundary between oral narratives and written literature.

In an essay on the use of the anecdote in medieval Arabic literature, Abdelfattah Kilito describes the literary forger as a trickster: he "presides over the game and pulls the strings from somewhere offstage."⁴⁸ This characterization also works for 'Attar. Kilito states, "Far from being the prisoner of genre. . . [he] can leap mischievously from one genre to another. He can pilfer any treasure with a casualness born of instinctive mastery of texts and the rules of attribution."⁴⁹ 'Attar displays these skills in his chapter on Rabi'a. Following Kilito, we can say that when 'Attar forges a tradition, he serves as the "occasion" or "pretext" for a narrative that someone else might have produced. Although 'Attar is in fact the *true author* of the stories that he passes off to his readers as oral traditions, he pretends that they originated far back in history. In narrative terms, he is the *true author* posing as the *implied author*. As it turned out, this ruse was very successful. Succeeding generations of Muslims have taken 'Attar's fictional stories for fact so completely that today the authenticity of his stories of Rabi'a are rarely questioned. To go back to Barthes' discussion of the reality effect, with respect to his *vita* of Rabi'a in *Tadhkirat al-awliya'*, posterity has turned 'Attar's fictions into fact by saying, "Let it be so."

With respect to its subsequent reputation, it is also important to add that 'Attar's *vita* of Rabi'a is different from the works of his predecessors because it was written both for Sufis and for the general public. One of the major reasons why 'Attar wrote *Tadhkirat al-awliya'* was to popularize the institution of Sufi sainthood. This meant that the language of the text had to be accessible to both Sufis and non-Sufis alike. One of the ways that he accomplished this goal was to write his book in Persian rather than in Arabic. In the region of Khorasan, Persian was the vernacular language of discourse. Another rhetorical device that 'Attar used was to follow Sulami's example by making Rabi'a respresent all Sufi women. Significantly, she is the only woman to merit her own chapter in *Tadhkirat al-awilya'*. Thus, 'Attar was very concerned to demonstrate how different she was from ordinary women. His desire to portray Rabi'a as an authentic Sufi saint also led him to create

---

47 Barthes, "Introduction to the Structural Analysis of Narratives," in *A Barthes Reader*, p. 286.
48 Kilito, *The Author and His Doubles*, p. 64.
49 Ibid.

miracle stories as proofs of her sainthood. He also added commentary to the text to tell the reader how he wanted her example to be understood. Because of these rhetorical techniques, the level of verisimilitude attained by 'Attar's depiction of Rabi'a is unequaled by any other Sufi work on Rabi'a before or since. For the vast majority of Muslims, including Sufis, 'Attar's version of Rabi'a's *vita* has become the "true" and authentic account of the life of Rabi'a al-'Adawiyya.

When we turn to the contents of 'Attar's text, we can see that because it was written as the outline or backstory for a myth, his "emplotment" of Rabi'a's life is both teleological and theological. It is a measure of 'Attar's skill as a writer and his mastery of Sufi doctrine that the theological message of this work can be read on more than one level. This aspect of 'Attar's depiction of Rabi'a has been remarked upon by Jean Annestay, a French writer who recently published a detailed reflection on Rabi'a's spirituality. His book, *Une Femme Sufi en Islam: Rabi'a al-'Adawiyya* (*A Sufi Woman in Islam: Rabi'a al-'Adawiyya*, 2009), cannot be treated as a historical study because he treats 'Attar's stories as authentic traditions, just as 'Attar intended. However, Annestay does not consider this a fault. As a follower of the Traditionalist philosophy of René Guénon (1886–1951) and Frithjof Schuon (1907–98), he argues that the findings of historical research should not be allowed to contaminate the spiritual message of a saint's life. For Annestay, the truth-value of Rabi'a's sainthood is not to be found in the historical details of her *vita* but in its "principial" (*sic*) or theological meaning:

> In such a perspective, the life of Rabi'a or of any saint, in order to be understood in all of its fullness, must not only be related to a given historical epoch but also to a strictly prehistoric or if one prefers, non-historic reality—that is to say, prior to all history and all temporality—in which it finds its principle and its end and which is its true reason for existence. It consists, if you will, of an anteriority that is neither horizontal nor temporal but vertical or principial. It is a vestige that refers back to the instantaneity of the eternal present and which can be anecdotally or literally nothing but a trace recounted in a temporal moment. Such a perspective is rigorously the inverse of that of modern history.[50]

---

50 Jean Annestay, *Une Femme Soufie en Islam: Rabi'a al-'Adawiyya* (Paris: Éditions Entrelacs, 2009), pp. 27–8; Annestay is not an academic but a cartoonist, who made a living for himself in France by designing stage sets and drawing panels for graphic novels.

Although Annestay's Traditionalist approach to Rabi'a al-'Adawiyya is very different from the perspective of the present study, his depiction of 'Attar's authorial intent is largely accurate. Virtually all of Rabi'a's hagiographers since 'Attar have sought to convey her "principial" meaning, or as Hendrik Vroom might say, the "religious truth claims" of her story. Indeed, the "principial" meaning of the anchoring name of Rabi'a al-'Adawiyya has always been an important part of her mythical identity. However, one must also add the caveat that in modern times, the principial meaning of her name has not always been theological, nor has it always been religious. For example, Widad El Sakkakini regarded Rabi'a as a religious figure but she also regarded her as a feminist icon: "Today I come, the last of the searchers, not to dispel this precious memory, not to clutch a handful of sand, but to release long-hidden pages in the East and West. I stretch out with loving hand to gather them together, as they do the mementoes of a Heroine fallen in the struggle, so as to enshrine them in a worthy place."[51] Although El Sakkakini's secular view of Rabi'a's "principial" meaning is different from that of Annestay, both authors remain true to the hagiographical tradition of portraying Rabi'a as an icon. In addition, El Sakkakini's depiction of Rabi'a, though secular, is still teleological: "I was a star in the heavens, then I became an idea on earth."[52]

It is appropriate to think of 'Attar as portraying Rabi'a as an icon because in composing her *vita* he attempted to create an image of her with words. In Greek or Russian Orthodox icons, the "principial" meaning of the icon is expressed through the composition of the painting and the form and details (i.e., the contents) of the main figure. Because icons are symbols, they serve as visual references to *paratexts*; these are folk tales, hagiographic narratives and scriptural texts that exist beyond the "narrative" of the painting itself.[53] References to paratextual materials and intertextual materials can similarly be found in written hagiographic portraits like 'Attar's chapter on Rabi'a.

---

51   El Sakkakini, *First Among Sufis*, p. 9; *al-'Ashiqa al-mutasawwifa*, p. 10. Here, as in many other places, the English translation of El Sakkakini's text is more of a paraphrase than an exact rendition of the Arabic.
52   El Sakkakini, *First Among Sufis*, p. 7; *al-'Ashiqa al-mutasawwifa*, p. 7.
53   See Gérard Genette, *Paratexts: Thresholds of Interpretation*, trans. Jane E. Lewin (Cambridge and New York: Cambridge University Press, 1997). For a detailed analysis of a Russian Orthodox icon, see Boris K. Knorre, "Icon of the Last Judgment: A Detailed Analysis," ed. Kent Russell, ed. and trans. Catherine Le Gouis, *Journal of Icon Studies*, occasional paper, n.d. This icon is in the collection of the Museum of Russian Icons, Clinton, Massachussetts: http://www.museumofrussianicons.org/pdf/JournalOfIconStudies/KnorreLastJudgmentFinal.pdf

In medieval Latin Christianity, the iconic status of a saint was expressed in hagiography through the trope of *admiranda*, "something to be wondered at." According to Aviad M. Kleinberg, "medieval female saints tended to belong more to the admirable than to the imitable pole of the spectrum."[54] 'Attar's depiction of Rabi'a also follows the trope of *admiranda*. She is more of an icon to be wondered at than an example to be followed. Although her *vita* reflects many of the doctrines of Sufism, she is not portrayed by 'Attar as teaching a systematic spiritual method. Rather, she stands symbolically for a predetermined set of spiritual ideals. Because she is in the category of *admiranda*, 'Attar portrays her more passively than Sulami, who portrays her through the trope of *imitanda*, an example to be followed. For Sulami, Rabi'a is an active teacher and moral exemplar. By contrast, in 'Attar's text people come to pay their respects to Rabi'a, just as they would to an icon. Those who come to ask her advice do so in a formal and even ritualistic manner. When she goes on the pilgrimage to Mecca, the Ka'ba seeks her out rather than the other way around. In one pilgrimage story, she is depicted as a sort of mirage—suspended rhetorically between the beginning and the end of her journey, neither at her starting-point in Basra nor at her goal in Mecca. In many of 'Attar's stories, Rabi'a seems to be posed, as if she were a figure in a painting.

To better illustrate 'Attar's depiction of Rabi'a as an icon, I have reproduced below a translation of the two introductory paragraphs from his chapter on her in *Tadhkirat al-awliya'*. In this passage, 'Attar argues for Rabi'a's iconic status by comparing her with the two most famous iconic female religious figures in Sunni Islam—the Prophet Muhammad's wife 'A'isha and the Virgin Mary. To further establish her unique status, he also provides a doctrinal commentary, in which he claims that through her spirituality Rabi'a transcended the limitations of her gender. Because she is "illuminated by a special spark," she is so different from ordinary women that she should be considered an honorary man:

> This one [Rabi'a] is illuminated by a special spark, veiled with the veil of sincerity, consumed with love and longing, enamored of proximity and immolation, deputy of Mary the Pure, and accepted among men—Rabi'a 'Adawiyya (may God Most High have mercy upon her).

---

54 Aviad M. Kleinberg, *Prophets in Their own Country: Living Saints and the Making of Sainthood in the Later Middle Ages* (Chicago and London: University of Chicago Press, 1997), pp. 134–5.

If anyone asks why her memorial is placed among the ranks of men, we reply that the Most Honored of Prophets [Muhammad] (may God bless and preserve him) said, "God does not examine your forms." In other words, it is not about forms but about pure intentions. If the saying is correct that two-thirds of the religion is from [the Prophet's wife] 'A'isha the Righteous (may God be pleased with her), then it is also appropriate to take benefit from her maidservants (*kanizakani-u fa'ida garaftan*). When a woman is on the path of God Most High, she is a man: she cannot be called a woman. Thus it is that 'Abbasa (*sic*) Tusi said, "When on the morrow on the Plain of Resurrection they call out, 'Oh men!' the first person to step into the ranks of men will be Mary."

If Hasan [al-Basri] would not hold a gathering unless [Rabi'a] were present, there is no harm in recording her memorial among the ranks of men. Indeed, when it comes to the reality of what this folk [i.e., the Sufis] are about, all are without distinction in divine unity. In unity, how can your existence or mine remain, much less "man" or "woman"? As Abu 'Ali Farmadi (may God have mercy on him) said, "Prophecy is the essence of glory and sublimity. High status and low status (*mihtari va-kihtari*) are not part of it." Sainthood is the same. This is especially true of Rabi'a, who in her time had no equal in her behavior or knowledge of God (*ma'rifat*). She was considered one of the greats of her age and was a decisive proof for those who lived in her time.[55]

In the book *Early Islamic Mysticism*, Michael Sells remarks on the ambivalence of 'Attar's portrayal of women in his chapter on Rabi'a. However, in the end Sells concludes that 'Attar "leaves the issue of women as women

---

55 'Attar, *Tadhkirat al-awliya'*, p. 61, translation of the Persian text by Vincent J. Cornell. V. Cornell's translation of this passage from the Isti'lami edition of *Tadhkirat al-awliya'* differs from that of Losensky in Sells, *Early Islamic Mysticism*, p. 155. In the latter translation, Losensky misses the pronoun (-*u*) that identifies Rabi'a as one of the maidservants of 'A'isha. Instead, he refers to her as the maidservant of God. Some modern writers have taken even greater liberties when translating these passages. For example, Margaret Smith adds a sentence to the text that does not exist in the original: "As the Prophet said, 'The people are assembled (on the Day of Judgment) according to the purposes of their hearts.'" Smith, *Rabi'a* (Oneworld), pp. 19–20; (Rainbow Bridge), p. 2. As for Widad El Sakkakini, what she presents in her book on Rabi'a as a "translation" of these passages is in fact completely made up. Her version bears hardly any resemblance to the original. She even has Rabi'a refer to the German religion scholar Rudolf Otto's concept of "The Idea of the Holy." See El Sakkakini, *First Among Sufis*, p. 42.

open." Sells sees 'Attar's view of women as more positive than that of the early Christian theologian St Augustine, who saw women as reflecting God's image only when they were "dewomanized" (Sells' term) or divorced from their physical attributes. He also sees 'Attar's portrayal of women as more positive than that of medieval European Christian writers, who thought of ascetic women as viragoes, women in the guise of men. Overall, he views 'Attar as a relatively enlightened male for his time and concludes, "Almost every anecdote concerning Rabi'a is a refutation of implied attitudes toward the 'weak woman'."[56] In this opinion, he agrees with Margaret Smith, who makes a similar comment about 'Attar's view of women in *Rabi'a the Mystic*: "['Attar's] conception of the relations between the saint and his Lord left no room for the distinction of sex. In the spiritual life there could be 'neither male nor female.'"[57]

Although it is not unreasonable to draw a positive conclusion about 'Attar's view of women from the introduction to his chapter on Rabi'a, I believe that the text of the chapter as a whole leads to a different conclusion. First, to claim, as Michael Sells does, that "no theological statement is made about the status of women," by 'Attar is incorrect. 'Attar's assertion that gender distinctions do not matter in the mystical station of divine unity is clearly a theological statement. Second, comparing 'Attar's view of women with that of St Augustine, who was a Latin Christian theologian, and with the views of medieval European Christians, who were even farther removed from 'Attar culturally than St Augustine, is problematical. A more valid comparison with respect to gender distinctions would have been between 'Attar and premodern Middle Eastern Christian writers, who shared a more similar cultural background. Evidence suggests that if Sells had made this latter comparison he might have regarded 'Attar's views on women differently.

For example, the Gnostic Christian *Gospel of Mary*, which was written in Egypt in the third to fifth century CE, displays attitudes about gender distinctions that are very similar to those of 'Attar. According to the historian of early Christianity Karen King, three views of the relationship between gender and spirituality can be found in Gnostic Christian texts. Although these views are different, each reflects the World/Nonworld Dichotomy discussed in Chapter 2 and each regards sharply defined gender distinctions as the normal state of affairs:

---

56 Sells, *Early Islamic Mysticism*, p. 345 n. 9.
57 Smith, *Rabi'a* (Oneworld), p. 19 and (Rainbow Bridge), p. 1.

1. The ideal state (described as transcendent) is gendered as male, whereas the lesser state (described as material or passionate) is gendered as female.
2. The ideal state is portrayed as androgynous (both male and female), whereas the fallen state is divided into separate male and female spheres.
3. The ideal state is non-gendered, whereas gender and sexual differences are to be found only in the lower sphere.[58]

The third Gnostic view described by King above corresponds to the view of 'Attar: "When it comes to the reality of what [the Sufis] are about, all are without distinction in divine unity. In unity, how can your existence or mine remain, much less 'man' or 'woman'?" For Margaret Smith, the fact that 'Attar assigned to Rabi'a a high rank in the hierarchy of Muslim saints was enough for her to conclude that Sufi women were highly respected: "The high position attained by the women Sufis is attested... by the fact that the Sufis themselves gave to a woman the first place among the earliest Muhammadan mystics."[59]

At first glance, 'Attar's statement seems to support a relatively liberal approach to gender distinctions, just as Sells and Smith conclude. However, after researching gender relations in Gnostic Christian society in detail, King was unable to correlate the concept of the non-gendered ideal with any empirical differences in the actual social practices of Gnostic Christians. In other words, this relatively open-minded theory does not seem to have been observed on the ground. Because of this she concludes, "The mere fact of a woman in a position of leadership does not necessarily reflect a positive valuation of women."[60] King's findings suggest that scholars of medieval Sufism should also beware of overreading seemingly open-minded doctrinal statements. Just because gender distinctions do not apply in the Nonworld does not mean that Sufi women were treated differently in the real world. Given King's evidence of the discrepancy between late-antique philosophical doctrines and actual social relations, it would be wise for us

---

58 Karen King, "Why All the Controversy? Mary in the *Gospel of Mary*," in *Which Mary? The Marys of Early Christian Tradition*, ed. F. Stanley Jones (Atlanta: Society of Biblical Literature, 2002), p. 59. On view (3) above, see also Kevin P. Sullivan, "Sexuality and the Gender of Angels," in *Paradise Now: Essays on Early Jewish and Christian Mysticism*, ed. April D. DeConick (Atlanta: Society for Biblical Literature, 2006), pp. 211–28. Sullivan argues that angels in early Christianity and rabbinic Judaism were depicted as genderless because they belonged to the supernatural realm.
59 Smith, *Rabi'a* (Oneworld), p. 21 and (Rainbow Bridge), p. 3.
60 King, "Why All the Controversy?," p. 59.

to reserve judgment and ask instead the follow-up question that King proposes: "To what end was the argument for a non-gendered spiritual ideal actually employed?"[61]

This question becomes even more important when we discover that in his chapter on Rabi'a 'Attar uses not one but two of the views of gender and spirituality listed by King. Not only does 'Attar use the third view (the non-gendered ideal), but he also uses the first view (the male gendered ideal). This view can be seen in the most famous statement from his Introduction: "When a woman is on the path of God Most High, she is a man; she cannot be called a woman." This is clearly an expression of the view in which the ideal spiritual state (the Nonworld) is masculine and the lesser, non-spiritual state (the World) is feminine. If this were not the case, then why could a woman on the path of God not be called a "woman"? The implication of this statement is that because of her high spiritual state Rabi'a is a virago, a woman who has taken on the attributes of a man. This is the very perspective that Sells claims not to find in 'Attar's chapter on Rabi'a.[62]

A negative view of femininity is also visible in other passages in 'Attar's chapter on Rabi'a, which conflate women's physical and moral weaknesses. In one passage, the ascetic Ibrahim ibn Adham is shocked when the Ka'ba leaves its location in Mecca and goes to meet Rabi'a in the desert. Despite this sign of divine approval, 'Attar still describes Rabi'a as a "weak woman" (Pers. *za'ifa*).[63] In this case, one might argue that 'Attar is being ironic. However, no such ambiguity exists in another story, in which the male ascetic Salih al-Murri describes himself as "an ignorant man" (*mardi jahil*), in comparison to Rabi'a, who is "a weak but knowledgeable woman" (*zani za'ifa dana*).[64] Clearly, the

---

61   Ibid., p. 60.
62   This negative attitude toward femininity was just as common among Eastern Christian theologians as it was among their Muslim counterparts. For example, St Jerome (d. 420 CE) stated, "She who serves Christ will cease to be a woman and will be called a man." Frances Beer, *Women and Mystical Experience in the Middle Ages* (Woodbridge, Suffolk, UK and Rochester, NY: Boydell Press, 1992), p. 4. Gnostic Christians were no less prejudiced against women than Orthodox Christians. The Gnostic *Gospel of Thomas* states: "Simon Peter said to them, 'Let Mary leave us, for women are not worthy of Life.' Jesus said: 'I myself shall lead her, in order to make her male, so that she too may become a living spirit resembling you males. For every woman who makes herself male will enter the Kingdom of Heaven.'" *The Gospel of Thomas*, trans. Thomas O. Lambdin, in *The Nag Hammadi Library in English*, general editor James M. Robinson (San Francisco: Harper and Row, 1981), p. 130.
63   'Attar, *Tadhkirat al-awliya'*, p. 64, Sells, *Early Islamic Mysticism*, p. 158.
64   'Attar, *Tadhkirat al-awliya'*, p. 69, Sells, *Early Islamic Mysticism*, p. 164. This statement is an addendum to an account that originally came from Sulami, in which Rabi'a paraphrases Jesus' Sermon on the Mount. See R. Cornell, *Early Sufi Women*, pp. 80–1.

reversal of status in this story is more apparent than real. Although Salih is inferior to Rabi'a extrinsically because he knows less about Sufism than she does, he is still superior to her intrinsically because he is a man. The notion of woman's intrinsic inferiority is also confirmed in a third story, where a man of high social status is amazed at "the spiritual aspiration (*himmat*) of [Rabi'a] this weak woman (*za'ifa*)." Just as in the previous examples, 'Attar implies in this story that Rabi'a's spiritual orientation is contrary to woman's inborn nature.[65]

As noted previously, statements about gender are not the only contradictions to appear in 'Attar's chapter on Rabi'a. Equally significant are the many historical anachronisms in the text. The most noteworthy of these are the famous stories of Rabi'a's encounters with the ascetic and theologian al-Hasan al-Basri (d. 728 CE). No less than thirteen of these stories appear in 'Attar's chapter.[66] The first reference to Hasan in the introduction to the chapter provides a clue as to why 'Attar may have placed Hasan and Rabi'a in the same generation. He states, "If the saying is correct that two-thirds of the religion is from 'A'isha the Righteous (may God be pleased with her), then it is also correct to benefit from her maidservants." This statement indicates that 'Attar likely confused Rabi'a with the earlier woman ascetic Mu'adha al-'Adawiyya (d. 702 CE), who was a maidservant of 'A'isha and who transmitted hadiths from her. As we saw in Chapter 2, Mu'adha was the founder of the Basra school of women's asceticism of which Rabi'a was the most famous example. She also provided al-Hasan al-Basri with Hadith accounts that she had learned from 'A'isha. We know from early sources that Mu'adha taught classes for women in Basra and that she had a number of well-known students.[67] Given this information, it is easy to see how the fame and reputation of Rabi'a al-'Adawiyya, who came from the same clan as Mu'adha al-'Adawiyya in Basra, likely caused 'Attar to conflate these two figures. 'Attar's predecessor Sulami also made a similar mistake. In his Book of Sufi Women, he erroneously claims that Mu'adha al-'Adawiyya was Rabi'a's close companion.[68]

The intertextual references that 'Attar uses to develop the Rabi'a myth are taken not only from Sufi literature but also from Islamic scripture and

---

65 'Attar, *Tadhkirat al-awliya*', p. 71; Sells, *Early Islamic Mysticism*, p. 166.
66 'Abd al-Rahman Badawi also notes these anachronisms in his book on Rabi'a. For Badawi, Rabi'a's likely association with Hasan's students was what led to the impression that she associated with Hasan himself. See idem, *Shahidat al-'ishq al-ilahi*, pp. 11 and 22.
67 Ibn Sa'd, *al-Tabaqat al-kubra*, vol. 8, p. 483.
68 R. Cornell, *Early Sufi Women*, pp. 88–9.

Christian literature. Among the Islamic references that he uses, stories of the Prophets from the Qur'an are particularly important. In the chapter one can find allusions to at least three prophetic or semi-prophetic figures that are reflected in Rabi'a's iconic image. These are Moses, Jesus and the Virgin Mary. Moses is mentioned twice in the chapter. The first time he appears is in a divine address in which God speaks to Rabi'a through her heart, "without an intermediary" (*bi-vasita beh-dilash khitab kard*).[69] The setting of this account is in the desert (*badiya*) between Basra and Mecca, where Rabi'a has lost her way. She cries out, "My God! My heart is desolate. Where am I to go? I am but a clod of dirt (*kulukhi*) and that House [i.e., the Ka'ba] is but a stone (*sangi*). I need you!" Rebuking Rabi'a for her presumptuousness, God replies, "Oh Rabi'a! You bathe in the blood of 18,000 worlds! Don't you see that when Moses (peace and blessings be upon him) wanted a vision, we cast a small amount of divine manifestation (*tajalli*) at the mountain and it shattered into forty pieces?"[70]

The scriptural reference in this story is the story in the Qur'an that describes God's encounter with Moses on Mount Sinai. The key verse in the story is Qur'an 7:143, which portrays God as speaking directly to Moses, just as He does to Rabi'a. At first, Moses is not satisfied with this honor, just as Rabi'a is not satisfied in 'Attar's story. He wants to see God directly and says, "My Lord, show yourself to me, so that I may look upon you." God's address to Rabi'a in 'Attar's story recalls the ending of the Qur'anic account, in which God reveals himself to the mountain before Moses and it shatters into many pieces. This reference to the Qur'an constitutes a double recollection (*dhikr*). First, God speaks to Rabi'a without an intermediary, just as He did with the Prophet Moses. This token of divine favor serves rhetorically as proof of Rabi'a's sainthood because it shows that Prophets (*anbiya'*) and saints (*awliya'*) enjoy the same level of intimacy with God. Second, the Qur'anic reference illustrates a famous hadith of the Prophet Muhammad that describes a genealogical relationship between the "knowers of God" (i.e., the Islamic scholars and saints) and God's Prophets: "The Knowers of God are the heirs of the Prophets" (*al-'ulama' warathat al-anbiya'*).[71]

The second reference to Moses in 'Attar's chapter on Rabi'a is in one of the stories in which Rabi'a and al-Hasan al-Basri appear together. In this story,

---

69 'Attar, *Tadhkirat al-awliya'*, p. 63; Sells, *Early Islamic Mysticism*, p. 157.
70 Ibid.
71 This famous tradition appears in the Hadith collections of Bukhari (Kitab al-'Ilm, no. 10); Abu Dawud (Bab al-'Ilm, no. 1); Ibn Majjah (Muqaddima, no. 17); al-Darimi (Muqaddima, no. 32); Ibn Hanbal, 5:196.

Hasan comes to visit Rabi'a just as darkness falls. Because of her extreme poverty, she has no lantern to light her hut. So she blows on her fingers, which burn like a lantern until daybreak (*Rabi'a tafa bar angushtan-i khud damid. Ta ruz angushtan-uyi chiragh miyafurukht.*).[72] 'Attar provides the following commentary for the story:

> If someone should say, "What does this [story] mean?" We would say, "It is like the hand of Moses (peace and blessings be upon him)." If someone should say, "But he was a Prophet." We would say, "Whoever follows a Prophet shares in a portion of his miracles. If a Prophet is associated with a prophetic miracle (*mu'jiza*), the saint is associated with saintly miracles (*karamat*), through the blessings of following the Prophet (*beh-barakat-i mutabi'at-i payghambar*). As the Prophet [Muhammad] (peace and blessings be upon him) said: "He who rejects even a small portion of what is forbidden will attain a degree of prophecy." In other words, he who gives back to the Adversary [i.e., Satan] the smallest amount of the forbidden achieves a degree of prophecy. [The Prophet] also said: "The true dream is one-fourth of prophecy."[73]

According to this commentary, not only are the miracles of the saints derived from the miracles of the Prophets but the station of sainthood itself is also related to prophecy. The comparison of Rabi'a's miracle with the miracle of the hand of Moses refers to the text of Qur'an 20:22, which describes Moses' contest with Pharaoh's magicians. God instructs Moses to put his hand down at his side. When Moses draws it forth again, it is white or shining (*bayda'a*) and "without evil" (*min ghayri su'in*). In comparing Moses' white hand to Rabi'a's blazing fingers, 'Attar may have been thinking of white phosphorous, which burns spontaneously when it encounters air. However, the point of the story is not scientific but epistemological. As the intimate friends or protégés (*awliya'*) of God, Muslim saints are deputies (sing. *na'ib*) of the Prophets. 'Attar's intertextual references to Moses suggest that as a Sufi saint, Rabi'a plays a semi-prophetic role. A similar motif also appears in the introduction to the chapter, where 'Attar portrays Rabi'a as the deputy (*na'ib*) of "Mary the Pure."

---

72 'Attar, *Tadhkirat al-awliya'*, p. 67; Sells, *Early Islamic Mysticism*, p. 161; text translation by V. Cornell.
73 Ibid.

The analogy between Rabi'a and Moses also applies to Rabi'a and Jesus. In a story that appears just before the reference to Moses on Mount Sinai, Rabi'a is on a pilgrimage to Mecca when the donkey that carries her belongings dies in the desert. Although the other members of the pilgrimage caravan offer to carry Rabi'a's things, she sends them away, preferring instead to put her trust completely in God. She admonishes God, saying: "My God! Do kings treat an incapable woman in this way? You invited me to your House, but on the way you killed my donkey and left me alone in the desert!" Suddenly, the donkey comes back to life and Rabi'a continues on her way.[74]

The scriptural reference in this story is to the Qur'anic Jesus, who says in Qur'an 3:49: "I heal the blind and the leper and bring the dead back to life with God's permission." However, this story also has a gendered message. Rabi'a refers to herself in the story as "an incapable woman" (*'awrat 'ajiz*). This feminine lack of power is contrasted with the powerful miracle of reviving the dead, which is one of the most potent miracles of Jesus. In both Persian and Arabic the term *'awra* refers to the private parts of men and women or to any part of the body that is too shameful to view. Although its use as a synonym for "woman" is metaphorical, it is significant because it is far from the most flattering term that could be used. Once again 'Attar reveals his ambivalent attitude toward gender. Are we to understand the story as an ironic repudiation of the tendency of men to hold women in low esteem, as Michael Sells suggests? Or should we see it instead as an example of Rabi'a being the exception that proves the rule of woman's intrinsic inferiority? Is this merely a rhetorical way of stressing Rabi'a's uniqueness by showing how far she has transcended her intrinsic nature as a woman?

Apart from Rabi'a herself, only two other female figures appear in 'Attar's chapter. These are the Prophet Muhammad's wife 'A'isha bint Abi Bakr and "Mary the Pure" (*Maryam Safiya*). As we have seen, 'Attar erroneously describes Rabi'a as the maidservant of 'A'isha. However, before 'Attar compares her to 'A'isha, he describes her as the "Deputy (*na'ib*) of Mary the Pure."[75] According to Stephen J. Shoemaker, Gnostic Christian texts from the Middle East often depicted a "universal Mary," who took on the attributes of both

---

74 'Attar, *Tadhkirat al-awliya'*, p. 63; Sells, *Early Islamic Mysticism*, p. 157.
75 'Attar, *Tadhkirat al-awliya'*, p. 61; Sells, *Early Islamic Mysticism*, p. 155. Margaret Smith translates the phrase, *na'ib Maryam Safiya* as "a second spotless Mary." Her depiction of Rabi'a as a "Second Mary" had a major influence on later interpretations of Rabi'a in European languages. See Smith, *Rabi'a* (Oneworld), p. 21, (Rainbow Bridge), p. 4 and Annestay, *Une Femme Soufie*, p. 18.

the Virgin Mary and Mary Magdalene.⁷⁶ The obvious scriptural reference for "Mary the Pure" is Mary the Mother of Jesus in the Qur'an, who personifies chastity, divine election, and complete trust in God.⁷⁷ All of these characteristics can be found in 'Attar's depiction of Rabi'a al-'Adawiyya as well. The key reference that links Rabi'a to Mary the Mother of Jesus is the Qur'anic verse, "Verily the angels said: 'Oh Mary! Behold, God has elected you and made you pure, and raised you above all the women of the world'" (Qur'an 3:42). 'Attar's choice of Rabi'a as the only woman to merit a chapter in *Tadhkirat al-awliya'* similarly indicates that like Mary, she has been "elected" and raised "above all the women of the world."⁷⁸

However, 'Attar's association of Rabi'a with Mary does not necessarily end with Mary the Mother of Jesus. A trace of Mary Magdalene is also arguably present in the chapter. This may be one explanation for 'Attar's odd and unprecedented remark that a "group of people" claimed that Rabi'a fell into playing music but later repented.⁷⁹ The idea that Rabi'a may have been a fallen woman and a repentant sinner like Mary Magdalene is only a small part of 'Attar's story and the way that it is presented in the narrative indicates that he doubted its authenticity. Indeed, had it not been made the basis for a whole new chapter of Rabi'a's *vita* in the twentieth century, this part of the story could be dismissed as incidental. It may also have originated as an intertextual reference to the figure of the *qayna* (pl. *qiyan*), the slave-girl singer, who was a popular motif in the literature of the Abbasid period. In Gnostic Christian texts Mary Magdalene is called "The Pure Spiritual One," and Jesus is portrayed as marveling at her wisdom.⁸⁰ These motifs of Mary Magdalene are suggestive of 'Attar's depiction of Rabi'a. Even in Orthodox Christianity, Mary Magdalene was sometimes portrayed as the personification of divine love and the contemplative life. This is also suggestive of Rabi'a al-'Adawiyya. Gregory the Great's sixth-century CE *Homily on the Feast of*

---

76 Stephen J. Shoemaker, "A Case of Mistaken Identity? Naming the Gnostic Mary," in *Which Mary?*, ed. Jones, p. 8.
77 See, for example, Qur'an 19:16–33. See also Annestay, *Une Femme Soufie*, p. 191, who describes the Mary of the Qur'an as "the archetype of the holy woman par excellence."
78 According to Jean Annestay, "The miraculous power attributed to Rabi'a derives entirely from Mary." For Annestay, Rabi'a as the Second Mary reflects the Latin Christian archetype of *Mater Nutrix*, or "The Nurturing Mother." This is because like Mary, Rabi'a "turns herself into a channel of grace and blessings, and thus is a privileged intermediary between Earth and Heaven." Ibid., p. 192.
79 'Attar, *Tadhkirat al-awliya'*, p. 63; Sells, *Early Islamic Mysticism*, p. 157.
80 Ann Graham Brock, "Setting the Record Straight—The Politics of Identification: Mary Magdalene and Mary the Mother in *Pistis Sophia*," in *Which Mary?*, ed. Jones, p. 51.

St Mary refers to Mary Magdalene in a way that seems to prefigure the later trope of Rabi'a the Repentant Sinner: "Mary Magdalene, a woman of the city which was a sinner, washed out the stain of her sins with her tears by her love of the truth, and the word of truth is fulfilled which says her sins are forgiven and she loved much. She who had previously been cold through sin was afterwards aflame with love." [81]

Did 'Attar intentionally combine the figures of Mary the Mother of Jesus and Mary Magdalene when comparing Rabi'a to "Mary the Pure?" Although this is possible, it cannot be proven conclusively. However, it is clear that tropes related to both the Virgin Mary and Mary Magdalene can be found in 'Attar's chapter on Rabi'a. As Karen King has observed "The virgin-mother reinscribes the centrality of motherhood and women's subordination to men, while the depiction of Mary Magdalene... contests gender definitions, for example in promoting transcendence from sexuality and accompanying gender roles as the ideal."[82] Given 'Attar's ambiguity about gender, it is significant that his portrayal of Rabi'a al-'Adawiyya and his comparison of her to "Mary the Pure" perform similar narrative functions to those described by King. He also uses the narrative motifs of Rabi'a the Deputy of Mary, Rabi'a the Honorary Man, and Rabi'a the Repentant Musician to draw attention to her transcendence of sexuality and socially imposed gender roles. These motifs are more reminiscent of Karen King's Mary Magdalene than they are of Mary the Mother of Jesus as envisaged by Margaret Smith.

III. EVERY PICTURE TELLS A STORY: 'ATTAR'S EMPLOTMENT OF RABI'A'S *VITA*

'Attar's literary iconography of Rabi'a al-'Adawiyya would not have been so effective if his chapter on her in *Tadhkirat al-awliya'* were only made up of sayings and commentaries, as in the works of previous writers. None of the other writers or traditionists mentioned in this study comes to mind as readily as 'Attar does when Rabi'a's name is mentioned. In the large number of popular books and Internet entries that one finds on Rabi'a today, the author that is most frequently cited is Farid al-Din al-'Attar.[83] If, as the saying goes,

---

81 Ward, *Harlots of the Desert*, p. 12.
82 King, "Why All the Controversy?" in ibid., p. 57.
83 Popular works on Rabi'a in European languages often contain no source references at all, not even to 'Attar. For example, in the French work *La Vie de Rabi'a al-'Adawiyya*, Jamal Eddine Benghal only notes that such sources exist: "Nous raconterons la vie de Rabi'a

"Every picture tells a story," then Rabi'a as an iconic figure needed a story to make her myth come alive. Widad El Sakkakini makes the same point in justifying her feminist adaptation of Rabi'a's life: "Because she has not written her own biography, nor left for the ages to come very much evidence to make her familiar to us, Rabi'a needs some of her hidden story to be brought to life."[84] Aleksei Fyodorovich Losev might have added that Rabi'a the Icon needed more than just an image or a visage; she also needed an "outline" or backstory to make her image more meaningful. This is why the *vita* that 'Attar composed for Rabi'a must be considered his most important contribution to her myth.

However, the problem with 'Attar's *vita* of Rabi'a is that the outline or backstory he created is entirely a work of fiction. All current evidence suggests that he made up the story himself. Although a few of the anecdotes that he uses in his chapter on Rabi'a can be found in earlier works, none of the details of Rabi'a's life that he recounts can be found in any previous source.[85] Thus, we are forced to conclude that in this respect at least, 'Attar was a literary forger who passed off a work of fiction as a work of history. In contemporary terms we can characterize him as a purveyor of "fake news."

From a historiographical perspective, 'Attar's *Tadhkirat al-awliya'* is one of the clearest examples in Islamic literature of Hayden White's concept of "the content of the form." As we have seen above, much of the "content of the form" in this work can be found in the author's use of narrative tropes. Another important example can be found in his heavy use of anecdotes. These are arranged one after the other in the "string of pearls" format of the

---

al-'Adawiyya avec une petite romance sur une base de données historiques éparses dans plusieurs écrits" (We will recount the life of Rabi'a al-'Adawiyya with a small romance based on historical accounts scattered in numerous writings). p. 37. Popular works in Arabic usually include a short bibliography of medieval and modern sources that are mixed together without distinguishing one group from the other. See, for example, Ma'mun Gharib, *Rabi'a al-'Adawiyya fi mihrab al-hubb al-ilahi* (*Rabi'a al-'Adawiyya in the Prayer-Niche of Divine Love*) (Cairo: Dar Gharib, 2000), pp. 125–6. In such works, the main sources of information are most often 'Attar or modern works that rely on 'Attar as their main source.

84 El Sakkakini, *First Among Sufis*, p. 73; *al-'Ashiqa al-mutasawwifa*, pp. 117–18.
85 'Abd al-Rahman Badawi calls 'Attar a "highly imaginative man" (*rajulun jamih al-khayal*) and also states that he made up most of the chapter on Rabi'a himself (*Shahidat al-'ishq al-ilahi*, p. 12). However, he also makes the following comment: "But we cannot reject everything that 'Attar says in this respect entirely. For the new documents (*watha'iq*) that are revealed to us day after day support many of the accounts that 'Attar transmits to us (ibid.)." Unfortunately, Badawi gives no examples in his book to tell us what these alleged "documents" might be. I have not found any such documents in my research.

tabaqat genre of medieval Sufi prosopography.[86] Because the anecdotal basis of *Tadhkirat al-awliya'* mimics that of earlier *tabaqat* collections, it conveys a strong sense of verisimilitude. In terms of its form, the work resembles well-respected earlier collections of Sufi traditions, especially Sulami's *Tabaqat al-sufiyya*. For 'Attar's readers, the fact that the work looked like an authentic collection of Sufi traditions reinforced the impression that it too was authentic.

In *tabaqat* literature, the reader is not presented with a fully coherent and internally consistent narrative as in modern biography. With the exception of the story of Rabi'a's life and an appendix of aphoristic discourses with God (*munajat*), 'Attar's chapter consists of a collection of independent anecdotes that are presented without a stated common theme or chronological order. Unless the author provides an internal commentary (which he does from time to time), the reader must provide her own sense of coherence and meaning to the narratives. In reading this type of prosopography, one approaches the work in the way that a customer examines a pearl necklace in a jewelry shop. One can study each anecdote or narrative "pearl" by itself or one can reflect on the entire collection as a whole, such as when a shopper looks at the whole necklace to determine its overall workmanship and value. This type of reading can be seen in the reception of 'Attar's chapter on Rabi'a by later Sufi writers. Most often, the stories they recount are reproduced either singly or haphazardly but rarely as a coherent group. This reception suggests that their value was to be found more in their anecdotal significance than in their overall narrative coherence.

'Attar's predecessor Sulami, who organized his chapter on Rabi'a in his Book of Sufi Women in much the same way, provides the reader with chains of transmission for most of his accounts in order to prove their authenticity. This indicates that for Sulami, it was important to prove the factual accuracy of the accounts in order to establish the authenticity of their Sufi teachings. Sulami's concern for accuracy may have been due to the fact that his works were written primarily for practicing Sufis, who were expected to take famous figures such as Rabi'a al-'Adawiyya as behavioral examples. In this sense, his readers were somewhat like modern scholars, who demand to see footnotes in a text to prove the authenticity of its sources. In premodern Islamic historical works (which included the genres of Hadith and hagiography), chains of transmission (*asanid*) served much the same function as footnotes do in

---

86 The "string of pearls" motif is used in numerous premodern Arabic works. See also the previous discussion of *tabaqat* literature in Chapter 1.

modern scholarship. In the field of communications studies, such aspects of narrative discourse are called "category entitlements."[87] They help justify an author's choice of a report or a story.

By contrast, 'Attar, who wrote for a wider audience that included both Sufis and non-Sufis, did not need to provide category entitlements. Instead, like a preacher or popular storyteller, he presents the stories in his book as information that everyone ought to know. They are to be treated as authentic traditions simply because they are presented as such. Only a single name is mentioned as a source for any of the information in 'Attar's chapter on Rabi'a. This is Abu 'Ali al-Farmadi, who is cited as the source for a single statement and a single anecdote.[88]

Abu 'Ali al-Fadl ibn Muhammad al-Farmadi (also known as "al-Farmadhi," d. 1084 CE) was an important Sufi of Khorasan. However, little biographical information is available on him. Trained in Shafi'i jurisprudence, he was favored by the Seljuk Turkish rulers of Iran, who gave him the title, "Chief of the Sufi Masters of Khorasan" (*shaykh shuyukh Khurasan*). Some sources claim that he was a teacher of the famous Sufi and theologian Abu Hamid al-Ghazali (d. 1111 CE). However, according to other accounts, the latter's younger brother Ahmad al-Ghazali (d. 1128 CE) was his associate.[89] In his youth Farmadi studied under several well-known Sufis of Khorasan, including Abu al-Qasim al-Qushayri (d. 1073 CE).[90] Today he is considered one of the links in the "Golden Chain" of spiritual masters of the Naqshbandi Sufi order.[91] Naqshbandi traditions claim that he was a specialist in Love

---

87 On category entitlements, see Potter, *Representing Reality*, pp. 142–5. All types of category entitlements are referred to as "footing" (footnote-like), even when they occur in oral form or in premodern contexts.
88 'Attar, *Tadhkirat al-awliya'*, pp. 61 and 64; Sells, *Early Islamic Mysticism*, pp. 155, 158.
89 See, for example, J. Spencer Trimingham, *The Sufi Orders in Islam* (New York and London: Oxford University Press, 1998 reprint of 1971 original), pp. 32–3. According to Trimingham, Farmadi was Ahmad al-Ghazali's *shaykh al-suhba*, more of a spiritual associate than a master of personal training.
90 J.A. Boyle, *The Cambridge History of Iran* (Cambridge: Cambridge University Press, 1968), p. 297
91 The Tahiri and Ghafuri Naqshbandi Golden Chains list Farmadi as a disciple of Abu al-Qasim Gurgani and claim that he was the shaykh of Abu Ya'qub Yusuf al-Hamadani (d. 1140 CE). The Naqshbandi Haqqani Golden Chain lists him as a disciple of Abu al-Hasan 'Ali al-Kharaqani (d. 1034 CE). http://en.wikipedia.org/wiki/Naqshbandi_Golden_Chain. For a short summary of Naqshbandi-Haqqani traditions about Farmadi, see Shaykh Muhammad Hisham Kabbani, *Classical Islam and the Naqshbandi Sufi Tradition* (Washington, DC: Islamic Supreme Council of America, 2004), pp. 129–31.

mysticism.[92] Because Farmadi is the only person cited as a source for any of the stories in 'Attar's chapter on Rabi'a, it appears that 'Attar used Farmadi's name and alleged reputation as a teacher of Ghazali to add verisimilitude to his narrative.

In the epigraph to this chapter, I quote H. Porter Abbott as stating, "Wholeness is something that we impose on narratives, rather than something we find in them."[93] In *Tropics of Discourse*, Hayden White observes that biographers who draw on diverse sources of information—as 'Attar purports to do in his chapter on Rabi'a—often create plots for their narratives in order to tie up the loose ends of the story and develop their characters more fully. Hagiographers are no different. In fact, this tendency is just as common in sacred biography as it is in modern biographical works. Hayden White calls this process "emplotment."[94] Paul Ricoeur states that this narrative device originally came from Aristotle, whose treatise *Rhetoric* was well known in the medieval Muslim world.[95] Besides providing a backstory for a character, emplotment also creates an idealized image of the subject in the mind of the reader, which makes the subject's impact on future developments seem paradigmatic. We have seen this process at work throughout the history of the Rabi'a narratives.

Aristotle's *Poetics* was also a well-known work in the premodern Muslim world.[96] A widely read translation of this work was made under the title, *Fann al-shi'r* (*The Art of Poetry*), by the Christian scholar Abu Bishr Matta ibn Yunus (d. 940 CE). Matta ibn Yunus was also a philosopher and is best known as the teacher of the Islamic philosopher Abu Nasr al-Farabi (d. 951 CE). In the *Poetics*, Aristotle gives priority to action—the incidents in the narrative—over character in the composition of a story. This is stated clearly in his discussion of Tragedy:

---

92 On the Haqqani Nasqshbandi website, http://naqshbandi.org/chain/8.htm, Farmadi is referred to as "Knower of [God] the Merciful and Custodian of Divine Love."
93 Abbott, *The Cambridge Introduction to Narrative*, p. 101.
94 White, *Tropics of Discourse*, pp. 65–6, 73.
95 Paul Ricoeur, *Time and Narrative*, trans. Kathleen McLaughlin and David Pellauer (Chicago: University of Chicago Press, 1984), vol. 1, pp. 31–51. On Aristotle's *Rhetoric* (Ar. *Kitab al-balagha*) and medieval Arabic commentaries on this work, see Wen-chin Ouyang, *Literary Criticism in Medieval Arabic-Islamic Culture: The Making of A Tradition* (Edinburgh: Edinburgh University Press, 1997).
96 See, for example, Salim Kemal, "Arabic Poetics and Aristotle's Poetics," *British Journal of Aesthetics*, 26 (2), 1986, pp. 112–23.

Tragedy is an imitation, not of men, but of an action and of life, and life consists in action, and its end is a mode of action, not a quality. Now character determines men's qualities, but it is by their actions that they are happy or the reverse. Dramatic action, therefore, is not with a view to the representation of character: character comes in as subsidiary to the actions. Hence the incidents and the plot are the end of the tragedy; and the end is the chief thing of all. Again, without action there cannot be a tragedy; there may be without character.[97]

The prioritization of action over character is also a hallmark of hagiographic narratives. For example, we saw at the beginning of this chapter how Thomas Heffernan defines the purpose of sacred biography as portraying the actions of God through the actions of a saint. This was just as true for Islamic hagiography as it was for Christian hagiography. Aristotle also states, "The Plot then, is the first principle, and as it were, the soul of a tragedy: Character holds the second place. A similar fact is seen in painting. The most beautiful colours, laid on confusedly, will not give as much pleasure as the chalk outline of a portrait."[98] This painting metaphor can be used to draw a connection between hagiography, Aristotle's *Poetics*, and the image of the saint as a hagiographic icon, which has been described above using Losev's theory of myth. In fact, almost all the major elements of Tragedy described by Aristotle can be found in hagiography: there is a Plot (the course of the action); there is Character (the quality or moral purpose of the actor); there is Thought (the faculty of saying what is possible under certain circumstances); and there is Diction (the expression of meaning through words). The only classical element of Tragedy that is missing in hagiography is Song, which Aristotle defines as an embellishment of the above four elements.

Is it possible to call hagiography a form of Tragedy, according to Aristotle's definition? I believe that it is, and I also believe that Aristotle's theory of Tragedy can be discerned in 'Attar's *vita* of Rabi'a al-'Adawiyya in *Tadhkirat al-awliya'*. However, it should be noted in this regard that sometimes 'Attar seems more "modern" than Aristotle in his approach to narrative. This is because he gives more importance to character than is recommended by Aristotle in the *Poetics*. In 'Attar's portrayal of Rabi'a, character and action are inseparable. Not only do Rabi'a's actions illustrate

---

97   S.H. Butcher (ed. and trans.), *The Poetics of Aristotle* (London: Macmillan, 1902), p. 26 (1450a).
98   Ibid., p. 29 (1450b).

her character, but also her actions are often as important as those of God. As Henry James states in the article, "The Art of Fiction," "What is character but the determination of incident? What is incident but the illustration of character?"[99] Although Rabi'a is often posed formally by 'Attar like an icon in his narratives, at other times she shows real personality and agency. This can be seen in the passage quoted in the previous section, in which Rabi'a talks back to God saying, "My God! Do kings treat an incapable woman in this way? You invited me to your House, but on the way you killed my donkey and left me alone in the desert!"

One of the keys to understanding how hagiography is related to Aristotle's *Poetics* can be found in the way that Aristotle defines the character of the tragic subject. Contrary to what modern readers have come to expect with Tragedy, for Aristotle it is not necessary for the main character or subject of a tragedy to display a tragic flaw. This is because in the most general sense of the term, "Tragedy is the imitation of persons who are above the common level."[100] In other words, the purpose of Tragedy is to provide examples of extraordinary individuals and their behaviors. As we might say today, this is Tragedy's "redeeming social value." Not only does Aristotle's definition of Tragedy not exclude saints—who are undeniably above the common level—but it also includes the narrative tropes of *admiranda* and *imitanda*, the idea that the subjects of Tragedy are worthy of admiration or imitation. As we have seen above, these concepts were central components of sacred biography in medieval Europe and they can be found in 'Attar's *vita* of Rabi'a al-'Adawiyya as well.

The connection thus suggested between the narrative genre of hagiography and Aristotle's *Poetics* is further confirmed by Aristotle's rules of character development:

1. The character must be *good*. As Aristotle states, "The character will be good if the purpose is good... Even a woman may be good and also a slave; though the woman may be said to be an inferior being, and the slave quite worthless."
2. The character must have *propriety*. For Aristotle, the character of a Tragedy can be fully virtuous and even be an exemplar of virtue. As with goodness, this can apply to women as well as to men,

---

99   Henry James, "The Art of Fiction," quoted in Abbott, *The Cambridge Introduction to Narrative*, p. 131.
100 Butcher, *The Poetics of Aristotle*, p. 57 (1454b).

although it is inappropriate for a woman to display manly valor or unscrupulous cleverness.
3. The character must be *true to life*. That is to say, the character must be believable and relevant to the life-experiences of the audience.
4. The character must be *consistent*. "A person of a given character should speak or act in a given way, by the rule either of necessity or probability; just as this even should follow that by necessary or probable sequence."¹⁰¹

All the goals of character development—goodness, propriety, believability, and consistency—can be seen to apply to saints as the subjects of hagiography. The same goals are also realized in ʿAttar's portrayal of Rabiʿa al-ʿAdawiyya in *Tadhkirat al-awliya'*. But this is not all. Aristotle comes even closer to ʿAttar when he states that the model of a character of Tragedy should be composed like a fine portrait: "Again, since Tragedy is the imitation of persons who are above the common level, the example of good portrait-painters should be followed. They, while reproducing the distinctive form of the original, make a likeness which is true to life and yet more beautiful."¹⁰² This aspect of Tragedy is strikingly visible in the portrait that ʿAttar paints of Rabiʿa the Icon.

In an important article, Alberto Rigolio argues that the Arabic translation of Aristotle's *Poetics* published by Matta ibn Yunus differed significantly from previous Syriac translations of this work because he did not retain the Greek term *tragedia* in its original form. Instead, he translated the term into Arabic as *al-madih* (literally, "praise"). This is the term used in medieval Arabic literature for the genre of encomium (Gr. *enkomion*).¹⁰³ Although in medieval Arabic literary culture the *madih* genre was most often associated with poetry, it could also be used for prose. Thus, Matta ibn Yunus' intercultural translation of this term provides further evidence for the theory that Aristotle's *Poetics* influenced the writing of hagiography in medieval Islam. As we have seen, for Aristotle, Tragedy is "the imitation of persons who are above the common level." In Arabic literary culture, this definition applied both to the genre of encomium (*al-madih*) and to the genre of hagiography (*tarjamat al-awliya'*, literally, "translation of the saints"). The purpose of both encomium and hagiography was to memorialize extraordinary people.

---

101 Ibid., pp. 53–5 (1454a).
102 Ibid., p. 57 (1454b).
103 Alberto Rigolio, "Aristotle's Poetics in Syriac and Arabic Translations: Readings of 'Tragedy,'" in *Khristianskii Vostok 6* (Moscow: Russian Academy of Sciences, 2013), p. 142.

Matta ibn Yunus also rendered Aristotle's term for Narrative (Gr. *diegesis*), as *khurafa* ("narration" or "story"), and his term for Plot (Gr. *muthos*), as *hikayat al-hadith* ("the relation of an event").[104] These Arabic translations also correspond closely to 'Attar's understanding of Narrative and Plot. His chapter on Rabi'a al-'Adawiyya in *Tadhkirat al-awliya'* consists of a collection of stories (Ar. *khurafat*) and narrations of events (Ar. *hikayat al-ahadith*). Once again, the composition of this work conforms to Aristotle's theory of Tragedy. For theoretical purposes it does not matter whether the events that he relates are true or not.

Although the circumstantial evidence appears strong, at the present time, it is not possible to state conclusively that 'Attar followed Aristotle's *Poetics* to the letter when he composed his *vita* of Rabi'a al-'Adawiyya. To develop such a theory would require a detailed literary study of the text of *Tadhkirat al-awliya'* as a whole. However, there is enough evidence to suggest this as a hypothesis. There is also enough evidence to warrant further study of the relationship between Aristotle's *Poetics* and the literary genre of Islamic hagiography. With this in mind, in the remainder of this section, I will outline the major plot elements of 'Attar's *vita* of Rabi'a, with comments on the rhetorical functions that these elements perform in his narrative.

1. Rabi'a is the fourth child in a family of four daughters. This is why she is called *Rabi'a* ("The Fourth").[105]

This plot element is more likely to be true than other parts of 'Attar's *vita* of Rabi'a. Although there is no tradition with an *isnad* to support the claim that Rabi'a was the fourth of four daughters, it is not uncommon in Arab culture to give a fourth daughter the name of Rabi'a. A related emplotment by subsequent writers was to give Rabi'a's father the name of Isma'il. Thus, her name is frequently rendered as "Rabi'a bint Isma'il al-'Adawiyya." This plot element was probably due to the conflation of Rabi'a al-'Adawiyya of Basra and Rabi'a bint Isma'il of Damascus.[106] As noted in Chapter 1, there is some evidence that this conflation may have originated with Muhammad ibn al-Husayn al-Burjulani in the ninth century CE. Among the authors whose

---

104 Ibid., p. 145. The Arabic phrase, *hikayat al-hadith*, is a nearly literal translation of the basic meaning of the Greek term, *muthos* ("story," "report").
105 'Attar, *Tadhkirat al-awliya'*, p. 62; Sells, *Early Islamic Mysticism*, p. 155.
106 See, for example, Badawi, *Shahidat al-'ishq al-ilahi*, p. 15.

works are currently extant, Ibn al-Jawzi is the first to comment on this mistake. In *Sifat al-safwa* he attempts to correct it by noting that one Rabi'a was from Basra but the other Rabi'a was from Syria.[107] However, he still calls Rabi'a al-'Adawiyya's father Isma'il and incorrectly states that Sulami said that the two Rabi'as shared both their first names and their father's names.[108] Sulami does not make such a claim in his Book of Sufi Women. Instead, he discusses the two Rabi'as in separate notices and does not compare them. No extant source prior to Ibn al-Jawzi's *Sifat al-Safwa* mentions Rabi'a al-'Adawiyya's father, nor gives his name. Since Ibn al-Jawzi died about twenty years before 'Attar, the attention that he gives to this subject indicates that the idea of a backstory for the Rabi'a narrative was already "in the air" before 'Attar put pen to paper.

For some unknown reason most writers after Ibn al-Jawzi do not cite him as the source of Rabi'a's father's name, nor do they cite Sulami, to whom Ibn al-Jawzi attributes this information. Instead, they most often cite the Syrian historian Ahmad ibn Khallikan (d. 1282 CE), who refers to Rabi'a as "Rabi'a bint Isma'il al-'Adawiyya" in *Wafayat al-a'yan*.[109] Ibn Khallikan also refers to Rabi'a as *Umm al-Khayr*, "Mother (or Source) of Goodness."[110] This appellation may reflect the Syrian Christian practice of describing female saints as sources of goodness. For example, the Greek name *Agatha* is very close in meaning to *Umm al-Khayr*. Later on in the notice, in a section that recounts Rabi'a's teachings to Sufyan al-Thawri, Ibn Khallikan also calls Rabi'a *Umm 'Amr* (Mother of 'Amr).[111] He cites Ibn al-Jawzi's *Sifat al-safwa* as the source for this appellation. This citation is just as incorrect as Ibn al-Jawzi's citation of Sulami for the name of Rabi'a's father. Ironically, by calling Rabi'a "Umm 'Amr," Ibn Khallikan makes the same mistake as Sulami did more than 200 years previously and conflates Rabi'a al-'Adawiyya with the other famous woman ascetic from Basra, Mu'adha al-'Adawiyya. What Ibn al-Jawzi actually states in *Sifat al-safwa* is that Mu'adha al-'Adawiyya's son was named 'Amr. A copyist of this text might have mistaken Mu'adha for Rabi'a. Both 'Amr al-'Adawi and his father Sila ibn Ushaym al-'Adawi were martyred in

---

107 R. Cornell, *Early Sufi Women*, Ibn al-Jawzi, *Sifat al-safwa* Appendix, pp. 314–15.
108 Ibid.
109 Ahmad ibn Muhammad b. Abu Bakr ibn Khallikan, *Wafayat al-a'yan wa anba' abna' al-zaman*, ed. Ihsan 'Abbas (Beirut: Dar Sadir, 1978), vol. 2, p. 285.
110 Ibid.
111 Ibid., p. 286.

battle against the Byzantines at the end of the seventh century CE, before Rabiʿa al-ʿAdawiyya was born.[112]

As stated at the beginning of this chapter, the reputation of Ibn Khallikan was so great that the verisimilitude created by *Wafayat al-aʿyan* overcame all of its inaccuracies. For this reason, his erroneous reference to Rabiʿa al-ʿAdawiyya as "Umm ʿAmr" was taken by some later authors as evidence that she married and bore a child (see Chapter 3). Ibn Khallikan also embellished Rabiʿa's *vita* by adding an anecdote in which she reproaches her father for eating meat that was obtained in an unlawful manner. When her father asks, "Do you believe that I can obtain only what is forbidden?" She replies, "Being patient in the face of hunger in the World is better than being patient in the face of fire in the Hereafter."[113] This story suggests that Rabiʿa's father was a heretic or non-Muslim in origin. Were the situation otherwise, it would not have made sense for her to doubt the lawfulness of the food he obtained. It is possible that this account was also originally related about Muʿadha al-ʿAdawiyya. As discussed in Chapter 2, Muʿadha was a client (*mawlat*) of ʿAʾisha bint Abi Bakr and her father was taken captive before he converted to Islam. Such clients (*mawali*) were usually of non-Muslim origin. Thus, it would make sense that Muʿadha would not trust her father's ability to differentiate between wholesome (*halal*) and forbidden (*haram*) foods. By claiming that the story was about Rabiʿa al-ʿAdawiyya, Ibn Khallikan reinforces the earlier claim made by Sulami that Rabiʿa was a *mawlat* of non-Muslim origin.

2. When Rabiʿa is born, her family is so poor that they have nothing with which to wrap her, nor any oil for cleaning her. The night after her birth, her father has a dream of the Prophet Muhammad, who says that Rabiʿa is a noble lady (*sayyida*), who will intercede for 70,000 of his community. The Prophet also tells him to ask for 400 dinars from "'Isa Radan," the Emir of Basra.[114] After hearing about this dream, the Emir gives 10,000 dirhams as alms to the poor and gives 400 dinars to Rabiʿa's father, who takes the gold and spends it.[115]

---

112 For a full reproduction and translation of Ibn al-Jawzi's notice on Muʿadha al-ʿAdawiyya in *Sifat al-safwa* see the Ibn al-Jawzi Appendix in R. Cornell, *Early Sufi Women*, pp. 264–9.
113 Ibn Khallikan, *Wafayat al-aʿyan*, vol. 2, p. 285.
114 It is possible that in the original the name of the Emir was 'Isa Zadan and that "Radan" was due to a copyist's error. The difference between the letters *ra* and *za* in Arabic and in Persian is a single dot.
115 ʿAttar, *Tadhkirat al-awliya*', pp. 61–2; Sells, *Early Islamic Mysticism*, pp. 155–6.

This plot element is meant to show that Rabiʻa was predestined for greatness. It also shows that she has the gift of saintly intercession (*shafaʻa*) because the Prophet Muhammad tells her father in a dream that she will intercede for 70,000 members of her community. She also is the source of good fortune, which is often a sign of *karamat*, or saintly miracles in Sufi hagiography. Although the Prophet orders her father to ask for 400 dinars from the Emir of Basra, Rabiʻa's birth is the immediate cause of his dream. As we saw earlier, ʻAttar states in one of the commentarial sections of his chapter on Rabiʻa, "Whoever follows a Prophet shares in a portion of his miracles." Because Rabiʻa is predestined to become a saint and a devoted lover of God and the Prophet, her intercessory powers are apparent from birth.

Although later authors sometimes changed minor details of this portion of Rabiʻa's *vita*, for the most part they have preserved the story just as ʻAttar presented it. For example, in the book *Rabiʻa al-ʻAdawiyya fi mihrab al-hubb al-ilahi* (*Rabiʻa al-ʻAdawiyya in the Prayer-Niche of Divine Love*), the Egyptian writer Maʼmun Gharib only adds the detail that Rabiʻa was born in a reed hut (*kukh*).[116] As we shall see in the next chapter, this claim takes for fact a rhetorical flourish that ʻAbd al-Rahman Badawi makes when he sets the opening scene for his modern existentialist version of Rabiʻa's life story: "Come with me now, gentlemen, to a reed hut (*kukh*) that is lowly but full of holiness, where there lives a worn-out old woman who has reached 80 years of age."[117] When composing this passage, Badawi was apparently thinking of a reed hut similar to the huts of the Marsh Arabs, who lived not far from Basra in the marshlands of the Tigris and Euphrates rivers.[118] As we saw in Chapter 1, in Rabiʻa's time these people were looked down upon because of their poverty and non-Muslim background. For Badawi, this detail supported the contention that Rabiʻa was originally a *mawlat* from a non-Muslim background.[119]

---

116 Gharib, *Rabiʻa al-ʻAdawiyya fi mihrab al-hubb al-ilahi*, p. 25.
117 Badawi, *Shahidat al-ʻishq al-ilahi*, p. 10.
118 According to the text of *al-Basra al-fayha' ta'rikh wa hadarat al-ʻArab* (Basra the Fragrant: History and Culture of the Arabs), on the website "Ruh al-Iraq" (http://www.roo7iraq.com), the original name of Basra in the Chaldean language (*al-lugha al-Kaldiya*) was *al-Aqniyah* or *Basarah*, which meant, "Place of Reed Huts" (*mahall al-akwakh*). See the section titled, *Tasmiyat al-Basra* (Names of Basra), in ibid. On the Marsh Arabs, see Sam Kubba, *The Iraqi Marshlands and the Marsh Arabs: The Maʻdan Their Culture and the Environment* (Reading, UK: Ithaca Press, 2010); and Wilfred Thesiger, *The Marsh Arabs* (London: Penguin Group, 2008 reprint of 1964 original).
119 Badawi, *Shahidat al-ʻishq al-ilahi*, p. 13.

3. Around the time that Rabi'a attains puberty (*chun Rabi'a buzurg shud*), a famine takes the lives of her parents. She becomes an orphan (*bi-madar o pedar*) and she and her sisters are separated. She then becomes the captive (*asir*) of an evil oppressor (*zalimi*), who sells her for a few dirhams (*chand dirham*). Her new master works her very hard. One day she runs away from a stranger (*na-mahrami*) in the street, but falls and breaks her arm.[120] Helpless and desolate (*shekasteh*), she commits herself to God, who says to her, "Do not be sad. Tomorrow a grandeur will be yours such that you will be honored by my most intimate friends among the heavenly hosts (*muqarraban-i asaman*)."[121]

There are four key terms in 'Attar's Persian text in this part of Rabi'a's *vita*: "orphan" (*bi-madar o pedar*), "captive" (*asir*), "stranger" (*na-mahrami*, literally, "not a family member"), and "broken" (*shekasteh*). The purpose of this plot element is to set the stage for Rabi'a's eventual spiritual transformation.[122] In this portion of the narrative she is depicted as an orphan like the Prophet Muhammad and a captive like the Prophet Joseph. As in these Prophetic examples, no one but God can help her. As a "broken" or helpless person, she is also comparable to the Qur'anic Virgin Mary, who like Joseph, is a model in the Qur'an for *tawakkul*, complete trust in God. Rabi'a appears in this portion of the story as a stranger in her own land. As the Qur'an asks rhetorically of the Prophet Muhammad: "Did [Allah] not find you as an orphan and shelter you? Did He not find you lost and guide you? Did He not find you in need and make you self-sufficient?" (Qur'an 93:6–11).

The story of Rabi'a's captivity has become one of the most important plot elements of her *vita* for subsequent generations of hagiographers. Along with the claim that Rabi'a was a *mawlat*, or foreign client of an Arab tribe, it provides the basis for the popular trope of Rabi'a the Slave. Margaret Smith states in *Rabi'a the Mystic* that the "evil-minded man" who seized Rabi'a "sold her as a slave for six *dirhams*."[123] Given the importance of this trope to the

---

120 In Sells, *Early Islamic Mysticism*, p. 156, Paul Losensky translates *na-mahrami* as meaning that Rabi'a fled from the indignity of being worked too hard by her master. This appears to be incorrect.
121 'Attar, *Tadhkirat al-awliya'*, p. 62; Sells, *Early Islamic Mysticism*, p. 156.
122 For medieval Muslim tropes of conversion, see Mun'im Sirry, "Pious Muslims in the Making: A Closer Look at Narratives of Ascetic Conversion," *Arabica*, 57, 2010, pp. 437–54.
123 Smith, *Rabi'a* (Oneworld), p. 23 and (Rainbow Bridge), p. 6.

Rabi'a myth, it is significant that neither the word "slave," nor the phrase "six dirhams," appears in 'Attar's original Persian text. Instead, 'Attar describes Rabi'a as a captive (*asir*), perhaps to stress the injustice of a Muslim being forced into servitude by another Muslim.[124] Based on the original wording of the text, her plight is best understood not in terms of legal slavery but of criminality. Another way to interpret this plot element would be to see Rabi'a as subjected to indentured servitude, such as when poor girls are indentured to work as carpet weavers or family servants in some modern Muslim countries. This would allow her servitude to reflect the theological relationship in Islam between God and His subjects, which is depicted in the Qur'an as an indentured or contracted master-slave relationship.[125] Seen in this way, this plot element provides a good illustration of Hendrik Vroom's contention that in religious stories, a truth claim that is fictional can be better than empirical reality in reinforcing the deeper truth of a theological claim.

4. During her time as a captive, Rabi'a fasts continuously, works during the day, and spends her nights in prayer, remaining on her feet until daybreak. One night her master awakes and finds her praying. He sees a lantern suspended over her head without a chain and filling the room with light. Recognizing God's miracle in this, he frees Rabi'a from her service to him (*khidmat*) and allows her to leave, saying, "If you wish to stay here, we will serve you." Rabi'a then decides to leave.

The trope of the miracle of the lamp, which has figured prominently in nearly every version of Rabi'a's *vita* since 'Attar first introduced it, appears to have been taken from Sulami's Book of Sufi Women or an earlier work. In Sulami's book, a similar story is told of Hafsa bint Sirin, the sister of the early ascetic and dream interpreter, Muhammad ibn Sirin (d. 728–9 CE). According to Sulami, "Hafsa bint Sirin used to light her lamp at night, and then would rise

---

124 In Islamic Law, Muslims are not allowed to enslave other Muslims, nor are Muslims allowed to sell themselves or their children into slavery because of poverty. In cases where this has occurred, it was in violation of the Law or was justified as a legal fiction, such as when states enslaved rebels or political dissidents. In such cases, rebels were treated as heretics or apostates.
125 See, for example, Qur'an 9:111: "Verily God has purchased from the believers their persons and possessions in return for Paradise. They fight in the cause of God and slay and are slain. It is a binding promise on God stated in truth in the Torah, the Gospel, and the Qur'an. And who is more faithful to his promise than [God]? So rejoice in the sale of yourself which you have concluded, for it is the supreme achievement."

and pray in her prayer area. At times, the lamp would go out, but it would continue to illuminate her house until daylight."[126]

In both versions of this story, the religious meaning of the lamp is the same: the lamp symbolizes spiritual illumination and divine knowledge.[127] In his Book of Sufi Women, Sulami traces the account of Hafsa's miraculous lamp to Sa'id ibn 'Uthman al-Hannat (d. 906–7 CE), a disciple of the famous Egyptian Sufi Dhu al-Nun al-Misri (d. 859 CE).[128] This connection with Egypt also suggests another possibility, which is that the story of Rabi'a's lamp may have originated in the legend of the "Lamp of Umm Hashim" (*Qindil Umm Hashim*), a lamp that used to hang in the tomb of Sayyida Zaynab in Cairo. Egyptians have long believed that the oil of this lamp could miraculously replenish itself and that it could cure eye diseases.[129] In Shiite Islam, Zaynab, the granddaughter of the Prophet Muhammad, is a major female saint. Her most likely tomb is in the Syrian town of Sayyida Zaynab, some 12 kilometers south of Damascus. However, some early Sunni historians, such Muhammad ibn Jarir al-Tabari (d. 923 CE) claimed that she was buried in Cairo.[130] According to modern historians, the tomb attributed to Sayyida Zaynab in Cairo actually contains the remains of Zaynab the cousin of Sayyida Nafisa (d. 824 CE), the great-granddaughter of the Prophet's grandson Hasan. Whatever the empirical truth of the matter may be, the interment of the Egyptian Sayyida Zaynab dates to a time close to that of Dhu al-Nun al Misri and his disciple Sa'id al-Hannat. This at least suggests the possibility that 'Attar's story of Rabi'a's lamp may have started out as an Egyptian legend.[131]

---

126 R. Cornell, *Early Sufi Women*, pp. 122–3.
127 Margaret Smith interprets the light of the lamp as signifying the divine presence (Heb. *shekhina*; Ar. *sakina*) and compares it to the nimbus or halo that surrounds the heads of Christian saints in religious icons. Smith, *Rabi'a* (Oneworld), p. 24 and (Rainbow Bridge), p. 7.
128 See the biographial note on Sa'id al-Hannat by Roger Déladrière in Ibn 'Arabi, *La vie merveilleuse de Dhu-l-Nun l'Egyptien*, pp. 379–80.
129 The Lamp of Umm Hashim was recently removed from the tomb of Sayyida Zaynab by the Egyptian authorities. In 1944 the Egyptian novelist Yahya Haqqi (1905–90) published a novella with the title, *Qindil Umm Hashim*. For a recent translation of this work, see Yahya Hakki, *The Lamp of Umm Hashim and Other Stories*, trans. Denys Johnson-Davies (Cairo and New York: American University in Cairo Press, 2006), pp. 45–88.
130 Michelle Zimney, "History in the Making: the Sayyida Zaynab Shrine in Damascus," ARAM, 19, 2007, pp. 695–703.
131 Caroline Williams, *Islamic Monuments in Cairo, A Practical Guide* (Cairo: American University in Cairo Press, 1993), pp. 123–4 and 152–3. On Sayyida Zaynab see also, Nadia Abu-Zahra, *The Pure and Powerful: Studies in Contemporary Muslim Society* (Reading, UK: Garnet Publishing and Ithaca Press, 1997).

5. "A group of people say" (*garuhi guyand keh*) that Rabi'a fell into being a musician after she left the house of her master and that she later repented (*dar mutribi aftad va baz tawbeh kard*).¹³²

The trope of Rabi'a the Repentant Sinner that comes from this plot element of 'Attar's *vita* will be discussed in greater detail in the next chapter. However, in the present context we can say something about an important motif of this trope, which is that Rabi'a played the reed flute (*nay*). This detail appears to be of purely modern origin. The earliest example that I have been able to find comes from Margaret Smith's book *Rabi'a the Mystic*: "According to one account, Rabi'a at first followed the calling of a flute player, which would be consistent with a state of slavery."¹³³ Smith does not say which "account" she was thinking of or what she had in mind when she said that flute playing was consistent with the state of slavery. Most likely she was referring to the *qiyan*, female slaves who were trained as singers and musicians for the Abbasid court in Baghdad. As noted previously, the *qiyan* were common figures in Abbasid-era literature. Another interpretation is provided by the contemporary Egyptian writer Taha 'Abd al-Baqi Surur, who sees this motif as alluding to the use of flutes by Sufis in sessions of spiritual audition (*sama'*).¹³⁴

However, Surur erroneously traces the origin of the Rabi'a the Flute Player trope to 'Attar. As we have seen in the above summary of this plot element, although 'Attar reports the claim that Rabi'a was a musician (*mutribi*), he does not describe her as playing the flute in the Persian text of *Tadhkirat al-awliya'*. Apparently, Surur did not read 'Attar's account himself but relied on 'Abd al-Rahman Badawi's book on Rabi'a, which erroneously claims not only that 'Attar said that Rabi'a played the flute but also that he was the only medieval writer to do so.¹³⁵ Strangely, Badawi cites as evidence for this assertion the Persian passage from 'Attar's text, which he quotes verbatim and which does not mention a flute at all.¹³⁶ This mistake is especially surprising because the word for "reed flute" in Persian is *nay*, just as it is in Arabic; likewise, the Arabic word for "musician" is *mutrib*, just as it is in Persian.

---

132 'Attar, *Tadhkirat al-awliya'*, p. 63; Sells, *Early Islamic Mysticism*, p. 157.
133 Smith, *Rabi'a* (Oneworld), p. 24 and (Rainbow Bridge), p. 7.
134 Surur, *Rabi'a al-'Adawiyya wa al-hayat al-ruhiyya fi-l-Islam*, p. 47.
135 Badawi, *Shahidat al-'ishq al-ilahi*, p. 19.
136 Ibid., p. 19 n. 1; Badawi took his reference from the Persian text of Farid al-Din al-'Attar, *Tadhkirat al-awliya'*, ed. R.A. Nicholson (London and Leiden: Luzac & Co. and E.J. Brill, vol. 1, 1905).

The earliest antecedent to the modern trope of Rabi'a the Flute Player that I have been able to find in medieval Arabic literature is in the book *Rawdat al-ta'rif* (*The Garden of Knowledge*), by the Andalusian *littérateur* Lisan al-Din ibn al-Khatib (d. 1374 CE). However, even Ibn al-Khatib does not claim that Rabi'a played the flute. Instead, he quotes Rabi'a as saying that she played the tambourine (*kuntu adribu al-daffa bi-l-tabl*).[137] Ibn al-Khatib's account can also be found in a slightly later work from Egypt, *al-Rawd al-fa'iq* (*The Garden of Awareness*), by the preacher and storyteller Shu'ayb al-Hurayfish (d. 1398 CE). Most of what Hurayfish says about Rabi'a in this work is based on 'Attar's chapter in *Tadhkirat al-awliya'*. However, neither a flute nor a tambourine is mentioned in the original Persian text. Nevertheless, Hurayfish does give us a clue that may explain how 'Attar came up with the idea that Rabi'a was a musician. He traces one account in his chapter on Rabi'a to Salih al-Murri (d. 792–3 CE), who is often mentioned as Rabi'a's companion in the practice of asceticism. In this story, Murri speaks of a slave-girl (*jariya*), who sang and played an instrument called the *tar* (*tughanni bi-l-tar*).[138] Although in much of the Arab world the *tar* is a hand-drum (like a tambourine), in other parts of the Arab and Muslim world (such as Azerbaijan) the *tar* is a stringed instrument that resembles a long-necked '*ud* or lute. Although this account does not specifically identify the slave-girl as Rabi'a al-'Adawiyya, Hurayfish assumes that it is she. If this account originally came from an early hagiographical work that is now lost, it might explain the conflation of Murri's unidentified slave-girl and singer-musician with the figure of Rabi'a the musician as introduced by 'Attar.

> 6. Rabi'a makes the Hajj pilgrimage but 'Attar does not specify how often this happens. The six accounts that discuss Rabi'a's pilgrimage in *Tadhkirat al-awliya'* all revolve around the question of balance between the moral truth claims of the Law (*al-Shari'a*) and the religious truth claims of faith (*al-haqiqa*).[139] The experience of true faith is depicted as a form of intimacy with God that sometimes makes the letter of the Law superfluous. In one account, the Ka'ba is depicted as leaving its location in Mecca and coming to meet Rabi'a halfway on her journey. In two stories, Rabi'a seems to disparage the Ka'ba. In one story she says: "My God! My heart is desolate. Where am I to go?

---

137 Ibn al-Khatib, *Rawdat al-ta'rif*, p. 148.
138 Hurayfish, *al-Rawd al-fa'iq*, p. 184.
139 Sells, *Early Islamic Mysticism*, pp. 157–9; 'Attar, *Tadhkirat al-awliya'*, pp. 63–5.

I am but a clod of dirt (*kulukhi*) and that House (i.e., the Ka'ba) is but a stone (*sangi*). I need *you*!" In the other story she says: "I need the Lord of the House. What am I to do with the Ka'ba? I am not able to bear the Ka'ba (*man-ra istita'at Ka'ba nist*).[140] What delight is there in the Ka'ba's beauty? What I need to welcome me is the One who said, 'Whoever approaches me by a span, I will approach him by a cubit.'[141] What would I see in the Ka'ba (*Ka'ba-ra cheh binam*)?"

Both of these stories imply that the true "House of God" is not in the city of Mecca but in Rabi'a herself. In most Sufi works this abode is depicted as the heart, which is regarded as the locus of spirituality in the human body. In the final story of this section of the narrative Rabi'a is lost in the desert in an intermediate or ambiguous place, no longer at home in the worldly city of Basra, but also unable to reach her true spiritual home with God in Mecca. She says in despair, "At first, I did not prostrate to the House because I wanted you. Now I am not even worthy of your House." This story affirms how the moral truths of the Shari'a are inseparable from the greater spiritual goals of religion: even the lesser degree of awareness of those who are slaves to the Law is better than being cut off from God completely.

A full discussion of the pilgrimage stories in 'Attar's chapter on Rabi'a would take a chapter by itself. The Egyptian philosopher and historian 'Abd al-Rahman Badawi argues that these stories depict three stages of spiritual awareness. In the first stage, Rabi'a goes to the Ka'ba like any other pilgrim. It is enough for her to fulfill the obligation of the Hajj according to the rules of the Shari'a. In the second stage, Rabi'a tries to integrate her ascetic practices into the Hajj pilgrimage in order to perfect its observance. Badawi states, "She started to fulfill her pilgrimage on foot or crawling, or by practicing another form of bodily mortification that the Sufis make obligatory for themselves in order to multiply the rewards of the Hajj."[142] Badawi's statement refers to Rabi'a's first pilgrimage to Mecca in 'Attar's chapter, in which she is depicted as crawling on her hands and knees for seven years. However, it also pertains to 'Attar's contrasting description of the even longer pilgrimage of Ibrahim

---

140 'Attar, *Tadhkirat al-awliya*', p. 63. In Sells, *Early Islamic Mysticism*, p. 157, Losensky translates the Persian phrase *man-ra istata'at Ka'ba nist* as, "Its power means nothing to me."
141 For this Hadith reference, see Bukhari, *Tawhid*, p. 50; and Muslim, *Dhikr*, pp. 2, 3, 20–2.
142 Badawi, *Shahidat al-'ishq al-ilahi*, pp. 40–1.

ibn Adham, in which the famous male ascetic performed two prostrations of prayer for every step toward Mecca that he took.

These types of extreme ritualistic and ascetic behaviors—which are parodied by 'Attar in this passage—are examples of the early Islamic practices of ascetic ritualism (*nusk*) and instrumental asceticism discussed in Chapter 2. In instrumental asceticism the ascetic mortifies the flesh or performs extreme ritualistic acts in order to gain a tangible reward. The Syrian historian Ibn Khallikan, who lived two generations after 'Attar, similarly portrays Rabi'a as practicing *nusk*. He describes her as wearing a hair shirt (*jubba min sha'r*) under an outer wrap of wool (*khimar suf*).[143] However, as 'Attar demonstrates in these stories, the obsessive performance of ritual can become a form of madness and the self-satisfaction of fulfilling the onerous requirements of instrumental asceticism can lead to spiritual egoism. The Lebanese–Syrian writer Widad El Sakkakini describes the paradox of this kind of asceticism in the following way: "The greater the sacrifice, the greater the reward; therefore those who sacrificed the most were in fact the most greedy for rewards."[144] 'Attar clearly agrees with this view, for the moral of the story of Ibrahim Ibn Adham's pilgrimage is that despite seeking the Ka'ba for fourteen years through the ritual practices of *nusk*, he was unable to reach his goal. When he arrived in Mecca, he found that the Ka'ba had left its location and had gone to meet Rabi'a halfway on her journey from Basra. This story provides an excellent example of Hendrik Vroom's contention that a major goal of religious narratives is to make the audience "see more truly."[145]

Badawi's explanation of Rabi'a's attempt to complete her pilgrimage continues: "The ardor of her faith increased and her self-consciousness was raised by virtue of the austerities that she made obligatory for herself on the path of pilgrimage. Thus it was natural that she would magnify the meaning of the Hajj in her mind. After the first stage, she sought the Ka'ba in order to see the Ka'ba. Now she begins to flirt with the idea of seeking the Ka'ba in order to see the Lord of the Ka'ba."[146] This new motivation leads to the third and final stage of Rabi'a's spiritual growth, in which "the Ka'ba itself is deprived of all meaning and she comes to see no meaning at all in the Ka'ba." For Badawi, the realization that the meaning of the Ka'ba is merely symbolic is problematical because "it is the same idea that played

---

143 Ibn Khallikan, *Wafayat al-a'yan*, vol. 2, p. 287.
144 El Sakkakini, *First Among Sufis*, p. 28; *al-'Ashiqa al-mutasawwifa*, p. 40.
145 Vroom, "Religious Truth," pp. 126–7.
146 Badawi, *Shahidat al-'ishq al-ilahi*, p. 41.

a dangerous role in the sect of al-Hallaj and was one of the causes of his apostasy and crucifixion."[147]

The danger that Badawi refers to in his exegesis of this story lies in the statement that 'Attar ascribes to Rabi'a: "What am I to do with the Ka'ba? I am not able to bear the Ka'ba (*man-ra istita'at Ka'ba nist*)." This and other statements of an apparently unorthodox nature have led to accusations of heresy against Rabi'a by the opponents of Sufism. A recent accusation of this type was made by Safar ibn 'Abd al-Rahman al-Hawali, a Salafi scholar from Saudi Arabia, who was jailed by the Saudi authorities for supporting Osama Bin Laden. Responding to a question about the acceptability of Rabi'a's Islam in his Internet blog, he cites a statement by the well-known Hadith transmitter Abu Dawud al-Sijistani (d. 888 or 889 CE). This early account by Abu Dawud may be the first recorded accusation of heresy against Rabi'a al-'Adawiyya, and it appears to contradict the views of Rabi'a's Sunni orthodoxy by Jahiz and Ibn Abi Tahir Tayfur, who were his contemporaries. In this account, Rabi'a is accused of heresy because of her doctrine of Love. However, in his explanation, Hawali takes Rabi'a's heresy in a more modern direction and blames her doctrine of Love on the heresy of religious pluralism:

> We say about Rabi'a al-'Adawiyya what the Imams of Hadith science such as Abu Dawud, who was a student of Imam Ahmad [ibn Hanbal], said in his Hadith collection and in the book *al-Jarh wa-l-ta'dil* (*Hadith Criticism and Assessment*): "Rabi'a is the 'fourth' of them in heresy (*Rabi'a rabi'atuhum fi-l-zandaqa*)." That is to say, Rabi'a al-'Adawiyya was among the most misguided of the worshippers who went astray in their worship and deviated from the Sunna of their Prophet (may God bless and preserve him). She imagined that her entire purpose in life was Love, such that she abandoned the fear and hope of God in their entirety. She attached herself to the doctrine of Love and forbade what God the Most Blessed and Exalted mandated (*shara'a*) for women, such as marriage and the like. She practiced celibacy and monasticism like the Christians, not the [pre-marital] virginity that God the Most Blessed and Exalted mandated for His worshippers.[148]

---

147 Ibid., p. 42.
148 Safar ibn 'Abd al-Rahman al-Hawali, *Nubdha 'an Rabi'a al-'Adawiyya* (Selection on Rabi'a al-'Adawiyya) in the blog post *al-As'ila* (Questions), http://www.alhawali.com. If it is indeed genuine, this criticism by Abu Dawud provides further evidence of Rabi'a's notoriety in the century after her death. If she was a subject of debate among early Hanbali scholars, she must have been considered an influential figure in early Islam.

In another blog post Hawali adds that Rabiʿa and other early Sufis "took as their religion what remained of Christian monasticism, which itself was derived from the monasticism of the Hindus, who became extremists by saying that God, may He be Glorified and Exalted, loved them as they loved Him."[149] Such accusations of Christian or Hindu influences are common in modern Salafi polemics against Sufism and ironically reflect nineteenth-century Orientalist arguments more than the opinions of medieval Muslim writers. Charles Upton responds to this genre of polemics in his recent book on Rabiʿa, *Doorkeeper of the Heart*: "Rabiʿa was a devout Muslim, with no heterodox tendencies except those common to all mystics. There are always those who, failing to deeply enough grasp their own traditions, view their own esoteric lore as a pollution by foreign devils."[150]

Ironically, by accusing Rabiʿa of heresy, Hawali rejects the opinion of the Hanbali jurist and theologian Taqi al-Din ibn Taymiyya (d. 1328 CE), one of the most respected religious authorities for Salafi Muslims, who defended Rabiʿa against such accusations. In a fatwa that appears in *Majmuʿat al-rasaʾil wa-l-masaʾil* (*Collection of Letters and Opinions*), Ibn Taymiyya denies that Rabiʿa ever said that the Kaʿba was "an idol to be worshipped on Earth" (*al-sanam al-maʿbud fi-l-ard*). This statement does not exist in ʿAttar's original Persian text of *Tadhkirat al-awliyaʾ*. However, since medieval times it has often been appended to Arabic translations of the passage in which Rabiʿa asks, "What am I to do with the Kaʿba?" In his *fatwa* Ibn Taymiyya goes further than merely denying the authenticity of this statement. He argues that even if Rabiʿa had said that the Kaʿba was an idol to be worshipped on Earth, this would not make her a heretic or an unbeliever. Reaffirming the theological truth claim of ʿAttar's story, he states: "Muslims do not worship the House [i.e., the Kaʿba]; rather, they worship the Lord of the House by circumambulating it and by praying toward it."[151]

7. Rabiʿa has several encounters with al-Hasan al-Basri. Most of these stories involve gendered role reversals and portray Rabiʿa as teaching Hasan a lesson that a major religious figure and ascetic such as he should already know. Sometimes the roles that are reversed are those of teacher and student. At other times these stories reverse the superiority

---

149 al-Hawali, *Min asbab al-zandaqa fi al-ʿibad* (*On the Causes of Heresy among the Worshippers*), in the blog post, *al-Inhiraf fi-l-ʿibadat* (*Deviations in Worship*), ibid.
150 Upton, *Doorkeeper of the Heart*, p. xii.
151 Taqi al-Din ibn Taymiyya, *Majmuʿat al-rasaʾil wa al-masaʾil*, ed. Muhammad ʿAli Baydawi (Beirut: Dar al-Kutub al-ʿIlmiyya, 2000), vol. 1, p. 94.

of male over female. The most famous example of a teacher/student role reversal is the account that places Hasan and Rabiʻa together by the banks of the Euphrates River. Hasan throws his prayer-carpet (*sajjada*) on the water and says, "Oh Rabiʻa, come over here! Let us pray two prostrations together." Rabiʻa replies, "Oh Teacher (*ay ustad*)! Are you going to peddle the goods of the non-worldly (*akhirtiyan*) in the market of the worldly (*dar bazar-i dunya*)? If so, you must do what the worldly types are not able to do." Then Rabiʻa throws her prayer rug into the air and says, "Oh Hasan! Come here, so that you will be hidden from the eyes of created beings (*chashm-i khalq*)!" She explains: "Oh Teacher! What you have done a fish can do and what I have done a fly can do. The real affair is beyond both of these."[152] The gendered subtext of this role reversal is revealed in the account that follows this story, in which Hasan testifies to Rabiʻa's superior knowledge: "I was with Rabiʻa for a full day and night. We discussed the matter of the Sufi way and its inner reality (*tariqat va haqiqat*) such that the thought, 'I am a man,' never occurred to me and the thought, 'I am a woman,' never occurred to her. When I arose at the end of this session, I saw myself as a person of no consequence (*muflisi*) and I saw her as a person of true sincerity (*mukhlisi*)."[153]

As mentioned several times already, the Hasan and Rabiʻa stories in *Tadhkirat al-awliya'* are clearly anachronistic because Rabiʻa was a young girl when al-Hasan al-Basri died in 728 CE. It is also relevant to point out that nearly every one of these stories begins with the phrase, "It is related that" (*naql ast keh*). This Persian phrase is equivalent in rhetorical terms to the Arabic phrases *qila anna* ("it is said that") or *nuqila anna* ("it has been related that"), which signify that a given tradition is more likely to be hearsay than history. As Jan Vansina states in his influential historiographical study *Oral Tradition As History*, in order to be used as historical evidence, a tradition must establish one or more links between the later record of a report and the original observation on which the tradition was based.[154] ʻAttar does not provide any links of this kind in his chapter on Rabiʻa al-ʻAdawiyya. His prefacing of these alleged traditions with the Persian phrase *naql ast keh* is equivalent to passing on gossip with the English phrase, "Some people say." Statements

---

152 ʻAttar, *Tadhkirat al-awliya'*, p. 66; Sells, *Early Islamic Mysticism*, pp. 160–1.
153 ʻAttar, *Tadhkirat al-awliya'*, pp. 66–7; Sells, *Early Islamic Mysticism*, p. 161.
154 Vansina, *Oral Tradition As History*, p. 27.

such as these make no legitimate claims about attribution and put fiction on the same rhetorical level as fact. 'Attar's use of this device shows that even as a storyteller he could claim no more than hearsay status for his accounts. However, he wanted to give them an aura of verisimilitude because of the important lessons in Sufism that they contained.

From the time that 'Attar first wrote down the Rabi'a and Hasan stories in *Tadhkirat al-awliya'*, these two important figures of Islamic sacred history have existed in each other's shadow. The pairing of Hasan and Rabi'a even extends to their burial places. As we shall see in the final section of this chapter, the most likely location of Rabi'a's grave is in the vicinity of al-Hasan al-Basri's tomb in the al-Zubayr suburb of modern-day Basra. In death, Rabi'a lies in Hasan's shadow. However, in Sufi legends, it is more often Hasan who is in Rabi'a's shadow. As 'Attar's story of the flying prayer rug makes clear, Rabi'a's role as the protagonist of these stories is to strip away the veil of superficiality and uncover the deeper truths of the Sufi path. In a way that recalls the trope of Rabi'a the Lover discussed in Chapter 3, she appears in 'Attar's narrative as a Diotima-like figure to Hasan's Socrates, providing spiritual insights that her famous male colleague could not otherwise have learned.

In his recent study of al-Hasan al-Basri in Islamic literature, Suleiman Mourad observes that the earliest accounts of Hasan depict "a very pious figure who uttered valuable sermons and anecdotes about piety, which emphasize proper worship and the deceitful nature of the world."[155] This is also how Hasan is portrayed in the chapter on Rabi'a in *Tadhkirat al-awliya'*. However, the figure that 'Attar portrays in the chapter on al-Hasan al-Basri himself in this work is very different. In his own chapter, Hasan is depicted as a mystic and as a key link between Sufism and the wider tradition of Sunni Islam. As Mourad demonstrates, 'Attar was nearly as influential in creating the Sufi image of al-Hasan al-Basri as he was in creating the Sufi image of Rabi'a al-'Adawiyya. In fact, the same use of fictional anachronism that characterizes 'Attar's depiction of the encounters between Hasan and Rabi'a can be found in the chapter on Hasan. For example, in one episode Hasan is described as meeting the Prophet Muhammad, although the Prophet died ten years before the real al-Hasan al-Basri was born.[156]

---

155 Suleiman Ali Mourad, *Early Islam Between Myth and History: Al-Hasan al-Basri (d. 110H/728CE) and the Formation of His Legacy in Classical Islamic Scholarship* (Leiden and Boston: E.J. Brill, 2006), p. 63.
156 Ibid., pp. 113–14; 'Attar, *Tadhkirat al-awliya'*, pp. 26–41.

One of the most important early works to contain information on al-Hasan al-Basri is 'Abdullah Ibn al-Mubarak's *Kitab al-zuhd wa-l-raqa'iq* (see Chapter 2). Suleiman Mourad notes that in this work Hasan is depicted as being "overwhelmed by sorrow and the fear of eternal punishment and is preoccupied with constant worship."[157] This portrayal of Hasan is consistent with the image depicted in 'Attar's chapter on Rabi'a. However, some Hasan and Rabi'a stories discuss inner states of knowledge or spiritual attitudes that go beyond asceticism. For example, in one account Rabi'a tells Hasan's disciples that real spiritual sincerity depends on the constant remembrance of God (*dhikr*). One of the disciples says to Rabi'a: "Hasan says that if he is deprived from seeing the Truth (*haqq*) in Paradise for the moment of a single breath, he will weep and moan so much that all of the people of Paradise will take pity on him." Rabi'a replies: "This is a fine statement. However, if in this world [Hasan] is heedless of the remembrance of the Truth (*dhikr-i haqq*) for the moment of a single breath and the same anguish and weeping and sorrow come to him, only then will the same thing happen to him in the afterlife. Otherwise, it will not be so."[158]

As discussed in Chapters 2 and 3, Islamic ascetic practices in Rabi'a's time fell into three main categories. The first category, *instrumental asceticism*, was directed toward specific goals and was closely related to the practice of ascetic ritualism (*nusk*). Ascetics of this type tended to conceive of their relationship with God in terms of religious and moral obligations. The second category of asceticism was *reactionary asceticism*. This type of asceticism was also instrumental but added a moral dimension that ranked poverty above both wealth and ordinary life. The statements ascribed to al-Hasan al-Basri in the earliest sources depict him as a practitioner of both instrumental and reactionary asceticism. This is also true of 'Attar's depiction of Hasan in the chapter on Rabi'a in *Tadhkirat al-awliya'*. The story summarized in the previous paragraph reflects these categories of asceticism. By affirming the equivalence of spiritual states and their effects across both sides of the World/Nonworld Dichotomy, Rabi'a in this story is also thinking like an instrumental ascetic. However, when she is portrayed in other stories as teaching Hasan the difference between ascetic practices and their inner reality, or when she says to Hasan, "What you have done a fish can do and what I have done a fly can do. The real affair is beyond both of these," her understanding of asceticism comes closer to *essential asceticism*. In this latter story, Rabi'a's rhetorical purpose

---

157 Mourad, *Early Islam Between Myth and History*, p. 65.
158 'Attar, *Tadhkirat al-awliya'*, p. 68; Sells, *Early Islamic Mysticism*, p. 162.

is to convey the inner truth of moral and religious doctrines that Hasan can only approach from the outside. As such, she stands not only for essential asceticism but also for the transcendence of the path of asceticism itself. For 'Attar this makes Rabi'a a true Sufi because her teachings demonstrate that outward excellence in ritual and ascetic practices depends on deeper states of inner spiritual knowledge.

Widad El Sakkakini makes a similar point in *al-'Ashiqa al-mutasawwifa* (*The Sufi Lover*). In this book, which was influenced by both Freudian psychology and Existentialist philosophy, she depicts al-Hasan al-Basri as a reactionary ascetic. However, for El Sakkakini, all asceticism is reactionary. As she states in the following passage, the source of the ascetic impulse is in the sublimation of frustrated desires: "Asceticism is seldom known to be inborn. The natural disposition of man is desire and greed. Therefore, behind every ascetic rages a tumult, however deeply concealed this may be. The lack or loss of fortune, fame, or a loved one; any of these may lead to a wish to forget and seek the comfort of serenity."[159] According to El Sakkakini, because "ascetic tyrants" like al-Hasan al-Basri used religion to solve their psychological problems, they misrepresented the true meaning of Islam: "Islam is a religion of effort in the present as well as the ultimate worlds; a counsel of work toward the development of man and his well-being."[160] Ironically, despite her liberal and feminist outlook, El Sakkakini's view of Islamic asceticism was not very different from that of the Salafi writer Safar al-Hawali. In her view, because early Muslim ascetics were influenced by Christian, Indian, Platonic and even Zoroastrian doctrines, they were not able to see that "asceticism was a heresy and an innovation paralyzing to the soul: it lured heads into the noose, and then pulled tight the rope."[161]

However, El Sakkakini had a more positive view of Sufi spirituality beyond asceticism. In her view, the purpose of the Rabi'a and Hasan stories in *Tadhkirat al-awliya'* was to show how a more progressive form of spirituality could replace "primitive" practices of self-mortification. Rabi'a's role was to convince Hasan and his followers that their asceticism was self-centered and egoistic, and that it would ultimately lead to a distorted vision of the good. Ironically, ascetic practices "actually worked against all that they hoped to achieve—and against the fulfillment of those who followed in their

---

159 El Sakkakini, *First among Sufis*, p. 21; *al-'Ashiqa al-mutasawwifa*, p. 29; the Arabic text states literally, "[The ascetic] buries [i.e,. represses] this experience in the deepest part of his personality" (*wa qad yadfanu al-haditha fi a'maqi nafsihi*).
160 El Sakkakini, *First among Sufis*, p. 22; *al-'Ashiqa al-mutasawwifa*, p. 31.
161 El Sakkakini, *First among Sufis*, p. 22; *al-'Ashiqa al-mutasawwifa*, p. 32.

footsteps... They had, in effect, put themselves in a position where they believed that they were the center and source of action (*wada'u anfusahum fi markaz al-haraka*), with the whole world reacting to them; they never understood that they themselves were the reacting elements."[162]

> 8. The excellence of Rabi'a's spiritual knowledge is further illustrated by 'Attar through her intimate discourses (*munajat*) with God. Six of these discourses or supplications are included in a separate section of the chapter. They include Rabi'a's most famous saying, "Oh Lord, if I worship you out of fear of Hell, burn me in Hell. If I worship in the hope of heaven, forbid it to me. But if I worship you for your own sake, do not deprive me of your enduring beauty (*jamal baqi*)."[163]

The Sufi narrative tradition of ascribing intimate discourses with God to Rabi'a al-'Adawiyya appears to have begun with the Nishapur Sufi and orthodox mystic Abu al-Qasim al-Qushayri (d. 1074 CE). The earliest of these discourses appears in the following anecdote from his influential manual of Sufism, *al-Risala fi 'ilm al-tasawwuf*: "Rabi'a al-'Adawiyya said in one of her *munajat*: 'Oh my God! Will you burn in Hellfire a heart that loves you?' Then a voice from the unseen called out to her (*fa-hatafa bi-ha hatifun*): 'We will never do such a thing! So do not think ill of us!'"[164] 'Attar also reproduces this anecdote in *Tadhkirat al-awliya'* but with major revisions. In his version Rabi'a says, "By God, if tomorrow you put me in Hell, I will cry out, 'You have made me a friend. Is this how you treat your friends?' A voice calls out to her, 'Rabi'a do not think ill of us![165] Be assured that we will bring you into the circle of our friends, so that you may converse with us.'"[166]

Although 'Attar provides no *isnad* or chain of transmission for this account, one can speculate that he got it either from Qushayri's book directly or via a tradition from the latter's student Abu 'Ali al-Farmadi. It is impossible to know where Qushayri got the original version because he does not cite a chain of transmission either. Whatever its origin, this is one of the most widely quoted statements of Rabi'a in Sufi literature and must be considered Qushayri's

---

162 El Sakkakini, *First among Sufis*, pp. 22 and 27; *al-'Ashiqa al-mutasawwifa*, pp. 32 and 40.
163 'Attar, *Tadhkirat al-awliya'*, p. 74; Sells, *Early Islamic Mysticism*, p. 169.
164 Qushayri, *al-Risala*, p. 328; this saying is also reproduced and ascribed to Qushayri's *Risala* by Ibn Khallikan in *Wafayat al-a'yan* (vol. 2, p. 285).
165 This last sentence is in Arabic in 'Attar's text, just as it is in Qushayri's original.
166 'Attar, *Tadhkirat al-awliya'*, p. 74; Sells, *Early Islamic Mysticism*, p. 169.

most important contribution to the Rabi'a narrative. The *munajat* in 'Attar's chapter on Rabi'a convey insights into how the Sufi is to behave before God, a spiritual attitude that al-Harith al-Muhasibi called "being attentive to the rights of God" (*al-ri'aya li-huquq Allah*).[167] This practice is also related to Rabi'a's Love mysticism as portrayed by Abu Talib al-Makki in *Qut al-qulub*. In devotional terms, Rabi'a's intimate discourses express the selflessness and single-mindedness of the sincere worshipper. However, although the object of her love is divine, her *munajat* express emotional states that are familiar to lovers everywhere. In this sense, they illustrate Hendrik Vroom's contention that the truth-value of religious stories is partly grounded in their evocation of basic human experiences.[168] With respect to religious truth claims, they convey in a popular register the notion of a "Love that is truly worthy of God," which is the moral of Rabi'a's Poem of the Two Loves.

9. The final section of 'Attar's chapter on Rabi'a describes her death and testifies to her exalted status with God through dreams and visions in which she appears after death. At the moment when she dies a voice is heard reciting the Qur'anic verse: "Oh soul at peace! Return to your Lord well pleased and well pleasing. Enter among My worshippers and enter into my heaven!" (Qur'an 89:27–9)[169] Through these dreams and visions, Rabi'a is portrayed as a humble worshipper, who is never arrogant with her Lord, who wants nothing, and never asks of God, "Make me thus," or "Do this or that." After her death she appears in a dream in which she is asked about Munkir and Nakir, the two angels of death in Islam. She replies, "When those pure youths (*javanmardan*) came to me, they asked, 'Who is your Lord?' I said: 'Go back and say to the Divine Reality (*Haqq*): Out of so many thousands of people You have not forgotten an old woman (*pir zani*)? Out of all of the worlds I have only You. Never would I forget You such that you would have to send someone to me to ask, "My God, who are You?"'"[170]

Most of the dream visions of Rabi'a in medieval Islamic literature are attributed to the figure of 'Abda bint Abi Shawwal. Ibn al-Jawzi identifies her in

---

167 This concept provided the title for Muhasibi's most famous work, *al-Ri'aya li-huquq Allah*, discussed in Chapter 2.
168 Vroom, "Religious Truth," p. 122.
169 'Attar, *Tadhkirat al-awliya'*, p. 74; Sells, *Early Islamic Mysticism*, p. 169; the last part of this Qur'anic passage is not reproduced in the Sells–Losensky translation.
170 'Attar, *Tadhkirat al-awliya'*, p. 75; Sells, *Early Islamic Mysticism*, p. 170.

Sifat al-safwa as having been the servant of Rabi'a in the latter part of her life.[171] The earliest known source of information on 'Abda was the ninth-century traditionist Ibn Abi al-Dunya, who mentions one of her dreams of Rabi'a in *Kitab al-manamat (Book of Dreams)*.[172] According to an *isnad* provided by the fourteenth-century CE Hanbali prosopographer Muhammad al-Dhahabi, another early account of 'Abda came from Muhammad ibn al-Husayn al-Burjulani.[173] The dream conversation is a common trope in Islamic hagiography. In rhetorical terms, it confirms the divine acceptance of the person who speaks from beyond the grave.[174] Often, such conversations are not about the deceased, but about other famous people who were known to the deceased or her companions. In 'Attar's dream stories, Rabi'a acts as a messenger from the beyond, which confirms her status as a saint. 'Attar does not identify 'Abda bint Abi Shawwal as the source of these stories. Instead, he attributes them to two men, whose names do not appear in any other account that I have seen. These are Muhammad ibn Aslam al-Tusi and Ni'ma (*sic*) al-Tarsusi.[175] Ibn Aslam al-Tusi (d. 856–7 CE) was a well-known Hadith transmitter and ascetic. I have not been able to identify Ni'ma al-Tarsusi. Presumably, 'Attar used these names to add a sense of verisimilitude to the stories, just as he did previously with the name of Abu 'Ali Farmadi.

IV. POSTSCRIPT: WHERE IS RABI'A BURIED?

Some of the most important discrepancies in the accounts of Rabi'a's death concern the site of her burial place. As mentioned previously, her most likely resting place is in the vicinity of al-Hasan al-Basri's tomb in the al-Zubayr suburb of modern Basra. However, Ibn Khallikan states in *Wafayat al-a'yan*, "Her grave is visited regularly. It is outside of Jerusalem to the east on top of the hill known as Tor."[176] In this passage, Ibn Khallikan refers to

---

171 For Ibn al-Jawzi's references to 'Abda bint Abi Shawwal and her dream visions of Rabi'a, see R. Cornell, *Early Sufi Women*, pp. 280–2.
172 Ibn Abi al-Dunya, *Majmu'at Rasa'il*, vol. 3, p. 33 no. 21.
173 al-Dhahabi, *Siyar a'lam al-nubala'*, vol. 8, p. 242.
174 On this trope see Leah Kinberg, *Morality in the Guise of Dreams: A Critical Edition of Kitab al-manam by Ibn Abi al-Dunya* (Leiden: E.J. Brill, 1994); Nile Green, "The Religious and Cultural Role of Dreams and Visions in Islam," *Journal of the Royal Asiatic Society*, 13 (3), 2003, pp. 287–313; Özgen Felek and Alexander D. Knysh (eds.) *Dreams and Vision in Islamic Societies* (Albany, NY: SUNY Press, 2012).
175 'Attar, *Tadhkirat al-awliya'*, p. 75; Sells, *Early Islamic Mysticism*, p. 170.
176 Ibn Khallikan, *Wafayat al-a'yan*, vol. 2, p. 287.

the tomb known today as "The Station of Rabi'a al-'Adawiyya" (*Maqam Rabi'a al-'Adawiyya*), on the Mount of Olives in East Jerusalem. This tomb, which is located inside a cave, contains architectural features that date it to the Crusader or Mamluk periods of Jerusalem's history. In other words, the architecture of the tomb is more or less contemporary with Ibn Khallikan himself, who flourished in the second half of the thirteenth century CE. In light of the available evidence, it is possible to suggest that his mistaken assertion that Rabi'a was buried there may have been due to a local legend that associated Rabi'a with this site.

According to local legends in Jerusalem today, the *maqam* of Rabi'a has been associated with a woman saint throughout its history. What is in question is whether the woman saint was Jewish, Christian, or Muslim. The most likely answer is that the actual occupant of the tomb is the late fourth-century CE Christian St Pelagia of Antioch, who early sources agree was buried on the Mount of Olives. According to the Syriac *Life of Pelagia*, this famous ascetic and penitent lived in a cell on the Mount of Olives in the last years of her life.[177] Such cells were often located in caves. It is possible that the tomb was venerated as St Pelagia's in Crusader times but after the Muslim reconquest of Jerusalem it was "reassigned," so to speak, to Rabi'a al-'Adawiyya.

Apart from Ibn Khallikan's *Wafayat al-a'yan*, the most important pre-modern text to provide an alternate location for Rabi'a's tomb is *al-Kawakib al-durriyya fi tarajim al-sadat al-Sufiyya* (*The Pearly Spheres in the Biographies of the Sufi Saints*), by the Egyptian Sufi Muhammad 'Abd al-Ra'uf al-Munawi (d. 1621 CE). Most notably, this work claims that Rabi'a lived in Egypt.[178] In terms of the historiography of the Rabi'a al-'Adawiyya master narrative, Munawi's work is important because most subsequent Egyptian versions of the Rabi'a myth are based on it. For example, we saw in Chapter 3 how the modern Egyptian historian Su'ad 'Ali 'Abd al-Raziq used Munawi's narrative as evidence that Rabi'a was married. In addition, a tomb ascribed to Rabi'a can be found in the Qarafa ("City of the Dead") section of Cairo today. For many Egyptians, this tomb provides material proof of Munawi's contention

---

177 For the story of Pelagia of Antioch, see the translation of the Syriac *Life of Pelagia* in Brock and Harvey, *Holy Women of the Syrian Orient*, pp. 40–62; see also, Coon, *Sacred Fictions*, pp. 77–84, who notes that early versions of *The Life of Pelagia* also existed in Latin and Arabic.

178 Munawi, *al-Kawakib al-durriyya*, vol. 1, p. 285. Munawi calls Rabi'a "Rabi'a al-'Adawiyya al-Qaysiyya *then* the Egyptian (*thumma al-Misriyya*)." For a partial English translation of Munawi's notice on Rabi'a, see John Renard (ed.), *Windows on the House of Islam: Muslim Sources on Spirituality and Religious Life* (Berkeley, Los Angeles, and London: University of California Press, 1998), pp. 132–5.

that Rabi'a passed the second half of her life in Egypt. Munawi's work is also important because it provides an illustration of how the trope of Rabi'a the Sufi was understood in the late medieval period. For example, Munawi uses the trope of Rabi'a the Lover to critique the spirituality of the great Sufi master of Baghdad, 'Abd al-Qadir al-Jilani (d. 1166 CE). According to Munawi, both Rabi'a and 'Abd al-Qadir focused their spiritual devotions too intensely on God and therefore transgressed the limits on worship imposed by the Sunna of the Prophet Muhammad.[179]

From the perspective of critical scholarship and the modern rules of historical research, Munawi's chapter on Rabi'a is most notable for the number of rules that it breaks. Throughout the text, accounts from previous works are mixed together without attribution and without concern for logical consistency. For example, although Munawi claims that Rabi'a lived in Egypt, he also relates how the ruler of Basra in Iraq offered her a large sum of money if she would marry him.[180] In addition, in his notice on Rabi'a bint Isma'il, which follows the chapter on Rabi'a al-'Adawiyya in *al-Kawakib al-durriyya*, he erroneously states that Rabi'a bint Isma'il was not from Syria but from Iraq and that she was 'Adawiyya in her clan origin, even though the allegedly "Egyptian" Rabi'a was the person actually named Rabi'a al-'Adawiyya. Munawi also follows Ibn Khallikan in calling Rabi'a *Umm al-Khayr* and adds that she was a *mawlat* who belonged to the clan of "Al 'Aqil." This is in spite of the fact that Sulami and others called this clan "Al 'Atik." However, this is not all of the confusion that Munawi creates. According to his account, the *mawlat* attribution, the 'Adawi clan origin, and the appellation, *Umm al-Khayr* all belong not to Rabi'a al-'Adawiyya as in the earlier sources, but to Rabi'a Bint Isma'il![181] Not one of these assertions can be found in any source prior to Munawi's text.

It is clear from the confusion of his narratives that Munawi was not sure whether the two Rabi'a's were the same or different. For example, he includes the Poem of the Intimate Gift, which is most properly attributed to Rabi'a bint Isma'il, in the chapter on Rabi'a al-'Adawiyya.[182] However, he correctly states that Rabi'a bint Isma'il was married to Ahmad ibn Abi al-Hawari. Munawi was also of the opinion that Rabi'a bint Isma'il was the person buried in the tomb ascribed to Rabi'a al-'Adawiyya on the Mount of Olives (he calls it *Ra's*

---

179 Munawi, *al-Kawakib al-durriyya*, vol. 1, p. 290.
180 Ibid., p. 286.
181 Ibid., p. 291.
182 Ibid., p. 288.

Zayta) in Jerusalem.[183] Nonetheless, despite these numerous shortcomings, Munawi's work is important for the historiography of the Rabi'a al-'Adawiyya master narrative. Because his conflation of information on the two Rabi'as conforms closely to what is presently found in popular legends and literature, we can add his book to 'Attar's *Tadhkirat al-awliya'* and Ibn Khallikan's *Wafayat al-a'yan* as key premodern texts that helped shape the multifaceted image of Rabi'a the Icon as she is known today.

---

183 Ibid., p. 293.

Chapter 6

Rabi'a the Icon (II): the Secular Image

"The greatest legends are those that most resemble the truth."
—Widad El Sakkakini, *al-'Ashiqa al-mutasawwifa*

"Religions—and secular worldviews as well—live through stories (at present often films) that show how people have insight and live properly, know how to deal with difficulties, or else bungle things, make the wrong choices, and fail. Paradigmatic stories sketch a view of life and give direction."
—Hendrik M. Vroom, "Religious Truth"

I. FROM RELIGIOUS TO SECULAR NARRATIVES

In the previous chapter, I described how the medieval Persian Sufi Farid al-Din al-'Attar created a *vita* for Rabi'a al-'Adawiyya and became the most important agent of the Rabi'a myth. 'Attar's revisions of the Rabi'a master narrative were so effective that they are now regarded as facts by the general public and even by some historians. In the terminology of narrative studies, we can say that 'Attar transformed Rabi'a from a "flat character" into a "round character." Most of the characters in hagiography are flat characters because they have little human depth. They are limited to a narrow range of behaviors and seem to exist on the surface of the narrative; as H. Porter Abbott states, "They declare themselves through their motifs."[1] Round characters, however,

---

1   Abbott, *The Cambridge Introduction to Narrative*, p. 133. The terms "flat characters" and "round characters" were coined by the English novelist E.M. Forster.

have a greater degree of depth and complexity. They cannot be summed up in a single phrase or a limited set of tropes.[2] By giving Rabi'a a biography, 'Attar added a measure of realism to her character by turning her into a "real" person. His *vita* of Rabi'a also contributed greatly to today's image of her as an actual historical personage.

Using an analytical model created by the Dutch historian and theologian Hendrik M. Vroom, I also showed how religious narratives such as 'Attar's chapter on Rabi'a make truth claims that operate on several levels at once. The historical truth claims that such stories make are not always the most important; sometimes, they are the least important. Moral or theological truth claims are often the real point of these stories. Sometimes, fictional stories can express moral and theological truth claims better than facts, especially when the form in which they are presented conveys a strong sense of verisimilitude. The Arab writer Widad El Sakkakini makes this very point in the epigraph to this chapter: "The greatest legends are those that most resemble the truth."

Roland Barthes' concept of the "reality effect" provides a helpful explanation for the effectiveness of 'Attar's *vita* of Rabi'a. Now that the Rabi'a narratives have entered the modern era, the impression of factuality has become even more important than before. There are still some traditionalist writers, such as Jean Annestay, who are primarily concerned with the "principial" meaning of the Rabi'a narratives. However, most of the contemporary audience for these narratives are imbued with modern notions of empirical history and consider it important for the literary portrayals of Rabi'a to appear historically authentic. Most modern Muslims speak of Rabi'a al-'Adawiyya as a historical figure and consider 'Attar's accounts of her to be not only figuratively real but factually real as well. Even if they doubt the miracle stories that 'Attar and his successors have added to the Rabi'a narrative, they treat her life story and her teachings as accurate.

This modern emphasis on factuality is not only important for the religiously minded. Because historicism and empirical research have become modern cultural standards, since the beginning of the twentieth century academic and historical narratives have mostly replaced Sufi narratives as the main vehicles for the Rabi'a master narrative. Because of this, the audience for the Rabi'a narratives has expanded globally. Rabi'a is now an object of secular attention as well as religious attention and secular notions of objectivity have become inextricably bound up with religious truth claims. Modern secular authorities must now be considered along with Sufi authorities as important

---

2   Ibid., pp. 133–4.

agents of the Rabiʻa myth. When studying these secular agents of myth, one must approach them on their own terms and assess their works according to the historical methods they employ. On this new ground, a retreat into the primacy of "principial" truth claims over historical truth claims is not enough to save them from the critique that they too may become purveyors of the "falsely obvious."

In the first part of the twentieth century, Margaret Smith replaced Farid al-Din al-'Attar as the chief agent of the Rabiʻa myth, not only in the English-speaking world but globally as well. This was due to the scholarly reputation of her highly influential study, *Rabiʻa the Mystic* (1928). Although Smith wrote from a broadly Christian perspective, she should be considered a secular author because her book on Rabiʻa followed secular rules of academic scholarship. In Chapter 5, we saw how this well-respected English scholar added what Roland Barthes called "nostalgic reminiscences" to the Rabiʻa al-ʻAdawiyya narrative, such as when she portayed Rabiʻa as playing the flute. Smith's trope of the flute-playing Rabiʻa has since become an important "historical" detail of the Rabiʻa master narrative.

Smith's importance to the construction of the Rabiʻa master narrative illustrates another modern development that must not be overlooked. Not only are secularists and modern historians now contributing to the Rabiʻa narratives but also non-Muslims have become contributors as well. To return to Hendrik Vroom's typology of religious stories, we cannot speak of Islamic theological truth claims in regard to Margaret Smith because she was a Christian. The religious and theological observations that she makes in *Rabiʻa the Mystic* are not Islamic but comparative. In addition, they are based on a Christian worldview, such as when she compares Sufi ascetics to early Franciscan monks. Although Smith has arguably been Rabiʻa's most important agent of myth in the modern period, we cannot assess her work in the same way as we did for 'Attar. Strictly speaking, as an outsider to the Muslim and Sufi worldviews, Smith could not make theological and doctrinal truth claims about Rabiʻa; she could only make scholarly observations. Scholarly observations have less immediate impact than religious truth claims. Academically, the most legitimate claims that Smith could make about Rabiʻa were historical; hence, those who wish to study her book *Rabiʻa the Mystic* critically must approach it according to historical standards of evidence. As we have seen, her use of historical methodology did not prevent her from using tropes and other rhetorical techniques in her adaptation of the Rabiʻa narratives.

In the present chapter, we shall examine how shortly after Margaret Smith another important agent of the Rabiʻa myth emerged in the modern Arab world. This time Rabi'a's agent was neither a Sufi like 'Attar nor an Orientalist Christian scholar attracted to mysticism like Smith. Instead, this new agent of myth, 'Abd al-Rahman Badawi (1917–2002), was a radical Egyptian secularist, an Existentialist philosopher, and the most respected Arab scholar of Islamic philosophy in his time. Much as with Smith, the verisimilitude of Badawi's historical representation of Rabi'a al-'Adawiyya depended on his scholarly reputation. Badawi's reputation as an academic authority on Islam was so great that his imaginative and sometimes fictional additions to the Rabi'a narrative went unquestioned and were accepted as facts by most of his readers. Badawi's narrative also inspired the Lebanese–Syrian writer Widad El Sakkakini and the Egyptian screenwriter Saniya Qurra'a to add further adaptations to his reconstruction of Rabi'a's *vita* and popularize it through novel and film. Through the influence of Qurra'a's screenplay in particular, the image of Rabi'a that Badawi constructed spread across the Muslim world from Morocco to Indonesia. Ironically, this twentieth-century secular image has now been accepted by both Sufis and the Muslim public, such that few people today are able to distinguish Badawi's additions to the Rabi'a master narrative from what originally came from 'Attar.

II. RABI'A THE EXISTENTIALIST

'Abd al-Rahman Badawi's adaptation of Rabi'a's *vita* makes up the centerpiece of his book, *Shahidat al-'ishq al-ilahi Rabi'a al-'Adawiyya* (*Rabi'a al-'Adawiyya the Martyr of Divine Love*). Badawi first published this book in 1948 and revised it in 1960. The most recent edition was published in Kuwait in 1978.[3] Today, this book is something of an unwanted child among students of Badawi's works. Despite its importance to the development of the Rabi'a master narrative, it is often missing from lists of Badawi's publications because scholars do not know what to make of it. In this work, Badawi applies to hagiography some of the concepts that he would later address in his 1960 treatise on Existentialism, *Dirasat fi-l-falsafa al-wujudiyya* (*Studies in Existentialist Philosophy*).[4] In particular, he portrays the ascetics and

---

[3] 'Abd al-Rahman Badawi, *Shahidat al-'ishq al-ilahi Rabi'a al-'Adawiyya* (Kuwait: Wakalat al-Matbu'at, 1978 reprint of the 1960 revised edition); this work has been cited many times in the preceding chapters.

[4] 'Abd al-Rahman Badawi, *Dirasat fi-l-falsafa al-wujudiyya* (Beirut: Dar al-Thaqafa, 1978 reprint of 1960 first edition).

mystics of early Islam as anxious or "unquiet" souls.⁵ Rabi'a's spiritual life is portrayed as a quest to resolve the anxieties and inner conflicts that arise from her life experiences.

Badawi uses the Existentialist concept of anxiety or angst (Ar. *qalaq*) to explain the motive for Rabi'a's spiritual quest. He first discussed this concept in *Shakhsiyyat qaliqa fi-l-Islam* (*Anxious Personalities in Islam*), which was published in 1946, two years before his book on Rabi'a.⁶ *Anxious Personalities* is a collection of notes and translated passages from the lectures and writings of his most important mentors, the French Orientalist scholars Louis Massignon (1883–1962) and Henri Corbin (1903–78). In it, Badawi posits four ideal types of Islamic spirituality: *Iranian Islam*, which is symbolized by Salman al-Farisi (d. 656 CE), a Persian Companion of the Prophet Muhammad; *Sufi Islam*, which is symbolized by the Sufi martyr Abu Mansur al-Hallaj (d. 922 CE); and *Illuminationist Islam*, which is symbolized by another famous Sufi martyr, Shihab al-Din al-Suhrawardi (d. 1191 CE). The fourth type of Islamic spirituality, which Badawi does not name but consists of Islam's view of other world religions, is symbolized by the Treaty of Najran (ca. 631 CE), which the Prophet Muhammad concluded with the Christian inhabitants of this Arabian town. For Badawi, all of these types of Islamic spirituality create psychological anxieties because they are based on cultural, theological, or philosophical contradictions.

Badawi's approach to Existentialism is based on the belief that the human being is defined by her actions. In other words, "You are what you do." This connection between personal identity and behavior is so central for Badawi that he uses this principle to define Existentialism in general in *Studies in Existentialist Philosophy*:

> Existentialism is a very precisely defined approach to being (*wujud*). It is founded on a very basic and simple principle, which is that a person's being consists of his actions (*wujud al-insan huwa ma yaf'aluhu*). The actions of the person are what define and form his being; for this

---

5 See Richard Kieckhefer, *Unquiet Souls: Fourteenth-Century Saints and Their Religious Milieu* (Chicago and London: University of Chicago Press, 1984); Kieckhefer takes the title of his book from St Augustine's concept of *inquietum*, the restlessness of the soul that searches for God (p. 181). As we shall see below, this concept is similar to Søren Kierkegaard's concept of restlessness, which provided the basis for Badawi's theory of existential anxiety.

6 'Abd al-Rahman Badawi, *Shakhsiyyat qaliqa fi-l-Islam* (Cairo: Dar al-Nahda al-'Arabiyya, 1964 reprint of the 1946 first edition).

reason the person is measured by his actions. Thus, the being of each person is [defined] according to his actions. This approach is the opposite of Essentialism (*al-mahiyya*). This [latter philosophy] is the approach of those who posit a prior essence for the human being out of which his actions grow, in accordance with which he is judged and by which he is defined.[7]

Elsewhere Badawi states, "In Existentialism, every point of view (*nazariyya*) develops from one's life experiences."[8] This statement helps us understand why in *Martyr of Divine Love* he felt the need to ground every aspect of Rabiʿa's spiritual career—from her asceticism, to her Love mysticism, to her effectiveness as a teacher—in specific life experiences, even if he had to make up these experiences himself. His attempt to ground Rabiʿa's worldview in her life experiences also helps explain the verisimilitude of his portrayal of her: if a writer portrays a character in a way that reminds us of ourselves, we are more likely to believe it.

According to Badawi, the father of Existentialism was the Danish philosopher Søren Kierkegaard (1813–55). The essence of this philosophy can be found in the following statement by Kierkegaard: "Verily, I have found Truth; truth, but in regard to myself. For I have found the Idea (*al-fikra*) to be that for the sake of which I wish to live and die."[9] Badawi explains that the Idea to which Kierkegaard refers is life itself, which is lived through life experiences and whose goal is the realization of life's ultimate possibilities. Because the realization of life's possibilities can only be attained through action, the human being must at all times be prepared to engage in struggle (*nidal*):

> [Struggle] between the self (*al-dhat*) and the Absolute, between God and the world, between reality and appearance, between the present moment and the totality of one's life, between time and eternity, and between knowledge and faith. This struggle will imprint upon being (*al-wujud*) its most fundamental characteristics: [freedom of] choice (*al-ikhtiyar*), [freedom of] change (*al-taghayyur*), [freedom of] individuality (*al-infirad*), and autonomous selfhood (*al-dhatiyya*).[10]

---

7   Badawi, *Dirasat fi-l-falsafa al-wujudiyya*, Preface before p. 1.
8   Ibid., p. 42.
9   Ibid., p. 2. This is my translation of Badawi's Arabic translation of Kierkegaard. Kierkegaard is one of the most discussed modern philosophers, and any interpretation of his views is potentially open to criticism. The discussion in this section reproduces Badawi's views of Kierkegaard and Existentialism, not my own.
10 Ibid.

In *Martyr of Divine Love*, Badawi bases his adaptation of Rabi'a's *vita* on his understanding of Kierkegaard's philosophy. In *Studies in Existentialist Philosophy*, he explains that for Kierkegaard,

> [T]he self is constantly preoccupied with itself; this [preoccupation is expressed through] the feeling of freedom, which is accompanied by sin (*khati'a*). This constitutes present existence, "face-to-face before God." The human being is free and unique, without the possibility of duplication. He cannot be placed in a generalized category and he cannot be defined by an abstract concept. Existence is struggle (*tanaqud*); it is the point of encounter between the finite (*al-mutanahi*) and the infinite (*al-lamutantahi*) and between the temporal (*al-zamani*) and the eternal (*al-sarmadi*). It is found in its finite individuality (*fi fardiyatihi al-mutanahiyya*) and immersed in time. It returns to itself and revolves around itself, certain in itself of its concreteness (*'ayniyatiha*) and its individuality. However, existence, insofar as it can be described as present in infinitude and eternality, also returns to God or the Absolute. In this rupture between an individuality comprised of the self and a present shared in conjunction with God, existence confirms itself as living, but in a condition of danger, impulsiveness, or sin.[11]

For Badawi, the meaning of life is found in the experiences that form the self. The human being confronts reality through an active and passionate (*infi'ali*) engagement with life. Badawi observes that some of the greatest and most passionate struggles that human beings undertake are associated with religious faith, where the desire for freedom and autonomy is confronted by the limits imposed by God and the world. The person is thus forced to find a balance between her desires and her limits; this creates a state of tension because not all of her desires can be fulfilled. Out of these tensions arise the existential states of despair (*ya's*) and anxiety (*qalaq*). These states arise from the feeling of isolation that occurs when the struggle of the self to live autonomously leads to error, sin, and the frustration of one's hopes and desires.[12]

Following Kierkegaard, Badawi identifies three key personality types according to Existentialist philosophy. These are Aesthetic Man (*rajul jamal*), Ethical Man (*rajul akhlaq*), and Religious Man (*rajul din*).[13] These three ideal

---

11   Ibid., pp. 2–3.
12   Ibid., pp. 3–4.
13   Ibid., p. 42.

types correspond to three paths of existence—the Aesthetic Path (*al-madraj al-jamali*), the Ethical Path (*al-madraj al-akhlaqi*), and the Religious Path (*al-madraj al-dini*).[14] The Aesthetic Path is lived immediately and in the present; the Ethical Path is lived through a series of self-assessments over time; and the Religious Path is lived through the quest for eternity.

Badawi describes Aesthetic Man as something like an Epicurean. He lives through the body for the sake of sensual gratifications. His motto is *carpe diem* (seize the day) and he avoids personal attachments because he fears that they will restrict his personal freedom. However, unlike the true Epicurean he is always restless and is unable to find inner peace. He rejects marriage and companionship because he values his independence but also because he is not able to tolerate stability for very long. Aesthetic Man is ambitious and sees life as a battle. For him, relationships are purely instrumental: they are valuable only to the extent that they help him attain his goals.[15] The moral emptiness of this existence makes Aesthetic Man subject to the moods of frustration and despair.

By contrast, Ethical Man seeks a meaningful life through moral duties and obligations. He seeks fulfillment not by means of material wealth but through reputation (*dhikra*) and consistency (*tikrar*). Because Ethical Man finds satisfaction in the fulfillment of moral duties and obligations, he lives his life as a social being and is dedicated to the improvement of his society, country, or humanity in general. Unlike Aesthetic Man, he values companionship and marriage because he finds pleasure in sociability and because he knows that living with a partner aids in the formation of the self. Because he is inspired by moral ends Ethical Man is not Epicurean but Aristotelian. He lives according to the mean and judges the value of all things according to the standards of fairness and balance: "The Ethical type advocates the establishment of the mean and discriminates between good and evil according to it; he judges everything according to the principle of the mean and balance."[16] In his life, Ethical Man strives to attain justice, security, and personal stability. However, this path also creates anxiety because the price of success in society is the loss of personal autonomy and individuality.

The aspiration of Religious Man is to transcend both time and the World and live timelessly in eternity (*bi-l-sarmadiyya*). This is different from Aesthetic Man, who lives selfishly in the moment, and Ethical Man, who

---

14 Ibid.
15 Ibid., p. 43.
16 Ibid., p. 44.

carefully constructs his social life by building a reputation over time (*bi-l-zamaniyya*). Because he views existence from a higher perspective, Religious Man is detached from both time and the World. In *Studies in Existential Philosophy* Badawi describes Religious Man in hagiographic terms: "[Religious Man] desires the discourse that is spoken in Heaven and touches the hand of the Spirit of those spirits that are born in the supernal."[17] Perhaps alluding to Rabi'a al-'Adawiyya he states,

> If [Religious Man] is a woman, her speech calls out to God for her to gain satisfaction and [divine] acceptance (*rida'*), and to reach the level of the Soul at Peace (*martabat al-nafs al-mutma'inna*). All of [her] efforts are toward attaining the eternal and everlasting life that the mind imagines to be lived within the divine embrace. In general, these states are the states and stations that are well known among the Sufis.[18]

In *Martyr of Divine Love*, Badawi depicts Rabi'a as embodying each of these ideal personality types in turn. Following the general outline of her *vita* as composed by 'Attar, he divides her life into three phases, each of which corresponds to a particular stage of development. The early period of her youth, captivity, and liberation sets the stage for his depiction of Rabi'a as Aesthetic Woman. In order for her to conform to this type, Badawi composes an entirely new narrative about her early life that stresses her physical beauty, restlessness, and desire for independence. Because the Aesthetic personality type is both artistic and sensual, he adds to her *vita* the narrative trope of the Reformed Sinner by combining 'Attar's depiction of Rabi'a as a musician with the Christian trope of saints who had dramatic conversion experiences, such as St Paul of Tarsus, St Augustine of Hippo, and St Teresa of Avila. He also adds another early Christian trope—that of the fallen woman saint. Although this latter trope is not foregrounded by Badawi in his book, it would become a major part of the Rabi'a master narrative in the hands of the novelist Widad El Sakkakini and the screenwriter Saniyya al-Qurra'a.

Badawi next depicts Rabi'a as Ethical Woman by focusing on her period of repentance, asceticism and conversion to Sufism. For Badawi, the Ethical personality type was best exemplified in early Islam by the students of al-Hasan al-Basri, who associated with Rabi'a in the community of ascetics in and around Basra. To create a background for Rabi'a's transformation from

---

17   Ibid., p. 45.
18   Ibid.

Aesthetic Woman to Ethical Woman, he depicts Basra as a city with a split personality. He portrays the city as containing contradictory attributes that hampered the development of a harmonious social life: rural values competed against the values of sophisticated urban culture; world-denying asceticism opposed world-affirming hedonism; and the religious practice of renunciation stood opposed to the artistic life of the senses.

For the third and final phase of Rabiʿa's life, Badawi uses the personality type of Religious Woman to symbolize the resolution of her inner conflicts. According to Badawi, Kierkegaard regarded poetry and Love mysticism as typically female expressions of spirituality. Therefore, in his adaptation of Rabiʿa's *vita*, he makes much of her Love mysticism and her purported writing of poetry. These are depicted as evidence of Rabiʿa's attempt to find ultimate fulfillment through transcendence of the World. Badawi saw the spirituality of Religious Woman as more passive than that of Religious Man. In his view, Religious Woman can find her true self only by surrendering her ego completely and by merging her identity with that of another, higher being. Because it is passive, woman's spirituality is based on submission. Through submission, Religious Woman achieves the transcendence of self by sublimating her identity. She surrenders herself to a divine male spouse, who is free of the imperfections of ordinary men. According to Badawi, Religious Woman's sublimation to a higher self is why Sufi women typically express their spirituality through Love mysticism.

Badawi's depiction of early Abbasid Basra in *Martyr of Divine Love* provides the background for Rabiʿa's career. In his article, "The Reality Effect," Roland Barthes notes the importance of realistic description in creating what he calls "aesthetic verisimilitude."[19] This impression is achieved through the literary technique of realism—an artificially constructed but seemingly natural description of objects and events. To illustrate this technique, Barthes uses Gustave Flaubert's depiction of the city of Rouen in the novel, *Madame Bovary*. The care taken by Flaubert in choosing only the most necessary elements for his description of Rouen was crucial for the sense of realism that he created. Realistic description is constructed to make the reader feel as if the depiction of the place in the narrative is linked to a painting that can be found in an art gallery. As Barthes states, "It is a painted scene which the language takes up."[20] In the following passage from *Madame Bovary*, the character of Charles Bovary has been sent to school in Rouen as a teenager.

---

19 Barthes, "The Reality Effect," in idem, *The Rustle of Language*, p. 144.
20 Ibid.

His mother finds him a room on the fourth floor of a building that overlooks a small river called Eau de Robec. In this passage, Flaubert uses the rhetoric of realism to paint a naturalistic picture of what Charles Bovary sees when he leans out of his window:

> The river, which makes this part of Rouen a kind of miserable little Venice, flowed beneath, yellow, violet or blue, between its bridges and its railings. Workmen, kneeling on the bank, were washing their arms in the water. On poles, jutting out from the attics, skeins of cotton were drying off in the air. Facing him, over the roofs, there was the pure wide-open sky, red from the setting sun. It must be grand over there! So cool under the beeches! And he opened his nostrils to breathe down the sweet smells of the country, smells that never reached this far.[21]

In *Martyr of Divine Love* Badawi uses the rhetoric of realism in a similar way to describe the city of Basra in the late Umayyad and early Abbasid periods. In doing so, he creates a sense of aesthetic verisimilitude that closely resembles the realism of Flaubert's depiction of Rouen:

> The Arab Venice: shimmering like a resplendent jewel to the eyes of hungry and fatigued travelers coming from the depths of the desert in the heart of the Arabian Peninsula. As they reach their destination and their camels kneel at al-Mirbad, they enter the Great Mosque at the Desert Gate (*Bab al-Badiya*), dazzled by the fine cylindrical columns and intricate craftsmanship that Ziyad ibn Abihi bestowed on this magnificent architectural monument of early Islam. Their eyes, covered with desert sand, wander about in this luxuriant godliness. They feel a touch of what awaits them on the eastern side of the city, in the northern and southern regions, where great ships come from Baghdad to the north via the Ma'qil Canal and vessels from the Persian Gulf to the south plow the waters of the al-Ubulla Canal in a dignified way, entrusted with the most valuable cargoes from India and China.[22]

Although Badawi's resplendent "Arab Venice" of Basra is far from the "miserable little Venice" of Flaubert's Rouen, it is clear that he is trying to create

---

21 Gustave Flaubert, *Madame Bovary*, trans. Geoffrey Wall (London: Penguin Books, 2003), pp. 9–10.
22 Badawi, *Shahidat al-'ishq al-ilahi*, p. 7.

a similar aura of aesthetic verisimilitude. I cannot determine conclusively whether the style of Flaubert's *Madame Bovary* directly influenced Badawi when he wrote *Martyr of Divine Love*. However, it is not impossible because much of his education was in France. In any case, he uses the rhetoric of realism in much the same way as Flaubert does to convey the sense of "being there." For Badawi, Basra in the time of Rabi'a al-'Adawiyya was a meeting-place of extremes: it was a newly created city, in which Bedouins from the Arabian desert rubbed shoulders with sophisticated Persian urbanites. In this clash of cultures, an austere religious ethic came face-to-face with worldly indulgence and excess. Making a pun out of the title of Abu Talib al-Makki's Sufi work *Qut al-qulub*, Badawi sums up this conflict of cultures in early Basra by stating that one half of the city yearned for the worldly nourishment of the senses (*qut al-hawass*), whereas the other half yearned for the otherworldly nourishment of hearts (*qut al-qulub*).[23]

In Badawi's narrative, the split personality of eighth-century Basra was mirrored in the lives and personalities of its inhabitants, including Rabi'a al-'Adawiyya. Within her, there raged a struggle between opposing extremes, with the worldly and otherworldly fighting to overcome each other. Badawi openly admits that his vision of a struggle in Rabi'a's soul is only a matter of conjecture because the historical details of her life are lacking:

> The deeper I looked and the more documents and manuscripts I consulted, the more I saw her personality disappear into a cave of myths. The more I scrutinized reports about her the more they faded into oblivion, such that I became disappointed and lost all hope of finding any information about her life or any of her statements that would allow me or any other serious historian to confirm them with ease. Everything that was attributed to her was like water running through the fingers of the researcher who tries to establish a systematic and scientific method of inquiry.[24]

Badawi concludes that because so much vital information about Rabi'a is lacking, her "real" story cannot be the subject of history; rather, it can only be the subject of myth (*ustura*). Because in his opinion the objectives of myth and scientific history cannot be reconciled, the modern scholar must seek a third way: he should turn to the rationalistic discipline of philosophy to "open up a light onto the unknown" and reveal the "existential essences"

---

23 Ibid., p. 8.
24 Ibid., p. 11.

(*dhawat wujudiyya*) of Rabiʿa and her contemporaries. In this way, he says, the methodology of the philosopher can guide the footsteps of the historian.²⁵

Because he uses Existentialist philosophy as a tool for historical investigation, Badawi's approach can be compared methodologically to that of the Russian mythologist Aleksei Fyodorovich Losev. In *The Dialectics of Myth* Losev states, "Myth is not the substantial, but an *energistic* self-affirmation of a person. It is the assertion of a person not in her deepest and ultimate root, but in her *manifestational* and *expressive* functions."²⁶ Badawi would agree with the first part of this statement: the individual identity of Rabiʿa al-ʾAdawiyya is indeed established through her myth. However, he would most likely argue against the second part of the statement by saying that Rabiʿa's self-affirmation through myth *reveals* her identity rather than constructs it in the way that Losev believed. The existentialist Rabiʿa that Badawi portrays in *Martyr of Divine Love* is a paragon of self-realization. Losev might have responded that the problem with such a portrayal is that a character based on a philosophical ideal type is not a real person at all; rather, she is just an alternative type of myth. Instead of shining a light on Rabiʿa's real self, depicting her in terms of Kierkegaard's ideal personality types would merely add another "face" to the various images in which Rabiʿa the Icon has appeared throughout history.

Badawi's most significant contribution to the master narrative of Rabiʿa al-ʾAdawiyya was to depict Rabiʾa as the female embodiment of Kierkegaard's Aesthetic Man. In *Martyr of Divine Love*, he depicts her as traveling figuratively "on the road to Damascus," according to the trope first established for St Paul of Tarsus in Acts of the Apostles.²⁷ The key motif of this trope is a life-changing experience. In Badawi's story, Rabiʿa's first life-changing experience occurs as a child, when she falls down while fleeing an evil man in the street and implores God to protect her.²⁸ This reliance upon God in a state of fear causes her to look inward rather than outward for her salvation. For Badawi, Rabiʿa's attempt after this to seek communion with God in prayer fits both the existential reality of her condition as a captive and the Aesthetic personality type, which seeks to find itself in solitude rather than in companionship with others.

---

25 Ibid., p. 8.
26 Losev, *The Dialectics of Myth*, p. 93.
27 Badawi, *Shahidat al-ʿishq al-ilahi*, p. 18; Badawi uses this phrase several times. See also, William S. Kurz, S.J., *Acts of the Apostles* (Grand Rapids, MI: Baker Academic, 2013), pp. 150–8 (Acts 9:1–22).
28 Badawi, *Shahidat al-ʿishq al-ilahi*, p. 16.

The second life-changing experience occurs when Rabi'a's master frees her from captivity. Escaping from her master's house, she now turns toward the World and abandons her former pious worship.[29] At this point, says Badawi, Rabi'a "followed the path of her life in any way that she wished."[30] In this part of the narrative, he rounds out her character by combining 'Attar's statement that Rabi'a "fell into playing music" with Margaret Smith's trope of Rabi'a playing the flute.[31] This act of creative license sets the stage for Badawi's most dramatic portrayal of Rabi'a. In this plot adaptation, Rabi'a as a newly liberated woman tries to discover herself by earning her living as a performer. It is fitting, Badawi claims, that she should turn to such pursuits, for it is through the arts that women best express their personalities.[32]

According to Badawi's interpretation of Existentialist philosophy, the lessons of life are learned through the body. Thus, he speculates that not only did Rabi'a experience her freedom through worldly pursuits but she also indulged in them wantonly. "We can only imagine," he writes, "that she devoted a long period of her life to the path of intentional sin (*tariq al-ithm*), drowned herself in the sea of lusts, and gorged herself on the pleasures of the senses (*iqtatat bi-qut al-hawass*) until she was satiated."[33] Badawi concludes that Rabi'a must have passed part of her life in sin because she later repented, "and this repentance by itself is clear proof for us of her compulsion to reach the furthest limit in the path of lust."[34] Why should she repent, he asks, if she has committed no sin? In this part of the story, Badawi compares Rabi'a explicitly to St Paul, "whose excessive [Christian] faith was the result of his [formerly] excessive hatred for Christianity, or St Augustine's excessive life of subterfuge [as a Manichaean], which led him naturally to excess in the sensuous life that he lived before his conversion to the [Christian] faith."[35]

Badawi's Existentialist adaptation of Rabi'a's life story was the inspiration for the Lebanese-Syrian writer Widad El Sakkakini's depiction of Rabi'a in *al-'Ashiqa al-mutasawwifa* (*The Sufi Lover*), a quasi-novelistic biography

---

29   Ibid., p. 19.
30   Ibid.
31   Ibid. See also, 'Attar, *Tadhkirat al-awliya'*, p. 63; Sells, *Early Islamic Mysticism*, p. 157.
32   Badawi, *Shahidat al-'ishq al-ilahi*, p. 19.
33   Ibid., p. 20.
34   Ibid. The examples of Rabi'a's repentance cited by Badawi consist for the most part of general statements of remorse for the human condition. None of these statements refers explicitly to acts of lust or other major sins that would require repentance for her behaviors.
35   Ibid., p. 21.

that was first published in 1955.³⁶ As noted previously, El Sakkakini adds a feminist twist to Badawi's Existentialist portrayal of Rabi'a. In her portrayal of Rabi'a's life story, she agrees that the newly liberated Rabi'a rejected the life of poverty that she had suffered in captivity, and in response she indulged the life of the senses. For El Sakkakini, "After her escape from slavery and servitude into the gay life of liberated women (*hayat al-ghid al-mutaharrirat*), Rabi'a discovered a new kind of existence, engulfed in nights of perfume and tenderness. She turned toward pleasure and away from the austerity and chastity to which she had become accustomed."³⁷

However, El Sakkakini's portrayal of the "Aesthetic Rabi'a" differs from Badawi's in that she portrays Rabi'a's hedonism as being prompted by the abuse she suffered from men during her captivity. Unlike other writers, El Sakkakini depicts Rabi'a as suffering from both physical and sexual abuse by her male captors. In her version of the story, the first time Rabi'a is abused is when a slave trader captures her: "She was followed and chased by a vicious thief, from whom she ran screaming and calling for help. She fell to the ground; he grabbed her like a despised object; and soon after she was sold to a wealthy merchant for six pieces of silver."³⁸ Another time Rabi'a is abused by a man is when her master sends her out into the street to buy something at the market: "On the way back she was confronted by a vicious man, a human animal; and running from him, frightened and shocked, through the winding streets of Basra, she escaped—though with injury. She had fallen and broken her arm."³⁹ The most radical of El Sakkakini's additions to the narrative is her suggestion that Rabi'a's captor raped her: "Was she able to rid herself of the memory of her first captor, who used her as he willed? No one but the victim can really tell of the effects of being violated and robbed of her chastity. This alone may have changed her approach to life completely."⁴⁰

---

36 The most recent edition of this work is Widad El Sakkakini, *al-'Ashiqa al-mutasawwifa, Rabi'a al-'Adawiyya* (Damascus: Dar Tlas li-l-dirasat wa-l-tarjama wa-l-nashr, 1989 reprint of the 1955 Cairo first edition). The work was translated into English by Nabil Safwat as Widad El Sakkakini, *First Among Sufis: The Life and Thought of Rabi'a al-'Adawiyya*, with an Introduction by Doris Lessing (op. cit.).
37 El Sakkakini, *First Among Sufis*, p. 16; *al-'Ashiqa al-mutasawwifa*, p. 22.
38 El Sakkakini, *First Among Sufis*, p. 13; *al-'Ashiqa al-mutasawwifa*, p. 17. In the original Arabic text Rabi'a is sold by the thief for a "low price" (*thaman bakhs*). This is an allusion to *Surat Yusuf* of the Qur'an (12:20). The trope of six pieces of silver used by the translator comes from Margaret Smith's *Rabi'a the Mystic*, where Rabi'a is sold for six dirhams. See idem, *Rabi'a* (Oneworld), p. 23 and (Rainbow Bridge), p. 6.
39 El Sakkakini, *First Among Sufis*, p. 13; *al-'Ashiqa al-mutasawwifa*, p. 17.
40 El Sakkakini, *First Among Sufis*, p. 15; *al-'Ashiqa al-mutasawwifa*, pp. 20-1. The Arabic text specifically uses the term, "rape" (*ightisab*).

Apart from speculating on her abuse, El Sakkakini's emplotment of Rabi'a's life follows Badawi's quite closely. However, she compares Rabi'a's "Road to Damascus" conversion not with that of St Paul, St Augustine, or St Theresa of Avila as Badawi does, but rather with that of St Thaïs of Alexandria, a fourth-century CE courtesan whose legend became popular in Europe through the 1890 novel *Thaïs* by Anatole France.[41] Recalling this novel, El Sakkakini states, "As I write this, I am imagining the ancient story of Paphnutius the priest, who wandered out from Thebes in central Egypt. He traversed the desert barefoot until he reached Alexandria, where he prostrated himself before the naked Thaïs. Thaïs, whose gathering was intoxicated with wine and the fragrance of incense, and whose palace was notorious for licentiousness and dissipation—did she not change and become a saint as she approached her death?"[42]

This passage recalls the scene in Anatole France's novel *Thaïs* where Paphnutius, the Abbot of Antinoë, first encounters the courtesan Thaïs relaxing with her female companions in the Grotto of the Nymphs.[43] For El Sakkakini, the figure of Paphnutius was comparable to that of Ibrahim ibn Adham, the male Sufi ascetic and foil for Rabi'a in 'Attar's narrative. In 'Attar's story Ibn Adham struggles for years to cross the desert to Mecca, only to discover that the Ka'ba had left its location to make a miraculous pilgrimage to Rabi'a.[44] A major theme of the novel *Thaïs* is that Paphnutius could not free himself from his worldly attachments, despite his extreme austerities. After meeting Thaïs, he tries to compensate for his shortcomings by becoming the agent of Thaïs's conversion. However, even in this role he does not succeed. Because Thaïs had formerly been baptized into Christianity as a child, she was able to attain salvation on her own, despite the fact that she had fallen into sin. Because her repentance to God was sincere, she attained forgiveness without the need for rigorous austerities or outside help. For Paphnutius, however, who harbored secret lusts and the sin of spiritual pride, neither his asceticism nor his other pious actions earned him any credit in the Hereafter. Just as with Ibrahim ibn Adham in 'Attar's *Tadhkirat al-awliya'*, in the novel *Thaïs* ascetic austerities do not necessarily lead to salvation. Salvation can only be earned through God's grace. At the end of the novel, the spiritually reborn

---

41   Anatole France, *Thaïs*, trans. Robert B. Douglas (Rockville, M.D.: Wildside Press, 2005). For the legend of St Thaïs, see Ward, *Harlots of the Desert*, pp. 76–84.
42   El Sakkakini, *First Among Sufis*, p. 16; *al-'Ashiqa al-mutasawwifa*, p. 21; my translation of the Arabic text.
43   France, *Thaïs*, pp. 57–8.
44   'Attar, *Tadhkirat al-awliya'*, p. 64; Sells, *Early Islamic Mysticism*, p. 158.

Thaïs becomes more beautiful as she approaches her death, while Paphnutius becomes increasingly ugly because his desire for the World still remains.[45]

In her depiction of Rabiʿa as Aesthetic Woman, Widad El Sakkakini reflects on the paradox of "the wandering singing-girls and the maiden lovers described by Pierre Louÿs in *Thaïs* and *The Songs of Bilitis*. Despite their disrespect for piety, and immersed as they were in debauchery, they were nevertheless inclined to piety. The Cypriot singer Mnasidika hoped that despite spending many years in licentiousness and sin, the following words would be written on her tomb: 'Here lies the most pious of women.'"[46]

In this passage, El Sakkakini incorrectly attributes the authorship of the novel *Thaïs* to the Belgian Orientalist writer Pierre Louÿs (1870–1925). In actuality, Louÿs was the author of *Les Chansons de Bilitis* (*The Songs of Bilitis*), a collection of erotic poems that was published in 1894.[47] Although this work was quite popular among *Fin-de-Siècle* feminists, it is most notable today as a literary fraud. Rather than bringing to light an important literary artifact as he claimed, Louÿs composed all of the poems in *The Songs of Bilitis* himself.[48]

In the Introduction to *The Songs of Bilitis*, Louÿs claims that the poems came from the tomb of a courtesan named Bilitis on the island of Cyprus.[49] In the *vita* that he composes for her, he states that she was raised as a shepherdess (she was supposedly the daughter of a Greek father and a Phoenician mother) and that her life passed through three stages—her childhood in Asia Minor, her youth on the island of Lesbos where she was a lover of the poet Sappho (d. 570 BCE), and her maturity as a courtesan on Cyprus, where she was the lover of a female singer named Mnasidika. This is the Mnasidika that El Sakkakini mentions in the passage quoted above. Louÿs even provides false documentary evidence to support his claim of the historicity of Bilitis and her poems.[50] His division of Bilitis' life into three stages seems to foreshadow the three-stage story of Rabiʿa's life as outlined by Badawi and El Sakkakini.

---

45 France, *Thaïs*, pp. 138–41.
46 El Sakkakini, *First Among Sufis*, p. 17; *al-ʿAshiqa al-mutasawwifa*, p. 23; my translation of the Arabic text.
47 For a reproduction of the original work, see Pierre Louÿs, *Les Chansons de Bilitis* (Paris: Nabu Press, 2010). Many translations of this work can be found in English. In what follows I use Pierre Louÿs, *The Songs of Bilitis*, trans. Alvah C. Bessie (Mineola, NY: Dover Publications, 2010 reprint of the 1926 translation).
48 For historical background information on *The Songs of Bilitis*, see the Wikipedia article at: http://en.wikipedia.org/wiki//The_Songs_of_Bilitis.
49 Louÿs, *Songs of Bilitis*, pp. 13–20; *Les Chansons de Bilitis*, pp. i–xii.
50 See Louÿs, *Songs of Bilitis*, pp. 19–20, where the reader is told that Bilitis' tomb was discovered by the German archeologist "Herr G. Heim." Such an archeologist seems never to have existed. See also, *Les Chansons de Bilitis*, pp. x–xi.

However, the eroticism of Louÿs' work goes beyond what Badawi imagined for Rabiʿa. In Louÿs' narrative, although Bilitis trades in sex with men, her real lovers are women and she makes love to both men and women without distinction. Widad El Sakkakini seems tempted to go in a similar direction in *The Sufi Lover*, although she does not address the issue of Rabiʿa's sexuality directly. However, by recalling in her book Bilitis' lover Mnasadika and the other "maiden lovers" of *The Songs of Bilitis*, she seems to suggest that Rabiʿa might have had lesbian relationships.

Because of Badawi's belief that Rabiʿa had love affairs with men and El Sakkakini's speculations on rape and lesbian relationships, it is not surprising that more conservative and religiously minded writers strongly objected to their adaptations of Rabiʿa's life story. For example, in *La Vie de Rabiʿa al-ʿAdawiyya* (2000), the French North African writer Jamal-Eddine Benghal comments that speculations such as these are "difficult to admit. Everything about Rabiʿa refutes this."[51] With respect to Badawi's version of Rabiʿa's life story in particular he states, "This version is apparently not founded on historical realities but is based on a phantasmagoric imagination."[52]

One of the earliest critics of Badawi's adaptation of Rabiʿa's *vita* was the Egyptian writer Taha ʿAbd al-Baqi Surur, who in 1957 attempted to set the record straight in the book *Rabiʿa al-ʿAdawiyya wa-l-hayat al-ruhiyya fi-l-Islam* (*Rabiʿa al-ʿAdawiyya and the Spiritual Life in Islam*). Noting the many discrepancies between ʿAttar's chapter on Rabiʿa and Badawi's narrative in *Martyr of Divine Love*, Surur accuses Badawi of lying about what ʿAttar related (*kadhdhaba al-ʿAttar fi-ma rawahu ʿan Rabiʿa*). He argues that because of this act of academic dishonesty Badawi's book is worthless as a scholarly product. It "neither attains the level of true scholarship nor corresponds to historical reality nor the experience of faith."[53]

However, other modern Egyptian writers have not been as quick as Surur to dismiss Badawi's speculations completely. One way to retain Badawi's Existentialist framework and yet preserve Rabiʿa's reputation for virtue was to marry her off. As we saw in Chapter 3, the Egyptian historian Suʿad ʿAli ʿAbd al-Raziq uses this tactic in her 1982 book, *Rabiʿa al-ʿAdawiyya bayn al-ghinaʾ wa-l-bukaʾ* (*Rabiʿa al-ʿAdawiyya Between Song and Tears*). According to ʿAbd al-Raziq, Rabiʿa found a husband after she attained her freedom from captivity. Although she remained as pious as before, she attended to her

---

51 Benghal, *La Vie de Rabiʿa al-ʿAdawiyya*, pp. 48–9.
52 Ibid., p. 49.
53 Surur, *Rabiʿa al-ʿAdawiyya wa-l-hayat al-ruhiyya fi al-Islam*, pp. 44 and 46.

husband's physical needs for many years and only turned to celibacy after he died. As noted previously, this plot element originally came from Ibn al-Jawzi's prosopography *Sifat al-safwa*, where the original story was not about Rabi'a al-'Adawiyya but about the wife of Riyah al-Qaysi (d. 796 CE).⁵⁴ 'Abd al-Raziq apparently believed that Rabi'a and the wife of Riyah al-Qaysi were the same person. Paraphrasing Ibn al-Jawzi's narrative, she states: "Every night [Rabi'a] used to cook and attend to her husband, saying, 'Do you have a need?' When she had fulfilled them and left him, she would purify herself and bend her knees in prayer."⁵⁵ Although 'Abd al-Raziq accepted Badawi's theory that the "Aesthetic" portion of Rabi'a's life must have included sexual experiences, her conservative view of Islamic morality did not allow her to imagine that a sexually active unmarried woman could ever attain sainthood.

Another Egyptian work written in response to Badawi's *Martyr of Divine Love* is *al-'Abida al-khashi'a, Rabi'a al-'Adawiyya, imamat al-'ashiqin wa al-mahzunin* (*The Submissive Worshipper: Rabi'a al-'Adawiyya, Leader of the Lovers and the Sorrowful*), by 'Abd al-Mun'im al-Hifni (1991).⁵⁶ Hifni was a student of Badawi at the University of Cairo. He disapproved of the atheism of Badawi and the Existentialist philosophers and tried to restore the reputation that medieval hagiographers had established for Rabi'a as a chaste and pious Sufi.⁵⁷ Despite its polemical tone, *The Submissive Worshipper* is actually one of the more careful historical studies of Rabi'a in the Arabic language. Overall, Hifni is concerned to maintain a high standard of historical scholarship. In particular, he criticizes Badawi (justifiably, in my opinion) for failing to live up to the academic standards that he upholds in his other scholarly works. For the most part, Hifni reproduces Badawi's arguments accurately and struggles to find a proper balance between the demands of his Islamic faith and objective scholarship.

However, Hifni's book suffers from some key factual errors that undermine his attempt to portray the "true story" behind Badawi's narrative. For example, he states that Badawi's Existentialist approach to Rabi'a's life story was based on the philosophy of Martin Heidegger (1889–1976). Although Badawi probably taught about Heidegger in his courses on philosophy at

---

54 See Ibn al-Jawzi, *Sifat al-safwa*, vol. 2, p. 721.
55 'Abd al-Raziq, *Rabi'a al-'Adawiyya*, p. 57.
56 'Abd al-Mun'im al-Hifni, *al-'Abida al-khashi'a: Rabi'a al-'Adawiyya, imamat al-'ashiqin wa al-mahzunin* (Cairo: Dar al-Irshad, 1991).
57 See, for example, ibid., p. 73, where Hifni describes Existentialism as an "atheistic methodology" (*madhhab ilhadi*) and claims that Badawi taught that "there was no existence outside of time, which means that he denied the Afterlife."

the University of Cairo, this assertion is inaccurate with respect to *Martyr of Divine Love*. As we have seen, Badawi based his interpretation of Rabiʿa's life on the philosophy of Søren Kierkegaard.[58] Because of this mistake, Hifni also fails to recognize Badawi's reliance on Kierkegaard's Aesthetic, Ethical and Religious personality types. Instead, he attributes Badawi's portrayal of the hedonistic period of Rabiʿa's life to the influence of the feminist Existentialist philosopher Simone de Beauvoir (1908–86).[59] In this case, Hifni's mistake of attribution is compounded by anachronism. It is unlikely for Badawi's book on Rabiʿa to have been influenced by Simone de Beauvoir's theories because *The Second Sex*, the only work on which such influence could have been based, was first published in 1949, one year after the publication of *Martyr of Divine Love*.

Likewise, Hifni's assertion that Badawi's depiction of Rabiʿa's sexual activity was influenced by de Beauvoir's discussion of "erotomania" is also without foundation.[60] Although Simone de Beauvoir discusses this psychological condition in *The Second Sex*, she disparages it as "a kind of professional derangement," in which a woman tries to increase her self-worth by fantasizing that important men are in love with her. Erotomania could not have been relevant to Rabiʿa's life story because its pathology contradicts the Existentialist belief in the truth-value of life experiences. For de Beauvoir, the narcissistic erotomaniac "looks at herself too much to see anything."[61] It would have made little sense to apply this condition to Rabiʿa al-ʿAdawiyya, even in the "Aesthetic" stage of her life.

Although Simone de Beauvoir's *The Second Sex* could not have influenced Badawi's book on Rabiʿa, the situation was different for Widad El Sakkakini. First published in 1955, six years after de Beauvoir's book, *The Sufi Lover* clearly reflects de Beauvoir's feminist view of Existentialism. When El Sakkakini states that Rabiʿa al-ʿAdawiyya "used her asceticism as a way to establish her reputation, assert her intellect, and avenge her past," she echoes Simone de Beauvoir's views on women's mysticism.[62] According to de Beauvoir, "The [woman] mystic will torture her flesh to have the right

---

58 Ibid., p. 69.
59 Ibid., p. 75.
60 Ibid., p. 76.
61 De Beauvoir, *The Second Sex*, pp. 678–80.
62 El Sakkakini, *al-ʿAshiqa al-mutasawwifa*, pp. 43–4. In *First Among Sufis* (p. 30), Nabil Safwat translates this passage as follows : "She used her asceticism as a way to freedom—to avenge her past."

to claim it; reducing it to abjection, she exalts it as the instrument of her salvation."[63]

We hear another echo of Simone de Beauvoir when El Sakkakini compares the "Aesthetic Rabi'a" to the courtesans Thaïs and Bilitis. When de Beauvoir discusses the social independence of the Greek courtesan (Gr. *hetaera*) in *The Second Sex*, she observes that the tragic irony of the courtesan's independence is that it can only be a negative form of freedom: "Her independence is the reverse side of a thousand dependencies."[64] Psychologically, the price that the courtesan pays for her autonomy is a "systematic nihilism."[65] In other words, the alleged freedom of the courtesan is in reality a form of self-alienation, not of self-affirmation. In a similar way, El Sakkakini speculates on the emptiness and despair that Rabi'a must have felt during the Aesthetic period of her life. How, she wonders, can a woman realistically seek salvation from the abuses of men in the arms of other men? For El Sakkakini, the hopelessness of Rabi'a's situation eventually led her to seek greater self-awareness through the process of self-criticism. "And if she did succumb so young, from a need to survive and a fear of struggle; if she did become tempted by the pull of beauty and the promise of security and happiness, and was indeed swept away by the stream which had carried off many others like her, then no alternative would later have been left to her but self-analysis, self-reflection, and self-assessment."[66]

We have already seen how in Badawi's interpretation of Existentialist philosophy the quest for an independent identity requires immersion in all forms of experience, including sin. We have also seen how the self is inseparable from the body and thus can only be affirmed through the experiences of the body. Both Badawi and El Sakkakini argue that the inability of the self to attain complete freedom due to the body's limitations leads to despair and the recognition of sin. For both authors as well, Rabi'a's "Aesthetic" excesses created "dark nights of the soul" (*al-layali al-zalma'*), which led to prolonged episodes of despair and suffering.[67] These episodes culminated in a "spiritual revolt" (*inqilab ruhi*), which eventually compelled Rabi'a to turn away from the Aesthetic life toward the Ethical life and take up once again her former practices of piety and asceticism.[68] As El Sakkakini views the matter, this was a healthy development because Rabi'a found her way back to God on her

---

63 Simone De Beauvoir, *The Second Sex*, p. 714.
64 Ibid., p. 616.
65 Ibid., p. 618.
66 El Sakkakini, *First Among Sufis*, p. 16; *al-'Ashiqa al-mutasawwifa*, pp. 21–2.
67 Badawi, *Shahidat al-'ishq al-ilahi*, p. 23.
68 Ibid., p. 22.

own: "Alteration of the self is a natural phenomenon. No one was ever born who remained the same person until he died; because life is like the earth itself, it has mountains and valleys, and we travel upon its surface, high and low, no one knowing what his or her destiny might be."[69]

For Badawi, Rabi'a's transformation from the Aesthetic personality type to the Ethical personality type occurred when she realized that her attempt to find liberation through the body had failed. However, he would have disagreed with El Sakkakini that returning to God in repentance was a positive thing. For Badawi, instead of finding her true self in God, Rabi'a created a new form of self-delusion by fleeing from the World a second time. Far from being a type of spiritual liberation, her renewed state of pious repentance was even more destructive than the earlier state of enforced servitude.[70] Because as an atheist he was not able to conceive of a healthy form of religiosity, he speculates that one of the causes of Rabi'a's repentance was a failed love affair. After the breakup of this affair, her hopelessness and anxiety caused her to wander about the city of Basra visiting mosques and oratories, where she listened nostalgically to sermons and attended Sufi sessions of invocation. According to Badawi, the disciples of al-Hasan al-Basri conducted the most important of these sessions. He suggests that at one such gathering Rabi'a met Riyah al-Qaysi, whom he identifies (without giving textual evidence) as her spiritual mentor.[71]

In Badawi's view, all of the statements on repentance (*tawba*) and sincerity (*ikhlas*) attributed to Rabi'a in Sufi literature are products of the Ethical stage of her life. These statements are pessimistic (*salbi*) because they advocate the surrender of the human will. Rather than assert her own self-worth in a proactive manner, Rabi'a instead begs God for forgiveness from her sins and then despairs of ever being worthy of it. Because Badawi viewed all forms of self-surrender negatively, his views on this issue differ from those of El Sakkakini, who viewed Rabi'a's search for salvation by seeking God's mercy more optimistically. For El Sakkakini, the notion of divine grace gives hope to Rabi'a that her sins can be forgiven. However, she agrees with Badawi that an excessive fear of punishment in the Hereafter can become a psychological illness.[72]

---

69 El Sakkakini, *First Among Sufis*, p. 16; *al-'Ashiqa al-mutasawwifa*, p. 22.
70 Badawi, *Shahidat al-'ishq al-ilahi*, p. 23.
71 Ibid., p. 22.
72 El Sakkakini, *First Among Sufis*, pp. 27–8; *al-'Ashiqa al-mutasawwifa*, pp. 40–1.

When he discusses divine grace, Badawi uses the Arabic term *rida'*, which is most often translated as "satisfaction."[73] For him, this concept has more to do with Christian mysticism (*al-tasawwuf al-masihi*) than with Islam, and its use by Rabi'a proves her reliance on Christian models of spirituality.[74] According to Badawi, one of the hallmarks of the Ethical personality type is an obsessive concern with time. The fact that Rabi'a is depicted in hagiography as repeating her supplications for forgiveness obsessively is proof for him that she suffers from this condition. As we have seen in Chapter 2, obsessive-compulsive religiosity is a characteristic of instrumental asceticism and the ascetic ritualist (*nasik*). Although Badawi does not discuss Rabi'a's behavior in these terms, he observes that her constant repetition of supplications means that she fears her time on earth will run out before she reaches her goal. This too is a hallmark of instrumental asceticism.[75]

To set the stage for Rabi'a's final transition from the Ethical personality type to the Religious personality type, Badawi creates the trope of the "True Sufi" (*al-sufi al-haqq*), which he defines as "the Sufi in the Existentialist sense of the term" (*al-sufi bi-l-ma'na al-wujudi*).[76] In doing so, he sets up a distinction between optimistic and pessimistic forms of spirituality, which correspond to the different states of mind that he sees reflected in Rabi'a's statements on repentance. For Badawi, the True Sufi approaches her faith optimistically rather than pessimistically, dynamically rather than statically, and actively rather than passively. To illustrate what he means by these types of spirituality, he quotes two dicta attributed to Rabi'a that have often been taken to mean the same thing. In the first dictum Rabi'a says: "I seek God's forgiveness for my lack of sincerity in saying, 'I seek God's forgiveness'" (*Astaghfir Allah min qillati sidqi fi qawli astaghfir Allah*).[77] In the second dictum Rabi'a says, "Our supplication for forgiveness needs its own supplication for forgiveness because of the lack of sincerity in it" (*Istighfaruna yahtaju ila istighfarin li-'adami al-sidqi fihi*).[78]

---

73 Badawi, *Shahidat al-'ishq al-ilahi*, p. 24.
74 Ibid., Badawi even suggests that Rabi'a al-'Adawiyya may have had a Christian background.
75 Ibid., p. 25.
76 Ibid.
77 See Kalabadhi, *al-Ta'arruf*, pp. 72–3 and Arberry, *The Doctrine of the Sufis*, p. 83.
78 Badawi incorrectly attributes this quotation to Ibn al-Jawzi, when in fact Ibn al-Jawzi quotes the previous version given above. Badawi, *Shahidat al-'ishq al-ilahi*, p. 25 and R. Cornell, *Early Sufi Women* (Ibn al-Jawzi Appendix), pp. 278–9. For the actual source of this saying, see Munawi, *al-Kawakib al-durriyya*, vol. 1, pp. 285–93.

Badawi considers the first dictum pessimistic because to him it reflects Rabiʿa's moral anxiety about her previous sins of the body. By contrast, he sees the second dictum as optimistic because it affirms more abstractly a general moral truth about the human condition.[79] For Badawi, the point of the second dictum is that true repentance cannot be achieved either quickly or easily. In fact, "A person cannot achieve it even if it takes all of his life."[80] In his view, the key difference between optimistic and pessimistic forms of spirituality is in the approach one takes to the Existentialist concept of temporality (*al-zamaniyya*). Repetitive actions that others might see as obsessive-compulsive are signs for Badawi that Rabiʿa is not pessimistic in this stage. She is not caught in an endless cycle of remorse and self-recrimination but instead seeks Eternal life through righteous actions that are antithetical to her previous sins. Her apparent compulsiveness is due to the reasonable fear that she will not attain her goal in the limited time that is left to her.

For Badawi, the compulsive attention to worship that characterizes the ascetic ritualist is a sign of the transition from Kierkegaard's Ethical personality type to the Religious personality type. For Widad El Sakkakini, however, this transition depends on the development of spiritual maturity. In Rabiʿa's case, this maturity can be found in the abandonment of her former hatred of the World and her new embrace of "the tolerant teachings of [true] Islam" (*taʿalim al-Islam al-samha*).[81] This optimistic perspective requires one to accept the World as it is and realize that everything exists just as God intended it to be. For El Sakkakini, Rabiʿa's acceptance of a more forgiving form of spirituality opens the way to what she calls "practical Sufism" (*al-tasawwuf al-ʿamali*).[82] This term is her version of Badawi's notion of Sufism in its Existentialist meaning.

However, as Religious Woman, Rabiʿa is still not completely free of her former life, including her emotional states and experiences. These remain with her throughout her life. To illustrate this point, Badawi introduces another new plot element to her *vita*, which would eventually become part of her depiction on film. He suggests that Rabiʿa's transitions through the various stages of her life were prompted by a failed love affair. The proof of this, he claims, can be found in her mystical poetry, whose allegorical statements about divine love recall the memory of an actual relationship. For Badawi,

---

79 Badawi, *Shahidat al-ʿishq al-ilahi*, p. 25.
80 Ibid.
81 El Sakkakini, *al-ʿAshiqa al-mutasawwifa*, p. 41; *First Among Sufis*, p. 28.
82 El Sakkakini, *al-ʿAshiqa al-mutasawwifa*, p. 85; *First Among Sufis*, p. 55. In his translation of El Sakkakini's book Nabil Safwat calls this concept "authentic Sufism."

the love that Rabi'a expresses for God in her poetry is a form of compensation for this failed affair. Through the psychoanalytic process of sublimation, in her poems she replaces an imperfect human lover with a more perfect divine lover. In Badawi's view, virtually every statement by Rabi'a on the subject of Love represents an attempt to compensate for the bitter experience of lost loves. Among the many examples that he gives of this is the statement first transmitted in the ninth century CE by Muhasibi: "Night has come, the darkness has mingled, and every lover is left alone with his beloved. Now I am alone with you, my Beloved!"[83]

Along with her Love poetry, Badawi also suggests that Rabi'a tried out a new type of spirituality during the "Religious" stage of her life. This was *khulla*—the practice of friendship or intimacy as a spiritual method. He suggests that she learned this method from her Sufi mentor Riyah al-Qaysi.[84] According to Badawi, the Sufi doctrine of *khulla* provides a bridge between asceticism and Love mysticism by allowing the ascetic to progress from a pessimistic form of spirituality based on remorse and withdrawal to a more optimistic form of spirituality based on Love. As part of this process, the Sufi practices her altruistic love for God by loving and behaving altruistically toward her Sufi colleagues. Although Riyah al-Qaysi had a generally good reputation among Sufi writers, some non-Sufi heresiographers, such as the Hanbali Khushaysh ibn Adram an-Nasa'i (d. 867 CE), accused him of teaching the doctrine that intimacy with God allows the Sufi to take liberties with the moral teachings of Islam. According to Khushaysh, such practices included licentiousness with women and young boys.[85]

Badawi agreed with this suspicious view of *khulla*. According to his view of Existentialist philosophy, Love is an experience or feeling (*shu'ur*) that transcends both good and evil. By seeking a higher form of love, the Sufi practitioner of *khulla* goes beyond conventional morality. According to Badawi, some Sufis sought to approximate the ecstasy (*ladhdha*) of intimacy with God by becoming sexually intimate with other Sufis.[86] "In this state,

---

83   Muhasibi, *al-Qasd wa-l-ruju' ila Allah*, p. 104. See also, Badawi, *Shahidat al-'ishq al-ilahi*, p. 29.
84   Badawi, *Shahidat al-'ishq al-ilahi*, pp. 64–6.
85   Carl W. Ernst, *Words of Ecstasy in Sufism* (Albany, NY: SUNY Press, 1985), pp. 100 and 118–22.
86   As used by Sufis and some of their opponents, the meaning of the Arabic term *ladhdha* ("enjoyment" or "ecstasy"), closely approximates the French term *jouissance*, made famous by the literary theorist Roland Barthes and the French psychiatrist Jacques Lacan (1901–81). For Sufis, *ladhdha* also approximates the meaning given to *jouissance* by the Algerian–French feminist writer Hélène Cixous (b. 1937), for whom it is a form of

they are beyond the need for ordinary moral values; in other words, they are above their level." [87] For Badawi, the outward manifestation (*zahir*) of *khulla* is disrespect for the Shariʿa; its inward aspect (*batin*) is disrespect for all worldly objects of veneration. This view sets the stage for Badawi's interpretation of the stories in ʿAttar's narrative where Rabiʿa seems to disparage or disrespect the Kaʿba in Mecca. Here he comes close to suggesting, as Widad El Sakkakini does in *The Sufi Lover*, that Rabiʿa al-ʿAdawiyya may have engaged in socially inappropriate or homoerotic forms of intimacy, even after becoming a famous Sufi.

Badawi's fascination with *khulla*, like his attempt to revise the narrative of Rabiʿa's life, was based on his Existentialist belief that the development of the self depends on outward bodily experiences. In *Martyr of Divine Love*, he tries to link the concept of *khulla* to Religious Man by using two of Rabiʿa's poems as illustrations. These are the famous Poem of the Two Loves (see Chapter 3) and another poem attributed to Rabiʿa that originally came from the Qur'an commentary of the early Sufi Ahmad Ibn ʿAta' (d. 922 CE). In the original version, this poem was not attributed to Rabiʿa al-ʿAdawiyya but to Ibn ʿAta' himself.[88] Besides mistakenly attributing the poem to Rabiʿa, Badawi uses a version that is worded differently from the original. Presumably, this revised version was better suited for his argument that Rabiʿa's Love mysticism was based on intimacy with a human lover:

> You have become one with the way of my soul;
> This is why the Friend (*al-khalil*) is called, "The Intimate."
>
> You are in my thoughts, my hopes, and my speech,
> And in my repose, whenever I desire a place to rest.[89]

For Badawi, this poem expresses mutual possession or ownership (*milk*), which reflects the affection that ardent human lovers feel for each other. As the wording of the poem suggests, the relationship between the lover

---

pleasure or rapture that combines mental, physical and spiritual experiences, bordering on mystical communion.
87   Badawi, *Shahidat al-ʿishq al-ilahi*, pp. 65–6.
88   See Paul Nwiya, *Trois Oeuvres inédites*, p. 46.
89   Badawi, *Shahidat al-ʿishq al-ilahi*, p. 63. In Ibn ʿAta's original version of the poem the second verse states: "Whenever I utter a word, you are in my speech / and when I am silent, you are my ardent desire (*al-ghalil*)." Nwiya, *Trois Oeuvres inédites*, p. 46.

of God and God himself is one of co-dependency. Although the poet feels that she possesses the divine Beloved in her heart, in reality she is the Beloved's possession. Because she feels that the Beloved is "one with the way of her soul," all of her actions (even those that transgress the Shari'a) are the Beloved's actions and thus are permitted to her because of the rules of *khulla*.[90] For Badawi, the danger of the Love mysticism expressed by Rabi'a and like-minded Sufis lies in the obsessive tendencies of the Religious personality type. He interprets this poem as foreshadowing the heresy of the Sufi martyr Abu Mansur al-Hallaj (d. 922 CE), whose practice of *khulla* caused him to equate his human self with the divine Self, and led to his torture and execution. According to Badawi, had Rabi'a not kept the full details of her Love mysticism secret, she too might have been executed for her beliefs.[91]

By contrast, Widad El Sakkakini is not worried about Rabi'a's mystical excesses. For her, Rabi'a's mysticism was a form of mature or "practical Sufism" (*al-tasawwuf al-'amali*). This type of Sufism is not excessively mystical but rather is pragmatic and down-to-earth. El Sakkakini rejects "theoretical Sufism" (*al-tasawwuf al-nazari*), which is based on "ecstatic experiences, fantasies, and mysteries, lost in raptures and the unknown."[92] However, she agrees with Badawi that Rabi'a must have had multiple lovers in her life. By substituting an inner mystical love for these outer loves, Rabi'a could reach new levels of understanding and deeper ways of introspection. As El Sakkakini writes in *The Sufi Lover*, "[Rabi'a] did not seek her true self outside of herself at all. Rather, she sought her true self within herself (*fa-innaha lam tanzur kharija nafsiha fa-hasb wa innama nazarat fi nafsiha dhatiha*)."[93] Through the process of introspection that is part of the spirituality of "practical Sufism," El Sakkakini's Rabi'a is able to realize the truth of the early philosophers, who said, "Know thyself," and the truth of the Qur'an, which states, "In the Earth are signs for the faithful, as well as in yourselves; will you not then see?" (Qur'an 51:20–21)[94]

---

90 Badawi, *Shahidat al-'ishq al-ilahi*, p. 63.
91 Ibid., p. 67.
92 El Sakkakini, *al-'Ashiqa al-mutasawwifa*, p. 85; *First Among Sufis*, p. 55.
93 El Sakkakini, *al-'Ashiqa al-mutasawwifa*, p. 84; *First Among Sufis*, p. 54. The translator Nabil Safwat gets a bit carried away in his rendering of this passage: "She moved in search of her own lost self, which had far preceded her. With extended wings in a higher timeless world, her Self appeared, signalling her to follow."
94 El Sakkakini, *al-'Ashiqa al-mutasawwifa*, p. 84; *First Among Sufis*, p. 54.

III. RABIʿA THE FILM ICON

In 1960, the Egyptian screenwriter Saniya Qurraʿa (d. 1990), explored the tropes of Rabiʿa the Ascetic and Rabiʿa the Lover in a book titled, ʿArus al-zuhd: Rabiʿa al-ʿAdawiyya (*The Bride of Asceticism: Rabiʿa al-ʿAdawiyya*). This work, published by the Egyptian National Press Office, was written because of the popular acclaim of Qurraʿa's radio drama on the life of Rabiʿa, which was broadcast over Radio Cairo in 1955. As part of the book, she adapted the script for her radio play into the plot outline for a movie. This outline, titled "The Long Story" (*al-Qissa al-tawila*), comprises more than half of Qurraʿa's book.[95] It was later developed into the 1963 movie, *Rabiʿa al-ʿAdawiyya*, directed by Mostafa Niazi (1911–86), with screenplay by Saniya Qurraʿa and Mustapha Abdel Fatah.[96] The film, which features songs by the Egyptian singer Umm Kulthum (1898–1975), has since become so famous that it now provides most of the information on the life of Rabiʿa known by the Muslim public, not only in the Arab world but also as far away as Indonesia.[97]

According to Roland Barthes, much of the effectiveness of the reality effect in literature is due to the illusion of "having been there."[98] This is why realistic literary portrayals of locales such as Flaubert's Rouen in *Madame Bovary* or Badawi's Basra in *Martyr of Divine Love* are so important. The sense of "having been there" in nineteenth-century Rouen or eighth-century Basra enhances the reality effect in the reader's mind and increases the verisimilitude of the author's portrayal. Barthes also notes the importance of photographs in conveying an impression of verisimilitude.[99] The realism of the photograph enhances the sense of "having been there" even more than a literary description. This effect confirms the truth of the saying, "A picture is worth a thousand words."

In the essay, "Leaving the Movie Theatre" (1975), Barthes discusses how the "lifelikeliness" (*sic*) of a narrative is enhanced even further by being made into a film. The verisimilitude of the film's depiction of events is conveyed through a phenomenon that Barthes calls "cinematographic

---

95   Saniya Qurraʿa, ʿArus al-zuhd: Rabiʿa al-ʿAdawiyya (Cairo: Maktab al-Sahafa al-Dawli [National Press Office], 1960), pp. 91–228.
96   For a short description of this film, see Viola Shafik, *Arab Cinema: History and Cultural Identity* (Cairo: American University in Cairo Press, 1998), p. 173.
97   At the time of this writing, Indonesian posts of the film in segmented form could be found on YouTube.
98   Barthes, "The Reality Effect," in idem, *The Rustle of Language*, pp. 146–7.
99   Ibid., p. 146.

hypnosis."[100] For Barthes, the audience member who watches a movie in a theater is like a voyeur who peers through a keyhole in a door. Cut off from the rest of the world in the dark theater, the moviegoer feels that she uniquely perceives what is "really going on" in the film. The darkness of the theater creates contradictory feelings of involvement and detachment with respect to what is happening on screen. As Barthes explains it, "I must be in the story (there must be verisimilitude), but I must also be *elsewhere*... like a... fetishist, that is what I require of the film and of the situation in which I go looking for it."[101]

The image on film acts as a powerful lure that draws the viewer into the scene: "I fling myself upon it like an animal upon the scrap of 'lifelike' rag held out to him."[102] Because of the attractiveness of this lure, the moviegoer is "glued" to the story and the characters on film and experiences the story's "coalescence, its analogical security, its naturalness, its 'truth.'"[103] If the film being watched is historical, the story on the screen is often an interpretation of a book. In Barthes' terminology, this is an interpretation "in the second degree." That is to say, it is an interpretation of an interpretation of actual or alleged events. Thus, the historical film is even further removed from objective reality than the book on which it is based. However, because of the "lifelikeliness" imparted by the cinematic genre, the "truth" of the story recounted in the film seems even more natural (and hence more real) than the truth of the original book. Because of the power of cinema to involve the viewer in its symbols and representations, the "misreading" of objective reality that the film imparts creates an aura of verisimilitude that is even harder to resist than the verisimilitude of a work of literature. For this reason, says Barthes, film as a medium of communication is inherently ideological. Hence, he concludes that every movie is a vehicle of propaganda.[104]

In 1957, more than a decade before Barthes first introduced the concept of the reality effect and nearly two decades before the essay, "Leaving the Movie Theater," Mircea Eliade made a similar observation about the cinema in his classic work of Religious Studies, *The Sacred and the Profane*. However,

---

100 Barthes, "Leaving the Movie Theatre," in idem, *The Rustle of Language*, p. 347.
101 Ibid. Italics in the original. Jonathan Potter refers to this experience as the perception of "out-there-ness." See idem, *Representing Reality*, "Constructing Out-there-ness," pp. 150–75.
102 Barthes, "Leaving the Movie Theatre," in idem, *The Rustle of Language*, p. 347.
103 Ibid.
104 Ibid., pp. 340–9.

Eliade's view of the relationship between the cinema and literature was based on his concept of myth:

> The cinema, that "dream factory," takes over and employs countless mythical motifs—the fight between hero and monster, initiatory combats and ordeals, paradigmatic figures and images (the maiden, the hero, the paradisal landscape, hell, and so on). Even reading includes a mythological function, not only because it replaces the recitation of myths in archaic societies and the oral literature that still lives in the rural communities of Europe, but particularly because, through reading, the modern man succeeds in obtaining an "escape from time" comparable to the "emergence from time" effected by myths. Whether the modern man "kills" time with a detective story or enters such a foreign temporal universe as is represented by any novel, reading projects him out of his personal duration and incorporates him into other rhythms, makes him live another "history."[105]

The 1963 Egyptian movie *Rabi'a al-'Adawiyya* is an excellent example of what Barthes and Eliade are talking about. When viewed as a form of historical representation, the movie illustrates how the reality effect of cinema can turn the dramatic "misreading" of a prior text into an accepted fact. Viewing the film as a historiographical document also provides a good illustration of Aleksei Losev's phenomenological theory of myth. In fact, the feature film is one of the clearest examples of Losev's comment, "[Myth] is always a manifestation, immediate and naïve reality, a seen and tangibly felt sculptural quality of life."[106] Losev would agree with Barthes and Eliade that because of its power to evoke an immediate sense of reality, a movie is better at creating myths than a book. To say, as Barthes does, that film as an artistic medium is ideological, is similar to saying that film is mythological. What Barthes calls "ideology," Losev calls "absolute mythology." As a result of her depiction on film, Rabi'a al-'Adawiyya has become what Losev calls an *absolute myth*. What this means is that the myth of Rabi'a as an iconic figure has become self-referential: because her depiction on film is fixed in the collective imaginary, everyone knows what the name "Rabi'a al-'Adawiyya" refers to. This is because the "truth" of Rabi'a that the film portrays is tautological. The

---

105 Mircea Eliade, *The Sacred and the Profane: The Nature of Religion*, trans. Willard R. Trask (San Diego, London, and New York: Harcourt, Brace, Jovanovich, 1987), p. 205.
106 Losev, *The Dialectics of Myth*, p. 100.

"historical" Rabi'a and the film version of Rabi'a are co-dependent; they are caught up forever in a vicious cycle of referentiality. After the moviegoer sees Rabi'a as portrayed on film, she thereafter compares the "historical" Rabi'a with the film version. From this point on, says Losev, "No one can ever set any obstacles or boundaries either to this being or to this myth."[107]

Absolute myths are constructed out of what Losev terms *relative myths*. The most important relative myths used to construct the absolute myth of Rabi'a al-'Adawiyya are the tropes and master narratives that have been discussed in this book—Rabi'a the Teacher, Rabi'a the Ascetic, Rabi'a the Lover, and Rabi'a the Sufi. The present chapter has added three more relative myths to the Rabi'a master narrative—Rabi'a the Existentialist, Rabi'a the Feminist, and Rabi'a the Reformed Sinner. According to Losev, through the proliferation of such relative myths, the absolute myth becomes "crowned" by a *magical name*.[108] The fact that a myth is symbolized by a magical name tells us that the logic of history has surrendered to the logic of myth: all categories of description applied to the myth must now be understood in light of this name. The magical name, "Rabi'a al-'Adawiyya," enjoys an exalted status throughout the Islamic world. Today, the mere mention of her name cannot fail to evoke one or more of the relative myths associated with it.

However, as Losev also points out, for a magical name to have this kind of power, an outline or *vita* must exist behind it. The myth of Rabi'a al-'Adawiyya as it is known today could not have existed without the construction and reconstruction of her *vita* undertaken by 'Attar in *Tadhkirat al-awliya'*, Margaret Smith in *Rabi'a the Mystic*, 'Abd al-Rahman Badawi in *Martyr of Divine Love*, Widad El Sakkakini in *The Sufi Lover*, and Saniya Qurra'a in her screenplay for the movie *Rabi'a al-'Adawiyya*. By introducing the story of Rabi'a to radio and cinema, Qurra'a added new tropes to Rabi'a's story that increased the power of her magical name.

An important observation should be made at the outset about Qurra'a's adaptation of Rabi'a's *vita*: historical accuracy had little importance for her. Although she cites so-called "consulted sources" (*masadir al-kitab*) in the bibliography of the book *Bride of Asceticism*, she seldom makes use of them. This leaves the impression that she is name-dropping the references in her book rather than truly consulting them. This impression is further reinforced by the fact that she gets many of her references wrong. For example, she cites a purported work by the medieval scholar Ibn Qayyim al-Jawziyya

---

107 Ibid., p. 190.
108 Ibid.

(d. 1350 CE) called *Safwat al-safwa* (sic), when she clearly means Ibn al-Jawzi's *Sifat al-safwa*.[109] Ibn Qayyim did not write a book called *Safwat al-safwa*. Even more problematical is that Qurra'a sometimes cites titles that do not exist in any form whatsoever. For example, under the name (Louis) "Massignon" she cites a work titled, "The History of Miracles in Islamic Lands" (*Tarikh al-khawariq fi-l-bilad al-Islamiyya*). The bibliography of Massignon's works on the website of the Association des Amis de Louis Massignon does not mention any work by this title. However, the most glaring example of Qurra'a's historiographical carelessness is in her reference to Margaret Smith's *Rabi'a the Mystic*. Instead of providing the actual title of the book in Arabic, she calls it "Rabi'a the Mysterious" (*Rabi'a al-ghamida*).[110] Even worse, she states that the author is not Margaret Smith but "Margaret Mitchell."[111] Imagine the reader's surprise to find that the author of *Rabi'a the Mystic* is the same person who wrote *Gone with the Wind*!

Another important point to be mentioned about Qurra'a's *Bride of Asceticism* is that although she relies heavily on Badawi's narrative for the historical parts of the book (the historical section is titled, "Rabi'a... In Reality" [*Rabi'a... fi al-haqiqa*]), she does not adhere as closely as Badawi does to 'Attar's version of Rabi'a's *vita*. Instead, she changes much of the narrative and adds new events and characters to better round out Badawi's depiction of the Aesthetic Rabi'a. She also adds the figure of the Egyptian Sufi Dhu'l-Nun al-Misri (d. 859 CE) to the story in order to establish the notion that the "real" Rabi'a had something to do with Egypt. Perhaps because of the strong feeling of Egyptian nationalism that prevailed in the Nasser era when her book and screenplay were written, Qurra'a appropriates Rabi'a for Egypt by making her a disciple of Dhu'l-Nun, the most important Sufi of early Islamic Egypt.[112] Surprisingly, however, the seventeenth-century Egyptian

---

109 Qurra'a, *'Arus al-zuhd*, p. 231; *Sifat al-safwa* is commonly misrendered as *Safwat al-safwa* in the modern Muslim world.
110 "Rabi'a the Mystic" would be translated in Modern Standard Arabic as *Rabi'a al-mutasawwifa*.
111 Qurra'a, *'Arus al-zuhd*, p. 231.
112 Qurra'a's use of Dhu'l-Nun replaces Badawi's use of Riyah al-Qaysi. Dhu'l-Nun al-Misri died more than fifty years after Rabi'a al-'Adawiyya and accounts of him, whether autobiographical or written by others, never mention that he met Rabi'a in person. If he met any ascetic named Rabi'a, it most likely would have been Rabi'a bint Isma'il of Damascus. Viola Shafik points out that the depiction of famous Islamic figures in Egyptian movies of the 1950s and early 1960s coincided with the nationalization of the Suez Canal, the Suez Crisis of 1956, and the attempt by the Nasser regime to make Egypt a major player on the world stage. See idem, *Arab Cinema*, pp. 170–3.

hagiographer 'Abd al-Ra'uf al-Munawi, who originally made the claim that Rabi'a al-'Adawiyya lived in Egypt, is not mentioned in her bibliography.

A film adaptation of Rabi'a's life story that adheres somewhat more closely to 'Attar's narrative can be found in another Egyptian movie that is now all but forgotten because of the fame of the film *Rabi'a al-'Adawiyya*. This film is *Shahidat al-hubb al-ilahi* (translated in English as *Witness to the Divine Love* and in French as *Amour Divin*), a black-and-white movie that was released in 1962, one year before its more famous Technicolor competitor. Directed by Abbas Kamel and starring the Lebanese actress Aida Helal (1925–87) as Rabi'a al-'Adawiyya, the debt of this film to Badawi's book is apparent in its title, which is almost identical to Badawi's title *Shahidat al-'ishq al-ilahi*. Today, the print of this film appears to be lost and all that remains of it is a recorded version of the soundtrack, which was rebroadcast on Radio Cairo in Ramadan of 2008. Apart from this recording, the only remaining artifacts of the film are posters, which can be found in collections of Arab film-poster art in the US and the Middle East.

Although this movie follows earlier versions of Rabi'a's life story more closely than the film *Rabi'a al-'Adawiyya*, it also takes significant liberties with the plot for dramatic purposes.[113] The moral of *Shahidat al-hubb al-ilahi* is that spiritual love is superior to worldly love. Rabi'a's father is portrayed as a fisherman in order to set the scene for his poverty and allow him to reflect on the wealth flowing into Basra through the port of al-Ubulla. Rabi'a's three sisters are named Fatima, Buthayna and Sukayna. These names do not appear in 'Attar's *Tadhkirat al-awliya'* or in any other extant source. The most important new character in the film is the "Emir Rabi' ibn Ziyad," who takes over as Emir of Basra when Ibn Zadan, the Emir of the medieval accounts, dies. During Rabi'a's captivity, Ibn Ziyad hears of her beauty and musical talents and purchases her. This makes Rabi'a's owner and the Emir of Basra one and the same person, thus resolving a contradiction in post-'Attar accounts of how she could be a captive slave and the love interest of the Emir of Basra at the same time.

Rabi'a meets the ascetic Riyah al-Qaysi (called "Rabah" in the film) when he comes to visit the Emir's palace. She asks him, "What is the way to God?" Following Sufi teachings, he informs her that the way to God is based on renunciation (*zuhd*), desire (*'ishq*), intimacy (*uns*), repentance (*tawba*), thankfulness (*shukr*), Love (*mahabba*), certainty (*yaqin*), satisfaction (*rida*),

---

113 For the soundtrack of the film *Shahidat al-hubb al-ilahi* see the website : egyzaman.com/post.php?(the rest of the address is in Arabic)=r-shahidat-alhubb-alilahi-Rabi'a-al'adawiyya-rushdi-abaza-wa-a'ida-hilal-istima'-awnlayn-tahmil.

and inspiration (*ilham*). Then Rabi'a asks him how to obtain a vision of God. He replies, "Can you see a rose (*ward*) in the [Arabic] letters *waw, ra', or dal*? Go and seek God in the reality of His Name. Seek the moon in the heavens, not in its reflection in water. Purify yourself with the remembrance and worship of God to reach the Divine Light."

After meeting "Rabah" al-Qaysi, Rabi'a spends her free time singing and composing poems about Love. When the Emir wants to be with her, she tells him to go to his wife instead. Rabi'a then begins to go out of the palace at night to pray, study and perform invocations with her Sufi teacher. When she leaves the palace she takes a companion named 'Abda with her. This character is based on the figure of 'Abda bint Abi Shawwal, who, as we have seen, first appears in accounts of Rabi'a transmitted by Ibn Abi al-Dunya. Another palace servant named Khalid informs the Emir of Rabi'a's nightly sojourns. When the Emir finally confesses his love for Rabi'a, he hears a voice telling him to free her. Becoming jealous, he accuses her of practicing magic and punishes her in his anger. When he hears the voice again, he now believes that it has come from Satan. Rabi'a perseveres under the Emir's repeated torture and composes new verses about the misery of a sinful life. When the Emir hears the voice again, he finally realizes that it is from God and releases Rabi'a from captivity.

The figure of Rabi'a the Ascetic is depicted in *Shahidat al-hubb al-ilahi* as living in a hermitage (*sawma'a*) in the desert. Several of the miracles that are related of her in later medieval accounts are depicted in the film, including one in which she turns a thief toward righteousness. These episodes repeat the trope of dramatic conversion narratives that Badawi originally incorporated into her story. The first dramatic conversion in the film is when Rabi'a is converted to the path of righteousness through the influence of her teacher "Rabah" al-Qaysi. Afterwards, Rabi'a converts the servant-spy Khalid, the Emir of Basra, and finally her female companion 'Abda. The Emir Ibn Ziyad comes to visit Rabi'a at her hermitage in the desert, professing his love for her and offering whatever she might want if she marries him. Rabi'a tells the Emir that she belongs only to God and says, "How can I ask for the world from one who does not own it?"[114] When Rabi'a dies, a supernatural voice announces, "The grave possesses her body but her soul is with God." The film ends with the recitation of the same Qur'anic verse that 'Attar uses at

---

114 This saying first appears in Jahiz's *al-Bayan wa-l-tabyin* and *Kitab al-hayawan*. See Chapter 1.

Rabi'a's death: "Oh soul at peace, return unto your Lord, well pleased and well pleasing" (Qur'an 89:27–29).

The 1962 movie *Shahidat al-hubb al-ilahi* conveys a more consistently religious message than the more famous movie *Rabi'a al-'Adawiyya*. However, both films were produced in order to create a greater level of popular interest in the moral teachings of Islam. According to the Egyptian film historian Mahmud Qasim, although both movies were made in the secular Nasser era, they were part of a response to fears about the loss of religious values among the Egyptian public.[115] Most other religiously oriented films in this period dealt with famous battles and other events in the history of Islam. Several, however, starting with the film, *al-Sayyid al-Badawi* in 1952 and ending with *Shayma'* in 1972, dealt with the lives of Islamic religious personalities. The scripts of these films were not concerned with historical accuracy but rather with how their characters incorporated the Islamic creed and moral values in their lives. In some films, including the two movies about Rabi'a al-'Adawiyya, Sufis appear as exemplars of piety and spirituality. The films also included music and dancing to capture the public's attention. The most common motifs in these films included suffering for one's beliefs, the struggle of Islam versus unbelief, dramatic conversion experiences, repentance, the depiction of women as temptresses, and the depiction of male religious figures as women's moral guides. Film production in Egypt in the Nasser era was both multi-religious and multinational. The producers, directors and actors of religious films about Islam included Muslims, Christians and Jews, and their nationalities included Egyptians, Sudanese, Lebanese and Syrians.

It is still rare today for women to play major roles in Egyptian film production other than as actors. Saniya Qurra'a was not only one of the first women to write a screenplay for the Egyptian cinema but she also claims to have been the first person of any gender to adapt the story of Rabi'a al-'Adawiyya for radio and cinema. She wrote her first script on Rabi'a in 1952 and submitted it to Studio Misr in 1953. The radio play based on this script

---

115 See the blog, *Cinema Tripoli* by Salim Ramadan (cinematripoli.blogspot.com). See blogpost_13html, "al-Malamih al-'amma li-l-sharit al-dini fi al-sinima al-'arabiyya (General Aspects of Religious Motifs in the Arab Cinema). Most of the information in this blog is taken from the book by Mahmud Qasim, *Surat al-adyan fi-l-sinima al-Misriyya* (*The Image of Religions in the Egyptian Cinema*) (Cairo: Wizarat al-Thaqafa al-Markaz al-Qawmi li-l-Sinima [Ministry of Culture, People's Center for Cinema], 1997). The text of this book is accessible through the website of the Biblioteca Alexandria in Alexandria, Egypt. See also, Shafik, *Arab Cinema*, pp. 170–4.

aired in August 1955.¹¹⁶ Qurra'a writes in her book *Bride of Asceticism* that one of her main goals in popularizing Rabi'a's story was to provide a taste of the Sufi experience for the Egyptian public. However, her knowledge of Sufism was minimal. Ironically, most of what she says about Sufism in her book is based on the anti-Sufi views of the Hanbali scholar Ibn Taymiyya. Like 'Abd al-Rahman Badawi before her, she regarded Sufism as contrary to the pietistic and ascetic ethos of early Islam.¹¹⁷

In the 1963 movie *Rabi'a al-'Adawiyya*, the character of Rabi'a is based on Badawi's depiction of her as a restless spirit (*nafs qaliqa*) in *Martyr of Divine Love*. The film begins with Rabi'a as an orphan (a sort of Arab version of Little Orphan Annie), who lives with an old beggar woman in the countryside of southern Iraq. She becomes interested in seeking a more exciting life for herself when she hears the stories of 'Aliyya, a courtesan who returns to her village from Basra wearing fine clothes and jewelry. In the draft of the script that appears in *Bride of Asceticism*, Rabi'a states that her life in the village is beset by three woes: poverty, misery and bad luck. However, using a pun that foreshadows what is to come, she predicts that her luck will change in the fourth part of her life (*hayatuha al-rabi'a*).¹¹⁸ She resolves to leave for Basra and on the way she finds thieves plotting to rob a rich man named 'Isam al-Din. Rabi'a warns him of the plot and saves his life. 'Isam admires Rabi'a's courage and her dreams of a better life, so he gives her some money to help her. Farther down the road, the thieves try to capture Rabi'a and steal her money but the Sufi Thawban (Dhu'l-Nun) appears to save her and predicts that one day she will attain a high station in the way of repentance.

The next section of the film follows Badawi's portrayal of Rabi'a as Kierkegaard's "Aesthetic Woman" and depicts her as a performer and courtesan. Rabi'a goes to Basra to look for 'Isam al-Din, with whom she is infatuated. Reflecting Badawi's evocation of Basra's split personality, the movie depicts Rabi'a as wandering through the streets of the city, amazed by bazaars filled with goods of every description. Belly-dance music plays in the background. In the bazaar, she sees religious preachers competing with slave dealers for attention. She encounters the wife of a procurer of dancers and singing-girls, who invites her home. There she is trained in dancing

---

116 Qurra'a, *'Arus al-zuhd*, p. 6.
117 Ibid., pp. 9–16; the reference to Ibn Taymiyya is on p. 10.
118 Ibid., p. 96.

and singing. The woman becomes jealous when she sees how easily Rabi'a captures the hearts of men with her beauty and grace. 'Isam al-Din finds Rabi'a at a party where she is performing and pays all of the money he has to possess her. Later, he is called upon to lead a caravan and leaves Rabi'a with his friend, the merchant Khalil of Al 'Atik. 'Isam gives Rabi'a to Khalil as collateral for a loan. Rabi'a is heartbroken and begins to dress modestly because she yearns for 'Isam al-Din.

The character of Rabi'a al-'Adawiyya was played in the film by the Egyptian actress Nabila Ebeid (b. 1945), who still remains one of Egypt's most popular celebrities. In 2005, the Egyptian Internet linked her romantically with 'Amr Musa, the former head of the Arab League and candidate for President of Egypt. Nabila began her career as a belly dancer and the first half of the film shows off her dancing abilities. Unlike the posters for the movie *Shahidat al-hubb al-ilahi*, which depict Rabi'a as veiled, posters for the film *Rabi'a al-'Adawiyya* depict Nabila unveiled and in a romantic pose with the actor who plays 'Isam al-Din. The choice of the voluptuous Nabila Ebeid for the lead role in the film highlights the importance of Badawi's characterization of Rabi'a as Aesthetic Woman. There is also a hint that Saniya Qurra'a might have taken material from Widad El Sakkakini's book *The Sufi Lover* for the screenplay. Although it is not mentioned in the bibliography of the book *Bride of Asceticism*, it seems to have been influential because the movie portrays the merchant Khalil of Al 'Atik as trying to rape Rabi'a. As noted above, the rape scenario was first introduced into the story of Rabi'a al-'Adawiyya by El Sakkakini.

Khalil of Al 'Atik is the villain of the movie. He lusts after Rabi'a and gives her money and jewels, but to no avail. When he tries to molest her, she fights him off. While Rabi'a is confined in his house, she leans out of the window and listens to religious singers (*munshidin*) in the street, singing songs about the love of God. However, her heart still belongs to 'Isam al-Din. When 'Isam returns he comes to Khalil to pay back his loan. Although Khalil allows 'Isam to see Rabi'a, his jealousy causes him to refuse the payment and he resolves to murder his friend. Rabi'a is heartbroken once again. A fellow singing-girl tells her to forget 'Isam by living a carefree life of singing, dancing and drinking. Rabi'a succumbs and finally surrenders her body to Khalil. Later, the courtesan 'Aliyya meets Rabi'a once again and warns her that her physical beauty will be lost when she becomes an old woman. To help her, she tries to ransom Rabi'a from Khalil. Khalil refuses the offer and takes Rabi'a with him on a hunt. When they stop to rest, the Sufi Thawban

(Dhu'l-Nun) appears once again and preaches to her. Rabi'a answers him disrespectfully, saying, "[Physical] love is my religion and the wine-glass is my spiritual path" (*al-Hubb dini wa al-ka's madhhabi*). Thawban patiently preaches to her about the virtues of a life of asceticism. When she returns to Basra and again hears the religious singers in the street, she begins to weep out of remorse for her sinful way of life. Rabi'a resolves to reform her life and takes "Rabah ibn 'Amr" (Riyah al-Qaysi) as her teacher.

Rabi'a al-'Adawiyya is depicted in the movie as studying under several figures drawn from the medieval hagiographical record. These include the male teachers al-Hasan al-Basri, Sufyan al-Thawri, and 'Abd al-Wahid ibn Zayd, as well as the woman teacher Hayyuna. As we have seen in the previous chapters, the "real" Rabi'a could not have studied under al-Hasan al-Basri and Sufyan al-Thawri was more likely Rabi'a's student than her teacher. Of these figures, only Hayyuna could possibly have been Rabi'a's teacher. Just as in the earlier film *Shahidat al-hubb al-ilahi*, a woman named 'Abda is also portrayed as Rabi'a's companion. When the other women of Khalil's house inquire about Rabi'a's nightly sojourns, 'Abda replies, "She is conversing with her beloved." The women think that Rabi'a has found another lover and inform Khalil that she is cheating on him. Khalil finds Rabi'a praying and reciting the words related by Muhasibi: "Night has come, the darkness has mingled, and every lover is left alone with his beloved. Now I am alone with you, my Beloved." Hearing this, Khalil strikes her and tries to force her to dance and sing, but she continues to pray. He then tries to force her to drink alcohol, but she refuses. Finally, Khalil lashes her with a whip. The other women of the house take their revenge on Rabi'a by humiliating her and forcing her to perform menial tasks. A woman named Dalal (an Arabic word meaning "spoiled" or "indulgent") is particularly jealous of her. When Rabi'a tries to pray, Dalal releases poisonous snakes and scorpions, but Rabi'a is undeterred. She continues to pray and asks God for a miracle to help her.

One night, while Khalil of Al 'Atik is sleeping with Dalal, a voice comes to him and tells him to release Rabi'a from her captivity. Upon awakening, he still hears the voice and recalls how Rabi'a has endured his abuse. At this point the plot of the film returns to 'Attar's narrative. A servant comes and informs Khalil that a light is suspended in the air and illuminates Rabi'a's room as she prays. When Khalil goes to see this miracle for himself, the soundtrack of the movie plays Umm Kulthum singing the Poem of the Two Loves. Khalil leaves the room, weeping. Later he beseeches Rabi'a to forgive him and confesses his love for her. He says, "If you were to fall in love with a human being I would kill him.

But because it is God, you are free to go or stay in my home and worship as you wish." Rabi'a decides to leave.

After she leaves Khalil's house, Rabi'a does not turn to religion but decides to earn her living as a musician by playing the lute. People come from all around to hear Rabi'a's beautiful music. The religious scholar, 'Abd al-Wahid ibn Zayd, comes to see her and asks her to marry him. However, he is a religious extremist and berates Rabi'a for her lute playing. He breaks all of her musical instruments and throws her out into the street. Once again, the Sufi Thawban (Dhu'l-Nun) appears in order to save her. He takes her back to her village to live with the old woman who had raised her in her youth. However, the suspicious villagers now accuse Thawban and Rabi'a of being lovers. They chase Rabi'a into the street and try to stone Thawban as a libertine. However, because he is a Sufi saint, those who try to stone him become paralyzed and repent of their suspicions.

Soon afterwards, Rabi'a's miracles begin to appear and people flock to see her just as they did for her singing, dancing and lute playing. Khalil of Al 'Atik, who has been driven mad by his love for Rabi'a, dies of a broken heart. The next part of the film portrays Rabi'a's life of piety. The once beautiful courtesan has now metamorphosed into a famous Sufi. She attracts the attention of the Abbasid Caliph Harun al-Rashid, who seeks out her wisdom and asks her to pray for his victory in a war against the Romans (i.e., the Byzantines). By this time, Rabi'a has become an old woman and when Harun returns victorious from battle she is at the point of death. She looks forward to her end and is happy at the prospect of finally uniting with God, her divine lover. Her friend the Sufi Thawban and her faithful companion 'Abda are by her side when she dies and a flame, representing her love for God, burns beside her. When Rabi'a dies, the ghost of a beautiful young woman emerges from her body as Umm Kulthum sings in the background. Surrounded by Houris, she rises up to Heaven. After a short time, her spirit returns and informs her friends that she has fulfilled God's promise. The movie ends with Thawban and 'Abda smiling.

Although neither film about Rabi'a al-'Adawiyya was good enough to be considered for an academy award, the audience experience of the color film *Rabi'a al-'Adawiyya* was clearly superior to that of the black-and-white film *Shahidat al-hubb al-ilahi*. It also has a richer and more compelling plot line, despite the fact that the screenwriter Saniya Qurra'a took many liberties with Rabi'a's *vita*. However, in the realm of myth, historical accuracy is not a major consideration. When a film is made from a book or a collection of narratives, it becomes in a sense the eye of the text. As Roland Barthes reminds us, neither historical detail nor the original text is able to "contaminate" the verisimilitude of a film. This is because the public, who are seldom familiar with the original sources, "see" the story only through the film. For the average moviegoer in Egypt, Turkey, Malaysia, or Indonesia where the film *Rabi'a al-'Adawiyya* has recently been most popular, who would not prefer to imagine Rabi'a as the beautiful Nabila Ebeid? Who cares that Saniya Qurra'a's screenplay was faithful neither to history nor to 'Attar's original *vita*? In the end, all that matters is the verisimilitude imparted by the magic of the film. As William Shakespeare states in *Hamlet*, "The play's the thing."

IV. POSTSCRIPT: RABI'A, THE PHANTOM OF THE TELEVISION SERIES

In 1996, a television series aired in Egypt under the title, *Rabi'a ta'ud* (*Rabi'a Returns*). The screenplay for the series was written by Yousry El Guindi (b. 1942), a well-known Egyptian playwright and former official of the Ministry of Culture who had previously written a radio play called *Rabi'a al-'Adawiyya* in 1980.[119] Although the title of El Guindi's series is *Rabi'a Returns*, its story is not so much about Rabi'a the person, whether historical or legendary, but about Rabi'a the Icon. The main character is not Rabi'a al-'Adawiyya but a girl named Badr, who grows up in the region of Basra around the time of Rabi'a's death. The actress who played Badr in the series was Iman El Toukhy (b. 1957), an actress and singer whose career spanned the years 1982–2003. According to rumors that appeared after the Egyptian revolution of 2011, she secretly married Egyptian President Hosni Mubarak and bore him a daughter.[120] The actress who played Rabi'a was Samiha Ayoub (b. 1930), a famous Egyptian actress whose career has covered more than five decades.[121]

The life of the character Badr in the series draws heavily from medieval accounts of Rabi'a al-'Adawiyya and the modern adaptations of her story by 'Abd al-Rahman Badawi and Saniya Qurra'a. For example, Badr is orphaned during a famine, which is a trope about Rabi'a that goes back to 'Attar's *vita*. Like Rabi'a in Qurra'a's screenplay, an old beggar cares for Badr as a child; however, this time the beggar is male instead of female. As a young girl,

---

[119] For information on Yousry El Guindi, see the Arabic Wikipedia site, ar.wikipedia.org/wiki/yusri al-jundi.
[120] See the website, ar.wikipedia.org/wiki/iman al-tukhi (in Arabic).
[121] In Egypt, Samiha Ayoub is called *Sayyidat al-Masrah*, "The Lady of the Theater." See ar.wikipedia.org/wiki/Samiha 'Ayub (in Arabic).

Badr sees Rabi'a in person and is fascinated by her. She watches her secretly through the window of her house and follows her to the house in which she performs her devotions. In the series, Rabi'a is cared for by another elderly woman named Shawla, who recalls the character 'Abda bint Abi Shawwal. The series also depicts Rabi'a teaching both male and female disciples. After Rabi'a dies and Badr grows up, her life begins to follow the pattern of Rabi'a's life, much as depicted in the film *Rabi'a al-'Adawiyya*. At moments of crisis, Rabi'a appears like a phantom to Badr from beyond the grave, informing her of future events and giving her moral and spiritual advice. This explains the title of the series, *Rabi'a Returns*.

It is not necessary to discuss the entire plot of this television series in detail. Despite some differences, it follows Badawi's *Martyr of Divine Love* and the film *Rabi'a al-'Adawiyya* fairly closely, except that the main character is not Rabi'a but Badr. In the series, Badr falls into a life of sensual dissipation, just as Rabi'a does in the movie and in Badawi's narrative. In addition, Badr's personality is characterized by restlessness and anxiety (*qalaq*), which is a key Existentialist motif in Badawi's book. The series *Rabi'a Returns* is an important postscript to the present chapter because it exemplifies the relationship of narrative to myth as discussed in the theories of Roland Barthes and Alexei Fyodorovich Losev. For Barthes, myth is the expression of "what goes without saying," in a historical narrative. Myth is a type of meta-discourse, in which meaning derives from the semiotic relationship between sign, signifier and signified.[122] The premise of the Egyptian series *Rabi'a Returns* is that the figure of Rabi'a al-'Adawiyya is a mythical meta-discourse of the type described by Barthes. This is why she is depicted as a phantom or apparition; she returns periodically to remind the viewer that Badr's story is based on Rabi'a's model. At more than one point in the series, Rabi'a even calls Badr "Rabi'a."

As the visual portrayal of a meta-discourse, the series *Rabi'a Returns* also illustrates Losev's phenomenological theory of myth, in which myth "is not the substantial, but an *energistic* self-affirmation of a person. It is the assertion of a person not in her deepest and ultimate root, but in her *manifestational* and *expressive* functions."[123] The phantom of Rabi'a that appears to Badr is the "energistic and expressive manifestation" of Rabi'a al-'Adawiyya as

---

122 See Barthes, *Mythologies*, pp. 11 and 131. To be accurate, however, for Barthes the relationship between meaning and image is the other way around: the meaning does not derive from the image; rather, meaning is *transformed into* the image. In the statement above, I interpret Barthes through Losev.
123 Losev, *The Dialectics of Myth*, p. 93.

an iconic image. For the screenwriter Yousry El Guindi, the apparition of Rabi'a stands for the mythologized Rabi'a of popular memory. In Losev's terminology, the mythological figure of Rabi'a as depicted in the series is a "pictorial emanation," or the idealized expression and personification of Rabi'a's teachings.

To put it another way, the phantom Rabi'a who keeps returning to Badr in the series is an *icon*. She not only manifests herself on screen as *visage, form* and *image*, but also as a paradigm or model for the main character. Through Badr's eyes, the viewer participates in "seeing" Rabi'a the Icon through a series of tropes, taken from a variety of premodern and modern narratives. As Widad El Sakkakini states in her book *The Sufi Lover*, the viewer looks at Rabi'a "as if through eternity, or at the door of the infinite."[124] And the story continues...

---

124 El Sakkakini, *First Among Sufis*, p. 9; *al-'Ashiqa al-mutasawwifa*, p. 10.

Epilogue

Rabiʿa, the Myth and the Narrative

"I see Rabiʿa as an apparition, shimmering like a wave—not unsteady with a walking stick and in old and worn-out garments and sandals but running toward the shores of heaven in a halo of light."
—Widad El Sakkakini, *al-ʿAshiqa al-Mutasawwifa Rabiʿa al-ʿAdawiyya*

"In passing from history to nature, myth acts economically. . . it organizes a world which is without contradictions because it is without depth, a world wide-open and wallowing in the evident, it establishes a blissful clarity; things appear to mean something by themselves."
—Roland Barthes, "Myth Today," in *Mythologies* (1957)

A Google Internet search of the name, "Rabiʿa al-ʿAdawiyya," turns up numerous visual images of Rabiʿa of Basra, which mostly follow a similar pattern. There is the famous medieval manuscript illustration of Rabiʿa from a Persian dictionary that shows her grinding grain. There are also images of women in languid poses from Mughal-era South Asian manuscripts that have been ascribed to Rabiʿa in modern times. Some images show Rabiʿa with a halo around her head and one modern image has her carrying a torch and a pitcher, like a female Muslim version of Diogenes the Cynic. Other images show her in attitudes of prayer, usually making supplications. Sometimes she is depicted as playing the lute or another traditional instrument, such as the *buzuq* or the *bendir*. The last time I looked these images up on Google, I noticed that the search engine also turned up pictures of Orthodox icons in similar pious poses, especially of the Virgin Mary. And of course, the cinematic story still continues. In 1973 two movies about Rabi'a were produced in Turkey. In that year the director, screenwriter and producer Osman Seden (1924–98) came out with a film called *Rabi'a-i Adviyye* (*Rabi'a al-'Adawiyya*). In the same year Süreyya Duru (1930–88) produced *Rabia ilk Kadin Evliya* (*Rabi'a the First Woman Saint*). Both films can be viewed today on YouTube.[1]

These Turkish films, like their Egyptian predecessors and the television series *Rabi'a Returns*, draw both on literary depictions of Rabi'a and the images that can be found in manuscript illustrations and modern paintings. As such, they serve as important examples of Rabi'a the Icon. They also serve as illustrations of Rabi'a the Myth. As representations of a myth, they no longer have much to do with the Rabi'a al-'Adawiyya of historical scholarship, or even with Rabi'a the Sufi or Rabi'a the Teacher. As Roland Barthes indicates in the above epigraph, these representations tell us that the myth of Rabi'a has now passed from the realm of history into the realm of nature. She now occupies a naturalized world, "which is without contradictions because it is without depth, a world wide-open and wallowing in the evident," where "things appear to mean something by themselves."[2] In terms of narrative discourse this is to say that with Rabi'a the Myth, the literary character that was rounded out so thoroughly over the centuries by 'Attar, Smith, Badawi and El Sakkakini has become "flatter" once again.

In 1994 Denise A. Spellberg published an important book about 'A'isha the wife of the Prophet Muhammad titled, *Politics, Gender, and the Islamic Past: The Legacy of 'A'isha Bint Abi Bakr*. Much like the present book, this work was not so much a biography as it was a study of 'A'isha's legacy in light of questions that were raised by her portrayal in Islamic history. Topics of the book included the construction of 'A'isha's historical persona, the memory of her in early sectarian debates between Sunni and Shiite Muslims, the role of gender in accounts of her political leadership, and the use of her image in shaping the Islamic feminine ideal. Spellberg's book was one of my inspirations for writing this book about Rabi'a al-'Adawiyya. Part of my inspiration came from our shared experiences in approaching our subjects of research. First, it took Spellberg ten years to write her book. This book took more than ten years for me to write as well. More importantly, however, we both shared

---

[1] For *Rabi'a-i Adviyye*, see https://www.youtube.com/watch?v=dFYB9gp_04Y; for *Rabia ilk Kadin Evliya*, see https://www.youtube.com/watch?v=wolzeusGA0Q. Accessed May 22, 2017.
[2] Roland Barthes, "Myth Today," in idem, *Mythologies*, p. 143.

a similar problem of trying to say something meaningful about "a difficult woman."³ 'A'isha bint Abi Bakr is a difficult woman to write about because she was a politically polarizing figure. Rabi'a al-'Adawiyya is a difficult woman to write about because—like 'A'isha but for different reasons—her historical persona has been portrayed in different and sometimes contradictory images. How, for instance, can one reconcile the ascetic moralist and spiritual master depicted by the Sufi Sulami with the existentialist rebel depicted by the modern writers Badawi and El Sakkakini, or the romantic lover immortalized by the Egyptian movie *Rabi'a al-'Adawiyya*?

The main historiographical problem that Spellberg had to face was to choose between 'A'isha's life or legacy as the focus of her study. She writes, "A life and a legacy are not always the same. Time and perspective collude to shape the latter, promoting a definitive semblance of the former. Yet of any life, the legacy is only a semblance—a vision of reality generated by those who thought and wrote about their subject, for their own reasons, after the life to be told has ended."⁴ On the surface, this statement also seems to be true of Rabi'a al-'Adawiyya. However, in reality, one cannot pose the historiographical problem of writing about Rabi'a in exactly the same way. Because 'A'isha was the Prophet Muhammad's wife and an important political figure after the Prophet's death, there is more empirically verifiable information on her life than on the life of Rabi'a. As Spellberg demonstrates in her book, the figure of 'A'isha appears often in Islamic history: she is a major protagonist in the Prophet Muhammad's biography; she is a figure of political contention between Sunni and Shiite Muslims; she is a major source of Hadith reports; and she is even alluded to in the Qur'an. No comparable method of verification is available for Rabi'a al-'Adawiyya. Although both 'A'isha and Rabi'a as they are known today are the products of literary representation, it is still possible to call 'A'isha a "historical figure." For Rabi'a however, her historicity is still an open question.

Because 'A'isha is a well-attested historical personage, the historiographical issues that Spellberg had to deal with were more conventional than those that I had to deal with in this study. Whether the issue in question was about gender, Islamic sectarianism, or another subject, Spellberg could still make a meaningful distinction between 'A'isha as a historical personage and the figure of 'A'isha as a literary representation. As the historiographer Frank

---

3   Spellberg, *Politics, Gender, and the Islamic Past*, p. ix.
4   Ibid., p. 1.

R. Ankersmit might say, 'A'isha's reality is still "on the outside."[5] In other words, a "real" 'A'isha exists that is at least partly independent of her textual representation.

As the present study has demonstrated, this is not the case with Rabi'a al-'Adawiyya. In Rabi'a's case, her legacy is not the semblance of her life, as it is with 'A'isha. Instead, it is the other way around. Rabi'a's life—as people know it today—is the semblance of her legacy. In composing a *vita* for Rabi'a, 'Attar composed a backstory for a pre-existing legacy. The modern writers Smith, Badawi, El Sakkakini and Qurra'a did much the same. Although Rabi'a is a major figure of both Islamic and modern literature, she does not have a historical identity apart from her representation in literature. No extant source from her lifetime mentions her and even the purportedly eyewitness accounts that can be found in some early sources are open to question. Even by Jan Vansina's relatively liberal standards for oral tradition as history (see Introduction), accounts about Rabi'a are testimony at second or third hand at best. As sources for empirical history, they count as little more than hearsay.

The intractability of this historiographical problem is why I chose to title this book *Rabi'a from Narrative to Myth*. As a work of history, it is primarily a work of literary history because it examines the most important tropes or themes of the Rabi'a master narrative. The "historical Rabi'a" apart from the text can only be inferred, not found. As I explained in the Introduction, I tried to approach the sources that were available to me pragmatically and with an open mind, using the theoretical tools that were best suited for the job at hand. Often, the best tools for the job came from the field of literary theory. This explains my reliance on Roland Barthes and his student Abdelfattah Kilito. Similarly, when I turned to historiography, the most useful theorists were those who drew on literary theory for their ideas, such as Hayden White, Elizabeth Clark and Frank Ankersmit. Sometimes, I was able to rely on scholars influenced by anthropology or the *Annales* tradition of historiography, such as Jacques Maquet, Jan Vansina, or Thomas Heffernan. The concept of the master narrative comes from the field of Communications Studies and scholars of narrative such as H. Porter Abbott. Finally, if I had not discovered by chance the Russian phenomenologist Aleksei Fyodorevich Losev and his seminal work, *The Dialectics of Myth*, I would not have thought of describing the mythical figure of Rabi'a as an icon.

---

5   For a detailed discussion of this issue, see Ankersmit, *Meaning, Truth, and Reference*, pp. 54–63.

Although the details of Rabi'a's representation in various forms of narrative differ widely, certain tropes have remained constant. First, the four main tropes of the premodern Sufi narratives—Rabi'a the Teacher, Rabi'a the Ascetic, Rabi'a the Lover and Rabi'a the Sufi—remain relevant in the modern era, although the trope of Rabi'a the Lover now takes pride of place. In addition, another constant of representation has remained since the premodern period. This is the depiction of Rabi'a as a figural image, like the subject of a painting. One can see this in Widad El Sakkakini's vision of Rabi'a in the epigraph: "I see Rabi'a as an apparition, shimmering like a wave—not unsteady with a walking-stick in old and worn-out garments and sandals but running toward the shores of heaven in a halo of light."[6] Because of the prevalence of such visual metaphors, following Losev I characterized the mythologized Rabi'a as "Rabi'a the Icon." The icon is an appropriate metaphor for Rabi'a as a "mythicized historical figure" (to use Mircea Eliade's term) because like a religious icon Rabi'a the Myth is a naturalized and hence "flattened" image as Barthes states, and yet is pregnant with multiple meanings and associations.

In terms of empirical history, Rabi'a al-'Adawiyya is no more than what Frank Ankersmit has called "a proper name attached to a number of narrative substances."[7] That is to say, her empirical reality is limited to a name and a collection of narratives associated with that name. Even though she likely existed, her name refers only vaguely to a real person or identity beyond the level of narrative. In Sufi and other genres of literature, she stands for particular "views or representations of the past," or "a common denominator to be discerned in a number of roughly comparable representations."[8] This means that when we study Rabi'a historically, we cannot study the "real person." All we can study is *the historical reality of her narrative representations*. This is why so much of the present work has been about "Rabi'a the Narrative."

Ankersmit explains that historical representation involves three distinct levels of reality: (1) the past itself; (2) the empirical description of the past; (3) the representation of the past.[9] In Rabi'a's case, the level of "the past itself" is the domain of the "real" Rabi'a al-'Adawiyya—i.e., the Rabi'a that is prior to historical representation. In empirical terms, this level of historical

---

6   El Sakkakini, *al-'Ashiqa al-Mutasawwifa*, p. 98. This is a direct translation from the original Arabic text and is somewhat different from Nabil Safwat's translation in *First among Sufis*, p. 62.
7   Ankersmit, *Historical Representation*, p. 57.
8   Ibid.
9   Ibid.

reality does not exist. There are no early sources of information on Rabi'a apart from aphorisms, dicta, or other forms of narrative representation. The purportedly first-hand accounts and descriptions of Rabi'a that can be found in some early sources (such as in the works of Muhasibi, Jahiz, Ibn Abi Tahir Tayfur, and Ibn al-Junayd) belong to the second level of historical reality—"the empirical description of the past." However, as we have seen, even these examples are few and far-between. The vast majority of what exists with respect to the historical reality of Rabi'a al-'Adawiyya are "representations of the past." These include all representations of Rabi'a that make a claim of truth, whether they are "principial," historical (as in modern academic studies), figural, or symbolic.

According to Ankersmit's model, a truly empirical historical study of Rabi'a al-'Adawiyya would have to limit its investigation only to the first two levels of historical reality—i.e., to (1) the level of the past itself (which does not exist in this case) and (2) the level of empirical descriptions of the past. In the present study, this would take us only through Chapter 1, "Rabi'a the Teacher," and Chapter 2, "Rabi'a the Ascetic." One might also consider the discussion of Rabi'a's celibacy in Chapter 3 as part of such an empirical study as well. Given such limitations, we would be able to conclude relatively little about the historical Rabi'a al-'Adawiyya: She was an ascetic from Basra; she was most likely celibate; she was known for her eloquence; she was a teacher of religiously inspired ethics; and she talked about the love of God in at least some of her teachings. We could also conclude on the basis of available evidence that she was a respected Arab and Sunni Muslim but not a slave or a *mawlat*—a client-convert to Islam. Most importantly, we could not call her a Sufi. No extant source prior to the tenth century CE describes Rabi'a al-'Adawiyya as a Sufi. Therefore, on the basis of empirical evidence alone, we would only be able to argue that the "real" Rabi'a was an ascetic, not a Sufi.

Such a bare-bones description of the "real" Rabi'a al-'Adawiyya would probably be enough to satisfy a strictly empirical historian. However, it would not make up a book and it would not be sufficient to explain why the figure of Rabi'a al-'Adawiyya has captured the imagination of millions of Muslims for over 1,000 years. What has mattered most for her legacy—including her historical legacy—is her representation in literature, which is more figural or "principial" than empirical. Thus, we must ask a further historiographical question: Which "truth" is more important for understanding Rabi'a al-'Adawiyya as a historical figure? Is it the empirical truth of the historian or the figural truth that has been carried in different forms of literary representation? In light of the undeniable importance of her figural image, we must conclude that the history of Rabi'a that is most significant is not her empirical history (although this is still important) but the history of her literary representation from narrative to myth.

In the previous chapters, much has been said about Rabi'a as a subject of narrative. But what does it mean to say that she is a myth? I started to answer this question in the Introduction by approaching myth as a narrative and I shall attempt to finish it here by approaching myth as a symbolic form of representation. For Alan Dundes, Mircea Eliade and Robert A. Segal, a myth is primarily a story. These scholars of folklore and religion may differ over which subjects myth can cover, but they all agree that myth is a type of narrative. In the Introduction I used Segal's broad definition of myth as a starting-point for thinking about how the master narrative of Rabi'a al-'Adawiyya could be viewed as a mythological representation: (1) A myth is a story about something significant; (2) the main figures of myths are personalities; (3) the function of a myth is to accomplish something significant for its adherents; (4) to qualify as a myth, a story must be held tenaciously by its adherents. As this book has demonstrated, the narratives that make up the Rabi'a myth all fit Segal's definition of myth: (1) the stories have significance (i.e., they have a moral or a point); (2) they are about a personality (i.e., Rabi'a al-'Adawiyya); (3) they accomplish something significant for their adherents (i.e., they have a didactic purpose); (4) they are believed tenaciously by their adherents down to the present day.

Not only has the master narrative of Rabi'a al-'Adawiyya become a myth but certain sub-narratives have developed into myths as well. For example, the suggestion by 'Attar that Rabi'a may have been a musician was embellished by the English Orientalist Margaret Smith in the early twentieth century. In later decades of the twentieth century, this image of Rabi'a became transformed into the musician, dancer and singing-girl of the Egyptian movie *Rabi'a al-'Adawiyya* under the influence of 'Abd al-Rahman Badawi's book *The Martyr of Divine Love*. With this trope and others, the story of Rabi'a went beyond the original narratives and became a second-order construct. To better understand the importance of second-order constructs to the development of myths, I introduced in Chapter 5 Alexei Fyodorovich Losev's notion of the "dialectics of myth" and Roland Barthes' concept of the "reality effect."

Although Losev's and Barthes' theories of myth are similar in many ways, they differ in that Losev approaches myth phenomenologically while Barthes theorizes myth from the perspective of structural linguistics and semiotics.

Both theorists conceive of myth more as a mode of representation than as a story. Losev would have agreed with Barthes that "everything can be a myth provided it is conveyed by a discourse. Myth is not defined by the object of its message, but by the way in which it utters this message."[10] Losev would also have agreed with Barthes that although a myth contains a message, the message of the myth is primarily a form of signification or representation. As such, with respect to its form, myth is not only limited to narrative: "[Myth] can consist of modes of writing or representations; not only written discourse, but also photography, cinema, reporting, sport, shows, publicity, all these can serve as a support to mythical speech. Myth can be defined neither by its object nor by its material, for any material can be arbitrarily endowed with meaning."[11] As discussed in Chapter 5, Losev illustrates the wide variety of modes of mythical representation by using the Russian myth of the Blossoming Fern of St John's Eve.[12] For both Barthes and Losev, a myth is not a story but a form of representation distilled into an *image*, which is given a historically determined meaning or mode of signification.

However, although a myth does not have to be a story, every myth must have a story behind it. As Barthes states in his book *Mythologies*, "Mythical speech is made of a material which has *already* been worked on so as to make it suitable for communication."[13] This explains in theoretical terms the significance of Abu Talib al-Makki's construction of the trope of Rabi'a the Lover, Abu 'Abd al-Rahman al-Sulami's construction of the trope of Rabi'a the Sufi Woman, and Farid al-Din al-'Attar's construction of Rabi'a's *vita*. For Barthes, "metalanguage constitutes a kind of preserve for myth."[14] That is to say, each of these medieval writers "worked on" the material of the Rabi'a narratives and created new tropes and other forms of metalangauage in order to make the myth of Rabi'a al-'Adawiyya more suitable for communication. Each adaptation of Rabi'a's identity through these tropes sharpened her image for subsequent generations of readers, listeners and devotees. This process of narrative construction was made easier by the fact that there was little or no empirical information on Rabi'a to contradict the tropological image created by these representations. If, as Barthes says, "Myth deprives the object

---

10 Barthes, "Myth Today," in *Mythologies*, p. 109.
11 Ibid., p. 110.
12 See Losev, *The Dialectics of Myth*, pp. 101–2.
13 Barthes, "Myth Today," in *Mythologies*, p. 109; italics in the original.
14 Ibid., p. 144.

of which it speaks of all History," it is easier to create a myth out of tropes if there is little history to get in the way in the first place.[15]

When making up Rabiʻa's life story in *Tadhkirat al-awliya'* Farid al-Din al-ʻAttar realized that he did not need to be concerned with facts, except as they could be endowed with tropological significance. For ʻAttar, the spiritual and moral values associated with the character of Rabiʻa al-ʻAdawiyya were more important than the historical details of her life. The alleged "facts" of Rabiʻa's life story, as expressed through his narrative, were made to support the values he advocated. In Barthes' terminology, these narrative elements were "tokens for something else."[16] It is important to recall in this context how ʻAttar abandoned the use of the *isnad*, or chain of narrative transmission, that was so important for Sulami's chapter on Rabiʻa in his Book of Sufi Women. This was a sign that for ʻAttar the meaning of Rabiʻa al-ʻAdawiyya as a *magic name* (Losev) or as a *representative form* (Barthes) was more important than the historicity of her sayings and actions. At this level of representation, where "ideas-in-form" (Barthes) take precedence over content, or when a "pictorial emanation" (Losev) or *image* is created—we are no longer in the territory of history but of mythology.[17] Rabiʻa al-ʻAdawiyya has now become Rabiʻa the Icon.

For Barthes, myth is both a *semiology*—a metalanguage of forms and meanings—and an *ideology*—a metalanguage of ideas-in-form. It is a "second-order semiological system," constructed out of the relationship between present signs and prior significations.[18] In other words, despite the fact that (as Barthes says) history "evaporates" in myth, every myth is a product of history.[19] As such, it should be possible to study the narrative construction of myths historically, just as I have done with the myth of Rabiʻa al-ʻAdawiyya in this book.[20] Especially important for the historiography of myth is that the process of myth-making includes both the past and the future in a potentially

---

15   Ibid., p. 151.
16   Ibid., p. 111.
17   Ibid., p. 112. See also, Losev, *Dialectics of Myth*, p. 93.
18   Barthes, *Mythologies*, p. 114.
19   Ibid., p. 151.
20   In a recent article in *Journal of the American Academy of Religion*, Mary Dunn has suggested in a similar way that the study of narratives can provide a new approach to William James' notion of "radical empiricism" in the history of religions: ". . . a well-researched and carefully crafted narrative can work for the historian to evoke the rich texture of an extinct lifeworld. It is however, the historian's juxtaposition of a multiplicity of incommesurate narratives. . . that facilitates the dialectical encounter between scholar and subject and creates the epistemological conditions for attending to and accounting for abundant historical realities." Mary Dunn, "What Really Happened: Radical Empiricism

never-ending developmental chain: the constructed materials of past myths become the raw materials for a new mythological system that is fashioned dialectically out of the previous system.[21] Although Barthes does not discuss the historiography of myth in detail in *Mythologies*, he seems to suggest that this would involve the study of the "waves of amplification" of a myth, as it develops through successive rhetorical forms, "according to which the varied forms of the mythical signifier arrange themselves."[22] I have tried to follow his advice in this book and I hope that *Rabi'a from Narrative to Myth* helps point the way to similar mythical–historical studies of other iconic figures of Islam.

Barthes also asserts that myth plays a constant game of hide-and-seek between meaning and form.[23] When I first read this statement, I understood what he meant because as a child, whenever I thought of Rabi'a al-'Adawiyya, I could never picture myself sitting with her as a real person. Instead, she was a distillation of moral teachings, values and feelings. Her stories were important to me but for some reason I could never think of Rabi'a as embodied. For me, she represented a particular kind of wisdom rather than a human being. She was less a protagonist in her stories than a name attached to a concept. Barthes apparently felt the same way about myths. For him, the form of a myth is completely absorbed in the concept it represents: "What is invested in the concept is less reality than a certain knowledge of reality; in passing from the meaning to the form, the image loses some knowledge: the better to receive the knowledge in the concept."[24] Just as in my childhood attempts to envision Rabi'a, "the concept... appears in global fashion, it is a kind of nebula, the condensation, more or less hazy, of a certain knowledge. Its elements are linked by associative relations... its mode of presence is memorial."[25]

In writing Rabi'a's life as a semblance of her mythological legacy, 'Attar understood—as Barthes put it—that "myth is a *value*, truth is no guarantee for it; nothing prevents it from being a perpetual alibi: it is enough that its signifier has two sides for it always to have an 'elsewhere' at its disposal. The meaning is always there to *present* the form; the form is always there to

---

and the Historian of Religion," *Journal of the American Academy of Religion*, 84 (4), 2016, p. 895.
21 This contradicts Barthes' assertion that myth is not dialectical. See Barthes, *Mythologies*, p. 143.
22 Ibid., p. 150.
23 Ibid., p. 118.
24 Ibid., p. 119.
25 Ibid., p. 122.

outdistance the meaning. And there never is any contradiction, conflict, or split between the meaning and the form."[26]

Also like Barthes, 'Attar and his successors understood that myth as ideology is inherently conservative. Like the icon, myth *eternalizes* the world that it conserves, utilizing all of the tropes and other rhetorical devices of narrative that seem to fit—morality, spirituality, legal and philosophical ethics, aesthetics, entertainment.[27] These tropes and rhetorical devices are the building-blocks of the "principial" meaning of Rabi'a al-'Adawiyya that Jean Annestay and other traditionalist readers of her narratives find within them. Toward the end of the essay, "Myth Today," in *Mythologies*, Barthes states that another sign of the conservative nature of myths is that they "tend towards proverbs."[28] This, of course, is one of the most important aspects of the Rabi'a myth: today, apart from her movies, she is best known through her proverbs and aphorisms. For Barthes, proverbs, aphorisms and maxims are the tokens of a circular logic or a tautology. In the case of Rabi'a al-'Adawiyya, their existence tells us that from the very beginning of her narrative history, she has tended toward an essentialized type. That is to say—if Barthes is right—from the the very beginning, she has tended toward becoming a myth. To return one more time to the historiographical problem with which I began this book, this is to say that the most important history to be written about Rabi'a al-'Adawiyya is what I have attempted to write here—the story of the myth of Rabi'a as The Woman Who Never Dies.

---

26 Ibid., p. 123; italics in the original.
27 Ibid., pp. 148–9.
28 Ibid., p. 154.

Bibliography

I. SOURCES IN ARABIC AND PERSIAN

'Abd al-Raziq, Su'ad 'Ali, *Rabi'a al-'Adawiyya bayn al-ghina' wa al-buka'* (Cairo: The Anglo-Egyptian Book Shop, 1982)
'Abd al-Wahid, Mustafa, *Dirasat al-hubb fi-l-adab al-'arabi* (Cairo: Dar al-Ma'arif, 1972)
Amin, Ahmad, *Duha al-Islam* (Cairo: Egyptian National Book Organization, 1997 reprint of 1933 first edition)
'Attar, Shaykh Farid al-Din Nishapuri (d. 1220 CE), *Ilahi nama*, ed. Fu'ad Ruhani (Tehran: Intisharat Zawar, 1961)
———*Tadhkirat al-awliya'*, ed. Muhammad Isti'lami (Tehran: Intisharat Zawar, 2005 reprint of 1967 edition)
———*Tadhkirat al-awliya'*, ed. R.A. Nicholson (London and Leiden: Luzac & Co. and E.J. Brill, vol. 1, 1905)
Badawi, 'Abd al-Rahman, *Dirasat fi-l-falsafa al-wujudiyya* (Beirut: Dar al-Thaqafa, 1978 reprint of 1960 first edition)
———*Shahidat al-'ishq al-ilahi Rabi'a al-'Adawiyya* (Kuwait: Wakkalat al-Matbu'at, 1978 reprint of the 1960 revised edition)
———*Shakhsiyyat qaliqa fi al-Islam* (Cairo: Dar al-Nahda al-'Arabiyya, 1964 reprint of the 1946 first edition)
Al-Basra al-fayha': ta'rikh wa hadarat al-'arab, on the Iraqi website *'Ashiqat al-ward* (Lover of Roses). [Online]. (http://www.a3ashk.com/vb/showthread.php?t=529)
Dayf, Shawqi, *al-Ritha'* (Cairo: Dar al-Ma'arif, 1968)
Al-Dhahabi, Shams al-Din Muhammad ibn Ahmad b. 'Uthman (d. 1374 CE), *Siyar a'lam al-nubala'*, ed. Shu'ayb al-Arna'ut and Salih al-Sumr (Beirut: Mu'asasa al-Risala, 1996)
Gharib, Ma'mun, *Rabi'a al-'Adawiyya fi mihrab al-hubb al-ilahi* (Cairo: Dar Gharib li-l-Tiba'a wa al-Nashr wa al-Tawzi', 2000)
Al-Ghazali, Abu Hamid Muhammad (d. 1111 CE), *Ihya' 'ulum al-din* (Beirut: Dar al-Ma'rifa reprint, n.d.)
Al-Hawali, Safar ibn 'Abd al-Rahman, "Nubdha 'an Rabi'a al-'Adawiyya," *al-As'ila*. [Online]. (http://www.alhawali.com). (Accessed July 12, 2018)
Al-Hifni, 'Abd al-Mun'im, *al-'Abida al-khashi'a: Rabi'a al-'Adawiyya, imamat al-'ashiqin wa-l-mahzunin* (Cairo: Dar al-Irshad, 1991)

Al-Hurayfish, al-Shaykh ['Abdullah Shu'ayb ibn Sa'd] (d. 1398 CE), *al-Rawd al-fa'iq fi-l-mawa'iz wa-l-raqa'iq* (Cairo: Maktabat al-Jumhuriyya al-'Arabiyya, 1970)

Ibn 'Abd Rabbih, Abu 'Umar Ahmad ibn Muhammad al-Andalusi (d. 940 CE), *Kitab al-'iqd al-farid*, ed. Ibrahim al-Abyari (Beirut: Dar al-Kitab al-'Arabi, 1990)

Ibn Abi al-Dunya, Abu 'Abdullah Muhammad ibn 'Ubayd al-Baghdadi, *Kitab al-tahajjud wa qiyam al-layl*, ed. Mus'ad 'Abd al-Hamid Muhammad al-Sa'dani (Cairo: Maktabat al-Qur'an, n.d.)

——*Majmu'at rasa'il Ibn Abi al-Dunya*, ed. 'Abd al-Qadir 'Ata, 5 volumes (Beirut: Mu'assasat al-Kutub al-Thaqafiyya, 1993)

Ibn Abi Tahir Tayfur al-Khurasani, Ahmad (d. 893 CE) *Balaghat al-nisa'*, ed. Muhammad Tahir al-Zayn (Kuwait: Maktabat al-Sundus, 1993)

Ibn Dawud al-Isfahani, Abu Bakr Muhammad (d. 910 CE) *al-Nisf al-awwal min Kitab al-zahra*, ed. Louis Nichol Al Bouhaymi and Ibrahim 'Abd al-Fattah Tuqan (Beirut: Jesuit Printing House, 1932)

Ibn Hanbal, Ahmad (d. 855 CE), *Kitab al-Zuhd*, ed. 'Abd al-Rahman ibn Qasim (Beirut: Dar al-Kutub al-'Ilmiyya, 1976)

Ibn Hazm al-Andalusi (d. 1064 CE), *Tawq al-hamama fi-l-ulfa wa-l-alaf*, ed. Ihsan Abbas (Sousse, Tunisia: Dar al-Ma'arif li-l-Taba'a wa al-Nashr, reprint of 1980 first edition, n.d.)

Ibn 'Imran, Abu Mas'ud al-Mu'afa al-Mawsili (d. 801 CE), *Kitab al-zuhd*, ed. 'Amir Hasan Sabri (Beirut: Dar al-Bashir al-Islamiyya, 1999)

Ibn al-Jawzi, Abu al-Faraj 'Abd al-Rahman (d. 1201 CE), *Sifat al-safwa*, ed. Mahmud Fakhuri and Muhammad Rawwas Qal'anji (Beirut, 1986)

Ibn al-Junayd al-Khuttali al-Samarra'i, Abu Ishaq Ibrahim b. 'Abdullah, *al-Mahabba li-llah Subhanahu*, ed. 'Adil ibn 'Abd al-Shakur al-Zarqi (Riyadh: Dar al-Hadara li-l-Nashr wa-l-Tawzi', 2003)

Ibn Khallikan, Ahmad ibn Muhammad b. Abu Bakr (d. 1282 CE), *Wafayat al-a'yan wa anba' abna' al-zaman*, ed. Ihsan Abbas (Beirut: Dar Sadir, 1978)

Ibn al-Khatib, Lisan al-Din (d. 1374 CE), *Rawdat al-ta'rif bi-l-hubb al-sharif*, ed. 'Abd al-Qadir Ahmad 'Ata (Beirut: Dar al-Fikr al-'Arabi, n.d.)

Ibn al-Khatib al-Baghdadi, Abu Bakr Muhammad 'Ali (d. 1071 CE), *Tarikh Baghdad wa Madinat al-Salam*, ed. Mustafa 'Abd al-Qadir 'Ata (Beirut: Dar al-Kutub al-'Ilmiyya, 1997)

Ibn Manzur, Abu al-Fadl Jamal al-Din (d. 1321 CE), *Lisan al-'Arab* (Beirut: Dar al-Sadir, reprint of 1883 first edition, n.d.)

Ibn al-Mubarak, 'Abdullah al-Marwazi (d. 797 CE), *Kitab al-zuhd wa yalihi Kitab al-raqa'iq*, ed. Habib al-Rahman al-'Azmi (Beirut: Dar al-Kutub al-'Ilmiyya, n.d.)

Ibn al-Nadim, Abu al-Faraj Muhammad ibn Abi Ya'qub Ishaq al-Ma'ruf bi-l-Warraq (d. 995 or 998 CE), *Kitab al-Fihrist li-l-Nadim*, ed. Rida ibn 'Ali ibn Zayn al-'Abidin al-Ha'iri al-Mazandarani Tajaddud (Beirut: Dar al-Masira, 1988)

Ibn Qutayba, Abu Muhammad 'Abdullah al-Dinawari (d. 889–90 CE), *Kitab 'Uyun al-akhbar*, ed. Muhammad al-Iskandarani (Beirut: Dar al-Kitab al-'Arabi, 1999)

Ibn Sa'd, Muhammad (d. 845 CE), *al-Tabaqat al-kubra*, ed. Riyad 'Abdullah 'Abd al-Hadi (Beirut: Dar Ihya' al-Turath al-'Arabi, 1985)

Ibn Taymiyya, Taqi al-Din (d. 1328 CE), *Majmu'at al-rasa'il wa-l-masa'il*, ed. Muhammad 'Ali Baydawi (Beirut: Dar al-Kutub al-'Ilmiyya, 2000)

Al-Isfahani, Abu Nu'aym (d. 1038–9 CE), *Hilyat al-awliya' wa tabaqat al-asfiya'*, ed. Abu Hajr al-Sa'id ibn Basyuni Zaghlul (Beirut: reprint of 1938 edition, n.d.)

Al-Jabr, Muwaffaq Fawzi, *Diwan Rabi'a al-'Adawiyya wa akhbaruha* (Damascus: Dar Ma'd and Dar al-Namir, 1999)

Al-Jahiz, Abu 'Uthman 'Amr ibn Bahr (868 CE), *al-Bayan wa-l-tabyin*, ed. Ibrahim ibn Muhammad al-Daljamuni (Beirut: reprint of 1900 edition, n.d.)
———*Kitab al-hayawan*, ed. 'Abd al-Salam Muhammad Harun (Beirut: Ihya' al-Turath al-'Arabi, 1969 reprint of 1949 first edition)
Al-Kalabadhi, Abu Bakr Muhammad ibn Ishaq al-Bukhari (d. 990 CE), *Kitab al-ta'arruf li-madhhab ahl al-tasawwuf*, ed. A.J. Arberry (Cairo: Maktabat al-Khanji, 1994 reprint of the 1933 edition)
Khamis, Muhammad 'Atiyya, *Rabi'a al-'Adawiyya* (Cairo: Dar Karam, 1955)
Al-Khargushi, 'Abd al-Malik ibn Muhammad (d. 1016 CE), *Tahdhib al-Asrar*, ed. Bassam Muhammad Barud (Abu Dhabi: al-Majma' al-Thaqafi, 1999)
Al-Makki, Abu Talib Muhammad ibn 'Ali b. 'Atiyya (d. 996 CE), *Qut al-qulub fi mu'amalat al-Mahbub wa wasf tariq al-murid ila maqam al-tawhid*, ed. Basil 'Uyun al-Sadr (Beirut: Dar al-Kutub al-'Ilmiyya, 1997)
Al-Malati, Abu al-Husayn Muhammad ibn Ahmad (d. 987–88 CE), *Kitab al-tanbih wa-l-radd 'ala ahl al-ahwa' wa'l-bida'*, ed. Sven Dedering (Istanbul: Matba'at al-Dawla, 1926)
Malik ibn Anas (d. 795 CE), *Kitab al-muwatta'*, ed. Faruq Sa'd (Beirut: Dar al-Afaq al-Jadida, 1981)
Al-Mas'udi, Abu al-Husayn 'Ali ibn al-Husayn b. 'Ali (d. 956 CE), *Muruj al-dhahab wa ma'adin al-jawhar*, ed. Mufid Muhammad Qumayha (Beirut: Dar al-Kutub al-'Ilmiyya, 1985)
Al-Muhasibi, Abu 'Abdullah al-Harith ibn Asad (d. 857 CE), *al-Masa'il fi a'mal al-qulub wa-l-jawarih wa al-Makasib wa al-'Aql*, ed. 'Abd al-Qadir Ahmad 'Ata (Cairo: 'Alam al-Kutub, 1969)
———*al-Qasd wa-l-ruju' ila Allah*, ed. 'Abd al-Qadir Ahmad 'Ata (Cairo: Dar al-Turath al-'Arabi, 1980)
———*al-Ri'aya li-huquq Allah*, ed. 'Abd al-Qadir Ahmad 'Ata (Beirut: Dar al-Kutub al-'Ilmiyya, fourth printing, n.d.)
———*al-Rizq al-halal wa haqiqat al-tawakkul 'ala Allah*, ed. Muhammad 'Uthman al-Hasani (Cairo: Maktabat al-Qur'an, 1984)
———*al-Tawba*, ed. 'Abd al-Qadir Ahmad 'Ata (Cairo: Dar al-Islah, 1982)
Al-Munawi, Muhammad 'Abd al-Ra'uf (d. 1621 CE), *al-Kawakib al-durriyya fi tarajim al-sadat al-sufiyya* (Beirut: Dar al-Sadir, 1999)
Al-Nisaburi, al-Hasan ibn Muhammad ibn Habib (d. 1016 CE), *'Uqala' al-majanin*, ed. Muhammad Bahr al-'Ulum (Najaf, Iraq: al-Maktaba al-Haydariyya, 1968)
Nwyia, Paul, *Trois Ouevres inédites de mystiques musulmans, Šaqīq al-Balhī, Ibn 'Atā, Niffarī* (Beirut: Dar al-Machreq, 1972)
Pourjavady, Nasrollah, *Majmu'at Athar Abu 'Abd al-Rahman al-Sulami* (Tehran: Tehran University Publishing Center, 2000)
Al-Qadi 'Iyad, Abu al-Fadl ibn Musa al-Yahsubi (d. 1150 CE), *al-Shifa' bi-ta'rif huquq al-Mustafa* (Beirut: Dar al-Kutub al-'Ilmiyya, 1979)
Qasim, Mahmud, *Surat al-adyan fi-l-sinima al-Misriyya* (Cairo: Wizarat al-Thaqafa: al-Markaz al-Qawmi li-l-Sinima, 1997)
Qurra'a, Saniya, *'Arus al-zuhd: Rabi'a al-'Adawiyya* (Cairo: Maktab al-Sahafa al-Dawli, 1960)
Al-Qushayri, Abu al-Qasim 'Abd al-Karim ibn Hawazin (d. 1072 CE), *al-Risala al-Qushayriyya fi 'ilm al-tasawwuf*, ed. Ma'ruf Zurayq and 'Ali 'Abd al-Hamid Baltarji (Beirut: Dar al-Jil, 1990)
Al-Sakkakini, Widad, *al-'Ashiqa al-mutasawwifa, Rabi'a al-'Adawiyya* (Damascus: Dar Tlas li-l-dirasat wa al-tarjama wa al-nashr, 1989 reprint of the 1955 Cairo first edition)

Al-Sarraj, Abu Nasr 'Abdullah b. 'Ali al-Tusi (d. 988 CE), *The Kitab al-Luma' fi'l-Tasawwuf*, ed. Reynold Alleyne Nicholson (London: Luzac & Co. Ltd., 1963 reprint of 1914 first edition)

Al-Sarraj al-Qari', Abu Muhammad Ja'far ibn Ahmad b. al-Husayn (d. 1106 CE), *Masari' al-'ushshaq* (Beirut: Dar Sadir, n.d.)

Al-Sharqawi Mahmud, *Rabi'a al-'Adawiyya* (Cairo: Matbu'at Dar al-Sha'b, 1971)

As-Sulami, Abu 'Abd al-Rahman (d. 1021 CE), *Dhikr al-niswa al-muta'abbidat al-Sufiyyat*, ed. Mahmud Muhammad al-Tanahi (Cairo: Maktabat al-Khanji, 1993)

——*Jawami' adab al-sufiyya*, ed. Nasrollah Pourjavady (Tehran: Markaz Nashr Daneshgahi, 1991)

——*Tabaqat al-sufiyya*, ed. Nur al-Din Shurayba (Cairo: Maktabat al-Khanji, 1986)

Surur, Taha 'Abd al-Baqi, *Rabi'a al-'Adawiyya wa-l-hayat al-ruhiyya fi al-Islam* (Cairo: Dar al-Fikr al-'Arabi, 1957)

al-Suyuti, Jalal al-Din, *Nazm al-'iqyan fi a'yan al-a'yan*, ed. Philip Hitti (Beirut: al-Maktaba al-'Ilmiyya, 1927)

——*Tanbih al-Ghabi fi Takhti'at Ibn 'Arabi*, ed. 'Abd al-Rahman Hasan Mahmud (Cairo: Maktabat al-Adab, 1990)

Al-Thawri, Abu 'Abdullah Sufyan ibn Sa'id ibn Masruq al-Kufi (d. 778 CE), *Tafsir Sufyan al-Thawri*, ed. Imtiyaz 'Ali 'Arshi (Beirut: Dar al-Kutub al-'Ilmiyya, 1983 reprint of the 1965 edition)

Al-Zayn, Samih 'Atif, *Rabi'a al-'Adawiyya* (Beirut: al-Sharika al-'Alamiyya li-l-Kitab, Dar al-Kitab al-Lubnani, 1988)

II. SOURCES IN EUROPEAN LANGUAGES

Abbot, Nabia, *Aishah the Beloved of Mohammed* (London: Al Saqi Books, 1985 reprint of 1942 first edition)

——*Two Queens of Baghdad: Mother and Wife of Harun al-Rashid* (Chicago: University of Chicago Press, 1974 reprint of 1946 first edition)

Abbott, H. Porter, *The Cambridge Introduction to Narrative* (Cambridge, UK: Cambridge University Press, 2008)

Abd-Allah, Umar F., "Creativity, Innovation, and Heresy in Islam," in *Voices of Islam, Volume Five: Voices of Change*, ed. Vincent J. Cornell (General Editor), Omid Safi (Westport, CT and London: Praeger Publishers, 2007), pp. 1–22

Abrahamov, Binyamin, *Divine Love in Islamic Mysticism: The Teachings of Al-Ghazali and Al-Dabbagh* (London and New York: Routledge Curzon, 2003)

Abu-Zahra, Nadia, *The Pure and Powerful: Studies in Contemporary Muslim Society* (Reading, UK: Garnet Publishing and Ithaca Press, 1997)

Adamson, Peter and Pormann, Peter E., *The Philosophical Works of al-Kindi* (Karachi: Oxford University Press, 2012)

Ahmed, Leila, *Women and Gender in Islam* (New Haven and London: Yale University Press, 1992)

Ali, Samer M., *Arabic Literary Salons in the Islamic Middle Ages* (Notre Dame, IN: Notre Dame University Press, 2010)

Allen, Graham, *Intertextuality* (New York and London: Routledge, second edition, 2011)

Andrae, Tor, *In the Garden of Myrtles: Studies in Early Islamic Mysticism*, trans. Birgitta Sharpe, and Introduction by Eric Sharpe (Albany, NY: State University of New York Press, 1987)

Ankersmit, F.R., *Historical Representation* (Stanford, CA: Stanford University Press, 2001)

——— *Meaning, Truth, and Reference in Historical Representation* (Ithaca, NY: Cornell University Press, 2012)
Annestay, Jean, *Une Femme Soufie en Islam: Rabi'a al-'Adawiyya* (Paris: Éditions Entrelacs, 2009)
Asad, Muhammad, *The Message of the Qur'an* (Gibraltar: Dar al-Andalus, 1980)
Awn, Peter J., "Sufism," in *The Encyclopedia of Religion, Second Edition*, ed. Lindsay Jones and Charles J. Adams (Mircea Eliade) (Detroit: Macmillan Reference USA, 2005), 13:8809–8825
Barthes, Roland, *A Barthes Reader*, ed. Susan Sontag (New York: Hill & Wang, 1998)
——— *Mythologies*, trans. Annette Lavers (New York: Hill and Wang, 1972)
——— *New Critical Essays*, trans. Richard Howard (Evanston, IL: Northwestern University Press, 2009)
——— *The Rustle of Language*, trans. Richard Howard (New York: Hill and Wang, 1986)
Bashir, Shahzad, "Islamic Tradition and Celibacy," in *Celibacy and Religious Traditions*, ed. Carl Olson (New York: Oxford University Press, 2007), pp. 133–50
Beer, Frances, *Women and Mystical Experience in the Middle Ages* (Woodbridge, Suffolk, UK and Rochester, NY: Boydell Press, 1992)
Bell, Catherine, *Ritual Theory, Ritual Practice* (New York and Oxford: Oxford University Press, 1992)
Bell, Joseph Norment, *Love Theory in Later Hanbalite Islam* (Albany, NY: State University of New York Press, 1979)
Benghal, Jamal-Eddine, *La Vie de Rabi'a al-'Adawiyya, une sainte musulmane du VIIIème siècle* (Paris: Editions Iqra, 2000)
Berkey, Jonathan, *Popular Preaching and Religious Authority in the Medieval Islamic Near East* (Seattle: University of Washington Press, 2001)
Biblical Hebrew E-Magazine [Online]. (http://www.ancient-hebrew.org/emagazine/). Ancient Hebrew Research Center. (Accessed July 9, 2018)
Booth, Wayne, *The Company We Keep: An Ethics of Fiction* (Berkeley, CA: University of California Press, 1988)
Böwering, Gerhard, *The Mystical Vision of Existence in Classical Islam: The Qur'anic Hermeneutics of the Sufi Sahl At-Tustari (d. 283/896)* (Berlin and New York: Walter de Gruyter, 1980)
Bowers, Alfred W., *Mandan Social and Ceremonial Organization* (Lincoln, NE and London: University of Nebraska Press, 2004 reprint of 1950 University of Chicago Press first edition)
Boyle, John Andrew, *The Cambridge History of Iran* (Cambridge, UK: Cambridge University Press, 1968)
——— *The Ilahi-nama or Book of God of Farid al-Din 'Attar* (Manchester, UK: Manchester University Press, 1976)
Brock, Sebastian, *Syriac Perspectives on Late Antiquity* (London: Variorum Reprints, 1984)
——— and Harvey, Susan Ashbrook, *Holy Women of the Syrian Orient* (Berkeley, Los Angeles, and London: University of California Press, 1987)
Brown, Peter, *The Body and Society: Men, Women, and Sexual Renunciation in Early Christianity* (New York: Columbia University Press, 1988)
Butcher, S.H. (ed. and trans.), *The Poetics of Aristotle* (London: Macmillan & Co., 1902)
Bynum, Caroline Walker (ed.), *Fragmentation and Redemption: Essays on Gender and the Human Body in Medieval Religion* (New York: Zone Books, 1992)
Cixous, Hélène and Clément, Catherine, *The Newly Born Woman*, trans. Betsy Wing (Minneapolis and London: University of Minnesota Press, 1986)
Clark, Elizabeth A., *History, Theory, Text: Historians and the Linguistic Turn* (Cambridge, MA and London: Harvard University Press, 2004)

―――― *Reading Renunciation: Asceticism and Scripture in Early Christianity* (Princeton, NJ: Princeton University Press, 1999)

―――― "The Lady Vanishes: Dilemmas of a Feminist Historian after the 'Linguistic Turn,'" *Church History*, 67 (1), 1998, pp. 1–31

Coon, Lynda L., *Sacred Fictions: Holy Women and Hagiography in Late Antiquity* (Philadelphia: University of Pennsylvania Press, 1997)

Cooperson, Michael, *Classical Arabic Biography: The Heirs of the Prophet in the Age of al-Ma'mun* (Cambridge, UK: Cambridge University Press, 2000)

―――― "Ibn al-Muqaffa'," *Dictionary of Literary Biography Volume 311: Arabic Literary Culture, 500–925*, ed. Michael Cooperson and Shawkat M. Toorawa (Farmington Hills, MI: Thomson Gale, 2005), pp. 156–8

―――― "Probability, Plausibility, and Spiritual Communication in Classical Arabic Biography," in *On Fiction and Adab in Medieval Arabic Literature*, ed. Philip F. Kennedy (Weisbaden: Harrassowitz, 2005), pp. 69–84

Cornell, Rkia E., "Death and Burial in Islam," *Voices of Islam Vol. 3, Voices of Life: Family, Home, and Society*, ed. Vincent J. Cornell (General Editor) and Virginia Gray Henry-Blakemore (Westport, CT and London: Praeger Publishers, 2007), pp. 153–72

―――― "Rabi'ah al-'Adawiyyah (ca. 720–801)," in *Dictionary of Literary Biography Volume 311: Arabic Literary Culture, 500–925*, ed. Michael Cooperson and Shawkat M. Toorawa (Farmington Hills, MI: Thomson Gale, 2005), pp. 292–8

―――― "'Soul of A Woman Was Created Below': Woman as the Lower Soul (*Nafs*) in Islam," in *Probing the Depths of Evil and Good: Multireligious Views and Case Studies*, ed. Jerald D. Gort, Henry Jansen and Hendrik M. Vroom (Amsterdam and New York: Editions Rodopi, 2007), pp. 257–80

―――― "The Muslim Diotima? Traces of Plato's *Symposium* in Sufi Narratives of Rabi'a al-'Adawiyya," in *Religion and Philosophy in the Platonic and Neoplatonic Traditions: From Antiquity to the Early Medieval Period*, ed. Kevin Corrigan, John D. Turner and Peter Wakefield (Sankt Augustin, Germany: Akademie Verlag, 2012), pp. 235–56

Cornell, Vincent J., *Realm of the Saint: Power and Authority in Moroccan Sufism* (Austin, TX: University of Texas Press, 1998)

―――― *The Way of Abu Madyan, Doctrinal and Poetic Works of Abu Madyan Shu'ayb ibn al-Husayn al-Ansari (c. 509/1115–1—594/1198)* (Cambridge, UK: Islamic Texts Society, 1996)

Corrigan, Kevin and Glazov-Corrigan, Elena, *Plato's Dialectic at Play: Argument, Structure, and Myth in the Symposium* (University Park, PA: Pennsylvania State University Press, 2004)

Crone, Patricia, *The Nativist Prophets of Early Islamic Iran: Rural Revolt and Local Zoroastrianism* (Cambridge, UK: Cambridge University Press, 2014)

Al-Daylami, Abu'l-Hasan 'Ali b. Muhammad (d. ca. 1001–2 CE), *A Treatise on Mystical Love*, trans. Joseph Norment Bell and Hassan Mahmood Abdul Latif Al Shafie (Edinburgh, UK: Edinburgh University Press, 2005)

De Beauvoir, Simone, *The Second Sex*, trans. Constance Borde and Sheila Malovany-Chevallier (New York: Vintage Books, 2011)

De Bei, Marie-France, *Rabi'a entre Ciel et Sable* (Paris: Les Deux Oceans, 2005)

De Certeau, Michel, *The Writing of History*, trans. Tom Conley (New York: Columbia University Press, 1988)

Delooz, Pierre, *Sociologie et Canonisations* (Liège, Belgium: Université de Liège Faculté de Droit, 1969)

Diamond, Eliezer, *Holy Men and Hunger Artists: Fasting and Asceticism in Rabbinic Culture* (Oxford and New York: Oxford University Press, 2004)

Dodge, Bayard, *The Fihrist of al-Nadim: A Tenth-Century Survey of Muslim Culture* (New York: Columbia University Press, 1970)
Dols, Michael W., *Majnun: The Madman in Medieval Islamic Society*, ed. Diana E. Immisch (Oxford, UK: Clarendon Press of Oxford University Press, 1992)
Dundes, Alan, *Sacred Narrative: Readings in the Theory of Myth* (Berkeley, Los Angeles, and London: University of California Press, 1984)
Dunn, Mary, "What Really Happened: Radical Empiricism and the Historian of Religion," *Journal of the American Academy of Religion*, 84 (4), 2016, pp. 881–902
El Badawi, Emran, *The Qur'an and the Aramaic Gospel Traditions* (London: Routledge, 2013)
Eliade, Mircea, *Myth and Reality*, trans. Willard R. Trask (Long Grove, IL: Waveland Press, 1998)
——— *The Myth of the Eternal Return or, Cosmos and History*, trans. Willard R. Trask (Princeton, NJ: Princeton University Press, 1974)
——— *The Sacred and the Profane: The Nature of Religion*, trans. Willard R. Trask (San Diego, London, and New York: Harcourt, Brace, Jovanovich, 1987)
El Sakkakini, Widad, *First among Sufis: The Life and Thought of Rabia al-'Adawiyya the Woman Saint of Basra*, trans. Nabil Fatih Safwat (London: Octagon Press, 1982)
Elm, Susanna, *Virgins of God: The Making of Asceticism in Late Antiquity* (Oxford, UK: Clarendon Press, 1996)
Embree, Ainslee, *Alberuni's India*, trans. Edward C. Sachau (New York: W.W. Norton and Company, 1971)
Ernst, Carl W., *The Shambhala Guide to Sufism* (Boston and London: Shambhala Books, 1997)
——— *Words of Ecstasy in Sufism* (Albany, NY: State University of New York Press, 1985)
Al-Farabi, Abu Nasr (d. 950 CE), *On the Perfect State (Mabadi' ara' ahl al-madinah al-fadilah)*, ed. Richard Walzer (Chicago: Kazi Publications, 1998 reprint of 1985 Oxford University Press original)
Felek, Özgen and Knysh, Alexander D. (eds.), *Dreams and Vision in Islamic Societies* (Albany, NY: State University of New York Press, 2012)
Fierro, Maribel, "Women as Prophets in Islam," *Writing the Feminine: Women in Arab Sources*, ed. Manuela Marin and Randi Deguilhem (London and New York: I.B. Tauris, 2002), pp. 183–98
Fisher, Walter R., *Human Communication as Narration: Toward a Philosophy of Reason, Value, and Action* (Columbia, SC: University of South Carolina Press, 1989)
Flaubert, Gustave, *Madame Bovary*, trans. Geoffrey Wall (London: Penguin Books, 2003)
Flood, Gavin, *The Ascetic Self: Subjectivity, Memory, and Tradition* (Cambridge, UK: Cambridge University Press, 2004)
Foucault, Michel, *The Archaeology of Knowledge and the Discourse on Language*, trans. A.M. Sheridan-Smith (New York: Pantheon Books, 1972)
Fowden, Garth, *Before and after Muhammad: The First Millennium Refocused* (Princeton and Oxford: Princeton University Press, 2014)
——— *Empire to Commonwealth: Consequences of Monotheism in Late Antiquity* (Princeton, NJ: Princeton University Press, 1993)
France, Anatole, *Thaïs*, trans. Robert B. Douglas (Rockville, MD.: Wildside Press, 2005)
Francis, James A., *Subversive Virtue: Asceticism and Authority in the Second-Century Pagan World* (University Park, PA: Pennsylvania State University Press, 1995)
Fromherz, Allen, "Tribalism, Tribal Feuds, and the Social Status of Women," in *Gulf Women*, ed. Amira El Azhary Sonbol (Doha, Qatar: Bloomsbury Qatar Foundation Publishing, 2012), pp. 48–68

Geary, James, *The World in a Phrase: A Brief History of the Aphorism* (New York and London: Bloomsbury Publishing, 2005)

Genette, Gérard, *Palimpsests: Literature in the Second Degree*, trans. Channa Newman and Claude Doubinsky (Lincoln, NE and London: University of Nebraska Press, 1997)

Al-Ghazali, Abu Hamid (d. 1111 CE), *Love, Longing, Intimacy, and Contentment: (Kitab al-mahabba wa'l-shawq wa-l-uns wa'l-rida), Book XXXVI of The Revival of the Religious Sciences (Ihya' 'ulum al-din)*, trans. Eric Ormsby (Cambridge, UK: Islamic Texts Society, 2011)

Gilman, Carolyn, *Lewis and Clark: Across the Divide* (Washington, DC and London: Smithsonian Books, 2003)

The Gospel of Thomas, trans. Thomas O. Lambdin, in *The Nag Hammadi Library in English*, General Editor James M. Robinson (San Francisco: Harper and Row, 1981)

Green, Nile, *Sufism, A Global History* (Malden, MA and Oxford, UK: Wiley-Blackwell, 2012)

——"The Religious and Cultural Role of Dreams and Visions in Islam," *Journal of the Royal Asiatic Society*, 13 (3), 2003, pp. 287–313

Grote, George, *Plato and the Other Companions of Sokrates* (London: John Murray, 1888)

Guillaume, Arnold, *The Life of Muhammad: A Translation of Ibn Ishaq's Sirat Rasul Allah* (Lahore, Pakistan: Oxford University Press, 1970 reprint of 1955 first edition)

Gutas, Dimitri, *Greek Philosophers in the Arabic Tradition* (Aldershot, Hampshire, UK and Burlington, VT: Ashgate-Variorum, 2000)

Gwynne, Rosalind Ward, *Logic, Rhetoric, and Legal Reasoning in the Qur'an; God's Arguments* (London and New York: Routledge Curzon, 2004)

Hadot, Pierre, *Philosophy as a Way of Life*, ed. Arnold L. Davidson, trans. Michael Chase (Oxford, UK and Malden, MA: Blackwell Publishers, 1995)

——*Plotinus or the Simplicity of Vision*, trans. Michael Chase with Introduction by Arnold I. Davidson (Chicago and London: University of Chicago Press, 1993)

Hafsi, Ibrahim, "Recherches sur le genre 'Tabaqat' dans la litérature arabe," *Arabica*, xxiii, 1976, pp. 228–65; xxiv, 1977, pp. 1–41, 150–86

Haider, Najam, *The Origins of the Shi'a: Identity, Ritual, and Sacred Space in Eighth-Century Kufa* (Cambridge, UK: Cambridge University Press, 2011)

Hakki, Yahya, *The Lamp of Umm Hashim and Other Stories*, trans. Denys Johnson-Davies (Cairo and New York: American University in Cairo Press, 2006)

Halman, Hugh Talat, *Where the Two Seas Meet: The Qur'anic Story of al-Khidr and Moses in Sufi Commentaries as a Model of Spiritual Guidance* (Louisville, KY: Fons Vitae, 2013)

Halperin, David M., *One Hundred Years of Homosexuality and Other Essays on Greek Love* (New York and London: Routledge, 1990)

Halverson, Jeffry R., Goodall, H.L., Jr, and Corman, Steven R., *Master Narratives of Islamist Extremism* (New York: Palgrave Macmillan, 2011)

Hammond, Marlé, *Beyond Elegy: Classical Arabic Women's Poetry in Context* (Oxford: British Academy and Oxford University Press, 2010)

Harpham, Geoffrey Galt, *The Ascetic Imperative in Culture and Criticism* (Chicago and London: University of Chicago Press, 1987)

Heffernan, Thomas J., *Sacred Biography: Saints and Their Biographers in the Middle Ages* (New York and Oxford, UK: Oxford University Press, 1988)

Hermansen, Marcia, "The Female Hero in the Islamic Religious Tradition," in *The Annual Review of Women in World Religions*, ed. Arvind Sharma and Katherine K. Young (Albany, NY: State University of New York Press, 1992), pp. 111–43

Hervieu-Léger, D., *Religion as a Chain of Memory*, trans. Simon Lee (New Brunswick, NJ: Rutgers University Press, 2000)

Hitti, Philip K., *History of the Arabs from the Earliest Times to the Present* (London: Macmillan Press, 1970 reprint of 1937 first edition)
Hodgson, Marshall G.S., *The Venture of Islam: Conscience and History in a World Civilization* (Chicago and London: University of Chicago Press, 1977), 3 volumes
Hollywood, Amy, *The Soul as Virgin Wife: Mechthild of Magdeburg, Marguerite Porete, and Meister Eckhart* (Notre Dame, IN and London: University of Notre Dame Press, 1995)
Honerkamp, Kenneth Lee, "Sufi Foundations of the Ethics of Social Life in Islam," in *Voices of Islam, Volume Three, Voices of Life: Family, Home, and Society*, ed. Vincent J. Cornell (General Editor) and Virginia Gray Henry-Blakemore (Westport, CT and London: Praeger Publishers, 2007), pp. 181–96
Hourani, Albert, *A History of the Arab Peoples* (Cambridge, MA: Belknap Press of Harvard University Press, 1991)
Al-Hujwiri, 'Ali B. 'Uthman al-Jullabi (d. 1071 CE), *The Kashf al-Mahjub, the Oldest Persian Treatise on Sufiism*, trans. Reynold A. Nicholson (London: Luzac and Company, 1976 reprint of 1911 first edition)
Humphreys, R. Stephen, *Islamic History, a Framework for Inquiry* (Princeton, NJ: Princeton University Press, 1991)
Hunt, Hannah, *Joy-Bearing Grief: Tears of Contrition in the Writings of the Early Syrian and Byzantine Fathers* (Leiden and Boston: E.J. Brill, 2004)
Ibn 'Arabi, Muhyiddin Muhammad (d. 1240 CE), *La Vie merveilleuse de Dhu-l-Nun l'Égyptien*, trans. Roger Deladrière (Paris: Éditions Sindbad, 1988)
Ibrahim, Ezzeddin and Johnson-Davies, Denys (trans.), *Forty Hadith Qudsi* (Cambridge: Islamic Texts Society, 1999)
Ibrahim, Mahmood, *Merchant Capital and Islam* (Austin, TX: University of Texas Press, 1990)
Isaac, St of Nineveh, *On Ascetical Life*, trans. Mary Hansbury (Crestwood, NY: St Vladimir's Monastery Press, 1989)
Izutsu, Toshihiko, *God and Man in the Koran: Semantics of the Koranic Weltanschauung* (Salem, NH: Ayer Company, 1987)
Jones, F. Stanley (ed.), *Which Mary? The Marys of Early Christian Tradition* (Atlanta, GA: Society of Biblical Literature, 2002)
Judd, Steven C., "Competitive Hagiography in the Biographies of al-Awza'i and Sufyan al-Thawri," *Journal of the American Oriental Society*, 122 (1), 2002, pp. 25–37
Kabbani, Shaykh Muhammad Hisham, *Classical Islam and the Naqshbandi Sufi Tradition* (Washington, DC, Islamic Supreme Council of America, 2004)
Karamustafa, Ahmet T., *Sufism: The Formative Period* (Edinburgh, UK: Edinburgh University Press, 2007)
Kemal, Salim, "Arabic Poetics and Aristotle's Poetics," *British Journal of Aesthetics*, 26 (2), 1986, pp. 112–23
Kermani, Navid, *The Terror of God: Attar, Job, and the Metaphysical Revolt* (Cambridge, UK: Polity Press, 2011)
Khalidi, Tarif, *Arabic Historical Thought in the Classical Period* (Cambridge, UK: Cambridge University Press, 1994)
Khalil, Atif, "Abu Talib al-Makki and *The Nourishment of Hearts* (*Qut al-Qulub*) in the Context of Early Sufism," *The Muslim World*, 102 (2), 2011, pp. 335–56
——— "*Tawba* in the Sufi Psychology of Abu Talib al-Makki (d. 996)," *Journal of Islamic Studies*, 23 (3), 2002, pp. 294–324
Kieckhefer, Richard, *Unquiet Souls: Fourteenth-Century Saints and Their Religious Milieu* (Chicago and London: University of Chicago Press, 1984)
Kilito, Abdelfattah, *The Author and His Doubles: Essays on Classical Arabic Culture*, trans. Michael Cooperson (Syracuse, NY: Syracuse University Press, 2001)

Kinberg, Leah, *Morality in the Guise of Dreams: A Critical Edition of* Kitab al-manam *by Ibn Abi al-Dunya* (Leiden: E.J. Brill, 1994)
Kingsley, Peter, *Reality* (Inverness, CA: Golden Sufi Center, 2003)
Kleinberg, Aviad M., *Prophets in Their own Country: Living Saints and the Making of Sainthood in the Later Middle Ages* (Chicago and London: University of Chicago Press, 1997)
Knysh, Alexander, *Islamic Mysticism: A Short History* (Leiden and Boston, MA: E.J. Brill, 2000)
Kubba, Sam, *The Iraqi Marshlands and the Marsh Arabs: The Ma'dan, Their Culture and the Environment* (Reading, UK: Ithaca Press, 2010)
Lane, E.W., *Arabic–English Lexicon* (Cambridge, UK: Islamic Texts Society, 1984 reprint of 1863 first edition)
Lassner, Jacob, *The Shaping of 'Abbasid Rule* (Princeton, NJ: Princeton University Press, 1980)
Lewisohn, Leonard (ed.), *Classical Persian Sufism: From its Origins to Rumi* (London and New York: Khaniqahi Nimatullahi Publications, 1993)
Lincoln, Bruce, *Theorizing Myth: Narrative, Ideology, and Scholarship* (Chicago: University of Chicago Press, 1999)
Lombard, Maurice, *The Golden Age of Islam*, trans. Joan Spencer (Princeton, NJ: Markus Wiener Publishers, 2004)
Losev, Aleksei Fyodorovich, *The Dialectics of Myth*, trans. Vladimir Marchenkov (London and New York: Routledge, 2003)
Louÿs, Pierre, *Les Chansons de Bilitis* (Paris: Nabu Press, 2010)
——— *The Songs of Bilitis*, trans. Alvah C. Bessie (Mineola, NY: Dover Publications, 2010 reprint of the 1926 edition)
Mahmud, 'Abd al-Halim, *Al-Muhasibi: Un Mystique Musulman Religieux et Moraliste* (Paris: Librairie Orientaliste Paul Geuthner, 1940)
Maquet, Jacques, "The World/Nonworld Dichotomy," in *The Realm of the Extra-Human, Volume 2, Ideas and Actions*, ed. Agehananda Bharati (The Hague: Mouton, 1976), pp. 55–68
Marin, Manuela, "Abû Sa'îd Ibn al-A'râbî et le développement du soufisme en al-Andalus," *Revue du monde musulmane et de la Mediterranée: Minorités religieuses dans l'Espagne médiévale*, 63/64, 1992, pp. 28–38
Martin, Dale B., *Slavery as Salvation: The Metaphor of Slavery in Pauline Christianity* (New Haven, CT and London: Yale University Press, 1990)
——— and Miller, Patricia Cox, *The Cultural Turn in Late Ancient Studies: Gender, Asceticism, and Historiography* (Durham, NC and London: Duke University Press, 2005)
Massignon, Louis, *Essay on the Origins of the Technical Language of Islamic Mysticism*, trans. Benjamin Clark (Notre Dame, IN: Notre Dame University Press, 1997)
McGuckin, John Anthony, *The Book of Mystical Chapters: Meditations on the Soul's Ascent, from the Desert Fathers and other Early Christian Contemplatives* (Boston, MA and London: Shambhala Books, 2003)
Melchert, Christopher, "Basran Origins of Classical Sufism," *Der Islam*, 82, 2006, pp. 221–40
———"Exaggerated Fear in the Early Islamic Renunciant Tradition," *Journal for the Royal Asiatic Society*, 21 (3), 2011, pp. 283–300
———"Origins and Early Sufism," in *The Cambridge Companion to Sufism*, ed. Lloyd Ridgeon (Cambridge, UK: Cambridge University Press, 2014), pp. 3–23
Mojaddedi, Jawid, *The Biographical Tradition in Sufism: The* Tabaqat *Genre from Sulami to Jami* (Richmond, Surrey: Routledge Curzon, 2001)

Montgomery, James E., "Al-Jahiz," in *Dictionary of Literary Biography, Volume 311: Arabic Literary Culture, 500–925*, ed. Michael Cooperson and Shawkat M. Toorawa (Farmington Hills, MI: Thomson Gale, 2005), pp. 231–42
——"Al-Jahiz's *Kitab al-Bayan wa al-Tabyin*," in *Writing and Representation in Medieval Islam: Muslim Horizons*, ed. Julian Bray (London and New York: Routledge, 2006), pp. 91–152
Mooney, Catherine M. (ed.), *Gendered Voices: Medieval Saints and Their Interpreters* (Philadelphia: University of Pennsylvania Press, 1999)
Morony, Michael G., *Iraq after the Muslim Conquest* (Princeton, NJ: Princeton University Press, 1984)
Motzki, Harald, "Dating Muslim Traditions: A Survey," *Arabica*, 52, 2005, pp. 204–53
Mourad, Suleiman Ali, *Early Islam Between Myth and History: Al-Hasan al-Basri (d. 110H/ 728CE) and the Formation of His Legacy in Classical Islamic Scholarship* (Leiden and Boston: E.J. Brill, 2006)
Mueller, Gert H., "Asceticism and Mysticism: A Contribution Towards the Sociology of Faith," in *International Yearbook for the Sociology of Religion 8: Sociological Theories of Religion/Religion and Language*, ed. Günter Dux, Thomas Luckman and Joachim Matthes (Opladen: Westdeutscher Verlag, 1973), pp. 68–132
Muslim ibn al-Hajjaj al-Nisaburi (d. 875 CE), *Sahih Muslim*, trans. 'Abdul Hamid Siddiqi (New Delhi: Kitab Bhavan, 1978), 4 volumes
Nicholson, Reynold A., *A Literary History of the Arabs* (Cambridge, UK: Cambridge University Press, 1969 reprint of 1914 first edition)
——*The Mathnawi of Jalaluddin Rumi* (London: Luzac & Co., 1977 reprint of 1926 first edition), 3 volumes
Nietzsche, Friedrich, *The Genealogy of Morals*, trans. Horace B. Samuel (New York: Boni and Liveright, 1918)
Ogén, Göran, "Did the Term '*ṣūfī*' Exist before the Sufis?," *Acta Orientalia*, 43, 1983, pp. 33–48
Orr, Mary, *Intertextuality: Debates and Contexts* (Malden, MA and Cambridge, UK: Polity Press, 2003)
Oudaimah, Mohammed and Pfister, Gérard, *Rabi'a: Les Chants de la Recluse* (Mesnil-sur-l'Estrée, France: Éditions Arfuyen, 2006)
Ouyang, Wen-chin, *Literary Criticism in Medieval Arabic-Islamic Culture: The Making of A Tradition* (Edinburgh: Edinburgh University Press, 1997)
Parens, Joshua, *An Islamic Philosophy of Virtuous Religions: Introducing Alfarabi* (Albany, NY: State University of New York Press, 2006)
Patton, Kimberley Christine and Hawley, John Stratton (eds), *Holy Tears: Weeping in the Religious Imagination* (Princeton, NJ and Oxford, UK: Princeton University Press, 2005)
Pellat, Charles, "Djahiz," in *The Encyclopedia of Islam (Second Edition)*, vol. 2, pp. 385–7
——*Le Milieu Basrien et la formation de Gahiz* (Paris: Librarie d'Amérique et d'Orient Adrien-Maisonneuve, 1953)
——*The Life and Works of Jahiz*, trans. D.M. Hawke (London: Routledge and Kegan Paul, and Berkeley: University of California Press, 1969)
Peters, Virginia Bergman, *Women of the Earth Lodges: Tribal Life on the Plains* (Norman, OK: University of Oklahoma Press, 2000)
Picken, Gavin, *Spiritual Purification in Islam: The Life and Works of al-Muhasibi* (London and New York: Routledge, 2011)
Pitschke, Christoph, *Skrupulöse Frömmigkeit im frühen Islam: das "Buch der Gewissenfrömmigkeit"* (Kitab al-Wara') *von Ahmad b. Hanbal: annotierte Übersetzung und thematische Analyse* (Weisbaden: Otto Harassowitz, 2010)

Plato, *The Dialogues of Plato in Four Volumes*, ed. and trans. B. Jowett (Boston and New York: Jefferson Press, 1871)
——— *The Republic*, trans. Desmond Lee (London: Penguin Group, 1955)
Potter, Jonathan, *Representing Reality: Discourse, Rhetoric, and Social Construction* (London: Sage Publications, 2012)
Radtke, Bernd (ed.), *Materialien zur alten islamischen Frömmigkeit* (Leiden: E.J. Brill, 2009)
———"Von den hinderlichen Wirkungen der Extase und dem Wesen der Ignoranz," in *Neue kritische Gägne. Zu Stand und Aufgaben der Sufikforschung (New Critical Essays: On the Present State and Future Tasks of the Study of Sufism)* (Utrecht: M. Thn. Houstma Sichting, 2005), pp. 251–92
Ramadan, Salim, *Cinema Tripoli* [Online]. (http://cinematripoli.blogspot.com). (Accessed July 12, 2018)
Reid, Megan R., *Law and Piety in Medieval Islam* (Cambridge, UK: Cambridge University Press, 2013)
Reinhart, Benedikt, *Die Lehre vom Tawakkul in der klassischen Sufik*, Studien sur Sprache, Geschichte und Kultur des islamischen Orients 3 (Berlin: W. de Gruyter, 1968)
Renard, John, *Knowledge of God in Classical Sufism: Foundations of Islamic Mystical Theology* (New York and Mahwah, NJ: Paulist Press, 2004)
———*Windows on the House of Islam: Muslim Sources on Spirituality and Religious Life* (Berkeley, Los Angeles, and London: University of California Press, 1998)
Ricoeur, Paul, *Time and Narrative*, trans. Kathleen McLaughlin and David Pellauer (Chicago: University of Chicago Press, 1984)
Ridgeon, Lloyd, *Moral and Mysticism in Persian Sufism: A History of Sufi Futuwwat in Iran* (London: Routledge, 2010)
——— (ed.), *The Cambridge Companion to Sufism* (Cambridge, UK: Cambridge University Press, 2014)
Rigolio, Alberto, "Aristotle's Poetics in Syriac and Arabic Translations: Readings of 'Tragedy,'" in *Khristianskii Vostok 6* (Moscow: Russian Academy of Sciences, 2013), pp. 140–9
Rippin, Andrew (ed.), *The Qur'an: Formative Interpretation* (Aldershot, UK: Ashgate Publishing and Variorum, 1999)
Rist, John M. (ed.), *The Stoics* (Berkeley and Los Angeles: University of California Press, 1978)
Ritter, Helmut, *The Ocean of the Soul: Men, the World, and God in the Stories of Farid al-Din 'Attar*, trans. John O'Kane and Bernd Radtke (Leiden and Boston, MA: Brill, 2013)
Roberts, Nancy N., "Voice and Gender in Classical Arabic *Adab*: Three Passages from Ibn Abī Ṭayfūr's 'Instances of the Eloquence of Women,'" *Al- 'Arabiyya*, 25, 1992, pp. 51–72
Roded, Ruth, *Women in Islamic Biographical Collections: From Ibn Sa'd to Who's Who* (Boulder, CO and London: Lynne Rienner Publishers, 1994)
Rosenthal, Franz, *A History of Muslim Historiography* (Leiden: E.J. Brill, 1968)
———"Ibn Abi Tahir Tayfur," in *The Encyclopedia of Islam (Second Edition)*, vol. 3, pp. 692–3
Ruprecht, Louis A., Jr, *Symposia: Plato, the Erotic, and Moral Value* (Albany, NY: State University of New York Press, 1999)
Sanders, Julie, *Adaptation and Appropriation* (London and New York: Routledge, 2006)

Sayeed, Asma, *Women and the Transmission of Religious Knowledge in Islam* (Cambridge, UK: Cambridge University Press, 2013)

Schimmel, Annemarie, *Mystical Dimensions of Islam* (Chapel Hill, NC: University of North Carolina Press, 1986 reprint of 1975 first edition)

Schleiffer, Aliah, *Mary the Blessed Virgin of Islam* (Louisville, KY: Fons Vitae, 1998)

Schoeler, Gregor, *The Written and the Oral in Early Islam*, ed. James E. Montgomery, trans. Uwe Vagelpohl (London: Routledge, 2006)

Segal, Robert A., *Myth: A Very Short Introduction* (Oxford, UK: Oxford University Press, 2004)

——*Theorizing about Myth* (Amherst, MA: University of Massachusetts Press, 1999)

Sells, Michael A., *Early Islamic Mysticism: Sufi, Qur'an, Mi'raj, Poetic, and Theological Writings* (Mahwah, NY: The Paulist Press, 1996)

Sheikh, Saʿdiyya, "In Search of *al-Insan*: Sufism, Islamic Law, and Gender," *Journal of the American Academy of Religion*, 77 (4), 2009, pp. 781–822

——*Sufi Narratives of Intimacy: Ibn 'Arabi, Gender, and Sexuality* (Chapel Hill, NC: University of North Carolina Press, 2012)

Sirry, Munʿim, "Pious Muslims in the Making: A Closer Look at Narratives of Ascetic Conversion," *Arabica*, 57 (4), 2010, pp. 437–54

Sizgorich, Thomas, *Violence and Belief in Late Antiquity: Militant Devotion in Christianity and Islam* (Philadelphia: University of Pennsylvania Press, 2009)

Smith, Jonathan Z., *To Take Place: Toward Theory in Ritual* (Chicago: University of Chicago Press, 1987)

Smith, Margaret, *An Early Mystic of Baghdad: A Study of the Life and Teaching of Harith B. Asad al-Muhasibi, A.D. 781–857* (London: Sheldon Press, 1977 reprint of 1935 first edition)

——*Rabi'a: the Life and Work of Rabi'a and Other Women Mystics in Islam* (Oxford, UK: Oneworld Publications, 1994)

——*Rabi'a the Mystic A.D. 717–801 and Her Fellow Saints in Islam, Being the Life and Teachings of Rabi'a al-'Adawiyya al-Qaysiyya of Basra, Sufi Saint ca. A.H. 99–185, A.D. 717–801, Together with Some Account of the Place of Women in Islam* (Cambridge, UK: Cambridge University Press, 1928)

——*Rabi'a the Mystic A.D. 717–801 and Her Fellow Saints in Islam, Being the Life and Teachings of Rabi'a al-'Adawiyya al-Qaysiyya of Basra, Sufi Saint ca. A.H. 99–185, A.D. 717–801, Together with Some Account of the Place of Women in Islam* (San Francisco: The Rainbow Bridge, 1977)

——*Studies in Early Mysticism in the Near and Middle East* (Whitefish, MT.: Kessinger Publishing Company, reprint of 1931 first edition, n.d.)

Sobieroj, Florian, *Ibn Ḥafīf aš-Šīrāzī und seine Schrift zur Novizenerziehung (Kitāb al-Iqtiṣād): biographische Studien, Edition, und Übersetzung* (Stuttgart: Franz Steiner Verlag, 1998)

Sonbol, Amira El Azhary (ed.), *Gulf Women* (Doha, Qatar: Bloomsbury Qatar Foundation Publishing, 2012)

Spellberg, Denise A., *Politics, Gender, and the Islamic Past: The Legacy of 'A'isha Bint Abi Bakr* (New York: Columbia University Press, 1994)

Stowasser, Barbara Freyer, "Women and Politics in Late Jahili and Early Islamic Arabia: Reading Behind Patriarchal History," in *Gulf Women*, ed. Amira El Azhary Sonbol (Doha, Qatar: Bloomsbury Qatar Foundation Publishing, 2012), pp. 69–103

Strong's Concordance with Hebrew and Greek Lexicon. [Online]. (http://www.eliyah.com/lexicon.html). (Accessed July 12, 2018)

As-Sulami, Abu 'Abd al-Rahman (d. 1021 CE), *Early Sufi Women*: Dhikr an-niswa al-muta'abbidat as-sufiyyat, ed. and trans. Rkia E. Cornell (Louisville, KY: Fons Vitae, 1999)

——— *The Book of Sufi Chivalry: Lessons to a Son of the Moment*, trans. Futuwwah, Sheikh Tosun Bayrak al-Jerrahi al-Halveti (New York: Inner Traditions International, 1983)

Sullivan, Kevin P., "Sexuality and Gender of Angels," in *Paradise Now: Essays on Early Jewish and Christian Mysticism*, ed. April D. DeConick (Atlanta: Society for Biblical Literature, 2006), pp. 211–28

Sviri, Sara, "The Early Mystical Schools of Baghdad and Nishapur: In Search of Ibn Munazil," *Jerusalem Studies in Arabic and Islam*, 30, 2005, pp. 450–82

Thesiger, Wilfred, *The Marsh Arabs* (London: Penguin Group, 2008)

Toorawa, Shawkat, "Ibn Abi Tahir Tayfur," in *Dictionary of Literary Biography Volume 311: Arabic Literary Culture, 500–925*, ed. Michael Cooperson and Shawkat M. Toorawa (Farmington Hills, MI: Thomson Gale, 2005), pp. 141–9

Trimingham, J. Spencer, *The Sufi Orders in Islam* (New York and London: Oxford University Press, 1998 reprint of 1971 original)

Tucker, William F., *Mahdis and Millenarians: Shi'ite Extremists in Early Muslim Iraq* (Cambridge, UK: Cambridge University Press, 2008)

Upton, Charles, *Doorkeeper of the Heart: Versions of Rabi'a* (New York: Pir Press, 2003)

Valentasis, Richard, *The Making of the Self: Ancient and Modern Asceticism* (Eugene, OR: Cascade Books, 2008)

Van Ess, Josef, *Die Gedankenwelt des Harith al-Muhasibi* (Bonn: Selbstverlag des Orientalischen Seminars des Universität Bonn, 1961)

Van Gelder, G.J.H., "Rabi'a's Poem of the Two Kinds of Love: A Mystification?" in *Verse and the Fair Sex: A Collection of Papers Presented at the 15th Congress of the UAEI*, ed. Frederick de Jong (Utrecht, The Netherlands: 1993), pp. 66–76

Vansina, Jan, *Oral Tradition as History* (London and Nairobi, Kenya: James Curry and Heinemann Kenya, 1985)

Voobus, Arthur, *History of Asceticism in the Syrian Orient* (Louvain, Belgium: Catholic University of America and Catholic University of Louvain, 1958)

Vroom, Hendrik M., "Religious Truth: Seeing Things As They Really Are, Experience, Insight, and Religious Stories," in *The Question of Theological Truth: Philosophical and Interreligious Perspectives*, ed. Frederiek Depoortere and Magdalen Lambkin (Amsterdam and New York: Rodopi Press, 2012), pp. 115–35

Ward, Benedicta, *Harlots of the Desert: A Study of Repentance in Early Monastic Sources* (Kalamazoo, MI: Cistercian Publications, 1987)

——— *The Sayings of the Desert Fathers* (Kalamazoo, MI and Oxford, UK: Cistercian Publications and A.R. Mowbray, 1984)

Ware, Kallistos, *The Orthodox Way* (Oxford, UK: Oxford University Press, 1979)

Watt, William Montgomery, *The Formative Period of Islamic Thought* (Oxford: Oneworld Publications, 2002). (This is a revised version of idem, *Free Will and Predestination in Early Islam* (1949).)

Weber, Max, *The Protestant Ethic and the Spirit of Capitalism*, trans. Talcott Parsons (London and New York: Routledge & Co., 1996)

White, Hayden, *The Content of the Form: Narrative Discourse and Historical Representation* (Baltimore, MD.: Johns Hopkins University Press, 1987)

——— *Tropics of Discourse: Essays in Cultural Criticism* (Baltimore and London: Johns Hopkins University Press, 1978)

Williams, Caroline, *Islamic Monuments in Cairo, A Practical Guide* (Cairo: American University in Cairo Press, 1993)
Wimbush, Vincent L. and Valentasis, Richard (eds), *Asceticism* (Oxford, UK and New York: Oxford University Press, 1998)
Wolterstorff, Nicholas, *John Locke and the Ethics of Belief* (Cambridge, UK: Cambridge University Press, 1996)
Yazaki, Saeko, *Islamic Mysticism and Abu Talib al-Makki: The Role of the Heart* (London and New York: Routledge, 2013)

Index

Abbas, Ihsan 186-8
Abbasids 49, 64, 65-6, 141-3, 186-7
Abbot, Nabia 124
Abbott, H. Porter 279-80, 298
'Abd al-Raziq, Su'ad 'Ali 167-8, 169, 342-3
'Abda bint Abi Shawwal 44-5, 137-8, 320-1
Abu Hashim "al-Sufi" 225-6, 256-7
Abu Madyan 120-1
action 298-300
adab (discipline of the mind) 60, 70-2, 75, 76-7
'Adi ibn Qays 45, 47
Aesthetic Man 331-3, 337, 345-6
'Afiya 160-1
'A'isha bint Abi Bakr 23, 122-5, 368-70
'Ajrada the Blind 140-1
Al 'Atik 48
'Ali ibn Abi Talib 64, 122-3
Amin, Ahmad 50
'Amir ibn 'Abd Qays 160-1
Ankersmit, Frank 370, 371, 372
Annestay, Jean 282-3, 326
aphorisms 58-60
Arab tribes 45-8
Arberry, A.J. 199-200
Aristotle 298-9, 300-2
Ascetic 27, 28-9
asceticism 73-4, 84-91, 150-3

and 'A'isha 123-5
and ethical precaution 96-103
and *faqr* 114-21
and Mu'adha al-'Adawiyya 125-8
and mysticism 158-9
and *nusk* 104-14
and reactionary 141-4
and renunciation 92-6
and ritual 52-4, 104-14
and Weeping Women 129-36
and women 121-2
see also essential asceticism; instrumental asceticism
al-'Ashiqa al-mutasawwifa (*The Sufi Lover*) (El Sakkakini) 20, 338-9
askesis (training) 79-80, 87
al-'Attar, Farid al-Din 10, 17-18, 22, 23, 30
and celibacy 176-7
and knowledge 252-3, 254
and love 179-80
and myth 375, 376-7
and plot 295-6, 299-300, 302, 304-7, 310-12, 315-16, 319-21
and Rabi'a al'Adawiyya 278-96
and reality effect 266-7, 325-6
'Awarif al-ma'arif
(*The Ways of Discernment*)
(al-Suhrawardi) 211
Ayoub, Samiha 364
Azd tribe 46, 48

Badawi, ʿAbd al-Rahman 18, 20, 30, 269, 305–6
  and Existentialism 328–34, 337–8, 343–4, 345–51
  and Hajj 310–13
  and realism 335–7
Banu ʿAdi 123
Banu Amghar 2
al-Baqir, Muhammad 64
Barthes, Roland 5, 9, 59, 373–6
  and film 352–3, 363–4
  and reality effect 262–4, 266–7, 269–70, 326, 334–5
Basra 14, 35, 46
  and asceticism 121–2
  and Badawi 334, 335–6
  and lovers 158–66
  and tomb 264–6
  and Weeping Women 129–36
Basser, Herbert W. 134–5
al-bayan (demonstrative argument) 53–7, 58
Bedouins 100
Bell, Catherine 90–1, 99
blossoming fern 271–2
body, the 97–8
Brown, Peter 97–8
al-Burjulani, Muhammad ibn al-Husayn 12–13, 17, 35, 38

Caliphates 64–5
Camel, Battle of the 122–3
Cameron, Averil 151–2
celibacy 53, 98, 167–79
chains of transmission 15, 17, 296–7
Chittick, William 130
Christianity 73, 106–8, 128, 242–3
  and asceticism 205–6
  and the body 97–8
  and celibacy 167, 168, 170–3, 175–6
  and Gnostics 286–7
  and heart metaphor 236, 238–9
  and icons 270–2
  and weeping 135–6
  and wisdom 214–15
  see also saints, Virgin Mary
cinema, see film
Clark, Elizabeth A. 88–9, 117, 261–2
  and saints 213, 214–15, 217, 218
combative ascetics 112–13

cultural memory 5, 33–4
Cynics 78–9

Dabʿi, Jaʿfar ibn Sulayman 43, 57
al-Darani, Abu Sulayman 96, 173–4, 241–6, 259–60
Daygham, Malik ibn 133–4
De Beauvoir, Simone 344–5
deconstructive reading 272–3
dhikr (invocation) 259–60
Dhikr al-niswa al-mutaʿabbidat al-sufiyyat (*Memorial of Female Sufi Devotees*) (al-Sulami) 17
Dhuʾl-Nun 206–7, 260, 356–7
Dialogues (Plato) 182
Diamond, Eliezer 109, 126–7, 129, 144
Diogenes 78–9
Diotima of Mantineia 183–4, 188–9, 192–5
Duha al-Islam (*The Mid-Morning of Islam*) (Amin) 50
Dundes, Alan 20–2, 23
Duru, Süreyya 368

Ebeid, Nabila 361
Egypt 322–3, 359–60
El Guindi, Yousry 366
El Sakkakini, Widad 20, 149, 167, 283
  and asceticism 318–19
  and Badawi 328
  and De Beauvoir 344–5
  and Rabiʿa 338–42, 351
  and reality effect 326
El Toukhy, Iman 364
Eliade, Mircea 5, 8–9, 23, 24–5, 353–4
Ernst, Carl W. 179–80
eroticism 249–50
essential asceticism 144–6, 153, 317–18
Ethical Man 331–4, 346, 348
ethical precaution 91, 96–103
exemplary figure 273–7
Existentialism 328–34, 336–8, 343–4, 345–51

faqr (poverty) 91, 114–21
al-Farmadi, Abu ʿAli al-Fadl ibn Muhammad 297–8
fasting 118–21
Fatah, Mustapha Abdel 352

Fatima 64
figures 35-6
film 352-64, 368
Flood, Gavin 90, 91, 109
folklore 20-2, 23-4
food 98-100, 118-21
Fowden, Garth 81-2
Fudayl ibn 'Iyad 66-7
futuwwa (young manliness) 74-5

Gaster, Theodore H. 22-3
al-Ghazali, Abu Hamid 201-2, 297
Ghufayra al-'Abida 126, 131-2
al-Ghulam, Utba ibn Aban 112
government 100-1
Green, Nile 222, 226-7
Gregory of Nyssa 214, 215, 217
Gutas, Dimitri 184-5, 188
Gwynne, Rosalind 105

Habib al-'Ajami 161
Hadith, *see* Qur'an
Hadot, Pierre 35-6, 58, 79, 87, 88, 178
Hafsa bint Sirin 307-8
Hajj pilgrimage 310-15
al-Hajjaj, Shu'ba Ibn 43
Harpham, Geoffrey Galt 90, 95, 152
al-Hasan al-Basri 43, 101-2, 148-9, 318-19
  and al-'Attar 289, 290-1, 315-18
  and celibacy 168-9, 176-7
  and heart metaphor 239, 240-1
Hasanids 65
al-Hawali, 'Abd al-Rahman 313-15
Hayyuna 138-9, 164-6, 248
heart metaphor 234-49
Heffernan, Thomas J. 263-4, 271, 299
Heidegger, Martin 343-4
Helal, Aida 357
Hellenism 78-82, 87-9;
  see also Aristotle; Plato
Hermansen, Marcia 253
al-Hifni, 'Abd al-Mun'im 343-4
hilm (reason) 72-3, 77, 87
Hilyat al-awliya' (*The Adornment of Saints*) (al-Isfahani) 60, 63, 241-3
Hodgson, Marshall 71
Hollywood, Amy 249, 250-1, 253-4
Holy Women 2

Hourani, Albert 136
al Hujwiri, 'Ali 97, 106, 234, 257-8
Hukayma 208, 247
al-Hurayfish, Shu'ayb ibn Sa'd 168-9, 207-8, 310
hurra (free Arab women) 49-50

Ibn 'Abd Rabbih 73, 78-9
Ibn Abi al-Dunya, Abu 'Abdullah Muhammad 13-14, 16, 35, 39
Ibn Abi al-Hawari, Ahmad 208, 210-11, 241-3
Ibn Abi Tahir Tayfur, Ahmad 13, 14, 35, 36-7, 57
  and celibacy 169-70
  and poverty 116
Ibn Adham, Ibrahim 164-5, 173, 246-7
Ibn al-A'rabi, Abu Sa'id 17
Ibn al-A'rabi, Muhammad 206-7
Ibn al-Jawzi, Abu al-Faraj 44-5, 302-4, 355-6
  and 'Abda 137-8
  and celibacy 175
  and femininity 277-8
  and Poem of the Intimate Gift 209-10, 212
  and poverty 116
  and weeping 131, 136
Ibn al-Junayd, Ibrahim 13, 14, 35, 38-9
Ibn al-Khatib, Lisan al-Din 201, 310
Ibn al-Mubarak, 'Abdullah 93, 117, 119, 124-5, 130
Ibn al-Muqaffa' 70-1
Ibn al-Nadim 39
Ibn Dinar, Malik 43, 132, 161-2, 173
  and heart metaphor 239-40, 241
Ibn Khallikan, Abu al-'Abbas Ahmad 265, 266, 303-4, 321-2
Ibn Manzur, Jamal al-Din 105-6
Ibn Salman, 'Abd al-'Aziz 132
Ibn 'Uyayna, Sufyan 67
Ibn Wasi', Muhammad 43
Ibn Zayd, 'Abd al-Wahid 157
Ibn Zayd, Hammad 41
iconography 9-10, 27-8, 30, 270-1
  and al-'Attar 283-5, 294-5
'ilm (outer knowledge) 256-8
implied author 272-3
impurity 97-9

instrumental asceticism 126–7, 129, 140–1, 152, 317–18
Iraq 16; *see also* Basra
Isaac of Nineveh 238
al-Isfahani, Abu Nu'aym 60–1, 230–1, 241–2
'ishq (love) 156–8, 182–3
Islam 15, 25, 47, 329, 359
  and celibacy 174–5, 176
  see also Qur'an; Shiite Muslims; Sufism; Sunni Muslims
Izutsu, Toshihiko 72–3, 77
'iyy (inexpressiveness) 56

al-Jahiz, Abu 'Uthman 13, 14, 16, 35, 36
  and Arabs 45, 46–7
  and *al-bayan* 53–6, 58–9, 255, 256
  and combative ascetics 112–13
  and exemplary figure 274–5
  and Rabi'a 83
  and renunciation 104
  and Sufism 229–30
  and Sunni women 51–2
Jakobson, Roman 262–3
Jerusalem 265, 266, 268, 321–2, 323–4
Judaism 127–8, 129, 134–6, 176, 235–6
al-Junayd, Abu al-Qasim 202–3

Kaelber, Walter O. 89, 90
al-Kalabadhi, Abu Bakr 91, 197, 198–9, 202
Kamel, Abbas 357
al-Kamil, 'Abdullah 65
Kashf al-mahjub (*Unveiling the Veiled*) (al-Hujwiri) 234
Kermani, Navid 278–9
Khalidi, Tarif 38
al-Khargushi, 'Abd al-Malik 101, 115, 210–11, 247–9
al-Khidr (The Green One) 5
Khorasan 16
al-Khuldi, Ja'far 17
khulla (intimacy) 349–50
Kierkegaard, Søren 330–1, 334, 344
Kilito, Abdelfattah 273–5, 281
al-Kindi, Abu Ishaq 80, 187
King, Karen 286–8, 294

Kirk, G.S. 22
Kitab al-bayan wa-l-tabyin (*On Demonstrative Proof and Elucidation*) (al-Jahiz) 13, 35, 36
Kitab al-bukhala' (*Book of Misers*) (al-Jahiz) 274–5
Kitab al-hayawan (*The Book of Animals*) (al-Jahiz) 13, 35, 36
Kitab al-mahabba li-llah (*Book of the Love of God*) (Ibn al-Junayd) 13, 38–9
Kitab al-ruhban (*The Book of Monks*) (al-Burjulani) 12–13, 38
Kitab al-Shifa' bi-ta'rif huquq al-Mustafa (*The Antidote in Recognizing the Rights of the Chosen One*) (al-Yahsubi) 76
Kitab al-zuhd (Al-Mu'afa) 142–4, 152–3
Kitab al-zuhd wa-l-raqa'iq (*The Book of Renunciation and the Refinements of Worship*) (Ibn al-Mubarak) 93
Kitab Baghdad (*The Book of Baghdad*) (Tayfur) 36
Kitab balaghat al-nisa' (*Book of the Eloquence of Women*) (Tayfur) 13, 36–7

lamp miracle 307–8
Latić, Džemaludin 147–8
legends 21–2
Lewis and Clark expedition 1, 3
Lombard, Maurice 141
Losev, Aleksei Fyodorovich 30, 295
  and myth 267–8, 269–70, 271, 337, 354–5, 373–4
Louÿs, Pierre 341–2
love 16, 27, 29, 148–50
  and Basra 158–66
  and God 154–8
  and al-Makki 189–96
  and mysticism 150–3, 158–60, 179–83
  and poetry 196–208
al-Luma' fi-l-tasawwuf (*Flashes of Insight into Sufism*) (al-Sarraj) 40–1

Madame Bovary (Flaubert) 334–6, 352
mahabba (love) 154–8
al-Mahdi 63

Majmu'at rasa'il Ibn Abi al-Dunya
(*The Collected Letters of Ibn Abi al-Dunya*) 14, 39
Makarios the Great 237
al-Makasib (al-Muhasibi) 227-8
al-Makki, Abu Talib 16, 209, 212
and celibacy 177-8
and exemplary figure 273-4
and knowledge 254-5
and love 184, 189-98, 216-18
manasik rituals 104-5, 108, 109
Mandan people 1-2, 3
manliness 72-5, 76
al-Mansur, Abu Ja'far 65, 66
al-Maqdisi, 'Izz al-Din ibn 'Abd al-Salam 180-2, 183-4
Maquet, Jacques 84-5
Marcrina, St 214, 215, 217
ma'rifa (inner knowledge) 256-60
marriage 139, 173-4, 176-7, 249-50
Mary, *see* Virgin Mary
Mary Magdalene 292-4
Maryam of Basra 44, 137
masa'il (topics) 77-8
Masari' al-'ushshaq (*Battlefields of the Lovers*) (al-Sarraj) 204-5
Massignon, Louis 101, 130, 157-8, 229, 356
al-Mas'udi, 'Ali ibn al-Husayn 186, 187-8
Matta ibn Yunus, Abu Bishr 298, 301-2
mawlat (non-Arab client) 47, 48
Mecca 49-50, 310-15
Mnasadika 341, 342
monasticism 95, 170-3
Mooney, Catherine M. 249-50
Moses 290-2
Mourad, Suleiman 316-17
mu'addiba (trainer) 60, 70
Mu'adha al-'Adawiyya 51, 52-4, 98-9, 122, 125-8
al-Mu'afa ibn 'Imran, Abu Mas'ud 117-18, 124-5, 142-4
Mudar 45-6, 48
Muhammad, Prophet 75-6, 122, 155, 181-2
al-Muhasibi, al-Harith ibn Asad 12, 13, 14, 34, 39-40

and fasting 118-19
and Sufism 226-8
and *wara'* 102-3
mujahada (disciplined struggle) 106, 112
al-Munawi, Muhammad 'Abd al-Ra'uf 322-4
murabitin (holy people) 2
al-Murri, Salih 69, 130
muruwwa (manliness) 72-5, 76-7, 87
Musonius Rufus 79
mysticism 150-3, 158-60
myth 4-12, 20-7, 30-1, 267-72, 373-7
and film 354-5

al-Nadim, Muhammad ibn 64
narrative 8-12
Niazi, Mostafa 352
Nicholson, Reynold A. 199, 200
Nietzsche, Friedrich 151
al-Nisaburi, al-Hasan ibn Muhammad 138-9, 202-4
nusk (ascetic ritualism) 91, 104-14

Old Woman Who Never Dies 1-2, 3
oral traditions 14-15, 37-8

Pelagia of Antioch 205-6, 277
"Person of *Bayan*" 16
philosophy 87-8
Piety-Minded 61, 71, 77, 86
Plato 182, 183-8, 192-6, 201, 203-4
Poem of the Intimate Gift 208-12, 252
Poem of Two Loves 196-208
Poetics (Aristotle) 298-9, 300-2
poverty 114-21
principled celibacy 175-6
prosopography 37-42
Protestantism 95
Proto-Sufism 231-3
purity 97-100, 105-6

al-Qasd wa-l-ruju' ila Allah (*God as the Goal and the Return*) (al-Muhasibi) 12, 13, 39-40
Qays 45-6, 48

al-Qaysi, Riyah 44, 168
Qur'an 2, 43, 85–6
   and *al-bayan* 54, 55
   and celibacy 170–3
   and heart metaphor 234–5
   and *hilm* 73
   and love of God 154–8
   and poverty 115
   and prophets 290–3
   and renunciation 95–6
   and rituals 109–10
   and wara' 101
   and weeping 130
Qurra'a, Saniya 328, 352, 355–7, 359–60
al-Qushayri, Abu al-Qasim 91, 100, 101–2, 319–20
Qut al-qulub (*The Nourishment of Hearts*) (al-Makki) 16, 17, 177–8, 189–96

Rabi'a al-'Adawiyya 3, 56–7
   and al-'Attar 278–96
   and Arab tribe 45–8
   and asceticism 73–4, 86–8, 144–6
   and associates 42–5
   and Badawi 328–34, 336–8, 345–51
   and caution 96
   and celibacy 167–79
   and El Sakkakini 338–42
   and exemplary figure 274–7
   and flute 309–10
   and Hajj 310–15
   and heart metaphor 246–7, 248–9
   and hunger 120–1
   and Ibn al-Jawzi 277–8
   and Ibn Dinar 239–40
   and identity 33–42, 302–4, 305–6
   and images 367–8
   and knowledge 251–60
   and leadership 50–2
   and love 148–50, 159–60, 163–4, 179–81, 183–4
   and love poetry 196–212
   and al-Makki 189–96
   and marriage 342–3
   and myth 4–12, 20–7, 268–9, 371–7
   and poverty 114, 116
   and purity 99–100
   and reality effect 266–7
   and ritual 109–11
   and slavery 162–3, 306–7
   and sources 12–14
   and Sufism 213–22
   and Sunni Islam 52–3
   and teaching 57–60, 77
   and al-Thawri 67–9
   and tomb 264–6, 321–4
   and weeping 136
   and writers 16–20
   and writings 15–16
   see also iconography; Sufism
Rabi'a al-'Adawiyya (film) 352, 354–7, 360–4
Rabi'a al-'Azdiyya 44
Rabi'a bint Isma'il 208–9, 210–11, 212
Rabi'a-i-Adviyye (film) 368
Rabia ilk Kadin Evliya (film) 368
Rabi'a ta'ud (*Rabi'a Returns*) (TV series) 364–6
Rabi'a the Mystic (Smith) 18–19, 40
al-Rashid, Harun 70
Rayhana 162–3
reactionary asceticism 141–4, 152–3
reality effect 262–4, 266–7, 269–70, 326, 334–5
reason 72–3
Religious Man 331–3, 334, 347–8
renunciation 92–6
repentance 107–8
ribats (Sufi teaching centers) 2
Rigolio, Alberto 301
ritualism 104–14

sacred biography 263–4, 299
sacrifice 52–3, 104–5
St John's Eve 271–2
saints 21–2, 213–14, 263–4, 278
al-Salaf al-Salih ("Righteous Predecessors") 25, 38, 60, 61–2
Salih ibn 'Abd al-Jalil 228–31
al-Sarraj, Abu Nasr 40–1, 76, 91
   and celibacy 175
   and Poem of Two Loves 204–5
   and ritual 110–11
   and Sufism 222, 224–5
Schimmel, Annemarie 223, 224
Second Sex, The (De Beauvoir) 344–5

secularism 326-8
Seden, Osman 368
Segal, Robert A. 25-7
Sells, Michael 285-6
Shahidat al-hubb al-ilahi (*Witness to Divine Love*) (film) 357-9
Shahidat al-'ishq al-ilahi (*The Martyr of Divine Love*) (Badawi) 18, 20, 269, 328-34
   and realism 335-7
Shakhsiyyat qaliqa fi-l-Islam (*Anxious Personalities in Islam*) (Badawi) 329
Shaqiq al-Balkhi 78, 94, 150-1
Sha'wana of al-Ubulla 44, 132-5, 166
al-Shibli, Abu Bakr 97
Shiite Muslims 64-5, 67
Shirin of Iraq 206
Sifat al-Safwa (Ibn al-Jawzi) 302-4
Smith, Margaret 18-19, 40
   and celibacy 167, 168
   and Christianity 82, 327
   and mysticism 158
   and Poem of Two Loves 199, 200
   and poverty 114
   and Sufism 219-20
Socrates 80-1, 192-3
Songs of Bilitis, The (Louÿs) 341-2
Spellberg, Denise 123, 368-9
Stoics 55, 58, 79
Stowasser, Barbara 50
Submissive Worshipper, The (al-Hifni) 343-4
Sufism 2, 3, 27, 29-30, 222-33
   and asceticism 87-8, 91
   and exemplary figure 275-7
   and *khulla* 349-50
   and knowledge 251-60
   and love 182-3
   and manliness 74-5
   and marriage 173-4
   and Naqshbandi 297-8
   and poverty 114, 115
   and pre-Islamic civilization 81-2
   and Rabi'a 16-17, 37-42, 213-22
al-Suhrawardi, Abu Hafs 'Umar 211
Sukayna bint al-Husayn 49
al-Sulami, Abu 'Abd al-Rahman 3, 16-17, 41-2
   and *al-bayan* 58
   and Arabs 48
   and asceticism 91
   and associates 43, 44
   and chains of transmission 296-7
   and exemplary figure 275-7
   and heart metaphor 247
   and knowledge 253
   and lamp miracle 307-8
   and *nusk* 113-14
   and *ta'dib* 75
   and al-Thawri 43, 68-9
   and weeping 130
Sunni Muslims 43, 51-4
Surur, Taha 'Abd al-Baqi 170, 342
Symposium (Plato) 183-8, 192-6, 201, 203-4
Syria 16, 106-8

ta'abbud (servitude) 125-6
tabaqat (generations) 37-8, 41, 295-6
tabattul (celibacy) 171-2
Tadhkirat al-awliya (*Memorial of the Saints*) (al-'Attar) 17-18, 278-96
ta'dib (training) 60, 69-82, 87
Tahdhib al-asrar (*The Primer of Secrets*) (al-Khargushi) 210-11, 247-9
tawakkul (providence) 93-4
Teacher 27, 28, 57-60
television 364-6
Thaïs (France) 340-1
al-Thawri, Sufyan 41, 42-3, 51
   and Rabi'a 59, 60-9, 192-3
tradition 60-2; *see also* oral traditions
Tragedy 298-9, 300-2
transparent anecdote 275
Turkey 368

'Ubayda bint Abi Kilab 132
al-Ubulli Shayban ibn Farrukh 57-8
'Umar, Caliph 123
Umayyad Caliphate 47-8, 75
Umm al-Darda' 51, 52-4
Umm Kulthum 352
Upton, Charles 149, 252
'Uqala' al-Majanin (al-Nisaburi) 138-9

Valentasis, Richard 80, 81, 89-90, 95, 128
   and celibacy 178
   and transformation 139-40

Vansina, Jan 14–15
Virgin Mary 23, 154, 292–4
vocational celibacy 176–7
Vroom, Hendrik M. 270–1, 326

Wafayat al-a'yan (*Death Notices of the Notables*) (Ibn Khallikan) 265, 266
Walbridge, John 185
wara' (ethical precaution) 91, 96–103, 108–9
Weeping Women (*al-Bakiyat*) 129–36
White, Hayden 213–14, 215–16, 262–3, 298
women 49–51, 129–36
  and al-'Attar 285–9
  and asceticism 121–2, 174
  and film 359–60
  and nusk 113–14
  and saints 213–15
  and stereotypes 249–51, 253–4
  and *wara'* 97
World/Nonworld Dichotomy 84–7, 92, 93, 143, 244–5

al-Yahsubi, Qadi 'Iyad ibn Musa 76
Yemenis 46

al-Zabidi, Muhammad Murtada 202
Zaydi Shiites 64–5, 67
Zaynab, Sayyida 308
Zubayda 49–50
zuhd (renunciation) 91, 92–6, 104

www.ingramcontent.com/pod-product-compliance
Lightning Source LLC
Chambersburg PA
CBHW032023290426
44110CB00012B/650